WORLD WIDE WEB

Your Personal Guide to the Best of the Web

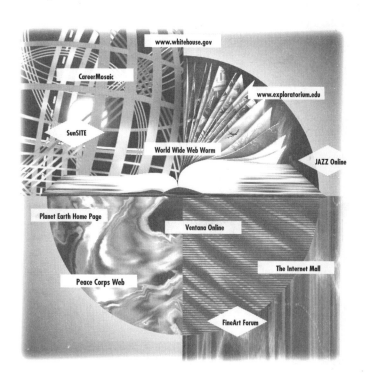

WALKING THE
WORLD WIDE WEB

Your Personal Guide to the Best of the Web

Second Edition

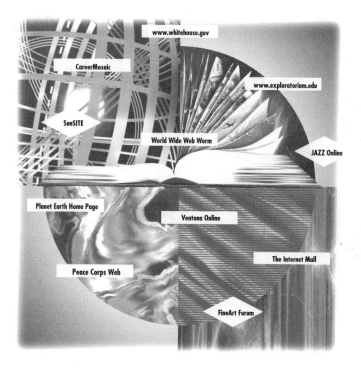

Shannon Turlington

VENTANA

Walking the World Wide Web: Your Personal Guide to the Best of the Web, Second Edition
Copyright © 1995 by Shannon Turlington

Library of Congress Cataloging-in-Publication Data

Turlington, Shannon R.
　　Walking the World Wide Web : your personal guide to the best of the Web /
　Shannon R. Turlington.— 2nd ed.
　　　p.　cm.
　　Includes index.
　　ISBN 1-56604-298-4
　　1. World Wide Web (Information retrieval system)　2. Computer network resources.
　I. Title.
　　TK5105.888.T88　1995
　　025.04—dc20
                                                95-25995
                                                    CIP

Sega back cover screen shot used with the permission of Sega. HotWired back cover screen shot copyright © HotWired Ventures LLC. All rights reserved.

Second Edition 9 8 7 6 5 4 3 2 1
Printed in the United States of America

Ventana Communications Group, Inc.
P.O. Box 13964
Research Triangle Park, NC 27709-3964
919/544-9404
FAX 919/544-9472

Limits of Liability and Disclaimer of Warranty
The author and publisher of this book have used their best efforts in preparing the book and the programs contained in it. These efforts include the development, research and testing of the theories and programs to determine their effectiveness. The author and publisher make no warranty of any kind, expressed or implied, with regard to these programs or the documentation contained in this book.

The author and publisher shall not be liable in the event of incidental or consequential damages in connection with, or arising out of, the furnishing, performance or use of the programs, associated instructions and/or claims of productivity gains.

Trademarks
Trademarked names appear throughout this book and on the accompanying compact disk. Rather than list the names and entities that own the trademarks or insert a trademark symbol with each mention of the trademarked name, the publisher states that it is using the names only for editorial purposes and to the benefit of the trademark owner with no intention of infringing upon that trademark.

President / CEO
Josef Woodman

Vice President of Content Development
Karen A. Bluestein

Managing Editor
Pam Richardson

Marketing Product Manager
Diane Lennox

Production Manager
John Cotterman

Print Department
Dan Koehler

Art Director
Marcia Webb

Editorial Staff
Bradley King, Amy Moyers, Beth
Snowberger, Melanie Stepp

Design Staff
Charles Overbeck, Jennifer Rowe

Acquisitions Editor
Cheri Robinson

Project Editor
Jessica Ryan

Copy Editor
Nancy Crumpton, Pam Upton

Assistant Editor
Bradley King

Technical Reviewer
Max Leach

Technical Director
Max Leach

Desktop Publishers
Patrick Berry, Scott Hosa,
Lance Kozlowski,
Jaimie Livingston

Cover Illustration
Williamson-Green, Inc.,
Charles Overbeck

Proofreaders
Vicky Wells

Indexer
Dianne Bertsch, Answers Plus

Acknowledgments

I would first like to thank my husband, Dykki Settle. He was instrumental in coming up with the idea for this book, and he continued to support and advise me throughout the process of writing it. For that, he has my unending love and gratitude.

I would also like to thank everyone at Ventana for making the whole publishing process smooth and painless. Special thanks go to Cheri Robinson and Jessica Ryan for their great skills at coordinating the editing and production end. Many thanks to Heather Valli and Laura Poole for their help in compiling the secondary sites. Thanks to Max Leach for his superb technical editing. Thanks to Luke Duncan, Eric Coker, Max Leach, and everyone in the "Batcave" for creating the wonderful CD-ROM and Online Companion. And deep thanks to Elizabeth Woodman for helping bring this book to life and for her continued support. Thanks also to the readers of the first edition who took the time to send me comments; I have made a special effort to incorporate your suggestions for improvements into this second edition.

Finally, I would like to acknowledge all the terrific World Wide Web site designers and Webmasters whose works are represented in these pages—without their efforts, this book would not have been possible. Most of these people are unpaid volunteers, and they often go without recognition despite the wonderful contributions they make to the Internet. True pioneers in cyberspace, they definitely deserve our gratitude.

About the Author

Shannon R. Turlington is a writer and World Wide Web publisher. She was the links editor for the first trade book, *Bless This Food* by Adrian Butash, to be published on the World Wide Web; as links editor, she researched and incorporated World Wide Web resources into the text of that book. She also completely edited and produced the hypertext edition of *Bernice Chesler's Bed & Breakfast in New England*, Massachusetts version, including HTML coding and formatting and editing external links. She currently edits and publishes *Cyberkind*, a World Wide Web magazine of Net-related fiction, nonfiction, poetry, and art and maintains a literature and writing resource archive on the World Wide Web. She has also contributed to *Internet Roadside Attractions* (Ventana). Shannon lives in Chapel Hill, NC, with her husband, two dogs, and two ferrets.

E-mail: shannon@vmedia.com

Home Page: http://www.vmedia.com/shannon/shannon.html

Contents

Introduction

You've heard all the buzzwords—the Net, cyberspace, online. You've been invited to surf the Net, to jack in, to drive the Information Superhighway. Perhaps you've already ventured into the Internet and found it to be a vast, confusing, fast-paced, foreign place. It's all too easy to get lost or feel left behind—there are no road signs along the Information Superhighway.

The World Wide Web (WWW) was made for people like you. You don't want to learn confusing Unix commands or try to feel your way through unfamiliar software programs, but you do want to access the vast information resources within the Internet. Through the World Wide Web, you can navigate the far reaches of cyberspace easily, using software that looks and acts like the other familiar programs on your Windows system.

Think of Web walking as taking a pleasant stroll through cyberspace. A Web walk lets you slow down and enjoy the multimedia scenery. Take the time to explore—you'll find museums, shops, magazines, games, research labs, cities, countries, even entire alternate worlds, all linked in.

The purpose of this book is to get you started on your Web walking tour. Inside, take a trip to the best and brightest World Wide Web sites, carefully chosen to introduce the newcomer to the Web. When you finish this book, you'll be an expert Web-walker, ready to venture out on your own into the vast world of the Net.

What You Need

You need only four things to start Web walking: a computer, a modem, a direct Internet connection, and special software, called a *client*, that allows you to interface with the Web.

First, let's consider the computer and modem. You'll be able to appreciate the WWW experience most fully using a Windows or XWindows computer with a color monitor and a lot of free memory and disk space. You'll also get the most enjoyment with a faster modem, 14.4 Kbps or better. However, the Web was designed to be available to almost anyone—from the person sitting at a terminal and connecting to the Internet through a dial-up account to one with the latest and most advanced multimedia machine. Specific requirements to run a graphical WWW client are described in Appendix C, "Netscape & the World Wide Web, but rest assured that if you have a computer and a modem, you can access the Web.

You've probably noticed the CD-ROM that comes with this book. If you don't have a CD-ROM drive on your computer, don't worry—you can still make the most of this book using its online companion. More about that later. For CD-ROM users, the CD-ROM provides some value-added features that will make understanding and using the WWW easier. (The CD-ROM and its use are described in more detail later in the introduction.)

You'll also need a direct Internet connection. The most common type, especially for home-computer users, is a SLIP or PPP connection that can be accessed through a modem from an Internet service provider. If you've already got one, great. If you don't have a SLIP or PPP connection but connect to the Internet through a dial-up account, you can still access many of the information resources on the WWW (you'll find out how to do this in Section 1)—you just can't get the multimedia, graphics, and other fun stuff. The best way to experience the WWW is through a direct Internet connection, using one of the many graphical WWW clients available. Talk to your Internet service provider about upgrading to a SLIP or PPP connection.

If you don't have an Internet connection at all, it's easy to get. I suggest you purchase a product like Ventana's *Internet Membership Kit, Windows Edition*. This kit will connect you to an Internet service provider, provide you with everything you need to create a SLIP account, introduce you to the Internet, and walk you through the steps of downloading Netscape Navigator, the most popular WWW client and the one I recommend. After that, you'll be ready to start cruising the WWW.

The final component you need to begin exploring the WWW is a software program that will enable your computer to interact with the Web. Netscape Navigator is, in my opinion, the best way to navigate the Web. With Netscape, you can access the latest, greatest features the Web has to offer. You'll find Netscape for Windows on the CD-ROM. Or you can instantly download it to your computer through the Internet. Use your FTP client to FTP to Ventana; the address is *ftp.vmedia.com*. Once you're there, follow the directories to find the latest version of Netscape for your system.

What's Inside

You've got your computer, a direct Internet connection, and a WWW client. Now you're ready to start exploring a universe of multimedia information resources. When you first get onto the WWW, you'll notice how much "stuff" is out there. It's all too easy to get lost in the maze of documents that make up the WWW. This book helps make your explorations easier by guiding you to the most useful, most beautiful, and most advanced Web sites.

Just like the Web itself, this book contains something for everyone. Beginning WWW users can tour the best-designed and most innovative places on the Web. Think of it as a familiarization tour, to show you what the Web is, what it can do, and how to navigate it. Internet wizards will likely discover new sites or hot spots they didn't know existed. Administrators of WWW servers and designers of Web presentations will also profit from touring the sites featured in this book, which were chosen to represent the best and most imaginative of the WWW's many features, such as multimedia, hyperlinks, and interactive elements.

The listings in this book, which follow the brief introduction to the WWW in Section I, are divided into six sections, each of which has more than one hundred Web sites for you to explore. Section II, "See the World," takes you on an around-the-world tour through the WWW, stopping at different countries, cities, and tourist spots along the way. Section III, "Get Cultured," introduces you to arts and humanities resources on the WWW, including art galleries, museums, libraries, reference sources, and schools. Section VI, "Experiment," explores science and math resources; here you'll find fun ways to learn about astronomy, computing, physics, zoology, and much more. Section V, "In Your Free Time," covers entertainment—games, news, movies, television, music, hobbies, sports, books, magazines, and the bizarre. Section VI, "Taking Care of Business," tours the commercial offerings on the WWW, including business resources, financial sites, Internet advertising, and publishing services, as well as virtual malls and storefronts where you can shop 'til you drop. Section VII, "Just for Kids," is a place where all kids can hang out, with clubs, video games, cartoons, homework help, and loads of other fun sites especially for kids.

Each site listing has four parts. A listing begins with the title of the Web page and the WWW address for the site. The review then thoroughly describes the site, outlining what is available there and emphasizing the highlights. These comprehensive reviews enable you to narrow your WWW tour to what truly interests you. The reviews also note innovative Web features, including inventive uses of multimedia. Beneath the review is contact information for the site, including the server where the site is located and the maintainer of the site. This tells you exactly who is creating these WWW gems.

At the end of every subsection, you'll also find several more resources to lead you to alternative sites on that subject. These secondary listings are not as fully reviewed. If you are craving more information on any one specific subject, check out these alternative listings for even more great sites.

By purchasing this book, you've also gained access to an online companion, located on the WWW itself and accessible only to Ventana customers. The *Walking the World Wide Web Online Companion* contains a full, hypertext version of the book and an archive of all the software mentioned in the book that is freely available through the Internet. This is your one-stop shop for everything you need to start touring the Web (and there's even a help center for advice in downloading and configuring the software). Hyperlinks in the online version will connect you instantly with all the sites reviewed in the book. Keep in mind that the Web is not a static place—it is continually changing and evolving. Old sites die or move, and new, better sites come online. If you cannot connect to any sites listed in this book, check the Online Companion for news of what's happened to them. You can also get periodic updates of all the information in the book and reviews of exciting new WWW sites. See Appendix A, "About the Online Companion," for instructions on connecting to the Online Companion.

Appendix B, "About the Companion CD-ROM," describes the enclosed CD-ROM, which contains a hypermedia version of this book to introduce you to hypertext and the WWW. It also has Netscape Navigator, a WWW browser that you can move to your hard drive and begin using right away. Using the CD-ROM, the included copy of

Netscape, and a direct Internet connection, you can connect instantly to the sites reviewed in the book by clicking on highlighted—*hyper-linked*—words. The CD-ROM will familiarize you with moving around the WWW and give you quick access to all the listings found in the book. Since the CD-ROM has a complete index, you can search for the site you want. Use the CD-ROM to prepare an itinerary of Web sites you want to visit offline, then fire up your Internet connection to begin Web walking. See Appendix B, "About the Companion CD-ROM," for more information. Appendix C, "Netscape & the World Wide Web," introduces you to the Web client, Netscape. You'll learn how to browse the Web, navigate in the document window, and discover the beauty of links—the core of the WWW. You'll also take a quick tour through the Web and learn how to set up your own home pages. Accessing FTP, Gopher, Usenet, and e-mail using Netscape is also addressed.

Appendix D, "World Wide Web Search Tools," describes the many sites located on the WWW that enable you to search the Web and the Internet interactively for specific resources. These tools are essential for scanning the huge amount of information on the Internet for resources that will be useful to you. To save you time, I have chosen the best of these search tools and listed them in one place.

Let's Get Started

Section I, "How to Get There From Here," introduces you to the WWW—its history, current status, and future directions. It provides an overview of hypermedia, including hyperlinks, the unique form of documents published on the Web. It also introduces you to Netscape Navigator and explains Uniform Resource Locators (URLs), the addressing system for sites and documents on the WWW. I recommend this section particularly for readers who have little or no experience with the Internet or the WWW. You'll find it doesn't take long to gain enough expertise to enable you to move around the Web with confidence.

If you already know this information or are eager to begin, skip straight to the listings, organized in sections as outlined earlier: geographical, cultural, and travel sites in Section II; educational, arts, and humanities sites in Section III; science, math, and computing sites in Section IV; news and entertainment in Section V; business and shopping resources in Section VI; and kids' sites in Section VII. Or just browse—you're sure to find something to snag your interest on just about every page. With all the listings counted, there are 1,800 sites for you to explore, and each one will lead you to new discoveries. So hook up your Internet connection, fire up your WWW client, and have a blast on your tour of the World Wide Web.

Shannon Turlington
shannon@vmedia.com

Section I

How to Get There From Here

Section I

How to Get There From Here

The Internet is a vast frontier of information resources, ripe for exploring and plundering. Best described as a "network of networks," the Internet connects thousands of computer networks all over the world. Computers in the networks that make up the Internet provide information to the Internet public on an unimaginable variety of topics. You can find free software and games, huge libraries of archived information, and facts and opinions on every subject under the sun.

As the Internet has grown in popularity, new tools have been developed to navigate the Net and access its many resources. The simplest of these is *Telnet*, which allows you to log in to another computer directly and look at information archived there. The need to move files from computer to computer led to the development of *File Transfer Protocol* (*FTP*). With FTP you can download text, software, and graphics from another machine to your own computer. The next evolution, *Gopher*, attempted to make navigating information resources more user-friendly by organizing them as menus of directories. These tools—Telnet, FTP, and Gopher, among others—are called *Network Information Discovery and Retrieval* (*NIDR*) tools. Their aim is to make exchanging information over the Internet quicker and easier.

The Internet is also useful for speedy communication between users. Electronic mail (e-mail) discussion lists, and Usenet news permit group discussion on thousands of different subjects. Many of these exchanges are archived, adding to the information resources available.

As long as you have a fair idea of what you are looking for and where to find it, Telnet, FTP, Gopher, and the other Internet tools may suit your needs. As the Internet grows, however, this isn't always possible. And knowing which tools to use to access the various archives can be confusing. The *World Wide Web* (*WWW*) formed as a way to solve these problems.

The World Wide Web is not a tool, like Telnet, FTP, and Gopher, but is rather an invisible network within the larger network of the Internet. Several WWW *browsers* have been developed to navigate the WWW. Using one of these browsers, you can access FTP, Gopher, and Usenet archives by typing an address for the resource. Essentially, the WWW links all the resources on the Internet into an interconnected net of information.

WWW files are encoded with *HyperText Markup Language* (HTML), which creates *links* to different parts of the same document or to other documents. Links transform HTML files into three-dimensional documents, with threads leading to other resources at the same site, and even to other sites. Every document on the WWW eventually links to every other document through HTML links, putting the "web" into World Wide Web.

The Web, as it is often referred to, has grown rapidly since it was introduced, and the number of WWW servers—computers providing HTML information—has mushroomed. As of this writing, there are several hundred thousand Web servers, and more are connecting every day.

One reason for the WWW's wide popularity is its ease of use. Most WWW browsers enable the user to navigate links with the point-and-click method, using the mouse, in place of difficult-to-remember commands. Through the WWW, all of the Internet can be accessed with the click of a button.

And for the first time on the Internet, true multimedia documents can be created and displayed. Most WWW browsers support full-color graphics, sound, and video. This makes the WWW particularly attractive to businesses, who have set up virtual storefronts and catalogs for the potentially vast Internet market, as well as to researchers and scientists, who can share graphics, videos, and interactive demonstrations of their research with others in their fields all around the world.

The WWW offers more than just multimedia—it also makes interactivity possible. With interactive forms, you can order products from one of these virtual stores or provide feedback to a Web site designer. Another innovation is image mapping, in which points on a graphic become links to other documents.

Even with the best of tools, though, it can be all to easy to get lost on the Web. Following the links can take you down confusing back alleys and meandering side roads, as well as main paths. That's where this book comes in. It will introduce you to the WWW and teach you necessary skills for finding information on it. The sites reviewed here represent a cross-section of the WWW and are a good place to begin your Web tour. Check out Appendix D for search tools and subject databases to help you find even more resources on the Web.

What Is the World Wide Web?

Earlier I described the WWW as an invisible network within the network of the Internet. The WWW is not a network of computers, however, but is instead a network of information. Information served through the WWW in HTML format is linked to other HTML documents, enabling you to traverse the WWW by following a trail of links. If you have enough time, it is possible for you to travel from one "end" of the WWW to the other along these links. Perhaps the best way to begin to understand this information web is to look at how and why the Web was put together.

A Brief History of the WWW

The WWW project was first proposed in 1989 by the European Particle Physics Laboratory (CERN), a high-energy physics laboratory in Switzerland. CERN developed the first WWW prototype in 1990. The developers initially envisioned the WWW as a means of sharing papers and data among physicists all over the world through the Internet.

The developers of the WWW had several goals in mind. The most important was to create a seamless network in which information from any source could be accessed in a simple and consistent way. Before the WWW was developed, researchers had to use many different computer programs to access all the information they needed. To overcome problems of incompatibility between different sorts of computers, the WWW introduced the principle of *universal readership*, which states that networked information should be accessible from any type of computer in any country, with one easy-to-use program. (See Figure 1-1 for an illustration of universal readership.) Universal readership makes the WWW the ultimate research tool.

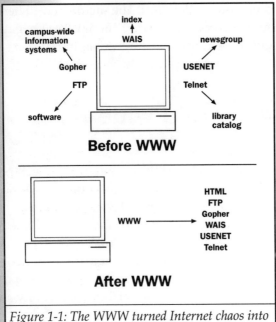

Figure 1-1: The WWW turned Internet chaos into universal readership.

As conceived by the developers at CERN, the WWW should embrace most information in previously networked information systems, including FTP, Gopher, and Usenet. This meant that information already available on the Internet would not have to be redesigned for the WWW. An addressing system, called *Uniform Resource Locators* or *URLs*, can reference any type of document on the Internet, including text, graphics, and video. This setup permits the WWW to extend into multimedia.

Mindful of the quickly evolving nature of the Internet, the developers of the WWW were careful to build in flexibility and the capacity for growth. The Web is designed to encompass future developments in technology, including new networks, protocols, and data formats. This includes advanced multimedia and virtual reality systems.

A final goal of the original developers was ease of use. They believed that the WWW should be accessible to the average computer user, not just to experts. With this in mind, they developed HyperText Markup Language (HTML) as the special code for documents on the WWW. Although the WWW embraces documents in many formats, the most powerful of these are hypertext documents (encoded with HTML formatting), which contain links to other documents or sections within the same document. Following a link requires only a simple point-and-click of the mouse or a keystroke. The WWW also allows you to search huge indices of information by simply entering one or two keywords, and the searches respond with hypertext links that take you directly to documents of interest.

Because of its user-friendly nature and its ability to encompass all the different sorts of information on the Internet, the WWW has grown dramatically since its initial development. Web traffic rose an incredible 2,500 percent between June 1993 and June 1994. Information over the WWW has been made available by many other organizations, besides research laboratories, including universities, elementary schools, city, state, and national governments, libraries, museums, corporations, and small businesses.

Exciting directions for future developments of the WWW have already been mapped out. We may soon see more communal publishing of books and research findings; for instance, this book has been published on the WWW, where it can be easily and regularly updated as the Web changes. In the future, vast hypertext libraries will be available through the WWW. Developers are already working on better tools for collaborative work, one of the original purposes of the WWW. In the not-too-distant future, researchers in a particular field should be able to work together as a group to modify, annotate, and contribute to WWW documents. Finally, the development of object-oriented databases within the Web will enable the user to manipulate objects other than documents, such as scientific data and simulated worlds. Perhaps this will be the first practical, widespread version of virtual reality.

At many sites, documents called FAQs (short for "frequently asked questions") give a quick overview of the site and its offerings and philosophy. These documents, originally developed on Usenet to describe different newsgroups, are organized in a question-and-answer format. For example, a World Wide Web FAQ was written by Thomas Boutell to answer questions most people have about the WWW. To read the WWW FAQ, open the following URL: http://sunsite.unc.edu/boutell/faq/www_faq.html.

Servers & Clients

The WWW has no central overseeing facility. Ideally, anyone can publish information on the Web and anyone can read that information, but there are technological restrictions. Publishing a document on the WWW requires a computer called a *server*. A server is a computer that is configured to communicate with other computers, such as those that provide documents or search mechanisms. Retrieving and displaying information from a server requires a software program called a *client* that is installed on your home or office computer. Client software makes requests of the server computer and provides an interface between the server and the user. The Internet connects all servers and clients, wherever they are located, and WWW protocols enable all clients to communicate with all servers.

The reality of the Internet is that documents are stored in many different data formats, and usually a different tool is required to read or view each one. The number of different graphic formats—GIF, TIFF, and JPEG, for example—can be a nightmare in itself. A client, however, sends a list of all the data representations it understands to the server, and the server responds suitably, all within a few seconds. For instance, some WWW clients may not support graphics, and so the server sends text only to them. The client-server model overcomes the frustrating incompatibilities of data formats because the client and the server talk the same language.

To give a practical illustration of this client-server relationship, suppose you want to use Netscape Navigator, a WWW client program, to access the documentation provided by CERN on their WWW server to learn more about the Web. Using the Open URL command on your WWW client, you enter CERN's URL—the address of the information on the server—and the client begins to communicate with CERN'S server over the Internet. The client tells the server that it supports inline graphics as well as hypertext, and so, within a matter of seconds, the server has sent your client the document you requested, complete with graphics. You are connected to the server only for those few seconds it takes to fulfill your request; after that, the document you are reading resides on your machine in a temporary file. When you click on a link to go to another document, the conversation between client and server begins again.

WWW Servers Around the World

Are you interested in finding out just how many WWW servers are out there? The WWW project at CERN, the developers of the Web, has a list of registered servers, "registered" meaning that the site's maintainer has sent e-mail to CERN describing his or her Web site. (A server does not have to be registered with CERN—there are currently no regulations governing the WWW—so this list may not reflect everything that's available.) Because the list is broken down alphabetically by continent, country, and state, it is a good place to find answers to certain kinds of questions you may have about the Web, such as, "Are there any WWW servers in Africa?" or, "How many WWW servers are there in Croatia?" The list is also a good place to check out servers that are geographically local to you, wherever you might be. To access the list, use the Open URL command on your WWW browser, and type this URL: http://www.w3.org/hypertext/Data-Sources/WWW/Servers.html.

Home Pages

You will often hear the term *home page* bandied about when discussing the WWW. For instance, someone may say to you, "Take a look at my home page," or, "Ventana has a terrific home page." After a while, it may seem to you that the term *home page* is being used to describe several different things.

The term *home page* has two basic meanings for dedicated users of the WWW: one is a client definition, and the other is a server definition. The client definition of home page is the document that first appears when you start up your WWW client. This kind of home page serves as a home base for exploring on the WWW; you move out from there, but whenever you get lost or want to go back, you can click on a button or enter a key that will take you "home." Usually, the client home page is one that has a lot of links that are useful for you, or it can be the information page for your company or school. The choice is up to you.

The server definition of a home page is a document on the WWW that represents a person, company, or organization. The term *page* on the WWW refers to any document that is represented by one URL— a document that you can scroll through without following any links. Generally, an organization's home page furnishes information about the organization and who works there, includes links to local documents, such as research projects or product catalogs, and provides links to other documents of interest throughout the WWW.

If you know how to write HTML and have access to a server, you can write your own home page. Personal home pages have become a trend on the Internet. They usually provide personal and professional information about the person who wrote the home page, including photographs, and list links of particular interest to that person. Many people who create their own home pages, use them as their client home pages as well, since the links they list are those that they use most often to get into the WWW. This gives them a personal view of the Web. (See Figure 1-2 for an example of a personal home page.)

Figure 1-2: A typical personal home page.

Hypertext & Hyperlinks

Most documents on the WWW are *hypertext* documents interconnected by *hyperlinks*. Hypertext simply means text with links. This idea of links is actually much older than computers. A printed book, for example, contains cross-reference links, links to footnotes, and links between the table of contents or index and the text. There are even links to other books, as in a bibliography or suggested reading list. To follow these links, you must turn pages in the book or go to a library or bookstore to look at other books.

Hypertext, however, breaks out of the linear arrangement found in printed documents. Hyperlinks provide multiple paths through the same information. In a hypertext document, the links are the words or phrases that are either highlighted or shown in a different color from the rest of the text, depending on the client you are using. These links enable you to pursue the information you're most interested in, bypassing the rest.

For example, suppose you connect to the online version of this book to find some cool games on the Web. You connect to the section on games by following a link in the table of contents. You see a listing for a game that interests you and follow another hyperlink to connect directly to that game, elsewhere on the Internet. In two clicks of your mouse, you've found just what you wanted. (See Figure 1-3 for a comparison of linear text and hypertext.)

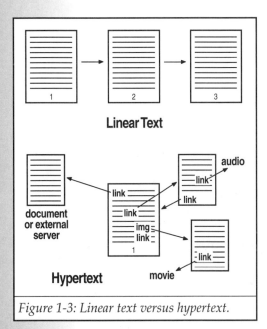

Figure 1-3: Linear text versus hypertext.

Documents interconnected by hyperlinks don't have to be text—they can be graphics, video, or audio as well. From this we get the term *hypermedia*. In the WWW environment, hypermedia refers to the ability to incorporate a variety of media in one document through hyperlinks.

Netscape Navigator: Your Tool for WWW Travel

Now that you know what the World Wide Web is, you need to know how to access it. First you need a direct Internet connection. The most common type, especially for home computer users, is a SLIP or PPP connection that can be accessed through a modem from an Internet service provider. If you've already got one, great. If you don't have a SLIP or PPP connection but already connect to the Internet through a dial-up account, you can still access many of the information resources on the Web. (See "Other Ways to Travel" later in this section.) You just can't get the multimedia, graphics, and other fun stuff. The best way to experience the WWW is through a direct Internet connection, using one of the many graphical Web clients available. Talk to your Internet service provider about upgrading to a SLIP or PPP connection.

CD-ROM

You also need a WWW browser, or client. A variety of WWW clients are available for downloading over the Internet. (See "Other Ways to Travel" later in this section.) The most popular of these, and the one included on the Companion CD-ROM, is Netscape Navigator.

Netscape has several exciting features that have made it the most popular of the WWW browsers. Versions are available for most common computer platforms. It is easy to use, with a user-friendly button bar, and pull-down menus. It can simultaneously load graphics and text, significantly speeding up transfer time and making it perfect for use with slower SLIP or PPP connections. As well as supporting FTP, Telnet, Gopher, and WWW protocols, it is also a full-service Usenet browser that allows you to read and post articles to newsgroups. You can even send Internet e-mail using Netscape.

Netscape is a commercial software product of Netscape Communications Corporation. The program is based on NCSA Mosaic, the original graphical WWW browser, but Netscape adds a lot of unique features that you'll read about later in this section. Netscape is available for three platforms: Macintosh, Windows, and XWindows. Appendix C gives detailed instructions for configuring and using Netscape, but read on for a quick beginner's tutorial.

A Beginner's Guide to Netscape

Netscape uses button bars and pull-down menus to make navigating the WWW as easy as pointing and clicking. Figure 1-4 shows the button bars and pull-down menus for Netscape for Windows (version 2.0). Netscape has two button bars. The buttons on the top bar, the *toolbar*, activate Netscape features that you'll use most frequently. The lower bar has directory buttons that link to online information about Netscape and to useful Internet resources. The pull-down menus activate the same features as the two button bars, plus additional features that you'll use less frequently.

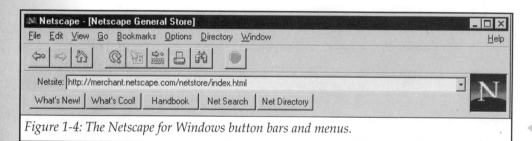

Figure 1-4: The Netscape for Windows button bars and menus.

Following are some of the basic features of the Netscape toolbar. Clicking on the Back button takes you back to the last document you visited. Clicking on the Forward button takes you forward if you have traveled back. The Home button takes you to the home page you configured to start Netscape with. Click on the Images button to load inline graphics for the page you are currently viewing. The Reload button allows you to reload the document you are currently viewing. The Open button brings up a dialog box that allows you to enter a new URL for a document you want to open. The Print button prints out a hard copy of the document you are currently viewing. The Find button lets you search the current document for a keyword. Use the Stop button to stop loading a document that is currently in transfer;

this feature is particularly useful if you are loading a very large document, the transfer is taking too long, or the server you are loading from is slow.

The directory button bar serves as a mini-guide to Netscape and the Internet. Link to the Netscape home page and introductory material about the program by clicking on Welcome. The What's New and What's Cool buttons guide you to the latest, coolest resources on the Internet. Follow the Questions button for answers to your basic questions about Netscape. Net Search goes to a list of popular Internet search tools. The Net Directory button links to a master directory of Internet resource databases.

In addition to the button bars and pull-down menus, there are some other standard features of the Netscape window. The status indicator (the "N" in the top corner) animates when Netscape is transferring data. The title bar at the top of the window displays the title of the document you are viewing. The Location or Go to text field displays the address, or URL, of that document. Along the side and bottom of the window are scroll bars that you can use to move down or across a document that is larger than your window. At the bottom of the window is a status message field that displays information about a hyperlink or transfer in progress; when you position the pointer over a highlighted link, this field displays the URL of the page or image that that link goes to. Also at the bottom of the window is a security indicator, which shows whether or not the WWW page you are accessing is secure for data transfer. A broken key and gray colorbar means that the document is insecure; a whole key and blue colorbar means it is secure. This indicator can be useful when using forms or ordering with your credit card over the WWW. You'll also see a progress bar at the bottom of the window that fills with color when a data transfer is complete.

Another useful feature of Netscape is the pop-up menu. Holding down the right mouse button brings up the pop-up menu. This pop-up menu contains some key commands. You can use it to navigate backward and forward among documents. If you position the pointer over a highlighted link and bring up the pop-up menu, you can use it to open the link, add the link to your Bookmarks, open a new window with the link, save the link to your hard drive, or copy the link location or URL. If you position the pointer over an image, you can use the pop-up menu to view the image, save it to your hard drive, copy the image URL, or load the image. (See Appendix C for further explanation of these commands.)

There are many ways you can use Netscape to open a new document. Click on the Open button on the toolbar to pull up a dialog box in which you can type in the URL, then click on OK or press Return to access that document. Choose Open Location from the File menu to perform the same operation. As a shortcut, you can type the URL directly into the Go to or Location field and hit Return (or Enter). These methods are useful only if you already know the URL you want to go to. For example, if you wanted to read the Online Handbook for Netscape, you would enter the following URL exactly as shown:
http://home.netscape.com/home/1.1/online-manual.html

You can also click on a hyperlink in a document to follow that link to a new URL. Hypertext links are displayed in a different color from the rest of the text. (See Figure 1-5 for an example of a hypertext document with links.) The default color for links is blue, but you can change the color under the Options menu. When you see a link you want to follow, position the pointer over the highlighted word. The URL for the link appears in the status message field at the bottom of the window. Click on the link, and Netscape begins downloading the document. Links you have already explored appear in a different color (the default color is purple) from unexplored links. Displaying links you've already explored in a different color reminds you of where you've already been.

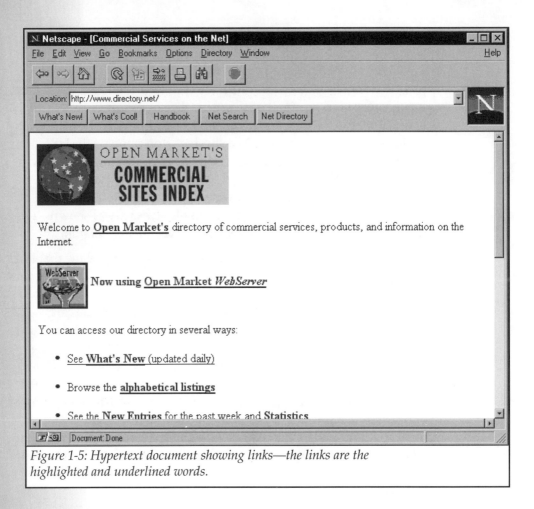

Figure 1-5: Hypertext document showing links—the links are the highlighted and underlined words.

Once a page has been downloaded to your computer for display in Netscape, it is cached after you move to another document. That means that the document is temporarily stored on your hard drive. If you leave the page and return again, it appears practically instantaneously, with no downloading time. This is also true of inline graphics.

Netscape has many useful features that make traversing the WWW easier. The most valuable of these is the *Bookmarks* feature. You can add the URL of the document you are reading to your personal hotlist by selecting Add Bookmark under the Bookmarks window. The URL stays in the Bookmarks list until you remove it. Open the Bookmarks menu, and you'll see a list of the Bookmarks you have added. Any time you want to return to one of your Bookmarks, even in another Netscape session, simply open the menu, and select the Bookmark you want. This saves you the trouble of having to write down or re-member URLs. Use this feature to add documents you want to access frequently or return to look at in greater detail at a later time.

Another useful feature is the History list, located under the Go menu. Netscape maintains a "history" of the documents you have opened during one session. Any time you want to return to a URL you've already been to, you can select it from the History list. Unlike Bookmarks, the History list is not maintained after you quit Netscape.

Use your mouse to click on a name in the History list to return instantly to that document.

Under the Options menu is another useful feature—toggling on and off the auto-load of inline images. Documents with lots of inline graphics can take a long time to load, especially over a SLIP or PPP connection and a slow modem. When this option is turned off, a stan-dard image icon is provided in place of the actual image, and down-loading of the document is greatly speeded up. To see the image, click on the icon, and Netscape downloads it. You can load all the images in a single document by clicking on the Images button or choosing Load Images from the View menu.

Netscape supports both GIF and JPEG images, so you do not need a separate viewer to load them. Often an inline image is a *thumbnail*, or a smaller version, of a full-size image. This thumbnail is linked to the larger image. To see the image, simply click on the linked image. Netscape opens a new document showing just the full-size image. After doing this, you must use the Back button to get back to the origi-nal page. Don't forget that images can be hyperlinks just as text can, linking to other text pages, videos, audio files, and graphics.

When you position your pointer over the image icon, notice that a separate URL for the image appears in the status message field. You can use the pop-up menu to save the image to your local disk by holding down the right mouse button. When you see the pop-up menu, choose Save the Image to save it as a graphics file on your own computer.

Also under the Options menu, you can set preferences for your Netscape session. You can choose whether to show certain window items, such as the toolbar, the directory button bar, and the location field; by removing these, you can increase your window "real estate," or the amount of space for displaying WWW documents.

Choose Preferences under the Options menu to see a lot more preferences. One of these is the home page that appears when you start the program. The default home page is the Netscape Welcome Page. (Figure 1-6 shows the default home page for Netscape for Windows.) Since this page gets a lot of traffic and may be difficult to connect to, you'll probably want to set your own home page. Choose Windows and Links Styles under Preferences. There you'll see a field where you can enter the URL for your home page. Your home page can be any page on the Internet for which you have the URL. Once you've entered the URL for your home page, Netscape automatically opens it whenever you start the program. You can also travel directly to your home page by clicking on the Home button or choosing Home from the Go menu.

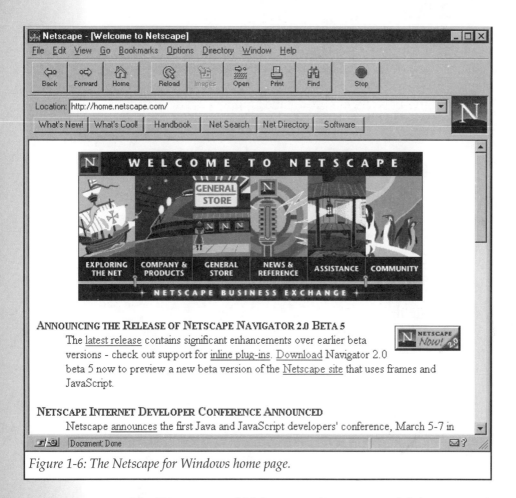

Figure 1-6: The Netscape for Windows home page.

The Directory and Help menus list some useful documents for using Netscape and for learning about the Internet. Some of these are also provided as shortcuts in the Directory toolbar buttons. You can jump to these resources immediately by clicking on them. Directory menu items include those items on the toolbar plus Internet white pages (resources for finding someone on the Internet), links to Internet information sites, and Go to Newsgroups, which connects you to Usenet news. (See Appendix C for more help on using Usenet with Netscape.) Help menu items include a handbook for using Netscape, frequently asked questions about the browser, and help on creating your own Web services. You should also find information about the version of Netscape you are using. Remember to check frequently for updated versions of Netscape.

This description should give you enough know-how to start using Netscape Navigator. To become a Netscape expert, get *The Netscape Quick Tours*, in-depth documentation for the Macintosh and Windows versions of Netscape, published by Ventana. Also read Appendix C in this book for a more detailed guide to using Netscape.

Other Ways to Travel

Lynx: An Alternate Route

Even if you have only a dial-up connection to the Internet, hypertext documents are still available to you, using a program called Lynx. With Lynx, you can access the WWW, although you cannot view the multimedia aspects, such as inline graphics.

Lynx was developed by Lou Montulli, Charles Rezac, and Michael Grobe at the University of Kansas. It grew out of efforts to build a campus-wide information system at the University of Kansas but was improved to give full access to all WWW servers. Although it does not support graphics, video, or sound, Lynx does provide many of the other features of Netscape, such as hyperlinks, a history list, and bookmarks. Like all WWW browsers, Lynx can access HTML documents as well as FTP archives, Gopher servers, and Usenet newsgroups.

If you are dialing in to another computer to access the Internet, such as through a university or a commercial service provider, it is easy to check if Lynx is available to you. Simply type **lynx** at the Unix prompt, and the Lynx screen should appear. If Lynx is not available, check with your service provider to see if they'll install it. Otherwise, you can use Telnet to access Lynx. Telnet to **ukanaix.cc.ukans.edu**, and login as **www** for a full-screen Lynx client. Alternatively, Telnet to **sunsite.unc.edu** and login as **lynx**. Both Telnet sites require a VT100 terminal or VT100 emulator to use Lynx.

If your home or office computer is directly connected to the Internet and you want to install a personal copy of Lynx, it is available free through anonymous FTP at the Ventana Visitor's Center. (See Appendix A for more information on connecting to the Ventana Visitor's Center.) Current versions of Lynx run on Unix and VMS terminals, and a DOS version called DosLynx has recently been developed.

Lynx is easy to learn and use. Hyperlinks are highlighted or appear as a different color, depending on your computer. Use arrow keys to move to different links forward and back, then press Return to follow a link. A simple coding system takes you "home" or enables you to enter URLs.

A Sampler of WWW Clients

A number of other WWW clients are available free of charge over the Internet. Netscape is probably the most advanced of these, but if Netscape does not satisfy you for one reason or another, try one of these. Once you find a client you are comfortable with, remember to check often for updates, as the clients change almost as often as the WWW itself.

Like Netscape, all these clients support point-and-click links and graphics. As with Netscape, all of them require a direct Internet connection. They are all freeware and are available through FTP over the Internet. You can also download any of these programs through the Ventana Visitor's Center.

Cello: An early competitor of Mosaic, this client operates on the Windows platform only. It was developed by Thomas R. Bruce at Cornell Law School. Connect to **ftp://ftp.law.cornell.edu/pub/LII/Cello/** to download the program; get the file cellofaq.zip for more information.

Chimera: Chimera is a newer WWW client for Unix-based systems, developed by John Kilburg at the University of Nevada, Las Vegas. Download the Chimera program and documentation from **ftp://ftp.cs.unlv.edu/pub/chimera/**; get the README file for more information.

MacWeb and WinWeb: This Mosaic clone for Macintosh and Windows platforms was developed by EINet. Connect to **ftp://ftp.einet. net/einet/pc/winweb/** for WinWeb software and documentation or to **ftp://ftp.einet.net/einet/mac/macweb/** for MacWeb software and documentation.

NCSA Mosaic: Mosaic is the original graphical Web browser, developed by the National Center for Supercomputing Applications (NCSA). You'll find versions of Mosaic for Windows, Macintosh, and XWindows at NCSA's FTP site: **ftp://ftp.ncsa.uiuc.edu/Mosaic/**.

tkWWW: This Unix-based client has the distinction of being the only one that includes an HTML editor, particularly useful for WWW designers writing hypertext documents. It is available in the XWindows format only. Get the tkWWW-0.17.README file, located in the FTP archive at **ftp://ftp.aud.alcatel.com/tcl/extensions/** for more information.

Viola: Viola is an early WWW client developed for XWindows, the Unix platform, by O'Reilly & Associates. Connect to **ftp://ftp.ora.com/pub/www/viola/** to download Viola; get the README file for more information about the program.

URLs: The Keys to the WWW

Uniform Resource Locators (URLs) are the addressing system of the WWW. They are as fundamental to the Web as hypertext. The protocol was developed to allow the WWW to access any information currently available on the Internet, not only HTML documents but also files available through FTP, Gopher, Telnet, and Usenet. The addressing system is designed to incorporate future developments in Internet technology as well. If you understand how a URL breaks down into its composite parts, you can navigate anywhere on the WWW.

A URL is the network-wide address of any document you can read with a WWW client. A URL can describe any file on the Internet, even though different files may require different protocols to access them.

A URL allows a user, with the help of a client program, to retrieve a document from its server. The URL instructs the client program how to contact the server, tells the server to perform an operation and return the result, then directs the client program where to locate the document. All of these actions require just one action on the part of the user: typing in the URL or clicking on a link. The rest of the process is invisible to the user.

Dissecting a URL

A URL consists of three distinct parts. All parts of a URL must be present for the client program to communicate effectively with the server that the URL addresses. Here is an example of a typical URL (the URL for the author's personal home page):

http://www.vmedia.com/shannon/shannon.html

The first part of the URL is called the protocol. It is always followed by a colon (:) and usually by two slashes (//), although that varies depending on the type of protocol being employed. The URL can address a number of different protocols, which can be thought of as aliases for different tools on the Internet. The one above, *http*, stands for HyperText Transfer Protocol, and the documents it addresses are the HTML documents typically associated with the WWW. All of the sites reviewed in this book are accessed with HTTP protocols because it is the native language of the WWW.

Another protocol is *gopher*, which addresses information provided by Gopher servers. The following Gopher URL would take you to the top level of the Gopher server called the Internet Wiretap:

gopher://wiretap.spies.com/

Gopher was developed at the University of Minnesota prior to the WWW. It does not supply styled text, such as italics or bold, and it does not support embedded hyperlinks. Gopher information is always served in a menu format, with file texts located on directory trees.

The protocol for File Transfer Protocol (FTP) is either *ftp* or *file*. This refers to any files available in FTP archives. The protocol *file*, followed by three slashes (///), can also be used to specify local files on your personal computer. The following FTP URL accesses the top directory of NCSA's anonymous FTP server:

ftp://ftp.ncsa.uiuc.edu/

The Telnet protocol instructs the WWW client to connect directly to another machine. It is expressed as *telnet*. For example, to telnet to the University of Kansas, you would enter the URL:

telnet://ukanaix.cc.ukans.edu/

The Usenet protocol enables the client to access a Usenet newsgroup directory and read posted articles. It is expressed as *news*, without the two slashes. To read the newsgroup *alt.hypertext*, for example, you would enter the URL:

news:alt.hypertext

The second part of the address refers to the server that contains the information you are trying to access, the home of the document.

Consider the URL for my home page:

http://www.vmedia.com/shannon/shannon.html

The server here is *www.vmedia.com*, the part between the double slash and the first single slash. The actual name of the server computer is *www*; it is located at *vmedia* or Ventana Media; and the type of connection is a commercial one, *com*. Another example of a server's URL is **http://sunsite.unc.edu**, the University of North Carolina's WWW server. The name of the server is *sunsite*; it is located at *unc* or the University of North Carolina; and it is an educational, or *edu*, connection. The number of slashes after the colon is determined by the type of access protocol used. Generally, two slashes indicate that the part that follows is a machine name (which is why Usenet URLs do not have slashes).

Often, the protocol and the server address are all you need to access that server. For example, if you entered the URL, **http://sunsite.unc.edu/**, your WWW client would access the top page for SunSITE's WWW server. Then you could follow links from page to page to access the documents you wanted to see.

The third part of the address is the full pathname of the file that you are trying to access. This includes not only the document name but also the names of every directory it sits in. Look at my home page URL again:

http://www.vmedia.com/shannon/shannon.html

Everything after the first single slash is the pathname of the file. The file itself is located in a directory, *shannon*, found in the main Ventana Media directory. The name of the file is *shannon.html*. The part following the period indicates what kind of file it is. This file is written in hypertext, so it is an HTML file. A plain text file would have the extension *.txt*, and a graphic would probably have the extension *.gif* or *.jpg*.

URLs have to be entered exactly as they are named. Uppercase, lowercase, separating slashes, and numbers cannot be ignored. Also, many filenames contain hyphens (-), underscores (_), or tildes (~), which must be entered. If the URL is not entered exactly as named, your WWW client returns an error message when you try to access it.

Once you understand what the different elements of a URL refer to, navigating the WWW becomes transparent. You can tell what type of information you are accessing (FTP, HTML, or Gopher, for example), where that information is located, and what the filename is. Understanding this turns URLs from complex conglomerations of letters, numbers, and slashes into addresses as easy to grasp as postal addresses with post office boxes, city names, and zip codes.

The Best of the Web

Want to know where the absolute best of the WWW can be found? The Best of the Web, a competition originated in 1994 by Brandon Plewe at the State University of New York at Buffalo, is like the Oscars of the World Wide Web. The nominees are those sites that best demonstrate the quality, versatility, and power of the WWW. The awards were selected in a two-week voting period, open to the entire WWW population. The first round of winners was announced at the International W3 Conference held in Geneva on May 26, 1994. This site also includes the Web Hall of Fame, which honors important overall contributors to the WWW. Other categories include the following: Best Overall Site, won by NCSA; Best Entertainment Site, won by the Sports Information Server; Best Navigational Aid, won by the WWW Worm; and Best Document Design, won by Travels With Samantha. All of these sites are reviewed later in this book. To check out the Best of the Web winners yourself, enter the URL: http://wings.buffalo.edu/contest/.

World Wide Web Must-Sees

It's not easy to narrow down the vast resources of the WWW to a top thirty (or even a top hundred) sites. But because the WWW is so huge, it can be difficult for new users to judge just what sites are worth their time. That's why I've put together the following list of "must-sees" on any Web tour. These thirty sites, five from each of the following sections of listings, have established themselves as landmarks on the

WWW. No Web tour would be complete without a stop at each one of them. If you want a quick introductory tour to the WWW, let these sites be your guide—you won't go wrong.

A Tourist Expedition to Antarctica: This diary of a trip to Antarctica, told in text, photographs, and audio recordings, is a prime example of what hypermedia publishing can be.
http://http2.sils.umich.edu/Antarctica/Story.html

City.Net: Enter the most comprehensive guide on the Internet for destinations around the world, with travel, entertainment, business, and government information on thousands of worldwide cities.
http://www.city.net/

The White House: Get the lowdown on the executive branch of government through this interactive citizen's handbook, loaded with fun graphics and free White House information.
http://www.whitehouse.gov/

Friends & Partners: This site joins the peoples and societies of the United States and Russia to create a mega-educational resource on both countries, truly demonstrating the power of the Internet to link different cultures.
http://solar.rtd.utk.edu/friends/home.html

Travels With Samantha: Tour North America, visiting interesting places and meeting fascinating people, through this hypermedia exhibit, completely illustrated with full-color photographs.
http://www-swiss.ai.mit.edu/samantha/travels-with-samantha.html

OTIS Project: Visit a meeting place for artists on the Web, where you can view a variety of exhibits of original art or create collaborative pieces with other Internet artists.
http://sunsite.unc.edu/otis/otis.html

The WebMuseum: Wander through the endless galleries of the Web's most famous art museum, viewing great works of art, sampling classical music, or taking a guided tour of Paris.
http://sunsite.unc.edu/louvre/net/

American Memory: A primary source of American culture and history materials, this site presents multimedia exhibits that make for a fun way to learn history.
http://rs6.loc.gov/amhome.html

Internet Public Library: This huge online library is the primary source for online literature and reference. It even has a fun, interactive kids' library. It also provides a virtual meeting place and exhibits from Internet users.
http://ipl.sils.umich.edu/

The English-Server: A gigantic reference center, this site collects, organizes, and distributes texts on an unimaginable variety of subjects, from art to film and television, from philosophy to law and government.
http://english-server.hss.cmu.edu/

The Nine Planets: Take a virtual tour of the solar system through this resource, incorporating tons of photographs, videos, audio files, and scientific information about the nine planets, their moons, and other bodies in our solar system.
http://seds.lpl.arizona.edu/nineplanets/nineplanets/nineplanets.html

Global Network Navigator: A principal source of Internet news and resources, the Global Network Navigator has mega-resource centers, Internet guides, and fun magazines.
http://nearnet.gnn.com/gnn/gnn.html

University of California Museum of Paleontology: View dinosaur fossils, follow the course of geologic time or learn about the theory of evolution at this huge multimedia museum.
http://ucmp1.berkeley.edu/welcome.html

JASON Project: Take an electronic field trip with a scientific expedition to rain forests, volcanoes, and marine habitats using this unique, multimedia, educational resource.
http://seawifs.gsfc.nasa.gov/JASON.html

Electronic Zoo: Organized in an easy-to-use, graphical format, this "zoo" helps you connect to all kinds of Internet resources on all kinds of animals. This huge site also covers veterinary medicine, as well as animals from cats to dogs to rodents to invertebrates.
http://netvet.wustl.edu/e-zoo.htm

Doctor Fun: You'll laugh at the Web's most famous daily cartoon, read with the morning coffee by millions of Internet users worldwide.
http://www.unitedmedia.com/comics/drfun/

HotWired: This multimedia magazine pushes the boundaries of electronic publishing, providing gossip, news, and interactive talk forums for readers.
http://www.wired.com/

Internet Movie Database: A vast database of movie trivia allows you to search interactively for any information you desire about the movies, so you can finally answer that question, "What else has he been in?"
http://www.cm.cf.ac.uk/Movies/

Internet Underground Music Archive: Sample the latest in all kinds of music, from indie rock to folk to instrumental jazz to Japanese experimental noise, at the WWW's largest free hi-fi music collection.
http://www.iuma.com/

World Wide Web of Sports: Get the latest scores, schedules, news, and video highlights on any major sport through this mega-resource that satisfies even the most avid fan.
http://www.tns.lcs.mit.edu/cgi-bin/sports/

Internet Business Center: This helpful resource points you toward the latest business news, hot commercial Web sites, and other handy nuggets of information related to doing business online.
http://www.tig.com/IBC/

Ventana Online: Need computer books or software, some help with a Ventana product or just want to see the "nifty site of the week"? Then visit Ventana's graphical, interactive catalog that is as much fun to browse as it is easy to use.
http://www.vmedia.com/

CareerMosaic: Browse job openings, post your resume, or get some handy tips on making your job search easier with this giant employment resource.
http://www.careermosaic.com/

CDnow!: One of the Internet's largest music resources, here you can shop for over 140,000 CDs, cassettes, and vinyl, plus tap into a free All-Music Guide, the world's largest music database project.
http://cdnow.com/

Downtown Anywhere: More than just an online shopping mall, in this "virtual city" you'll find stores, services, and public resources to suit any need.
http://www.awa.com/

Disney Pictures Home Page: Virtual "theaters" give you sneak peeks at previews and production processes of current and upcoming Disney movies, plus lots of activities, sound files, and video clips from old favorites.
http://www.disney.com/

FishNet: This cool online hangout is for teens only. Here you can read an electronic magazine, talk with other teens online, and find information about the subjects teens are most interested in.
http://www.jayi.com/jayi/

KidsCom: Visit a communications playground for kids ages 8 to 14. Activities include online games, story writing, contests, and places to talk with other kids on the Internet. Restricted to kids only.
http://www.kidscom.com/

Children's Literature Web Guide: This well-organized site is chock full of Internet resources related to books for children and young adults, including children's book events, online children's stories, home pages for favorite authors and characters, book awards, and must-reads.

http://www.ucalgary.ca/~dkbrown/index.html

Uncle Bob's Kids Pages: A huge guide to Internet resources for kids and young-at-heart adults, this page has everything. Sports, ASCII art, games, space, bizarre sites—it's all here.

http://gagme.wwa.com/~boba/kids.html

Moving On

The following sections review some of the most interesting and diverse examples of what the WWW has to offer. Many of the sites you visit will lead you to other exotic places as links there strike your interest. The sites reviewed here offer interesting jumping-off places into the WWW, as well as reliable pages packed with information to return to again and again. You can either flip to a subject you're interested in or browse through the book to get an overall view of the WWW.

Here's how to use the listings. A listing begins with the title of the Web page and the WWW address for the site. The review of the site follows, describing the WWW site, hitting the highlights, and outlining what makes the site stand out as a model of hypermedia design. Beneath the review is contact information for the site, including the server at which the site is physically located, the person or organization that publishes the information and maintains the site, with e-mail addresses (if available) so you can contact the maintainer directly if you wish. Note that many sites provide a "feedback form," so that you can e-mail the maintainer directly from the site. To get to the site, simply type the URL listed under the name of the page into the Open URL box on Netscape, and you're on your way.

As an alternative, you can use the included CD-ROM to follow hyperlinks directly through Netscape to the reviewed site on the Internet. Look in Appendix C for full instructions on how to use this interactive tool.

While the sites listed in this book are chosen because they are some of the best the WWW has to offer, these listings are not meant to be comprehensive. The WWW is in a constant state of flux, and new sites come online every day. Old sites fade away, and by the time you read this book, some may no longer exist or the URL may have changed. Check the online version of this book at the Ventana Visitor's Center (available only to purchasers of the book) for up-to-date listings and reviews of new sites. See Appendix A for more information about the online version. In the meantime, go ahead and dive into the WWW—you're ready to surf the Net.

References

Berners-Lee, Tim, editor. Uniform Resource Locators. **http://www.w3.org/hypertext/WWW/Addressing/URL/Overview.html**

Berners-Lee, Tim. WorldWide Web Seminar. **http://www.w3.org/hypertext/WWW/Talks/General.html**

Blythe, Garrett, Lou Montulli, Michael Grobe, and Stephen Ware. Lynx User's Guide version 2.3. **http://www.cc.ukans.edu/lynx_help/Lynx_users_guide.html**

Boutell, Thomas. World Wide Web Frequently Asked Questions. **http://sunsite.unc.edu/boutell/faq/www_faq.html**

CERN. World Wide Web Client Software Products. **http://www.w3.org/hypertext/WWW/clients.html**

CERN. World Wide Web Initiative. **http://www.w3.org/hypertext/WWW/TheProject.html**

CERN. World Wide Web: Summary. **http://www.w3.org/hypertext/WWW/Summary.html**

Cornell Law School. Cello Home Page. **http://www.law.cornell.edu/cello/cellotop.html**

EINet. MacWeb Home Page. **http://galaxy.einet.net/EINet/MacWeb/MacWebHome.html**

EINet. WinWeb Home Page. **http://galaxy.einet.net/EINet/WinWeb/WinWebHome.html**

Macintosh Devlopment Team, NCSA. NCSA Mosaic for Macintosh User's Guide. **http://www.ncsa.uiuc.edu/SDG/Software/MacMosaic/MacMosa.0.html**

Macintosh Development Team, NCSA. NCSA Mosaic Home Page for Macintosh. **http://www.ncsa.uiuc.edu/SDG/Software/MacMosaic/ MacMosaicHome.html**

NCSA. Mosaic for Microsoft Windows Home Page. **http:// www.ncsa.uiuc.edu/SDG/Software/WinMosaic/Homepage.html**

NCSA. NCSA Mosaic Copyright. **http://www.ncsa.uiuc.edu/SDG/ Software/Mosaic/Docs/copyright.html**

NCSA. NCSA Mosaic for the XWindows System User's Guide. **http:// www.ncsa.uiuc.edu/SDG/Software/Mosaic/Docs/UserGuide/ XMosaic.0.html**

Netscape Communications Corporation. The Online Handbook for Netscape Navigator. **http://home.netscape.com/home/1.1/ online-manual.html**

Netscape Communications Corporation. Questions About Netscape Navigator. **http://home.netscape.com/home/faq.html**

Netscape Communications Corporation. Welcome to Netscape Navigator. **http://home.netscape.com/home/welcome.html**

University of Nevada at Las Vegas. Chimera Home Page. **http:// www.unlv.edu/chimera/**

Section II

See the World

Geographical, Cultural & Travel Sites

Section II
See the World: Geographical, Cultural & Travel Sites

With only the World Wide Web and a mouse as transportation, the armchair tourist can journey to exotic locations all over the globe. The multimedia nature of the WWW makes electronic travel the next best thing to being there—you can see pictures of faraway places, watch videos of foreign events, and listen to the music of other cultures. Countries, states, cities, and regions have taken advantage of the Web to publicize themselves. If you are planning a trip, the WWW can also be your own personal travel agency, providing access to many tourist guides and travel services.

This section reviews some of the best destinations on the Web, from Antarctica to the North Pole, Slovakia to the White House. You'll begin your around-the-world journey in Africa and then tour all of the continents, stopping at faraway countries, cosmopolitan cities, and exotic tourist locations. You'll also find sites to help you get around, from maps to travel agencies. And you'll explore governments in the United States and throughout the world. Finally, you'll visit many different cultures, from Native Americans to a global organization of women. Every place has something new and different to offer, so don't overlook a less popular destination. You may be surprised at what you find.

Buckle your seat belts and return your trays to the upright position—you're about to see the world!

Africa & the Middle East

African Art

http://www.lib.virginia.edu/dic/exhib/93.ray.aa/African.html

This electronic exhibition catalog introduces you to the history, beauty, and meaning of African art. Displaying the finest pieces in the African art collection at the Bayly Art Museum of the University of Virginia, the online exhibit teaches you African aesthetic principles. The exhibition consists of thumbnail photographs with short descriptions of each piece; click on the thumbnail for a larger view. The fourteen pieces in the online exhibit include masks, headdresses, and statues. One highlight is an exhibition of the beautifully decorated pulleys that are used in Africa to hold heddles onto looms. As you progress through the exhibit, text commentary explains the purpose and meaning of each piece.

Contact: Bayly Art Museum, Christie D. Stephenson, University of Virginia Libraries, *cds2e@virginia.edu*

African National Congress

http://www.anc.org.za/

The African National Congress (ANC) is the major political party in South Africa's new government of national unity. At the ANC's Web site, you can look up the mailing addresses for President Mandela, members of parliament, and other ANC leaders. Get information about the ANC, including the party's structure, relevant historical documents, maps, photographs and symbols, and publications like the *Constitution News*. You'll also find the latest news from South Africa. Access a database of South African governmental information, including governmental structure, speeches, legislation, and national anthems. Follow local government elections and connect to other South African Web sites and political sites. Learn about other South African political organizations, such as the Congress of South African Trade Unions and the Communist Party in South Africa. Come to this site first for complete South African governmental information under the new regime.

Contact: African National Congress, *info@anc.org.za*

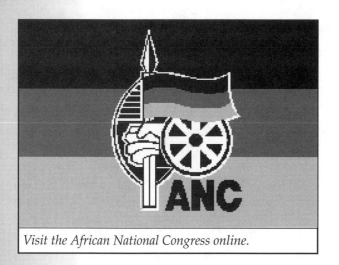

Visit the African National Congress online.

Ethiopia: A Country Study

http://rs6.loc.gov/et_00_00.html

This is a true hypertext textbook, set up like a printed book with a table of contents, sections, and chapters. The table of contents links directly to the chapters, giving the reader the choice of moving straight through the text or jumping directly to particular sections. You can also search the entire text of the book using keywords, accessing immediately a list of section titles that contain the keyword in order of relevance. This feature is similar to an index in traditional books but is more comprehensive and flexible than a printed index would be. Intended to be a "handbook" of information about Ethiopia, this site covers the history, society, economy, government, and military of the country, and the text is updated regularly. The Ethiopia "book" is the first of a series of hypertext country studies to be published on the WWW by the Library of Congress; look for more to follow.

Contact: American Memory Collection, Library of Congress, *lcweb@loc.gov*

The Jerusalem Mosaic

http://www1.huji.ac.il/jeru/jerusalem.html

Take a tour of one of the world's most venerated cities. Start in the Main Hall, where text, song, and photographs introduce you to Jerusalem. Then enter one of four "gates," each of which opens onto a pictorial tour of a different aspect of the culture, history, and people of Jerusalem. When you enter a gate, you are greeted by a poetic introduction or a quote from a traveler, as well as a text introduction describing what the gate represents. The first is the Faces Of Jerusalem gate, a collection of photographs of the ethnic and cultural mix of people who call Jerusalem home. The second is the Maps Of Jerusalem gate, a collection of maps made through the ages by people with differing emotional, spiritual, and political attitudes toward Jerusalem. You can even view maps created before the advent of printing. The third is the Views Of Jerusalem gate, where you can see the city from all angles, including general views, views of the old city, and views of the new city. Each picture, taken by a different photographer, portrays Jerusalem in a unique perspective. The final gate is the Painting Of Jerusalem gate, which leads to twenty "steps." Atop each step is a painting of Jerusalem by a different artist with a unique outlook on the city. From here, you can also get general information about the city, find out important events in the history of Jerusalem, and take a city tour.

Contact: Dana Barnes and Dudu Rashty, Hebrew University of Jerusalem, *Rashty@WWW.HUJI.AC.IL*

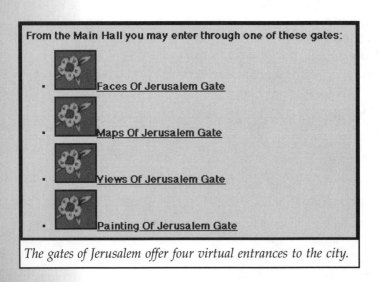

From the Main Hall you may enter through one of these gates:

- Faces Of Jerusalem Gate
- Maps Of Jerusalem Gate
- Views Of Jerusalem Gate
- Painting Of Jerusalem Gate

The gates of Jerusalem offer four virtual entrances to the city.

South Africa

http://osprey.unisa.ac.za/0/docs/south-africa.html

Learn all about South Africa using the interactive map at this site. Click on any portion of the map to travel to different regions of the country, accessing photographs and regional information. Travel all around to learn facts and figures about the country and the peoples of South Africa, both the native and Afrikaner cultures. Access a database of tourist attractions and accommodations. Tap into a medical web, including a medical service for travelers to the country. To help plan your jaunt in South Africa, access current weather conditions through a satellite image that is updated every thirty minutes.

Contact: Aleksandar Radovanovic, Department of Computer Science and Information Systems, University of South Africa, *web@osprey.unisa.ac.za*

**For more information on Africa and
the Middle East, visit these sites:**

Abyssinia Region

http://www.cs.indiana.edu/hyplan/dmulholl/exodus.html

Includes many links to Africa-related sites, including news sites, Net services, people, groups, and other information.

Africa on CharmNet

http://www.charm.net/~compro/africa.html

Includes links to people, news, events, religions, and art of Africa. This site is still under construction, but it has a nice design and is a good starting place without an overwhelming amount of links.

Africa Page

http://kahn.interaccess.com/intelweb/africa.html

Includes links to related news pages, country information, and maps, plus other regions.

African Flags

http://www.adfa.oz.au/CS/flg/col/R-Africa.html

Includes flags and current names, plus other information about African nations.

African Information Center

http://darkwing.uoregon.edu/~karimi/AIC.html

Includes country flags, country information, and "The African Story" as well as some African American links and resources.

African Links on the Web

http://www.cis.yale.edu/swahili/afrilink.html

Nice list of Africa-related links, including maps, flags, archives, and African studies links. Also has links organized by country.

Kwanzaa Information Center

http://www.melanet.com/melanet/kwanzaa/kwanzaa.html

Contains the history and other information about the African holiday Kwanzaa.

Maps, Pictures and Culture of Middle East Countries

http://menic.utexas.edu/menic/subject/culture.html

Includes information about maps, language, and culture—even recipes.

Mennonite Central Committee Page on Africa

http://www.mennonitecc.ca/mcc/regions/africa.html

Look up news articles and resources by individual country or the region as a whole. Useful for news, but not necessarily for history and culture. The site also has links to different regions in the world for futher information.

Middle East

http://kahn.interaccess.com/intelweb/mideast.html

Middle East resources by country; includes a mailing list, news services, and general categorical links.

Travel World's Guide to the Middle East

http://www.theworld.com/travel/PLACES/MIDDLEE/
CONTNENT.HTM

Commercial travel service, but the Web page lists maps, airlines, and "things to do in the Middle East." Links to individual country information as well. Quite a good page, actually.

Antarctic & Arctic Regions

Byrd Polar Research Center

http://www-bprc.mps.ohio-state.edu/

The Byrd Polar Research Center is a leader in polar and alpine research; learn all about the center at its jam-packed Web site. Look at research imagery of Greenland and the Antarctic. You can also access research groups like the Polar Meteorology Group and the Remote Sensing Laboratory. Polar and weather pointers take you to interesting sites all over the Web. Be sure to play with the XEarth server before you leave; this is a program that lets you create computer images of the earth by entering variables into an online form.

Contact: Tim Davis, Byrd Polar Research Center,
tim@polarmet1.mps.ohio-state.edu

Arctic Adventours

http://www.oslonett.no/html/adv/AA/AA.html

Arctic Adventours is a Norwegian travel company that specializes in expeditions to the Arctic area. At this WWW site, you can read about tour packages and even book reservations. Or create your own expeditions. Sail aboard the yacht *Arctic Explorer* to areas of the Arctic that are inaccessible by other means. Many different expeditions are available, such as sail and ski, whale safaris, fishing, and definitely sightseeing. All expeditions are described in detail, and hundreds of photographs enliven the descriptions. The site provides the latest information available about destinations, prices, and availability. After reading through the expedition descriptions, use an interactive form to request more information or book your trip.

Contact: Arctic Adventours, Oslonett, *arcadv@oslonett.no*

After seeing this guy at Arctic Adventours, you won't be able to resist booking a trip to the Arctic.

Gateway to Antarctica

http://icair.iac.org.nz/

The Gateway to Antarctica is a visitor's introduction to Antarctica and its environment. An opening image map links to many different subject areas, including news, education, science, environment, history, and tourism. Use a clickable map and a catalog of digital map data to learn about the Ross Sea area. Other exciting activities include learning how to rent a helicopter to Antarctica, viewing floor plans of Scott Base, and accessing daily weather reports. Learn about the Antarctic Treaty and the Protocol on Environmental Protection. Order educational resources, including posters, postcards, books, and videos, directly through e-mail at the site. You can request a catalog that features forget to pick up a brochure for Southern Heritage Expeditions so you can take your own expedition to Antarctica.

Contact: Dean Ashby, International Centre for Antarctic Information and Research, *ashby@icair.iac.org.nz*

New South Polar Times

http://www.deakin.edu.au/edu/MSEE/GENII/NSPT/
NSPThomePage.html

The New South Polar Times is a bi-weekly newsletter written by the staff at the Amundsen-Scott South Pole Station in Antarctica. Every issue discusses life at the research station, scientific research going on there, and Antarctica in general. At the site, you can read current and back issues or access polar science reports, including ones on meteorology, ozone measurements, the climate, and astronomical events. Learn a little history by reading about the first expeditions to Antarctica and other peoples' visits there in their own words, a collection of stories you won't find in history books. From the site, you can submit questions about the South Pole; some will be answered in the newsletter. You can also submit poetry, stories, articles, art, or puzzles to be published on the server. Learn more by following links to other Antarctica resources. Although the site is under development, you'll find a lot of information about the South Pole here.

Contact: Katie Wallet, Deakin University, *kwallet@pen.k12.va.us*

International Arctic Project

http://scholastic.com/public/Network/IAP/IAP-Home.html

On March 7, 1995, veteran explorer, author, and educator Will Steger and his international team of explorers and scientists began a four-month trek across 2,000 miles on an expedition to the North Pole. Their mission was to raise awareness of the global importance of the Arctic. This historic journey was the first surface crossing of the Arctic Ocean by dogsled in a single season and the first expedition use of canoe-sleds. You can see a map of the route and read a project overview, including information about diet, clothing, dogs, gear, and supplies. You can also access daily reports, organized by week, of the expedition's progress as it happened, including reports of the team's position, the temperature and wind speed, and events along the way. Look at photographs and read biographies of the members of the expedition, or visit a photo gallery related to the project. *Scholastic News* articles are linked in to give more background information about the Arctic. This site was also an experiment in education, as students worldwide studied the Arctic and interacted with team members in conjunction with the expedition.

Contact: Scholastic Network, Shaklee Corporation and the International Arctic Project, *arcproject@aol.com*

Specially trained dogs pull a team of explorers across the North Pole.

A Tourist Expedition to Antarctica

http://http2.sils.umich.edu/Antarctica/Story.html

This hypermedia exhibit is a travelog of a cruise to Antarctica, presented as a combination of journal entries and full-color photographs. The site opens with a beautiful photograph of the approach to Ross Sea and some introductory material. The exhibit consists of pre-cruise materials from Orient Lines (who sponsored the expedition), the author's personal journal entries and photographs, and audio recordings of lectures presented by eminent explorers, biologists, and others during the cruise. First, tour the cruise ship by viewing deck plans. Then proceed through the fully hyperlinked journal entries. You can search the entries for something in particular or choose a chronological listing with a short description of each entry, so that you can jump directly to what interests you. A geographically organized list links to the various destinations of the cruise. A highlights section lists the best parts of the trip, including landings at points of interest and unexpected events along the way. Another list covers the lectures; eventually, recorded versions will be linked in. This unique organizational style takes full advantage of hypertext to allow for many ways to move through the published information.

Contact: Lee Liming, School of Information and Library Studies, University of Michigan, *Lee.Liming@umich.edu*

You'll feel like you've been transported to Antarctica by photographs like this one. (Copyright 1994 University of Michigan.)

For more information about Antarctic and
Arctic regions, visit these sites:

Alfred-Wegener Institute

http://www.awi-bremerhaven.de/

This is a center for polar and marine research. Visit a research station in the Antarctic and access a hydrographic atlas of the southern ocean.

Arctic Circle

http://www.lib.uconn.edu/ArcticCircle/

Includes information on history and culture as well as natural resources and other links. Very nice design. Special report on national wildlife refuge.

Live from Antarctica Project

http://quest.arc.nasa.gov/livefrom/livefrom.html

Includes photos of Antarctica, teacher's resources, field journals, weekly newsletters, a bibliography, and links to other pages. Possibly very useful for information on Antarctica.

The Polar Regions Homepage

http://www.stud.unit.no/~sveinw/arctic/

Includes links to information on both polar regions, including wildlife, travel, and a polar newsletter. Also ranked in the top 5 percent of Web sites. Nice design.

World Wide Wally

http://www2.gol.com/users/wally/

Includes a scrapbook of a trip to Antarctica.

Asia

Asian Art

http://www.webart.com/asianart/index.html

This online gallery of Asian art features fine exhibits from private galleries, new or rare color publications, and new discoveries in Asian art. It offers a forum for the study and exhibition of arts from Asia. The fascinating exhibit, Early Tibetan Mandalas, features thirteen fine Tibetan paintings of mandalas, dating from the thirteenth to the sixteenth centuries. A Mongolian exhibit introduces you to the art of that mysterious region. The exhibit, Images of Faith, displays religious images from all over Asia. View displays of Laotian and Chinese textiles. Notes and articles enhance the educational experience. After browsing the gallery, you can chat about what you've seen with other visitors or connect to other online Asian art sources.

Contact: Ian and Andrew Alsop, Web Arts Publishing, *asianart@rt66.com*

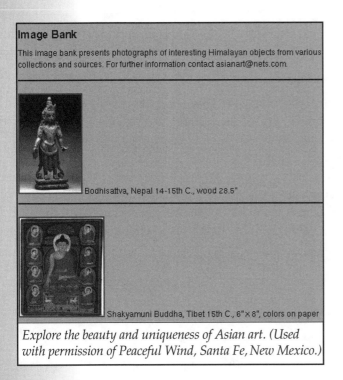

Image Bank

This image bank presents photographs of interesting Himalayan objects from various collections and sources. For further information contact asianart@nets.com.

Bodhisattva, Nepal 14-15th C., wood 28.5"

Shakyamuni Buddha, Tibet 15th C., 6"×8", colors on paper

Explore the beauty and uniqueness of Asian art. (Used with permission of Peaceful Wind, Santa Fe, New Mexico.)

Asian Studies

http://coombs.anu.edu.au/WWWVL-AsianStudies.html

This online library for Asian studies is part of the WWW Virtual Library, but this site is so complete that it is worth reviewing separately. The library documents leading information resources on the Internet for Asian studies. You can look up resources by region or country. Regions covered include the Middle East, all of Asia, Australia, New Zealand, and the South Pacific. The library links to online resources such as mailing lists, e-journals, infoservers in Asia, databases, and more. Locate business, academic, religious, language, environmental, social, arts, political, and geographical Internet resources for any Asian region. Many countries also have a separate library with even more pointers. You can use the library to study Asia from an academic or business viewpoint or to get a complete overview of any Asian country. No resource is overlooked in this very complete and well-organized site.

Contact: Coombs Computing Unit, Australian National University, Dr. T. Matthew Ciolek, *tmciolek@coombs.anu.edu.au*, and John A. Brubaker, *brubaker@e-mailhost.ait.ac.th*

Asia-Pacific Information

http://sunsite.sut.ac.jp/asia/

Tap into a huge library of resources about the Asia-Pacific region, including specific resources on India, Russia, South Korea, Japan, and China. You'll also discover many general Asian resources here. For each country, find images, general information, maps, FAQs, academic studies, and specifics, such as business practices, governmental policies, and technology. You can also connect to all the Internet servers in that country from this site. The Asia-Pacific information here is collected from all over the Internet, making a complete library at one site.

Contact: SunSITE Japan, *ftpadmin@SunSITE.sut.ac.jp*

The Beauty of India

http://www.cs.clemson.edu/~nandu/india.html

This personal home page provides general information about the world's second most populous country, including facts about India's population, languages, economy, religions, and history. One feature that makes this site stand out from many others is that the links are built into the text rather than listed in a menu format. Through these "context" links, you can connect to a variety of relevant Internet resources on India. For example, read the verses of the *Bhagavad Gita* or travel to the Zen WWW page. Did you know that the first percussion instrument was invented in India? Learn about Indian classical music, and check out audio archives of Hindi movie songs here. For tourists, a guide to India explains the philosophy of travel in India and gives tips about what to bring with you and what to buy when you're there. You can also see India in pictures, read a travelog by a recent visitor or check out adventure tours you can take. Don't leave India without sampling the cuisine through a collection of recipes.

Contact: Nandakumar Sankarian, Computer Science Department, Clemson University, *nandu@cs.clemson.edu*

A Brief Introduction to Penang

http://www.cs.usm.my/penang_island/tourist.html

This guide to the popular Malaysian tourist spot is arranged as one WWW page, with a hyperlinked table of contents at the top so that you can easily skip to the subject that most interests you. After reading each section, return to the table of contents through a link at the end of the section, and then jump to any other subject you want. Throughout, you can follow links to view full-screen photographs (there are no inline graphics). Highlights include full-color maps of Malaysia and Penang. The shopping section reveals where to buy Penang's local crafts, including batik, pewter, and pottery. The food section describes local dishes that should not be missed. Visit clan houses and places of worship through full-color photographs. This site is an example of what can be done in one WWW page instead of using interlinked, nested pages, so you have to download a trove of information only once.

Contact: G. C. Sodhy, University of Malaysia at Penang, *sodhy@cs.usm.my*

China Home Page

http://solar.rtd.utk.edu/~china/

This home page imparts mainly scientific, technological, and business information about China. It outlines the computer networks in China, contains links to Chinese research institutes and universities, and lists scientific conferences in China. But don't despair if none of this interests you—look under Chinese Regional Information to tour the various provinces and cities of China. Get inside information, such as what to see in Beijing, or visit the birthplace of Chairman Mao in Hunan. You can also visit Shanghai, Inner Mongolia, Tibet, and many other famous places within China, all without having to apply for a visa. Under Chinese Culture and Art, you'll find an art gallery and an archive of Chinese music. You can also learn about Chinese dialects and linguistics. Or get a daily report on scientific and cultural happenings in China.

Contact: Institute of High Energy Physics in Beijing and University of Tennessee at Knoxville, *webmaster@www.ihep.ac.cn*

China News Digest

http://www.cnd.org/

The China News Digest (CND) is a voluntary, nonprofit organization aimed at providing news and other information services to readers concerned about affairs relating to China. CND publications highlight recent Chinese news and information of interest. The InfoBase has information on important historic events, scenic pictures of the country, classic Chinese literature, and scholarly organizations. Get a catalog of Chinese software. You'll even find giant panda pages. Plus connect to other China home pages, general educational information, and seasonal news elsewhere on the Internet.

Contact: Chinese News Digest, *webmaster@cnd.org*

Himalayan Expeditions

http://lykos.netpart.com/che/

Craving adventure? Canadian Himalayan Expeditions offers an adventure-tours service, accessible through the WWW. Here you will find environmentally conscious adventure expeditions for small groups of travelers, free-form tours that specialize in venturing off the beaten track. Access summaries of all the adventure offerings, including tours in Nepal, India, and Pakistan, among other destinations. Go on a camping safari to Africa or see Everest in Hillary's footsteps. You can even customize your own adventure. Descriptions of tours include cost, grading (a system that indicates the level of difficulty of the tour through graphic icons), and detailed, day-by-day itineraries. You can't book a trip online, but the site tells you who to contact to reserve a tour.

Contact: Canadian Himalayan Expeditions, NetPartners, *webmaster@netpart.com*

Kulu-Zanskar-Ladakh Adventure

This trip explores two of the most spectacular and varied regions of the Indian Himalayas; the lush Kulu Valley, and the high desert plateau of Zanskar and Ladakh, known as "Little Tibet". Also included is time in Delhi and a visit to the Taj Mahal, for a comprehensive look at two very different central Asian societies: Hindu Northern India, and Buddhist Zanskar and Ladakh. 28 days total: 4 days in Kulu / Manali, 10-day Manali-Zanskar trek, 3-day Ladakh vehicle safari, 4 nights in Delhi, 1 night in Agra (Taj Mahal) 1 night in Jaipur.

Trip grading: Good rhythm.

Land Cost: CDN$2390 (including domestic airfare in India).

Customize your own adventure at the Himalayan Expeditions site.

Japanese Information

http://www.ntt.jp/japan/index.html

The Living Manual in Japan includes information on living or traveling in Japan, such as medical care, recreation, shopping, driving, and children's schools. Of special interest is the section on food, which has restaurant listings and explanations of Japanese cuisine. You'll also find tourist guides to several fun Japanese cities. Another highlight is the Traveler's Japanese Manual, which teaches essential expressions for traveling around Japan, using audio examples. A section of basic advice for tourists includes electronic "brochures" with titles like Your Traveling Companion—tips for budget travel and planning your trip—and Exploring Japan With Maps. Look here too for miscellaneous information about the country on geography, holidays, sports, government, law, the Internet, and news. There's even an interesting collection of Japanese proverbs.

Contact: Nippon Telephone and Telegraph, *www-admin@seraph.ntt.jp*

Indonesian Homepage

http://mawar.inn.bppt.go.id/

The home page for Indonesia publishes an enormous amount of information about the country, enhanced by lots of inline graphics. One of the best links is to the government information page, where you can learn about the Republic of Indonesia "at a glance." You'll find a background of Indonesian history, the proclamation of independence, the constitution of 1945, the national anthem, and an overview of governmental organization. Another good link is to the business page, with information on the Bank of Indonesia's current conversion rates, as well as links to companies in Indonesia. Click on an image map of Indonesia to get information about a particular region on the Cultural Life page. You can also connect to an Indonesian travel guide. Visit various universities and technological institutes from the education page. Finally, you can jump from here to other Indonesian home pages, such as the Indonesian Muslim Network page.

Contact: BPPT-DTEI Indonesia, *webmaster@inn.bppt.go.id,* Indonesian Homepage

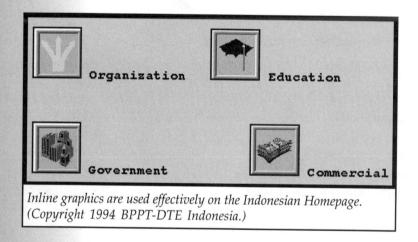

Inline graphics are used effectively on the Indonesian Homepage. (Copyright 1994 BPPT-DTE Indonesia.)

Korea

http://cair-archive.kaist.ac.kr/korea/index.html

Visit Korea through this information server. Find out what to do on a trip to Korea, such as annual events to attend and natural vistas to see. Travel around all of the country by clicking on regions on a huge image map. Take in Korea at a glance by learning facts about the population, government, history, religion, climate, and more. Get useful touring information or connect to network services available in Korea. You can even download Hangul software.

Contact: Center for Artificial Intelligence Research, *cair-tech@cair.kaist.ac.kr*

Online Guide to Bangladesh

http://camelot.cif.rochester.edu:80/users/outcast/tour/index.html

The Online Guide to Bangladesh provides comprehensive information about the country of interest both to tourists and to natives. For those who are returning home but don't want to lose touch with friends overseas, a list of organizations in Bangladesh providing Internet services is given. A section on the Bangladesh Internet Relay Chat (IRC) channel has links to documents on IRC chat and an interesting experimental gateway from the WWW to IRC in which you can capture a window of what is currently going on in the channel. Don't miss the detailed tour guide of Bangladesh, in which you can visit tourist attractions, archaeological sites, and monuments. In the tour guide, you can take in Bangladesh "at a glance" by linking to important factual information, as well as find out A Visitor's View of Dhaka, learn about Dhaka City sight-seeing tours, and find out currency regulations and visa requirements. Also at this site is a gallery of pictures of Bangladesh and links to home pages of various Bangladeshies resident on the WWW.

Contact: Rajib Rashid, University of Rochester Computer Interest Floor, *outcast@cif.rochester.edu*

Singapore Online Guide

http://www.ncb.gov.sg/sog/sog.html

Enhanced by humorous drawings on every page, this electronic guide is the way to visit Singapore. An innovative feature of the guide is the Interactive Tour Agent, which uses interactive forms to give you a customized tour of Singapore. Fill out a form with details about your trip, such as when you want to visit, how long you will stay, and what you are most interested in seeing. Choices include activities for children, shopping, food, entertainment, and places of worship, among many others. Send the form off, and within seconds you'll get back a personalized tour guide of Singapore, with a tour schedule that you can follow in the time frame of your visit. The guide, which you can also page through in its entirety, tells you what to expect from a trip to Singapore, advises on what to see and do, and gives useful information on subjects ranging from feasting to formalities. With photographs throughout, you'll learn facts about Singapore history, climate, religion, language, and people. If you're interested in one particular subject, you can search the guide for keywords, or get a list of the top ten articles to see where the most popular spots are. Also download images and maps of Singapore, or get a list of travelers' essentials.

Contact: Singapore Tourist Promotion Board, *chowwei@ncb.gov.sg*

Online Museum of Singapore Art and History

http://www.ncb.gov.sg/nhb/museum.html

If you want to learn more about Singapore's culture and history, this is just the place to visit. One of the finer examples of an online museum, this site includes many exhibits on Singapore art and history, each of them a pleasure to wander through. The Fall of Singapore in 1941 chronicles the surrender of Singapore to the Japanese in World War II. The multimedia exhibit includes a timeline of day-to-day events of the campaign, a textbook with an authoritative account of the war, a glossary with descriptions of key people and places, images of the Battle of Malaya, and radio broadcasts of wartime speeches. Pont des Arts: Nanyang Artists in Paris examines the influence of French study on Singapore artists. A large collection of color plates can by viewed by thumbnail or title; just click on the link to see the full-size version. The exhibit of historical postcards provides a visual study of the history of Singapore. Revisit the founding of the country in Raffles Revisited and learn all about the exploits of Sir Thomas Raffles. Don't leave out the exhibit of Balinese art, From Ritual to Romance. The art is spectacular, and text commentaries educate you on the important influence of Bali on Singapore art. You can search the entire museum to find just what you're looking for.

Contact: Digital Media Center, National Computer Board, *shaopin@ncb.gov.sg*

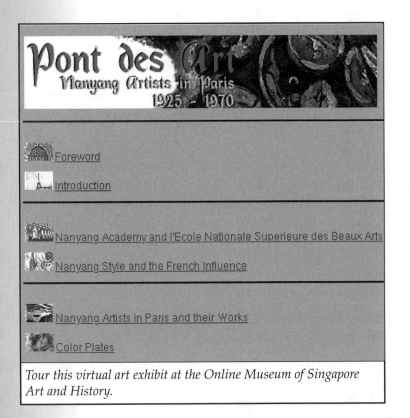

Tour this virtual art exhibit at the Online Museum of Singapore Art and History.

SunSITE Singapore

http://sunsite.nus.sg/

This SunSITE provides lots of Asian resources with a focus on Singapore and Southeast Asia. Access a trove of information about Singapore, including a general guide, a photo album, and links to many Singapore servers. Visit the countries of Southeast Asia through a clickable map, or connect to other important Asian information resources online. Find a general overview of each country and links to more in-depth information on many different subjects. You'll travel to countries like Brunei, Burma, Cambodia, Indonesia, Laos, Malaysia, the Philippines, Thailand, and Vietnam. You'll also find information on Asia-Pacific networking, marketing, business, research, and more.

Contact: SunSITE Singapore, *sunsite@sunsite.nus.sg*

Shangri-La Home Page

http://aleph0.clarku.edu/rajs/Shangri_La.html

Visit the tallest mountains in the world and explore a paradise on earth by virtually traveling to the Himalayas. Here you can learn about the Asian countries where the Himalayas are located, sail along the entire range with a list of more than 200 peaks, and see the vistas of the Himalayas from scenic spots. Climb the top ten highest mountains in the Himalayas, from K2 and Mt. Everest on down, by hopping along the mountain tops. Just click on any picture for an enlarged view of the mountain, and get facts by clicking on the mountain's name. You can also look at paintings of famous peaks and the best-ever picture of Everest taken from space. Get a view of the entire mountain range, and click on an individual peak to see a picture and to get information about it. You'll feel like an experienced explorer after scaling these impressive peaks.

Contact: Rajesh B. Shrestha, Clark University, Department of Mathematics and Computer Science, *rajs@aleph0.clarku.edu,*

Virtually scale Mt. Everest, the highest mountain on earth.

TravelASIA

http://silkroute.com/silkroute/travel/

TravelASIA strives to consolidate Internet information related to traveling in Asian countries into a well-organized and attractive online guide. So don't leave home without getting the Asia travel essentials from this site. Essential information you'll find here includes general facts about the climate, entry regulations, getting around, eating out, customs, where to stay, shopping, and other miscellaneous tidbits, such as currency, banking hours, post offices, and more for selected Asian countries. The guide is organized by country; some countries you'll find are Australia, China, Hong Kong, India, Japan, Nepal, the Philippines, Taiwan, Vietnam, and many more. When you visit each country, you'll get links and descriptions of information found elsewhere on the Internet. For instance, visiting India links you to the India home page, clickable maps, culture and life resources, essential travel information, a currency converter for the rupee, and tours of Indian cities. And if you click on Indonesia, you can go to hotel listings, a travel guide, an introduction to Indonesian music, an exhaustive list of the provinces, and Bali FastFacts. Every country has different resources, all of them useful. You can also connect to travel resources for all of Asia, such as a currency converter, the money abroad FAQ, a guide to hostelling, travel health information, Asia travel book lists, weather, and world maps. Send e-mail to the Online Coolie to suggest other relevant links.

Contact: Asia Online, Branch Mall, *coolie@silkroute.com*

A Visit to Nepal

http://enigma.phys.utk.edu/~syost/nepal.html

In the fall of 1994, Scott A. Yost, the author of this site, spent six weeks visiting Nepal. He made a twenty-day trek in the Everest region and climbed two 18,000-foot mountains. He also visited the Royal Chitwan National Park for elephant rides and jungle walks. At this unique site, you can read his travel journal, which contains a detailed account of his trip, and look through his photograph album. See the countryside and mountains of Nepal, plus pictures of elephants, rhinos, and crocodiles. Interactive trek maps provide an interesting way to follow along as Scott trekked across Nepal. Click the numbers on the maps to connect to the journal entry for that day; clicking anywhere else finds the photo taken closest to that selected point. You can also meet his guide, look at Scott's packing list and find out his expenses, and see what guidebooks he used—all useful if you're going to Nepal yourself.

Contact: Scott A. Yost, University of Tennessee at Knoxville, Department of Physics and Astronomy, *syost@enigma.phys.utk.edu*

For more information on Asia, visit these sites:

Asia Library

http://lib-221.lib.umich.edu/eindex.htm

The collections at the online Asia Library hold materials relating to the culture and history of China, Japan, and Korea. You'll also find news, electronic periodicals, and conference announcements relating to Asian countries.

Editions Didier Millet

http://www.ncb.gov.sg/EDM/

This is the page of an Asian publishing company that specializes in non-fiction books on Asian subjects. It includes a catalog and ordering information.

Japan Window

http://jw.stanford.edu/

Japan Window is a U.S.-Japan collaboration for Internet-based information about Japan. Here you'll find a directory of Japan resources, including a WWW server list, tourism information, a telephone directory, and an event calendar.

Southeast Asia Studies

http://garnet.berkeley.edu:4252/seascalinformation.html

Contains plenty of links to other servers and resources about Southeast Asia studies.

South Asia

http://library.adelaide.edu.au/information/socsci/southasia.html

This site outlines the available resources on South Asia at the University of Adelaine. Its contents are well organized, but don't expect to follow the links for more than one layer.

Thailand WWW Services

http://www.inet.co.th/thaiwww.html

Here you can link to information about the country of Thailand, including educational sites, a business directory, news and society, and cultural resources.

Australia & New Zealand

Australia National Botanic Gardens

http://155.187.10.12/anbg.html

Take a fascinating tour of Australian plants and wildlife through this site. There's something here for the browser, the serious botanist, and even the botanic gardens manager. Here you can read about plant identification, taxonomy, frogs, conservation, and birds, or access botanical and horticultural databases. Take a tour through the gardens, where you can read about eucalyptus on the Eucalyptus Lawn, or follow the Aboriginal Trail to learn how the Aborigines use plants. Get the latest issue of the garden newsletter, *In Flower This Week*, or search back issues for the past year. Another highlight is a page on common birds found in the gardens, accompanied by their calls. You can also see images of Australian flora and hear sounds of Australian wildlife. This is just a bare skimming of the large amount of wonderfully diverse information you will find here. If all of this information overwhelms you, don't worry—the whole site is searchable.

Contact: Jim Croft, Australia National Botanic Gardens, *jrc@anbg.gov.au*

Australian Water Resources

http://www.dwr.csiro.au/

Interested in Australia's key water and environmental issues? Find out ways to use and manage the country's most precious resources at this environmental site. The CSIRO Division of Water Resources is seeking ways to provide solutions to Australia's water and environmental problems. Read about the division's geography and structure. Find out about the division's research programs in water management, irrigation, and protecting rivers and wetlands. Learn about the consulting and research services the division offers, and even about the software and products it produces. You'll find scientific publications and project information sheets. There is also a photo gallery of Australia's water resources and links to related sites in Australia and around the world.

Contact: CSIRO Division of Water Resources, *Web@per.dwr.csiro.au*

Guide to Australia

http://www.csu.edu.au/education/australia.html

The goal of this site is eventually to grow into an online hypertext encyclopedia of Australia, and the editors have already progressed a good way toward that end. The number of subjects covered is immense, but don't miss some of these highlights. Learn the history of the national flag and other Australian flags, including the Aboriginal flag, with accompanying illustrations. Interactive and static maps of the continent provide geographic information about Australia. Download travel information, such as airline timetables and U.S. State Department notices. Telnet to the Bureau of Meteorology for the latest weather forecast. Even get earthquake reports or learn about vegetation monitoring from satellite. Other subjects covered include the states and territories, communications, culture, law, environment, and government. Although most of the links connect to external sources, the information is well-organized in one place, creating a handy, all-in-one guide.

Contact: Charles Sturt University, David Green, *David.Green@csu.edu.au*, and Jim Croft, *jrc@anbg.gov.au*, editors

Koalas are just one of the topics you'll find in the Guide to Australia.

Museum of New Zealand

http://hyperg.tu-graz.ac.at:80/DFOC637C/CNew_Zealand/

Learn the history, view the art, and experience the culture of New Zealand in this online museum. The site consists of information provided by the National Art Gallery of New Zealand and the National Museum and is intended as a gateway to New Zealand itself. When you first arrive, you will hear a musical piece as an introduction. The collections include a Maori culture exhibit, the natural environment, New Zealand history, and art exhibits. The Maori exhibit has audio, photos, and video depicting the native peoples of New Zealand. The natural environment exhibit, which introduces you to some of New Zealand's animal life, also has audio, photos, and video. The art collection displays several hallmarks of New Zealand art.

Contact: W. Schinn, Graz University

New Zealand/Aotearoa

http://nz.com/NZ/

This information database arms you with little-known facts about New Zealand—its society, culture, and geography. Greeted with a graphic of New Zealand's flag, you can click on the flag to learn its history. A unique format displays New Zealand news—click on the highlighted dates of a calendar to read the news for that day. Take an illustrated tour of New Zealand, starting at North Island and working your way down the country. Or click on an interactive map to visit any spot in New Zealand you wish. In addition, you'll find a lot of varied information about tourism and travel in New Zealand that is invaluable to anyone planning a trip. For instance, learn how to travel cheaply to New Zealand, or read about the popular sport of "tramping." Visit native New Zealanders, the Maori, by listening to audio clips of Maori speech. Tour New Zealand volcanoes, or learn about the national government. Also come here to meet other New Zealanders on the Web. This hodgepodge of information is fun to browse through, with new discoveries at the end of every link.

Contact: Akiko International, *akiko@nz.com*

For more information on Australia and New Zealand, visit these sites:

AusArts Home Page

http://www.anu.edu.au/ITA/AusArts/

Mainly links to other art schools in Australia, but includes online galleries and publications of Australian art.

Australia and New Zealand

http://www.webworkshop.com/gallery/gallery.html

Contains images from and about Australian and New Zealand artists.

The Australian Outback

http://matahari.tamu.edu/People/Ewen/Outback.html

Photos by Ewen Bell.

Down Under Travel

http://www.market.net/travel/anz/index.html

Information on places to go and what to do once you get there, with special emphasis on outdoor activities (walking tours, etc.). Of special interest—How to Travel Free.

Education Abroad Programs

http:/www.psu.edu/research/anzsc/ctr/edu.html

This page lists locations of study-abroad programs in Australia and New Zealand that are available through Penn State.

IIS Web Server Melbourne

http://webnet.com.au./koori/homekori.html

This site has information about many aspects of Australian Aboriginal life, culture, and history. The text is oriented toward the casual reader as much as the academician.

Makin' Waves Studios

http://cyberzine.org/html/Waves/wavepage.html

This site contains Australia-related sounds available for downloading and using on and off the computer.

Mountain Biking in New Zealand

http://www-swiss.ai.mit.edu/~philg/new-zealand/nz-mtn-bike.text

This page discusses the wonderful people, sights, biking opportunities, and prices in New Zealand. If this page doesn't get you to book a flight to New Zealand, nothing will.

National Library of Australia

http://www.nla.gov.au/

At this reference resource, you'll find information about Australian government, Internet guides, navigation assistance, and Australian electronic journals. You'll also find information about government's role in the Information Superhighway and links to other government sites all over the world.

New Zealand Government Home Page

http://www.govt.nz/

Might be more useful to check out the national history link. Lots of government-related links.

Penn State Australia New Zealand Studies

http://www.psu.edu/research/anzsc/

With links to information and other resources for Australia, New Zealand, and "Oceania." Most of the information pertains to their study abroad programs and this particular research institute, but this site might be useful if you are interested in these countries.

The "Worldwide" Australian & New Zealand Scientists Connection

http://flowcyt.cyto.purdue.edu/flowcyt/oz.html

This site is an attempt by Australian and New Zealand scientists to set up a dialogue with the worldwide scientific community. So far the site includes lists of scientific, industrial, and governmental connections; a short list of Australian scientific collequiums; and a long discussion of phone service changes in Australia.

Canada

The Atlas of Canadian Communities

http://ellesmere.ccm.emr.ca/ourhome/home.html

This unique digital atlas is a tool for Canadian students to show their perspectives of the communities in which they live. Written in both English and French, the atlas takes you on an exploration of some of the smaller communities in Canada. A clickable map lets you select from towns in Alberta, Manitoba, Saskatchewan, British Columbia, Ontario, the Yukon Territory, Newfoundland, Quebec, and Nova Scotia. You can even visit Indian reserves, take a look at towns like Moose Jaw, Owlseye, and Whitehorse and learn how they got their names. When you journey to a community, you'll find pictures, maps, and written information, including general facts, the best features of the community, and the aspects of the community that the students want to change. Read about plant and animal life, weather, places, people, and daily life in each community, even inspired poems, all written by students. Be sure to check out the pick of the month, and keep coming back for new entries that are added all the time.

Contact: National Atlas Information Service, *atlasinfo@nais.ccm.emr.ca*

Canada Open Government

http://info.ic.gc.ca/opengov/

This site is a pilot project to provide greater access to government through information networks. The site opens with a photograph of the Parliament Building and an audio clip of the national anthem. From there visit the main institutions of Canadian government. Look in on the Senate and House of Commons for an overview of their organization and function, or get contact information for each member. The section on the Supreme Court supplies recent rulings of the court, historical information, and home pages for individual judges. Important government documents are also published here, including NAFTA and GATT and documents relating to NATO and the United Nations. There are also links to various government departments, such as the National Library, health-care groups, and the Department of National Defense. You can also search for keywords across all Canadian government information on the Internet. The site even includes a Development Kit, which other governments can use to build their own online governmental information system, with software and instructions that can be downloaded from the site.

Contact: Communications Development Directorate, Industry Canada, *ogp@info.ic.gc.ca*

Canadian Business Index

http://cban.worldgate.edmonton.ab.ca/

This is Canada's premier online business directory and the place to come if you're looking for business in Canada. The Canadian business directory provides a listing of all kinds of Canadian companies and is searchable by keyword. You'll also find online "business cards" for individual Canadian consultants, a magazine about running an Internet information server, and even resources for job-seekers. From here, connect to many other international business sites.

Contact: Andrew Stanley-Jones, Canadian Business Advertising Network, *webmaster@cban.com*

Canadian Heritage Information Network

http://www.chin.gc.ca/

The Canadian Heritage Information Network (CHIN) provides services for museums, libraries, and other heritage institutions in Canada. Find out more about CHIN's services in the online brochure, or catch up on recent developments in the latest issue of the newsletter. The network provides many databases on the humanities, art, architecture, and heritage of Canada. There is a natural sciences database and there are Canadian Society of Zoologists' collections. Make a survey of Canadian newspapers, learn about Canadian artists, and take a tour of national archaeological sites. From this site, you can also access the Conservation Information Network, databases for the conservation community. Check out multimedia heritage projects, such as Canada's Visual History or Charting a New World. You can also explore other sites of interest in Canadian heritage from here.

Contact: Canadian Heritage Information Network, *WebMaster@www.chin.gc.ca*

Environment Canada

http://www.doe.ca/envhome.html

What: Drive down the "green lane" on the Information Superhighway at Environment Canada. Here you can read about the organization, environmental acts administered, and programs to protect and conserve Canada's environment. Learn all about Canada's environment, including endangered species, pollution, water quality, and more. Explore news, actions, speeches, and issues in recent environmental events, such as climate change, the Great Lakes, wildlife, and what you can do for the environment. You can also check out weather services or visit the Minister of the Environment here.

Contact: Environment Canada, *stpierrec@ncrsv2.am.doe.ca*

Canadian Museum of Civilization

http://www.cmcc.muse.digital.ca/cmc/cmceng/welcmeng.html

Wander through this unique museum collection to view artifacts of historic and cultural significance that help define Canada's national heritage. An interactive floor plan lets you tour the virtual galleries housing a mix of permanent and changing exhibits. A large portion of the museum is devoted to the study of Canada's first peoples—their history, cultural identities, artistic expression, and traditional and contemporary ways of life. Another floor of the museum re-creates in the Canada Hall the sights and sounds of the country's past, beginning with the arrival of Norse explorers. Other galleries to visit include the Arts and Traditions Hall, the Indian and Inuit Art Gallery, the Children's Museum, and the National Postal Museum. Also, browse a cyber-boutique at the Museum Marketplace. French and English versions of the museum are available; switch back and forth with the push of a button.

Contact: Digital Equipment of Canada, Ltd. and Canadian Museum of Civilization, *alsford@muse.cmc.doc.ca*

Totem pole on display in the Grand Hall of the museum.

National Library of Canada

http://www.nlc-bnc.ca/index.htm

The National Library of Canada gathers, preserves, and promotes Canada's published heritage. From the library's Web site, you can access lots of resources to learn about Canada's history, literature, and culture. A virtual tour of the library points out features of the building and stops at interesting art and architecture features. Then go back to the front lobby to read the latest annual report of the library and a message from the national librarian. Wander through the collections, focusing on Canadiana, and learn about the services available to researchers, libraries, and publishers. Explore the ever-changing exhibits, including an exhibit on Canadian science fiction and fantasy. You can also learn about the library's publishing program and read some of the library-related publications, such as *National Library News* and the Canadiana brochure. Learn about the electronic publications pilot project, which identifies issues that libraries will encounter in handling electronic publications and online collections. Connect to other sources of Canadian information from here as well, including a project that organizes Web sources of Canadian information by subject.

Contact: National Library of Canada, *Webmaster@nlc-bnc.ca*

Touring Guide of New Brunswick

http://www.cuslm.ca/tourist/welcome.htm

"You've come to one of the friendliest places in the world," this site proclaims when you first arrive, and after a tour through the photograph- and information-rich guide, you'll believe it. Get into your virtual automobile, and travel through New Brunswick along your choice of several scenic drives (through text and photographs), stopping at towns along the way for sightseeing. Every drive has places to stop and things to do, or you can opt for the Discovery Byway along lesser-traveled back roads. Several "pamphlets" are provided to enhance your trip to New Brunswick. For example, there's a handbook of things to do for free in New Brunswick and one listing attractions for children. View The World's Highest and Wildest Tides, or take a whale-watching expedition. There are also guides to shopping along the drives, general travel information, and a list of Tourist Information Centers.

Contact: Jocelyn Nadeau, Centre Universitaire Saint Louis-Maillet *Jocelyn_Nadeau@cuslm.ca*

For more information on Canada, visit these sites:

Canada

http://www.clo.com/~canadainformation/

Almanac and lots of other information about Canada. Very cool design.

Canadian Permanent Residence FAQ

http://www.abdn.ac.uk/~opt018/Immigration/FAQ.html

A simple FAQ for those interested in immigrating to Canada. No real links to anything interesting or to other sites.

Canadiana: The Canadian Resource Page

http://www.cs.cmu.edu/afs/cs.cmu.edu/user/clamen/misc/Canadiana/README.html

This site provides access to almost everything a tourist would need to visit various parts of Canada. There are facts and figures, governmental information, and a discussion of Canada's new $2 coin. (It has a polar bear on it, if you're interested—apparently lots of Canadians were.) There are some surprising holes in the information. For example, information on Vancouver was not easily found, nor was information on anything except sports. The information that is there—and there's a lot of it—seems pretty thorough.

National Atlas on the Net

http://www-nais.ccm.emr.ca/schoolnet/

With French and English versions, this site includes maps, geographical facts and names, and a quiz. Aimed at kids, I believe, but useful for all ages.

Protect Canada's Biodiversity

http://www.web.apc.org/wcwild/biodiver.html

A site with an agenda—but a well set-up site with an agenda. There is a lot of good information, spiced with some very nice graphics, at a *Scientific American* level of readability, with slightly less scientific jargon. A couple of links take you to closely related sites—I suspect that they are separate to keep the Net surfer from tapping his/her fingers too much while the pictures load.

Central & South America & the Caribbean

Caribbean Home Page

http://caribbean-www.lcs.mit.edu/caribbean-www/

Take a Caribbean vacation without leaving your computer. At this home page, you can use an interactive form to get Caribbean information, including time zones, government resources, languages, currencies, population, airport locations, and other basic facts, on places like Barbados, Jamaica, Martinique, and many other Caribbean countries. Look in country profiles for more in-depth information (not all of these have been completed). These profiles incorporate photographs of sunny skies, clear oceans, and white beaches as well as more factual information including maps, travel guides, and links to other information sources. Visit De Shop Corner for a hodgepodge of Caribbean connections, including links to home pages of West Indians, the Usenet newsgroup *soc.culture.caribbean,* and the cricket home page. This Caribbean information source is just getting started but has lots of growth potential.

Contact: Geoff Lee Seyon, Massachusetts Institute of Technology, *gseyon@mit.edu*

Haitian Art Gallery

http://www.iis.com/egallery/haiti.html

Haiti has a well-earned reputation for great art, with a cadre of talented artists emerging from that Caribbean country. As you'll see at this gallery, Haitian art is rich with color and texture, depicting themes ranging from politics to voodoo. The gallery features paintings that hang permanently in galleries and museums as well as a selection of original art for sale. From the lobby, go on a walking tour of the exhibits, learn the history of Haitian art, or view selected paintings by artist or title. On the walking tour, you'll pass through rooms where you can view thumbnails of paintings. Purchase paintings you like by connecting directly to an online order form. If you want additional information about Haiti, you can jump straight to the Haiti Web page.

Contact: Electric Gallery, Internet Information Services, *rwpb11@pipeline.com*

Latin American Information Center

http://lanic.utexas.edu/

The Latin American Information Center is the most complete library of Latin American studies on the Web. Find lots of resources about countries in Latin America and the Caribbean, including pointers to home pages, newsgroups, maps, and tourism information. Almost every Latin American country is represented, from Argentina to Venezuela. For each country, get information about the economy, government, education, news, science, and technology. Connect to other Internet servers in that country. Or access Latin American information by subject, such as art, anthropology, libraries, and publications. You'll also find information about Latin American history, politics, and studies.

Contact: Latin American Network Information Center at the University of Texas, *info@lanic.utexas.edu*

MayaQuest Learning Adventure

http://mayaquest.mecc.com/

MayaQuest is a wholly kid-directed bicycle expedition into the Mayan world of Guatemala, Mexico, Belize, and Honduras. The goal of the three-month expedition is to engage kids and teachers in unraveling one of the greatest mysteries of all time—the collapse of the ancient Mayan civilization. Go to General Information to learn about the expedition's goals and participants and to learn more about the Maya. Expedition photographs and updates are linked in to the site regularly. At the MayaQuest Student Home Page, discover activities and information related to the expedition and designed especially for young people, including facts about the Maya and the expedition, pictures, maps, and a scavenger hunt. There are also educational activities and resources under The Quest, as well as a teacher's study guide. Look in Resources for images, maps, multimedia tools, and electronic field trip resources. You'll even find theme-based projects on flora and fauna in the area of the Maya, Mayan hieroglyphics, math and astronomy, natural disasters, the Spanish language, and many more interesting topics.

Contact: MECC, TIES and InforMNs, MayaQuest Internet Center, *webmaster@mecc.com*

Bicycling through Central America.

WWW of Peru

http://www.rcp.net.pe/peru/peru_ingles.html

Learn about Peru from a number of different cultural perspectives. Even though some of the information at this site is in Spanish, there is plenty here to interest the English speaker. See the country in over 79 photographs that can be viewed in a "slide show." Or listen to selections from an archive of Peruvian music. Read about ecotourism (in Spanish), then become a tourist yourself as you travel to different provinces via an interactive map. Each province provides tourist calendars, listings of principal attractions, general facts, and information on how to get there. Some provinces also include photographs and music from that region of the country.

Contact: Internet Network of Peru, *www@rcp.net.pe*

An interactive map of Peru links you to photographs and music from all over the country.

For more information on Central and South America and the Caribbean, visit these sites:

Brazil Web

http://www.escape.com/~jvgkny/culture.html

An armchair tourist guide to Brazil. This site has pictures, museums, and pop culture information. Note: Some of the text is in Portugese.

Central America

http://www.theworld.com/travel/PLACES/CENTRAL/CONTENENT.HTM

Basically under construction. Click on a link and you'll find yourself in a maze of "object not found" and "go back to ____" that don't take you back to anything. Might be worth rechecking in a couple of months.

The Institute of Caribbean Studies

http://www.microstate.com/pub/micros/ics/

Although officially "under construction," this site already has some good academic information on Caribbean studies. This site is not a tourist guide, but an educationally oriented spot with an emphasis on Caribbean social studies.

Mexico, Central and South America

http://www.gorp.com/gorp/location/latamer/latamer.html

Provides access to several different types of Central and South American information: tourism, environmental concerns, schools, a Spanish-speaking countries page, archaeology, books, and Internet resources by country. Very thorough and well organized.

Project Central America

http://informationrmns.k12.mn.us/~eroberts/pca/

Project Central America's home page includes maps and other information on Central America, including photos and an electronic textbook.

South America

http://grafton.dartmouth.edu:8001/lrc/culture/samerica/

A good overview of the socio-political situations in South American countries. Several different points of view are covered, with special emphasis on Brazil. Also a good place to discover Dartmouth's South American studies program.

South American Archaeology

http://spirit.lib.uconn.edu/ArchNet/Regions/South_Americal.html

An in-depth look at specific archaeological studies, along with some rather nice pictures of pre-Columbian art. This is a small site at the moment, but if it gets more information along the present lines, it should be very good.

Ten-Day Precipitation Outlook for South America

http://grads.iges.org/pix/prec8.html

This site contains exactly what the title promises—the South American precipitation outlook for the next week and a half. There is a link to a GIF file for further map information, although a reasonably detailed map loads with the rest of the site. There are also several other special purpose GIFs available for aviators, El Nino forecasts, and related items. A good jumping-off place for those with a special interest in Western hemisphere weather conditions.

Three Weeks in the Wilds of South America

http://www.solutions.mb.ca/rec-travel/south_america/
peru_ecuador.trip.leeper.html

Travelog from a 1986 trip to South America. Might be interesting or helpful for those planning to travel there.

Europe

All About Turkey

http://www.ege.edu.tr:80/Turkiye/

This site is packed with information about Turkey, mostly external links that are gathered together in one easy-to-navigate setting. The site is organized by subject, such as art, cuisine, government, sports, and tourism. Online books provide an illustrated tour of Turkish architecture and sculpture. The Turkey in Pictures archive takes you through Izmir (the birthplace of Homer), the Mediterranean region, Ankara, the Black Sea region, Istanbul, and the Yayla. Explore Turkish comics, music, poetry, and theater, or learn Turkish for travelers. Don't miss one of the highlights of the site, Izmir: The City of Fairs, for a general introduction covering subjects such as traveling in Turkey, the climate, and the importance of the fair to the Turkish economy. The descriptions of the fairs are in Turkish, but an English fair schedule extends to the year 2000 so you can plan your next trip.

Contact: Ozgur Balzoy, Ege University, *e73894@mozart.ceng.metu.edu.tr*

The Amsterdam Channel

http://www.channels.nl/adam.html

This site offers several ways to virtually visit Amsterdam: take a tram, walk around, or be guided through town on a virtual tour, or take a shortcut by zooming to a particular point of interest on a clickable map. You start your tour in the center of Amsterdam, in front of the Central Station. If you choose to walk, there are nearby destinations you can choose from. Tram riders can board the different lines from the site and ride around following the tram maps provided. You can even take a taxi and go anywhere in the city instantly. Everywhere you stop, whether traveling by tram, taxi, or foot, you find out what you can see, do, or buy in that area. Pictures accompany you every step of the way. As an alternative, try the tours, all of which have themes. A culture and history tour explores galleries, museums, theaters, and concert halls, as well as the beautiful sites of Amsterdam. The business tour takes you to the best hotels, restaurants, and other places a business visitor might want to know about. Follow a fun tour to the red light district, coffee shops, bars, and discotheques. The low-budget tour is a guide to cheaper hotels, restaurants, and other bargains. There's also a shopping tour if that's your obsession. The Amsterdam Channel provides a unique way to get to know a far-away city online.

Contact: The Channels, *basvreek@channels.nl*

Czech Republic

http://www.eunet.cz/

From this one server, you can connect to lots of information about the Czech Republic and Eastern Europe. Find general resources on tourism, culture, news, business, and finance at the commercial Internet server. Access a free daily news service for those interested in Central and Eastern Europe. Check out an e-bulletin covering Czech business news. Read the *Prague Financial* for up-to-date information on Czech financial markets, stock listings, and late-breaking news. You can also access the Internet network in the Czech Republic, including servers in the Czech language.

Contact: EUnet Czechia, *info@EUnet.cz*

EUnet

http://www.EU.net/

EUnet is Europe's major Internet network, and when you connect to its Web page, you can tour Europe through its main Internet backbone. From here, learn more about EUnet, connect to interesting European Web sites, and find out the latest news about the European Internet. Visit the countries that EUnet serves, from Algeria to Uzbekistan. Find out about the services that the Internet service provider offers, including EUnet Traveler, which allows you to have a connection to the Internet even when you're traveling in Europe. Find useful information, including EUnet news, links to interesting sites, and a map of EUnet's connections. As a bonus, a new, random hotlink to a EUnet server appears every time you reload this page.

Contact: EUnet Communications Services, *webmaster@EU.net*

Germany

http://www.chemie.fu-berlin.de/adressen/brd.html

Here a range of information about Germany is arranged in a menu format. Subjects covered include geography, people, economy, government, and communications. A long version of the textual information links to relevant references, such as information on geographic regions and German texts of important historical documents and photographs. Alternatively, a short version condenses this information for quick fact-finding. An interactive map of Germany links to information on various regions of the country. You can also get news about Germany through the German News Service or access a map of German WWW servers to enter even further into the country.

Contact: Burkhard Kirste and Heiko Schlichting, Department of Chemistry, FU Berlin*kirste@chemie.fu-berlin.de*

Iceland Tour Guide

http://www.rfisk.is/iceland/rest_of_iceland.html

This fun server is an informal tour guide to a usually overlooked country, Iceland. The site opens with an interactive map of Iceland. Click on a region on the map of Iceland for local photographs and tourist guides. For example, journey to West Iceland to view inline photographs that you can transform into full-screen graphics just by clicking on them with your mouse. Or you can go to the Southern Westfjords to get detailed information and maps. There isn't a lot of information here—the guide is being built slowly by volunteers—but it is definitely worth a quick stop.

Contact: Mark Townley, Icelandic Fisheries Laboratories, *mark@rfisk.is*

Mirror of Lithuania

http://www.mcs.com/~thomas/www/lt/

This site creates a single unified access point for electronic resources on the Republic of Lithuania. The "mirror" server gives a superior connection speed and increased availability. Connect to the Parliament for an inside look at Lithuanian government. Or check out academic research inside the country. There are a lot more stops on this round-up of Lithuanian servers.

Contact: Thomas Baltis, MCSNet, *thomas@mcs.com*

Overview of Belgium

http://www.iihe.ac.be/hep/pp/evrard/BelgCul.html

This site opens with maps and a general overview of the country of Belgium. Further information covers the geography, politics, government, art, and languages. Find tourism information or virtually visit major cities and regions. Connect to servers and home pages in Belgium. There's even a beer guide for the country. A hypertext essay on Belgian culture offers a personal viewpoint on Belgium and its people, providing very entertaining and informative reading. Links in the text travel side roads to new and interesting places related to the subject at hand.

Contact: F. Heylighen, Brussels University, *fheyligh@vnet3.vub.ac.be*

Polish Home Page

http://info.fuw.edu.pl/pl/poland-text.html

The Polish Home Page is actively experimenting in online publishing. One project draws from the *Gazeta Wyborcza*, the largest daily newspaper in Poland. The Donosy Liberal Digest, a daily electronic news bulletin from Warsaw, is also served here. Several other Polish electronic journals are accessible. Visit the Warsaw Stock Exchange for the latest quotes, get information on Polish satellite television stations, and walk through an exhibit about the Warsaw Uprising of World War II. Or check out Polish movies, art, poetry, and music. You can also get complete information about Poland on the Internet, from a clickable map of Polish WWW servers to a database of Polish e-mail addresses to Usenet news in Poland. The entire site is organized by subject for easy browsing. Although this site is mostly in Polish, enough is in English to make it well worth a visit.

Contact: Wojtek Bogusz, Marcin Gromisz, Michal Jankowski, and Kacper Nowicki, Physics Department, Warsaw University, *Wojtek.Bogusz@fuw.edu.pl*

Portuguese Home Page

http://s700.uminho.pt/homepage-pt.html

Travel to Portugal through this site that opens with a huge graphical map of the Portuguese Internet; click on symbols to access Gopher, WWW and FTP servers, or travel information in Portugal. Get facts about the country in both English and Portuguese, with links to pages about the geography, people, economy, and government. Useful information for Portuguese people includes cultural events, news, and Portuguese contacts in the world. Useful information for non-Portuguese includes travel tips, exchange rates, and human rights practices. This site is valuable not only for the information it provides about Portugal but also for the many links to the continent of Europe through the Europe home page and the European Commonwealth home page.

Contact: Jose Eduardo Pina Miranda, University of Minho, *pinj@di.uminho.pt*

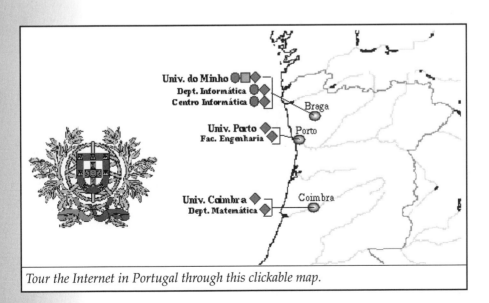

Tour the Internet in Portugal through this clickable map.

Sí Spain

http://www.civeng.carleton.ca/SiSpain/

Sí Spain is an interactive service promoting the free exchange of data on Spanish current affairs and cultural development. The site offers handy basic information on everyday life in Spain and on Spanish history, language, and culture. You can access the guide in either English or Spanish. Learn about Spain's geography with a map, climate information, and facts about vegetation, minerals, and hydrography. Get facts about Spanish population and society, with lots of demographics on the family, women, ethnic minorities, Catholicism, and traditions. Download a full overview of the history of the country, from the first human settlements to the present. Read about the Spanish language throughout the world and the evolution of Spanish culture in art, literature, music, and film. Delve into the political system in Spain, and learn about Spanish foreign relations and policies. You'll find an economic history and the current positions of the Spanish financial system and stock market. There are also overviews of the Spanish infrastructure, environmental policy, health system, educational system, science and technology research, and the media. Find out about traveling to Spain, with general information on passports, currency, social customs, shopping, and suggested itineraries. You can even download a Spanish course for beginners or connect to other Web sites in Spain. After visiting this loaded site, you'll feel like you've been to the country itself.

Contact: Dr. Jose Luis Pardos, Embassy of Spain in Canada, *aj765@freenet.carleton.ca*

Slovakia Document Store

http://www.eunet.sk/slovakia/slovakia.html

This site opens with the quote, "There's something to be said about being number two," and then goes on to demonstrate what—the ability to create a unique culture without having to live up to a lot of expectations. This attitude makes the Slovakia home page a fun place to explore. There are so many unique things to see at this site. Access recipes for Slovak cuisine, a traveler's guide, or notes on Slovak business practices. You can't miss the picture tour around Slovakia. An interactive map links to photographs (including satellite photographs) and brief histories of different places in Slovakia. Visit the capital through the link, Bratislava Navigator, which provides maps, listings of theaters, galleries and museums, and a picture tour of the city. All in all, the Slovakia site is a good example of how a "number-two" country can make itself number one on the WWW.

Contact: Slovakia Document Store, EUnet Slovakia, *SDS@Slovakia.EU.net,*

Tour of Paris

http://sunsite.unc.edu/wm/paris/

Get to know one of Europe's most famous cities. From this site, you can walk around Paris on your own, take an historical guided tour, or explore the Catacombs underneath the city. The tour lets you visit Paris's famous landmarks in text and pictures. You can see the Louvre, the Champs-Elysées, the Royal Palace, and the Eiffel Tower. When you're finished, look at Paris from the sky, or follow the Seine to more interesting places. The guided tour provides a lot of historical commentary on the places you visit. The walking tour is more relaxed and informal. (Try them both out!) Don't skip a trip into the Catacombs where you can see the skeletons of the five to six million people who were buried there.

Contact: Nicholas Pioch, WebMuseum, *Nicholas.Pioch@inf.enst.fr*

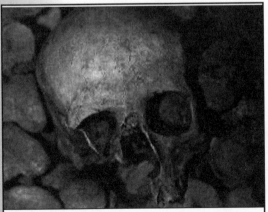

Say hi to the inhabitants of the Catacombs in Paris. (Photo credit: C.A. Merriman.)

Yugoslavia

http://www.umiacs.umd.edu/research/lpv/YU/HTML/yu.html

This site opens with a musical introduction and a short text with embedded links to information on regions of the new Yugoslavia. A clickable map leads to a tour of particular regions, enhanced by photographs, videos, and audio clips. You can visit little-known but interesting attractions, such as monasteries, ancient archaeological sites, the Montenegrin Riviera, and the Kopaonik Mountain Resort. Interesting photographs, such as of the frescoes in the monasteries, make you feel as if you are actually there. Learn about the language and the Cyrillic alphabet by taking a reading drill with audio examples. Meet important Yugoslav politicians, artists, and writers through photographs and biographies. Sample traditional cuisine through recipes and holiday foods. This educational and engaging site helps you learn all about this region of Europe.

Contact: Nina Milosevk and Yojislav Lalich-Petrich, Institute for Advanced Computer Studies, University of Maryland, *lpv@umiacs.umd.edu*

For more information about Europe, visit these sites:

The Bitricci Gardens

http://www.uidaho.edu/vb/theGardens.html

This page describes the history of these Italian gardens from the late sixth century to 1982.

Europa

http://www.cec.lu/

Europa is a WWW server that offers information on the European Union's goals and policies. Find out more about the Union's history and politics, download official documents, and access a citizen's guide to the European Union.

Project Runeberg

http://www.lysator.liu.se/runeberg/

Project Runeberg publishes free electronic editions of classic Nordic literature and art. You can access the site in many different Nordic languages, as well as English, and connect to related electronic text projects.

German Resources

http://www.rz.uni-karlsruhe.de/Outerspace/VirtualLibrary/

You want to find information about Germany? Come here first. This library of German resources on the Web is organized by subject, with pointers to culture, sports, law, economics, science, medicine, engineering, and art resources.

Switzerland Home Page

http://heiwww.unige.ch/switzerland/

Tour Switzerland through an interactive map that lets you visit different regions and cities. You can also connect to nonprofit and commercial institutes, events, general information, miscellaneous directories, and other Switzerland resources.

Geography

CIA World Factbook

http://www.odci.gov/cia/publications/95fact/index.html

The CIA's World Factbook contains statistical information on every country in the world. If you're researching a country, this site probably offers more complete information than an encyclopedia, and it's free. Get maps and information about the government, people, economy, transportation, communications, and defense of any country you're interested in. The Factbook also has information about organizations such as the United Nations, international environmental agreements, and maps of the world. You can even find out exchange rates for local currencies if you're planning on traveling abroad.

Contact: Central Intelligence Agency, Office of the Director of Central Intelligence

City.Net

http://www.city.net/

City.Net is the most comprehensive guide on the Internet to city information sites around the world. The guide provides easy and timely access to everything you would want to know about any city, including travel, entertainment, local business, and government information. You have lots of choices for navigating the database: browse an alphabetical listing of cities, browse entries by country, access a country and city hierarchy (which lists all entries alphabetically by country, then breaks them down into region and city), visit by world region, search the database for a keyword, or access it through a world map. City information includes city guides, community organizations, transportation information, maps, travel and tourism info, tourist attractions, and whatever else can be found on the Internet. Hundreds of cities are listed, including Alexandria, Aspen, Amsterdam, Aix-en-Provence, Athens—and that's just the A's. All information in the guide is gathered from local resources on the Internet; if you maintain city or regional information, you can register your site with City.Net here. Extras include country and government information and maps for every world region. You can also access an around-the-world journal. The City.Net browser check-up will even keep your WWW browser up-to-date for you.

Contact: City Net Express, Kevin Altis and Rowland Smith, *altis@city.net*

Finding Your Way

http://info.er.usgs.gov/fact-sheets/finding-your-way/finding-your-way.html

Learn how to read maps and use a compass to find your way almost anywhere. This site helps you build skills to use when camping, hiking, or just exploring an area. The easy-to-understand instructions show you how to use a topographic map and how to find the distance on a map using scales. You'll also learn how to use a compass and map to determine direction. There's even a picture gallery of examples.

Contact: U.S. Geological Survey, *webmaster@www.usgs.gov*

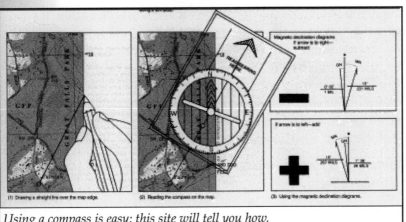

Using a compass is easy; this site will tell you how.

Geographic Information Systems

http://info.er.usgs.gov/research/gis/title.html

Geographic Information Systems (GIS) is a technology used for scientific investigations, resource management, and development planning. GIS is capable of assembling, storing, manipulating, and displaying geographic reference information—data identified through their locations. At this site, you can learn about the technology and access data collected in this way, such as digital airborne and satellite imagery, national water conditions, and mineral investigations resource maps. Follow all the steps in a typical GIS operation, including data capture, integration, and modeling. Find out how to use GIS for mapmaking, emergency response planning, and simulating environmental effects, among other applications. An online software archive provides tools to help collect geographic data.

Contact: U.S. Geological Survey, *webmaster@info.er.usgs.gov*

Geographic Nameserver

http://www.mit.edu:8001/geo/

Interactive forms are a powerful application of the WWW. A unique use of interactive forms is the Geographic Nameserver. Here you can instantly obtain down-and-dirty information on many geographic locations. All you do is enter the name of the place you want to know about into the interactive form and press the Search button. If you enter the name of a city, the server instantly returns facts such as the county, state, and country location, area code, latitude and longitude, elevation, and zip code. The information you get varies widely depending on what you're searching for. For a state or country entry, for example, you get less information, sometimes just latitude and longitude. U.S. cities return the best results. But as a quick and easy geographical tool, the Geographic Nameserver is invaluable.

Contact: Student Information Processing Board, Massachusetts Institute of Technology

How Far Is It?

http://gs213.sp.cs.cmu.edu/prog/dist

Enter the names of two cities in the United States, and this program tells you how far apart they are as the crow flies. The program also automatically draws a map showing the two places you've asked about. You can enter a city name, a zip code, or a city and state. The program also returns general facts about the places you selected, such as latitude and longitude, population, county, elevation, and zip codes. Be sure to go from here to the Xerox PARC Map Viewer (a description follows), which draws maps of the world according to the coordinates you set. Or connect to the Geographic Nameserver (see the previous listing), which helps you locate U.S. cities.

Contact: Darrell Kindred, Carnegie Mellon University, *Darrell.Kindred@cmu.edu*

The Perry-Castañeda Library Map Collection

http://rowan.lib.utexas.edu/Libs/PCL/Map_collection/ Map_collection.html

On any trip, it's a good idea to bring a map along. This WWW library archives detailed, full-color maps of many locations around the world. The collection itself holds more than 230,000 maps; over 300 are accessible here, and more are being added all the time. The maps are formatted as JPEGs and GIFs. You'll always find maps of current interest highlighted. The Islands, Oceans, and Poles link lists maps of diverse locations like Antarctica, Easter Island, and Fiji. You can visit international hot spots like Paris, Vienna, and Abu Dhabi through a large collection of city maps. Visit U.S. national parks, monuments, and historical sites through a complete library of government maps. Connect to other cartographic resources online. This collection demonstrates how the WWW can be used effectively as a library resource, storing collected materials that any user can "check out," or access.

Contact: General Libraries, University of Texas at Austin, *www@lib.utexas.edu*

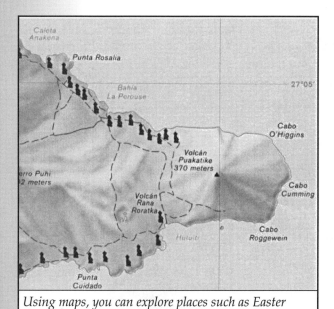

Using maps, you can explore places such as Easter Island, with its mysterious giant statues.

The Virtual Tourist

http://wings.buffalo.edu/world/

Visit the Virtual Tourist to view a full-color, clickable map of the world that tells you at a glance what's on the Web. The map links to Web servers all around the world. By visiting Web servers, you get an inside look at companies, universities, and governmental agencies anywhere you want to go. Or look up your own hometown to find local Web servers. Map symbols tell you at a glance what you're linking to.

Contact: Brandon Plewe, State University of New York at Buffalo, *plewe@acsu.buffalo.edu*

World Tour

http://wings.buffalo.edu/world/vt2/

Use this world map to travel anywhere in the world. This site is the companion to The Virtual Tourist (see previous listing). The map connects to a database of world information. You can use it to find general information, tourist guides, and pictures for thousands of places around the world. Clicking on a continent takes you to a more detailed map where you can visit countries and cities, just by clicking on them. For example, I went to France, visited many cities, found out general facts about the country itself and information about the language and government, and viewed maps, photographs, and travel guides. You can also visit schools, parks, tourist attractions, TV and radio stations, and much more. This WWW page is a fun and easy way to explore anywhere in the world.

Contact: Brandon Plewe, State University of New York, *plewe@acsu.buffalo.edu*

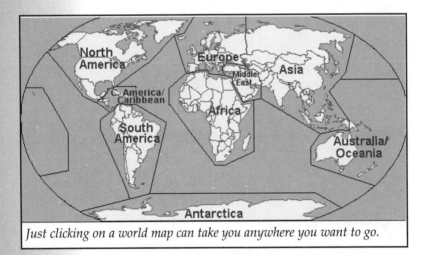

Just clicking on a world map can take you anywhere you want to go.

Xerox PARC Map Viewer

http://pubweb.parc.xerox.com/map/

You can create your own map at this site. An experiment by Xerox in dynamic information retrieval, the Map Viewer won Best of the Web awards for technical merit and best use of interaction. Through the interface, you request maps of specific latitude and longitude; the program returns an HTML document including an inline GIF image of the map. Control the map rendering by panning across the map, zooming in to a particular point, or changing the level of detail the map provides. A color display with an accompanying legend draws in rivers, borders, roads, lakes, ferries, railroads, pipelines, parks, and Indian reservations. This is one of the best examples of interactive multimedia on the WWW. Many of the sites listed in this section have used the Map Viewer to create the maps included in their travel guides.

Contact: Steve Putz, *putz@parc.xerox.com*, Xerox Palo Alto Research Center

---

For more information on geography, visit these sites:

Ancient World Home Page

http://atlantic.evsc.virginia.edu/julia/AncientWorld.html

Contains information on ancient world geography, breaking news on research, and other useful links.

Around the World in Eighty Clicks

http://www.coolsite.com/arworld.html

Click on highlighted spots of a big map. Uncertain what information is in each link—it took wayyyyy too long to connect.

Cartography Resources

http://geog.gmu.edu/gess/jwc/cartogrefs.html

Here you'll find a ton of cartography links, including map companies, museums, and software, as well as government and education sites.

Geography Reference

http://www.worldweb.net/~abrody/new.html#LST

Index to various sites, including 23 links to geography sites. Also includes biology, employment, astronomy, weather, travel, news, computer references, and lots more!

Government, International

Electronic Embassy

http://www.embassy.org/

The Electronic Embassy provides resources from the Washington, D.C., embassy community on business and industry, education, the press, and government in countries all around the world. From here, connect to the Web sites for countries that have embassies in the United States. Or find basic contact information for all the embassies in Washington, and link to American embassies abroad. For each embassy listed, you'll find out how to contact it by telephone, fax, or e-mail, locate other consulates from that country in the U.S., read about the services of the embassy, and discover foreign relations facts. You'll also find a comprehensive list of resources about that embassy's country online. Link to indices of media, cultural, commercial, and trade resources of participating embassies. Find out about foreign education exchange programs, or visit a consular office for help when traveling abroad. Locate travel and tourism opportunities from foreign embassies, or find job openings in Washington and in the foreign affairs community. There's also a Washington events calendar and a monthly newsletter about the embassy community, as well as information on foreign affairs in general.

Contact: TeleDiplomacy, Inc., Electronic Embassy, *director@embassy.org*

Flags

http://155.187.10.12/flags/flags.html

Get in the spirit of traveling to a distant country by looking at its national flag. This site has them all. You can view the flags as inline thumbnails or click on one of these to get a full-screen graphic. There are also international maritime signal flags, in case you get lost at sea during your voyage. For automobile-racing fans, racing flags are included. You can even polish your semaphore skills in a section that graphically demonstrates flag positions for the semaphore alphabet. If you didn't get enough, you can connect to other flag databases from here.

Contact: Australian National Botanic Gardens, Jim Croft, *jrc@anbg.gov.au*

Oceania

http://oceania.org/

If you're itching to visit somewhere new and different, go to this site to learn all about a movement to construct Oceania, a brand-new country. The Atlantis Project is an attempt to create a new country devoted to the value of freedom. The project intends to build a country literally where none existed before—on an artificial island constructed off the coast of Panama—and create a government structure from scratch. You can read all about it at this site, including the constitution and laws of Oceania, and learn how you can become involved.

Contact: Bob Bickford, Oceania Organization, *wmaster@oceania.org*

Voices of Youth

http://www.iisd.ca/linkages/un/youth.html

Young people from 81 countries sent over 3,000 messages to the World Summit for Social Development hosted by the United Nations. You can read those messages indexed by country or topic, or search for messages by the sender's name. You can also read messages from world leaders in response. Although you can't send your own messages right now, you'll be able to do so soon, so keep coming back. Go to the original home page to find out what the Social Summit was, and get more information about the outcome of the World Summit. Kids have a right to express their views; the power of the Internet makes their voices heard.

Contact: World Summit for Social Development, MBNet, *gopher@undp.org*

Children of the world make their voices heard.

For more information about international government,
visit these sites:

Campaign for World Government

http://www.bath.ac.uk/~adsjrc/eu/dt-cam.htm

This site has been put up to start debate about the pros and cons of a
world government campaign.

The Fourth World Conference on Women

http://www.iisd.ca/linkages/women.html

Contains information on the women's conference in Beijing, China.

United Nations Online

http://www.un.org/

Very nicely designed, this site includes news clips, basic information,
conferences, publications, documents, etc.

World Government Home Page

http://www.webcom.com/~worldgov/

Dedicated to grassroots activism and discussion of future world government, including an e-mail list, a link to an upcoming newsgroup,
and articles. A little bare, but with a funky background design.

Government, U.S.

CapWeb

http://policy.net/capweb/congress.html

This is a guide to the United States Congress from an outsider's point
of view. Meet all of the senators and representatives organized by
state, political party, and committee. You'll find each senator's and
representative's first election date, office phone number, and committees. You can also connect to related resources for that congress-

person's state. Visit the Library of Congress and learn about congressional support agencies. Search recent congressional legislation. Get an overview of the Constitution. Connect to other related resources, or explore the judiciary and executive branches of government. Go to the Political Page to learn more about the different political parties and party organizations. You can also connect to presidential candidates' home pages, political groups and PACs, other lists with information on political campaigns, and, for a laugh break, political parodies. You'll find lots more good government resources on this page, including guides to getting to, from, and around Capitol Hill. Be sure to check out CapWeb before the next election, and get informed.

Contact: Chris Casey and Jeff Hecker, PolicyNet, *info@idi.net*

Department of Energy

http://www.doe.gov/

The Department of Energy provides an easy-to-use server with information organized in several different ways to simplify finding the information you want. You'll find news and hot topics on energy, such as upcoming meetings, conferences, speeches, education, and training. Follow a link to OpenNet, which lets you access all the department's declassified information, including the National Environmental Policy Act. Visit the Electronic Exchange Initiative for software, papers, encoding, and SGML-related information. Get telephone and contact information for employees throughout the department. This is an excellent example of a government information server.

Contact: Department of Energy Office of Scientific and Technical Information, *webmaster@apollo.osti.gov*

Department of the Treasury

http://www.ustreas.gov/

At the Department of the Treasury, you can learn everything you could care to know about the treasury mission and responsibilities. Through a link on the page, visit the Treasury Electronic Library, which contains speeches, press releases, and news relating to the department. Look in Who's Who for photographs and biographies of treasury officers. Learn more about the twelve bureaus through this site. Other useful resources you'll find here include information on small business opportunities, a historical photo archive, savings bond information, financial statistics, and a bulletin board system for exchanging messages on treasury topics.

Contact: Department of the Treasury, *wwwadmin@www.ustreas.gov*

Federal Bureau of Investigation

http://www.fbi.gov/

At this site, you can virtually visit the FBI and get an inside look at the United States' most famous law enforcement agency. Read the mission statement, learning how the FBI performs its duties of criminal law enforcement, foreign counterintelligence, investigative and operational support, and consulting services for other law enforcement agencies. You can also find out the bureau's jurisdiction, specialties, and functions. Follow along with current FBI investigations, such as the search for the Unabomber, an investigation of a series of unsolved bombings. Here you can find out why the information is being made available to the Internet community and get a description and chronology of the crimes, including a sketch of a suspect. Also read about rewards being offered and how to contact the task force. There isn't a lot of information at the FBI's home page now, but everything that is here is interesting, and the server is growing.

Contact: William L. Tafoya, Federal Bureau of Investigation, *btafoya@orion.arc.nasa.gov*

FedWorld

http://www.fedworld.gov/

This extremely useful site links to all the government information servers on Web, FTP, Gopher, and Telnet sites, organized by subject category and forming a complete guide to U.S. government. You can also locate recent U.S. government reports, the national technological information service with scientific, technical, and business-related files, and the commerce information locator service. Or access the FedWorld libraries with more than 10,000 files on business, health, environment, and more. FedWorld is the fastest and easiest way to find government information online.

Contact: FedWorld, FedWorld Information Network, *webmaster@fedworld.gov*

The Supreme Court
http://www.law.cornell.edu/supct/

At this one site, you'll find everything you would want to know concerning the judicial branch of U.S. government. Check out recent Supreme Court decisions either indexed by topic or searchable by keyword. Topics you can investigate include civil rights, capital punishment, drugs, guns, schools, the environment, and taxation. For each case, you can access the background of the case, the judges' opinions, and the decision. Also check out significant pre-1990 decisions such as *Roe v. Wade* and those concerning school prayer. Learn about the establishment of the Supreme Court, get biographies of the current justices, and read about the court's jurisdiction and organization as well.

Contact: Legal Information Institute, Cornell Law School, *lii@lii.law.cornell.edu*

THOMAS: Legislative Information on the Internet
http://thomas.loc.gov/

THOMAS introduces you to the congressional branch of U.S. government and keeps you up-to-date on current bills and legislation. The full text of all bills introduced by Congress are available at this site, searchable by keyword. You can limit your search to only bills for which floor action has occurred or bills sent to the president, or you can search all bills; also search by bill number, or get a full list of all bills by type. Access the full text of the Congressional record, a daily account of proceedings on the House and Senate floors searchable by keyword. Find out about hot legislation—major bills receiving floor action, listed by subject, popular and/or short titles, and bill number and/or type. How Our Laws Are Made provides an explanation of the process from the origin of a legislative proposal through its publication as a law. Connect to Gopher info about the House of Representatives and the Senate, including committee hearing schedules, the current floor schedule and visitor information. Find out how to correspond with your congressperson or senator using an e-mail directory for House and Senate members and specific committees. THOMAS provides a very easy way to keep in touch with what's going on in Congress.

Contact: THOMAS, Library of Congress, *thomas@loc.gov*

In the spirit of Thomas Jefferson, the THOMAS service makes legislative information easily available through the Internet.

U.S. Census Bureau Home Page

http://www.census.gov/

Here, public census information is laid out in an attractive, easy-to-use format. You can find out the projected resident population of the United States for the current day and time. Also order census information on CD-ROM, video, and maps directly through the Internet. Demographic information on subjects ranging from education to retirement to buying the first home can be downloaded. Find useful resources on geography and the economy. Get tips on genealogy research. You can also retrieve free statistics software. If you need a break from all these numbers, visit the art gallery to view a variety of census posters with Native American themes.

Contact: U.S. Census Bureau, *WebMaster@Census.GOV*

Posters in the Census Bureau's art gallery.

U.S. Constitution

http://www.law.cornell.edu/constitution/
constitution.overview.html

This hypertext version of the Constitution was nominated in the Best of the Web awards for Best Document Design. This style of presentation is particularly useful both for in-depth research and for quickly answering questions. Read the sections and amendments in order, paging through using hyperlinks, or skip straight to the section that you are most interested in. Sections of the original document that were later amended are linked directly to the appropriate amendment. This well-planned use of hypertext makes the Constitution site a valuable place for students and researchers to visit.

Contact: Peter W. Martin, Legal Information Institute, Cornell Law School, *martin@law.mail.cornell.edu*

U.S. Government Hypertexts

http://sunsite.unc.edu/govdocs.html

This is the official Web archive for documents of the Clinton-Gore administration. All of the White House press releases are stored here. Browse, search, or retrieve documents, including, for example, a complete copy of the proposed budget for the upcoming fiscal year. Or read the National Performance Review, completely hyperlinked and enhanced with audio clips of statements from both the president and vice-president, as well as an archive of supporting documents. The National Information Infrastructure Proposal, President Clinton's proposal for building the Information Superhighway, is available here, complete with video and an audio clip from Secretary of Commerce Ron Brown. Tap into the most comprehensive source of world trade data. You can also read through the original health care plan and supporting documents or search the audio clips of the Saturday radio addresses by President Clinton. Or find news on other current subjects like tax reform and telecommunications policy.

Contact: Office of Information and Technology, SunSITE, University of North Carolina at Chapel Hill, *webmaster@sunsite.unc.edu*

The White House

http://www.whitehouse.gov/

On the Internet, the front door to the White House is literally always open. Use this Interactive Citizen's Handbook to learn all about the executive branch of government, including the office of the president, the cabinet, and independent federal agencies and commissions. Take a virtual tour of the White House, and meet the First Family. Browse through a library of White House publications, including press releases (up to today's), policy briefings, speeches, executive orders, and Congressional testimony. Listen to welcome messages from the president and vice-president, and "speak out" by sending e-mail to either the president or vice-president directly from the site. You can even browse a gallery of Vice President Gore's favorite political cartoons.

Contact: Office of Science and Technology Policy, The White House, *feedback@www.whitehouse.gov*

For more information about U.S. government, visit these sites:

All Things Political

http://www.federal.com/Political.html

This site covers what's new in politics, presidential primaries (including details on those running), political speeches, and the latest scandals. This site covers a very wide spectrum in considerable depth.

Democratic National Party

http://www.democrats.org/

From this site, visit government branches, political sites, and other online resources of interest to Democrats. You'll also find information about Democratic National Party campaigning, history, and events.

FDA and Food Safety

http://vm.cfsan.fda.gov/index.html

Contains links to documents on food safety and nutrition.

FedWeb Locator

http://www.law.vill.edu/fed-agency/fedwebloc.html

A very, very, very handy resource for looking up government agencies on the Web. Includes quick reference by branch, plus lists of new information. Very comprehensive, ranked in the top 5 percent of Web sites.

Grand Old Page Directory of Political Sites

http://www.berkeleyic.com/gop/sites.html

All acronyms aside, this site has links to all kinds of political sites. It also has links to government servers, so if you want to log onto the Department of the Treasury's server, this is a good spot to check out.

Hope for the Politically Homeless

http://www.self-gov.org/hope.html

This site is pretty Libertarian oriented. It's useful for anyone who wants to know what a Libertarian is and for the "world's smallest political quiz."

Links Where You Can Participate

http://www.vote-smart.org/other/participate.html

Ever wonder why those polls never take your opinion into account? Here's your chance to be heard! This site has links to sites where you can give your opinion on presidential candidates, issues, and politics.

National Archives

http://www.nara.gov/

Includes links to genealogy, online exhibits, the federal register, and other National Archives-related stuff. Looks interesting!

PIN: Online Political Information Network

http://www.ai.mit.edu/projects/ppp/news.html

This site has links to newsgroups from all sections of the political spectrum, from Newt Gingrich to Clinton and from white nationalism to progressivism. A good place for the politically interested to start their Net search.

The Progress & Freedom Foundation "Democracy in Virtual America" Conference

http://www.glocom.ac.jp/WhatsNew/PFFLisa.html

A text-only discussion of the Progress & Freedom Foundation, its goals, and its political alignments, with special attention to its Newt Gingrich connections. No graphics, one link to Cyberspace and the American Dream: A Magna Carta for the Knowledge Age.

The U.S. Army Online

http://www.army.mil/

A rather testosterone-laden page, but probably a good resource for army information.

U.S. Department of Commerce

http://www.doc.gov/

Includes information and news, plus a link to the White House.

Russia

Dazhdbog's Grandsons

http://sunsite.unc.edu/sergei/Grandsons.html

Here you'll find culturally oriented resources from Russia. Much of the information on this server is in Russian, but you can download the software you need to read it from the site. Access daily Russian news, hot topics, and political materials here. There is also information on law, science, and day-to-day life in Russia. Get some culture through an archive of Russian literature and music, plus electronic exhibitions. There's even Russian humor. This site also serves as a gateway to Russian networks.

Contact: Sergei Naoumov, SunSITE, University of North Carolina at Chapel Hill, *serge@sunsite.oit.unc.edu*

Friends & Partners

http://solar.rtd.utk.edu/friends/home.html

At this site, citizens of the United States and Russia have linked together to educate each other about their cultures, histories, and societies. The aim of the site is to provide a common "meeting place" where meaningful communication can be established. The two principal designers actually never met face-to-face; their friendship and collaboration developed entirely over the Internet. To better understand this experimental project, stop in the Global Lecture Hall for a slide presentation accompanied by a recorded talk. Once you've heard the lecture, return to the interactive map of the United States and Russia that connects to a wealth of information about the two countries collected from all over the Internet. By clicking on the button border of the map, you can move to different subject areas. Take time to explore the many hidden gems. For example, you can hear selections from the Slavyanka

Men's Slavic Chorus compact disc or take a course in Russian through graphics and audio examples. End your visit by relaxing in the interactive coffeehouse, where you can talk with other visitors to the site.

Contact: Greg Cole, Office of Research Services, University of Tennessee at Knoxville, *gcole@solar.rtd.utk.edu*, and Natasha Bulashova, *natasha@ibpm.serpukhov.su*

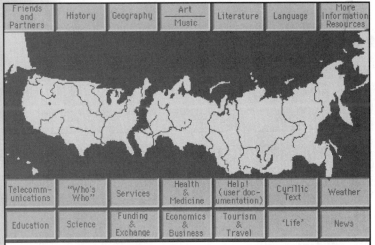

American and Russian culture is linked through this interactive map at Friends & Partners.

Moscow Kremlin Online Excursion

http://www.kiae.su/www/wtr/kremlin/begin.html

This beautiful exhibit is set up as though you were actually taking a walking tour of the Kremlin, listening to talks about the history and layout of the historic Moscow site along the way. The first stop is a map of the Kremlin. Then you have a choice of walking through Red Square or Cathedral Square. In the squares, you can look at the surrounding buildings and choose which one to visit. Every stop on the tour is accompanied by full-color photographs. Take the tour in any order you like and stay as long as you like in any of the buildings. If you're in a hurry and want to visit a specific place, a hyperlinked list links directly to every destination on the tour.

Contact: State Museums of Moscow Kremlin, COMINFO Ltd., and Relcom Corporation, *cdguide@cominf.msk.su*

Soviet Archive Exhibit

http://sunsite.unc.edu/expo/soviet.exhibit/soviet.archive.htm

This fascinating exhibit makes available online for the first time the top-secret archives of the Central Committees of the Communist party of the former Soviet Union. Follow the "golden footsteps" on the floor of the exhibit halls for a guided tour of documents from the archive. The first floor archives documents on the workings of the Soviet system, including internal politics and aspects of Soviet reality hidden or falsified in the official propaganda. The second floor holds documents on the relations of the Soviet Union and the United States during the Cold War. Documents on display include letters, speeches, reports, memos, and testimonials. You can see the original documents, such as private letters from Lenin and Gorky, in inline GIFs. An accompanying text commentary provides historical background on topics such as Soviet anti-religion campaigns, attacks on the intelligentsia, Chernobyl, and the Cuban Missile Crisis, among many other fascinating subjects.

Contact: EXPO, Frans van Hoesel, SunSITE, *Hoesel@chem.rug.nl*

St. Petersburg

http://www.spb.su/

Visit another of Russia's historic cities through this gateway to St. Petersburg. Read the St. Petersburg Press, an HTML version of St. Petersburg's English newspaper. A new issue is published online every week, with the latest news as well as cultural and business features and a classifieds section. For lighter fare, access the St. Petersburg Press Culture and Lifestyle Guide, which features cultural attractions, maps, restaurant listings, and travel tips updated weekly. The Other St. Petersburg is a guide to special nuances of living in the city, with short stories and line drawings. You can also check out business and travel resources and even comics from St. Petersburg. For a closer look at the city, visit the picture gallery to view photographs of main attractions.

Contact: Nevalink, Relcom, and the St. Petersburg Press, *webmaster@arcom.spb.su*

SunSITE Russia

http://sunsite.cs.msu.su/

This SunSITE multimedia server contains a lot of local information on Russia. Read all about the REDLab, a research, education, and demonstration laboratory that was developed in conjunction with Moscow State University and Sun Microsystems. You can access its research programs and educational services. Connect to Moscow State University itself or take a tour of the city of Moscow. Here you'll learn about Moscow's history, visit museums and art galleries, and get tourism information along with lots of pictures of the city. Connect to all the Russian Web servers, including research organizations, universities, government sites, and commercial companies. Visit a Moscow WWW Art Gallery, with an electronic photo gallery and many other exhibits related to Russian culture and art. And find information on the international space station project in which Russian and many other countries are collaborating to build a space station.

Contact: SunSITE Russia, Moscow State University, *webadm@cs.msu.su*

Treasures of the Czars

http://www.times.st-pete.fl.us/treasures/TC.Lobby.html

Learn all about the czars of Russia by exploring this online exhibit. Begin with an audio welcome from the Russian Embassy. The czar timeline takes you from the beginning of the Romanov Dynasty in 1613 to the Bolshevik Revolution of 1917; clicking on the timeline brings you face to face with the czar that ruled during that time with a picture and a short history. Take a tour through twelve galleries, exploring the history of the czars' reign in Russia by subject. See the treasures of the church, learn about royal parades and ceremonial arms, experience court life, and explore many more aspects of the era of the czars. Each gallery shows one featured item from the actual museum, such as a painting or an artifact, that you can learn about in detail. Be sure to take the kids to the playground of the czars; here you can play the name game, learn some fun facts, access a bibliography of Russian history and literature, and explore activities from the education guide. Go to the Czar Bazaar for Russian goods like nesting dolls and the official KGB watch. On the way out, stop by the Forum of the Czars to interactively discuss what you've seen in the museum.

Contact: Times Publishing Company and the Florida International Museum, *Comments@Times.St-Pete.FL.US*

For more information about Russia, visit these sites:

Armenian Research Center Home Page

http://www.umd.umich.edu/dept/armenian/

This site has some balanced, if dated, information about Armenia, a Transcaucasian country that was formerly in the Soviet Union. A good spot to study the effects of the break-up of the Soviet Union on a small scale. Still, someone needs to update the fact sheets so that they don't have references such as, "President Bush is..."

Country Information—Russia

http://www.cudenver.edu/psrp/eurr.html

This site gives a basic overview of present-day Russia.

Gateway Travel

http://www.magna.com.au/~gatrav/

Tours and trips through Russia, Latvia, etc., booked via the Web.

Gelleflint

http://www.otm.fi/nowerail/gelleflint.html

Offers information on a private commercial railway in Russia. Gives some commercial information.

Pictures from Central Russia

http://www.cs.toronto.edu/~mes/russia/centr/main.html

This site covers parts of Russia that are often overlooked, including Vyatka, Saratov, and Ryazan. It includes pictures and warnings that the site is a little hard to access at times. Suggestion: Check it out on a weekend.

REESweb: Russian and East European Studies

http://www.pitt.edu:81/~cjp/rshist.html

With links to news articles and other information pages. There's a lot here!

Rules and Regulations in Russia

http://www.spb.su/rulesreg/3/

This site concerns the legal aspects of doing business in Russia. It seems more oriented to the potential investor in Russian business than a tourist heading to Russia.

Russia and the Other States of the CIS

http://www.cliffordchance.com/rosc_e00.htm

This site provides information on current social, legal, and economic conditions in Russia.

Russia Online

http://www.online.ru/

This service has an acronym similar to America Online, and I doubt that's an accident. It seems to be an Internet access provider for Russia.

A Russian Phototrack

http://www.cs.toronto.edu/~mes/russia/photo.html

This site breaks Russia down into geographical areas and provides a photographic virtual tour of the different sections. While several areas, such as Moscow and St. Petersburg, are familiar from the TV news, other areas are not as common a sight.

Russian Portfolio

http://world.std.com/~rusport

A subscrition-only newsletter that covers Russian financial and investment information.

Russian Reminiscence Gallery

http://www.wfu.edu/~david/russia/

Provides information about Russia, including places, people, and The Schudel Collection.

Sprint Russia

http://www.rosprint.ru/

This site provides Internet access to some people in Russia. It has a great deal of Russian-language content.

Trento Bike Pages

http://www-math.science.unitn.it/Bike/Countries/Russia/

This site discusses the issues involved in trying to take a bike tour of Russia.

Window-to-Russia Home Page

http://www.kiae.su/www/wtr/

This site contains an overview of current Russian culture, business, science, and technology. It is hosted by Relcom.

Travel

American Airlines

http://www.amrcorp.com/

This site contains lots of useful travel information that you'll want to check out. First, link to the AMR Corporation (owners of American Airlines) to find news releases about its businesses. Then go to the Airline Group, where you can check flight schedules, get information about reservations and maintenance, find out more about the travel awards program, visit the virtual Admirals' Club, and check out special products and programs. You'll also find employment opportunities here. Even see what movie is playing on your flight. From the main page, you can also go to the Sabre Group to find travel products and services. Learn more about the leading provider of software and consulting to the travel and transportation industries. Make travel arrangements online, and get travel news and bargain fare information. You can also quickly access every page on this huge site from a comprehensive index.

Contact: AMR Corporation, *webmaster@amrcorp.com*

Canadian Airlines International

http://www.cdnair.ca/

Canadian Airlines was the first airline to offer WWW services. Through the Internet, you can access the latest information on travel services and schedules. Using an interactive form, choose your points of departure and arrival, and a complete flight schedule is returned to you. Another form provides the latest departure and arrival times for specific flights, updated every half hour from a live feed. Even find out what movie is playing on your flight, or get a map of the airport you're journeying to. Finally, Canadian Airlines connects you through hyperlinks to travel and accommodation services to help make planning your trip even easier.

Contact: Grant Fengstad, Canadian Airlines, *webmaster@www.CdnAir.CA*

Costa Travel Online

http://mmink.cts.com/mmink/kiosks/costa/costatravel.html

Costa Travel is a full-fledged travel agency that offers online services, specializing in cruises. Its Web page provides information about different cruises, including discount tour packages and Club Med specials. It also offers a unique "Internet cruise discount" if you decide to order after visiting the site. You can access international airfare specials and get an "Internet computer coupon" to save on airline fares. Also download travel brochures from destinations all over the world. A form is provided for booking trips and taking advantage of discounts. Although the form is not interactive, you can print it and fax or mail it to make reservations.

Contact: Costa Travel Online, Multimedia Ink Designs, *costatvl@aol.com*

GNN Traveler's Center

http://nearnet.gnn.com/gnn/meta/travel/index.html

This is not a travel agency but rather a center of information resources for travelers, gathered from outside sources and from all over the Internet. The information in the center is updated every week with new columns, Internet resources, and marketplace additions. The bulk of the center is organized like a magazine with travel columns and features. Check out Notes from the Road for ongoing journal reports of road trips all over the world. In addition to the magazine sections, the center serves as a gateway to travel resources on the Internet. Each section contains links to a variety of information centers, including a guide for planning your next trip over the Internet. The reading room points to travelers' journals all over the Internet. One highlight is the Currency Converter, updated weekly with the latest currency rates. A large shopping center for travel goods includes maps and atlases, guidebooks, literary travel anthologies, and time-sensitive travel information.

Contact: Morris Dye, editor, NearNet, *morris@gnn.com*

International Traveler's Clinic

http://www.intmed.mcw.edu/travel.html

Visit this virtual clinic for a useful resource concerning health when traveling. The good stuff is located under Travel Health Information. Here you'll find a wealth of health tips for traveling abroad, especially in developing countries. Learn what to pack and what first-aid supplies you need in a travel medicine kit so you can be prepared. Get tips for traveling while pregnant, especially special precautions you should take. Find out about diseases, such as cholera, diphtheria, hepatitis, malaria, rabies, typhoid, and even ebola, that you could be at risk for when traveling and the immunizations for them. You'll find an overview of where recent outbreaks have occurred and what you can do to keep from contracting these diseases. Also learn about high-risk countries for disease and vaccinations you should get before you start your trip. The directory even contains information about environmental hazards such as altitude sickness, motion sickness, and automobile accidents. Learn how to prevent them or what to do if the situation occurs. From the clinic, you can access a directory of physicians who offer consultative services in tropical medicine, medical parasitology, or travelers' health. And find out more about the International Travelers' Clinic, which provides comprehensive health care services for travelers planning trips abroad. Check here first before embarking on any journey.

Contact: International Travelers Clinic, Medical College of Wisconsin, *barnas@post.its.mcw.edu*

Onward

http://sunsite.unc.edud/onward/home.html

Roadtrips, pilgrimages, nomadisms, and secret missions—the e-zine Onward publishes real stories from real people about real places and unreal situations. Read travel stories and road journals here that take you across the United States in text and pictures. Also connect to The Crash Network, a cool travel zine, and to other travelog resources on the Internet.

Contact: Onward, SunSITE, *ed@sunsite.unc.edu*

Rec.Travel Library

http://www.digimark.net/rec-travel/

This is one of the Web's most extensive databases of travel information, culled from the *rec.travel* newsgroup. Check out the featured travel site of the week, or search all the articles posted to the newsgroup in a complete archive. Then get traveling—you can choose any destination in the world. Each destination links to valuable travel information on the Internet, including how to get there, what to do once you're there, travelogs, and other tips. General articles share travelers' impressions of each area. Learn who to call for travel arrangements, including tour operators, travel agents, accommodations, vendors of travel-related products, airlines, buses, car rental agencies, and trains, all with sites on the Internet. Find out fun things to do and helpful travel information about camping, flying, cruises, diving, health, languages, skiing, white water rafting, and traveling around the world. You can also connect to further sources of online information, including tourism offices worldwide and other Internet collections of travel-related information.

Contact: Internet Solutions, Inc., DigiMark Center

Travel Information

http://galaxy.einet.net/GJ/travel.html

Visit a one-stop shop for travel information found on the Internet. You'll find airline information, FAQs about tourism, specifics on countries and cities around the world, travel guides, and newsletters. The resources are arranged in alphabetical order and are searchable.

Contact: Gopher Jewels, TradeWave Galaxy, *galaxy@tradewave.com*

Travels With Samantha

http://www-swiss.ai.mit.edu/samantha/travels-with-samantha.html

This Best of the Web award winner (for Best Document Design) is an online travelog about the summer the author spent traveling across North America. As the trip progresses, the work becomes a retrospective of American people and places, illustrated along the way with maps and photographs. The site features over 250 full-color photographs taken during the trip, which can be viewed in their entirety through a "slide show." Click on any photograph to get a 100 KB JPEG view, or click on the link BIG to get a 250 KB poster. An index of maps for all the places the author visited is also included. Samantha, by the way, is the author's Mac Powerbook computer, which he recorded his journal on. You can even send him e-mail using an interactive form.

Contact: Philip Greenspun, Switzerland (Project MAC) Home Page, Massachusetts Institute of Technology, *samantha@mit.edu*

Photographs like this make the author's experiences traveling through America come alive in Travels With Samantha.

TravelWeb

http://www.travelweb.com/

If you're traveling and need a place to stay, you'll find all the information you could want at TravelWeb. The site features hotels, motels, inns, resorts—every facet of the lodging world. Soon you'll even be able to check availability of rooms and book your room via this online guide. Right now, you can search only the collected brochures from hotels and chains around the world, a useful service in itself. Pick a hotel you want to get information about. The electronic brochure lists check in and check out times, the local airport, room rates, services, facilities and amenities, and a description of the location of the hotel. More links take you to further information, such as chain info, area info, rooms, rates, restaurants, meeting sites, and weather. This very complete guide even includes international hotel locations, so you should find it invaluable in planning your next business trip or vacation.

Contact: THISCO and Cyber Publishing, Inc., TravelWeb, *cyber1@enet.net*

U.S. State Department Travel Warnings

http://www.stolaf.edu/network/travel-advisories.html

Do you want to vacation in Cuba? Need to do business in Kuwait? Planning to visit friends or relatives in North Korea? You'd better check here first. Travel warnings are issued when the State Department recommends that Americans avoid traveling to a certain country. Search the entire database of recent travel warnings for specific keywords or browse by country name. You'll also find here Consular Information Sheets, available on every country in the world, that provide information on the location of the U.S. embassy consulate, unusual immigration practices, crime and security, drug penalties, minor political disturbances, health conditions, and unusual currency and entry regulations. There are also links to a collection of detailed maps, international flags, and excerpts from the CIA World Factbook. From here, you can learn how to subscribe to the travel advisories mailing list or link to related travel information, such as the international travelers' clinic and the travelers' tales resource center. This site is a good first stop when planning any trip abroad.

Contact: Craig D. Rice, St. Olaf College, *cdr@stolaf.edu*

For more information about travel, visit these sites:

Blueheart Tours

http://www.blueheart.com/tours/

Includes tours to Ireland, Russia, Eastern Europe, China, Turkey, and Greece.

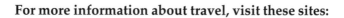

Cruise Review Library

http://www.webcom.com/~jbd/rtc/rtc.html

Listings and descriptions of cruises all over the watery sections of the world. A straightforward, one-issue site.

Down the Garden Path...

http://www.prairienet.org/ag/garden/downpath.htm

This site provides a virtual tour of gardens all over the world. Each link includes pictures from the garden specified.

Internet Travel Network

http://www.itn.net/cgi/get?itn/index/

Book your vacation via the Internet, and this service will register it with a local agency.

Lonely Planet Travel Guides

http://www.lonelyplanet.com/

Guides to traveling, including first-person stories by travelers, researchers, and authors. Free quarterly newsletter.

United Kingdom

The Alien's Guide to Oxford

http://www.comlab.ox.ac.uk/archive/ox/guide/PRG-TR-12-90.html

If you need to journey to Oxford, home of Oxford University, this witty guide will help you survive the trip. The authors warn that the guide may be a little out-of-date, but it still makes for good hypermedia reading. Written in an informal, humorous style, the guide presents a large amount of information about Oxford. One of the best places to start reading is the Local Sights section. This page lists sights not usually found in tour books, such as the house with the shark through the roof. Another useful section, entitled The Boring Bits, is actually full of useful information, such as where Oxford is (a map), how to get to Oxford by car, taxi, coach, and train, how to stay in Oxford (a listing of hotels), and how to get out of Oxford. The text becomes more fun when you follow links just to see where they take you—to photographs, related documents, even a glossary of Oxford vocabulary words. This guide is a fun read, whether you're planning on visiting Oxford or not, and is also a good example of hypertext publishing.

Contact: Jonathan Bowen and Peter Breuer, Oxford University Computing Laboratory, *Jonathan.Bowen@comlab.ox.ac.uk*

Brit Chat

http://www.fer.uni-lj.si/~iztok/england.html

England is a regular channel on Internet Relay Chat (IRC), described as "The Friendly Channel." At the Web page, England enthusiasts can find a list of frequent visitors to the channel, as well as a collection of pictures of the channel users. Such WWW pages expand the community feeling of IRC channels, and this one does the job very well. In fact, some call it the best IRC-channel Web page. Visit and decide for yourself.

Contact: Iztok Umek, Faculty of Electrical and Computer Engineering, University of Ljubljana, *iztok@fer.uni-lj.si*

Gaelic and Gaelic Culture

http://sunsite.unc.edu/gaelic/

This unique site is one of the few language home pages I know about on the WWW. The term *Gaelic* includes Irish Gaelic, Manx Gaelic, and Scottish Gaelic, spoken in places you can visit through the United Kingdom Guide and the Virtual Tourist Guide to Ireland. Here, listen to audio examples of all three forms of Gaelic or access today's news spoken in Irish. Hear the works of Scottish poet Robbie Burns read aloud, or read the poetry of 1995 Nobel laureate Seamus Heaney. There is even a collection of tartans. Don't forget to check out the information on Celtic music. If this home page stirs your heart for Gaelic, a Gaelic mailing list and newsgroup can lead you to even more information.

Contact: Shawn Mehan, Godfrey Nolan, and John Walsh, SunSITE, *webmaster@sunsite.unc.edu*

London Information

http://www.cs.ucl.ac.uk/misc/uk/london.html

An in-depth guide to everything you wanted to know about the city of London, this site is a must for exploration. It combines a range of information, from BBC television and radio schedules to descriptions of city museums. First travel to London by air, land, or rail using full-color maps, or zoom in from orbit by clicking on a satellite photograph of the city. Two particularly innovative attractions at this site make it a good stop on your Internet tour. One is a huge, full-color, interactive map of central London. Click on any area of the map to receive detailed information about London's many historic sites, illustrated by photographs. The second is the Tube Journey Planner Index, an experimental system to find the best route between two places on the London Underground. You can also visit London restaurants and pubs, be entertained by music and theater, and see statues and street art.

Contact: Mark Handley, University College, London, *mhandley@cs.ucl.ac.uk*

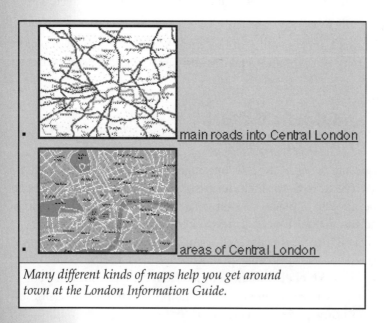

- main roads into Central London
- areas of Central London

Many different kinds of maps help you get around town at the London Information Guide.

United Kingdom Guide

http://www.cs.ucl.ac.uk/misc/uk/intro.html

Tour the British Isles in one easy-to-use guide. The guide opens with an interactive map of the United Kingdom and Ireland. You can jump around from place to place through the map or take a guided tour, starting with London. (The London tour has so much information that I reviewed it separately.) After London, move first through the cities of England and then out to Scotland and Wales. Every one of the many stops has tourist information, and many provide photographs and clickable maps of the region. The tour also guides you to WWW servers at every destination, in case you need even more information about the place. Another highlight for the virtual tourist is the Better Accommodation Guide, a unique listing of recommended (by the people who live there) places to stay in the United Kingdom. Also connect to recreational and governmental information here.

Contact: Mark Handley, University College, London, *mhandley@cs.ucl.ac.uk*

Virtual Tourist Guide to Ireland

This guide to Ireland is unique because of the genealogical information provided. This service will help you track your Irish ancestors. Another unique feature is RTÉ to Everywhere, which serves audio clips of news headlines from Dublin daily in both English and Irish. Arts buffs will enjoy poetry by Yeats, short stories by Joyce, Bram Stoker's *Dracula*, or a visit to the Druid Theater Company to see what's playing. Music lovers can listen to the Irish National Anthem in either English or Irish or visit Irish bands on the Web. Visit the capital, Dublin, and explore the four provinces of the country. Learn about Irish economics, politics, and current affairs. You'll find everything you'd want to know about Ireland in this tourist guide.

Contact: Paddy Waldron, Department of Economics, Trinity College, *pwaldron@tcd.ie*

For more information about the United Kingdom, visit these sites:

BBC Homepage

http://www.bbcnc.org.uk/

Includes links to a TV index and a radio index.

CityNet's Page on the U.K.

http://www.city.net/countries/united_kingdom/

Includes division by country (and territory!) and information based on topic, such as general facts, and hotel and restaurant information, all easily navigated.

Guide to Offbeat Britain

http://vvv.com/adsint/freehand/britain/

A nicely organized, slightly out-of-kilter guide to the offbeat stuff in Britain. Interesting!

Ireland

http://www.misty.com/ulysses/

With a very cool design, this site includes a virtual guide to Ireland and a Virtual Irish Pub.

National Arts Guide

http://www.national-arts-guide.co.uk/uk/home.html

Guide to art galleries and exhibits in the United Kingdom. Includes all of the U.K., not just Britain, with previews of shows.

Travel Diary

http://Alpha.Solutions.Net/rec-travel/europe/uk/scotland-trip-bates.html

Travel diary of a personal trip to Scotland and Northern Ireland. Might be interesting for those who are traveling.

United Kingdom

http://www.emg.com/uk/index.html

The site looks pretty bare when you get there, but there's some useful information buried behind the blue letters. The guide to English money will make understanding pre-twentieth-century English Lit monetary terms much easier, and the U.K. guide has several active maps.

United Kingdom Geography

http://www.adfa.oz.au/CS/flg/wf93/uk.html

Long text file of facts and figures including geography, climate, and other technical information about the U.K. Also includes outside links to the CIA World Factbook and other related info.

United Kingdom Information

http://www.cs.ucl.ac.uk/misc/uk/wfb.html

Contains basic information, mostly text, but cleanly organized and with a few outside links. Possibly an excerpt of the CIA World Factbook? Lots of good information here.

Wales Page

http://www.data-wales.co.uk/

Provides information on Wales, with a nice design—looks helpful.

United States

American South Home Page

http://sunsite.unc.edu/doug_m/pages/south/south.html

This regional home page opens with greetings from Elvis and some mood music—the "dueling banjos" sequence from the motion picture *Deliverance*. From the home page, you can enter the Center for the Study of the American South, which publishes *Southern Cultures*, a quarterly that examines the folk, popular, and historical cultures of the South. Get submission and subscription information, or read the table of contents and editor's introduction. You can also access the Southern Focus Poll, a public opinion poll that samples Southern opinions. Another highlight of this site is the Southern Historical Collection, where you should definitely pay a visit to the Doc Watson Multimedia Exhibit. There you can wander through an exhibit of photographs while listening to samples of Doc's music. Current satellite weather images of the Southeast are available, and an interactive map connects directly to Internet resources and home pages by state.

Contact: Doug Matthews, SunSITE, University of North Carolina at Chapel Hill, *rdm@unc.edu*

Atlanta!

http://www.gatech.edu/studlife/travelink/homepage.html

This experimental project is a complete guide to Atlanta, including transportation, entertainment, universities, parks, and architecture. Travel to Atlanta and all around the city by clicking icons for air, bus, rental car, taxi, and train transport. The airport section, for instance, provides a list of airlines, a layout map of the airport, and a list of the airport's amenities. The Buckhead Information Guide is a fun bar guide, where you can choose a bar either from an interactive map or an alphabetical listing. You can even locate a bar with a particular specialty or atmosphere. Two highlights of this site that shouldn't be missed are the '96 Olympics Guide and the Music Guide. The Olympics Guide connects to information about events—where they will be held, where to buy tickets, and information about participating countries. The Music Guide provides a listing of music happenings in Atlanta, including album releases, upcoming concerts, music festivals, and concert series. There is also information about local radio stations, clubs, and artists, all accessible through a handy interactive map.

Contact: Georgia Tech Students, Georgia Institute of Technology, *studmain@www.gatech.edu*

Big Island of Hawaii

http://bookweb.cwis.uci.edu:8042/Books/Moon/moon.html

This experimental travel guide is based on J.D. Bisignani's *Big Island of Hawaii* handbook, published by Moon Publications. The guide explores the land, culture, history, and recreation of Hawaii through text, maps, photographs, and audio clips. If you are interested in scenery, access a repository of all the images in the guide. If thoughts and impressions of Hawaii intrigue you, a directory of sound files recorded by the author is available. Or thumb through the guide, reading about the land, flora and fauna, people, sports and recreation, and seasonal festivals, among many other topics. All pages are illustrated with full-color photographs. A beautiful, interactive map makes for easy travel across the island. Clicking on the Hawaii Volcanoes National Park, for example, takes you to the Visitor's Center, where you can get a crash course in geology while viewing photographs of the volcanoes or walk Devastation Trail over a lava field.

Contact: Moon Publications and University of California at Irvine Bookstore, Jonathan Cohen, *jkcohen@uci.edu*

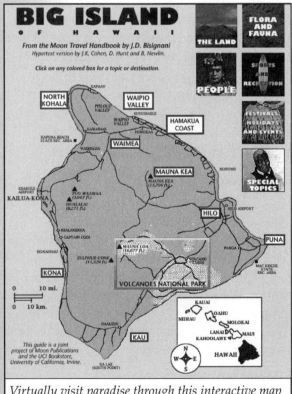

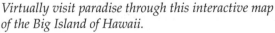

Virtually visit paradise through this interactive map of the Big Island of Hawaii.

Blacksburg Electronic Village

http://www.bev.net/

This is the ideal model of a community network, based in Blacksburg, Virginia. The Electronic Village is a cooperative project that links the citizens of Blacksburg to each other and to the Internet. Explore the town through a photo album or learn more about local history, commerce, and activities at the Chamber of Commerce. Go to the Village Mall for shopping at almost a hundred local businesses. Online event calendars updated weekly give scheduling information for arts and entertainment, public meetings, health-related events, senior citizen activities, and community activities. Browse the guide to local organizations for a club to join. Learn about students and activities of local schools, published by the students themselves. Get home health care tips from a medical database composed by a local doctor. All departments in the town government post and update useful information for citizens. Read about recreation programs, send e-mail to the police chief, or use the Fire Department's information to teach your children fire prevention and safety. You can also link to other Virginia resources from here.

Contact: Virginia Tech, Bell Atlantic of Virginia and the Town of Blacksburg, Blacksburg Electronic Village, *webmaker@bev.net*

City of Cambridge, Massachusetts

http://www.ci.cambridge.ma.us/

Explore this historic city starting from the Cambridge Common. Find maps of the city, visit libraries and museums, or learn about education. Every other facet of the city is included here as well. Also from this site, you can enter City Hall and learn all about local government. If history is your interest, a historical profile of the city is linked in. If you're planning to travel to Cambridge, tourist information and a restaurant guide are available. Finally, from Cambridge you can venture out into Massachusetts, with links to educational resources, Boston information, and a graphical map of Massachusetts WWW servers.

Contact: City of Cambridge, Massachusetts, *webmaster@ci.cambridge.ma.us*

City of San Diego

http://www.nosc.mil/planet_earth/sandiego.html

Visit what this site calls "America's finest city" in an information-packed resource. There are a lot of links here, all connected to resources elsewhere on the Internet. For instance, connect to a map of San Diego at the Xerox Map Server or a census total at the U.S. Census Bureau's site. The information provided is varied and useful, including weather forecasts, employment opportunities, military information, and earthquake and disaster information. Colleges and universities, K-12 schools, businesses, and research institutes are all linked in. For fun, stop at coffeehouses and restaurants, get the San Diego hiker atlas, or see the San Diego Padres in action. Tourist attractions that you can visit include the San Diego Zoo, Sea World, and historic Spanish missions. This site is an example of how a lot of information from all over the WWW can be gathered in one place to thoroughly cover a narrow subject, such as the author's home town.

Contact: Richard Bocker, Naval Command, Control and Ocean Surveillance Center, *bocker@nosc.mil*

City of West Hollywood

http://www.ci.west-hollywood.ca.us/cityhall/

Tour the city of West Hollywood from this virtual city hall. Here you can access inaugural remarks from the mayor, a directory of city officials, and a city council profile. Get a schedule of upcoming events. Check out art and entertainment guides for listings of restaurants, night life, galleries, and bookstores. You'll even find West Hollywood film facts. You can also access general information, like important city hall phone numbers, a social services guide, landmark legislation, city council agendas, and city statistics. Visit the city departments, including public safety, human services, and transportation and public works. Access the city budget and comprehensive annual financial report. A West Hollywood fact sheet gives a quick overview of attractions, shops, architecture, events, population, and government. You can also connect to other general community interest and government resources on the Internet from here.

Contact: City of West Hollywood Government, Delta Internet Services, *wehoweb@deltanet.com*

The Connecticut Guide

http://www.atlantic.com/ctguide/

This complete guide has tourism info, news, a Web server list, and facts about the New England state. Read current news stories from the *Hartford Courant*. Access tourist guides, a census, economic and industrial information, official state and town government information, and climate and current weather reports. A complete list of WWW servers and other resources connects you to anything you would want to find in Connecticut. Even Connecticut's winning lottery numbers are linked in to the site.

Contact: Atlantic Computing Technology Corporation, *ct-guide@atlantic.com*

Grand Canyon

http://www.kbt.com/gc/

Let this site be the starting point for your explorations of the grandest canyon on earth, one of the seven natural wonders of the world. Here you can learn general information about the Grand Canyon, including facts about geology and history. See flora, wildlife, rocks, and water in an online photograph album of the canyon. Want to take a trip? The site tells you how to get there and where to camp. You'll also find names of hotels, restaurants, and other services available in the area. What do you do when you're there? You can go hiking on back country trails or river running; get tips from the online guide. You can also find out what the weather is like there or download free maps of hiking trails. Visit other attractions in the area through the site, such as national parks, monuments, museums, craters, observatories, caverns, and more. You'll even find tips for making your trip a green one. Access a list of books and guides for further research.

Contact: Bob Ribokas, Knowledge Based Technologies, *bob@kbt.com*

Greetings from the Grand Canyon.

Hoboken X

http://www.stevens-tech.edu/hobokenx/

Hoboken, New Jersey, may not be your first pick for a glamorous travel destination, but it is a worthwhile stop on your WWW tour. This online guide showcases "one of the coolest towns in the U.S.," focusing on local arts, eating, and entertainment. Hoboken restaurants are listed by ethnic type, such as Italian, Korean, Thai, and Middle Eastern. Some listings include menus or reviews. (You can even review Hoboken restaurants yourself by filling out an interactive form with your comments on entree, dessert, price, and other details.) The guide also connects to the local record label, Bar None, where you can purchase Hoboken's finest music directly through the Internet. Another worthwhile stop is a gallery of art by local Hoboken artists. Follow the Literary Scene link to read published extracts from books by Hoboken writers. You'll also find transit information, demographics, and feature articles about the experience of living in Hoboken.

Contact: David Belson and Paul F. Peacock, Stevens Institute of Technology, *dbelson@web.cc.stevens-tech.edu*

Home of Everything That's Cool in Austin

http://www.quadralay.com/www/Austin/Austin.html

With that title, how can you go wrong? This is a complete directory of goodies to be found in Austin, Texas, including listings of bed and breakfast establishments, pubs, a community calendar, businesses, education opportunities, restaurants, and even movie show times. The main attraction is the music information, including listings of live music and road shows. Read about such Austin musicians as Stevie Ray Vaughn, the Fabulous Thunderbirds, Edie Brickell, and Willie Nelson. Visit the Austin film production center, where you can read about movies filmed in Austin. You can learn everything there is to know about armadillos. A large picture archive is also available, but bear in mind the warning that these photos may cause an uncontrollable urge to move to the heart of Texas.

Contact: Quadralay Corporation, *webmaster@quadralay.com*

Information About Alaska

http://info.alaska.edu:70/1s/Alaska/

Get an introduction to one of the United States' most remarkable states through this informative site. The introductory text, which explains a little of the history of Alaska, contains lots of links of side interest. The introduction is followed by a wealth of menued information, all completely hyperlinked, on subjects ranging from the Constitution to criminal statutes to public radio. Read historical documents, such as the Statehood Act and the treaty with Russia, or download a Jack London novel. Monitor dog sled races with photographs and daily progress updates, aurora borealis activity reports, and weather news. You can even search for Alaskan place names, which returns lists of files on the server containing that name, a useful geographic tool. Finally, there may be no real Cicely, Alaska, but there is a "Northern Exposure" link that provides episode guides, a music guide, photos, FAQs, and quotes about the popular television show.

Contact: Douglas Toelle, University of Alaska, *sxinfo@orca.alaska.edu*

Las Vegas

http://www.vegas.com/vegascom/vegdir.html

Visit the tackiest city in America in all its glory on the WWW. See the Las Vegas strip in neon-rich graphics. Take a tour of the city's casinos, learning the basics of every casino game (a fee-based service), visiting casino shops, and checking show and event schedules. A section of gambling information has lots of articles, including an inside look at the cutting edge of gambling technology, Native American gambling information, current casino stock quotes, expert opinions by gambling professionals, and gambling news. The Las Vegas Sports Club introduces you to the "future of sports information." Take a look at computerized sports betting services, and find out how you can place bets through your computer. Or visit the other side of Las Vegas through a listing of city businesses with stops on the Information Superhighway. You'll also find information on other points of interest in southern Nevada as well as listings of airlines, car rental agencies, tour operators, and national parks and recreation services. You can even plan your dream Las Vegas wedding through this site.

Contact: On Ramp Internet Computing Services, Vegas.Com, *mktng@vegas.com*

North Carolina Encyclopedia

http://hal.dcr.state.nc.us/nc/cover.htm

This site is an evolving information repository about the state of North Carolina. New text and graphics are added to the site daily, making return visits a must. The online encyclopedia gives an overview of the people, government, history, and resources of the Tar Heel State. Some interesting tidbits include historical and governmental summaries of all one hundred of North Carolina's counties and a chronology of four hundred years of North Carolina history. You can visit North Carolina historic sites in text and photographs, including the governor's mansion and the state capitol. The site includes a description of the evolution of the government system in North Carolina. North Carolina's geography is outlined with embedded hyperlinks to photographs illustrating the text. For fun, access a list of all the state emblems, including the state beverage (milk) and the state dog (the Platt Hound).

Contact: Bob Coats, Juedi Kleindienst and Joel Sigmon, State Library of North Carolina, *SLIS.RBC@NCDCR.DCR.STATE.NC.US*

The Paperless Guide to New York City

http://www.mediabridge.com/nyc/

This graphical, easy-to-use guide takes you all around the Big Apple (concentrating on Manhattan). Use the clickable map to explore the different areas of the guide. Go to How for history, facts, and general information. A transportation link provides a guide to subways, buses, car rentals, taxis, air transportation, helicopters, and bridge crossings. Use the navigator to interactively find cross streets in Manhattan. The survival guide gives tips for getting through not-so-safe situations in the city and alerts you to many scams. Visit Wow for information about food and dining, shopping, sightseeing, hotels, and museums. Get dining tips, find out how to locate the most famous New York restaurants, critique a restaurant, or use the FoodPhone, one of the best ways to find restaurants in the city. At Now, you'll find info about current events, sports and fitness, entertainment, and media. Learn where to party in the city, get a comprehensive listing of talk shows and live tapings, or look at theater, concert, and movie schedules. Headlines tells you what's happening in the city today and are automatically refreshed every hour. At the marketplace, locate various services such as those of attorneys, moving companies, car rental agencies, and theater ticket vendors. Whether you're visiting the city for sightseeing, shopping, or business, this guide can help you survive the trip.

Contact: Mediabridge Infosystems, Inc., *nyc@mediabridge.com*

Philadelphia LibertyNet

http://philadelphia.libertynet.org/

This is a well-organized site covering everything in the Philadelphia region from fun and community to business and education. Here you can learn where the action is in Philadelphia, from sightseeing to sports. Get information about local businesses. Join the community with medical and transportation information, and a list of local service and religious organizations. Visit the area's universities, K-12 schools, and libraries. Discover government home pages and a directory of elected officials. You'll also find everything you need to know about exploring the Internet here.

Contact: LibertyNet, *webmaster@libertynet.org*

Salt Grass Trail Ride

http://www.cybersim.com/sgtr/

Ride across Utah on virtual horseback when you join the annual Salt Grass Trail Ride at this site. Here you can look at daily photos taken from the most recent ride. All of the beautiful scenes were shot from horseback. You can also see pictures from past trail rides. Follow along with a schedule and trail ride map. Meet the trail guide, CyberJoe, who sends back daily reports and photos from the annual trail ride. Participate in every day of the eight-day ride from the comfort of your own home.

Contact: Cybersim Communications, Inc., *sgtr@cybersim.com*

South Florida Environmental Reader

http://envirolink.org/florida/index.html

This electronic newsletter, which covers South Florida environmental concerns, including the Everglades, is a good example of electronic communal publishing. Read the current issue, or access an archive of back issues to 1991. You can also submit articles through the site. The newsletter is made up of short articles, mostly describing Internet resources of interest, such as mailing lists or FreeNets. The articles also announce relevant documents that can be retrieved through the Internet. Issues appear to be published weekly, but publication dates are sporadic. A separate page links to other environmental resources for Florida. All in all, this newsletter represents a good use of HTML for communal publication and quick, inexpensive distribution of information.

Contact: EnviroWeb, EnviroLink Network, Andrew Mossberg, editor, *sfer@symbiosis.ahp.com*

State of South Dakota

http://www.state.sd.us/

The clickable opening graphic leads to pages of information about this often-overlooked state. Interactive "buttons" on the map access such items as a South Dakota Internet Resource Map or tourist information from the Department of Tourism and Economic Development. Get information, with photographs, on attractions like Mt. Rushmore, the Crazy Horse Memorial and the Badlands. You can even view a South Dakota road map or fill out an interactive form to request more information. The Government button opens an interactive map that connects to government agencies, the state capitol complex, and legislative bills. From the Cities button, visit Pierre, Madison, and Rapid City, among others, to access local government information, resources for families, popular attractions, motel listings, weather forecasts, and local radio stations.

Contact: Network Services Group, State of South Dakota, *webmaster@is.state.sd.us*

Texas, Texans and the Alamo

http://www.lib.utexas.edu/Libs/CAH/texas/cah_texas1.html

You can't visit Texas without a stop at its most famous historic site—the Alamo. This educational exhibit is composed of items in the Barker Texas Historical Collection at the Center for American History. The exhibit features the earliest photograph taken in Texas, an 1849 daguerreotype of the Alamo. Paging through the exhibit uncovers many other items of interest, including Sam Houston's handwritten draft of his inaugural address after being elected first president of the Republic of Texas and General Santa Anna's battle map for the assault on the Alamo. Read the reminiscences of an early settler as she describes her journey to Texas; two pages of the actual journal are reproduced in the exhibit for you to view. A hand-colored lithograph gives an early view of the city of Austin. Other historic documents, paintings, and photographs featured here are a great source of early Texas history.

Contact: Center for American History, University of Texas at Austin, *www@lib.utexas.edu*

Early photograph of the Alamo featured in the Texas Historical Collection exhibit. (Used with permission of the General Libraries and the Center for American History, University of Texas at Austin. May not be reproduced without permission.)

For more information about the United States, visit these sites:

Alaska Web Site

http://www.corcom.com/

Here you'll find a complete directory to business, educational, and cultural resources in Alaska.

Arizona Web Servers

http://www.eas.asu.edu/az/servers.html

This site provides a list of all Web servers in Arizona. This resource directory will lead you to businesses, universities, and government resources in that state.

Boulder Community Network

http://bcn.boulder.co.us/

An excellent example of a community information center, this one about Boulder, Colorado. Find out about business, news, weather, community, and more for Boulder County.

California Environmental Resources Evaluation System

http://resources.agency.ca.gov/

This electronic data center describes California's rich and diverse environmental resources. You'll also find environmental impact reports, information about water resources, and information about wildlife.

Center for the Study of Southern Culture

http://imp.cssc.olemiss.edu/

This is an outlet for the wide variety of cultural events in the southern United States. Find out about conferences for Southern studies and read about periodicals, videos, and books published by the Center. This is also a great place for learning about Southern music (Elvis, blues, gospel) and literature (Faulkner).

World Cultures

American Indian Computer Art Project

http://aicap.s21.com/

The American Indian Computer Art Project allows the exchange of ideas and art relating to Native Americans. Here you can look at a variety of Native American paintings, masks, and pottery. Be sure to read the poems or text associated with each work to learn more about it and its place in Native American culture. See a gallery of

sacred pipes, and read about the tribes that use the pipes traditional-
ly. Walk through a gallery of original art by tribal artists. View art
from different tribes and in different styles and mediums. Wander
through a large digital art gallery by Turtle Heart, an Ojibway artist.
There's also an exhibit of original songs created spontaneously on
the computer. Read about the rituals and history of certain Native
American tribes with photographs to illustrate the text. This project
is a unique blending of Native culture and traditions with computer
and Internet technology.

Contact: Turtle Heart, Massachusetts Institute of Technology,
turtle@aicap.s21.com

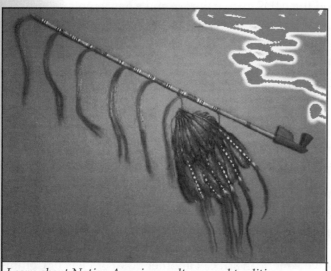

*Learn about Native American cultures and traditions
through their art.*

Anthropology Resources

http://lucy.ukc.ac.uk/

This site exhibits lots of anthropology research projects for many locations around the world as well as general anthropology resources.
Explore the research projects in Turkey, the Cook Islands, Thailand,
and more places around the globe. Find software for anthropologists

and reviews of books and software. Connect to anthropology exhibits all over the Web. Also find a lot of other anthropology resources on the Internet, including the anthropology WWW virtual library, the archives of the anthropology mailing list, and anthropology-related Gophers and Usenet newsgroups.

Contact: Michael D. Fischer, University of Kent at Canterbury, *M.D.Fischer@ukc.ac.uk,* Centre for Social Anthropology and Computing

Gay and Lesbian Resource Center

http://www.actwin.com/queerindex.html

Here you'll find the AIDS virtual library and a gay events calendar. Connect to gay organizations online, such as the Massachusetts Gay and Lesbian Political Caucus. The site is also linked to lots of online resources of interest to the gay and lesbian community.

Contact: Active Windows Productions, *mar@actwin.com*

Indigenous Peoples' Literature

http://kuhttp.cc.ukans.edu/~marc/natlit/natlit.html

Lots of literature and art is available here for studying the history and culture of native peoples. You'll find stories, fables, poetry, myths, and music offering a fascinating look into native cultures. The collection reflects tribes from all over the Americas. Take a look at Internet collections of Native American art. Get another point of view of Columbus's discovery of America. Read great speeches from famous Native American leaders. Access prayers to the Great Spirit and Mother Earth, and learn about spiritual dances. Read famous documents in Native American history, and find out about sacred geography, Thanksgiving, and the origin of names of American states. When you leave here, you can connect to Internet resources for other native peoples in Europe, Africa, Asia, and the Pacific for further study.

Contact: Glenn Welker, University of Kansas, *gwelker@mail.lmi.org,* and Marc Becker, *marc@ukanaix.cc.ukans.edu*

Enter the world of Native Americans through stories, songs, and art.

Oneida Indian Nation

http://nysernet.org:80/oneida/

The Oneida Indian Nation exists as a sovereign political unit that pre-dates the U.S. Constitution. It is also the first Native American nation to establish a WWW site. The site shares the culture, history, and progress of the Oneida with an international audience. Listen to an audio welcome message, and read an introduction to the Oneida Nation. Access ongoing projects where you can find out little-known historic facts about the Oneida, including the unique role they played in supporting America's fight for independence. You can also read historic treaties, hear audio samples of the Oneida language, visit the Shako: Wi Cultural Center for an art exhibit, and learn about Native American education issues. Finally, take a tour of the Oneida Nation, or link to other Native American information sites.

Contact: Dan Umstead, NYSERNet, Inc., *oneida1@transit.nyser.net*

Powersource Native American Art and Education Center

http://www.powersource.com/powersource/gallery/default.html

At this online Native American center, you can explore the artwork of featured Native artists and learn more about Native culture, history, and beliefs. Visit the Powersource art collection for exhibits of art pieces by leading Native American artists. Be sure to take a look at the gallery of nature photographer Harry Bowden, which contains lots of animal photographs. Learn about powerful places in Native American legends, and find a travel guide to important Native American sites. Read about powerful Native Americans in history and in the present. Get reference guides to symbols of power and to ceremonial dances. Visit the Cherokee National Historical Society, and link to related sites. All the educational resources are illustrated with Native American art, which you can buy online. You can also purchase Native American-related gifts and books through interactive catalogs.

Contact: Powersource, *sestrapp@powersource.com*

WomensNet

http://www.igc.apc.org/womensnet/

WomensNet is a global community of women activists and organizations using networks to increase women's rights, and it offers lots of information resources for women. Women on WomensNet share their ideas, access vital information, and highlight their own work. Here you can explore projects such as world conferences on women, global computer training, and women online. Access a directory of the WomensNet community, organized by regions. Find out about electronic conferences sponsored by WomensNet. Connect to other online resources for women, including the National Organization for Women, Planned Parenthood, and domestic violence resources.

Contact: WomensNet, The Progressive Directory at the Institute for Global Communications, *womensnet@igc.apc.org*

For more information about world cultures, visit these sites:

African-American Home Page

http://www.sas.upenn.edu/African_Studies/Home_Page/
mcgee.html

Contains links to other pages and documents for issues affecting the
African American community.

Asian-American Resources

http://www.mit.edu:8001/afs/athena.mit.edu/user/i/r/irie/
www/aar.html

Includes organizations, publications, newsgroups, and personal home
page links. I'm not certain if this contains Asian American studies
documents, but it is a good resource for those wanting to find out
more about this community.

Feminist and Women's Resources

http://www.ibd.nrc.ca/~mansfield/feminism.html

Neatly organized, with plenty of outside links for people interested in
feminism and women's issues.

FourthWorld Documentation Project

http://www.halcyon.com/FWDP/othernet.html

A very comprehensive list of Internet resources on "fourth world"
topics, organized by country/region.

Index of Native American Resources on the Web

http://hanksville.phast.umass.edu/misc/NAresources.html

Links are organized by category, including a link to the WWW Virtual
Library index of Aboriginal resources.

Insitute for Hispanic-Latino Culture

http://www.acprog.ifas.ufl.edu/~lacasita/

Contains outside links and information on the University of Florida campus.

Mennonite Central Committee

http://www.mennonitecc.ca/mcc/programs/development.html

This site includes links to discussions of socio-economic issues around the world, with special emphasis on Canadian problems. Spotty covereage—the overemphasis of Canadian poverty problems, compared to, say, Bangledesh, was rather disconcerting. The present leader is apparently Canadian, but still...

The National Organization for Women

http://now.org/now/home.html

This site describes the history and present-day activities of NOW. It includes ways of joining and who to contact in the organization.

Native Web

http://kuhttp.cc.ukans.edu/~marc/native_mail.html

This site is still being developed, but it already has lots of information. There are links to different nations/peoples, maps, literature, and even an online store. It contains some well-chosen, appropriately placed graphics, too. If your opinion of Native Americans was molded by *Dances with Wolves*, this site will be a good reality check for you.

On the Issues

http://www.echonyc.com/~onissues/

Women's issues magazine, looks great. Links to other women's pages.

OutNOW! Alive

http://www.zoom.com/outnow/

This is an online magazine for gays and lesbians. While not sexually explicit, it does cover world/national/local issues from a gay and lesbian perspective.

Queer Frontier

http://www.usc.edu/Library/QF/

From a conference on queer studies, includes paper, abstracts, and other neat stuff.

Queer Resources Directory

http://www.qrd.org/QRD/

Massive amounts of archived information, searchable by keyword or browsable by topic. Looks very useful, but has a boring design.

Shaman and Native American Resources

http://sojourn.com/~jjarrell/web/links.html #sham

Includes shaman stories, pharmaceuticals, and other Native American resources. Looks cool! In the middle is a list of other resources such as Tarot links, etc.

Sources in Anthropology

http://www.geminisystems.com/ARN/ARNNC/ARNNC.html

This site is essentially a list of what the Fogelman Library of the New York School for Social Research has available. If you're going to go to NYC to do some anthropology research, this site would be worth visiting first.

The Web of Culture

http://www.earthlink.net/~webofculture/

This nifty site contains information on cultures around the world and tests and games to help you become more "worldly wise."

Westmont Hilltop

http://westy.jtwn.k12.pa.us/~mjr/WorldCultures.html

Hotlist to world cultures resources, including magazines and lots of other Web sites. A great starting place.

Women's Resources

http://mevard.www.media.mit.edu/people/mevard/women.html

A very impressive page of resources and links for women's interests and issues. Lots of links, including one to the "geekgirl" page.

World Cultures to 1500: Internet Resources List

http://www.wsu.edu:8080/~dee/InternetResources.html

I believe this page is for a specific class, but this list is quite long and has lots and lots of links, organized by category (such as Jewish culture or Islamic culture). Quite complete, efficiently organized, with one-line descriptions of the links. Each category includes Web page links, FTP site links, text document links, and newsgroup links.

Moving On

You've been around the world, and you're probably not even tired. These sites have shown you the huge amount of geographic and cultural information available on the WWW; it is possible to virtually visit foreign countries and exotic locales you may never get to in real life. Now we're going to switch gears and visit a wide variety of resources for the humanities and social sciences: art, literature, religion, law, and education, to name a few. So prepare for the ultimate field trip, multimedia-style.

Section III

Get Cultured

Arts & Humanities Sites

Get Cultured: Arts & Humanities Sites

The potential educational applications of the World Wide Web are infinite. From interactive multimedia exhibits for elementary school students to scholarly texts for college students to searchable databases for professionals, the WWW, with its capacity for multimedia and hypertext, imparts information in a multitude of ways. All across the Internet, elementary and high schools, universities, libraries, and research institutes are taking advantage of the Web to make their resources available to an international audience.

The sites in this section represent the best humanities and arts resources on the Web. They make good use of hypertext, multimedia, and interactive applications to publish information on a variety of subjects, for both the casual browser and the serious researcher. In this section, you'll visit art galleries exhibiting all kinds of art, from a panorama of fine art to very specialized exhibits. You'll tour schools and universities that have created a WWW presence and visit resources just for educators. You'll also find history museums, literature collections, libraries, photography studios, and law institutes, among many other interesting stops.

Whether you're a professional engaged in serious research or a casual browser looking for something fun on the Web, you'll find a site in this section to capture your attention. Put on your artist's beret, your reading glasses, and your old school tie—we're searching for culture on the WWW.

Archaeology

ArchNet

http://spirit.lib.uconn.edu/ArchNet/ArchNet.html

ArchNet is a huge database that provides access to archaeological resources available on the Internet, categorized by geographical region and subject. An attractive button bar enables you to move quickly through an immense amount of information. Visit archaeological regions in North America, Central America, South America, Europe, Africa, the Near East, Asia, Australia, and the Pacific. Or access information by subject, including historical archaeology, ceramics, educational material, and archaeological software. ArchNet also contains links to many external resources, such as academic departments, museums, electronic journals, and newsgroups.

Contact: Alumni/Library, University of Connecticut, Thomas Plunkett and Jonathan Lizee, *archnet@spirit.lib.uconn.edu*

This graphical button bar makes it easy to locate archaeological information at ArchNet.

Cave Paintings

http://www.culture.fr/culture/gvpda-en.htm

A vast underground network of caves decorated with paintings and engravings dating from the Paleolithic age (17,000–20,000 years ago) was discovered recently in Vallon, in Southern France. You can read about this important archaeological discovery and what was found there at this fascinating WWW site. Inline graphics show the ancient cave paintings. It is very rare to find totally intact decorated cave systems, but the WWW lets you visit this unusual archaeological site first-hand.

Contact: French Ministry of Culture

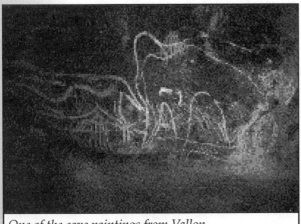

One of the cave paintings from Vallon.

Museum of Archaeology

http://classics.lsa.umich.edu/Kelsey/Outreach.html

If you've always wanted to be an archaeologist, digging up ancient artifacts like Indiana Jones, this online museum will give you the real picture. Go to the Greek and Roman gallery to see archaeological items such as portraits and a sarcophagus. Visit the Egyptian and Near Eastern gallery to view a mummy's mask and tomb portraits. Travel on an archaeological expedition to Egypt where you can view objects of daily life discovered during a real excavation. A library of maps will help you find your way around the ancient Mediterranean world—visit ancient Greece, Italy, and Germany. Also connect to other online resources to further your studies of the ancient world.

Contact: Sebastian Heath, Classics and Mediterranean Archaeology Home Page, *sfsh@umich.edu*

For more information on archaeology, visit the following sites:

Archaeology Consortium

http://www.brad.ac.uk/acad/archsci/tltp/tltp.html

Main link is to newsletters.

Archaeology on the World Wide Web

http://avebury.arch.soton.ac.uk/NetStuff/archplaces.html

This may just be a collection of links to archaeologically oriented Web sites, but what a collection. Well organized and designed, this site is a fun place to ramble through, finding whatever archaeological information interests you.

ArchNet North American Archaeology Net

http://spirit.lib.uconn.edu/ArchNet/Regions/North_America.html

Contains links to various resources by region. Nicely designed and looks very handy. Sub-page of ArchNet as previously reviewed.

Diogenes' Links to the Ancient World

http://www.snider.net/lyceum/

This site provides links to several, mainly academically oriented, Western mythological sites. It is a beautifully designed Web site.

French Archaeology

http://www.culture.fr/culture/daf/dafac-en.htm

Links to French archaeology, in English and French. Minimal links.

List of Anthropology and Archaeology Resources on the Web

http://www.aau.dk/~etnojens/etnogrp/anitaslist.html

Fairly complete list of archaeology resources organized coherently by subject. Includes links to Yahoo and the WWW Virtual Library.

The Perseus Project

http://www.perseus.tufts.edu/

A project on ancient Greece, this site includes links to art and archaeology. It might be of interest to archaeologists.

University of Connecticut Archaeology Page

http://spirit.lib.uconn.edu/archaeology.html

Contains links to museums, archaeological areas (look up information by region) and subjects, plus other useful-looking links.

University of Missouri Museum of Art and Archaeology

http://www.missouri.edu/~c655264/museum.html

Not certain if it contains exhibits online, but it does have information on programs, exhibits, and other things related to the museum.

Art

The Andy Warhol Museum

http://www.usaor.net:80/warhol/

A visit to the Andy Warhol Museum is essential to the understanding of the most influential American artist in the second half of the twentieth century. The museum is also a primary resource for anyone wanting to gain insight into contemporary art and popular culture. At the site, take a guided tour through all seven floors where you can view the layout, walk through the galleries, and see a listing of the works on each floor. View art samples, including general works like Marilyn and Jackie, or look at floor shots. Shop at the museum store for books, CDs, note cards, T-shirts, and posters. Access general museum information, a calendar of upcoming events, a FAQ, press releases, and a complete catalog of the Warhol works at the museum, featuring paintings, sculpture, drawings, prints, and photographs. Also check out education resources, such as workshops and programs designed for students, and learn about the museum patronage program.

Contact: The Andy Warhol Museum, USA Onramp, *www@warhol.org*

Art Crimes

http://www.graffiti.org/

This unique gallery depicts street art—graffiti—from all around the world, including Prague, Sao Paulo, Toronto, El Paso, and Paris. The online exhibit allows you to view many terrific pieces of this "illegal" art, some of which no longer exist in the real world. There is also a FAQ on graffiti art and a listing of graffiti shows and events. View the pieces as inline graphics, and click on the ones you like for a more detailed image. The WWW has made possible an exhibit that would have been impossible to create in a conventional gallery.

Contact: Susan Farrell, Art Crimes Index, *winsom@graffiti.org*

An example of the "illegal" art you'll find at Art Crimes. (Copyright 1994 Susan Farrell, Art Crimes.)

ANIMA

http://www.anima.wis.net/

The Arts Network for Integrated Media Applications (ANIMA) calls itself "the creative cultural information source." Now you know where to go online for creative culture. ANIMA is divided into sections covering events, art zines, online art projects and tools and technologies used in contemporary art. A Guide to Online Galleries reviews many different kinds of art sites and provides hotlinks to them.

Contact: WebWeavers, Arts Network for Integrated Media Applications, *anima@artworld.com*

Art Hole

http://www.mcs.net/~wallach/arthole.html

Visit the Art Hole for a unique collection of art. One great feature is the exhibition of pinhole photography. Another unique exhibit is a collaborative piece based on images of the Levy-Shoemaker comet (the comet that collided with Jupiter in summer 1994). Many artists from all over the Internet contributed to the piece in a process called *cornflaking*. Many other pieces created by the same process are also on display. If static art is not your thing, an exhibit of animations might be. Or you can go to the temporary gallery for "real-life" art—emoticons found on the streets of Paris. (Emoticons or *smileys*:-) are a peculiar Internet invention for expressing emotion in e-mail.) Also check out the Conceptual Art Gallery for a unique piece about the WWW, called "Web."

Contact: Harlan Wallach, MCSNet, *wallach@mcs.com*

Art Links on the Web

http://amanda.physics.wisc.edu/outside.html

It may seem like there are so many art galleries on the Web that you'll never get to them all. Possibly you'll never even find them all. Don't worry any longer about locating online art sites. This page links to most of the major, and minor, Internet galleries. Use this as a launching pad to discover new and innovative art, music, video, photography, and 3D renderings.

Contact: John E. Jacobsen, Strange Interactions, *jacobsen@amanda.physics.wisc.edu*

Art Navigator

http://www.uiah.fi/internetguide/navigator.html

This collection of hotlinked sites will get you started on your quest for art on the Web. From here connect to fun and fantastic art sites, such as the Off the Wall Gallery, the Cybercafe, the Art Noir Exhibition, Art on the Edge, the Finnish National Gallery, and many more. Each site listed is described briefly so you know where you're going before you start.

Contact: University of Art and Design at Helsinki, *joel.ortila@uiah.fi*

ArtNetWEB

http://da.awa.com:80/artnet/artnetweb/

ArtNetWEB is the third phase of a process to establish an art colony in cyberspace. Phase one, The Internet Reading Room, is where artists and art writers gather to learn about the online environment. In the second phase, the ArtNetBBS, art content is selected and organized. (Information about both phases is linked to this site.) ArtNetWEB is the end result of the communal effort to present art content to a worldwide audience. There are four areas for you to explore. On display in Web Projects are art projects created specifically for the WWW. The Slide Registry is a fast and inexpensive way to get art on the Web; look through the exhibits already stored in the registry, or learn how to get your work registered. The registry makes it fast and easy to browse many presentations with a thumbnail browser page that contains small images and a brief explanation of the artists' works. *Views* is

ArtNetWEB's online art magazine, with reviews of current exhibits, interviews with art critics, an experiment in participatory art history, and essays on art-related subjects, such as the censorship of art or the age of digital reproduction. Art Resources presents a hotlist of online art-related sites, such as exhibits, museums, galleries, magazines, and commercial vendors. You'll also find Internet tools and interesting non-art-related sites.

Contact: ArtNet, Downtown Anywhere, *remo@awa.com*

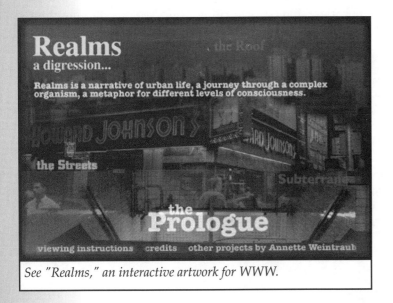

See "Realms," an interactive artwork for WWW.

Art on the Net

http://www.art.net/

At Art on the Net, artists share their works with other artists over the Internet. The site offers space where artists can have studios and gallery rooms accessible via the WWW. Also artists can find out how to get their works exhibited on the Internet and learn about art happenings online. Studios and galleries you can visit include visual arts, music, performance art, poetry, sculpture, video, animation, audio art, and hacker art. Also find out how to submit your own artwork and connect to other interesting art sites.

Contact: Network Wizards, Art on the Net, *webmasters@art.net*

Art Serve

http://rubens.anu.edu.au/

Art history and architecture students will appreciate this immense database of over 16,000 art and architecture images. Art lovers will also enjoy the variety of exhibitions located at this site. The prints database contains prints dating from the fifteenth to the nineteenth centuries. Accompanying that is a collection of classical architecture images. While the databases are the star attraction at this site, don't miss the exhibits, including one on Islamic architecture and another on contemporary architecture in Hong Kong. Other exhibit highlights include a survey of Western art and 250 images of prehistoric ritual monuments within the British Isles.

Contact: Michael Greenhalgh, Art History Department, Australian National University, *gremarth@fac.anu.edu.au*

Explore the history of art and architecture at Art Serve.

ArtsEdge

http://artsedge.kennedy-center.org/artsedge.html

ArtsEdge links the art and education worlds through technology. Search the entire ArtsEdge database or find browsable indices of conferences, organizations, funding resources, and more. Get news and features about arts and education, including professional development opportunities. Visit spotlighted sites in the arts, education, and cultural places. There is also a collection of sites for and by students. Go to the Community Center to meet the guest of the week, read announcements, or join a mailing list. In the Curriculum Studio, teachers can find curriculum examples, goals, and standards. This huge resource is invaluable for arts educators and art lovers alike.

Contact: ArtsEdge, *editor@artsedge.kennedy-center.org*

Arts Quiz

http://www.mtn.org/MIA/germ00_quiz_intro.html

Take a fun, interactive quiz that will help you learn something about art. The quiz focuses on a specific work of art from the Minneapolis Institute of Arts. Scroll through, looking at the artwork and reading about it and the artist. Additional pictures show details of the painting with text describing the meaning of the details. Then take the quiz by clicking on the answers to multiple choice questions. There are ten questions and a bonus brainteaser. You'll learn the story behind the painting by taking the quiz. The questions teach you about the ideas surrounding the work and encourage you to think about it in new ways. After finishing the quiz, you may want to go to the main menu and explore the museum's online exhibitions and galleries.

Contact: Minneapolis Institute of Arts, The River Project, *miagen@mtn.org*

Who Painted *The Death of Germanicus?*

Take the Quiz.

Chesley Bonestell Art Gallery

http://www.secapl.com/bonestell/top.html

Artist Chesley Bonestell probably is best known for his contributions to the field of astronomical art. His illustrations of space explorations and solar scenes, painted during the 1940s and 1950s, were his most influential and far-reaching contributions. These sketches illustrated concepts of space at the time and still influence our perceptions of the solar system today. Tour this online exhibit of Bonestell paintings that show the artist's conceptions of Earth, Mars, Jupiter, and the moon. Click on the thumbnails of each painting to get a larger view as well as information about the painting, including the date, medium, museum showings, and notations. The paintings are interspersed with commentary on Bonestell's astronomical conceptions. Highlights that shouldn't be missed are the star series, which depicts famous stars in the galaxy, and the Jupiter series, noteworthy for its stunning images.

Contact: Kathryn Humm, Security APL, *kathyh@secapl.com*

Fine Art Forum

http://www.msstate.edu/Fineart_Online/home.html

This electronic news service covering art and technology issues is of use to all artists and art students. Fine Art Online is the news service of the Art, Science, and Technology Network, a virtual organization whose board members meet in cyberspace. The forum serves the interests of artists and other creative people interested in applications of technology to art. In the index of services, you'll find the group's electronic newsletter, an online gallery, and a WWW resource directory. The gallery, which includes exhibits by diverse artists, will appeal to all interests; some unique exhibits are Mathematics in Stone and Bronze and performance-art displays. The Fine Art Open Gallery shows work selected from across the Internet by open submission. Finally, the directory of WWW art resources is a good jumping-off point for much more online information about art.

Contact: Paul Brown, editor, Mississippi State University, *paul_brown@siggraph.org*

Folk Art & Craft Exchange

http://www.folkart.com/~latitude/index.htm

This site is dedicated to art made by native folk artists and craft persons in the Americas. Through the site, find folk art for sale indexed by where it was made, how it was made, or a short description. Choose between baskets, glass, quilts, religious items, toys, and more. Artists, museums, and private collectors can learn how to exhibit or sell their Native American artwork at the site. You can also locate folk art and crafts events all over the Americas, link to online museums and private collections, and even read some Mayan folk tales.

Contact: Latitude International, Folk Art & Craft Exchange, *webmaster@folkart.com*

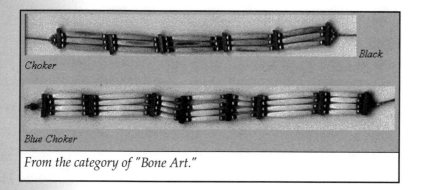

Choker

Black

Blue Choker

From the category of "Bone Art."

Internet Arts Museum for Free

http://www.rahul.net/iamfree/

This online music, art, and literature museum presents complete, downloadable, free exhibits created expressly for the museum. The project is an experimental system for the creation and distribution of art, allowing the artist to create solely for artistic expression and not for commercial value. Here you'll find an ever-changing series of exhibitions in modern art, music, and writing, all in high-resolution JPEGs and complete audio files, not just thumbnails and sound bites. There are seven areas to explore: sound, words, photos, lectro-art, motion, archive, and information. Among the exhibits, you can access the first complete album to be archived on the Internet and the first album created exclusively for the Internet. Wander through the photography and art exhibits, or download and keep individual pieces. You can also download complete original prose. An archive of software applications and players is available to use for viewing or listening to the featured exhibits.

Contact: Artists for Revolution Through Technology on the Internet, a2i Communications, *info@artnet.org*

Krannert Art Museum

http://www.art.uiuc.edu/kam/

This electronic guide to the permanent collections of the Krannert Art Museum at the University of Illinois at Urbana-Champaign introduces you to many fine art pieces. The guide takes you through exhibits of sculpture, European and American paintings, twentieth-century art, Asian art, Medieval and Near Eastern art, decorative art, Old World antiquities, African art, and pre-Columbian art. In each exhibit, you can view thumbnail images of selected pieces. Click on the graphic to get a much larger inline image and a description of the piece. Be sure to visit the Krannert Art Museum Explorer, a selection of hypermedia displays from the permanent collection that changes periodically. An education resources center offers a collection of art instructional materials. After wandering through the museum, stop at the Palette Cafe and Bookstore for a light lunch or pastry.

Contact: NCSA Publications Group, University of Illinois at Urbana-Champaign, *pubs@ncsa.uiuc.edu*

A guide to the
Krannert Art Museum

Introduction
  About the Krannert Art Museum building including floorplans.

Sculpture

Follow this electronic guide to view online art exhibits at the Krannert Art Museum. (Copyright 1994 University of Illinois at Urbana-Champaign.)

Internet for the Fine Arts

http://www.iaex.com/

This is a network of online artists, galleries, museums, and resources for the fine arts. Look here for the most complete collection of fine arts links. Visit several online galleries, including galleries of international artists and commercial galleries. The main gallery contains many pieces categorized by medium, and new pieces are added all the time. You can join art organizations or access art events, including worldwide competitions. Find art publications to read. Join a fine-arts-related mailing list, or connect to interesting art sites. You'll also find a bulletin board where individuals and organizations can post services that provide resources and information for artists.

Contact: Internet for the Fine Arts, *ifa@fine-art.com*

Leonardo da Vinci Museum

http://www.leonardo.net/main.html

Visit the Leonardo da Vinci online museum for a complete collection of images and information relating to the great painter, designer, scientist, futurist, and thinker. You can explore four wings of the gallery. View the famous paintings, including the *Mona Lisa* and *The Last Supper*, in the oil paintings gallery. The engineering and futuristic designs gallery exhibits sketches of fantastic weapons and flying machines. Look in the drawing and sketches gallery for illustrations, anatomical sketches, and unfinished works. There is also an historical exhibit of the life and times of Leonardo da Vinci, with a short background of his life and contributions. See individual works in detail by clicking on the thumbnail; you'll also get a short description of each work. This online museum provides an opportunity to see diverse works by the original Renaissance man.

Contact: Jim Pickrell, Leonardo Internet, *jimp@leonardo.net*

The OTIS Project

http://sunsite.unc.edu/otis/otis.html

The OTIS (Operative Term Is to Stimulate) Project is an online gallery and experiment in collaboration among artists. Here, image-makers and image-lovers meet, exchange ideas, and collaborate. The archives are the highlight of the site—you can access a large number of exhibits cataloged by either medium or content. The media catalog in the gallery runs the entire gamut, from collages, morphs, drawings, and paintings to puppets, dolls, math art, raytraces, and even jewelry, body art, and performance art. Any art fan can find something to interest him or her here. Be sure to check out the Collaborative Grid Gallery, which presents a unique form of art made possible by the Internet. Each piece is the collaborative effort of several artists, creating over the Internet a grid of squares filled with images that interconnect and play off one another. Another section of the site, called Synergy, presents a wide range of art projects created interactively through the Internet by several artists working together. You can also meet the OTIS artists, get tips and tricks for image compression, and access a random image from the OTIS archive.

Contact: Ed Stastny, SunSITE, University of North Carolina at Chapel Hill, *ed@sunsite.unc.edu*

Strange Interactions

http://amanda.physics.wisc.edu/show.html

Experience a one-person art show of drawings, paintings, etchings, and lithographs, using the Internet as a publicly accessible gallery with a potential audience of over 25 million. John E. Jacobsen created the exhibition himself as a way of expanding art out of the locally accessible sphere of conventional galleries and into the globally accessible one of the Internet. View Jacobsen's works through GIFs and read descriptions of each work written by the artist. This one-person show is a pleasure to tour and a great application of the Web.

Contact: John E. Jacobsen, Strange Interactions, *jacobsen@amanda.physics.wisc.edu*

The WebMuseum

http://sunsite.unc.edu/louvre/net/

This online version of the world-famous museum, the Louvre, is a must-see on any WWW tour. First, switch to the mirror site closest to you, with mirrors in North America, South America, Australia, Asia, and Europe. Then explore many interesting exhibits, including French medieval art, well-known paintings from famous artists, art of the twentieth century, and a Cézanne exhibit. At the famous paintings exhibit, view paintings from the Gothic period to twentieth-century art. One of the best sections is Impressionism, where you can see large collections of works by Manet, Degas, Cézanne, and Monet, among many others. Another highlight is Les Très Riches Heures, a classic example of a medieval book of hours. The exhibit features twelve beautiful, full-color illustrations, one for each month, from the calendar. Visit the museum auditorium for some background music. Or leave the museum to take a historical guided tour of Paris.

Contact: Nicholas Pioch, SunSITE, University of North Carolina at Chapel Hill, *Nicholas.Pioch@inf.enst.fr*

Examine in detail famous paintings like Raphael's Maddelena *at the WebMuseum.*

World Art Treasures

http://sgwww.epfl.ch/BERGER/

World Art Treasures is a vast online archive dedicated to spreading the love and knowledge of art. The collection contains 100,000 slides showing the art of the major civilizations of the world. Download any of the art slides to your computer and use the art in classroom projects, term papers, and for personal art projects. The resources are divided into different programs to help you understand the period and history of the art. Look at Roman portraits from Egypt. Click on the portrait to zoom in on details. Click on the text beneath the portrait to get information about the different aspects of the portrait and its place in history. Visit the ancient site of Abydos in Egypt on a virtual journey. Your trip to the online site retraces the pilgrimage undertaken 3,300 years ago. Also look at art from all over the world, including Egypt, China, Japan, India, and other Asian countries. You'll see a clickable map of the art from that country. Just click on the piece you want to see in more detail and learn more about it. You'll not only explore art, but you'll also learn about the history and culture of other countries at this site.

Contact: Francis Lapique, Support Silicon Graphics, *Francis.Lapique@sic.adm.epfl.ch*

World of Escher

http://www.texas.net/escher/

The artist M.C. Escher is generally recognized for his works incorporating spatial illusions, impossible buildings, and repeating geometric patterns called tessellations. Explore the world of Escher through art and stories in this unique online gallery. Go to the Reading Room for further information about the artist and his art. Here you can read a collection of essays and stories about Escher, as well as notable quotes by the artist himself. Be sure to check out the story of the month and a biography of Escher. On display in the Escher Art Museum are some of his best artworks. You can explore four galleries or skip directly to favorite pieces by clicking on the title. Study Escher's famous optical illusions, like Drawing Hands, House of Stairs, and Reptiles. Underneath each artwork are quotes about it by art critics and scholars. In the Escher store, you can shop for posters, jewelry, books, clothing, puzzles, and even computer software, all based on Escher's designs.

No one is really sure if Escher was an artist, mathematician, or visionary. Visit the Escher online gallery and decide for yourself.

Contact: Paul Schofield, Texas Networking, Inc., *escher@texas.net*

View an Escher painting online.

For more information on art, visit the following sites:

American Studies Web

http://pantheon.cis.yale.edu/~davidp/art.html

This site contains links to art and material culture sources on the Web. It's one of those good jumping off places. Each link has a short description.

ArtAIDS Link Project

http://artaids.dcs.qmw.ac.uk:8001/

Here you'll find out about and see exhibits from a collaborative art project where digital artists commemorate and celebrate the fight against AIDS.

Art Galleries

http://www.comlab.ox.ac.uk/archive/other/museums/galleries.html

This site has links to Web services connected with art galleries and archives. Many of the links are to sites with online art; others links go to sites hosted by museums and galleries.

The Art of Raku

http://www.aloha.com/~cobweb/rc/

This page describes the pottery-making technique known as raku. It also contains pictures of a potter's work and ordering information.

ArtsNet

http://artsnet.heinz.cmu.edu/

ArtsNet provides services and information related to arts management and cultural resources on the Internet. Here you can access information about career opportunities in the arts, art sites online, the ArtsNet development database, and many more resources.

Arts Publications: World Wide Arts Resources

http://www.concourse.com/wwar/pub.html

This site has links to online arts publications and galleries.

Arts USA

http://www.artsusa.org/

This site contains information on expanding support for the arts, art education, a discussion group, a catalog of art-related books and tools, and links to other art and culture sites. A lot of the information seems more oriented to supporting the arts than the arts themselves.

ArtsWire Current

http://artswire.org/Artswire/www/current.html

This is a magazine for the arts community. It contains news about staff cuts at the National Endowment for the Arts, art awards, conferences, and links to other art information on the Web.

Binary Newsgroups

http://www.cis.ohio-state.edu/hypertext/faq/usenet/pictures-faq/fine-art/faq.html

Wondering how to post your own artistic creations or download others from the many binary newsgroups on Usenet? This FAQ will help you out. It explains picture formats and instructions for uploading and downloading binary pictures to Usenet.

The Civilized Explorer

http://www.crl.com/~philip/Arthome.html

This site lists selected art and culture sites and has links to both.

College of Fine Arts, University of South Florida

http://arts.usf.edu/

Get information at this site about the University of South Florida's fine arts program, including theater, music, visual arts, and dance. You can also visit the university's contemporary art museum and graphic studio.

The Galeria El Dorado

http://www.interart.net/shops/list.html

This site includes a linked list of shops offering various craft items over the Net. Items range from music to pottery to textiles.

Gallery Walk

http://www.ECNet.Net/users/mfjfg/galwalk.html

A virtual excursion through some of the world's finest art museums and galleries.

Iron Age Arts and Crafts

http://ifu.net/html/culture/celts/crafty.htm

This site discribes The Celts, a U.K. group that specializes in Iron Age arts and crafts. Included is a list of future display dates.

The Israel Judaica Emporium: Silversmith's Shop

http://www.macom.co.il/emporium/silver/index.html

This site contains a display of David Cohen's modern Jewish silver-work. His silverwork is a good example of a combination of Judaic ritual silver art and a modern smithing style.

Los Angeles County Museum of Art

http://www.lacma.org/

This online museum publishes catalogs of masterpieces and pho-tography in the L.A. County Museum and an exhibition schedule, plus a special education section. From here, you can also link to other art museums.

The Online Arts and Crafts Resource Directory

http://www.ragtime.org/ragtime/Ragtime_Resources.html

This site serves as a yellow pages of crafts pages. The links are broken down into topics and include specific snail mail addresses and phone numbers. This is not a guide to arts and crafts on the Web.

What's New @ Art on the Net

http://www.art.net/whats_new.html

This site contains recent (organized by date) sites to hit the Web and provides links to most of them.

Whitney Museum of American Art Online

http://mosaic.echonyc.com/~whitney/WMAA/INT4.html

Includes exhibits. Has a very nice home page design.

The World Library: Arts and Crafts

http://www.scescape.com/worldlibrary/business/companies/artscrf.html

This is a listing of different art-related Web sites, most of which are commercial or catalogs.

Education

Ask ERIC

http://ericir.syr.edu/

ERIC (Educational Resource Information Center) is a federally funded system that provides access to an extensive body of education-related literature at all educational levels. This valuable Internet resource provides an online library of materials for teachers and educators. The Ask ERIC service answers questions for anyone involved in K-12 education, responding within forty-eight hours after receiving the question in e-mail. The Ask ERIC staff specializes in questions about K-12 education, information technology, teaching, educational administration, and learning. You can learn more about this service and Ask ERIC through a slide show at the WWW site. You don't have to use the Ask ERIC service to make use of the resources available through the Web site, however. Visit the Ask ERIC toolbox for a set of Internet resources used by the staff in answering e-mail queries. You'll also find lots of lesson plans for the sciences, mathematics, language arts, social studies, and more specialized curricula; these include course guides for NASA's SIR-C educational program and the PBS series, "Newton's Apple." ERIC Digests will catch you up on hot topics in the field of education. From here, you can also link to archives for education listservs, educational conferences, electronic journals, books and reference tools, Internet guides and directories, and online library catalogs. The entire Ask ERIC database is searchable for keywords, titles, authors, publication dates, language, and many other criteria. Don't skip a visit to the amazing Cow Gallery. The Ask ERIC library probably will become a daily online stop for all educators.

Contact: Ask ERIC Virtual Library, Virtual Dave Lankes, *rdlankes@ericir.syr.edu*

CAUSE

http://cause-www.colorado.edu/

CAUSE is the association for managing and using information resources in higher education. This site functions as a clearinghouse on issues related to managing and using campus information resources. Read CAUSE publications online, including professional papers, *Campus Watch,* and *Best Practices in Campus Networking.* Access CAUSE information resources, including an information resources library, a job posting service, and a list of Internet servers at higher education organizations. Also find out how to contact CAUSE's members and about training and professional support programs.

Contact: CAUSE, *info@cause.colorado.edu*

Chronicle of Higher Education

http://chronicle.merit.edu/

This site provides free summaries of recent articles from the *Chronicle of Higher Education.* Access a guide to the top stories of the week and the complete table of contents. Special sections include information technology in academe, finances and personal planning, notable Internet resources, best-selling books, events and deadlines, the facts and figures on U.S. higher education, and jobs in and out of academe.

Contact: Chronicle of Higher Education, *editor@chronicle.merit.edu*

Cisco Educational Archives

http://sunsite.unc.edu/cisco/edu-arch.html

This educational resource center provides information to help educators and schools connect to the wealth of resources on the WWW. The catalog also connects to resources worldwide that demonstrate the power of networking in education. Get an introduction to the project through a link that describes the Cisco educational program and Cisco's efforts to improve educational networking. Search the entire educational archives quickly. Visit the school of the month, or access a meta-library of K-12 links categorized by subject. You can also learn about one of the coolest software programs available for educational networking.

Contact: Cisco Systems and David McConville, SunSITE, University of North Carolina at Chapel Hill, *id@sunsite.unc.edu*

Garner information about K-12 or education reform, or see pages by and for Blair students and classes with these two links.

Discover frightening and little-known secrets of life as you learn about some of the insane and/or paranoid students which go here to Blair. Be warned: we are not responsible for the contents of these pages, nor for your reaction to these pages. Tax, Tags, and Freight May Apply.

Cisco Educational Archives helps educators and schools connect to the wealth of resources on the Web.

Cyberspace Middle School

http://www.scri.fsu.edu/~dennisl/CMS.html

At the Cyberspace Middle School, travel the Internet in style. Take a spin on the Information Superhighway by clicking on street signs. Find the most interesting links on the Web in Surf City. Topics of Interest points to activities and information that help with studies. Visit home pages of middle schools on the Web and educational resources for teachers using the Web in their classrooms. The Cyberspace Middle School is designed for middle school and junior high students who are using the WWW to help get an education.

Contact: Larry Dennis, Supercomputer Computations Research Institute at Florida State University, *larry@fsulcd.physics.fsu.edu*

Education Central

http://www.ehhs.cmich.edu/

Education Central is a vast electronic center for education professionals. Broaden your collegial associations by linking to higher-education associations. Access vast Internet educational resources in many subjects, including departments of education, the humanities, math and science, and even setting up a Web server. Visit resources covering all aspects of the school district, state government, and world events, and knowledge. Also connect to many useful education resources all over the Net.

Contact: Richard Lamb, EdCentral, *helpdesk@edcen.ehhs.cmich.edu*

EdWeb

http://k12.cnidr.org:90/

This hyperbook explores the worlds of educational reform and information technology. Using this book, you can find online educational resources, learn about trends in educational policy, examine success stories of computers in the classroom, and more. Explore K-12 Internet and the role of the WWW in education. Take an HTML crash course, or join in the Information Superhighway debate. Learn about educational reforms for the twenty-first century and what schools are doing with computers today. Finally, link to tons of online K-12 educational resources.

Contact: Andy Carvin, CNIDR Educational Servers, *acarvin@k12.cnidr.org*

Eisenhower National Clearinghouse

http://www.enc.org/

The Eisenhower National Clearinghouse helps improve science and math education by offering curriculum resources and links to math and science sites. Access a catalog describing a comprehensive collection of curriculum materials in print, audio, video, electronic, and Internet formats. A virtual reference desk answers questions about locating math and science resources. Students and teachers will find lots of science and math sites linked in, including curriculum resources, school-based sites, and reference materials. Also many sites on education research, grants, professional development, school reform, testing, and standards are referenced here. You'll even find Internet software and information you can access or download immediately. Be sure to check out the Digital Dozen, which displays the twelve best educational sites of the month.

Contact: Eisenhower National Clearinghouse for Mathematics and Science Education, *web@enc.org*

Visit the Eisenhower National Clearinghouse for links to math and science sites.

Engines for Education

http://www.ils.nwu.edu/~e_for_e/

This hyperbook demonstrates a unique use of hypertext while imparting valuable information about education. The book discusses what's wrong with our educational system, how to reform it, and the role of technology in that reform. The author introduces the book in an audio link. The text itself is organized as a network of snippets interconnected through hyperlinks by the questions they raise. This set-up provides an infinite number of ways to move through the material, so that you can truly follow your own interests. Click on a question that interests you, and read the answer, which raises even more questions. You can always access an outline to find out where you are in the book or follow a linear path through the text by clicking on a special link. This unique hyperbook will interest both educators and hypertext designers.

Contact: Roger Schank and Chip Cleary, Institute for Learning Sciences, *engines@ils.nwu.edu*

Explorer

http://unite2.tisl.ukans.edu/

This site contains a huge archive of curriculum resources for science and math education. The resources are organized by subject in a handy outline and labeled with grade levels, so it's easy to find what you want. You can either browse through the subjects or search the entire archive. Or, for fun, play Edulette and receive a random resource. In the mathematics folder, you'll find resources for general mathematics, problem solving, tools, numeration, measurement, geometry, statistics, and algebra. The science resources are extensive, broken down into general science, life science, physical science, earth science, and common themes. Types of resources available include software, lab activities, instructional aids, lesson plans, and news, and most are instantly downloadable.

Contact: Great Lakes Collaborative and University of Kansas UNITE Group, Explorer at University of Kansas, *explorer@unite.tisl.uk ans.edu*

Global Schoolhouse

http://k12.cnidr.org/gsh/gshwelcome.html

The Global Schoolhouse project connects schools and students nationally and internationally using the Internet. Students involved in the project conduct collaborative research and interact using Internet tools and video conferencing. At the Global Schoolhouse's Web page, you can find out what schools were involved in the project and connect to a school spotlight for each. You'll also meet students and teachers who participated in the project. Explore the student projects, including research in alternative energy sources, solid waste management, space exploration, and weather and natural disasters; discover how each project was conducted; and follow student conversations through mailing list archives. Here you can also get technical tips for using the Internet as a research tool and access a list of popular Internet searching tools. Explore an archive of K-12 Internet resources and opportunities. Download Internet software used by the Global Schoolhouse, including CU-SeeMe, Web browsers, and other useful freeware. The Global Schoolhouse demonstrates how the Internet can be used effectively in K-12 education.

Contact: Global Schoolhouse, Center for Networked Information Discovery and Retrieval, *webmaster@k12.cnidr.org*

Globewide Network Academy

http://uu-gna.mit.edu:8001/uu-gna/

Visit the world's first completely online university. The goal for the school is to create a fully accredited online university. At the site you can learn all about the university, including its background and programs, and review a list of frequently asked questions. Then take a look at some of the special projects here, such as the plan to generate hypertext textbooks on various subjects for teaching over the Internet. Visit the GNA Library for course-specific resources; there's even a campus bookstore. The campus is entirely virtual, with classes and office hours taking place in participating MOOs (MOOs are virtual-reality, text-based environments where users can interact in real time). By sending in an interactive form through e-mail, you can join the Globewide Network Academy mailing list, volunteer to teach a course, or sign up as a student.

Contact: Globewide Network Academy, *gna@mcmuse.mc.mericope.edu*

GNN Education Center

http://nearnet.gnn.com/gnn/meta/edu/index.html

This huge educational resource is dedicated to providing curricula, projects, and connections to education professionals. The resources cover all aspects of education and focus on using the Internet in education. At the Curriculum Centers, explore resources available for K-12 in reading, language arts, mathematics, and social studies. Feature articles cover the impact of information technology on K-12 education. Also check out the latest Internet and education happenings, or browse a student gallery of kid-generated, online publications. When you've finished, take a break with some humorous tales and inspirational quotes.

Contact: Global Network Navigator, NearNet, *melissa@ora.com*

Honolulu Community College

http://www.hcc.hawaii.edu/

Honolulu Community College, the site of many WWW "firsts," has produced a model campus-wide information system (CWIS) using the

Web. This was the first college to develop an interactive, clickable map of its campus. The interactive map connects to buildings on campus, including the bookstore, cafeteria, and campus center, as well as to classroom buildings. Some buildings have photographs and movies along with the text information. From the CWIS, you can connect to a dinosaur museum, the library, special programs, and the provost. Features include the Berlin Wall Freedom Monument and information about Hawaii. You can also access a unique archive of videos of campus life, including videos of the harbor skyline and the Dinosaur Exhibit.

Contact: Honolulu Community College, *webmaster@hcc.hawaii.edu*

NASA K-12 Internet Initiative

http://quest.arc.nasa.gov/

This NASA site for K-12 education provides support for schools to use the Internet as a basic tool for learning. Get in touch with NASA scientists, researchers, and engineers. Find grant information, or download a tutorial for using the Net in the classroom. Collaborate with teachers and kids online. Then enter the universe of NASA online resources that are useful for any educational project.

Contact: Steven Hodas, Quest: NASA K-12 Internet Initiative, *hodas@nsipo.nasa.gov*

Enter the universe of NASA online resources at this educational site.

IBM Kiosk for Education

http://ike.engr.washington.edu/

This educational resource has news, software, and Internet pointers for higher education. Download free software, or find out more about IBM products and services useful for higher education. Connect to higher education resources on the Internet. Read technical journals, redbooks, and Usenet newsgroup archives. This online "kiosk" is a helpful place to learn more about the role of technology in higher education.

Contact: IBM Kiosk for Education, *ike@ike.engr.washington.edu*

The Open University

http://www.open.ac.uk/

Established twenty-five years ago, the Open University is the largest and certainly the most innovative university in the United Kingdom. It is genuinely open because there are no entry requirements, and the courses come to students by mail, television broadcasts, and online, wherever they live. The courses are constructed for independent learning; students earn bachelor's, master's, and doctoral degrees from the university. At this site, you can get detailed course descriptions and learn how to enroll in and take classes. The site allows you to visit all the departments and student organizations, including the Open University library. For those interested in distance education itself, a link connects to the International Center for Distance Learning, based at the Open University.

Contact: Open University, *WebMaster@open.ac.uk*

Ralph Bunche School

http://mac94.ralphbunche.rbs.edu/

Visit this Harlem elementary school for a good example of what schools can do when they join the WWW community. Here you can access two student newspapers and read articles written by the students. Or connect to the school's Gopher to see student work and science projects and to read about the background of the school. Access interesting school projects, such as the Pineapple Project, Halloween stories, and the Great Penny Toss. Be sure to check out the illustrated

Spanish alphabet, created by the students of the school. A menu of Spanish vocabulary words for every letter in the alphabet connects to original artwork by the students illustrating each vocabulary word. At this site, elementary-school students have the chance to show off their special projects while learning through the Internet.

Contact: Ralph Bunche School, Hamidou Diori, *hamidoud@ralphbunche.rbs.edu,* and Paul Reese, *preese@ralphbunche.rps.edu*

Learn Spanish vocabulary words, and view student art at the Ralph Bunche School. (Art by Chris Glover and Felipe Paulino, P.S. 125, 1993-1994.)

Scholastic Central

http://www.scholastic.com/

Scholastic, a leading publisher of children's books, classroom and professional magazines, technical products, and other educational materials, provides a great educational resource at this site. One attraction is the Education Store, an online shopping center for K-12 materials, including books, magazines, and instructional materials.

Visit the libraries for free lesson plans, activity guides, resource materials, and public-domain software. Read electronic newsletters for current information, ideas, and discussion of topics of particular interest to educators, including the integration of education and technology. Look at interesting projects, such as the Mt. Everest Adventure and the International Arctic Project. Or connect to home pages for popular children's book series, including *Goosebumps* and *The Baby-sitters Club.*

Contact: Scholastic, Inc., *staff@scholastic.com*

The Education Store, a great online shopping spot for educational resources.

U.S. Department of Education

http://www.ed.gov/

The Department of Education's Web site offers educational guides for teachers, researchers, and parents. Find information about applying for a grant or student loan. Check out programs sponsored by the department, such as Family Involvement, School-to-Work, and school-wide programs. A dynamic map of the United States lets you find Department resources and services in your area. Get useful pamphlets for parents, educational statistics, and resource directories. Keep up with national education goals. Be sure to look at the picks of the month for the latest and greatest educational resources.

Contact: U.S. Department of Education, *webmaster@inet.ed.gov*

Yale University

http://www.cis.yale.edu/FrontDoor/

Enter this huge "front door" to Yale University where you can tap into campus-wide information, including undergraduate admissions. Visit all the Yale departments, and see what they're doing online. Go to the School of Medicine for medical information, or check out research centers on earth observation, supercomputing, music technology, neuroscience, and more. Learn all about computing at Yale. Visit online galleries, museums, and music-related organizations at the university. Browse the entire library catalog. You'll also find a tour of New Haven, a genetic stock center, a speleology information server, and the Yale newspapers at this jam-packed CWIS for Yale.

Contact: Yale University, *Webmaster@yale.edu*

Check out the resources at the Yale University Library.

Web66

http://web66.coled.umn.edu/

The WWW is a catalyst that will integrate the Internet into K-12 school curriculums, and the Web66 project facilitates the introduction of this technology into K-12 schools. The goals of the project are to help educators learn how to set up their own Internet servers, to link K-12 WWW servers and the educators, and to help educators find and use K-12-appropriate resources on the WWW. The Web66 Classroom Internet Server Cookbook gives recipes with step-by-step instructions for setting up a web site, e-mail, and FTP server on a Macintosh computer, with hyperlinks to every ingredient you'll need. SharePages are useful HTML parts and pages, such as search engines, clip art, and images, that can be downloaded for use with your own pages, server programs, and databases. Join the Web66 mailing list where educators using WWW servers in their schools can share problems, questions, ideas, and successes. The What's New page contains new WWW items of interest to educators and students. The project also maintains a registry of K-12 schools on the Web, the most comprehensive list you'll find anywhere.

Contact: Web66, University of Minnesota College of Education, *WebMaster@web66.coled.umn.edu*

For more information on education, visit the following sites:

Education Virtual Library

http://www.csu.edu.au/education/library.html

This library of education resources is well-organized to help you find exactly what you're looking for. You'll find education pointers listed alphabetically, by education level, by resources provided, by type of site, and by country. You can also search the entire library.

Fullerton School District

http://host.fsd.k12.ca.us/

The packed pages of this school district's Web site contain resources for teachers, reference, curriculum, field trips, Internet use, and administrative support.

Global SchoolNet Foundation

http://gsn.org/

The Global SchoolNet Foundation is a major contributor to educational networking on the Internet and in the classroom. It supports free educational e-mail, the Global Schoolhouse, the Global SchoolNet newsgroup service, and many other interactive projects for education.

Mushing in the Classroom

http://www.polarnet.com/Users/Mushing/classrm.htm

In the unlikely event that you are called upon to talk to students about sled dogs, check out this page. The author tells you what information to get before stepping foot in a school, as well as what to take, how to prepare, and what to do in the classroom. A goodly amount of the information is useful for any non-teacher who has to speak in front of a class.

Patch American High School

http://192.253.114.31/

The first high school server in Europe features an ever-changing presentation of educational exhibits on history, Germany, current events, biology, computing, music, art, and much more.

Virtual Theater Project

http://www-ksl.stanford.edu/projects/CAIT/index.html

This site allows children to play all the creative roles involved in producing and performing plays in an improv theater company. This site is both an experiment and an educational experience.

History

The African American Mosaic

http://lcweb.loc.gov/exhibits/African.American/intro.html

Here you'll find a sampler of the African American collections in the Library of Congress. A rich resource guide for the study of black history and culture, the database covers five hundred years of black experience in the Western Hemisphere, broken down into three periods: colonization, abolition, and migration. You can also view a collection of works depicting African American history created by the Works Progress Administration during the Depression. Lengthy introductions to each section give historical background. The exhibit itself is composed of graphics and text from several different sources, including maps, treatises, memoirs, and historical photographs. You can click on the inline images for larger, more detailed views. Each section is several Web pages long, creating a huge, information-packed archive.

Contact: Library of Congress, *lcweb@loc.gov*

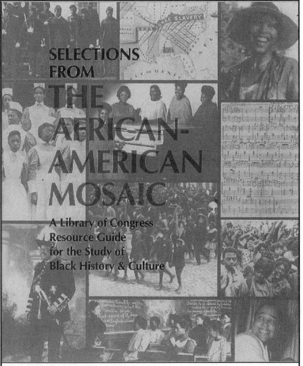

Learn about the African American experience at this information-packed archive.

American Memory

http://rs6.loc.gov/amhome.html

American Memory presents primary source and archival materials relating to American culture and history. One highlight is the Carl Van Vechten exhibit, which features photographs of literary figures, artists, and celebrities from 1932 to 1964. Using an interactive form, you can search the database of 1,395 photographs, accessing biographies, chronologies, and bibliographies. You'll also find photographs and films of turn-of-the-century America. Live history manuscripts from the Folklore Project offer the recollections of Americans from many walks of life. Other exhibits currently online are selected Civil War photographs and color photographs from the Farm Security Administration Office. This huge amount of material offers a fascinating trip into various aspects of American history.

Contact: American Memory Collection, Library of Congress, *lcweb@loc.gov*

The Biographical Dictionary

http://www.mit.edu:8001/afs/athena/activity/c/collegebowl/ biog_dict/intro.html

This online dictionary attempts to present in a concise format the basic facts about over 16,000 notable figures from ancient times to the present day. The searchable and completely free database constantly is being updated with ongoing events. Entries provide only the very basics; find out names, nationalities, claims to fame, created works (such as literature, movies, musical compositions, and visual artworks), and death and birth dates of historical figures. The database is useful for getting the most basic information about a person, "fast facts." You can perform a fast search for a last name or a slower search for a keyword. All the entries are also browsable in an alphabetical file. Be sure to consult the entry format and abbreviations files before you begin so you can understand the layout of the listings.

Contact: Eric Tentarelli, Massachusetts Institute of Technology, *tentarelli@iiiv.tn.cornell.edu*

Carlos Museum

http://www.cc.emory.edu/CARLOS/carlos.html

Visit a museum of classical art and history at this site. The Michael C. Carlos Museum at Emory University has a permanent collection of over 15,000 objects spanning nearly 9,000 years of history. The galleries in the Web site include exhibits on the ancient Americas, ancient Egypt, the ancient Near East, Asia, Greece, Rome, and more. Go to the Egyptian section to see a coffin, a fragment from the Book of the Dead, and a mummy, or visit the ancient Americas exhibit to view a whistle in the form of a crocodile and a vessel in the form of a jaguar, among other objects. Each exhibit includes inline images of selected pieces and a textual commentary with a brief history of the period covered by the exhibit. Click on the thumbnail image for more information about the piece, including the period, medium, and history.

Contact: Alison Nichols, Georgia Institute of Technology and Emory University, *gt8850b@prism.gatech.edu*

Go to the Egyption section of the Carlos Museum to see a coffin, a fragment from the Book of the Dead, and a mummy.

1492 Exhibit

http://sunsite.unc.edu/expo/1492.exhibit/Intro.html

Rediscover the New World through this online exhibit. The display first surveys the rich mixture of societies coexisting in the New World before the Europeans arrived, as well as the Mediterranean world at this dynamic turning point in its development. It goes on to explore the first sustained contact between Native American peoples and the European explorers. The exhibit is divided into six sections covering the New World, the Mediterranean world, Columbus, and Europe colonizing America. You can also access an outline of topics to jump directly to something of particular interest. Here you'll see drawings, manuscripts, books, maps, and other items. Exhibit pieces include such diverse items as a Mexican calendar, Venetian sailing directions, Columbus's coat of arms, and the first map of California. An extensive text provides a thorough history lesson on this important and controversial period in American history.

Contact: Library of Congress, EXPO and Jeff Barry, *lcweb@loc.gov*

Welcome to

1492: AN ONGOING VOYAGE

an Exhibit of the Library of Congress, Washington, DC

Rediscover the New World at the 1492 Exhibit.

Historical Text Archive

http://www.msstate.edu:80/Archives/History/

This site is a Web interface to one of the first FTP sites for historians. The resources here include ASCII files of historical documents and scholarly papers, GIF files, software, library search programs, diaries, and bibliographies, all of which can be easily downloaded to your computer. The most extensive resources are for American history, covering the United States up to the Gulf War, and including constitutional history and African American history. The Vietnam War archive is especially rich, with lots of photographs you can download. You'll also find materials on Europe, Asia, Africa, Canada, and Latin America. Other great finds include directories to databases of interest to historians, such as government sources and women's studies, freeware programs for historians, and address lists of others in the field.

Contact: Don Mabry, Mississippi State University, *djm1@ra.msstate.edu*

History Virtual Library

http://kuhttp.cc.ukans.edu/history/WWW_history_main.html

This virtual library of history resources is the central information server for historians online. Here you'll find a database of historical resources from antiquity to the twentieth century. Also access global news, conference announcements, and discussion lists for historians. The huge indices of history information are divided alphabetically, by era, region, and subject, to simplify browsing. There is also a huge section on Kansas history and life. An electronic library is linked in for reference purposes.

Contact: History Virtual Library, University of Kansas, *lhnelson@ukanaix.cc.ukans.edu*

Letters from a Civil War Soldier

http://www.ucsc.edu/civil-war-letters/home.html

These letters were written by a private in the Civil War over a three-year period. They give detailed accounts of the activities of one company in the Union army, filled with the rich details of the war and the living conditions in the Union army camps. The letters tell of disease and soldiers' frustration with politicians in Washington. They also give you a glimpse into the emotions of a soldier. The letters are a good way to learn about the Civil War first-hand. From the site, get more Civil War information, and learn how to make your own family history available on the WWW.

Contact: Bill Proudfoot, University of California at Santa Cruz, *pfoot@znet.com*

See the Civil War through the eyes of someone who was there.

U.S. History

http://www.msstate.edu/Archives/History/USA/usa.html

Explore the history of the United States through this library of documents. You can browse by period: colonial, the Revolutionary War, the early republic, the nineteenth century, and the twentieth century. Or examine wars in U.S. history such as the Philippines-U.S. war, the world wars, the Vietnam War, and the Gulf War. You can also look at history from the point of view of African Americans. Get a first-hand look at American history through speeches, important documents, photographs, manuscripts, important laws, diaries, and novels. Also take a look at bibliographies, constitutions, history databases, and book reviews for more info.

Contact: Don Mabry, Mississippi State University, *djm1@ra.msstate.edu*

U.S. Holocaust Memorial Museum

http://www.ushmm.org/

The Holocaust Museum in Washington, D.C., remembers and immortalizes the millions of victims of World War II, exhibiting the world's largest and most diverse collection of Holocaust-related items. The online version of the museum examines the Holocaust through multiple media. You can also get general information on the Washington museum. Many educational materials are available through the online site, including a guide to teaching about the Holocaust, a brief history, an article about children in the Holocaust, and an annotated videography. Through the site, connect to the museum's research institute for information about scholarly publications, programs, and archives. You can also link to the Web pages for member organizations of the Association of Holocaust Organizations.

Contact: U.S. Holocaust Memorial Museum, *web-administrator@ushmm.org*

The Viking Network

http://odin.nls.no/viking/vnethome.htm

If you're interested in the ancient Vikings, check out this charming WWW textbook researched, written, and illustrated entirely by school-age children. The Viking Network, created by students in ten countries, explores the Vikings' lifestyle, travels, and heritage. Read about the Viking ship and Viking exploration across the Atlantic Ocean. Take a look at a timeline of Viking history. Even find out what sports the Vikings played. One of the best ways to explore the site is by taking the Viking quiz. You'll have to go on a scavenger hunt everywhere in the site to find all the answers.

Contact: David Morley and Yngve Skramm, National Centre for Educational Resources, *dmorley@cityscape.co.uk*

Voice Library

http://web.msu.edu/vincent/index.html

The Vincent Voice Library houses taped voices—speeches, performances, lectures, interviews, and broadcasts—recorded over the past hundred years. Here you'll find an entire library of sound samples of

U.S. presidents, from Cleveland to Clinton, that you can download and listen to. These samples include speeches, informal talks, address-es to Congress, and more. Hear some of the most famous presidential speeches, such as Roosevelt's "Day of Infamy" speech and Kennedy's "Ask Not" speech. Also archived here is a collection of sound samples from interesting people such as writer Isaac Asimov, scientist George Washington Carver, pilot Amelia Earhart, nurse Florence Nightingale, and baseball player Babe Ruth. You can even hear Big Ben ringing-in the twentieth century.

Contact: Erik P. Larson, Michigan State University, *elarson@msu.edu*

The World According to Student Bloopers

http://www.mit.edu:8001/afs/athena.mit.edu/user/a/v/ avondale/Humor/SchoolHumor/HTML/WorldHistory.html

Did you know that Benjamin Franklin invented electricity by rubbing cats backwards or that the Revolutionary War was caused by the En-glish putting tacks in the colonists' tea? English and history teachers occasionally receive blooper gems in essays. Here Richard Lederer has pasted together an essay from the best of those student bloopers col-lected by teachers throughout the United States, from eighth grade through college level. This "alternate history" is very funny, even bet-ter than "America's Funniest Home Videos." Read carefully and you'll learn a lot.

Contact: Carl E. Snow, Media Librarian, Massachusetts Institute of Technology

World War II

http://192.253.114.31/D-day/

This exhibit, prepared and published online by high school students, commemorates the fiftieth anniversary of D-Day. A multimedia collec-tion of World War II materials includes historic documents, drawings, and photographs from government and military archives and *Stars and Stripes*, the official newspaper of the American troops. View vid-eos of invasion footage and the march into Paris, or listen to excerpts from famous speeches of the time. An archive of maps and battle plans is also available. All of this material can be downloaded from the site's FTP server by following a hyperlink.

Contact: Bill Dyer, Patch American High School, Stuttgart, Germany, *www@patch-ahs.dsi.net*

Remember D-Day at this diverse exhibit prepared by students at Patch American High School.

For more information on history, visit the following sites:

American Studies

http://pantheon.cis.yale.edu/~davidp/amstud.html

Man oh man, that's a lot of links. Links in nearly every conceivable category, organized so it's easy to find the desired link. I did a lot of research from this page, probably found twenty to thirty more sites of interest. It's easy to find what you're looking for—there are great descriptions of each link and lots and lots of links. I can't recommend it enough!

The Civil War Home Page

http://cobweb.utcc.utk.edu/~hoemann/cwarhp.html

This is rated in the top 5 percent of Web sites, with a great design and links to lots of Civil War resources. (It doesn't appear to favor a particular side, either.)

European Borders: History of Space/Space of History

http://english-server.hss.cmu.edu/ctheory/a-european_boarders.html

This page contains a fascinating discussion of the nature of history in a European context. Academic, but not too dry.

Europe, Russia, and Eastern Europe

http://execpc.com/~dboals/europe.html

This site contains links to resources on ancient and classical history through to modern history. Long and relatively comprehensive.

Gardens, Villas, and Social Life in Renaissance Florence

http://www.monash.edu.au/diva/kent.html

This page discusses the relationship between gardens and the life-styles of Renaissance Florentines.

Gateway to World History

http://neal.ctstateu.edu/history/world_history/world_history.html

Links to departments, discussions, archives, journals, etc.

Insects and Human Society

http://www.ento.vt.edu/IHS/

Did you know that an insect was primarily responsible for Napoleon's defeat in Russia? Or that insects affected the outcome of Xerces' invasion of Greece and the Great Crusades? Check out this site to find out how.

The LesBiGay History Month

http://www.cts.com/~drcarr/gay_travel/his.html

This page covers the development of Lesbian, Bisexual, and Gay History month, as well as listing some resources for those interested in learning more.

Rulers

http://www.geopages.com/Athens/1058/rulers.html

An index of world rulers, such as heads of state and heads of government.

The Society for Creative Anachronism

http://web.ce.utk.edu/departments/information_services_group/ mcnutt/SCA/

The Society for Creative Anachronism (SCA) is a nationwide group devoted to re-creating the more positive aspects of medieval life. Their Web site contains history, a discussion of the group, vendors of interest, and a newsletter. Does anyone else find the entire concept of an SCA Web site ironic?

WWW Virtual Library History Index

http://history.cc.ukans.edu/history/WWW_history_main.html

Gazillions of links, categorized nicely.

Language & Linguistics

Human Languages Page

http://www.willamette.edu/~tjones/Language-Page.html

This library of language resources is devoted to bringing together information about the languages of the world. You can view this page in many languages, including English, Dutch, German, French, and Portuguese. Resources include dictionaries, language tutorials, and spoken examples gathered from all over the Internet; the resources are endless. Some examples of what you'll find include: an audio tutorial of Arabic; a catalog of Chinese-language software; Bulgarian poetry; the news in Danish; a beginner's course in Dutch; a Middle English dictionary; a project to put French texts online; *Der Speigel*, a popular German magazine; the Hawaiian Language Center; audio and video Hindi lessons; the Quick and Dirty Guide to Japanese Grammar; a Latin study guide; a Polish daily newspaper; Project Runeberg, which publishes Scandinavian texts online; and a Welsh tutorial. You can even visit the Klingon (from "Star Trek") Language Institute. You'll also find links to multilingual resources, book collections, and communications resources. This library is great for the language scholar, the international tourist, or the non-English speaker looking for resources in his or her own language. There are also many general reference materials useful to anyone.

Contact: Tyler Jones, Willamette University, *tjones@willamette.edu*

Signing and Braille Guides

http://www.disserv.stu.umn.edu/AltForm/

Learn another language—sign language—with this fun, interactive guide. All you have to do is click on a letter, and you'll see the sign for that letter. The guide makes it easy to practice the signing alphabet. A spelling quiz tests your signing know-how. You can also learn all about Braille using the interactive guide. First, get some general information about Braille. Then enter the guide, where you click on a letter to see the Braille for it. The online guides are a fun and easy way to learn these languages. Expand your communication skills in no time with these interactive Braille and signing lessons.

Contact: Disability Services at the University of Minnesota, *webmaster@disserv.stu.umn.edu*

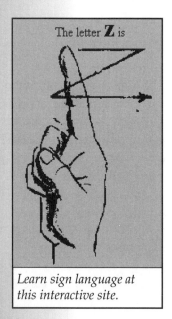

Learn sign language at this interactive site.

For more information on language and linguistics, visit the following sites:

Carnegie-Mellon Linguistics Page

http://english-www.hss.cmu.edu/langs.html

Contains lots of links to all kinds of language pages, including lots of foreign language and translation pages. A great starting resource.

Ethnologue Page

http://www-ala.doc.ic.ac.uk/~rap/Ethnologue/

Contains a database of information on 6,500 plus languages.

Foreign Languages for Travelers

http://insti.physics.sunysb.edu/~mmartin/languages/languageshtml

This site can help you learn useful words and phrases in seven different languages (eight, if you count English). All languages included are European.

Haskins Laboratories

http://www.haskins.yale.edu/

They do basic research in many areas, with a link to linguistics.

Hruodoperht's Heimpage

http://ukanaix.cc.ukans.edu/~eickwort/cv/hrd_main.html

This home page provides links to sites on Germanic, Nordic, and Celtic languages and culture, as well as pagan culture. Middle English literature is also covered.

Language Resources

http://www.pitt.edu/~groupev/Language/index.html

This site covers the interactions between language and daily life and other interesting linguistics information.

Linguistics

http://www.cog.brown.edu/pointers/linguistics.html

Very handy page of pointers to linguistics resources including universities, the WWW Virtual Library, journals, organizations, and e-mail lists. Worth looking into.

Linguistics Department at Stanford University

http://www-linguistics.stanford.edu/Linguistics/

Contains department information as well as many links to useful and informative documents.

Linguistics Resources

http://www.sil.org/linguistics/other.html

Provides links to various resources, discusion groups, papers, bibliographies, pubishers, booksellers, and so forth dealing with linguistics.

The Linguist List

http://www.ling.rochester.edu/linguist/contents.html

Home page for a linguistics mailing list, with archives, a database, contents, and articles of current issues, plus links to other pages of interest.

Newsletter for Researchers in Ethnomethodology & Conversation Analysis

http://www.comp.lancs.ac.uk/sociology/research/ethnonews/ethnonewsindex.html

This page includes a newsletter on ethnomethodology and conversation analysis. The newsletter contains topical information on academic events taking place around the world. Unfortunately, as of this writing only the Spring 94 version was posted.

Resources for Studying Human Speech

http://weber.u.washington.edu/~dillon/PhonResources.html

Links to phonetic information; looks very interesting!

The Sign Linguistics Resources

http://www.vuw.ac.nz/~nzsldict/

With information on sign language, including deaf resources on the Net, articles, and newsgroups. A good resource.

Law

Government, Law, and Society

How: http://english-server.hss.cmu.edu/Govt/

Explore this site to understand the impact of politics on everyday life. Look through directories concerning Congress, the courts, education, economics, history, international events, the law, and more. The diverse collection of files gives you a sense of American history and an understanding of current events. You can learn about recent election campaigns through speeches, news stories, and political party files. Access records from the White House, Congress, and the Supreme Court, or connect to other federal agencies to get a better understanding of government. There's even some political humor, with amusing headlines and quotations from famous politicians.

Contact: English-Server, *postmaster@english.hss.cmu.edu*

Human Rights Depository

http://www.intac.com/PubService/human_rights/

This site provides an educational resource on human rights around the world, including wartime, legal, and environmental resources related to human rights. Get updates on human rights campaigns, including human rights news and environmental information. War and peace archives keep track of current wars and peace movements throughout the world. There are also resources on laws concerning human rights. From here you can connect to human rights organizations such as the Red Cross and Amnesty International, as well as to a library of human rights resources on the Internet.

Contact: Martin Hogan, Intac Access Corporation, *hogan@intac.co*

Legal Domain Network

http://www.kentlaw.edu/lawnet/lawnet.html

This Web site is a repository for legal information on the Internet. It provides read-only access to law-related Usenet discussion groups, such as *alt.freedom.of.information.act* and *misc.legal,* as well as a number of Internet mailing lists on legal topics. All of the archives are searchable. Also connect to the Electronic Frontier Foundation, learn about intellectual property rights, and find a guide to legal resources on the Internet here.

Contact: Legal Domain Network, Chicago-Kent School of Law, *webmaster@chicagokent.kentlaw.edu*

Legal Information Institute

http://www.law.cornell.edu/

The Legal Information Institute is a huge legal resource, with access to *Cornell Law Review,* current legal new, special topics on information technology, the Supreme Court, state statutes, lawyers online, and more. The site offers a hypertext front-end to recent Supreme Court decisions and a collection of recent decisions of the New York Court of Appeals. You can also access a hypertext version of the full U.S. code and many other important legal documents. The material here is organized by either legal topic or type or Internet resource to make finding something specific very easy.

Contact: Legal Information Institute, Cornell Law School

Pepper & Corazzini

http://www.iis.com/p-and-c/

Visit an online law firm that specializes in communications law. Its practice covers radio, television, cable, online services, satellite, and cellular matters. At the online law offices, you'll find a useful series of articles on issues about telecommunications and information law. Also access an update on pending telecommunications legislation and links to other legal and telecommunications resources online.

Contact: Pepper & Corazzini, *pepcor@commlaw.com*

Venable, Baetjer, Howard, and Civiletti

http://www.venable.com/

Hire a full-service business law firm over the Internet. The firm specializes in business, labor, litigation, and government law, but they
also have a strong interest in information law. Even if you're not looking for a lawyer, you'll find the online periodicals interesting reading,
including the *NII Oracle*, an information law publication. Other articles featured here deal with labor law, including workplace, technology, environmental-protection, and information-law issues. Also check
out an article on why lawyers and law firms should be on the Internet.

Contact: Venable, Baetjer, Howard, and Civiletti, Venable Home
Pages, *info@venable.com*

Virtual Law Library Reference Desk

http://law.wuacc.edu/washlaw/reflaw/reflaw.html

At this large legal information database, you can access a number of
reference guides for law professionals and students, including U.S.
legislative history, the federal register, U.S. briefs, legal periodicals,
and worldwide treaties. Professor's Choice files include links to
Supreme Court decisions, Holt's stock market report, a list of legal
directories on the Internet, current foreign exchange rates, and historic
documents, speeches, and books. You'll also find archives for law-
related mailing lists, including files on family law, communications
law, clinical legal education, health law, and many other subjects.
Look in the reference corner for online law library catalogs, legal resources, and other online reference books. Also here you'll find directories of private law libraries, law deans, and legal academics, as well
as federal legislation documents, the congressional record, an e-mail
directory of legislators, and the entire U.S. code in searchable format.
Finally, a complete news source, updated daily via newswire, covers
bills and laws in the news, government speeches and announcements,
and election, media, business, banking, court, and international news.

Contact: Lissa Holzhausen, Washburn University School of Law
Library, *zzholz@acc.wuacc.edu*

For more information on law, visit the following sites:

ABA Network

http://www.abanet.org/

This is a good law-related site, with links to research sites and information on law-related events and technology. A worthwhile stop for both lawyers and paralegals.

Constitutional Law

http://www.einet.net/galaxy/Law/Constitutional.html

Page with information on the U.S. constitution, relevant law organizations, and a nonprofit organization.

The Consumer Law Page

http://www.seamless.com/talf/txt/resource.html

Contains lots of links to all sorts of law-related information—archives, related pages, statutes and codes, and U.S. government.

Criminal Justice Page

http://www.stpt.usf.edu/~greek/cj.html

An awesome page, with tons of links to criminal justice resources, including agencies, court cases, bills and legislation, and lots more, plus a really cool picture of Alcatraz. Great design.

Foreign and International Law Home Page

http://lawlib.wuacc.edu/washlaw/forint/forintmain.html

Contains links to the United Nations, treaties, foreign countries, archives, embassies, and e-journals.

Internet Crime Archives

http://underground.net/Art/Crime/

Slightly disturbing—has archives of mass murderers and serial murderers.

LawInfo Page

http://www.lawinfo.com/

Includes a lawyer location search, a self-help forum (for those who need help but not representation), an index of WWW legal resources, etc.

Law Schools and Legal Associations

http://lawlib.wuacc.edu/washlaw/lawschools.html

While dryer than static cling, this site does give you what it promises: links to law schools and legal associations. If you're researching potential law schools, check out this site. Some of the links are worth the visit: the American Bar Association (ABA) Network, for example.

LawServ

http://www.emedia.net/lawserv/legallinks.html

Claims to have the most comprehensive set of links to law-related pages. Contains links by categories, such as courts, agencies, law firms, and schools, libraries, news, journals, etc.

The Legal List

http://www.lcp.com/The-Legal-List/TLL-home.html

This is a complete list of law-related resources on the Internet. You can browse the list in HTML format by subject or download the entire list in ASCII format.

Legal.Net

http://www.legal.net/

This is a home page with a great design! It contains links to attorneys, legal services online, news, and articles, including something called "divorce online." There's also a non-attorney link.

Office of International Criminal Justice

http://www.acsp.uic.edu/index.htm

Information on criminal justice, including publications, conferences, training, and consulting.

Rape Victim Advocates

http://www.lib.uchicago.edu/~loakleaf/RVA.html

This site gives information on Rape Victim Advocates as well as information on rape and how to deal with it.

"Rate Your Risk" Page

http://www.Nashville.Net/~police/risk/

While digging for criminal law sites, I found this page sponsored by the Nashville police to "rate your risk" for certain crimes. Looks helpful, but didn't go into much detail.

Sexual Assault Information Page

http://www.cs.utk.edu/~bartley/saInfoPage.html

This site contains resources on what constitutes sexual assault, the victim's recourses, how to avoid it, and how to get help afterward.

Sexual Harassment: What Every Working Woman Needs to Know

http://www.cs.utk.edu/~bartley/other/9to5.html

This site outlines what constitutes sexual harassment and what one can do to counteract it.

University of Richmond Pre-Law Handbook

http://www.urich.edu/~polisci/prelaw.htm

This page has a good, step-by-step guide on preparing for and applying to law school.

U.S. House of Representatives Civil Law Library

http://www.pls.com:8001/d2/kelli/httpd/htdocs/his/93.GBM

Includes bills on civil rights from many states and other countries, plus links to other relevant law resources. Handy!

WWW Virtual Library Law Index

http://www.law.indiana.edu/law/lawindex.html

A most amazing list of Web links to law-related pages. This quite comprehensive list is a great starting point for beginners.

Literature

British Poetry Hypertext Archive

http://www.lib.Virginia.EDU/etext/britpo/britpo.html

This Internet-accessible electronic library of scholarly editions of British poetry has been made freely available for classroom and study use. The poetry archived here covers the period from 1780 to 1910. Each entry uses introductions, notes, and glosses as well as other scholarly materials to elucidate the works, including sample facsimiles of the original texts. Tennyson's "Charge of the Light Brigade" places scanned pages from the original manuscript beside the hypertext version. The Rossetti collection has digitized images of original documents, poetical manuscripts, printed texts (including proofs and first editions), and drawings and paintings, all supplemented with scholarly annotations and marked up for electronic search and analysis. Other useful editions linked in include poems by Oscar Wilde, John Keats, Lewis Carroll, Samuel Taylor Coleridge, William Wordsworth, Percy Bysshe Shelley, and many more.

Contact: Electronic Text Center, University of Virginia Libraries, *etext@virginia.edu*

Drama Archive

http://english-www.hss.cmu.edu/drama.html

This large archive contains many scripts of plays for reading and performing. You'll find dozens of scripts by both classic and contemporary playwrights. Look here for Shakespeare's complete works and the Oedipus trilogy by Sophocles. You can also download other classics, such as Goethe's *Faust* and Ibsen's *Peer Gynt*. Or read the scripts of new favorites such as *Into the Woods.* You can find lyrics to your favorite musicals or learn more about early theater by reading some classic criticism. If you want more general information on drama, try the theater FAQ, or connect to Theater Central for loads of drama links. If you want to talk about your favorite plays with other drama buffs, there are lots of newsgroups you can connect to. Theater techies will want to check out the stagecraft newsgroups for discussions of lighting, sound, stage managing, sets, and anything else related to producing a play.

Contact: Geoffrey Sauer, English-Server, *webmaster@english.hss.cmu.edu*

The ETEXT Archives

http://ftp.etext.org/

This vast, independent library of electronic texts has been online since 1992. All the files on the virtual shelves are either in ASCII text or compressed PostScript format, and all the materials are freely and legally redistributable. There are many different areas to explore. Check out an extensive collection of hypertext and ASCII electronic zines of all kinds. You can also access a large selection of electronic books from Project Gutenberg, archiving the classics and poetry, and from Project Libellus, archiving classical works. Political material ranges from zines to essays on subjects such as feminism, conspiracy, the environment, and current events. Browse through a selection of mainstream and not-so-mainstream religious periodicals and texts, or a variety of legal documents and essays. Access the Computer Professionals for Social Responsibility archives and the Computer Underground Digest archives, as well as archives of various electronic mailing lists. And don't miss the baseball archives.

Contact: Paul Southworth, The ETEXT Archives, *www@etext.org*

The Internet Poetry Archive

http://sunsite.unc.edu/dykki/poetry/home.html

This archive of selected works by contemporary poets makes poetry accessible to new audiences and gives teachers new ways of presenting and studying poetry. It features the poetry of Nobel Prize winners Seamus Heaney and Czeslaw Milosz. The Czeslaw Milosz exhibit has an introduction and two poems, all read aloud by the poet in both English and his native Polish. You can also read the poems yourself in English and then view GIF files of the Polish versions. The archive of Irish poet Seamus Heaney features nine poems and a bibliography of the poet's major works. Again, all of the poems are read aloud by the poet to accompany the text versions. The archive makes it possible to study poetry as both a written and a spoken art.

Contact: University of North Carolina Press and Paul Jones, SunSITE, University of North Carolina at Chapel Hill, *paul_jones@unc.edu*

The Internet Poetry Archive is a must-visit for poetry lovers.

Internet Public Library

http://ipl.sils.umich.edu/

Use image-maps to easily navigate the first Internet public library. In the reference section, ask a question at the reference desk, or search the collection of reference materials. Find reference materials on every subject, plus general reference tools such as dictionaries and encyclopedias. All of these are outside links to other Internet resources. Go to the reading room for online fiction. Librarians and information technology professionals should look under Services for the librarian of the week, Internet resources for librarians, a discussion of libraries and technology, contacts, events, and resources for professional development, readings and discussions on important issues such as copyright and intellectual freedom, and reviews of information resources. Educators should visit the Classroom for Internet tutorials and guides to using the Internet in education. The library also provides an environment for individuals and organizations to create displays and exhibits for the benefit of the Internet community. Soon you'll also be able to connect to the Internet Public Library Interactive Virtual Environment for a real-time reference desk and a chat room. The best part of the library is the Youth Division, where there are lots of activities for the kids. Enter one of two contests to get your story published on the WWW. At Story Hour, read multimedia stories. Explore science, math, and the Internet with Dr. Internet where you can ask science trivia questions using an online form, try a science project, and learn about the Internet. The book section provides a place to talk about books, read book reviews written by kids for kids, and answer trivia questions. Also learn about your favorite authors and illustrators here. There is something for everyone at the Internet Public Library.

Contact: Internet Public Library, *ipl@umich.edu*

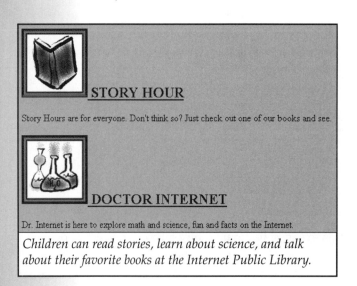

STORY HOUR

Story Hours are for everyone. Don't think so? Just check out one of our books and see.

DOCTOR INTERNET

Dr. Internet is here to explore math and science, fun and facts on the Internet.

Children can read stories, learn about science, and talk about their favorite books at the Internet Public Library.

Into the Wardrobe

http://SLEEPY.USU.EDU/~slq9v/cslewis/index.html

If you're a fan of C.S. Lewis' Narnia series, you have to make a stop here. This list of resources points you toward all things Narnian on the Internet. Find out more about Lewis' works in a chat group, a mailing list, and a Usenet newsgroup. Get an outline of C.S. Lewis' life. Connect to a bibliography of all of Lewis' writings—fiction, poetry, and nonfiction—with brief descriptions of each work. Find out about books written about Lewis, and read some papers about him that were published online. Read and listen to sound clips of Lewis quotes. A photograph gallery shows pictures of Lewis and his famous friends, maps, and photographs of important places in his life, and Narnian book covers. In the MereLewis archive, read past digests from the C.S. Lewis mailing list; find out how to subscribe to the mailing list here too. If you hunger for more, connect to other Lewis links or links on related topics such as Christianity and other great fantasy authors (such as J.R.R. Tolkien).

Contact: John Visser, DECthreads, Ohio State University, *slq9v@cc.usu.edu,*

Fly into the magical land of Narnia.

The Labyrinth

http://www.georgetown.edu/labyrinth/labyrinth-home.html

This global information network for medieval studies is well worth a visit for its WWW design alone. Venture into the vast, inter-connected network of information resources on medieval history, but don't worry about getting lost—you can always use "Ariadne's thread" to find your way back to the home page. An online library contains electronic texts in Latin, Middle English, French, Italian, and Old English. Subject menus link to information on a wide variety of topics, including national cultures, international culture, Arthurian studies, and Vikings. Another valuable service provides learning aids, projects, and syllabi for teaching. Also find professional news, publications, and organizations, as well as large medieval studies databases.

Contact: Martin Irvine and Deborah Everhart, Georgetown University, *labyrinth@gusun.georgetown.edu*

Welcome to the Labyrinth:

A World Wide Web Server for Medieval Studies

Follow Ariadne's thread to get around in the Labyrinth. (Copyright 1995 Deborah Everhart and Martin Irvine.)

Mark Twain Home Page

http://web.syr.edu/~fjzwick/twainwww.html

This fun home page contains a hotlist of resources relating to Mark Twain, one of America's best-known authors and humorists. The links range from texts of Twain's books to an analysis of his character's appearance on "Star Trek." Connect to a multimedia exhibit, Mark Twain on the Philippines, to see photographs, political cartoons, and texts that examine Twain's opposition to the Philippines-U.S. war. Read all of his works online, including *Huckleberry Finn, Tom Sawyer, A Connecticut Yankee in King Arthur's Court*, and *The Tragedy of Pudd'nhead Wilson*. You can also read short stories and speeches by Twain. Look at Pudd'nhead Wilson's Calendar for humorous maxims from the novel or search through an archive of Twain's witty quotes. Take a Twain tour of the world where you can visit his home town of Hannibal, Missouri, the Mark Twain National Forest, San Francisco, and the place where Twain once stayed in the Hawaii Volcanoes National Park. Mark Twain lovers will find much to explore at this unique home page.

Contact: Jim Zwick, Syracuse University, *fjzwick@mailbox.syr.edu*

Explore Mark Twain's writings, life, travels, and humor online.

The Legend of Sleepy Hollow

http://auden.fac.utexas.edu/~daniel/amlit/sleepy/sleepy.html

The Internet lets you interact with one of the best known ghost stories of all time—"The Legend of Sleepy Hollow" by Washington Irving. As you read through the story, you'll see buttons you can click on to make comments about what you have read or read the comments other people have written. The comments address themes that elucidate the story. When you click on the button, you'll find a passage to read and comment on, and questions to answer. Or you can check how others responded to the questions. Even if you don't want to participate, "The Legend of Sleepy Hollow" is still a great read.

Contact: Daniel Anderson, Computer Writing and Research Labs, University of Texas at Austin, *amdan@ccwf.cc.utexas.edu*

The Poe Page

http://www.et.byu.edu/~conradt/poepage.html

Long before Stephen King, there was Edgar Allan Poe, the original master of the horror story. You can read every one of his famous stories and poems here. Using hyperlinks, jump through a table of contents by initial letter to the title you want to read. For instance, if you want to read the well-known poem, "The Raven," just click on *R*, and download the complete text. Are you looking for that famous horror story, "The Fall of the House of Usher"? Jump to *F*—it's here too. Or you can page through the alphabet to read the complete works of Edgar Allan Poe.

Contact: College of Engineering and Technology, Brigham Young University, Jeff Wickel, *taper@yvax.byu.edu*, and Thomas Conrad, *conradt@caedm.et.byu.edu*

Representative Poetry

http://library.utoronto.ca/www/utel/rp/INTRO.HTML

Representative Poetry is an online textbook of English poetry that you can freely use for research, teaching, and study. The textbook covers poetry from the early medieval period to the beginning of the twentieth century. All of the poems have been edited for the ordinary reader. Easily access the poems through indices divided by poet, title, first line, and date. You can also search all of the works for a keyword. Poets whose works appear in the textbook include Blake, Byron, Coleridge, Donne, Keats, Rossetti, Pope, Tennyson, Spenser, Wordsworth, and many more, with a large volume of poetry by each poet. You can also access a full source bibliography. If you're interested in the encoding used for the HTML version of the textbook, check out the guidelines.

Contact: Ian Lancashire, University of Toronto, *ian@epas.utoronto.ca*

Shakespearean Insult Service

http://www.nova.edu/Inter-Links/cgi-bin/bard.pl

Experience the wrath of the Bard! All you have to do is reload the page for a new insult, straight from the pen of William Shakespeare. This isn't a very useful site, but it is a lot of fun.

Contact: Jerry Maguire, Nova Southeastern University

A Word A Day

http://lrdc5.lrdc.pitt.edu/awad/home.html

This is the Web page for the mailing list that mails out a new word and its definition every day. At the Web site, you can check out to-day's and yesterday's words, read a FAQ to find out more about the service and look at all past words of the day. Also find other word links such as Scrabble, crosswords, word play, word puzzles, and *The Devil's Dictionary.*

Contact: Anu Garg, The Haven, *anu@wordsmith.org*

For more information on literature, visit the following sites:

Alex

http://www.lib.ncsu.edu/stacks/alex-index.html

This is a catalog of online texts, with 1,800 plus searchable or browsable entries. The search engine is extremely simple.

Applied and Interactive Theater Guide

http://csep.sunyit.edu/~joel/guide.html

This site discusses the use of theater/drama techniques for non-entertainment purposes.

Authornet

http://www.authornet.com/auth/index.html

Authornet is a venue for information about literary authors. You can connect to information on authors from Shakespeare to Dickens to King (yes, that's Stephen King). Readers and writers will also find reference sources, online publishers, and bookstores.

Classics Archive

http://the-tech.mit.edu:80/Classics/

This site contains information on many classic authors and their works, as well as entire classic books, such as *The Prince* by Machiavelli.

Elysium

http://linex.com/~stephm/

This site provides links to mythology and science fiction sites, showing a certain relationship between the two enroute.

Mythology Sites

http://internetcafe.allyn.com/rod/myth1.html

This site gives links and a brief description of several different mythology-related sites. A good starting spot.

Norse Mythology

http://www.ugcs.caltech.edu/~cherryne/mythology.html

This page is essentially a Norse mythology FAQ. It covers the main gods and goddesses, the Norse creation myths, Ragnarok (Norse doomsday), and various Norse sagas.

The Online Books Page

http://www.cs.cmu.edu/Web/books.html

Includes a search or browse feature, links to other repositories, including foreign books, special exhibits celebrating women writers, and banned books.

The Tolkien Timeline

http://www.lights.com/tolkien/timeline.html

This site briefly outlines J.R.R. Tolkien's life and literary work, including non-Rings writing.

Walt Whitman's Leaves of Grass

http://www.cc.columbia.edu/acis/bartleby/whitman/index.html

Final edition of 800 plus poems, including an index of poem titles, an index of first lines, illustrations, and all the poems, searchable by section and title. Quite impressive.

Philosophy & Religion

The Bible Gateway

http://www.gospelcom.net/bible/

Instantly access the entire Bible over the WWW in this useful reference format. An interactive program produces HTML versions of Bible chapters on the fly, as you request them. Using a form, type in the passage you want to retrieve, for example, John 3:16. Within a few seconds, the passage is displayed on the screen. You can choose between several versions of the Bible or get pages from all versions. The interface also includes a concordance—type a search word into a field, and a hyperlinked list of verses containing the word is produced. If you specify a passage to search for specific words, the returning hypertext document will have all occurrences of the search word highlighted. Besides English, you can access German, Swedish, Latin, French, Spanish, and Tagalog versions of the Bible here.

Contact: Nick Hengeveld, Gospel Communications Network, *nickh@gospelcom.net*

Christus Rex

http://www.christusrex.org/

This Christianity site mostly provides information about the pope, Vatican City, the Sistine Chapel, and Vatican news. There is also Christian art on display here, with a worldwide tour of churches and images from the Vatican museums. Get the latest news and writings from the Vatican. Explore Vatican City, the Sistine Chapel, the Vatican museums, and many more places in images. You'll also find human rights news and links to many more Christian resources.

Contact: Michael Otleanu, Christus Rex, *root@christusrex.org*

See Christian art on display at Christus Rex.

Dead Sea Scrolls Exhibit

http://sunsite.unc.edu/expo/deadsea.scrolls.exhibit/intro.html

Learn the fascinating story of the Dead Sea Scrolls through this exhibit, which explores the ancient Qumran community, where the scrolls may have originated, and also relates the story of their discovery 2,000 years later. The exhibit is divided into five sections: an introduction to the world of the scrolls, the Qumran library, the Qumran community, the area in modern times, and a conclusion. As you travel through the exhibit, you'll see 12 scroll fragments and 29 other objects relating to the scrolls, mostly artifacts from the Qumran site. View the scroll fragments as inline images accompanied by English translations. A text commentary takes you through the story, backed up with secondary materials from the Library of Congress. You can also access an outline of topics and lists of selected resource materials for teachers.

Contact: Library of Congress, EXPO and Jeff Barry, *lcweb@loc.gov*

Gospel Communications Network

http://www.gospelcom.net/

The Gospel Communications Network provides many Christianity resources, with information on gospel software and videos, online Christian resources, and more. The International Bible Society provides scripture resources, an online Bible, and a call to prayer. You can also take a daily online Bible class or access a Bible hour for kids. Youth Specialties announces events for youth and has a resource mall. Download a collection of devotionals too, or explore many more Christian resources here.

Contact: Gospel Communications Network, *webmaster@gospelcom.net*

Principia Cybernetica Web

http://pespmc1.vub.ac.be/

The Principia Cybernetica Project (PCP) tackles age-old philosophical questions with the help of recent cybernetic theories and technologies. Here you'll find an overview of the evolutionary worldview that PCP is developing, as well as links to the major theoretical results of the project. A clickable outline lets you easily find local resources on cybernetics, philosophy, and evolution. Also connect to other resources on cybernetics, artificial intelligence, evolution, philosophy, memetics, systems science, and more, everywhere on the Web.

Contact: Principia Cybernetica Project, *fheyligh@vnet3.vub.ac.be*

Spirit-WWW

http://zeta.cs.adfa.oz.au/Spirit.html (Australia) or
http://www.protree.com/Spirit.html (United States)

Spirit-WWW is a fascinating online library of collected texts about many topics related to spirituality and paranormal phenomena. Topics covered include channeling, healing, reincarnation, UFOs, yoga, astrology, and many more interesting subjects. The searchable library catalogs in-depth, professionally written articles on every topic included; this is not just a hodgepodge of information but a useful research resource. Some examples of the variety of information you'll find here include Christ, Christians, and Krishna from a Vedic point of view, the lucid dreaming FAQ, highlights of Chicago's UFO Public Awareness Program, an overview of gemstones and spiritual healing, a discussion on Techno-Shamanism, and a crop circle gallery. Offerings in the library range from book excerpts, journals, and essays to Internet postings, FAQs, and photographs. Multimedia offerings include collections of related pictures, illustrations, paintings, videos, related sound clips, and a New Age music collection; there's also a collection of movie and music reviews. From this site, you can connect to related sites, networks, mailing lists, and Usenet newsgroups. You can also link to the Electric Mystic's Guide, the Mage's Guide to the Internet, and a separate library of New Age resources. Two sites are available, one in Australia and one in the United States; pick the one that's closest to you.

Contact: Spirit-WWW, Canberra or PAIC-WWW, Colorado, Rene K. Muller, *kiwi@iis.ee.ethz.ch*

Vatican Exhibit

http://sunsite.unc.edu/expo/vatican.exhibit/Vatican.exhibit.html

At this unique exhibit, you'll find 200 of the Vatican Library's most precious manuscripts, books, and maps, many of which played a key role in the recovery of the classical heritage of Greece and Rome. From the main hall of the exhibit, you can go to several rooms organized by subject, including archaeology, humanism, math, music, medicine, and biology. Each room has an extensive text introduction to the history of the topic. Then you can view images of the actual manuscripts from the Vatican Library, such as pages from early copies of texts and translations of Plato and Aristotle, among many other pieces. As you proceed through the exhibit, you'll learn the story of the Vatican Library as a driving force behind the emergence of Rome as a superpower during the Renaissance. If you don't want to take the time to travel through the exhibit, access a complete list of objects in the exhibit, and jump straight to those that interest you.

Contact: Library of Congress, EXPO and Frans van Hoesel, *lcweb@loc.gov*

Why visit Rome when you can visit the Vatican online?

For more information on philosophy and religion, visit the following sites:

About Witchcraft

http://www.crc.ricoh.com/~rowanf/COG/iabout.html

Includes links to definitions, basic philosophy, FAQs, general practices, holidays, and a bibliography.

Adam and the Snake

http://www.buffnet.net/~bb112/snakes.htm

This site covers one person's research into the function of snakes as religious symbols. It has an academic organization, but it covers an innately interesting subject.

Analytic Philosophy Page

http://college.antioch.edu/~smauldin/

This site has been set up by a person, not a university or group, and it shows. There are links to discussions on Nietschze, Marx, and Engles, but there are also links to the Church of the Sacred Aardvaark and cool quotes. This site is worth a visit by serious philosophers in as much as it has links to all kinds of philosophical debates and a whole slew of university philosophy department pages, but the average person who can't ever tell if Kierkegaard is spelled right can find a lot to enjoy here.

The Aquarian Age

http://www.sentex.net/~aquarius/

Information page for New Age and other resources.

Bjorn's Guide to Philosophy

http://www-und.ida.liu.se/~y92bjoch/

With a great design, this page was rated in the top 5 percent of Web sites. It has links to philosophers and other Web resources.

BUBL WWW Subject Tree

http://www.bubl.bath.ac.uk/BUBL/ReligPre.html

This site provides links to sites involving many of the Western and North African ancient religions.

Carnegie Mellon Philosophy Page

http://english-www.hss.cmu.edu/philosophy.html

With lots of useful links, this is another good starting page.

Catholic Resources on the Net

http://www.cs.cmu.edu/Web/People/spok/catholic.html

A veritable plethora of Catholic links, including liturgy, history, Vatican II documents, recent stories, and the Council of Trent.

Celtic Orthodox Religion

http://www.awod.com/gallery/rwav/robertg/relig.html

The links are a little bare, but include Celtic mythology, Celtic Christianity, myths and legends, and a religious calendar.

Chinese Philosophy Page

http://www.monash.edu.au/cc/staff/sas/sab/WWW/index.html

Intended to be the one page with links to everywhere. Includes links to documents, bibliographies, and mailing lists.

The Church Must Learn to Cope with the Computer Culture by Pope John Paul II

http://www.cs.cmu.edu/Web/People/spok/catholic/computer-culture.html

No, this is not the "Microsoft Buys the Catholic Church" text document. This is an actual statement issued by Pople John Paul II on the role the computer should play in the advancement of the Christian church.

Covenant of the Goddess

http://www.crc.ricoh.com/~rowanf/COG/cog.html

Links to various witchcraft and pagan resources, including student groups, organizations, articles, information links, etc.

CyberZen Page

http://www.indy.net/~bdmoore/cyberzen.html

Includes links to a Tao source page and a Zen source page, Zen teachings, and sutras. Really cool design, though the background is too busy.

The Department of Philosophy at the University of Gothenburg

http://www.phil.gu.se/Philosophy.html

This site provides information on philosophy and the available courses at the University of Gothenburg.

Documents of Jewish Beliefs

http://www.netaxs.com/~expweb/jewish_belief.html

Includes orthodoxy, reform, and classical texts as well as new articles and writings.

DreamLink

http://www.iag.net:80/~hutchib/.dream/index.html

This site provides tools for interpreting your dreams. It also lists the dreams of various other visitors to the site and gives you the chance to list your reactions to the posted dreams.

Facets of Religion

http://marvin.biologie.uni-freibury.de/~amueller/religion/general.html

This site is impressively balanced; while it certainly gives space to the dominent Western religions (Islam and Christianity), it also includes Buddism, Sikhism, Hinduism, Zoroastorism, and the Baha'i Faith.

Glossary of Confusing Religious Terms

http://www.kosone.com/people/ocrt/glossary.htm

Provides clear, precise definitions of certain religious terms such as "pagan." Not linked—this page is one long document.

Gnoses Archive

http://www.webcom.com/~gnosis/

Filled with piles of links to archived information on Gnosis and Gnosticism. Really helpful. Also links to other pages of interest.

A Guide to Chabad Literature

http://www.utexas.edu/students/cjso/Chabad/chabad.html

Rated in the top 5 percent of Web sites, this page has many useful links to Gophers, journals, online books, online galleries, and other useful pages relating to Chabad literature. There's a lot here!

Hare Krishna Home Page

http://www.webcom.com/~ara/

Includes philosophy, news, and other resources. Neatly organized.

The Haven

http://sfbox.vt.edu:10021/H/hshabana/index.html

A page with links to spiritual places and resources, such as Kahlil Gibran's *The Prophet*, the Spirituality Gallery, and the Ambiguity Corner.

The Hazel Nut

http://www.auburn.edu/~kerrlin/

A journal of Celtic spirituality and sacred trees. Interesting design, but doesn't seem to connect to much.

Hindu Universe

http://rbhatnagar.csm.uc.edu:8080/hindu_universe.html

Very nice design and graphics, with links to lots of neat stuff, including Scriptures.

The Hopkins Philosophy Pages

http://www.jhu.edu/~phil/subjects.html

A collection of philosophy-related resources.

Islam

http://mars.superlink.net/user/tashour/islamlnk.html

An Islam page with links to Koran translations, bibliographies, country information, and many other resources.

Islam: Come and Learn

http://linux.hartford.edu/~grant/islam/islam.html

Includes links to Koran translations, original Arabic texts, interesting articles, newsgroups, and a bibliography.

Islamic Resources

http://www.latif.com/

Includes a discussion on the personal meaning of Islam, community announcements, and links to other Islam sites.

Jain Home Page

http://www.vuw.ac.nz/~nzsldict/

With archived information on Jainism, links to newsgroups, and a brief historic overview.

Judaica World

http://www.nauticom.net/users/rafie/judaica-world.html

A packed page with lots of links to Judaica resources and information, including a kids' page, a Torah fax service for people on the go, a virtual Jewish community, and lots of links to Jewish resources as well as to Israel resources.

Leisa Goodman's Home Page

http://www.theta.com/goodman/

Leisa is an employee of the Church of Scientology and provides lots of information on this controversial church.

Light! Page

http://sojourn.com/~jjarrell/web/

Contains interesting links to Tarot, astrology, meditation, and spiritual journey.

Mithraism

http://www.io.org/~hermes3/Mithras.html

This page discusses Mithraism, a late-Roman pagan religion that strongly influenced Christianity. It is well worth a look by anyone interested in Greco-Roman mythology or the development of Christianity.

New Age Web Works

http://www.newageinfo.com/

Seeks to unite pagan, occult, and alternative spirituality communities. Really neat design and ranked in the top 5 percent of Web sites.

Nine Houses of Gaia

http://www.9houses.org/9houses/

This page is to promote earth-based religions. Includes links to resources, but many are inactive.

Philosophy

http://www.arts.cuhk.hk/Philo.html

This page covers philosophy, with an emphasis on Eastern philosophical studies. It also has links to lots of other philosophy-oriented sites.

Philosophy of Mind and Cognitive Resources Page

http://www.nd.edu/~alaser/philo.html

Still under construction, but lists many useful links to organizations, documents, publications, etc. Includes some really great graphics!

Philosophy-Related Resources on the Internet

http://www.liv.ac.uk/~srlsclark/list.html

This site outlines some of the philosophy-related resources on the Internet. The links are not established as widely as one could wish.

Plates of Brass

http://www.infohwy.com:80/church/lds/

This site is the Church of Latter Day Saints (aka Mormons) online. It includes Mormon hotlists, a place to order books and supplies, and a search function for both the Scriptures and the Book of Mormon.

Quan Yin Method

http://fiber.ieo.nctu.edu.tw:5000/

Meditation is the key to enlightenment.

Religion and Philosophy

http://wwwleinet.net/GJ/religion.html

This site is a searchable index of information on religion and philosophy.

Religions Working Together for a Better World

http://www.crc.ricoh.com/~rowanf/religion.html

While working with a different focus than the Facets of Religion site, this site also provides an overview of available religion sites. Also, unlike Facets of Religion, this site provides information on various pagan sites.

Richard Arnold's Home Page

http://www.clark.net/pub/rarnold/homepage.html

This site has a lot of non-mythological information, but it also contains links to several Judeo-Christian-oriented myth sites.

Routledge's Philosophy Page

http://www.routledge.com/philosophy.html

Contains links to publishers, associations, and other resource-filled pages. A great starting place.

Science Without Bounds

http://world.std.com/~swb/

"A synthesis of science, religion, and mysticism."

Sikhism

http://www.io.org/~sandeep/sikhism.htm

Resource page with a great design, this appears to have a lot of relevant information and links elsewhere.

Some Bible Resources

http://www.maths.monash.edu.au/~hyndman/bible.html

Includes links to organizations, Bible information documents, searchable Bibles, and lots of cool stuff with many interesting links.

Su Tzu's Chinese Philosophy Home Page

http://mars.superlink.net/user/fsu/philo.html

Excellent resource with plenty of links to information on Taoism and other important Chinese philosophy texts.

Themes in Contemporary Analytic Philosophy as Reflected in the Work of Monty Python

http://www.prairienet.org/rec/britcom/afmp.pythonphilo.html

This site is an analysis of different types of philosophy, using Monty Python as a descriptive medium. If you've been to twelve philosophy classes and you're still not sure what holism is, this page might clear it up for you.

Unitarian Universalist Church

http://www.qrd.org/QRD/www/UUA/uu-toc.html

Contains a table of contents page, with information on the Unitarian Universalist church and more.

Unitarian Universalist Theology Page

http://www.qrd.org/QRD/www/UUA/uu-theology.html

Links to principles, beliefs, and other information about the Unitarian Universalist church.

Virtual Christianity: Bibles

http://www.mit.edu:8001/people/aaronc/bibles.html

Links to all sorts of Bibles, including many English translations, such as the King James version, Bible search engines, and lots of foreign-language bibles.

The Voodoo Page

http://www.nando.net/prof/caribe/voodoo.html

Although still under construction and with few links, this page includes a bibliography, a mythological index, and other great stuff. It will be very cool when it's finished!

William James: The Varieties of Religious Experience

http://www.ultranet.com/~ngr2/JamesVRE

This page is essentially an extended outline showing the relationship between William James's religious views and Christian religious history, with some discussion of classic and modern philosophers. There are some links to other related sites, but not many.

Photography

Ansel Adams

http://bookweb.cwis.uci.edu:8042/AdamsHome.html

View a unique collection of the work of America's most famous photographer in this online exhibit, a hypermedia version of the book that Adams created to commemorate the centennial celebration of the University of California in 1968. This portfolio of 605 signed prints captures the university's nine campuses and its natural reserve system, research stations, and agricultural centers. You can access the exhibit either by following links in an introductory text or by moving through a menu format. If you like the exhibit, finish up in the exhibition bookstore, where you can purchase posters, note cards, and books of Ansel Adams photographs by phone, fax, mail, or e-mail.

Contact: UCI Bookstore, J. K. Cohen, University of California at Irvine Bookstore, *jkcohen@uci.edu*

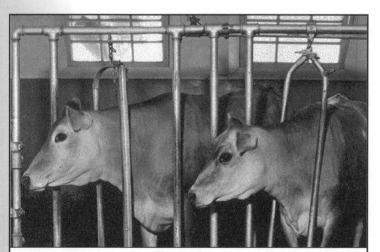

A collection of America's most famous photographer's works are available for viewing at the Ansel Adams site.

(Art)^n Laboratory

http://www.artn.nwu.edu/

(Art)^n—pronounced "art to the nth"—Laboratory is a collaboration of artists, scientists, mathematicians, and computer experts who invented PHSColograms, the museum-quality photography of virtual reality. PHSColograms are digital, full-color, high-resolution, 3D images created directly from three-dimensional data. This 3D can be viewed without special glasses (but not, unfortunately, on the computer screen). Applications for the images include scientific visualization, medical imaging, and video games. At this informative site for the laboratory, you can get technical details about the process, the history of the lab, a book list, magazine articles, and artists' and critics' statements about the photography. There are five different galleries to visit. The virtual photography gallery has sculpture, virtual portraits, science visualization, and computer-aided designs. There is also a video gallery and a commercial gallery of 3D images used in advertising.

Contact: Ellen Sandor, (Art)^n Laboratory at Northwestern University, *ellen@artn.nwu.edu*

Black Star Photography

http://www.blackstar.com/

Connect to an archive of resources for both amateur and professional photographers. The Web Resource Center has tools and tips for creating the best Web sites. The Photo Resource Center offers the latest photo stories and links. The Picture Collection Online provides stock photos. A photography database has information on film, paper, and photographic chemistry. Here you can also link to the International Center for Photography, view various photography studies, or visit the Michigan State University Online Photography Gallery. Other tidbits you'll find in the archive include FAQs on film and developing, exhibition information, and photography magazines.

Contact: Black Star Publishing, Black Star Photo and Web Resources

California Museum of Photography

http://cmp1.ucr.edu/

This virtual museum offers a range of contemporary art works and historical images prepared specifically for Internet exhibition. A unique feature is the Virtual Magnifying Glass, where all the photographs are image-mapped so that you can click on a portion of the picture to see it in greater detail. Look in Current Exhibitions for historical photographs and new art projects. Network Exhibitions cover several different historical topics, including historic Los Angeles, trains, Russia before the Revolution, and Japan circa 1880. Visit the Net Work Shop for projects by contemporary artists, offering a series of changing exhibitions designed for network distribution. You'll also find educational resources and children's projects in this unusual and fascinating museum.

Contact: Edward Earle, California Museum of Photography, University of California at Riverside, *edward.earle@ucr.edu*

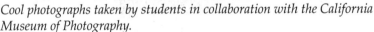
Cool photographs taken by students in collaboration with the California Museum of Photography.

Cloud Gallery

http://www.commerce.digital.com/palo-alto/CloudGallery/home.html

"Summon the angels to your desktop" from this gallery, where you'll find 32 photographs of various clouds, all copyright-free. Downloading and using the images is encouraged (or you can order a CD-ROM with all of the images directly through the site). Jump from an interactive map of all the selections to photographs you like, or select pictures by name, such as Cherubim, Repose, and Sandwich. Besides the images, you'll find some interesting information here. One valuable resource is a page of tips for using the cloud photographs for special effects, backgrounds, brochures, screen savers, and so forth. You can also read the photographers' comments on clouds as inspiration, how to summon angels, and how to watch clouds. This site is a fun place to laze away a summer afternoon, gazing up at the clouds.

Contact: Mary Bartnikowski and Michael John Price, Digital Equipment Corporation

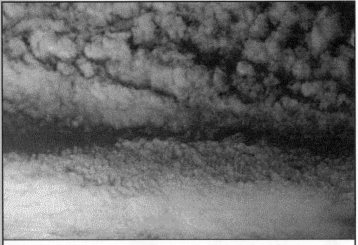

This cloud picture, Sandwich, is ready to download for your personal use from the Cloud Gallery.

For more information on photography, visit the following sites:

Andreas Zamperoni: Photography

http://www.wi.leidenuniv.nl/~zamper/photo.html

A nice photo gallery, but it will take a little longer to access than your average text file. Nicely organized.

California Virtual Tourist: Photography

http://www.research.digital.com/SRC/virtural-tourist/final/
CaliforniaRetail-photography.html

A listing and catalog of California photographers, along with tips and tricks for taking better pictures.

City Gallery

http://www.webcom.com/~cityg/

Includes online images, links to articles and guides, and other resources. Still under construction, but most links appear to be up and working.

Gallery 145

http://subee.com/145/145home.html

A gallery of fine-art photography.

George Eastman House in Rochester

http://www.it.rit.edu:80/~gehouse/

Museum, gallery, library, and other photo resources. Nice design!

History of Photography

http://www.primenet.com/~sos/history.html

This page describes the history of photography, from the daguerrotype to present-day photographic methods. Strangely enough, there are no pictures on this page.

Kodak

http://www.kodak.com/

Old Yeller's home page. Includes product information, digital imaging information, and general photography information, plus some nice design.

Jef's Photo Page

http://www.river.org/~jef/photos.html

Quite a lot of photos, actually, all taken by Jef. Probably not a good site for fine-art photos.

LightWork

http://sumweb.syr.edu/summon2/com_dark/public/web/L1.html

LightWork is a nonprofit artist-run organization. The page provides information on the organization, fellowships, and its publications (which are very cool).

150 Years of Photography

http://www.wingspread.com/fa/fa030.html

Includes a brief history of photography, a suggested reading list, a link to a glossary of photo terms, and collector's resources, plus some nice design. Limited usefulness.

Photography

http://www.lib.cortland.edu/photo.html

List of photo-related links. Not terribly extensive, but includes photo-related companies, individuals' pages, famous photogs, galleries and museums, and magazines.

Photography Film and Video

http://www.intellinet.com/~jdutton/photography.html

This site is essentially a catalog of videos on photography, many of which are by Kodak.

Photo Information Pages

http://www.southwind.net/~janet3/

Links to the photo of the month, galleries, searchable information databases, photo newsgroups, model information, and other photo pages. A good resource for the beginner who needs information and wants to poke around newsgroups and chat groups.

PhotoPLEX Online Bookshelf for Focal Press Books

http://www.directnet.com/wow/photo/kobre/focal/focal.htm

Provides online ordering of beautiful photography books by Focal Press. Includes a description, cover art, pricing, etc. To order, click on the book title link, scroll way down to the bottom of the next screen, and fill out the electronic order form. Useful for photogs who want these high-quality books.

Photo Sight

http://www.webcom.com/~zume/PhotoSight/

Includes new products, tips and techniques, and online galleries. Very nice design, this is another good starting place for beginners.

Plescia Photo Online

http://www.plescia.com/photo/index.html

Includes prices and descriptions of various photo and digital imaging services, as well as prices of photo products.

Santa Fe Workshop

http://www.nets.com/sfworkshop.html

One of the pre-eminent photo workshops in the nation, now online. Check course listings, information, and other cool stuff.

TimeLife's Photo Sight

http://pathfinder.com/@@iRahPwFvYwEAQC5H/pathfinder/photo/sighthome.html

Includes a photo gallery of their massive photography archives, a photo essay, and other links.

Yahoo Photography Exhibits

http://www.yahoo.com/Arts/Photography/Exhibits/

This site has lots and lots of links to differents photo-art galleries, discussions, and archives. A great place to wander and look at the pretty pictures.

Zone 1 Studio

http://www.gate.net/~eak3/

A forum for African American photography with a nice opening image.

Reference

Britannica Online

http://www.eb.com/

Forty-four million words long, the *Encyclopedia Britannica* has long been recognized as the world's most extensive reference product. Now with advanced search and retrieval capabilities and the power of hypertext formatting, Britannica Online becomes an even more powerful resource. This fully searchable and browsable collection of authoritative references includes Britannica's full encyclopedia database, a dictionary, Nations of the World, and more. The online resource is now available by subscription to colleges and universities and will soon be made available to libraries, businesses, and individuals. At the site, you can find out how to subscribe and get a free demonstration of the online resources available. The demonstration shows all the features of the service and lets you browse samples of the resources, including sample articles and searches. You can also get information about many other Britannica products. Subscribers to the service can search the entire encyclopedia through this site.

Contact: Encyclopedia Britannica, *sales@eb.com*

Dictionary Library

http://math-www.uni-paderborn.de/HTML/Dictionaries.html

This service, which points to many different English dictionaries, is endlessly useful. Access a number of literary, grammatical, and lexigraphical reference books from here, including *American English Dictionary, Webster's Dictionary, Roget's Thesaurus, The Oxford Dictionary of Familiar Quotations,* and an online hacker dictionary. You'll also find

German-English dictionaries, technical dictionaries, dictionaries for other languages, and an acronym dictionary. Be sure to explore the CyberDorktionary, Dan's Poker Dictionary, and the Unofficial Smiley Dictionary under the miscellaneous category.

Contact: Jürgen Péus, Universität Paderborn, *grobi@uni-paderborn.de*

The English Server

http://english-server.hss.cmu.edu/

This student-run cooperative publishes and distributes a huge library of resources for scholars working in the humanities: research, criticism, novels, hypertext, and miscellaneous writings. The amount of information archived and linked in at this site is so large it would be difficult to explore it all. The main menu is divided by subject, including archives of art, books, music, film and television, philosophy, poetry, reference, history, government, and drama. You'll also find resources for narrower fields, such as race studies, techno-culture, and gender studies. A collection of interactive hypermedia is included, and there is even a recipes folder. Some of the resources are links to external documents elsewhere on the Internet, and some are documents stored in the English Server archive itself. This site represents a vast library of scholarly resources collected from all over the Internet.

Contact: Geoffrey Sauer, The English Server, Carnegie Mellon University, *webmaster@english.hss.cmu.edu*

NCSU Libraries

http://www.lib.ncsu.edu/

Just like in a real library, here you can look up texts on all sorts of subjects in the humanities, life sciences, physical sciences, and social sciences. You can also visit a reference desk and a huge literature section. This virtual library is hosted at North Carolina State University in Raleigh. Search library catalogs, journal article indices, and book catalogs. Or access the library through subject resources, including agriculture, education, psychology, engineering, humanities, government, law, life sciences, medicine, physical and mathematical sciences, and natural resources. Find complete electronic books, anthologies, magazines, newsletters, scholarly journals, and more. To make your hunting easier, the entire online library is searchable.

Contact: North Carolina State University Libraries, *webteam@castor.lib.ncsu.edu*

UNCAT Database

http://www.sapphire.com/UNCAT/

Browse through an electronic catalog of "uncatalogued" titles not generally available in bookstores or libraries. Through this online catalog, you can access information on such publications as research reports, pamphlets, brochures, catalogs, newsletters, books, videos, audio cassettes, disks, and CD-ROMs, published by businesses, nonprofit organizations, trade associations, government agencies, museums, and self-published authors. Begin by selecting a subject of interest from a wide range, including the arts, education, history, social action, and travel. Then select a title that strikes you. You can get cataloguing information including medium, language, price, publication and revision dates, author, editor, illustrator, and a short description of the contents. You'll also find out where to order the publication or how to link to the publisher's WWW site. This great service is completely free to you.

Contact: Sapphire Press, Michael R. Prolman, *UNCAT@sapphire.com*

University of Virginia Library

http://www.lib.virginia.edu/

At this virtual library, access everything you would in a real library, including a reference room and online collections of texts, art, and music. In the Reference Room, you'll find an encyclopedia and dictionary, plus an Internet Reference Shelf, with useful reference information gathered from all over the Internet. Online Collections include a newspaper room, collections of literature, philosophy, and religion texts, a periodicals room, art and architecture images, maps and geographic information, music and media resources, and statistical databases. Access online publications, including an online atlas to Virginia. Electronic centers assist users with the online materials. Here you'll find a Social Sciences Data Center, a Geographic Information Center and many more useful resources. You're sure to find what you need in this all-purpose reference library.

Contact: James Campbell, *campbell@virginia.edu*, University of Virginia Library

---

For more reference materials, visit the following sites:

AT&T's Central Source Yellow Pages

http://www.telephonebook.com/

"Every business phone in America" online, searchable by name, number, or category, or look at an index. Handy reference!

AT&T's Toll Free Directory

http://www.tollfree.att.net/dir800/

AT&T's toll free directory online! Browse by category or search, plus find FAQs.

Bartlett's Quotations

http://www.cc.columbia.edu/acis/bartleby/bartlett/

Searchable by word and also includes an alphabetical listing of authors and a "hotlist" of oft-quoted authors by chronology right on the home page with links to their quotes. Very easy to use, it even breaks down Shakespeare's quotes by play. Really cool!

Census Bureau Lookup

http:// cedr.lbl.gov/cdrom/doc/lookup_doc.html

Got a "cool rating" from Yahoo. Look up census information from 1990.

General Information Desk Reference

http://www.america.net/ca/deskref.html

Includes links to the American English dictionary, *Roget's Thesaurus*, and many other (mainly Gopher) reference sites.

Global Encyclopedia

http://204.32.221.16/

A free online encyclopedia written by volunteers. Searchable by keyword or look up section by first letter. Anyone can contribute to the encyclopedia as well. Ranked in the top 5 percent of Web sites, so it must be growing.

Library of Congress

http://www.loc.gov/

A gold mine. Resources include exhibits and events, a searchable database of publications, digitized collections, and services and publications available to the public.

Phone Phinder

http://www.natltele.com/form.html

Look up area codes and prefixes anywhere in the United States or overseas country codes. Returns lists of cities by code and prefix. I don't think you can search for individuals.

Ready Reference

http://ipl.sils.umich.edu/ref/RR/LIB/readyref-rr.html

A companion page to the Reference Center (see the next listing). This site has links to other reference sites, such as the Purdue Virtual Reference Desk. Useful for crosschecking.

Reference Center

http://ipl.sils.umich.edu/ref/CenterNG.html

A combination dictionary and encyclopedia. Not a "fun" browse, but worth keeping in your hotlist, just as you keep a dictionary on your shelves.

Roget's Thesaurus Online

http://tuna.uchicago.edu/forms_unrest/ROGET.html

Accessed through word searches.

The Scholes Library of Ceramics Electronic Reference Desk

http://scholes.alfred.edu/Ref.html

Dictionaries, computing resources, phone books, area codes, geographical information, government information—this site is chock-full of links to useful reference information.

Teleport Internet Services Almanac

http://www.teleport.com/almanac/index.shtml

Includes daily weather, world news, this day in history, etc.

U.S. Postal Service

http://www.usps.gov/consumer/rates.htm

Provides a synopsis and tables of domestic and international mail rates. The URL for the USPS home page is simply **http://www.usps.gov/**.

Webster's Dictionary Online

http://c.gp.cs.cmu.edu:5103/prog/webster

In this hypertext version, you look up a word by entering a search term.

Social Sciences

Humanities Text Initiative

http://www.hti.umich.edu/

The Humanities Text Initiative is a project to provide networked hypertexts and multimedia exhibits in the humanities. Here you'll find lots of humanities texts for reference and research purposes. (Some texts are restricted to only the University of Michigan, but many are available to every WWW user.) Enter the stacks for publicly available editions of the Bible, the Book of Mormon, the Koran, and Middle English materials. You'll find many SGML resources, including guidelines, bibliographies, and tools. (SGML is the programming language that includes HTML.) You can also read about a collaboratory for the humanities and about the Humanities Text Initiative itself. An alphabetical index of all resources makes texts easy to find.

Contact: Humanities Text Initiative, *hti-info@umich.edu*

Institute for Advanced Technology in the Humanities

http://jefferson.village.virginia.edu/

Here you'll find a server full of texts and information of use to anyone interested in the humanities. The server offers many publications, including research reports, journals, technical reports, and software. Among these you'll find *Postmodern Culture,* an electronic journal of interdisciplinary criticism. You can also explore a large directory of related readings, collected from all over the Internet. These cover every aspect of the humanities, from art to literary studies, legal issues to philosophy, and religion. There is also a large reference shelf, information on electronic publishing, and teaching resources here. From the server, you can enter the Institute's MOO to discuss in real time projects of the Institute, or take part in an experimental Web chat program.

Contact: Institute for Advanced Technology in the Humanities, University of Virginia at Charlottesville, *iath@virginia.edu*

Smithsonian Institute

http://www.si.edu/

Now you don't have to make the trip to Washington, D.C., to see the Smithsonian Institute because it is all online. First you'll enter a welcome center to the online museum, where you can look at an overview of the Institute, get help navigating the electronic Smithsonian, search the site, read a FAQ about the Smithsonian, and plan a real visit. In Places, you can visit the many museums and galleries, such as the Air and Space Museum, the Museum of African Art, the Museum of American History, the Museum of the American Indian, and the National Zoo. Lots of museums and galleries have online multimedia exhibits that give you a taste of the museum itself. You can also link to research centers, such as the Archives of American Art, the Marine Station, the

Smithsonian Libraries, and the Smithsonian Environmental Research Center. Or poke your head in some offices, such as the Center for Museum Studies, the National Science Research Center, and the Office of Telecommunications. You'll find new and temporary exhibitions and events for each museum and gallery in Activities. Here you can also learn about traveling exhibitions. Perspectives looks at broad cultural, social, or political subjects, such as African American culture, Asian culture, activities for children, and topical areas such as computers, mammals, and oceans. Other resources include *Smithsonian Magazine*, discussion groups, and Radio Smithsonian. You can also go electronic shopping for Smithsonian items. Get ready to explore, but don't get lost in this gigantic, multimedia-filled site.

Contact: P. W. House, Smithsonian Institute, *webmaster@si.edu*

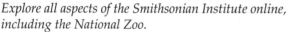

Explore all aspects of the Smithsonian Institute online, including the National Zoo.

Social Sciences Server

http://coombs.anu.edu.au/CoombsHome.html

This server provides a publicly accessible, free-of-charge research facility containing virtual libraries covering the social sciences and humanities. The huge social sciences virtual library catalogs Internet resources on every subject in social sciences. This is a great place to begin research efforts on the WWW. Here you'll find large collections of Asian studies, Aboriginal studies, Buddhist studies, Pacific studies, demographic and population studies, and Tibetan studies. There is also a large exhibit on the history of science, technology, and medicine. These large databases include current affairs, art, geography, anthropology, libraries, journals, and many more resources to make your research efforts easy.

Contact: Dr. T. Matthew Ciolek, Australian National University, *tmciolek@coombs.anu.edu.au*

For more information on the social sciences, visit the following sites:

Electronic Journals, Papers, and Books

http://archpropplan.auckland.ac.nz/misc/sources2.html

This site is academically oriented, yet still fun. The designers set it up to include academic facts and figures (schools, professors, who is hiring, etc.) and threw in a journal to boot. But they also included a section called Basilisk, which has all kinds of fun wierdness with a vaguely sociological slant.

The European Sociological Association

http://www.qub.ac.uk/socsci/miller/esaintro.html

This page describes the ESA and gives membership information.

Everton Publisher's Genealogy Help Page

http://www.everton.com/

Contains back issues of their magazine and links to other genealogy helpers. Good page; I'd recommend it.

Guide to Library Resources on Byzantine Studies

http://library.adelaide.edu.au/info/hum/classics/BYZREF.html

An extended bibliography on available material on Byzantine studies. The site doesn't really tell you where the material is, however. Since the URL mentions Adelaide, one might hazard a guess that the library is at the University of Adelaide in Australia. Similar sites include:

Guide to Library Resources for Classical Studies, **http:// library.adelaide.edu.au/info/hum/classics/CLASS.html** and Guide to Resources in the Barr Smith Library on Anthropology, **http:// library.adelaide.edu.au/info/socsci/anthro/ANTHROP.html.**

National Council for Social Sciences

http://www.ncss.org/online

Contains links to publications and other information. Nicely designed.

National Geneaology Society

http://genealogy.org/NGS/

Includes lots of links on geneaology information as well as many other genealogy resources.

Social Science Data System

http://www.stat.itd.umich.edu/data.html

This server provides a menu-driven means of extracting data from social sciences datasets, such as the General Social Survey, the National Health Interview Survey, and the Current Population Survey.

Social Science Information Gateway

http://sosig.esrc.bris.ac.uk/Welcome.html

This site is a resource for all the social sciences, from anthropology to statistics. Some of the areas are more fully developed than others, but they all seem to have something worth looking at.

Social Science International Gateway

http://www.sosig.ac.uk/

Includes links to United Kingdom and worldwide resources, plus links by subject. Useful starting place.

Voice of the Shuttle

http://humanitas.ucsb.edu/

About a zillion links to humanities-related pages—very useful, comprehensive, nice design.

WWW Virtual Library Humanities Index

http://www.hum.gu.se/w3vl/w3vl.html

Organized by category, easily browsable, lots and lots of links.

Moving On

With this section, you've received a well-rounded liberal arts education. But what about the scientific side of things? The next section
covers every aspect of science and mathematics as represented on the
Web, from astronomy to zoology, geometry to physics. If all this
sounds too boring, don't despair—when you explore these sites,
you'll find that math and science can be fun too. These sites incorporate multimedia, interactivity, and hyperlinks to enliven math and
science topics. Now that I've got you excited, let's dive into the wealth
of math and science sites on the WWW.

Section IV

Experiment!
Science, Mathematics & Computing Sites

Experiment! Science, Mathematics & Computing Sites

The World Wide Web offers infinite opportunities to study science and mathematics at all levels. Huge databases provide a wealth of scientific and technical information that anyone can access. Interactive applications transform abstract concepts into hands-on activities. And the WWW carries you far into outer space or deep inside the smallest organisms, as well as to laboratories and museums, without leaving your computer.

We'll start our scientific studies with a selection of fun astronomy sites that will send you to the stars. From there, we'll go on to the other science disciplines, including biology, physics, oceanography, paleontology, and zoology. We'll explore numerous computing and Internet sites that can help you solve personal computer problems, carry you into virtual reality, and teach you all about the Internet. We'll also visit virtual hospitals, get close to dinosaurs, tease our brains with geometry games, go on scientific expeditions, and more.

The Web creates such a powerful blend of hypertext, multimedia, and interactivity that it can make learning science and math fun and exciting. Roll up your sleeves—let's get online and experiment!

Astronomy

The Face of Venus

http://stoner.eps.mcgill.ca/bud/first.html

Learn all about the planet Venus at this fun and informative site. Get an overview of Venus, including images and descriptions of planetary features. The site illustrates and describes some of the surface features on Venus by using available images and information collected from NASA, scientific publications, and other sources. An interactive document describes volcanic and tectonic features and impact craters of Venus. There are also two research databases here, one of Venus' craters and one of its coronae. The crater database is the most complete version available. It contains 935 identified impact craters, listing the location and classification of each crater type and the origin of the crater. The database is searchable by size and/or type of crater. Selected craters are displayed on an interactive graphical map. The coronae database is searchable by size of corona, with an interactive graphical map allowing access to the whole database. This research tool is a unique example of hypertext publishing.

Contact: The Face of Venus Development Team, Department of Earth and Planetary Sciences, McGill University, *gnewton@alert.ccm.emr.ca*

Hands-on Astronomy Activities

http://www.c3.lanl.gov/~cjhamil/SolarSystem/education/index.html

Visit a library of easy and fun activities for learning about space and astronomy. Many of the activities can be done at home or directly on the computer. Some require ingredients that may not be easily obtainable, however. Find out about convection through images and animations. Learn about impact craters and eclipses. Complete an activity to determine if there is life elsewhere in the universe. Learn how to collect micrometeorites. You'll find activities for learning the phases of the moon and finding out what robots are. Learn how to observe the space shuttle as it orbits the earth. Find out how to look for sun spots. You can also download lots of fact sheets about space exploration and observations of our solar system.

Contact: Calvin J. Hamilton, Computer Research and Applications Group, Los Alamos National Laboratory, *cjhamil@lanl.gov*

Mapping the Earth and Heavens

http://portico.bl.uk/exhibitions/maps/overview.html

The oldest challenge facing the human mind is discovering the exact shape and extent of the earth and the cosmos that contains it. This problem has been addressed by religion, poetry, and myth, but science has confined itself to mapping the earth and heavens. At this site, visit an exhibition of maps, books, and artifacts that draws on 1,000 years of science and art. Follow the progress of scientific knowledge of the earth and universe over the centuries. Study the ways in which art and symbolism have been used to make statements about man's relationship to his world and the mysteries of the universe. Look at maps from A.D. 150 to the 1800s, each with a short explanation of what you're seeing and the context of the map. This is a fun way to learn the history of man's knowledge of the universe and earth's place in it.

Contact: Portico, British Library's Online Information Server, *portico@bl.uk*

Mt. Wilson Observatory

http://www.mtwilson.edu/

Visit a real space observatory through the WWW. First view a clickable map of the observatory, or go on a multimedia walking tour to get a feel for the grounds and find out the history of the observatory. On the virtual tour, you can visit places where tourists are not allowed to go, as well as a museum and astronomical exhibits. Then read about the telescopes and other astronomical equipment at the observatory. Professional services at the site include abstracts of scientific papers and resources for robotic observatories. A page for amateur astronomers has many fun features, including a constellation quiz in which you can test your knowledge of the night sky.

Contact: Bob Donahue, Mt. Wilson Observatory, *donahue@mtwilson.edu*

The Nine Planets

http://seds.lpl.arizona.edu/nineplanets/nineplanets/nineplanets.html

Take a multimedia tour of the solar system. This site contains an essay about the solar system enhanced by text, pictures, sounds, and an occasional movie. No special expertise or knowledge is needed to understand the essay; all of the technical and astronomical terms are defined in a glossary. First get a general overview of the solar system. Then tour the solar system, starting with the sun and journeying to all nine planets and their moons. You'll also visit small bodies such as comets, asteroids, and meteors. Find lots of facts about the solar system, the discovery of the planets, the names of astronomical bodies, and hypothetical planets. Learn about spacecraft involved in planetary science, and find out how you can support the continued exploration of space. Each page has a picture of a planet or its moons, some planetary facts, a list of pretty pictures found elsewhere on the Net, a table of data on any planetary satellites and links to their pages, links to more information about objects elsewhere on the Web, and a list of open questions about the planet for which we have no answers. In addition, there are music clips from Holst's *The Planets*, sound files of pronunciations of some of the more difficult names, and movies of a few objects. There's also a master picture list—an index of planetary images on the Internet. If you don't have time for the full tour, take the Express Tour of the ten most interesting bodies in the solar system. This fun site gives a complete overview of what we know today about our own solar system.

Contact: Bill Arnett, Students for the Exploration and Development of Space, University of Arizona, *billa@znet.com*

Tour the solar system in style at the Nine Planets.

Northern Lights Planetarium

http://www.uit.no/npt/homepage-npt.en.html

Connect to Norway's oldest public planetarium for information about the organization and its history, its activities, and technical installations. Then go to the real highlight of the site—information on the northern lights, or aurora borealis. Learn about the lights and their physics, and view an image collection. Or jump to a section highlighting the planetarium's special performances. The planetarium presents eight special programs, and you can read about all of them, including Arctic Light, Big Bang, and Star of Bethlehem. Some descriptions have multimedia enhancements, with sounds or excerpts from the performances accessible through hyperlinks.

Contact: Roger Larsen, University of Tromso, *nptweb@geronimo.uit.no*

Planetary Data Systems

http://stardust.jpl.nasa.gov/

Planetary Data Systems (PDS) archives and distributes data from past and present NASA planetary missions, astronomical observations, and lab measurements. At this site, you'll find lots of technical info about the planets and images from missions. Visit different organizations of PDS, such as the geosciences node, the atmospheres node, and the rings node. Each "node" provides varied and useful information about its research, including images, databases, online CDs, software, and links to related home pages. Access online catalogs, such as a database of images and information about small bodies from planetary missions. You'll also find other useful services, such as a software inventory and bulletin boards on current astronomical topics.

Contact: Tina Pauro, Planetary Data Systems, *pds_operator@jplpds.jpl.nasa.gov*

Solar System Live

http://www.fourmilab.ch/solar/solar.html

Using this interactive program, you can view the solar system live, as it looks at this moment. The online controls allow you to set the time and date, viewpoint, observing location, and many other parameters. Click on the title of any control for a help page describing it. The pictures you create show the positions of the planets in their orbits relative to each other. You can change the heliocentric view to look at the solar system from different angles. Also choose whether you want planets depicted as icons or images, and decide whether you want to see all the planets or just the inner ones. Go ahead and play with the parameters to see how many different views of the solar system you can make.

Contact: John Walker, Index Librorum Liberorum, *kelvin@fourmilab.ch*

Space Movies and Animations

http://marvel.stsci.edu/EPA/Anim.html

Download movies of objects in space, and see them in action. Each movie has a short text file that explains what you're seeing. You can see the Asteroid Vesta rotating or take a look at Mars's weather right on your computer. Search for evidence of oxygen on the moon Europa. Check out variable stars. See an animation of the collision of Comet Shoemaker-Levy with Jupiter. Fly into the Orion Nebula to see close-ups of protoplanetary disks viewed by the Hubble Space Telescope. Check out a storm in the atmosphere of Saturn. It's lots of fun to see these space events actually happen before your eyes.

Contact: Zolt Levay, Space Telescope Electronic Information Service, *levay@stsci.edu*

Stargazer Map

http://www.mtwilson.edu/Services/starmap.html

Just fill out an online form, and the computer will automatically create a star map for you to print out and use. All you have to do is put in the date and time you want to stargaze. Then choose from a list of pre-recorded locations, or enter your town's latitude and longitude. You can also decide whether you want to show constellations, meteor showers, reference lines, and other optional parameters. For more information about the star map computer program, look at the FAQ. The program automatically creates the map and saves it to the hard drive of your computer. You can then use it to locate stars, planets, moons, and astronomical events in the area where you live.

Contact: Mt. Wilson Observatory, *donahue@skepsis.com*

Stars and Galaxies

http://www.eia.brad.ac.uk/btl/

In this multimedia guide to the stars and galaxies, you can explore pictures, audio narrations, and movies to learn more about the universe we live in. Find out how stars behave, how their energy is generated, and about their origins and life cycles. Narrations explain each section that you are viewing. A wide range of interesting pictures of galaxies and star phenomena accompany the text. First study the origin of the universe and the Big Bang. Accompanying pictures and movies demonstrate the concepts of the creation of the universe. Then find out how stars are formed, and get close to our sun. Visit galaxies and nebulae through many pictures. You'll see some remarkable sights in the universe in this multimedia guide.

Contact: Mark J. Cox, Engineering in Astronomy, Bradford University, *m.j.cox@bradford.ac.uk*

Views of the Solar System

http://www.c3.lanl.gov/~cjhamil/SolarSystem/homepage.html

On this tour of the solar system, you'll learn all about our neighboring sun, planets, asteroids, comets, and meteoroids. Go to the history of space exploration for information about rocketry, space missions, astronauts, and traveling in space. Then start at the sun and work your way through all the planets. For each planet, you'll read an overview of the planet, jump to its moons, see photographs, study a chronology of the exploration of the planet, find out science facts, learn all about the planet's special features, and get statistics. You'll also find animations and lots of photos on every page. The planetary information browser is an interactive program that lets you tap into a database of facts about all the planets. Use it to get facts about our solar system quickly. Select the bodies in the solar system you want information about, and decide how you want the information sorted. You can organize the planetary facts by name, order, date of discovery, mass, density, distance, or many other ways. Then select the information to be included; you can choose from all sorts of statistical data. This online program is very easy to use and a good way to learn all about our solar system.

Contact: Calvin J. Hamilton, Computer Research and Applications Group, Los Alamos National Laboratory, *cjhamil@lanl.gov*

Virtual Trips to Black Holes and Neutron Stars

http://cossc.gsfc.nasa.gov/htmltest/rjn_bht.html

Virtually travel into a black hole or to a neutron star. (You've always wanted to, right?) All the movies found at this site are accurate and highlight the visual distortion effects you would see on such trips. The text explains the gravitational principles and mathematics behind the animations. Also get a trip description with technical explanations for each movie. Or just skip to the movies. You can journey into a black hole through five different animations and see firsthand the distorting effects of high gravity. Go to a neutron star, and follow the distortion effects caused by a high gravitational field with five different movies.

Circling the neutron star and approaching it are the most fun. Then travel to an ultracompact star to notice color changes and shifts. Of the eight movies, circling the star is the best.

Contact: Robert Nemiroff, Compton Observatory Science Support Center, *nemiroff@grossc.gsfc.nasa.gov*

Web Nebulae

http://seds.lpl.arizona.edu/billa/twn/

Nebulae are gas and dust clouds in space that sometimes form beautiful images on the night sky. At this site, take a look at the beauty of nebulae that usually can be seen only with a powerful telescope. Go to Types of Nebulae to learn more about nebulae. You'll see a large image of each different nebula and get some basic information about it. Find out what type of nebula it is, how far away it is, when and how it was discovered, its origin, and other interesting facts. A glossary explains difficult terms. Then you can follow links to other pictures of the object available on the Internet. Check out night sights such as the Pleiades, the Horsehead Nebula, the Crab Nebula, and supernova remnants. Web Nebulae takes you on a fascinating exploration of the universe.

Contact: Bill Arnett, Students for the Exploration and Development of Space, University of Arizona, *billa@znet.com*

WebStars

http://guinan.gsfc.nasa.gov/

WebStars is NASA's premium list of cool astronomy sites on the Internet; it also provides links to virtual reality, software, and more interesting sites. Link to many astronomy and astrophysics resources on the Internet, including articles, literature, conferences, data formats, and newsgroups. Find lots of virtual reality resources, such as articles, newsgroups, and FTP files. Locate style guides for online hypertext, downloading of necessary Web software, and WWW technical pages. You can connect to all of these astrophysics, cyberspace, and virtual reality resources through a huge image map.

Contact: Alan Richmond, WebStars

Welcome to the Planets

http://stardust.jpl.nasa.gov/planets/

Gathered at this one site is a collection of the best images from NASA's planetary exploration programs. Click on a planet's picture in the graphical menu to access statistical information such as the planet's distance from the sun, mass, and surface temperature, among other useful facts. These data are followed by images of the planet taken by NASA space probes and telescopes, complete with descriptions of how each photograph was taken and what it shows. Don't bypass our home planet—you will find pictures of Earth's surface from space and of the moon, including the moon landing. The Jupiter archive is one of the richest, with spectacular images of the giant planet and its moons, including the famous red spot. There is also a section on small bodies, with close-ups of asteroids and comets. Tour the solar system through this fascinating image gallery.

Contact: Ann Bernath, Planetary Data Systems, NASA, *abernath@stardust.jpl.nasa.gov*

A graphical menu takes you on a tour of the solar system at Welcome to the Planets.

For more information on astronomy, visit the following sites:

AstroWeb

http://www.w3.org/hypertext/DataSources/bySubject/astro/astro.html

AstroWeb is a virtual library of astronomy and astrophysics resources on the Web, divided by subject. Subjects include observations, data, publications, organizations, people, software, research areas, imagery, education, and history.

Cambridge Astronomy

http://www.ast.cam.ac.uk/

Visit observatories at Cambridge University, with research highlights, images, educational materials, and information on telescopes. You'll also find everything you'd want to know about the Hubble Space Telescope at this server.

Catastrophism

http://pubweb.acns.nwu.edu/~pib/catastro.htm

This page dicusses the function of stellar catastrophy in culture and modern folklore.

Green Bank Observatory

http://info.gb.nrao.edu/

Visit an observatory and learn all about the Green Bank telescopes.

University of Iowa Remote Telescope

http://inferno.physics.uiowa.edu/

This site contains images of stellar phenomena, examples of student research, automated telescope software, and a brief guide to sky display and image analysis.

Biology

AgriGator

http://WWW.IFAS.UFL.EDU/WWW/AGATOR/HTM/AG.HTM

This site gathers a collection of resources on the Internet containing agricultural and biological information. Here you'll find worldwide agricultural resources, including conferences, community groups, international locations, almanac servers, U.S. government and state sites, publications, mailing lists, and marketing services. The pointers are coded to let you know what type of resource you are accessing: WWW, Gopher, Telnet, FTP, or WAIS. They are also divided into sub-sections for easy browsing.

Contact: AgriGator, Institute of Food and Agricultural Studies, University of Florida, *AGRIGATOR@GNV.IFAS.UFL.EDU*

ANU Bioinformatics

http://life.anu.edu.au/

This huge "bioinformatics" service provides a large and varied amount of biological info. The complex systems section covers all aspects of artificial life, neural networks, fractals, and self-organizing systems. A landscape ecology section has information on ecology, biogeography, and fires. You'll find many medical resources, including large sections on neuroscience and viruses. A molecular biology section covers genetics, sequence analysis, and online access to all international databases. You can also get information on biodiversity, biochemistry, and biomathematics. Besides biological information, connect to a virtual library of educational resources, access a guide to Australia, and check out weather and global monitoring resources.

Contact: Australia National University Bioinformatics, *www-manager@life.anu.edu.au*

BioWeb

http://www.bioweb.com/g/p/bw/index.html

BioWeb is an information resource and virtual meeting place for the online community of biologists. A huge guide of resources for biologists located here is organized by branch of biology, organism studied, and kind of information, to make specific resources easy to locate. The detailed listings include a description of the resource, the organism studied, the biology subfield, and type of information. You'll also find a detailed list of biotechnology companies here, including a description of the resource, the biology subfield it covers, and the language of the resource. Or tap into a career center for all kinds of biology professionals. Different from traditional hotlists, BioWeb is a true library of online biology information.

Contact: Presence, *info@presence.com*

Game of Life

http://www.research.digital.com/nsl/projects/life/life.html

It's not the old board game that you'll find here, but rather a true game of life in which you try to reproduce generations of organisms. The game is played on a field of cells, each of which has eight neighbors. Each cell is either occupied by an organism or not. By clicking on cells, you determine deaths, births, and survivors, creating new generations from the previous ones. A variety of options at the beginning allows you to select an initial generation. This is a slow-paced game that will be fun for those who like brain teasers. One warning—if your generations get too big, the numerous large images can really slow downloading time over a modem connection.

Contact: John Conway and Stephen Stuart, DEC Corporate Research Group, *stuart@pa.dec.com*

International Interactive Genetic Art

http://robocop.modmath.cs.cmu.edu:8001/htbin/mjwgenforml

At this unique interactive site, you are presented with a series of pictures created by a genetic algorithm and then asked to vote on the "fitness" of each picture. Once ten people have voted on a particular series, the results are used by the genetic algorithm to create new pieces of art. The votes determine the fitness of a picture in a current generation. The more fit pictures are more likely to be used in the creation of the next generation, demonstrating an art-based version of "survival of the fittest." If you are interested, you can click on each picture to see the formula that created it, or you can just have fun voting. Be sure to revisit to see which pictures survived. You'll also find a gallery of even more genetic art here.

Contact: Computer Science Department, Carnegie Mellon University, Michael Witbrock, *witbrock@cs.cmu.edu*, and Scott Reilly, *wsr@cs.cmu.edu*

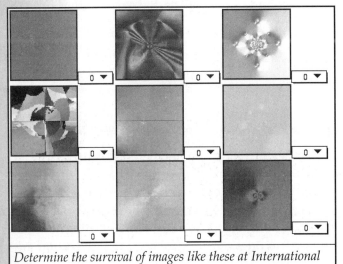

Determine the survival of images like these at International Interactive Genetic Art. (Copyright 1994 Scott Reilly and Michael Witbrock.)

Harvard Biological Laboratories

http://golgi.harvard.edu/

Harvard's biology Web site provides an index of lots of biology resources, including software, databases, journals, and conferences. You'll also find a listing, updated weekly, of biology seminars in the Boston area. Selected WWW biology resources include biotechnology resources, laboratories, educational programs, the National Institutes of Health, bioinformatics servers, and more. Find software documentation divided by analysis type and program name as well as online biological software directories. Selected model organism databases are included. You can also tap into other biomedical, biochemistry, and biological databases. There are even online biology job and career resources here.

Contact: Keith Robison, Harvard Biological Laboratories, *Krobison@nucleus.harvard.edu* and Steven Brenner, *S.E.Brenner@bioc.cam.ac.uk*

MendelWeb

http://netspace.students.brown.edu/MendelWeb/

MendelWeb is a unique and interesting educational resource for anyone interested in the origins of genetics, elementary plant science, or the history and literature of science. The resource is based on Gregor Mendel's original study of genetics. In the table of contents, you will find a background, Mendel's paper, essays and commentary, secondary sources, reference, and tools. Use the site as an archive for downloading and viewing Mendel's original paper. The hypertext version of the paper links to glossaries, introductory tutorials, biographical information, Mendel's German text, discussion questions, and exercises. You can also connect to Mendelroom, a MOO (a MOO is a multi-object orientation system where users can interact in real time) where you can join discussions with other users of MendelWeb. Whether your interests are biological, historical, or casual, you are sure to find many interesting paths through MendelWeb.

Contact: Roger B. Blumberg, Brown University NetSpace Project, *rblum@netspace.org*

Virtual Frog Dissection Kit

http://george.lbl.gov/ITG.hm.pg.docs/dissect/info.html

Squeamish about cutting up real frogs in biology courses? Don't like the idea of taking a frog's life for science? Real-life dissection may become obsolete with interactive virtual-dissection kits like this one, in which you can take apart an entire frog on your computer screen. The kit allows you to remove and replace organs and change the view on the frog so you can see it from all sides. A tutorial walks you through the process of online frog dissection; then you can go to it. Start with an external view of a whole frog. Select items in an interactive form to turn the frog or remove organs. An image-mapped version of the kit displays each organ's name and function when you click on it. You can even create movies of your dissection on the fly or access the kit in a variety of languages. This interactive kit is a fun way to learn biology, and when you're done, you can put the whole frog back together again. Try that with the real thing.

Contact: William E. Johnston and David Robertson, Lawrence Berkeley National Laboratory, *Webmaster@george.lbl.gov*

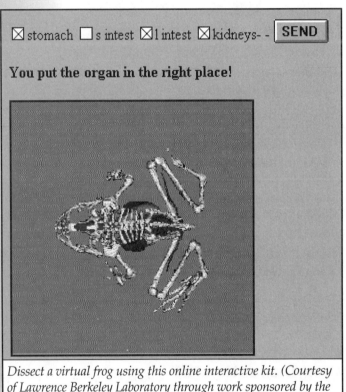

Dissect a virtual frog using this online interactive kit. (Courtesy of Lawrence Berkeley Laboratory through work sponsored by the U.S. Department of Energy, Energy Research Division, Office of Scientific Computing.)

For more information on biology, visit the following sites:

California State University Biological Sciences

http://arnica.csustan.edu/index.html

This site is an attempt to organize biological teaching resources and information. It would be helpful for anyone interested in teaching biology at anywhere from the high school to the grad school levels. It's worth a glance for the "fruit key," if nothing else. (Did you know that tomatoes are berries?)

Genome Database for Forest Trees

http://s27w007.pswfs.gov/

Just what it says, this site is for tree lovers only. You can also connect to other flora and forest biology resources and to the plant genome database collaboration.

Infomine

http://lib-www.ucr.edu/bioag/

This site is essentially a bibliography to different biological, medical, and agricultural resources on the Net. It's relatively fast and has several different organizational methods to choose from. A good spot to start research on biological topics.

Johns Hopkins University Bioinformatics

http://www.gdb.org/hopkins.html

Here you'll find a collection of protein databases, electronic biology publications, and many other biology-related databases.

Lawrence Berkeley National Laboratory Human Genome Center

http://www-hgc.lbl.gov/GenomeHome.html

This site is devoted to mapping the human genome, or genetic structure. The site includes studies of different mapping methodologies, as well as a genetic mapping-in-progress. The text is intended for people with a serious, professional interest in the topic.

University of Oklahoma Biological Sciences

http://obssun02.uoknor.edu/

This site allows the user to become involved in the University of Oklahoma biological survey by reporting finds of rare plants in Oklahoma. It also has other biology resources.

Virtual Genome Center

http://alces.med.umn.edu/VGC.html

This site provides access to new information on genetics, as well as tools for studying genetics. It's not for the casual, *Scientific American* type of biology fan, but it could be a very useful tool for people seriously studying the topic.

The Visible Embryo Multimedia Anatomy Tutorial

http://visembryo.ucsf.edu/

This site has a terrific tutorial on prenatal human development. The pictures are gorgeous and, although the text does have a lot of medical jargon, the tutorial would be useful for anyone from seventh grade up.

Chemistry

Fisher Scientific

http://www.fisher1.com/

Browse an online catalog of chemical products from Fisher Scientific. You'll find the general analytical reagents catalog and the Fisher Biotech reagents catalog, both of which are searchable. You can also get information about ordering chemical products from Fisher. Or connect to a large number of chemistry resources from here, including chemistry sites at academic, nonprofit, and commercial sites. You'll also find chemistry and biochemistry Usenet news, as well as resources for chemistry education, chemistry-related virtual libraries, and biochemistry and biomolecular resources.

Contact: Fisher Scientific Internet Catalog, *info@fisher1.com*

Web Elements

http://chemserv.bc.edu/web-elements/web-elements-home.html

Access a periodic table that's interactive and may make understanding chemistry easy. Just click on any element in the periodic table to learn more about it. You'll get the atomic number, atomic weight, symbol, group number, and other characteristics of that element. The table provides general information about the element as well, such as its color, how it was discovered, its physical state, and the meaning of its name. After playing with this online periodic table, you'll wow everyone with your elemental knowledge.

Contact: Dr. Mark J. Winter, Chemistry Department at Boston College, *M.Winter@sheffield.ac.uk*

For more information on chemistry, visit the following sites:

American Chemical Society

http://www.acs.org/

The American Chemical Society is the world's largest scientific society, with a membership of over 150,000 chemists and chemical engineers. The Society is recognized as a leader in scientific education and research and in promoting public understanding of science. Here get information about the Society, find out about upcoming events, and access a chemical abstracts service.

Chemistry at CSC

http://www.csc.fi/lul/csc_chem.html

Everything you want to know about chemical research and education in Finland, and more. But wait! There's really some interesting stuff here, such as pictoral representations of chemical properties, and anyone with a deep interest in chemistry should give this site a look.

Chemistry Virtual Library

http://www.chem.ucla.edu/chempointers.html

Here you'll find an extensive list of chemistry pointers, including chemistry sites at academic institutions, nonprofit organizations, commercial organizations, Usenet newsgroups, and other resources.

University of Sheffield Department of Chemistry

http://www2.shef.ac.uk/chemistry/chemistry-home.html

This site contains the usual university program faculty information, but it also has chemistry WWW publications, the Sheffield Macintosh archive of chemistry software, and other useful resources.

Computing

Animations

http://www.tc.cornell.edu/Visualization/contrib/cs418-sp94/cs418.html

Browse through a large archive of cool computer animations created by students at Cornell University. The animations incorporate computer graphics, 3D, and other technical stuff. Some animations that you can download and watch include an AT-AT from *Star Wars*, the opening battle of *Empire Strikes Back*, a "Knight Rider" automobile duel, a driver's view of a car race, a dogfight in the air, flight of the crash test dummies, a diver hunting for treasure, a car crash, a tank battle, spacecraft, a walk through a haunted house, and a space roller coaster. There are many more weird movies here as well. The video files are all very large, so make sure you have plenty of time to wait through the downloading.

Contact: Bruce Land, Cornell Theory Center, *doccomments@tc.cornell.edu*

Computer Professionals for Social Responsibility

http://www.cpsr.org/dox/home.html

Computer Professionals for Social Responsibility (CPSR) is a public-interest group interested in the impact of computer technology on society. The group provides the public and policymakers with realistic assessments of the power and limitations of computer technology. At this site, you can get basic information for prospective members, including chapters, discussion groups, conferences, and publications, as well as current hot topics in information technology. Learn about program areas such as the National Information Infrastructure, privacy, the Clipper Chip, gender issues, and more. An electronic archive includes information about computer crime, security, ethics, government, intellectual property, and more.

Contact: Computer Professionals for Social Responsibility, Sunnyside Computing, Inc. , *webmaster@cpsr.org*

Free Online Dictionary of Computing

http://wombat.doc.ic.ac.uk/

This online dictionary provides an invaluable resource for defining computing terms and acronyms. You can search the entire dictionary for a keyword. Or browse by subject, alphabetically, and by heading. You can even get a random definition. This great reference tool is available to Web users for free.

Contact: Denis Howe, Free Online Dictionary of Computing, *dbh@doc.ic.ac.uk*

The Icon Browser

http://www.cli.di.unipi.it/iconbrowser/icons.html

Need an icon for your home page, to use as clip art, or simply for fun? This is the one-stop online store for icons. Browse through 114 pages of icons, all available for downloading. Each page of icons has a clickable map of about 64 selections. Alternatively, you can search the icons by name using an interactive form. The icon selections cover everything imaginable, from James Bond to the weather. Click on one to view the icon and load it to a disk or hard drive on your computer. Maybe it isn't fine art, but it is a useful service made possible by the WWW. A warning: the image maps are very large—around 80 to 100 KB each—and can take a very long time to download through a slow modem connection.

Contact: Gioacchino La Vecchia, Department of Computer Science, Pisa University, *gio@virgilio.di.unipi.it*

Index to Multimedia Sources

http://viswiz.gmd.de/MultimediaInfo

The Index to Multimedia Sources is the place to go for cool graphics, nifty animations, and more impressive multimedia features on the Internet. This site provides hyperlinks to thousands of multimedia resources online. Connect to digital galleries, media archives, multimedia software, conference announcements, media-related companies, and much, much more. You'll also find online guides, FAQs, and newsgroups, all related to multimedia.

Contact: Simon Gibbs, Visualization and Media Systems Design, *Simon.Gibbs@gmd.de*

Interactive Graphics Renderer

http://www.eece.ksu.edu/IGR/intro.html

If you're getting ready to write some WWW pages or you just want to play around with a cool tool for making graphics, visit this site. This online program lets you design customized graphics and then downloads them to your computer to use in your own home pages. Read the license agreement first—you can only use the graphics in personal home pages. Also read the basic instructions for the lowdown on using the program (it's very easy). The online program makes bullets and those nifty lines you see everywhere. Use the online form to rotate the object, change the color, size, and shape, mix in new colors, and change the surface properties. There are many colors and shapes to pick from. Click on the Render button to see a preview of your new graphic, or hit Reset to wipe out the changes you've made. Click on Gimme to download the graphic to your hard drive. This interactive site provides a fun and easy way to make graphics. You'll also find a lot of useful resources for creating WWW pages, including an interactive generator of basic pages, a beginner's guide to HTML, and instructions for making advanced techniques like you've seen in many sites described throughout this book.

Contact: Patrick J. Hennessey, Department of Electrical and Computer Engineering at Kansas State University, *spectre@ksu.ksu.edu*

Internet Computer Index

http://ici.proper.com/

This site points to online resources for Macintosh, PC, and Unix users—a true equal-opportunity hotlist. Resources include mailing lists, newsgroups, FTP sites, FAQs, publications, and sales outlets. Get information about hardware and software. Download freeware and shareware online. Discuss your computer platform and problems in mailing lists and newsgroups. Also read online publications about operating systems and programming languages.

Contact: Proper Publishing, *comments@proper.com*

Macintosh Chat

http://disserv.stu.umn.edu/~thingles/PoundMac/

#macintosh is an Internet Relay Chat (IRC) channel discussing the Macintosh computing platform and anything relating to it. The official home page of the IRC channel features common channel topics, including PC bashing and Apple adoring. You'll find a list of ten commandments, a FAQ, and the policy and history of the channel. Meet regulars, read gems from discussions on the channel, and learn the channel theme song. From here, you can also access useful software archives and Usenet groups.

Contact: Jamie Thingelstad, Disability Services at the University of Minnesota, *thingles@disserv.stu.umn.edu*

Mac Resources

http://www.astro.nwu.edu/lentz/mac/home-mac.html

Robert Lentz, the maintainer of this useful Web site, has spent a lot of time searching the Internet for Mac-related resources. This site links to FAQs, software and hardware information, FTP sites, mailing lists, programming resources, publication archives, and just about everything Macintosh on the Internet for the benefit of Apple owners. Don't forget to take a break with Mind Candy, including QuickTime movies, Macintosh recreation, Mac humor, and the Unix Haters' Handbook.

Contact: Robert Lentz, Northwestern University Physics and Astronomy, *lentz@rossi.astro.nwu.edu*

MIT Artificial Intelligence Laboratory

http://www.ai.mit.edu/

This fun online lab provides research on artificial intelligence (AI), including learning, vision, robotics, and the development of new computers. Access research on robotics, learning systems, information access, software agents, virtual reality, and computing systems. Also locate all the lab's publications through a searchable database. A reference section includes a list of Net-wide artificial intelligence resources and a virtual reference desk. Lab information resources include a reading room, a novice's guide to the lab, and much more interesting information about the lab. There's even some fun stuff!

Contact: Robert S. Thau, Artificial Intelligence Laboratory at Massachusetts Institute of Technology, *webmaster@ai.mit.edu*

NCSA Virtual Reality Lab

http://www.ncsa.uiuc.edu/VR/VR/VRHomePage.html

The virtual reality laboratory at the National Center for Supercomputing Applications (NCSA) is a research facility exploring new methods of visualizing and interfacing with scientific data and simulations. The goal of the lab is to study and develop improved methods of viewing and interacting with information. At the Web site, you'll find papers related to the lab's research and project reports, with links to more Internet sites and Usenet groups devoted to virtual reality and other advanced imaging technologies. You'll also find information on virtual reality tool development and some visualization applications.

Contact: Bill Sherman, NCSA, University of Illinois at Urbana-Champaign, *wsherman@ncsa.uiuc.edu*

PC Lube and Tune

http://pclt.cis.yale.edu/pclt/default.htm

PC Lube and Tune is the PC owner's online service station and convenience store. The site provides usable introductions, tutorials, and education on communications, networking, and PC issues. An on-site newspaper, *Road and Hack*, reports on road conditions on the Information Superhighway. You'll also find articles on Windows and OS/2 operating systems, PC hardware, booting, DOS, client-technical issues, TCP/IP, Ethernet, and mainframes. This free service should become your pit stop for PC problems.

Contact: Howard Gilbert, Yale University Computing Information Systems, *Howard.Gilbert@yale.edu*

The final section discusses the various Internet services available and the programs that can be used to take advantage of them. FTP file transfer, Gopher menus, Web document browsing, E-mail, and searching tools will be described. Viewers for graphics, sound, and PostScript will also be reviewed.

Continue   Back   PCLT

Road signs guide you down the Information Superhighway at PC Lube and Tune.

Power PC News

http://power.globalnews.com/ppchome.htm

This free online newsletter publishes the latest news on the Power PC, along with some of the most up-to-date information about the Internet, personal computing, and technology in general. The newsletter is updated on the Web about two weeks after it comes out and is read by over 50,000 people. At the site, read the current issue and back issues, or search the entire archive. If you don't want to wait, find out here how to get the newsletter mailed to your e-mail account. You'll also find a computer bookstore here.

Contact: Chris Rose, APT Data Group, *chrisr@power.globalnews.com*

Quadralay Cryptography Archive

http://www.quadralay.com/www/Crypt/Crypt.html

On any computer network, security is an important issue. Whether you're a security-conscious network manager or a renegade hacker, you'll find this archive a good source of information collected from all over the Internet on cryptography and security, arranged by subject for easy reference. Some examples of what you can access here include an archive on the Pretty Good Privacy program for encrypting e-mail, including a list of frequently asked questions and references to appropriate newsgroups; encryption standards; National Security Agency information; and articles on the Clipper Chip, a proposed device that would enable the government to access all Internet files. Travel other links to FTP sites, journals, and cryptography sites elsewhere on the Internet. The Cryptography Archive is a worthwhile site to explore, whether for fun or research.

Contact: Quadralay Corporation, *webmaster@quadralay.com*

Rob's Multimedia Lab

http://www.acm.uiuc.edu/rml/

At this famous site for multimedia resources, you'll find downloadable graphics, movies, and sounds of all kinds. Tons and tons of GIFs are stored in the archive, sorted chronologically, alphabetically, or by subject category, such as Escher, *Jurassic Park*, raytraces, and *Star Wars*. Sound directories range from film and TV quotes to music and sound effects. You'll also find many MPEG movies, from MRI images to "Beavis and Butthead." A weather archive has satellite images and movie clips. Other links take you to even more sound, image, and movie archives on the Internet; icons tell you what kind of resources you're accessing. Amateur multimedia designers will find plenty to choose from at this online lab.

Contact: Rob Malick, Association for Computing Machinery, University of Illinois at Urbana-Champaign, *rmalick@www.acm.uiuc.edu*

Download publicly accessible GIF files like this one from Rob's Multimedia Lab.

TidBITS

http://www.dartmouth.edu/Pages/TidBITS/TidBITS.html

Adam C. Engst's TidBITS is one of the best documents for entering the world of computing. Published weekly, it covers a range of computing topics, including hardware, software, industry news, and product reviews (mostly from a Mac perspective). The Web site features an index of back issues and the current issue in hypertext form.

Contact: Adam C. Engst, Dartmouth College, *ace@tidbits.com*

UK VR-SIG

http://www.crg.cs.nott.ac.uk/ukvrsig/vr-sig.html

This site lets you access the UK Virtual Reality Special Interest Group (VR-SIG) and is a major jumping point to virtual reality archives and discussion groups all over the Internet. Get information on upcoming events, new research and development, and the latest software. You can even view demos. If you're a virtual reality fan, this is the place to connect with the online VR community.

Contact: Dave Snowdon, Communications Research Group, University of Nottingham, *d.snowdon@cs.nott.ac.uk*

The Virtual City

http://riceinfo.rice.edu/projects/RDA/VirtualCity/

Through the WWW, you can attend a virtual lecture series, such as this one on the "virtual city," even from a thousand miles away. This particular lecture series covers a topic of interest to any Netizen—the architecture of the city based in cyberspace. There are five lectures in the series. Cyberpunk author Bruce Sterling's talk is the only one published online, along with links to works by Sterling and biographical information about him. Biographical information and works by the other lecturers are linked in as well. Connected with the lecture series is a film series called Cinemarchitecture V: The Virtual City. You can access the film schedule and read information about each movie in the series, so that you can see the movies at home and follow along with the talks. This unique presentation of a lecture series on the WWW is presented by a nonprofit group called the Rice Design Alliance.

Contact: Kim Baumann Larsen, Rice University, Rice Design Alliance, *kiml@chico.rice.edu*

Virtual Computer Library

http://www.utexas.edu/computer/vcl/nindex.html

Tap into a large reference library of information sources regarding computers and computing. This library connects to many online computing resources, including academic computing from all over the country and the world. Check out reviews of the latest computing, networking, and Internet books. You'll also find links to online books, dictionaries, and guides to computing. Access research in computing areas such as artificial intelligence, graphics, multimedia, security, and virtual reality. Find out about upcoming computing conferences. Documentation and FAQs answer your computing questions. Get Internet information, including guides, products, services, and news. Link to computing journals and magazines, such as *MacWeek, PC Week,* and *MacWorld*. Read news and press releases from the world of computing. Learn about nonprofit and government computing organizations, as well as user groups. Find computer book and documentation publishers and vendors of hardware, software, information services, networking, and consulting. There's also information about the WWW, including resources on HTML, guides, products and services, magazines, and news. Whatever your computing question or interest, you'll find it here.

Contact: Christine M. Hale, Reference Services, Computation Center, University of Texas at Austin, *vclib@www.utexas.edu*

ZDNet

http://www.pcweek.ziff.com/

ZDNet offers information from a family of computing magazines, including *PCWeek, MacUser, Interactive Week, MacWeek, FamilyPC, Computer Shopper, Computer Gaming World, PC Magazine,* and *Computer Life.* Get subscription information, news, and sample articles from each magazine featured. A news desk provides breaking news collected from all the magazines. The Trailblazer charts the Web, picks the best computing sites, and reviews them. You'll find sites on a variety of subjects, including utilities, games, multimedia, operating systems, and networking, forming a powerful computing resource guide. You can even join a free service that delivers the hottest computing news from major news sources and filters only the stories you want to follow.

Contact: Ziff-Davis Interactive, *webmaster@ziff.com*

For more information on computing, visit the following sites:

Advanced Computing Center for the Arts and Design

http://www.cgrg.ohio-state.edu/

This is a center for instruction, research, and design in the use of computing in the arts. The work done here includes computer graphics and animation, scientific visualizations, software development, computer-mediated art, telecommunications, multimedia, and virtual reality.

The Alliance for Computers and Writing

http://prairie_island.ttu.edu/acw.html

This is a site for people interested in writing on the computer as a serious communications tool. That doesn't mean that the site is dust-bowl dry. Some of the Best E-mail Messages from the Lists (IMHO) are worth a read.

Army High Performance Computing Research Center

http://www.arc.umn.edu/

Learn about the national initiative in high performance computing and recent research.

Epic

http://epic.org/

Epic is a nonprofit organization that focuses on emerging civil liberties issues relating to the National Information Infrastructure. Here you'll find news about cryptography, telecommunications legislation, and privacy.

IEEE Computer Society

http://www.computer.org/

This is the world's leading organization of computing professionals. It is also a leading provider of technological services and information to computing professionals.

Interactive Cross Reference for Windows

http://www.kudonet.com/~ixfwin/ixfw/ixfw.html IXFW_WHATIS

This site gives you the chance to test drive Interactive Cross Reference for Windows.

Knowledge Media Institute

http://hcrl.open.ac.uk/

This Institute promotes a broad convergence of learning and cognitive sciences with computing and telecommunications technology. Read all about it and visit the Institute's research labs here.

Localization: Designing Software for Export

http://www.worldsimages.com/localise/commandshtm

This site addresses the problems in designing and merchandising products, especially software, for a world market. Check out the Eleven Commandments of Localization.

National Center for Supercomputing Applications

http://www.ncsa.uiuc.edu/

At this huge site you can get general information about the NCSA research groups. Also visit a variety of multimedia exhibits, learn about software developed at NCSA (including Mosaic), and connect to lots of computing resources.

Perl Programming Language

http://mox.perl.com/

Here you'll find a useful archive of resources about the programming language Perl.

School of Informatics

http://web.cs.city.ac.uk/

This site publishes lots of computing information on Unix, Logic, software, systems architecture, and human-computer interface design.

Sybex

http://www.sybex.com/

This site lists classes, tutorials, and books on computers, software, networks, and the Internet.

University of Cambridge Computer Lab

http://www.cl.cam.ac.uk/

This site connects to lots of useful computing resources, including resources on programming, graphics, security, artificial intelligence, and more.

Earth Science & Environment

CIESIN

http://www.ciesin.org/

The Consortium for International Earth Science Information Network (CIESIN) offers information about earth observations, global changes, human impacts on the environment, and more environmental resources. At the Web site, you'll find data about human interactions with the environment, information resources for social-environment studies, and tools that assist with environmental research.

Contact: Consortium for International Earth Science Information Network, *ciesin.info@ciesin.org*

Daily Planet

http://www.atmos.uiuc.edu/

This weather information site features current weather maps, satellite images, animations, forecasts, and more. The site also points to sources of local and global climate data. Electronic textbooks at the site are valuable tools for studying atmospheric features, including winds, clouds, storms, and weather maps. A special section furnishes curriculum resources for elementary-school teachers on weather subjects. You'll also find pointers to other useful weather and climate resources on the Internet.

Contact: Daily Planet, Department of Atmospheric Sciences at the University of Illinois, *web-masters@www.atmos.uiuc.edu*

Earth Viewer

http://www.fourmilab.ch/earthview/vplanet.html

This interactive online program lets you look at the earth in many different ways. You can view a map of the earth showing the areas of day and night at the moment. See the earth as it looks from the sun, the moon, or a satellite in earth orbit (even choose which satellite you want to view it from). Take a look at the night side of the earth. Or pick a view with a specific longitude, latitude, and altitude. You can also choose to see the earth with the current cloud cover. Go to the expert mode for additional control over the images you create. You may choose to play around with the variables, but it's fun just to look at the pictures too. You can also download astronomy software, such as Home Planet, which allows Windows users to create images of the earth, the solar system, asteroids, comets, and more.

Contact: John Walker, Index Librorum Liberorum, *kelvin@fourmilab.ch*

Get many different views of our planet using the Earth Viewer program.

EcoNet

http://www.igc.apc.org/econet/

EcoNet serves those people working for environmental preservation and sustainability. You'll find lots of environmental resources and organizations here. The environment Gopher provides a way for EcoNet members to disseminate information about their projects and research. Here you'll find an archive with information on biodiversity, climate, energy, environmental law, water, toxic waste, and much, much more.

You can also connect to important environmental news sources and organizations. A useful environmental issue resource center connects to outside resources on many activist subjects, including animal rights, endangered species, energy, forests, mining, and oceans.

Contact: EcoNet, The Progressive Directory, *econet@econet.apc.org*

EnviroWeb

http://envirolink.org/

The EnviroLink Network, the largest online environmental information service on the planet, reaches well over 450,000 people in 95 countries. It offers the world's largest environmental archive at this Web site. The library is a clearinghouse for all the Internet's environmental resources, divided into categories such as activism, events, green business, government, organizations, publications, and more. A Green Marketplace lists all the companies on the Internet who have passed a stringent screening process to ascertain their level of social responsibility. You can even express yourself in a free space that allows anyone to assert their ideas and opinions through art, debate, and writing.

Contact: EnviroLink Network, *admin@envirolink.org*

Smithsonian Gem and Mineral Collection

http://galaxy.einet.net/images/gems/gems-icons.html

The gem and mineral collection at the Smithsonian Institute is world famous. Now you can visit it without having to make the trip to Washington, D.C. The online exhibit shows 41 of the Smithsonian's most famous gem and mineral holdings. Here you can see the 98.6-carat Bismarck Sapphire, Marie Antoinette's diamond earrings, the Star of Bombay, the Spanish Inquisition necklace, and (of course) the Hope Diamond, among many other well-known pieces. View each item through an inline image followed by a short description of the piece and its history. Click on the image for a more detailed view. You can wander endlessly among these fabulous jewels.

Contact: EINet and Smithsonian Institute, EINet Galaxy, *galaxy@einet.net*

Solstice

http://solstice.crest.org/

Connect to a valuable online archive for information on energy effi-
ciency, renewable energy, and sustainable technology. You'll find
loads of documents on a variety of topics, including energy, education, the environment, environmental legislation, and renewable
resources. Resources located at this site are extensive, and if you want
more information, you can link to related resources on the Internet. If
you're at all interested in energy conservation or the environment,
this large archive should have something for you.

Contact: Solstice, Center for Renewable Energy and Sustainable
Technology, *www-content@solstice.crest.org*

Unidata Integrated Earth Information Server

http://atm.geo.nsf.gov/index.html

Unidata is a prototype of an Integrated Earth Information Server
(IEIS, pronounced "eyes"), provided by the Unidata Internet Data
Distribution network, a coordinated national effort among 125 universities. Follow a link to learn more about Unidata. The server provides
a wide variety of environmental information. Get current weather
reports and forecasts, including national and international weather
reports. You can access high and low temperatures, forecasts by cities
and states and weather maps. Other environmental data available at
the server include the latest sea surface temperature maps, polar
observations, and high resolution images of important environmental
events. Check out southern and northern ozone levels as soon as they
become available, or look at the most recent earthquake reports and
maps of epicenters. The server also provides instructional materials
created from environmental data for teachers, including lesson plans,
observation instructions, and an online cloud catalog.

Contact: Ben Domenico, Sally Bates, and Mike Wright, National
Science Foundation Geosciences, *support@unidata.ucar.edu*

U.S. Geological Survey

http://www.usgs.gov/

This United States government site provides information about governmental environment research, geographic information systems, education, and public issues. Get maps, reports, and information to manage, develop, and protect America's natural resources. Find educational resources on earth science, marine geology, earthquakes, and an Ask-a-Geologist resource to answer your earth science questions. Connect to a wealth of environmental resources covering natural hazards, water resources, risks, and more. Publications include CD-ROMs, books, fact sheets, reports, and maps that you can download online. You'll also find useful databases on water resources, geology, cartography, and more.

Contact: U.S. Geological Survey, *webmaster@www.usgs.gov*

VolcanoWorld

http://volcano.und.nodak.edu/

In this massive database, you can have fun finding out everything there is to know about volcanoes. Discover which volcanoes are erupting or getting ready to erupt right now. Learn how volcanoes work, where the world's volcanic regions are, and about historical eruptions. Find out how to become a volcanologist, or ask real volcanologists questions using an online form. You can also read other questions and answers about eruptions, volcano folklore, lava, studying volcanoes, the effects of volcanoes, terminology, and interesting facts. Visit volcanoes all around the world by viewing a slide show. Tour famous volcano parks in Hawaii, at Mount St. Helens, and elsewhere. You can also look at volcano art, read about volcanoes in the news, and visit the Volcano Mall to buy volcano merchandise. You can search the entire site for specific information, but you may just want to wander around—there's a lot to explore.

Contact: VolcanoWorld Development Team, University of North Dakota

Get close, but not too close, to erupting volcanoes like this one at VolcanoWorld.

WebWeather

http://www.princeton.edu/Webweather/ww.html

The University of Michigan Weather Machine provides weather information for almost any place in the United States. At the WebWeather interface to the Weather Machine, choose a state on the form provided (not all states are listed but most are). Then pick a city from four or five choices, usually the major cities in that state. The form instantly returns current weather conditions, including temperature, humidity, wind speed and direction, atmospheric pressure, and sky conditions (sunny, partly cloudy, etc.). You'll also find weather reports for selected cities in Canada, Europe, Asia, Central America, South America, and the Caribbean. And try out WebWaterWeather, which retrieves near-shore marine forecasts.

Contact: Ben Davenport, Princeton University, *bpd@princeton.edu*

For more information on earth science and the environment, visit the following sites:

Alaska Volcano Observatory

http://www.avo.alaska.edu/

Learn all about volcanism in Alaska, get highlights of recent eruptions, and see satellite images of volcanoes. There are also links to other volcanological sites.

Center for Landscape Research

http://www.clr.toronto.edu/

The Center explores ideas related to the design, planning, and policies of the environment. This site contains architecture and landscape architecture virtual libraries, as well as information about environmental resources and teaching.

Eco-Motion

http://cyberzine.org/html/Electric/ecomotion.html

This site tells you about electric cars, provides conversion information for existing cars, and gives information on how to buy original electric cars.

Global Change Master Directory

http://gcmd.gsfc.nasa.gov/

Directory source of information on earth science, the environment, the biosphere, climate, and global change data. You'll find a searchable database and links to other sites.

Greenpeace

http://www.greenpeace.org/

Out of Amsterdam. Nice design, aimed at the politically active.

Ground Truth Earthwatch Research Report

http://gaia.earthwatch.org/WWW/Gkammen.html

This is a good introductory site to sustainable energy use and alternative energy sources. Don't be fooled by the single link on this page—that link leads to dozens of others.

Institute of Geophysics and Planetary Physics

http://www.igpp.ucla.edu/

Here visit the Center for Earth Systems Research, the Center for the Study of Evolution and the Origin of Life, the Center for Planetary Chemical and Physical Study, and the Space Sciences Center.

Intellicast USA Weather

http://www.intellicast.com/icast/weather/usa/wxusa.html

A really cool page! Includes extreme temperatures from across the nation, a clickable map to get today's weather, constant updating, TV footage of events (including hurricane Roxanne), and other neat stuff.

The International Solar Energy Society

http://www.ises.org/

This page gives information on the ISES and provides links to some solar power information.

Mr. Solar Home Page

http://www.netins.net/showcase/solarcatalog/index.html

This site shows how one couple got off the energy grid and how you can too. Specs on household energy systems and a catalog are included.

Naval Research Laboratory

http://www.nrlssc.navy.mil/

Learn more about navy resources on atmospheric science, the environment, oceanography, geosciences, and more.

Project Nature Connect

http://www.pacificrim.net/~nature/

A discussion of nature's effect on human psychology. Provides access to courses on nature and psychology.

Renewable Energy and Sustainable Living

http://wwws.us.ohio-state.edu/~steen/sustain

A great page for anyone interested in ecologically friendly living. There are tips on everything from low-cost, energy-saving habits and projects to building an entire house in an energy-saving manner. There are also links to other eco-Web sites.

The Self-Sufficient Solar House

http://www.ise.fhg.de/
Institute.Projects.SelfSuffSolHouse.english.html

This site describes a self-sufficient solar house and lists resources for more information. Unfortunately, there are no links on this page.

Sierra Club

http://www.sierraclub.org/

Lots of linked information about Sierra Club, including the book club, with books organized by topic, including children's books.

Solar Energy

http://www.rt66.com/rbahm/

A good resource on the state of solar energy use and technology.

Solar Energy and Renewable Energy Related Servers

http://www.ise.fhg.de/Other_Solar.html

This site lists numerous other sites on alternative energy resources and ideas.

Solar Energy Applications Laboratory

http://princeton.lance.colostate.edu:8080/Solar.html

A good introduction to how solar energy works, possible applications, and why some people consider it a vital area of research.

Southern California Earthquake Center

http://scec.gps.caltech.edu/

This is a primary archive of seismological data in southern California. Find out about recent earthquake activity and seismic activity, and connect to other earthquake centers.

Taking Action for Endangered Species

http://www.the-body-shop.com/es.html

This site has been set up by the famous/infamous Body Shop and has information on the legal aspects of hunting endangered species.

U.S. Environmental Protection Agency

http://www.epa.gov/

Here you can get information about the Environmental Protection Agency (EPA), including news and events, contracts and grants, and employment opportunities. You'll also find information on environmental regulations and legislation, as well as huge libraries of environmental information.

The Weather Channel

http://www.infi.net/weather/index.html

A seriously cool page with a great design. Includes maps and daily weather updates, plus more about the channel and other "cool stuff."

Weather Processor

http://thunder.atms.purdue.edu/

This huge weather information source provides weather visualizations, satellite imagery, surface and upper air data, radar data, current forecast model data, and other resources for finding weather or earth information.

Wildlife Disappearing?

http://www.cris.com/~cheeta/

This site not only contains information on endangered species around the world but, it also provides contact information for those interested in working to stop species extinction.

Internet

(See Appendix D, "World Wide Web Search Tools," for specific tools and databases for help with finding Internet resources.)

ASCII Art Archives

http://gagme.wwa.com/~boba/ascii.html

ASCII art is an art form created on the Internet. ASCII art is made entirely with the characters on a computer keyboard. You've probably seen some examples of ASCII art in *sigs* (sigs are signature files, usually found at the end of an e-mail address or newsgroup posting). Now browse the best ASCII art in one archive. Follow the most requested art link for the best of the best, including ASCII animals, hearts, teddy bears, flowers, happy birthdays, Star Trek, spaceships, dragons, Snoopy, and more. You won't believe how good these pictures are until you see them. For more info about ASCII art, check out the ASCII art FAQs, with links to other ASCII art resources and many examples for reference. There is an archive of humorous ASCII art, a 3D gallery, and a gallery of the best sigs. Check out the BBS gallery for the best login and server screens for bulletin board systems and multi-user dungeons (MUDs). There's also a gallery of the best GIF-to-ASCII conversions, showing GIF files changed to ASCII fonts. You can even download ASCII pictures, fonts, GIFs, and sigs for your own use.

Contact: Bob Allison, WorldWide Access, *boba@wwa.com*

```
                 _\I/_
               (      )
             ( (/oo\) )
              ( \''/ )                                    ⱳⱳ
               ( \/ )          ⱳⱳⱳⱳⱳ                     /__\
             (        )     ⱳ"ⱳⱳ  ⱳⱳ"ⱳ              | oo |  _ⱳⱳⱳⱳ
            (          ) ⱳ   o""o    ⱳ    (o)(o)   (|_()_|) /  o o  \      (+)(+)
    oo               )ⱳ  ___   ⱳ  ⱳ"    "ⱳ    \_/ (| __o__ |)/        \
  ⱳ"()"ⱳ    (        ) "ⱳ \_\/_/ ⱳ" ⱳ  -====-  ⱳ  /!\/!\  \ \___/ /   \  -==- /
  ⱳ -===- ⱳ   '--'  ⱳ "ⱳ"ⱳⱳⱳⱳⱳ"ⱳⱳ "ⱳ       ⱳ"  ||||||||| /-------\   \    /
   "ⱳⱳⱳⱳ"     =  =    ||||||||||| ⱳ"""""""""""ⱳ |||||||||=========| <\/\/\/>
  ⱳ"     "ⱳ    =  =    |||||||||||ⱳ         ⱳ|||||||||=========| /        \
    Elmo     Big Bird    Oscar      Cookie       Bert      Ernie     Kermit
```

This ASCII picture can be found in the best of the best ASCII archive.

Best of the Net

http://src.doc.ic.ac.uk/gnn/wic/best.toc.html

Global Network Navigator annually gives awards for the overall best
Web pages. Every year 10 honorees are chosen, creating an eclectic
collection of useful, well-designed, and entertaining sites. At the Web
site, you can explore this year's nominations and recent years' honorees. Looking at these "best of" lists is very helpful when designing
your own WWW pages.

Contact: Global Network Navigator, SunSITE Northern Europe

Electronic Frontier Foundation

http://www.eff.org/

The Electronic Frontier Foundation (EFF) is a civil liberties organization working to protect privacy, free expression, and access to online
information. Access EFF's services here. Document and file archives
provide information on activism, censorship, civil liberties, cryptography, legal issues, security, and anything else having to do with information technology freedom. The EFF newsletter publishes alerts of
recent Internet censorship legislation and news and tells you what
you can do. You'll also find a huge guide to the Internet and a virtual
world tour of cyberspace here.

Contact: Electronic Frontier Foundation, *webmaster@eff.org*

EFF's Guide to the Internet

http://www.eff.org/papers/bdgtti/eegtti.html

Also known as Big Dummy's Guide to the Internet, this very complete guide tells you everything you could want to know about the Internet. Learn everything from the basics of connecting to the Internet to the secrets of the most advanced Net wizards. The guide includes sections on every basic Internet tool, including e-mail, Usenet, mailing lists, Telnet, FTP, Gopher, WWW, MUDs, and IRC. You'll also learn proper Netiquette (Internet manners) and even get a smiley dictionary. After reading this guide, you definitely won't look like a "newbie."

Contact: Electronic Frontier Foundation and EUNet, *info-admin@Germany.EU.net*

E-mail FAQs

http://www.cis.ohio-state.edu/hypertext/faq/bngusenet/comp/ mail/misc/top.html

This collection of FAQs, regularly posted to the newsgroup *comp.mail.misc*, will give you the lowdown on using all the functions of electronic mail. You'll learn how to find e-mail addresses and how to access Internet files in FTP, Usenet, Gopher, and WWW servers through e-mail. Discover how to subscribe to mailing lists and how to send e-mail to different networks. Check the Signature, Finger, and Customized Headers FAQ for useful e-mail information, including info about many popular e-mail programs, creating a signature, how to use finger, and many more basics.

Contact: Department of Computer and Information Sciences, Ohio State University, *webmaster@cis.ohio-state.edu*

FAQ Central

http://www.cis.ohio-state.edu/hypertext/faq/usenet/

Every experienced Netizen knows that you'd better read the FAQ before joining a new Usenet newsgroup. Newsgroup FAQs are also a good source of general information on any imaginable subject. You can find all of the FAQs at this archive just for Usenet FAQs. This

WWW site lets you search all the FAQs for a keyword or locate FAQs by newsgroup or title. This resource is also useful for finding newsgroups to join.

Contact: Thomas A. Fine, Department of Computer and Information Sciences, Ohio State University, *webmaster@cis.ohio-state.edu*

Fishnet

http://www.cs.washington.edu/homes/pauld/fishnet/

This is the site of a one-man newsletter providing an eclectic discussion of the Internet. Fishnet is a weekly publication that gleans some of the best and most interesting items from all over the Internet. The issues consist of tidbits collected from everywhere on the Internet covering an amazing variety of subjects. You can browse back issues by date or access a list of all the subjects that Fishnet has covered.

Contact: Fishnet Editor, Computer Science and Engineering Department, University of Washington, *fishnet-request@cs.washington.edu*

Global Network Navigator

http://nearnet.gnn.com/gnn/gnn.html

Global Network Navigator (GNN) is a series of publications and information services provided by O'Reilly & Associates, the computer book publishers. From the home page, you can access many useful services. Find a weekly publication of news from the Internet. Access the electronic version of the *Whole Earth Catalog*, with hotlinks to all its site listings, or learn what's best and what's new on the Net. Visit meta-centers such as the personal finance center, the travelers' center, the education center, and the sports center for articles and pointers to hot Web sites. You'll also find here the Internet center, which has a help desk for new Netizens. You have to subscribe, but the subscription is free.

Contact: Global Network Navigator, NearNet

Gopher Jewels

http://galaxy.einet.net/GJ/index.html

Gopher Jewels is a mailing list of interesting finds from all kinds of Gopher sites. This Web site organizes and lists all of the collected "jewels," with resources on everything from AIDS and HIV information to multimedia, museums, and travel info. If you primarily use the WWW, then you may not have delved into the troves of information that Gopher servers offer. This site provides an attractive and easy-to-use way to access all of them.

Contact: David Riggins and Bruce Speyer, Galaxy at EINet, *GopherJewels-Comment@EINet.net*

Internaut

http://www.zilker.net/users/internaut/index.html

An online magazine supplement to the *Online User's Encyclopedia,* Internaut offers a treasure trove of Internet information, including resource pointers and Internet tools. Go to the "latest" page to find the most current articles from Internaut. These include features on networking, software, the Information Superhighway, and technical issues. Check the index page for links to valuable Internet resources, such as search engines, the *net.happenings* mailing list, and InterNIC. You'll also find Internet-specific books for sale at this site, including the *Online User's Encyclopedia*; take a look at sample chapters, tables of contents, and reviews, and then find out where you can order the books online.

Contact: Bernard Aboba, Zilker Internet Park, *aboba@itnernaut.com*

The Internet Adapter

http://marketplace.com:80/tia/tiahome.html

The Internet Adapter (TIA) is an Internet access program that lets you use popular software programs such as Netscape and Eudora with a standard Unix dial-up account. (Normally you would need a SLIP or PPP account to use these software programs.) The Web site, maintained by the developers of TIA, provides background and ordering information for this useful software. You can also find TIA news, get a tutorial for installing it, and try it out for free.

Contact: Cyberspace Development, Marketplace.Com, *webmaster@marketplace.com*

Internet Glossary

http://www.matisse.net/files/glossary.html

Are you confused about the meanings of WAIS, BBS, MOO, or ASCII? Did you think Archie, Jughead, and Veronica were just comic book characters? Do you believe a "client" is a customer, a "server" is a waiter, and "fingering" doesn't sound very nice? What the heck is a URL anyway? Learn the real meanings of all those weird Internet terms and acronyms. After consulting this glossary, you'll toss around words like "bandwidth," "hypertext," and "TCP/IP" like a Net guru.

Contact: Matisse Enzer, Internet Literary Consultants, *admin@matisse.net*

Internet Tools Summary

http://www.rpi.edu/Internet/Guides/decemj/itools/ internet-tools.html

This huge list offers a complete overview of every tool you can use on the Internet. You'll learn where to find the tools, how to use them, and where to go for more information. Find tools for locating other Internet users, such as finger, Netfind, and Whois. Get information on basic Internet tools such as FTP, Telnet, Gopher, and the World Wide Web, including a list of WWW software that you can download. Learn how to search the Internet using tools such as Jughead, Archie, Veronica, WAIS, and spiders. You'll also find links to resources for learning about Usenet, IRC, MUDs, mailing lists, e-mail, CU-SeeMe, and the Mbone. This is a good basic resource to all of the tools used to access the Internet.

Contact: John December, Rensselear Polytechnic Institute, *john@december.com*

IRC Primer

http://www2.undernet.org:8080/~cs93jtl/irc_primer.txt

This primer tells you everything you need to know about using Internet Relay Chat (IRC). You'll find a guide to commands, hints for using IRC politely, information about different channels, and much more. You'll also learn where to get IRC software, about privacy on IRC, and other frequently asked questions.

Contact: Nicholas Pioch, Brunel University, *Nicolas.Pioch@grasp.insa-lyon.fr*

John December's Home Page

http://www.rpi.edu/~decemj/index.html

John December is famous for his many contributions to the Internet, especially his well-known summary of Internet tools and his hypertext index-guide to the Internet, the Internet Web Text. Connect to both those resources through his home page, or read about some of John's other publications. His home page is loaded with other useful links, especially to information on computer-mediated communications.

Contact: John December, Rensselaer Polytechnic Institute, *john@december.com*

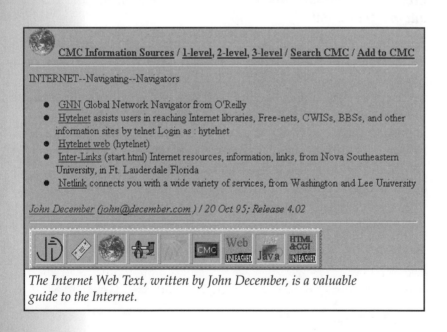

The Internet Web Text, written by John December, is a valuable guide to the Internet.

Kevin Hughes' Home Page

http://www.eit.com/people/kev.html

Kevin Hughes is a hypermedia software engineer and Webmaster for Enterprise Integration Technologies (EIT), but his fame extends back to the beginnings of the WWW. While Webmaster at Honolulu Community College, he invented the interactive map and wrote the famous text, Entering the WWW: A Guide to Cyberspace, now archived all over the WWW. At his links-heavy home page, you can connect to all of Kevin's WWW innovations. Jump over to Honolulu Community College, the first fully hyperlinked campus-wide information system, which featured multimedia on the Web for the first time. For this work, Kevin was inducted into the WWW Hall of Fame. You can also link to other WWW projects Kevin worked on, including EIT WWW software. For fun, lots of movies Kevin created are also linked in here.

Contact: Kevin Hughes, Enterprise Integration Technologies

Mailing List Search

http://www.nova.edu/Inter-Links/listserv.html

If you're looking for a new discussion group to join through electronic mail, try this site first to find just the right one. The site lets you search a master list of more than 5,900 e-mail discussion groups to find one on a subject that interests you, such as movies, music, "Star Trek," the environment, books, sports, or anything else. You can also learn how to subscribe, unsubscribe, and post to an e-mail list, as well as many other commands for Listserv.

Contact: Rob Kabacoff, Nova Southeastern University, *kabacoff@alpha.acast.nova.edu*

Netiquette

http://rs6000.adm.fau.edu/rinaldi/net/index.htm

Everyone who uses the Internet should follow some basic rules to make the Internet a friendlier and better place for everyone. After all, you don't pay anything for these Internet resources other than the cost of connecting, so you have a responsibility to follow these long-established rules. This guide to Netiquette (Internet etiquette) teaches you the proper behavior for using Internet resources. You'll find guidelines for using e-mail, Telnet, FTP, and the World Wide Web. Learn some common rules of behavior for participating in electronic mailing lists and Usenet newsgroups. This is also a good place to get tips on basic Internet usage.

Contact: Arlene H. Rinaldi, Florida Atlantic University, *RINALDI@ACC.FAU.EDU*

NetLand

http://sunsite.unc.edu/netland.html

NetLand provides resources on all sorts of networking geek topics. The communications archives feature IRC logs and virtual communications. Learn to be a server daemon and even a Webhead. Connect to the Linux documentation project. (Linux is a free Unix-type operating system for PCs.) You'll also find an excellent source of information about Usenet and the World Wide Web, including new developments in Web software.

Contact: SunSITE, University of North Carolina at Chapel Hill

Nexor List of Web Robots

http://info.webcrawler.com/mak/projects/robots/active.html

This page links you to most of the better *robots*—programs that automatically hunt the Web and index the results of their searches. Each robot listed includes a short description so you know what it does before you jump to it. Robots listed here include the World Wide Web Worm, JumpStation, Lycos, InfoSeek, and many more.

Contact: Martijn Koster, WebCrawler, *m.koster@webcrawler.com*

Paul Jones' Home Page

http://sunsite.unc.edu/pjones/pjones.html

You've probably noticed a lot of sites based at SunSITE reviewed in this book. Now meet the man responsible for all of that. Through a slide show on Paul's home page, you can learn about SunSITE, its history, access methods, and statistics. You can also read Paul's poetry chapbook, *What the Welsh and Chinese Have in Common,* currently out of print and available only on the WWW. You'll find many fun links to sound effects, graphics, and movies in Paul's introduction. From his home page, you can also link to all of SunSITE's services, including the WWW site, FTP archive, Gopher, and BBS.

Contact: Paul Jones, SunSITE, University of North Carolina at Chapel Hill, *Paul_Jones@unc.edu*

Scott Yanoff's Home Page

http://www.cs.uwm.edu/public/yanoff/index.html

Scott Yanoff is best known for his Internet Services List, a mega-resource of Internet sites that is widely distributed everywhere on the Internet. From his home page, you can connect to an HTML version of the list. You can also link to another famous Internet resource that Scott now maintains, the Inter-Network Mail Guide. You'll find some useful shell scripts that Scott has written, including Fingerinfo, a program that presents a menu of the Internet's best finger sites. Besides all these great Internet resources located on his home page, there is personal information, such as Scott's favorite television shows and musicians, all linked to their home pages. If you're really interested, you can even see pictures of Scott's trip to Des Moines.

Contact: Scott Yanoff, University of Wisconsin, *yanoff@alpha2.csd.uwm.edu*

3W Magazine

http://www.cityscape.co.uk/3W/

For a look at the Internet from a user's perspective, try this WWW magazine. 3W publishes useful articles on networking, the Internet, service providers, software, the WWW, electronic publishing, multimedia, and Internet resources. Columns include Absolute Beginners—information for beginning Internet users—and regular WWW coverage. One unique feature is Internet A-Z, an alphabetical list of Internet resources covering every subject in depth. You'll find lots of other useful resources here as well, including lists of service providers, zines, and virtual reality resources. Subscribe to the magazine, or check out sample articles. Be sure to follow the value-added link for sample goodies, such as a list of 99 zines, letters from the Internet, and other Internet-related articles.

Contact: 3W, Cityscape, *3W@ukartnet.demon.co.uk*

Tim Berners-Lee Bio

http://www.w3.org/hypertext/WWW/People/
Berners-Lee-Bio.html

Not really a traditional home page, Tim Berners-Lee's biography pages are still a necessary visit for anyone interested in the WWW. Tim originally created the WWW and is now the director of the W3 Organization, which coordinates WWW development. At this site, you can find basic information about the Web and presentations Tim has given. Tim was recently inducted into the WWW Hall of Fame, so any serious student of the WWW should pay him a visit.

Contact: Tim Berners-Lee, The World Wide Web Consortium, *timbl@w3.org*

URouLette

http://www.ukans.edu/uroulette.html

Gambling on the WWW? You only gamble on where you'll end up when you access this random URL generator. Click the floating roulette wheel to travel to a random location on the WWW. You won't know where you're going until you get there. In three spins of the URouLette wheel, I traveled to the Center for Integrative Studies at Michigan State University, the ARL Supercomputing User's Guide, and the Cornell University Institute for the Study of the Continents. The WWW is so big that it's unlikely you'll go to the same place twice, and you can make a real killing from spinning the wheel if you stumble on a particularly interesting site.

Contact: University of Kansas Campus Internet Association (KUCIA), *kucia@ukanaix.cc.ukans.edu*

The WELL

http://www.well.com/

Considered by many the birthplace of citizen-based virtual community, this service has over 260 conferences on diverse subjects, including media, art, literature, music, and spirituality. More than anything, this is a place to meet and interact with others. Learn about the WELL virtual community through community pages. Members will find lots of Internet services, including access services, classes, Web self-publishing, and Web software tools. From here you can also search the Internet, check out the WELL's favorite Net resources, and connect to cool lists of hot Web sites.

Contact: WELL Web Staff, The WELL, *web@well.com*

Who's Online

http://www.ictp.trieste.it/Canessa/whoiswho.html

Find out who's who on the Internet with this interactive guide. Who's Online is a collective attempt to create a hyper-biographical database of people on the Internet. Search for someone with a particular profession or specialty using a keyword index, or access by general category, from astronomers to writers, Webmasters to cyberneticians. Entries link to the person's curriculum vitae or similar information, including personal data and listings of publications by people online. The index is intended to help you hook up with others in your field or discover researchers who publish information on topics of particular interest. You can also enter yourself into the database by selecting your own profession from the list and then filling out an interactive form.

Contact: Dr. E. Canessa, International Center for Theoretical Physics, *cannessae@ictp.trieste.it*

World Wide Web FAQ

http://sunsite.unc.edu/~boutell/faq/

You love the WWW, but you want to know more about it. For instance, what exactly is SGML, HTML, and Java? Where can you find Web browsers, and how do you use them once you've got them? How can you make your own home page, with all of the most advanced

Web features? To get these and more questions answered, the only place to go is the WWW FAQ. If this very complete document doesn't answer your every question, it is sure to point to a resource that will.

Contact: Thomas Boutell, SunSITE, University of North Carolina at Chapel Hill, *boutell@netcom.com*

Zen and the Art of the Internet

http://www.cs.indiana.edu/docproject/zen/zen-1.0_toc.html

Another helpful basic guide to the Internet, this handbook explains such difficult concepts as domains, IP numbers, and networks. You'll also learn everything there is to know about e-mail, FTP, Usenet, and Telnet, as well as how to finger, ping, and talk. Follow the many pointers in the guide to places where you can find out more about the Internet.

Contact: Brendan P. Kehoe, Computer Science Department, Indiana University at Bloomington

For more information on the Internet, visit the following sites:

ASCII Art FAQ

http://www.cis.ohio-state.edu/hypertext/faq/usenet/ascii-art-faq/faq.html

This FAQ will answer all your questions related to creating, sharing, and finding ASCII art on the Usenet newsgroup *alt.ascii-art*. You'll even find tips for making great special effects.

Association of Internet Professionals

http://associp.org/

This nonprofit organization provides lots of useful stuff on their Web site, including basic Internet help, help with HTML, a shareware library, and pointers to Internet resources. Among these pointers, you'll find search engines, resource directories, news, legal resources, other Internet-related organizations, and Internet statistics.

CERFnet

http://www.cerf.net/

CERFnet is one of the oldest Internet service providers. Its Web site not only tells the company's fascinating history, but also provides many value-added exhibits, like the Interactive Media Festival, the Federation of American Research Networks, and the Supercomputer Teacher Enhancement Program.

Cinenet

http://www.cinenet.net/

So you've avidly explored the Internet, but would like a different form of access. Or you're interested in getting on the infobahn for the first time. Cinenet will help you get set up (for a price). They also have links to other cool pages.

FAQ Index

http://www.nsu.nsk.su/FAQ/index.html

A list of hundreds (if not thousands—I couldn't get the end of it) of FAQs on every conceivable topic, indexed alphabetically, with a one-line description of where the link goes (usually a Gopher site for a newsgroup).

Find it Fast!

http://www.webcom.com/~tbrown/findpage.html

Find information on the Web, searchable by category or by keyword. Looks handy! Does more than just find individuals.

InfoSeek Services

http://www.infoseek.com/

Provides a free search on keywords of up to 100 hits and, for a fee, you can get a subscription service to get lots and lots more hits plus access to members-only databases. A free one-month trial subscription is available.

Internet Search

http://twod.med.harvard.edu/labgc/roth/E-mailsearch.html

Index to several e-mail searches, finger searches, and other Web page search indices. Handy for trying several services.

LookUP!

http://www.lookup.com/

An Internet search for e-mail addresses.

Metacrawler

http://www.cs.washington.edu/research/projects/ai/metacrawler/www/

Searches the Web for keywords. However, it has nice features that allow for limiting the wait, domain, and accuracy of the search. Also includes instructions.

The Online World

http://login.eunet.no/~presno/

This site covers practical global aspects of using online information.

Savvy Search

http://www.cs.colostate.edu/~dreiling/smartform.html

A cool search engine that will find resources on a keyword query. You can limit sources and types of information (i.e., WWW resources, software, academic, etc.) and get information from a number of Internet search engines.

The Search Page

http://www_is.cs.utwente.nl:8080/cgi-bin/local/nph-susi1.pl

A page in the Netherlands that lets you search using all kinds of servers, such as InfoSeek, Archie, or Veronica, plus you can search lots of different databases by category. Definitely worth a look.

SGML Open

http://www.sgmlopen.org/

SGML Open is a nonprofit international consortium of suppliers whose products and services support the Standard Generalized Markup Language (SGML). Their mission is to promote and enable the widespread adoption of SGML, especially within the mainstream information technology market. Here you'll find a library of SGML resources, with information on getting started with SGML, uses of SGML, conversion, industry standards, and HTML.

Starting Point

http://www.stpt.com/

Designed to be the easiest starting point for Web access beginners, with button categories and a "hot site."

WWW Search Engines

http://ugweb.cs.ualberta.ca/~mentor02/search/search-all.html

Provides 128 links to search engines and includes a description of each one. This is really handy if you want to search multiple places from one starting point or find the most suitable search engine for your needs.

Mathematics

The Fractal Microscope

http://www.ncsa.uiuc.edu/Edu/Fractal/Fractal_Home.html

The Fractal Microscope is an interactive tool for exploring the Mandelbrot set and other fractal patterns. (Fractals are art created from recurring mathematical patterns.) It was created by the National Center for Supercomputing Applications (NCSA) as a practical way of teaching elementary-school students about fractals. The Microscope combines the creation of math art with the science of math for enjoyment and real learning. At the site, learn more about fractals; all text is illustrated with fractal images. Then read about the Fractal Microscope created by

NCSA. The Microscope enables the user to zoom in and out of the Mandelbrot set quickly, much quicker, in fact, than in most computer programs that create fractals. In this way, elementary-school students can experience firsthand the beauty and recurring patterns of fractals.

Contact: Education Group, National Center for Supercomputing Applications, University of Illinois at Urbana-Champaign, *rpanoff@ncsa.uiuc.edu*

Fractal Pictures and Animations

http://www.cnam.fr/fractals.html

Experience fractals in action. The fractal movie archive at this site is the largest online collection of fractal animations. Zoom in and out of the Mandelbrot set, soar over a fractal-generated landscape, or fast-fly over the earth's surface. You can also access a huge archive of fractal still images here. The complete Mandelbrot set is contained in nine directories, and there is an archive of miscellaneous fractals. Finally, you can connect to all sorts of information about fractals, including a fractal FAQ.

Contact: Frank Roussel, National Conservatory of Arts and Crafts, *RousselF@univ-rennes1.fr*

See the Mandelbrot set again and again at this fractal image archive.
(Used with permission of F. Roussel, CNAM.)

Fun Math

http://www.uni.uiuc.edu/departments/math/glazer/fun_math.html

Math can be fun when you include math jokes, fractals, paradoxes, logic puzzles, crystals, hyperbolics, and knots. These puzzles, problems, and pictures are educational as well as entertaining. Math jokes will make you laugh, and cool fractal pictures will relax you. Tease your brain with paradoxes and logic puzzles. You'll also find a gallery of interesting mathematical graphics, plus assorted fractals, hyperbolics, crystals, and knots.

Contact: Kumar Das, University Laboratory High School, *kdas@uni.uiuc.edu*

Gallery of Interactive Online Geometry

http://www.geom.umn.edu/apps/gallery.html

Make your own mathematical art through a variety of interactive tools at this site. Each of the tools includes a sample image and an explanation of how the image was created. Connect to the tool you want to play with through an interactive map. Then use forms to change variables and create your own images. One fun tool is Orbifold Pinball, which explores the effects of negatively curved space in a pinball-style game. Or try Cyberview, an interactive 3D viewer that works with most WWW browsers. Another favorite is Kali, an interactive edit or for symmetrical patterns in a plane, such as those used by M. C. Escher in some of his famous woodcuts. You'll have fun playing with possibilities at this engaging site.

Contact: Geometry Center, University of Minnesota, *webmaster@geom.umn.edu*

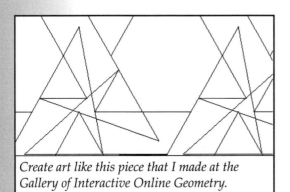

Create art like this piece that I made at the Gallery of Interactive Online Geometry.

Geometry Center

http://www.geom.umn.edu/

The Geometry Center features a variety of fun geometry information. Play around with interactive Web applications—math you can manipulate. Multimedia documents include research papers, educational materials, and a geometry forum. Serious geometry students, researchers, and teachers will find reference resources, downloadable software, and course materials. There is also a gallery of videos exploring mathematical concepts.

Contact: Geometry Center, University of Minnesota, *webmaster@geom.umn.edu*

Math Magic

http://www.scri.fsu.edu/~dennisl/topics/math_magic.html

Tap into a heap of magic tricks based on simple mathematics. The tricks are easy to learn and almost foolproof. Try out some baffling card tricks. Convince your friends that you have x-ray vision or a fantastic memory by performing the tricks in Calculational Wizardry. Learn some simple puzzlers based on geometry. Explanations in mathematical terms of all the tricks are included.

Contact: Larry Dennis, Supercomputer Computations Research Institute at the University of Florida, *larry@fsulcd.physics.fsu.edu*

Mega-Mathematics

http://www.c3.lanl.gov/mega-math/

Experience math the way mathematicians and scientists do. All the hands-on activities at this site will get you thinking mathematically. Every topic covered is important to current research; this is not outdated or boring stuff. In each section, read a background about the topic, learn about big ideas and key concepts, and try out fun activities. There's something to do at the end of every link. One activity you can try is the Most Colorful Math of All, where you color maps with as few colors as possible and learn about the theories behind this simple but difficult problem. You can also play Games on Graphs to learn about graphing, untangle the Mathematics of Knots through lots of activities, grapple with the concept of infinity, figure out word problems, and use logic to solve a mystery. There's lots more to explore here, such as math stories. From the site, you can send e-mail to ask questions, tell about things you find interesting, or make comments. There's fun for kids and math-impaired adults alike at Mega-Mathematics.

Contact: Nancy Casey, Los Alamos National Laboratory, *casey931@cs.uidaho.edu*

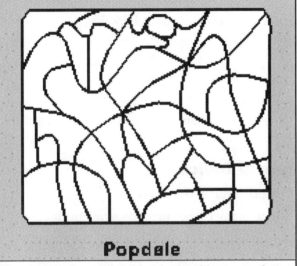

Popdale

How many colors will it take to color this map so that different colors touch on each border? This is only one of the math activities you'll find at Mega-Mathematics.

Number Trivia

http://acorn.educ.nottingham.ac.uk/cgi-bin/daynum

Connect to this page for some trivia concerning today's date. You'll find fun facts about the number of the day and the number of the month. What kind of facts? Well, mathematical trivia, measurements, places the number seems to turn up, and other significant uses of the number. Want to know more? Just come back tomorrow.

Contact: Richard Phillips, School and Faculty of Education at the University of Nottingham, *Richard.Phillips@nottingham.ac.uk*

Texas Instruments Calculators Page

http://dnclab.Berkeley.EDU/~smack/ti.html

If you are a nut about Texas Instruments calculators, you have to see this page. Visit a picture gallery of the calculators, and read about each one. Find out how to connect your calculator to your Macintosh or PC. Download programs for the calculator. Link to all sorts of resources on Texas Instruments calculators, including newsgroups, mailing lists, Web sites, FTP archives, Gopher sites, and Telnet sites (there are more than you may think).

Contact: Smack, University of California at Berkeley, *smack@dnclab.Berkeley.EDU*

For more information on mathematics, visit the following sites:

CSC Mathematical Topics

http://www.csc.fi/math_topics/General.html

This site links the user to many of the currently available math-oriented sites.

The Electronic Journal of Combinatorics

http://ejc.math.gatech.edu:8080/Journal/journalhome.html

This site contains papers and articles on high-level mathmatics. Definately for the serious mathematics enthusiast.

Florida State University Department of Mathematics

http://euclid.math.fsu.edu/

This site is more than its title would suggest. Yes, it contains lots of information about FSU's math offerings and recent publications, but it also has "fun stuff" and a weather link, both of which make this a site worth checking out, for both math junkies and the mathematically disadvantaged.

The MacTutor History of Mathematics Archive

http://www-groups.dcs.st-and.ac.uk:80/~history/

This site contains the biographies of most of the major mathematicians in history, as well as a birthplace map of the Western ones. There's lots of information for the mathematical historian in each of us.

Stephan Kaufmann

http://www.ifm.mavt.ethz.ch/~kaufmann/

This page covers Kaufmann's work on mathematics and tells something about the mathematician as a person.

Medicine & Psychology

Disability Services

http://www.disserv.stu.umn.edu/

Here you'll find lots of resources for the disabled, including Braille and American Sign Languge guides, a career database, and pointers to resources on the Internet. Link to any of the campuses of the University of Minnesota to learn about disability services there, including employee and student accommodations, informational brochures, a guide to access for students with disabilities, a staff directory, auxiliary services, research projects, and training.

Contact: Disability Services at the University of Minnesota, *webmaster@disserv.stu.umn.edu*

History of Medicine

http://www.nlm.nih.gov/hmd.dir/hmd.html

This invaluable archive contains a searchable database of nearly 60,000 images from the prints and photographs collection of the history of medicine housed at the National Library of Medicine. The database is designed as an online catalog to assist users in finding illustrative material for private study, scholarship, and research. A sampler of the online collection reflects its diversity, including a photograph of Lincoln visiting soldiers' graves and a recent poster from a medical film festival. Search the entire database by using text expressions, or browse by retrieving ten random items. (Warning: you can search the database only with certain WWW clients, including Netscape. NCSA Mosaic for Mac and Windows cannot currently access the database.) In addition to the database, you can take a look at many exhibitions, including Cesarean Section: A Brief History, Paracelsus: 500 Years, and The Art of Medicine at the Twenty-first Century.

Contact: HyperDOC, U.S. National Library of Medicine, *hyperdoc@nlm.nih.gov*

The Interactive Patient

http://medicus.marshall.edu/medicus.htm

Try out a fun interactive program that simulates an actual patient-doctor encounter. The program is used as a teaching tool for physicians, residents, and medical students, but anyone will be interested in playing with it. The program lets you interact with an imaginary patient, requesting information, performing a physical exam, and reviewing lab data and x-rays. First pick the case number you want to examine. Then proceed by taking the history. You actually ask the patient questions using an interactive form. During the physical exam, you can literally inspect, palpate, and auscultate. Then request reports and x-rays from the hospital laboratories. When you're finished, fill in your diagnosis and treatment plan; feedback is provided by the doctor who wrote the program. The Interactive Patient makes for a fun and different way to learn more about medicine.

Contact: Christoph U. Lehmann, MD, and Kent A. Hayes, Marshall University School of Medicine, *medicus@musom02.mu.wvnet.edu*

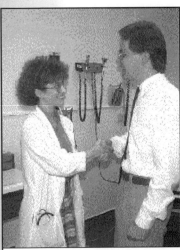

You can play doctor using the Interactive Patient.

Medical College of Wisconsin

http://www.intmed.mcw.edu/

The Medical College of Wisconsin provides lots of medical, drug, and bioethics information. Find extensive WWW resources, including medical indices, medical servers, and clinical information. Local resources are even more extensive, with an antibiotics guide, a bioethics online service, a medical information database, an international travelers' clinic, and a medical resource network, plus much more. This is a good place to begin your search for online medical resources.

Contact: Ron Kneuse, Medical College of Wisconsin, *rkneusel@post.its.mcw.edu*

OncoLink

http://cancer.med.upenn.edu/

Here you'll find a huge database of cancer news and information. This is the first multimedia oncology resource on the Internet, and it has received lots of recognition for the excellent service it provides. Access regularly updated cancer news and recent developments in cancer research. Learn about upcoming cancer conferences and meetings. Find cancer-related publications, including online journals. The service also provides extensive resources on cancer causes, screening, and prevention, financial issues, clinical trials, psychological support, and global resources for cancer information. Archives of specific cancer disease and specialties related to cancer treatment and prevention are also here.

Contact: OncoLink, University of Pennsylvania Cancer Resource, *editors@oncolink.upenn.edu*

The Virtual Hospital

http://indy.radiology.uiowa.edu/

The Virtual Hospital is a continuously updated database of multimedia information that provides patient-care support and distance learning to practicing physicians. The latest medical information is instantly available here. There are many great features. Health-care providers will find many training and reference tools. Several multimedia textbooks are online here, including Lung Anatomy and Gastrointestinal Nuclear Medicine, all illustrated with inline images that you can click on for relevant graphics and animations. Choose a patient simulation case from a large menu to virtually treat different kinds of patients. There is also information for nondoctors, such as patient instruction manuals that teach about basic medicine in layman's terms.

Contact: Electric Differential Multimedia Lab, Department of Radiology, University of Iowa College of Medicine, *librarian@vh.radiology.uiowa.edu*

For more information on medicine and psychology, visit the following sites:

The Abortion Rights Activist Home Page

http://www.cais.com/agm/

This site provides information on clinic violence, abortion, news and events, activist tools, and a reference library.

Abuse Pages

http://marie.az.com/~blainn/dv/index.html

This site was set up by a former domestic abuser and contains stories and resources for abusers and the abused. This is a good page for both men and women.

Acupuncture

http://198.150.8.9/acupuncture.html

A plain text document, with lots of information on the history of acupuncture and its uses, including a bibliography and two outside links to medical pages.

Acupuncture.Com

http://www.acupuncture.com/acupuncture/

Includes information on Chinese acupuncture, Chinese nutrition, and diagnostic methods. Very cool, but takes a long time to download.

American Medical Association

http://www.ama-assn.org/

The AMA's home page, with archived journals, press releases, news, information, and worldwide medical page links.

American Psychological Association

http://www.apa.org/

The American Psychological Association (APA) provides information on psychology for the general public, practice and education information, a psychology database service, and membership information for the association.

Ask the Dietician

http://www.hoptechno.com/cookhint.htm

This page has a series of questions and answers on subjects such as whether eating microwaved foods can be harmful and how to prepare round steak.

Centers for Disease Control

http://www.cdc.gov/

The Centers for Disease Control's home page has lots of information and a nice design.

ChiroPages

http://www.soflo.com/soflo/chiro/

For more information on chiropractic medicine, including a history and how to find a chiropractor near you. Also has information about conditions treatable by chiropractic medicine, but out of a long list of conditions, only two links are active. Possibly still under construction. The referral service is useful, though.

Chiropractic Resources

http://www.mbnet.mb.ca/~jwiens/chiro.html

Appears to be aimed toward people who are chiropractors, rather than beginner's information for the uninitiated.

Cognitive Science on the Internet

This site provides an overview of cognitive science sites—those involving issues such as psychology, neuroscience, and artificial intelligence—on the Internet.

Department of Health and Human Services

http://www.os.dhhs.gov/

Includes consumer information and some information on preventative medicine as well. Nice design.

Drama Therapy

http://csep.sunyit.edu/~joel/nadt.html

This page discusses the use of drama/theater processes as therapy to promote emotional integration and personal growth.

The Good Health Web

http://www.social.com/health/index.html

This site provides links to preventative, holistic, and alternative medicine pages and sites. It also hosts discussions on different aspects of preventative medicine.

Good Medicine

http://none.coolware.com/health/good_med/ThisIssue.html

This site is supposedly a preventative health magazine. What's there is worth looking at, but, as of this writing, the magazine had not been updated since the Nov/Dec issue of 1994.

Health and Longevity

http://www.sims.net/organizations/naturopath/naturopath.html

This site includes a recent edition of the homeopathy newsletter, past editions of the newsletter, a naturopathy mailing list, and a health-related products catalog. The newsletter has some thought-provoking articles.

Homeopathy Page

http://www.dungeon.com/~cam/homeo.html

This page contains lots of links to documents, newsgroups, publications, discussions, and more. I'd earmark this as the best homeopathy page, especially for people starting searches.

LifeLines Health Page

http://www.rain.org/idsolute/lifehome.html

Superb design! Links to medical servers, research libraries, newsletters, and more. Two thumbs up!

Medical Informatics Laboratory

http://ipvaimed9.unipv.it/homepage.html

This page discusses the medical research taking place at Pavia University in Italy. The page also discusses who's doing what work; interestingly enough, the page divides folks into "people" and "students."

Medscape

http://www.medscape.com/

Medscape provides access to peer-reviewed articles, graphics, literature, and annotated Internet links dealing with medicine. You'll find resources for infectious disease, AIDS, urology, surgery, managed care, and much more. You have to register to use Medscape, but it is free.

Multimedia Medical Reference Library

http://www.tiac.net/users/jtward/

Lots of great links, including journals, searchable databases, medical movies, and software downloads. Very nice design, probably a great starting place for beginners.

The National Network of Libraries of Medicine

http://www.nnlm.nlm.nih.gov/

This page provides information from many different medical libraries across the United States.

Natural Remedies Web Site

http://rampages.onramp.net/~nlhealth/

Get information on natural remedies of herbs. This appears to be a consumer service, selling products, but has minimal information on what they do. Marketing blurbs or unbiased info? You be the judge.

Noodles' Panic-Anxiety page

http://www.mtsu.edu/~sward/anxiety/

While not a doctor's or licensed counselor's site, Noodles' page has some great ideas and info on battling panic/anxiety attacks.

NOW and Abortion Rights/Reproductive Issues

http://now.org/now/issues/abortion/abortion.html

This page details what NOW (National Organization of Women) has been doing to preserve reproductive freedom for American women, as well as discussing social issues such as clinic violence and anti-abortion terrorists.

PharmInfoNet

http://pharminfo.com/

Pharmaceuticals information page with a FAQ, a browsable database, the PharmMall, newsletters, and other neat stuff. Nice design, too.

PharmWeb

http://www.mcc.ac.uk/pharmweb/

Another huge resource page for information on pharmaceuticals. A really awful background choice though; I can barely make out the text.

Stupid Questions Frequently Asked (of Paramedics and EMTs)

http://community.net/~sierra/stupid.htm

This page contains many of the questions you shouldn't ask the paramedics if you ever need their services.

Virtual Library: Medicine

http://golgi.harvard.edu/biopages/medicine.html

Virtual Library index to medicine information pages. A very good starting spot.

Virtual Library Pharmacy Page

http://www.cpb.uokhsc.edu/pharmacy/pharmint.html

This page links to pharmacy resources all over the Web and all over the world, including university departments, medical schools, associations, pharmacy reference resources, online drug stores, pharmaceutical companies, databases, software, mailing lists, and newsgroups.

Web Of Addictions

http://www.well.com/user/woa/

This site has very comprehensive information on drugs, described for non-medical professionals. Both legal and illegal drugs are discussed.

WelchWeb

http://www.welch.jhu.edu/

Online medical library from Johns Hopkins University.

Women's Health Page

http://www.best.com/~sirlou/wmhp.html

Includes archives of articles, mailing lists, and other links. Nice design, too.

World Health Organization

http://www.who.ch/

Press releases, publications, information for travelers, and other health-related links.

Oceanography

Safari Splash

http://oberon.educ.sfu.ca/splash.htm

For 10 days, a team of scientists, archaeologists, and kids explored the ocean environment of Barkley Sound, British Columbia. This site describes their experiments, discoveries, and experiences. During the expedition, they broadcast live via satellite into homes and schools. Viewers in downlink sites in North America and Japan could speak directly to the participants in the expedition. Scientists answered questions from students around the globe, and their exchange is archived here. You can browse the entire catalog of questions or look them up by subject, such as shipwrecks, diving, and invertebrates. The highlight of this site is the innovative, aquarium-like touch tank that you can click on, or "touch," to get information about the animals inside or view in motion through hyperlinked animation. You can also visit the 3D Icon Gallery of thumbnail photos of various marine plants and animals. Click on one to get a larger photograph and information about that specimen. From here, explore more marine biology information online.

Contact: Excite Center and Royal British Columbia Museum, Simon Fraser University, *cshields@cln.etc.bc.ca*

"Touch" fish and plant life in this touch tank at the Barkley Sound Expedition. (Used with permission of Excite Center, Simon Fraser University.)

Sea World

http://www.bev.net/education/SeaWorld/

In this database, you're sure to find everything you want to know about saltwater fish and mammals. The most complete section of the site is the Animal Information Database. Access this database for interesting facts about killer whales, bottlenose dolphins, manatees, polar bears, walruses, and other marine animals, plus many non-marine animals, from bald eagles to vampire bats. There's also information on coral reefs and endangered marine species. Learn about the scientific classification, habitat, physical characteristics, senses, water adaptations, behavior, diet and eating habits, reproduction and care of young, communication, longevity, and causes of death for any of these animals. There are many pictures to look at, and some files are enhanced by educational activities and multimedia. For quick facts go to Animal Bytes, where each file lists the scientific classification, fun facts, and biological value of different animals. If you have a question about marine life and ocean animals, ask the Sea World experts at Ask Shamu. Or find out about keeping aquariums as a hobby. Educators and parents will want to download the Teacher's Guides for fun hands-on activities to learn about marine life, all aimed at younger children. You can also get more information about the Sea World theme parks here.

Contact: Sea World and Busch Entertainment Corp., Blacksburg Electronic Village, *Sea.World@bev.net*

Stephen Birch Aquarium-Museum

http://aqua.ucsd.edu/

The Birch Aquarium-Museum of the Scripps Institute of Oceanography presents undersea creatures in realistic habitats and offers many interactive exhibits and educational activities for visitors. Read about current research at the aquarium, including the Sequoia 2000 project, a collaboration between earth scientists and computer scientists to develop computer tools for earth science research. A slide show explains the project's goals, and afterward you can visit participants in the project. You can also visit the Institute's library or connect to other oceanography institutions online.

Contact: Stephen Birch Aquarium-Museum, Scripps Institute of Oceanography, *Webmaster@aqua.ucsd.edu*

Whale-Watching Web

http://www.physics.helsinki.fi/whale/

Whales have had their own worldwide communication network for 70 million years. Now you can use the World Wide Web to learn all about them. Listen to Greetings from Whales for an introduction to the world of the whales. Find out places all over the world where you can go whale-watching, and connect to agencies that offer tours. Read about other people's experiences whale watching. Or go whale watching right now with lots of whale pictures and songs that you can download to your computer. Connect to related WWW resources about whales, dolphins, oceanography, and animal rights. Read literary works inspired by whales, and get a list of whale and dolphin books for further reading. Learn about efforts to communicate with whales and dolphins and about the whaling industry. You'll find much to look at and read when you go whale watching online.

Contact: Rauno Lauhakangas, Department of Physics at the University of Helsinki, *lauhakangas@phcu.helsinki.fi*

Go whale watching online!

**For more information on oceanography,
visit the following sites:**

National Ocean and Atmospherics Administration

http://www.noaa.gov/

Here you'll find research on oceanography and atmospheric science performed by this division of the federal government, as well as connections to environmental data, the National Marine Fisheries service, the National Ocean Service, and the National Weather Service. Besides oceanography information, you'll also find geophysical, space environment, and conservation data here.

Woods Hole Oceanographic Institution

http://www.whoi.edu/

The Woods Hole Oceanographic Institution is the largest independent marine science research facility in the United States. Here connect to the scientific community at Woods Hole, including research in marine biology, fisheries, and marine geology, and find a directory of WWW oceanographic information.

Paleontology

Charlotte, the Vermont Whale

http://www.uvm.edu/whale/whalehome.html

Visit a unique exhibit of the bones of a white whale found near Charlotte, Vermont. The fossils, and the exhibit, provide a handy way to study the geology and history of the Champlain Basin. Enter sections of the exhibit through questions raised by the finding of the whale bones, such as, "How did a whale get in Vermont?" and, "Where and how was it found?" Following the link that explains how a whale happened to be in Vermont, you will learn about glaciers, the history of the Champlain Basin area, and the preservation of the bones. You can also get information about the whale itself, how it was found, how it was studied, and what specific information it provided to researchers. Traveling further into the exhibit leads to additional hyperlinks that connect to more and more detailed information, making it a great educational tool.

Contact: Jeff Howe and Wesley Alan Wright, University of Vermont, *Wesley.Wright@uvm.edu*

Field Museum of Natural History

http://www.bvis.uic.edu/museum

At this online museum, you can study specimens and images of over 20 million objects selected from various research collections. The interactive DNA to Dinosaurs exhibit is the high point of the museum, though. The full tour explains the age of dinosaurs and includes photographs, explanatory text, and audio and video enhancements, even 3D. Trace the history of dinosaurs through to their extinction, learning facts about specific dinosaurs and other life forms of the period along the way. Fun features include a 100-million-year Triassic weather forecast and late-breaking news from the *Triassic Tribune*. You can also skip the tour and go straight to the multimedia fun stuff on the Media Page, with animation, sounds, scary pictures, and interactive games. Or check out Live Over Times for the latest evolution news, a great educational tool. Other exhibits are on display, such as a collection of Javanese masks that you can browse by icon or catalog number.

Contact: Mary Rasmusser, Biomedical Visualization Laboratory, University of Illinois at Chicago, *mary@evl.eecs.uic.edu*

Meet dinosaurs face-to-face at the Field Museum of Natural History.

Dinosaurs in Hawaii!

http://www.hcc.hawaii.edu/dinos/dinos.1.html

Another dinosaur exhibit, this one based at Honolulu Community College, is one of the first examples of multimedia publishing on the WWW. You can page through the exhibit, viewing a different dinosaur fossil on each page. Audio clips by dinosaur expert Rick Ziegler accompany the tour. Many enhancement links are included, such as a sculpture of a full Triceratops or a rendering of how Stegosaurus might have looked in its natural environment. You'll also find valuable scientific information on the dinosaur fossils.

Contact: Ken Hensarling, Honolulu Community College, *webmaster@pulua.hcc.hawaii.edu*

Natural History Museum of Los Angeles County

http://cwis.usc.edu/lacmnh/default.html

There are many activities in this museum filled with pictures and interesting facts. Pay a visit to Kid's Stuff for a Dinostore gift shop, games, a hands-on discovery center, and an insect zoo. Learn about endangered species and the La Brea Tar Pits through word searches. In the Virtual Exhibits, you can find out how DNA technology is applied to paleontology, just like in the movie *Jurassic Park*. Also read about mammoths, view cave paintings, and take a look at an encyclopedia of fantastic and mythical beasts. Finally, travel down some links to additional information and activities about dinosaurs and natural history.

Contact: Jim Angus, University of Southern California, *jangus@rcf.usc.edu*

PaleoPals

http://ucmp1.berkeley.edu/museum/pals.html

Anyone can post questions and responses about any aspect of paleontology in this discussion site. Get all your dinosaur questions answered here; no question goes unaddressed. You can also look at all the questions and answers already posted. This is a great resource for research and for would-be paleontologists.

Contact: Allen G. Collins, University of California Museum of Paleontology, *allenc@ucmp1.berkeley.edu*

University of California Museum of Paleontology

http://ucmp1.berkeley.edu/welcome.html

One of the most famous sites on the WWW, this exhibit offers hours of entertaining and instructional exploration. Enter the museum by way of one of three topics: phylogeny, or the family tree of life; geological time; or the history of evolutionary thought. The museum is also organized in an easy-to-use way that instantly connects you to any taxon, geologic period, or topic you choose. As you move deeper into one topic, you will discover crosslinks to other topics. The phylogeny section has exhibit halls of fossils, including dinosaur and mammal exhibits. One that you shouldn't miss is the Great White Shark exhibit. In the dinosaur exhibit—a must-see—an interactive map leads you down various hallways where you can view dinosaur fossils, with explanatory text every step of the way. A fossil specimen database links to an online catalog that can be searched for more specialized research on specimens in the museum.

Contact: David Polly and Robert Guralnick, University of California Museum of Paleontology, *robg@fossil.berkeley.edu*

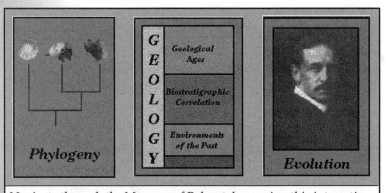

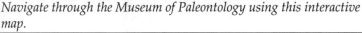

Navigate through the Museum of Paleontology using this interactive map.

For more information on paleontology,
visit the following sites:

Paleontological Society

http://www.uic.edu/orgs/paleo/homepage.html

This a WWW resource for paleontologists and those interested in paleontology. Contains society activities, society publications, and links to
many other paleontology resources.

Royal Tyrrell Museum

http://www.cuug.ab.ca:8001/VT/tyrrell/

Take a virtual tour of this paleontology museum, learn about what
paleontologists do, discover education resources, visit Dinosaur Pro-
vincial Park, and explore other paleontology resource on the Web, all
at this one site.

Physics

Brown High Energy Physics

http://www.het.brown.edu/

Here you'll find lots of physics resources, both locally and around the
Web. Connect to research, theory, and experimental groups. Or go to
the guide of Internet physics resources, including papers, job and conference announcements, news, and organizations. You'll also find
specific resources on high energy physics, condensed matter physics,
and astronomy.

Contact: Brown High Energy Physics, *webmaster@het.brown.edu*

Early Instruments of the Institute of Physics

http://hpl33.na.infn.it/Museum/Museum.html

This collection of early physics instruments from the Institute of Physics at the University of Naples dates from 1645 to 1900. Each instrument is shown in a full-color JPEG and accompanied by a detailed description. An introduction provides a background of the museum itself. You can wander through the entire exhibit or connect straight to exhibits of optics, heat, and electromagnetism instruments.

Contact: Luca Lista, National Institute for Nuclear Physics, University of Naples, *lista@na.infn.it*

Spacetime Splashes: Catching the Wave in Einstein's Equations

http://www.ncsa.uiuc.edu/Apps/GenRel/SC93/HOME_sc93.html

The Relativity Workbench is a tool for computing solutions to Einstein's equations through an intuitive visual user interface. At this site advertising the tool, you can learn about the physics of numerical relativity and the background of the project. A site demonstration called the CAVE shows gravitational waves propagating through space-time according to Einstein's equations for a gravitational field. You can interactively control the physics parameters of the simulation and navigate through the animating surface for a fun ride through the space-time continuum.

Contact: NCSA Relativity Group, University of Illinois at Urbana-Champaign, *jmasso@ncsa.uiuc.edu*

ZEBU at the University of Oregon

http://zebu.uoregon.edu/

ZEBU provides a huge archive of physics and astronomy resources for educational purposes. An astronomy library contains images, movies, educational materials, and demonstrations. Learn about earth sciences, including earthquakes, volcanoes, oceans, and hurricanes. Hypertext textbooks teach astronomy and physics principles. Study energy, the ozone layer, and global warming in the environment archive. Physics

Online features Web classes, demos, and lectures for teaching all aspects of physics. You'll also find a collection of resources useful to physics students as well as physics sites on the Web. And check out fun physics and astronomy animations. There's even more to explore here, including K-12 and Oregon resources.

Contact: Electronic Universe Project, ZEBU at the University of Oregon Physics Department, *nuts@moo.uoregon.edu*

For additional information on physics, visit the following sites.

The American Institute of Physics

http://www.aip.org/

You have to be a member of AIP to get the most out of this site, but it has some information on new developments in physics for the casual user as well.

Artificial Neural Networks in High Energy Physics

http://www1.cern.ch/NeuralNets/nnwInHep.html

This site covers applications of neural network techniques to experimental high energy physics. Included are recent news, experiments, conferences, and workshop information.

Crystallography

http://www.unige.ch/crystal/crystal_index.html

This site has vast amounts of information for anyone interested in the field of crystallography. Not only are there links to papers and data on crystallography, but there are also job listings, conferences, addresses of crystallographers, and lots of other information. Every field should be so well covered.

European Laboratory for Particle Physics

http://www1.cern.ch/

Here you'll find lots of physics information, a scientific information server, and, incidentally, the birthplace of the WWW.

Fusion Research at the University of Texas

http://hagar.ph.utexas.edu/

Get information about the Fusion Research Center and the Institute for Fusion Studies. There is also a magnetic fusion energy database at this site.

Physics and Astronomy at the University of Pittsburgh

http://www.phyast.pitt.edu/

This site has information on the University of Pittsburgh's physics and astronomy programs, as well as recent research, research tools, and suggested research engines.

The Plasma Physics Home Page

http://www.physics.auburn.edu/fusion.html

This page discusses Auburn's research into controlled fusion, with some discussion of related research elsewhere.

Plasma Science and Technology

http://www-plasma.umd.edu/

This site discusses the nature and uses of plasma. It has information across a broad spectrum of user knowledge, from the *Scientific American* reader to the physicist.

Purdue University's Society of Physics Students

http://tycho.physics.purdue.edu/~sps/spshome.html

This site introduces the user to Purdue University's physics students and promotes a lot of things that are primarily of interest to people near Purdue. However, there are FTPs that may be of interest to anyone working or playing with physics.

Research and Development in Physics Education

http://flatwater.unl.edu/

This site is not so much about physics as about how to teach physics. Included is a discussion of multimedia and its use in physics teaching.

University of Cambridge Department of Physics

http://www.phy.cam.ac.uk/www/physics.html

This site contains information on Cambridge's physics program and on the research that the college is currently pursuing.

The Wilson Group

http://www-wilson.ucsd.edu/wgabout.html

This page starts off as a high-level discussion of quantum and classical dynamics and goes deeper into the subject matter from there. A serious scientist may well find this page fascinating.

Science

The Exploratorium

http://www.exploratorium.edu/

This online science museum is always fun to visit, with interactive exhibits on light and color, sound and music, patterns of motion, and other natural phenomena. In the Learning Studio, you'll find a collection of exhibits for students, teachers, and science enthusiasts. These include Mutant Fruit Flies, for learning about genetics, and several interactive exhibits for learning about perception. These multimedia exhibits are always changing, so keep coming back. Teachers and parents can order museum publications, such as "cookbooks" that describe how to build the museum exhibits at home, or *Science Snackbook*, classroom versions of Exploratorium exhibits. A library includes still images of the museum exhibits, artist-in-residence pieces, and other interesting images, such as bubbles and prisms. Don't forget to stop by the Exploratorium store for gifts and learning tools that you can order through an online form.

Contact: Exploratorium, ExploraNet, *ronh@exploratorium.edu*

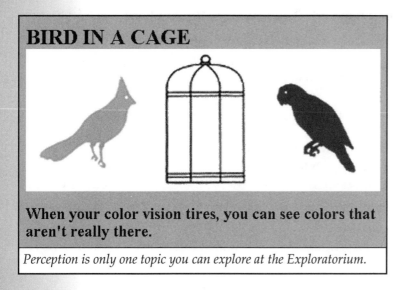

BIRD IN A CAGE

When your color vision tires, you can see colors that aren't really there.

Perception is only one topic you can explore at the Exploratorium.

Hands-On Science Guide

http://www.cs.cmu.edu/~mwm/sci.html

This page links to museums worldwide that emphasize interactive science education and are also on the Internet. Instantly connect to science museums in Asia, Europe, Australia, and North America for information, exhibits, and activities. From here you can virtually visit the Sciencenter in New York, the History of Science Museum in Italy, and the Singapore Science Centre, among many other science museums, for hours of interactive fun.

Contact: Mark W. Maimone, School of Computer Science, Carnegie Mellon University, *mwm@cs.cmu.edu*

The JASON Project

http://seawifs.gsfc.nasa.gov/scripts/JASON.html

The JASON Project is an educational experiment in "bringing the thrill of exploration and discovery live to students around the world as they participate in an amazing electronic field trip." Through the project, scientists journey to a region of the earth and study different aspects of it. Their activities are broadcast live through satellite to students all over the world, who can ask questions and actually perform experiments by remotely controlling the robot, JASON. This intensive, communications-based participation is called *telepresence*. Before you plunge into the expeditions, learn about the background of the project through a multimedia presentation, including talks by Dr. Robert Ballard, the founder. Then travel along on the available expeditions. Explore the rain forests, caverns, Mayan ruins, and coral reefs of Belize. The highlight of this expedition is Letters from the Rain Forest, journal-like, day-by-day descriptions of thoughts, experiences, and reflections that were made on the expedition. Voyage into the volcanoes of Hawaii. Or learn about conditions of life in the coastal marine habitats of southern Florida. After reading, participate by joining discussion groups or completing exercises.

Contact: Gene Carl Feldman, Goddard Space Flight Center, NASA, *gene@seawifs.gsfc.nasa.gov*

Photographs like this one heighten the rain forest experience of Letters from the Rain Forest.

Franklin Institute Science Museum

http://sln.fi.edu/

This science education museum is truly interactive; each of the online exhibits features things to do (interactive activities); things to see (videos and graphics); things to learn (graphics, timelines, and resources); things to hear (audio enhancements); and places to go (Internet sites relevant to the exhibit). Start with a video tour of the museum. Then go to the exhibits, such as Ben Franklin: Glimpses of the Man, which features videos, lots of graphics, and loads of links. At this exhibit, you can learn about electricity, try to interpret Ben's sayings from *Poor Richard's Almanack,* and hear Ben speak on subjects such as science, music, the economy, statesmanship, inventions, and printing. Another interesting exhibit features a tour of the heart, where you can watch movies of open-heart surgery, identify heart sounds, and write poetry about the heart. Other bonuses are an education hotlist that points to educational hot spots on the Internet and an exhibit hotlist that helps you find other online exhibits.

Contact: Franklin Institute Science Museum

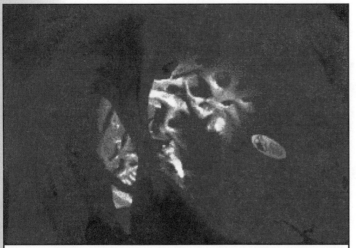

Look at the heart close up when you explore the heart exhibit at the Franklin Institute Science Museum.

Los Alamos National Laboratory

http://www.lanl.gov/

Here you'll find information on all departments of this huge lab, with physics, chemistry, astronomy, biology, medical, military, and computing resources. The science and technology section describes that organization, outlines its award-winning scientific research, and provides scientific and technical information in a variety of subjects. Read about the educational programs offered by the lab, and download resources for science education. A research library contains electronic databases, subject resources on every branch of the sciences, and hot topics from the lab. Visit a science museum with exhibits on the history of the laboratory and its research. Much more information about the Los Alamos National Laboratory is online here, including a look inside the lab.

Contact: Los Alamos National Laboratory, *www-board@lanl.gov*

National Science Foundation

http://www.nsf.gov/

The National Science Foundation (NSF) is an independent agency of the federal government that promotes the progress of science and engineering. Here you can learn all about the organization, including an overview, science education activities, and grant information. Enter the world of science and engineering to access results of NSF-funded research. You'll also learn about grant and research opportunities, science trends, and NSF news of interest.

Contact: National Science Foundation, *Webmaster@nsf.gov*

Natural History Museum

http://www.nhm.ac.uk/

Learn all about the Natural History Museum in London, including a schedule of exhibitions, special events, and other public activities. Go behind the scenes of the museum, and explore research in the earth and life sciences. Access the library catalog of one of the largest collections of earth and life sciences publications in the world. You can also research the museum's science holdings or connect to other earth and life science resources on the Internet.

Contact: Natural History Museum, Neil Thomson, *N.Thomson@nhm.ac.uk*, and Robert Bloomfield, *R.Bloomfield@nhm.ac.uk*

NCSA Digital Gallery CD-ROM

http://www.ncsa.uiuc.edu/SDG/DigitalGallery/DG_readme.html

At this site, you'll find a sample of scientific visualizations, movies, and software demonstrations developed by the National Center for Supercomputing Applications (NCSA). View animations in the Science Theater, or access image samples. On display are MPEG movies and GIF files submitted by researchers from all over the world, including images of Hurricane Bob, animations of fluid dynamics, eclipse and supernova images, and volume visualizations. You can even view an MRI image of a person's brain or a 3D image of a dog's heart in the medical sciences section. Click on a menu item to get scientific and technical information about the image or animation—what it is and how it was created.

Contact: Digital Gallery CD-ROM, National Center for Supercomputing Applications, University of Illinois at Urbana-Champaign, *sgoode@ncsa.uiuc.edu*

Oregon Museum of Science & Industry

http://www.omsi.edu/

The Oregon Museum of Science & Industry (OMSI) is a nonprofit museum with exhibits emphasizing interaction and participation. Hop on board the Subway of Science to explore different areas of the museum, including the Earth Science Hall, the Information Science Hall, the Sky Theater, the Life Science Lab, and the Science Store. Each stop features photographs and descriptions of exhibits. Also learn about educational programs the museum offers, and browse the OMSI magazine. One interesting exhibit, Waterworks, examines the science and engineering behind fountains; you can investigate fountains, create your own fountain, and look at a gallery of fountain pictures.

Contact: Oregon Museum of Science & Industry, *rjv@www.omsi.edu*

For more information on science, visit the following sites:

Community of Science

http://best.gdb.org/

This useful server helps you identify scientific researchers with expertise and interests similar to yours. You'll find an online inventory of inventions, researchers, and facilities. There's also information about federally funded research and the Canadian community of science.

Elsevier Science

http://www.elsevier.nl/

Elsevier is the leading supplier of scientific information. Learn about products and journals of the company. And find specific services for engineering, mathematics, computer science, nuclear physics, chemistry, and more.

The Office for Mathematics, Science, and Technology Education

http://www.mste.uiuc.edu/

This page describes the available programs at the University of Illinios at Urbana-Champaign and the ongoing research efforts in math, science, and technology. It also provides links to related Internet resources.

The Sci-Cop Story and Memoirs of an Agent

http://athena.athenet.net/~jlindsay/SciCop.shtml

This page chronicles the ongoing struggle of the Sci-Cops to enforce the laws of nature. Funny for anyone in the sciences.

Space Exploration

Air and Space Museum

http://ceps.nasm.edu:2020/NASMpage.html

Visit the Air and Space Museum in the Smithsonian Institute without leaving your computer. A map guides you to all the different exhibits; just click on where you want to go. In the Milestones of Flight exhibit, you'll learn about important achievements in the development of flight. Here you can see the Wright brothers' plane, the Apollo 11 Command Module, the Sputnik 1 Satellite, and much more. The Air Transportation exhibit shows planes used in commercial air travel. Learn the story of the first 40 years of jet aviation and the earliest flights. You can also study aviation during World Wars I and II. Visit the exhibit, Stars, for a history of the study of astronomy. See lunar exploration vehicles and equipment used to look at Earth from space.

Follow the history of space flight from the fantasy in the thirteenth century to modern achievements. The Space Hall displays large rockets, guided missiles, and manned spacecraft. Take a tour of the solar system, and learn about planetary exploration. There are many more exhibits to explore, each with lots of photographs, to help you learn the history of flight and spaceflight. Go to Resources for guides to air and space history, more photographs and *Air & Space* magazine. This huge online museum will take you through the history of flight, from the Wright brothers' plane to the latest craft used to explore space.

Contact: Smithsonian Institute, Center for Earth and Planetary Studies, *mtuttle@www.nasm.edu*

Basics of Spaceflight

http://oel-www.jpl.nasa.gov/basics/

Get a complete education in space flight with this online textbook. This is the first in a series of training modules for space flight operations and will give you a head start on astronaut training or a physics class. First learn all about the environment of space and the planets, including earth. Study gravitation and mechanics, interplanetary trajectories, and planetary orbits. Get into some space projects with scientific experiments, spaceflight classifications, and descriptions and illustrations of spacecraft. Learn about telecommunications, onboard subsystems, and typical science instruments. Find out about spacecraft navigation and the phases of spaceflight operations. The textbook is fairly technical and for major space buffs only. But it will teach you everything you want to know about spaceflight.

Contact: Jet Propulsion Laboratory, Operations Engineering Laboratory, NASA, *diane.f.miller@jpl.nasa.gov*

Astro-2 Live

http://liftoff.msfc.nasa.gov/archive/astro2/welcome.html

Astro-2 is a high-tech observatory that flew for 16 days in the payload bay of the Space Shuttle. The Astro-2 instruments allow astronomers to view stars, galaxies, planets, and quasars in ultraviolet light. At the Astro-2 home page, you can learn more about the experiment and share in discoveries made by astronomers. You'll find descriptions of the payload and Space Shuttle on the Hardware and Science page. Meet the Flight Crew on board, and learn about the NASA team who supported them on the ground. Read the Flight Log to find out what happened during the mission. On the Flight Deck, you can view and hear the downlink transmissions from orbit, experience a virtual reality trip around the Astro-2 payload, and use the Flight Computer to determine the Space Shuttle Endeavor's orbit speed and the time it takes to circle the earth. The interactive activities will give you a sample of what the crew does during the mission. Finally, pay a visit to the Visitor's Port, where you can ask questions of the Astro-2 Team and take the Astro-2 Quiz.

Contact: John Piner, Liftoff, Marshall Space Flight Center, *John_Piner@pobox.tbe.com*

Travel along on a Space Shuttle mission at Astro-2 Live.

Educational Space Simulations Project

http://chico.rice.edu/armadillo/Simulations/simserver.html

What is a space simulation exactly? Linked by telecommunications, a group of schools each pretend to be one aspect of an overall simulation of a space launch, sharing information, events, and activities. Different schools act as the Space Shuttle, landing sites, solar flare observatories, the Russian space station, reporters, and many other components. At this site, you can learn all about space simulations. Get a description of the project, read the official debriefing, look at sample space simulation communications, and learn about student roles in the simulation. You can also download activities and experiments, a space simulation starter kit, and IBM software for use in space simulations. Take a look at images and animations from real space launches and snapshots from simulations, or read *SPACESIM*, an electronic magazine for space simulation educators. This unique, hands-on activity is perfect for educators, students, and anyone interested in space exploration.

Contact: Chris Rowan, Rice University, *chris@tenet.edu*

Embry-Riddle Aeronautical University

http://macwww.db.erau.edu/

This aeronautical university publishes on the Web not only information about the university itself, but also valuable information about aeronautics and aviation. After you take a virtual tour of the campus and learn about student services, be sure to take a look at *Avion Online*, the first online aviation and aerospace newspaper. Inside you'll find aeronautical, space technology, and campus news, plus features on Shuttle launches, aviation trade news, and airshows. When you're finished there, go to Research Services where you'll find many useful resources, including an aviation and an aerospace virtual library and aviation and aerospace research information. There's also a special section on women in aviation.

Contact: Brian Gamage, Embry-Riddle Aeronautical University, *gamageb@db.erau.edu*

History of Space Exploration

http://www.c3.lanl.gov/~cjhamil/SolarSystem/history.html

Get a basic history of the exploration of space, from the earliest astronauts to the Space Shuttle, using this online textbook. A summary of space history introduces you to the development of the rocket, automated spacecraft, and the basics of space flight. Take a close look at all the manned missions from Mercury to the Space Shuttle. For each project, you'll read about the goals of the mission, the spacecraft, and the flight summary. You'll see lots of pictures of the spacecraft and astronauts, then follow along on the unmanned and manned missions. There are also guides to robotic spacecraft and spotting the Space Shuttle. And you'll learn when each planet in the solar system was explored. This very complete history will make you an expert in space travel.

Contact: Calvin J. Hamilton, Los Alamos National Laboratory, *cjhamil@lanl.gov*

How to Become an Astronaut

http://www.ksc.nasa.gov/facts/faq12.html

So you want to be an astronaut? This document tells you exactly how you can become one. You'll find descriptions of the Space Shuttle program and the astronaut professions, including pilot and mission specialist. You'll also find out basic qualification requirements for the astronaut candidate program and even pay and benefits. Hyperlinks take you to even more information about different parts of the process. Besides finding out what you need to do to become an astronaut at NASA, you can read about the Astronaut Candidate Program. Select the link that returns you to the FAQ page for even more info about NASA and NASA programs.

Contact: Jim Dumoulin, NASA Kennedy Space Center, *dumoulin@titan.ksc.nasa.gov*

Johnson Space Center Images

http://images.jsc.nasa.gov/html/home.htm

The library of space photographs at the Johnson Space Center offers press releases and Earth observation images from the manned space program, including images from the latest missions. There are about 10,000 image files available. Go into the Press Release Images Collection for photos from all the space programs, including the Mercury program, the Apollo program, Skylab, and the Space Shuttle program. You'll see pictures of Earth from space, astronauts in action, and scientific images taken during the missions. You'll also see images taken with video downlink from the Space Shuttle. Virtually explore space through this fascinating collection of images.

Contact: Kevin C. Marsh, Johnson Space Center Digital Images Collection, *KMarsh@ja6.jsc.nasa.gov*

Get a first-hand look at space exploration.

Mars Mission Research Center

http://www.mmrc.ncsu.edu/

The Mars Mission Research Center focuses on research and educational technology for planetary exploration, especially exploration of Mars. It is located at both North Carolina State University and North Carolina Agricultural and Technical State University. Get a general understanding of the project, and read the newsletter of ongoing events. Access current research and technical papers. Find detailed information about Mars. You can also connect to the North Carolina Space Grant Consortium here, as well as to resources for mechanical and aerospace engineering.

Contact: Mars Mission Research Center, *www-admin@mmrc.ncsu.edu*

Mission to the Moon

http://www.gsfc.nasa.gov/hqpao/apollo_11.html

Journey along with the Apollo 11 rocket on man's first trip to the moon. You'll learn all about the historic journey through this multimedia Web site. First, get some background by reading about NASA's history. Here you can study aeronautics and astronautics, learn about important people in the history of NASA, travel along a timeline of air and space developments, visit the different NASA centers, and enjoy a collection of mission patches. Then get information about the Apollo 11 mission with an overview, recollections of the astronauts, documents that were instrumental in the decision to go to the moon, and more. See the mission patch and the poster commemorating the twenty-fifth anniversary of the mission to the moon. There's lots of multimedia to look at here, including movies of the "one small step." Travel back twenty-five years in time by looking at images of all aspects of the moon mission, from pre-flight training to landing on the moon to re-entry into Earth's atmosphere. You can also listen to audio files of the moon landing. This fun site lets you relive the historic moon landing again and again.

Contact: Allen Clark and Woody Smith, NASA, *comments@www.hq.nasa.gov*

Walk on the moon with the Apollo astronauts.

NASA Home Page

http://www.gsfc.nasa.gov/NASA_homepage.html

NASA has lots of information available on the WWW, so much that it is often difficult to find just what you're looking for. You can connect to the whole NASA web through its home page here. Jump to any of NASA's 13 research centers through an interactive map. Use the subject index to link to topics of interest, such as aeronautics, earth science, computing, and space sciences. Or go through a searchable guide to find NASA resources on science, education, and government, among other subjects. Get an overview of NASA's history, or learn about sponsored educational programs. You'll find technical reports and information about NASA commercial technology here, too. The home page also links to other space agencies and aerospace resources on the Internet.

Contact: Archie Warnock and Jim Gass, Goddard Space Flight Center, NASA, *james.gass@gsfc.nasa.gov*

NASA News

http://space.mit.edu/nasanews.html

Get the latest news bulletins from NASA. Everything posted here was released by NASA during the most recent 24-hour period, so this is the place for up-to-date information. You can find out the newest results in NASA studies, the latest events in NASA exploration missions, current information on the Space Shuttle, and the very latest in astronomy discoveries. From here, follow links to additional information and pictures about the news announcements. Go to the archives for all the past news releases back to 1987. Regular visits here will help you impress your friends with your NASA newsworthiness.

Contact: Planetary Data Systems, Center for Space Research, Massachusetts Institute of Technology, *pds_operator@jplpds.jpl.nasa.gov*

The Search for Extra-Terrestrial Intelligence

http://altair.syr.edu:2024/SETI/seti.html

Have you ever wondered if someone else is out there? Join the search for alien life at this Web site. Learn about the present status of the search for extra-terrestrials. For more background information, go to the Beginner's Guide and SETI (Search for Extra-Terrestrial Life) overview. At Historical Notes, you'll find a history of the belief in ETs. Check out quotes on ETs from throughout the ages, ancient writings about ETs, and a history of speculation of life on Mars. We need to understand the principles of life on Earth before we can look for it elsewhere in the universe. Understanding Life gives you an overview of the essentials of life, how life began and evolved, and how strange life can be. Go to Looking for ETs to connect to information about aliens. Perhaps aliens have already visited Earth. Make up your own mind by reading a collection of documents about alien visits to Earth. To search for life elsewhere in the universe, first take an astronomy tutorial that transports you from the beginning of the universe to the origins of the solar system. You'll also get an overview of the birth and death of a star and summaries of the planets in the solar system. Then you can start your search for life in the solar system and outside it. Follow other Internet links for more information on astronomy, biology, physics, and UFOs.

Contact: Department of Physics at Syracuse University, *gvidali@mailbox.syr.edu*

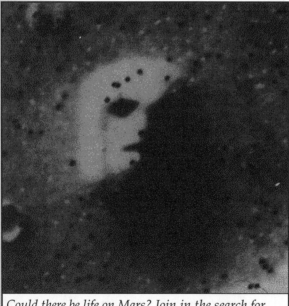

Could there be life on Mars? Join in the search for extraterrestrial intelligence.

Space Calendar

http://newproducts.jpl.nasa.gov/calendar/

The space calendar lists space-related activities and anniversaries for the coming year. You can also use it to find out what happened this month in space history. Check out celestial events for the current month. These tell you what's going on in the sky, including moon phases, planetary appearances, eclipses, neat stars to look for, and more. Find out launch dates, planetary and astronomical events, asteroid encounters, events in ongoing NASA missions, seasonal events (such as solstices, equinox, etc.), and meteor shower schedules. Hyperlinks take you to more information about the NASA event or astronomical occurrence. Checking the space calendar first will ensure that you are prepared for any space event or sky happening.

Contact: Ron Baalke, New Products Development Group, NASA, *baalke@kelvin.jpl.nasa.gov*

Space Shuttle Image Archive

http://shuttle.nasa.gov/sts-73/images/

Here you'll find official photos from the Space Shuttle and its missions, which take you through a mission of the Shuttle. Pre-flight photos depict the work required of the crew to prepare for the mission. In-flight video stills show daily activity on board the Shuttle during a mission. These images are selected from the Shuttle video downlink. You'll also see still camera photos taken in-flight by the crew. Finally, post-flight photos depict mission events after landing the Shuttle. These photos are updated with each new mission and provide an inside peek at a Space Shuttle flight that those of us on the ground wouldn't get otherwise.

Contact: Eric Nielsen, STS-73 Shuttle Page, *nielsen1@jsc.nasa.gov*

Space Shuttle Map

http://seds.lpl.arizona.edu/ssa/space.shuttle/docs/homepage.html

Learn more about the Space Shuttle by using this interactive map to explore it inside and out. Just click on a component of the Space Shuttle in the picture to learn more about it. You can find out more about the external tank, the solid rocket booster, the crew compartment, the cargo bay, and the main engine. The explanations are very detailed to make sure you know everything there is to know about the Space Shuttle. You can also get general information about the Shuttle, such as quick facts and questions and answers. Go to Orbiter Processing to follow step-by-step through a launch, mission in orbit, and landing. To find out more, go to Additional Resources for links to other space information.

Contact: Joshua S. Mussaf, Students for the Exploration and Development of Space, University of Arizona, *mussafj@db.erau.edu*

Climb aboard the Space Shuttle.

Space Settlements

http://wk122.nas.nasa.gov/NAS/SpaceSettlement/

At this site, you can find out the basics of space stations—who would live there, what they are, where they would be, how they would work, why we would have them, when we will start building them, and how much they will cost. Take a look at artists' renditions of space station designs. The Millennial Project images are particularly interesting because they show conceptions of what life might be like in the future. You can also see videos about living in a weightless environment. Browse through an archive of documents related to space settlements. Get info on space station designs, and connect to a contest for students to develop space stations. Finally, pay a visit to a playground for space stations designed by kids.

Contact: Al Globus, Numerical Aerodynmaic Simulation Program, NASA, *globus@nas.nasa.gov*

United Nations Office for Outer Space Affairs

ftp://ecf.hq.eso.org/pub/un/un-homepage.html

You can start your journey to the "final frontier" at the United Nations Office for Outer Space Affairs. This is a virtual office providing information about this office of the United Nations. Here you can learn all about international efforts to explore outer space and to find peaceful uses for space research. Access a fully hyperlinked listing of United Nations activities in promoting basic space science, including listings of workshops that link to transcripts of the proceedings, observations made, and final recommendations. Check out miscellaneous activities, including the search for extraterrestrial intelligence and astronomical efforts. This site doesn't have many multimedia gadgets, but it is a good example of how organizations can make information about their activities available to the public. From here, you can also jump to other space-related resources and to more United Nations information.

Contact: European Southern Observatory, H. J. Haubold, *haubold@ekpvs2.dnet.tuwien.ac.at*, and R. Albrecht, *ralbrech@eso.org*

UNITED NATIONS   NATIONS UNIES

VIENNA INTERNATIONAL CENTRE

Visit a virtual office through the United Nations Office for Outer Space Affairs.

For more information on space exploration, visit the following sites:

Canadian Astronauts

http://schoolnet2.carleton.ca/english/math_sci/astronauts/

Learn all about Canadian astronauts at this site, and find out how they prepare for missions. You'll also find information about the Canadian space station program.

Malin Space Science Systems

http://barsoom.msss.com/

Malin Space Science Systems designs, develops, and operates instruments on spacecraft. Here you can read about current projects and flight project participation.

NASA Jet Propulsion Laboratory

http://www.jpl.nasa.gov/

Here you'll find the center for robotic exploration of the solar system, learn about missions and programs, access image archives, and take an online tour of the lab.

Students for the Exploration and Development of Space

http://seds.lpl.arizona.edu/

You'll find lots of fun space stuff here, including a galaxy of images, a deep sky catalog, information about rocketry and space stations, and space events. This is also the home of a solar system tour and information about nebulae.

The University of New Hampshire Small Satellite Lab

http://burst.unh.edu/ssl.html

This site was originally designed so people could help design small satellite instrumentation, but there are links to NASA information and other items which might have a broader appeal.

Zoology

B-EYE

http://cvs.anu.edu.au/andy/beye/beyehome.html

See the world through the eyes of a honey bee. Or at least see what scientists think a bee's world looks like, based on anatomical and behavioral studies. First, there's a technical description of how bees see. Then pictures show the world as a bee would literally see it. You can either look at preprocessed images ready to download, hover at close range in front of a pattern, or set your own parameters for using the B-EYE computer program. Take a look at the original pictures, and then compare them to the same pictures through the bee's eyes. This very different view of the world will amaze you.

Contact: Andrew Giger, Centre for Visual Sciences, *giger@rsbs-central.anu.edu.au*

The Electronic Zoo

http://netvet.wustl.edu/e-zoo.htm

At this virtual zoo, explore an extensive list of animal-related online resources, such as mailing lists, Gophers, WWW sites, Usenet news-groups, FTP archives, and bulletin board systems. Look here for infor-mation about animals of all kinds: amphibians, birds, cats, cows, dogs, exotic animals, ferrets, fish, horses, marine mammals, pigs, primates, rabbits, reptiles, rodents, sheep, goats, and invertebrates, just to name a few of the many animals included here. For each link you choose, you'll find loads of resources on the Internet about that animal. Look for your pet, your totem, or a creature you're researching. In addition to the animal resources, there are many bonus hotlists. Travel along the images link to find picture collections of animals on the Internet. A fictional archive links to made-up animals such as cartoons, characters in stories, and mythological beasts. Under miscellaneous, look for general information on genetics, anatomy, sounds, species, and even animal games. Go to the veterinary section for a huge archive of veter-inary resources such as laws and regulations, organizations, and col-leges. You can also search all the resources, find out what's new, or look up resources by type. This one-stop information shop will get you started on your online hunt for any kind of animal.

Contact: Ken Boschert, DVM, NetVet, Washington University, *KEN@WUDCM.WUSTL.EDU*

You'll find any animal at the Electronic Zoo.

Insect Database

gopher://bluehen.ags.udel.edu:71/hh/.insects/.descriptions/entohome.html

Check this online insect database for fast facts on any insect in the world. The database is divided by insect order. You'll learn the meaning of each insect order's name and how to pronounce it. Match the order names with common names of insects that you already know. Then learn all about the insects in each order, including their body characteristics, where they are found, their practical uses, the size of the order, and a step-by-step explanation of metamorphosis. There's also a picture example of every order. This database contains lots of easy-to-understand information about all kinds of insects. Use it as a study aid or for extra research.

Contact: University of Dakota College of Agricultural Sciences

Everything you could want to know about insects can be found in the Insect Database.

Jane Goodall Institute

http://gsn.org/gsn/jgi.home.html

The Jane Goodall Institute for Wildlife Research, Education, and Conservation is committed to wildlife research, sharing knowledge through education, and conservation of the habitats that sustain life on Earth. Learn about Jane Goodall and her research with chimpanzees at the Institute's online site. Visit the Gombe Stream National Park in Tanzania where Dr. Goodall's work began. Go to chimpanzee sanctuaries, and find out about the ChimpanZoo program that studies chimpanzees in zoos. Discover how you can become a chimpanzee guardian or a member of the Jane Goodall Institute. This site doesn't have a lot of pictures, but it does provide some interesting reading about Jane Goodall and chimpanzees. You'll also find good contact addresses for Jane Goodall Institute programs.

Contact: Jane Goodall Institute, Global SchoolNet Foundation, *jgi@gsn.org*

The Penguin Page

http://www.sas.upenn.edu/~kwelch/penguin.html

Learn all about penguins and see some great pictures at this home page just for our favorite flightless sea birds. Here you can study penguin biology and learn about penguin behavior and reproduction. Get information about anatomy, where penguins live, diet, breeding, migratory patterns, and predators. There are lots of picture examples of every topic. Study fossils of extinct penguins, and learn about the links between them and modern-day species. Connect to a FAQ for penguin basics, including biology and behavior. Follow links to other Internet resources about penguins. There is even some penguin humor, including Far Side cartoons and an analysis of Opus.

Contact: Kevin Welch, School of Arts and Sciences, University of Pennsylvania

Meet every kind of penguin at the Penguin Page.

Raptors

http://www.raptor.cvm.umn.edu/

Visit the Raptor Center, an international medical facility for birds of prey, such as hawks, owls, eagles, and vultures. Here you'll learn what to do and who to contact if you find an injured bird, particularly if it needs emergency care. Get tips for handling injured birds. Read all about birds of prey and laws concerning raptors. Connect to information about the different raptor types and brief facts about each species. Jump to other Internet resources about raptors, including newsgroups. Finally, look at bird images, and hear sounds from different raptors. In my opinion, raptors are the most beautiful and fascinating birds of all; learn all about them at the Raptor Center.

Contact: Raptor Center, *raptor@umn.edu*

Taxon Information

http://ucmp1.berkeley.edu/taxaform.html

Get a close look at any kind of animal. Just click on the group of animals (called a taxon) that you're most interested in, then click on the button below it. Off you'll go to a hallway in the virtual museum of paleontology with information about the animals you chose. This museum links to scientific information on any kind of animal. You'll find animal groups all along the evolutionary scale, from one-celled creatures to the highest developed mammals. Or click on larger groups, such as mammals and birds, to learn more about animal families. You can even look up facts about the first animals. You'll see pictures and find out about that animal's place in the evolutionary scale. You can also learn about paleontology and fossils here.

Contact: University of California Museum of Paleontology

For more information on zoology, visit the following sites:

Birdlinks

http://www.phys.rug.nl/mk/people/wpv/birdlink.html

This site contains an index and links to bird- and birding-related sites around the world. It also contains links to software and book reviews/sources on the subject.

Center for the Integrative Study of Animal Behavior

http://www.cisab.indiana.edu:80/cisab.html

This site is a coffee klatch for animal behavioralists. There is a lot of good information on the topic here, but it is presented in a relatively casual style and would not intimidate the average reader. Some parts are specific to the physical location of the Center, such as events and visitors, but the papers posted are of a much wider interest.

Latrobe University School of Zoology

http://www.zoo.latrobe.edu.au/

This site has the usual information about Latrobe University's zoological offerings. It also has a Zebra Finch Page and some cool Animal/Nature GIFs.

The Los Angeles Zoo

http://www.ci.la.ca.us/dept/ZOO/

Includes archived articles and a gallery.

WWW Virtual Library Index of Animals

http://www.mindspring.com/~zoonet/www_virtual_lib/zoos.html

Links to all sorts of animals on the Web—plenty of links to explore.

ZooNet Links

http://www.mindspring.com/~zoonet/zoolinks.html

Links to just about every official and unofficial zoo Web page. Not all have photos; some just contain zoo park information. A jillion links, but could use some better design.

Moving On

You've gone through two whole sections being studious and educating yourself. Now you're ready to have some fun. That's what the next section is all about. If there's one thing any WWW tourist can tell you, it's that the Web is a lot of fun. Entertainment sites abound, ranging from general topics to very specific ones. Whatever your taste in books, magazines, movies, television, music, or sports, you'll find something out there to suit you. You'll also discover a whole mess of games, many of them created especially for the WWW, that encourage hours of wasting time. It's time to relax and let the Web entertain you.

Section V

In Your Free Time

News & Entertainment Sites

Section V

In Your Free Time: News & Entertainment Sites

It's not difficult to track down good entertainment on the World Wide Web. In this section, you'll find entertainment-rich sites to suit any interest. WWW programmers have taken advantage of the interactive elements of the Web to create new worlds of video games. WWW designers use the Web's multimedia format to publish magazines, books, and newspapers on all subjects. In what is quickly becoming a Web tradition, individuals are creating home pages for favorite televisions shows, movies, and musical groups. This tour of entertainment sites on the WWW will hit many of the highlights, but don't refrain from exploring. You may find fun gems hidden deep in someone's home pages or at the bottom of a server's directory.

In this section, you'll travel to some of the best-known and most useful entertainment resources on the WWW, and you'll also discover lesser-known sites that should not be overlooked. Enter some bizarre sites that could only be found on the Internet. Discover a wide range of books and magazines to suit any taste, from creative writing to lifestyle magazines. Find fun sites that should please just about any entertainment-seeking impulse. What computer network would be complete without an assortment of games? The WWW is no exception, with a range of interactive games and multimedia gateways to other online games, such as MUDs and MOOs, found on the Internet. Get information about your favorite sports and hobbies, from the latest scores in professional sports to unicycling, from quilting to pets. Laugh at cartoons and jokes archives. Music resources on the Web are vast, and a few of the best are described in this section. You'll stop in at virtual radio stations, music magazines, and band home pages. And television and film buffs will find movie information and guides to popular TV shows.

If you don't have a lot of free time, be warned: these entertainment sites have a way of enticing you for hours, distracting you from any real work to be done. But if that's just what you're looking for, read on, and let the WWW entertain you.

Bizarre

IguanaCam

http://iguana.images.com/dupecam.html

The IguanaCam shows you Dupree, the green iguana, live. The video camera takes a live picture of the iguana and broadcasts it over the World Wide Web. Wait a few minutes, then reload to download a new picture and follow Dupree's every move. You can also read about recent events in Dupree's life. The IguanaCam is just one of the many live cameras you'll find on the Internet, broadcasting live pictures of all sorts of things, such as coffee makers and Coke machines. Iguana-Cam just happens to be one of the more fun ones.

Contact: Iguana Images, *info@iguana.images.com*

Magic 8-Ball

http://resort.com/~banshee/Misc/8ball

Do you want to know your future or the answer to your deepest, most crucial questions? Just ask the WWW Magic 8-Ball. Type the question in the blank space provided, concentrate deeply, then ask the Magic 8-Ball your question. Based on the Magic 8-Ball toy, this online version is much better (and sillier) because it's on the Internet.

Contact: Banshee, The Resort, *banshee@resort.com*

Get answers to your deepest questions using the WWW's Magic 8-Ball.

Mr. Edible Starchy Tuber Head

http://winnie.acsu.buffalo.edu/potatoe/

Play Mr. Potato Head online. All you have to do is select the features you want by clicking on the buttons. Pick the eyes, ears, nose, mouth, hair, chin, and feet for your new creation. Then click on the Finished button to redraw the image and display your very own Mr. Potato Head. Also check out several animations of Mr. Potato Head played right on your Web browser (Netscape only). Take a look at the Potatoe Cam (spelled wrong on purpose) for fun Mr. Potato Head pictures. You're never too old to play Mr. Potato Head when it's this much fun.

Contact: Andy Kutner, Lisa's Toybox, *potatoe@acsu.buffalo.edu*

Ouija Board

http://www.math.unh.edu/~black/cgi-bin/ouija.cgi

 Let the spirits in your computer talk to you using this interactive WWW Ouija board. Ask a question, then close your eyes and let the pointer move on its own over the letters and numbers to answer your questions. Be sure to allow the spirits to guide your hand. Move the classic Ouija board into the twentieth century by contacting the spirits online.

Contact: Kelly Black, Department of Mathematics, University of New Hampshire, *black@vidalia.unh.edu*

Roadkills-R-Us News Network

http://www.rru.com/rru/

Roadkills-R-Us advertises itself as an "Internet-based disinformation center," but you'll probably find the site to be a fun side trip on your Web travels. The site represents a fictional company, Roadkills-R-Us, whose slogan is, "Recycling up the food chain as far as possible." Here you'll learn all about the company, formed on Usenet in 1988 and "known throughout the solar system for fine food and other products made from roadkill." Read company information, including a payment schedule for various roadkills, from armadillo to zebra to mouse (PC, serial, etc.). Download their most popular taco recipe, or even find a job within the company. Connect to the roadkill virtual library—it's bizarre how many roadkill sites are out there. Roadkills-R-Us is also a proud sponsor of the *talk.bizarre* newsgroup; from this site, you can connect to the newsgroup's home page and other bizarre pages on the WWW.

Contact: Miles O'Neal, Schober O'Neal, Inc., *meo@rru.com*

Rome Lab Snowball Cam

http://www.rl.af.mil:8001/Odds-n-Ends/sbcam/rlsbcam.html

The Rome Lab Snowball Cam is a prime example of the kind of fun, useless, interactive toys that can be found on the WWW. The object is to throw snowballs at unsuspecting persons working in the Rome Laboratory. (Of course, the snowballs are virtual, but it's still fun to imagine you may have beaned someone, especially in the middle of the summer.) A video camera is mounted on top of a workstation, offering a glimpse into the lab. When you "throw" a snowball from your WWW browser by clicking on a hyperlink, the camera takes a picture of the incident and sends it back to your WWW browser. If the picture returned shows a snowball over any part of target, you get a hit. You can aim the snowball to the left or right or shoot it straight down the middle. You can even download profiles of potential targets. Also check out the scores, see recent throwing attempts, visit the hall of fame, and look at the shot of the week. Over 80,000 snowballs thrown can't be wrong—try it today.

Contact: Rome Laboratory, *web@www.rl.af.mil*

Try to hit lab workers or superheroes with the Rome Lab Snowball Cam.

The Schwa Corporation

http://fringeware.com/SchwaRoot/Schwa.html

Bill Barker, an artist living in Reno, Nevada, became fascinated with the subject of alien invasion and abduction and with people's seemingly sincere tales of flying saucers and aliens among us. He became so fascinated that he began a series of stark drawings featuring an alien motif and published them on the Web behind the mask of a mysterious entity called the Schwa Corporation. He then developed a line of "alien defense products" based on his Schwa characters and themes. He's now creating a whole line of alien *objets d'art*. Explore Barker's bizarre alien creations and the Schwa Corporation at this fun site. Under Plagiarize, you'll find lots of bizarre texts, including Schwa Plans Space Defense and an alien invasion survival manual. Besides the alien drawings, there are also sounds and music, the Schwa magazine, and information on Schwa products. This site definitely invites you to explore.

Contact: Marcel Levy, FringeWare, *schwa@well.sf.ca.us*

Tarot Information

http://cad.ucla.edu/repository/useful/tarot.html

Get your fortune read by the WWW using this Tarot server. The interactive program provides an authentic Tarot card reading to answer all your pressing questions. Think about your problem, let your vibes travel through the mouse and over the Internet, and then hit the hyperlink to get a personal reading from a virtual Tarot deck. The computer randomly lays out graphics of Tarot cards and interprets the reading for you. A three-card reading tells you about your past, present, and future. Or chose a representative card as your querent, and get the full, sixteen-card, Celtic reading. Even if you don't believe in fortune-telling, this Tarot game is a fun and unique place to spend some time.

Contact: Jonathan Katz, UCLA Campus Information Online, *jonathan@ucla.edu*

Let the WWW tell your fortune at the Tarot server.

Trojan Room Coffee Machine

http://www.cl.cam.ac.uk/coffee/coffee.html

Coffee truly is the universal cure-all—it picks you up in the morning, it tops any meal, and you can get it in about a million different flavors and brews. Now you can even drink coffee on the World Wide Web—virtually, that is. A video camera is trained on this cyberspace coffee pot, taking a picture of it every second. When you reload the page, you'll get a current image that shows you how much coffee is in the pot.

Contact: Daniel Gordon, University of Cambridge, *Daniel.Gordon@cl.cam.ac.uk*

Vampyres Only

http://www.vampyre.wis.net/vampyre/index.html

Join other creatures of the night on the "Vorld Vide Veb" at this fun site packed with vampire stuff. Check out 35 plus FAQs on vampires, answering any question you could possibly have. Read electronically available fiction about vampires, including authors Bram Stoker and Anne Rice. Find lists of vampire books and movies, as well as lists of songs, role-playing books, nonfiction books, editions of *Dracula,* and so forth. You can also find out what's current in the world of vampires in books, zines, games, film, television, and conventions. A gallery displays portraits of vampires gathered from all over the Internet and connects to other online horror art. Link to an international listing of vampire shops, vampire book reviews, and other vampire sites. Or have fun taking the vampire probability test, the vampire vulnerability test, and the human-vampire compatibility test.

Contact: Vlad III, Wimsey Information Services, *bmiddlet@wimsey.com*

For more information about the bizarre, visit these sites:

Alien Online

http://www.crs4.it/~mameli/Alien.html

This site has several intriguing "alien" photos and links to other hot UFO-related sites. Most of the text is in Spanish, but there is a minimal amount of text compared to the pictures. And the links are in English.

Aliens

http://www.hk.super.net/~martins/alien.html

This page suggests that aliens have had a hand in human development and history for millenia.

The Audio Arts Page

http://www.rahul.net/renoir/

Sometimes weirdness isn't in the eye of the beholder—it's in the ear. This page contains sound clips ranging from the ejection of a larynx to Melznor snoring.

The Bizarre Bazaar

http://www.camtech.com.au/~virtart/clients/bb/

Refreshingly forthright, the Bizarre Bazaar claims that they will provide you with an Internet presence, if you just give them money.

Bizarre Central

http://www.aston.ac.uk/~coxgc/bizarre.html

Perhaps this site seems stranger in the U.K., where its maintainer lives. There is information on Eurovision, attractive women, and supposedly bizarre remotes. (CBS is bizarre?)

Building a Boatmobile

http://www.io.com/~twobit/boatmobile/boatmobile.html

This page shows you how to build, step by step, a boatmobile from a boat and either a volkswagon bug or Karmann Ghia. Pictures included.

Galactic Central

http://www.efn.org/~lcapt/

This site contains information on alien abduction, film footage, Canadian UFO information, and more. There are also links to related newsgroups. The entire site has a certain "X-Files" flavor.

Gabe Fankhauser's Home Page

http://www.uc.edu/~FANKHAG/

This site has several items of interest for seekers of the bizarre. Odd pictures (pig pottery on railroad tracks, at this viewing, but it may change). Interesting links. Gabe's resume.

The Godot Hierarchy

http://www.wolfe.net/~godot/

This site is devoted to the wisdom inherent in absurdity. It has links to other absurd sites.

Greetings Earthpeople!

http://osf1.gmu.edu/~rgoggans/

Beware! Our planet has long been observed by a potato-like alien race who plan to enslave us all. Check out this site for warnings, reasons behind the invasion, and potential redeeming human features.

How to Tell if Your Head's About to Blow Up

http://www.mit.edu:8001/people/mkgray/head-explode.html

This page gives a history of peoples' brains exploding. It also gives some of the warning signs to watch out for. Unfortunately, it doesn't tell how to prevent your head from exploding.

An Illuminati Outline of History

http://www.impropaganda.com/~street/detour/ill5.html

The Illuminati conspiracy is the granddaddy of all conspiracy theories. If you wonder what they were up to between 1950 and 1973, check out this page.

Mirsky's Worst of the Web

http://mirsky.turnpike.net/wow/Worst.html

Need I say more? A big hit all over the Web.

News of the Weird

http://www.cs.su.oz.au/~giovanni/humour/wierd.html

This site keeps track of the latest weirdnesses occurring all over the world.

Peeping Tom Page

http://www.ts.umu.se/~spaceman/camera.html

With links to photos of places, things, scenes, etc. Ranked in the top 5 percent of Web sites.

PEZ Candy Home Page

http://wwwcsif.cs.ucdavis.edu/~telford/pez.html

For us PEZ lovers. Includes history, ingredients, "PEZ quotes," and a PEZ art gallery.

The Pickled Trauma

http://weber.u.washington.edu/~jaysonm/index.html

I'm as fond of a site with a pickle for a mascot as the next person. But, for some reason, each time I tried to access the page called Hit the Books, I was kicked completely out of Netscape Navigator 1.1. Look at this site, but cautiously.

Prayers Heavenbound

http://www.primenet.com/~prayers/

This page provides information on sending your prayers directly into space via a microwave radio beam. As of this writing the cost was about $10.

Some "Good" Articles from *talk.bizarre*

http://www.funhouse.com/jfw/talk-bizarre.html

This page is related to, but not necessarily linked to, the Talk Bizarre site (listed below). It contains past postings with references to fire-breathing clue mosquitoes and sweet sensitive koala bears.

Strawberry Pop-Tart Blow-Torches

http://www.sci.tamucc.edu/~pmichaud/toast/

This site describes the use of Kelloggs Strawberry Pop-Tarts as incendiary devices. The writer fails to mention if this use of Pop-Tarts has Kellogg's approval.

Talk Bizarre

http://www.cybercom.net/~kristen/bizarre/bizarre.html

This site has a pet page containing a boy and his newt. It has bizarre art even stranger than that, including Kate's newt designs. It's one of those things that you don't have to understand to enjoy, which is just as well.

Too Weird

http://www.webcom.com/~jcurrie/weird.html

This site contains links to some truly bizarre pages, including time-lapse photography charting the development of a chia plant. Not all the links are suitable for kids.

The T.W.I.N.K.I.E.S Project

http://www.rice.edu/~gouge/twinkies.html

This site is the result of an exam period's worth of scientific testing on a readily available cake-like food substance. The scientific data was written up in proper lab note format and has been placed on the Net for your edification. For example, it has been conclusively proven that twinkies do burn if properly dried out.

The Unofficial Otter Pops Home Page

http://www.cs.washington.edu/homes/brad/op/o.pops.html

Otter Pops are a frozen, fruit-flavored food item. This page discusses their origin, uses, names, and other information vital to Otter Pops fans.

Useless Pages

http://www.primus.com/staff/paulp/useless.html

Just in case you weren't wasting enough time on the Net, Paul Phillips and Steve Berlin have collected and linked up as many completely useless sites as they could find. Check out the floating fish site, where fish tell you the Greenwich Mean Time. Find out what T-shirts Steve has in his dresser drawers. I'm not kidding—people actually put these things on the Net. And Paul and Steve will lead you to them.

Vanity License Plate

http://www-chaos.umd.edu/misc/plates.html

Ever wonder just what that vanity plate on the car ahead of you was supposed to say? This list gives a translation of many different plate cyphers.

Wacky Patent of the Month

http://colitz.com/site/wacky.htm

This page recognizes the inventors of things most people couldn't or wouldn't imagine. Example: US Patent 11,942 - The Tapeworm-Trap.

Weirdland

http://www.phoenix.net/~lsimon/writing/

This site contains a requiem for a headache, a map of weirdness, and other intriguing-looking pages.

Welcome to My World...

http://www.tezcat.com/~nrn/

This page provides useful information on good and bad service providers, classic cinema, Nixon links, and a word from Charles Bukowski. (Note: mild profanity.)

Books

BookWire

http://www.bookwire.com/

BookWire is the first place to look for book information on the Internet. This huge Web site has everything you want to know about books. Tap into a best-seller list database organized by title, author, and imprint, as well as historical top ten lists and *Publisher's Weekly* best-sellers complete with reviews. Visit the best bets—book sites that are really worth visiting. Laugh at the book cartoon of the day. Browse reviews from *The Boston Book Review*, covering fiction, children's books, poetry, the arts, CD-ROMs, and more, plus interviews and essays. Scan the gigantic lists of book publishers and booksellers on the Web, or connect to online libraries around the world. Find electronic books and additional online book resources in the Reading Room. You'll also find book events, insider information and resources for those in the book business. If you love books, publish books, or write books, you definitely need to put this site on your hotlist.

Contact: BookWire, *www@bookwire.com*

The Doomsday Brunette

http://zeb.nysaes.cornell.edu/CGI/ddb/demo.cgi

The Doomsday Brunette is "the first Internet-browsable, downloadable, interactive, science-fiction, humorous, satirical, mystery, electronic book," or so the introduction says. This WWW demonstration, in which you can read only the first three chapters of the book, gives you a good feel for the downloadable version of the entire book. Hyperlinked words within the futuristic text lead you to definitions of unknown terms, from either a realistic point of view or the main character's point of view, depending on which you choose. You also choose where the story goes at the end of every page. The entire book costs only $5.95 to access, and after reading through the WWW demonstration, you'll probably want to download it right away just to see what happens next—or, rather, what you can make happen.

Contact: John M. Zakour, Z Stuff on the Web, *support@zeb.nysaes.cornell.edu*

Internet Book Information Center

http://sunsite.unc.edu/ibic/IBIC-homepage.html

This useful resource provides access to general information about books culled from all over the Internet. The information is divided by subject, including readers, authors, poetry, publishers, booksellers, libraries, online books and magazines, and a reference shelf. Listings connect to Internet resources such as newsgroups, WWW sites, mailing lists, and Gophers. You'll find reviews and notes on current books at the top of the page. A unique feature, the Commonplace Book, is an edited collection of striking passages from writers, built by Internet users. Here you will find such quotes as those of science fiction author Gene Wolfe on sanity, Machiavelli on innovation and author H.P. Lovecraft on the nature of reality. Don't miss this meta-resource on books on the Internet.

Contact: Frederick Zimmerman, SunSITE, University of North Carolina at Chapel Hill, *ibic@sunsite.unc.edu*

Jayhawk

http://www.klab.caltech.edu/~flowers/jayhawk/

At this site, you'll find an archive for *Jayhawk*, a science fiction novel by Mary K. Kuhner that was originally posted to the Internet in 144 installments. Each part is available here separately. A background on the story is also available.

Contact: Dave Flowers, The Koch Lab, California Institute of Technology, *dflowers@caltech.edu*

Online Horror Classics

http://www.ee.pdx.edu/~caseyh/horror/online.html

Read the full text versions of all your favorite horror classics from this specialized horror library. You've probably seen all these spooky creatures in action on the movie screen. Now check out their original sources. Here you'll find links to your favorite monsters, such as Frankenstein, Dr. Jekyll and Mr. Hyde, Dracula, and the Invisible Man. Connect to Edgar Allan Poe stories, H.G. Wells's *The Island of Dr.*

Moreau, and Oscar Wilde's *The Picture of Dorian Gray*. Besides being chilling and thrilling, these books are also literary classics. There's even a short story by Stephen King linked in (it's sure to be a classic some day). These texts and other electronic novels were made possible by Project Gutenberg, an endeavor to put classic literature into free electronic format that everyone can access.

Contact: Casey Hopkins, Department of Electrical Engineering, Portland State University, *caseyh@ee.pdx.edu*

Meet the Invisible Man and other scary guys at this library of horror novels.

Science Fiction and Fantasy Archive

http://sf.www.lysator.liu.se/sf_archive/sf_main.html

Here you'll find a hypertext interface to a massive ASCII-text archive of science fiction and fantasy resources on the Internet. You'll find authors' biographies and bibliographies, book reviews, film commentaries, and a list of electronically available fiction. Special series stored here include some real gems: "belated reviews" of classic works; *Dragon Zine*, a fantasy fiction magazine; publisher's newsletters from Del Rey and Tor; and *Quanta*, a magazine of science fiction and fantasy. Comprehensive lists include books sorted by type, such as alternative history and transformations, as well as a list of musical science fiction works. You can even visit an art gallery created by science fiction and fantasy fans.

Contact: Mats Öhrman, Lysator Computing Society, *matoh@lysator.liu.se*

Umney's Last Case by Stephen King

http://www.eu.net/king/

Even the master of mass market fiction can be found on the WWW. This 21-page novella from King's anthology *Nightmares and Dreamscapes* was published electronically before it ever saw print—the first commercially published, hypertext short story. The bilingual WWW edition has versions in English and German. The opening page features a full-color graphic of the cover of the anthology. The table of contents follows, linking in each of the seven sections. You'll even find a few surprise links in the text to sound effects that enhance the story. Don't overlook this model of future trade publishing on the Internet and Stephen King's first appearance on the WWW.

Contact: Published by Online Bookstore, designed by Dykki Settle, EU Net, *Webmaster@EU.net*

For more information on books, visit these sites:

Comics FAQs

http://www.cis.ohio-state.edu/hypertext/faq/usenet-faqs/ bygroup/rec/arts/comics/info/top.html

The many FAQs in this archive introduce you to the *rec.arts.comics* newsgroups, give you a glossary of terms used in the newsgroups, tell you how to behave, and list other Net resources for comics information.

Hitchhiker's Guide to the Galaxy Home Page

http://www.galcit.caltech.edu/~jdavis/hhgttg.html

For us Zaphod Beeblebrox fans, lots of links to related pages on Douglas Adams, used bookstores, and other cool information pages, including the Vogon home page!

The Mysterious Homepage

http://www.db.dk/dbaa/jbs/homepage.htm

This page provides links to online mysteries, pages by and about mystery fiction writers, mailing lists, and more. Very comprehensive.

The Mysterious Web

http://www.slip.net/~cluelass/

This site has links to various mystery-related sites, mystery authors' home pages, criminalistic research, movie and TV mystery-related sites, and mystery games.

The Mystery Zone

http://www.mindspring.com/~walter/mystzone.html

This is an online magazine of short stories, reviews, pictures, essays, and featured authors.

The Mystery Zone's Fiction Spotlight

http://www.mindspring.com/~walter/fictspot.html

This site reviews recent releases of mystery novels.

The Mystery Zone's Non-Fiction Features

http://www.mindspring.com/~walter/features.html

This site contains interviews with popular mystery novelists and a "how to" section on writing mystery novels.

Neither Liberal Nor Communitarian: Feminism, Political Theory, Possibility

http://english-server.hss.cmu.edu/ctheory/r-either_liberal_nor.html

This page is a review of the book, *The Politics of Community: A Feminist Critique of the Liberal-Communitarian Debate*. The review is fascinating, for those with an interest in any of the three mentioned subjects, and the book looks even more so.

The New Mythology

http://www.sccs.swarthmore.edu/~dominic/new_myth.html

This page discusses the relationship between mythology and the more widely known science-fiction works (*Star Wars*, *Dune*, etc.).

Other Mysteries

http://www.eskimo.com/~bpaul/other.htm

This is the home page of Barbara Paul, a mystery novelist. She describes some of her work and how she developed it.

Pre-Release Comic Information

http://www.cam.org/~stoy/newcomics.html

This site will let you know what to expect from Marvel, DC, and Image comic companies in the upcoming months.

SF and Fantasy Author Bibliographies

http://julmara.ce.chalmers.se/SF_archive/Authorlists/

This site gives the bibliographical information on a large number of authors in the science fiction and fantasy genre. Also, many of the authors' bibliographies include links to further author information.

Fun

Anagram Server

http://lrdc5.lrdc.pitt.edu/awad-cgibin/anagram/

An anagram is a word made from the letters of another word. Discover the wisdom of anagrams by entering a word or words into the interactive form and then hitting return; the program returns a full list of possible anagrams. You'll also find out what an anagram is, get fun facts about anagrams, and visit the anagram hall of fame.

Contact: Anu Garg, The Haven, *anu@wordsmith.org*

Cool Site of the Day

http://cool.infi.net/

The Cool Site of the Day has become an Internet standard, so visit every day for a new fun site. You never know where you're going till you get there. Also visit Categorically Cool, providing new cool sites each day in different categories that change every week. The categories could include knowledge, art, music, bizarre, and commercial. Or see the past cool sites of the day, and explore the cool sites of the year.

Contact: Cool Site of the Day at InfiNet, *cool@infi.net*

CyberSight

http://cybersight.com/cgi-bin/cs/s?main.gmml

Wander through an online boutique of fun, interactive applications unique on the WWW. At the Real-Time Prattler, you can watch people chat just by reloading the page and even add your own comments to the discussion. Go to the Phlogotician's Corner to read postings on an infinite variety of topics; spout off yourself, or make up a new subject for future discussion. Take some polls, or try your hand at one of three trivia quizzes. Explore a random URL, participate in an add-your-own-adventure story, or play a game of Hangman. Scribble something on the graffiti wall, an image map of WWW graffiti; you just click on the part of the image where you want to leave your mark. The What You Want List is a collection of Internet resources on all sorts of entertaining topics such as TV, kitsch, art, music, cybersive, sports, and fun. Access a list of the most and least popular resources, or browse the resources and give them a thumbs up or thumbs down. You're guaranteed to waste a lot of time at this decidedly different site.

Contact: Internet Marketing, Inc., CyberSight, *imi@cybersight.com*

Kaleidospace

http://kspace.com/

At this jam-packed entertainment site, you'll find a little bit of everything: art, performance, music, fiction, news, and movies, to name a
few. An interactive kaleidoscope transports you to different places
within the site. The Art Studio displays original artwork, and Center
Stage features video clips of stand-up routines and dance. Go shopping at the Cyberfaire, or sample contemporary, alternative, and
world music at the Music Kiosk. The Reading Room holds hypertext
fiction and graphic novels, or visit the Screening Room for animation
and music videos. The site also spotlights high-profile artists who
demonstrate a concern for the future of art and its relationship to technology. You'll even get the opportunity to produce collaborative
works with these nationally known artists-in-residence, including
fiction, art, comics, videos, and music, or just chat with them interactively online.

Contact: Jeannie Novak and Pete Markiewicz, Kaleidospace,
editors@kspace.com

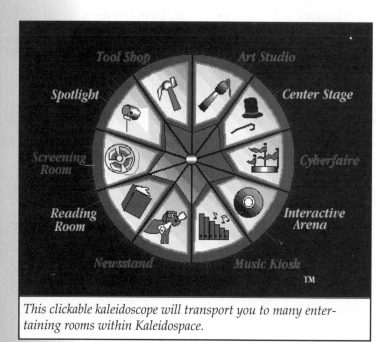

*This clickable kaleidoscope will transport you to many enter-
taining rooms within Kaleidospace.*

Lite-Brite

http://www.galcit.caltech.edu/~ta/lb/lb.html

"Lite-Brite, Making Things with Light"—that's exactly what you can do here, with the light from your computer screen, that is. The interactive program uses colored buttons to simulate the Lite-Brite toy you may remember from your childhood. The editor allows you to create your own Lite-Brite pictures using a virtual pegboard. Advanced picture-editing tools are even available. When you're done, post your art for all the world to see. Connect to the top ten pictures in the Lite-Brite Gallery, or see lots and lots of light art in a complete archive. While you're here, be sure to check out the rest of the Asylum, which hosts the WWW Lite-Brite toy, for more fun.

Contact: The Asylum, Graduate Aeronautical Laboratory, California Institute of Technology, Joe Cates, *joe@galcit.caltech.edu*, and Aure Prochazka, *aure@galcit.caltech.edu*

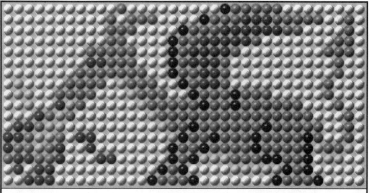

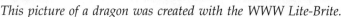
This picture of a dragon was created with the WWW Lite-Brite.

Miller Genuine Draft Taproom

http://www.mgdtaproom.com/

No, this is not a shameless plug for Miller beer. Rather, it is a fun lifestyle magazine, a place where you can find out what's happening. It has articles on art, fashion, sports, city life, social issues, and entertainment. Coverage centers on New York, Atlanta, Chicago, Austin, Los Angeles, San Francisco, Seattle, Miami, and cool happenings on the

Internet. Get stories from the music scene and from the world. You'll find news and notes from the worlds of sports and rock-n-roll. You can also get all your questions about beer and beer brewing answered by the Brew Master. This site is a great example of Web-based advertising, giving the user a lot of on-site information in exchange for product promotion.

Contact: Miller Genuine Draft, *mgdtaproom@mgdtaproom.com*

Rainbow Confusion

http://www.mps.org/~rainbow/

In this virtual toy box, you'll find unique playthings probably not available anywhere else on the Internet. Access the Written Word page for humorous essays, such as Fabio's Top Ten Pick-up Lines, Jack Handey's Deep Thoughts, and a nerdity quiz. A collection of fun images features cartoons and a personal photo album. Visit the Internet Candy Dish to receive a handful of Valentine candy hearts with inspiring messages. You can also shop for unique products and unusual gifts in Uncommon Connections, such as Rosencratz and Guildenstern banknotes and Nancy Drew clothing.

Contact: Mike W. Miller and Britton Smith, The Minnesota Preparatory Schools, *rainbow@mps.com*

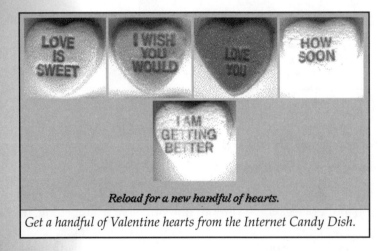

Get a handful of Valentine hearts from the Internet Candy Dish.

Robert Hartill's Fun Page

http://www.cm.cf.ac.uk/People/Robert.Hartill.html

Robert Hartill was inducted into the WWW Hall of Fame, mainly for his movie database interface, his most famous contribution to the WWW. Jump to it from his home page, or link to many other fun "bits 'n' bobs" he has worked on, such as a guided tour around South Wales or an interactive game of Hangman. You will also find the VOGON news service that Rob created, which serves United Kingdom news daily. Search an image finder for loads of images of all kinds. For fun, connect to Basil Fawlty quotes from the British comedy, "Fawlty Towers." Rob's work has shown how interactive servers can be implemented on the WWW, and most of his projects are very entertaining.

Contact: Rob Hartill, Computing Mathematics Information Server, Cardiff University, *hartill@lanl.gov*

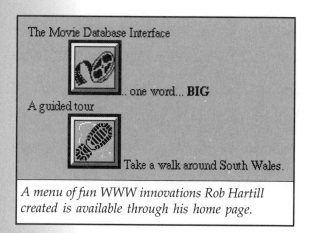

A menu of fun WWW innovations Rob Hartill created is available through his home page.

Roller Coaster World

http://tmb.extern.ucsd.edu/woc/

Whether you just like to ride roller coasters or you're a diehard fan, you'll find lots of news and pictures of coasters from all over the world at this site. Get the latest news, rumors, and gossip floating around the roller coaster and amusement park communities. This is a good place to find out about new parks and attractions opening up. Read reviews of coasters and parks, most with pictures. You'll find reviews of favorite parks such as Busch Gardens, King's Dominion, and Carowinds. If you're planning a vacation, check here first to see what amusement parks you should stop at. Check out statistics on the most awesome roller coasters made by man and a history of roller coasters in the Roller Coaster Almanac. You'll find out what the steepest, highest, fastest, and oldest coasters are, as well as the coasters with the longest drop, the biggest loop, the highest g-forces, and the most demented shuttle loop. Get a list of roller coaster events, or read a survey of favorite coasters. Visit a picture gallery of more than 200 coasters. You can also connect to more coasters pages and information sources online.

Contact: Jim Serio, University of California at San Diego, *jserio@sdcc10.ucsd.edu*

Stoli Central

http://www.stoli.com/

This site is for audiences of legal drinking age only. That being said, Stoli Central is a free-spirited place, where the freedoms of adventure, expression, and vodka always hold true. In Freedom of Vodka, you can be your own bartender by entering your favorite cocktail recipes into the mixology archives using an online form. Look at What's Your Pleasure to see others' vodka concoctions and vote on the best ones. In Specialties of the House, get recommendations from the horse's mouth—the Stoli experts—on the best vodka cocktails. Step out on the town with a list of good restaurants and bars in major American cities. In Freedom of Expression, you can create masterpieces on the Stoli Palette or try to master the Stoli Cipher. There is also a gallery of Russian art. Go to Freedom of Adventure to visit a random hot spot on the Web. Or take a fascinating tour of the spirits of the world. You can also order vodka or other spirits from the 800 Spirits Gift Catalog, learn about the charities that Stoli supports, and read about vodka events.

Contact: Stoli Central, *info@stoli.com*

16 Puzzle

*http://arachnid.cs.cf.ac.uk/htbin/AndrewW/Puzzle/
puzzle4x4image*

Do you remember the old favorite? The sliding puzzle in which you
push tiles around to form a picture? Now you can play it on the
WWW interactively. View the 16 tiles, and move them around either
singly or in groups by clicking on them. Once you solve the puzzle,
find out more about the WWW program and how it was created, or
send comments to the author of the program. If you like this, you can
also visit a collection of other sliding tile puzzles.

Contact: Andrew Wilson, Cardiff University,
Andrew.Wilson@cm.cf.ac.uk

*All you need to do is click on the sliding tiles to
solve this interactive puzzle.*

Spirograph

http://juniper.tc.cornell.edu:8000/spiro/spiro.html

When you were a kid, perhaps you had a Spirograph, a drawing toy used to create colorful spirals. Now it's available on the WWW for adult "kids" to play with anytime. The Spirograph draws pictures based on mathematical principles. Enter numbers in the blank boxes to make different pictures. Experiment with entering negative and positive numbers to see what kind of spirals you get. Then click on the Generate Image button to display the picture you made.

Contact: Jeffrey Cohen, The Junkyard, *jcohen@dri.cornell.edu*

Create geometrical pictures like this one with the Spirograph on the WWW.

The Web's Edge

http://kzsu.stanford.edu/uwi.html

Visit a "cultural playground" at this site. Here you'll find the home of Underworld Industries group, dedicated to linking underground music, art, and the Internet. There's lots of stuff to do here. You can read a poetry zine and road trip journals. Jump to hot and cool Web sites. Get stuff from the Shopping Maul, such as books and music. Visit sub-sites for specialized knowledge, such as the *Blade Runner* site, the Glossary of Mayhem, and *Factsheet Five*. Plus you'll find sites about fashion design, animation, and experimental music. Look at an odd-art archive and a video show, both of which you can be a part of. Finally, stare at a fun page, containing a "bunch of lame stuff," or at a page of ideas and propaganda. Take the time to explore this varied and eclectic site.

Contact: Underworld Industries, KZSU Radio at Stanford University, *jon@kzsu.stanford.edu*

For more fun, visit these sites:

Anagrams Insanity

http://www.infobahn.com/pages/anagram.html

A very cool anagrams page, with a nice design.

Anagram Solver

http://www.ssynth.co.uk/~gay/anagram.html

Enter a phrase or word and get a list of possible anagrams. You can limit the search by number of words in resulting anagrams and whether to include "a" and "I". Cool stuff.

CoolSite

http://www.coolsite.com/

Links to some cool stuff, some of which is mentioned elsewhere.

The Electric Postcard Rack

http://postcards.www.media.mit.edu/postcards/

One of my favorites. Send a virtual postcard to anyone or pick up one. Lots of fun to browse and see the images online.

Fun & Games Site

http://www.nova.edu/Inter-Links/fun_games.html

Several links, including an almanac, which has current information from several sources (including U.S. population), plus a horoscope and Tarot. Some humor links, such as cartoons and random quotes.

Lisa's Toybox

http://winnie.acsu.buffalo.edu/

You'll find lots of fun stuff here, including Mr. Potato Head and many online cameras like Fallscam (Niagara Falls), SnakeCam, and Fish Cam. There is also information about the visual arts and opera.

Netville

http://www.netville.de/netville.html

This site has information on music, movies, shopping, travel, art, and books. However, once you get a layer or two into it, much of the information is in German.

Point Communications

http://www.pointcom.com/

This is the page for the company that selects the top 5 percent of Web sites. Includes links to reviews and individual pages. You have to read the review for the page before you can link directly to it, and there seems to be an awful lot of menu navigation, but there's some cool top ten lists and new reviews for the day. A must for those who just have to be hip and current. Free subscription service.

Robert Lee Entertainment

http://www.rle.com/~rle/index.htm

This site has information on videos, mountain biking, and bands, as well as poetry, job listings, and humor.

Theme Parks FAQ

*http://www.cis.ohio-state.edu/hypertext/faq/usenet-faqs/
bygroup/rec/parks/theme/top.html*

This FAQ, from the newsgroup *rec.parks.theme*, discusses all amusement parks with trip reports, statistics, news, and arguments over the best roller coasters.

Underground

http://bazaar.com/

Get information about music, movies, and art, from Lollapalooza to the House of Blues to the Beatles. You'll also find bizarre stuff like the Psycho Friend's Network.

Games

Addventure

http://www.addventure.com/addventure/

Addventure is a choose-your-own-adventure game with a twist. The interactive capabilities of the WWW allow you to add your own creations to the game. Once you enter the game, proceed through various rooms, all of which were created by previous players. Because of its collaborative nature, the game moves into a variety of unknown plot twists. Room numbers tell you how far you have ventured into the game. If you reach a point where no one has ever been before, you get to create your own room for other players to use. At this site, there are lots of different Addventure games to choose from, including Kiddventure, the Red-Light District, and the Unending Addventure.

Contact: Allen S. Firstenberg, Addventure, *prisoner@addventure.com*

Atlantis Play-By-E-mail Game

http://www.cs.utexas.edu/users/orb/atlantis/

Atlantis is an open-ended fantasy game run by computer. In the game, you try to carve out huge empires and become a master magician, intrepid explorer, rich trader, or anything else you want to be. There's no winner in this interactive game, and players set their own goals. Go to the home page first to learn more about Atlantis. Here you can read all the rules, find out how to join, and download the software you'll need to play (it's free).

Contact: Norman Richards, University of Texas Computer Science Department

BU's Interactive Web Games

http://www.bu.edu/Games/games.html

Pay a visit to the first interactive multiplayer games page on the Web, and plan to stay awhile. Here you can play against a computer in a game of tic-tac-toe or pegs, try to solve a sliding tiles game, or risk your virtual life playing Hunt the Wumpus. Try out Minesweep, a Web version of the popular Windows game. The games are a bit more primitive than the average Sega or Nintendo video game, but this page is a harbinger of things to come.

Contact: Glenn Bresnahan, Scientific Computing and Visualization, Boston University, *glenn@www.bu.edu*

Risk your life playing Hunt the Wumpus at the first interactive, multiplayer game page on the Web.

Drool

http://www.mit.edu:8001/afs/athena.mit.edu/user/j/b/jbreiden/game/entry.html

In this text-based puzzle game, you get to be your favorite dog on a mission to retrieve a stick your master has thrown. The game usually takes a couple of hours to solve. First, choose your breed and gender from an interactive form. Then read descriptions of the action, and make choices about what to do by clicking on the hyperlinked options. You can follow other links to look at various objects in the game, such as the stick and the people and places you encounter along the way. Chase the stick over a fun hypertext journey in an effort to return it to your owner and win the game.

Contact: Jeff Breidenbach, Massachusetts Institute of Technology, *jbreiden@mit.edu*

The Game Cabinet

http://web.kaleida.com/u/tidwell/GameCabinet.html

This online game cabinet holds rules, reviews, and random information about board games from all over the world. When you first enter the site, you'll see the Living Room Floor, which has all the new items in the cabinet that haven't been cleaned up yet. Scroll to the bottom of the page for the cabinet itself. Access news about board games and announcements of new games. Read reviews of games, books, and magazines in the Review Drawer. You'll find game rules on the Game Shelf for interesting strategy, board, card, beer and pretzel, and pencil and paper games, as well as rules for traditional games such as Bridge and darts. Learn the rules to some games from other countries you may never have heard of. Look in Extra Bits for rules variations, additional rules, score sheets, and spells for specific games. Check out the Front Door for links to games companies or shops. Link to games to play on the Internet, as well as to other games-related places on the Web.

Contact: Ken Tidwell, Kaledia Labs, *tidwell@kaleida.com*

Games Domain

http://wcl-rs.bham.ac.uk/GamesDomain/

The Games Domain is your central reference point for all things game-related that can be found on the Internet. With over 350 links and growing, this site is low in graphics and rich in information, all easily located using a forms-based searching tool. The site covers all kinds of games, including video, board, card, role-playing, and online games. It specializes in games FAQs, with over 55 links, and in "walk-throughs" of favorite video games, such as Myst, Ultima, Bard's Tale, Space Quest, and more. In addition, you'll find connections to games-related FTP sites, magazines, and home pages. You can also connect to a wide array of miscellaneous gaming resources, such as game reviews, online gaming companies, software outlets, and top ten gaming home pages. This central hub of gaming information should be your first stop on any quest for online gaming resources.

Contact: Dave Stanworth, Wolfson Computer Laboratory, *djh@gamesdom.demon.co.uk*

From the game "Chronicles of the Sword" by Sony Psygnosis.

Games Domain Reviews

http://wcl-rs.bham.ac.uk/gdreview/

Here you'll find a user-supported gaming magazine with information about all your favorite computer and video games. Read reviews of recently released games, previews of new games, notes on the gaming industry, and news items. The magazine covers a wide range of game types, perfect for any video game lover.

Contact: Dave Stanworth, Wolfson Computer Laboratory, *djh@gamesdom.co.uk*

Hunt the Wumpus

http://www.bu.edu/htbin/wcl

This multi-player WWW game allows you to interact with other players as you track down the Wumpus in its lair. The Wumpus lives in a cave with interconnecting rooms; it is your job to move along various tunnels and shoot the Wumpus with one of your arrows, while avoiding bats, pits, and other players' arrows. You also lose if the Wumpus eats you before you can find it or if you grow too old to play, that is, don't move soon enough. The text provides clues to what is in the rooms around you, and graphics of the various tunnels show you where you can move next. As you track the Wumpus, you'll see the number of other players in the cave with you increase and decrease; you can even try to hit some of them with your arrows. Good luck with this simple but fast-paced and entertaining game.

Contact: Glenn Bresnahan, Boston University, *glenn@lobster.bu.edu*

Interactive Web Games

http://einstein.et.tudelft.nl/~mvdlaan/texts/www_games.html

This site connects you to tons of classic games, which you can play online. There's something for every interest and age level. Link to Web versions of Connect Four, Yahtzee, Hangman, TicTacToe, Othello, Name that Tune, Memory, Battleships, and Minesweeper. You'll find a WWW version of Mastermind, with four levels of play from beginner to expert. Check out several sliding tile puzzle games. Seven puzzles are available, and in one you can choose the pictures to make. Try out online brainteasers and crossword puzzles. You can also Telnet to games such as chess, Go, Scrabble, and Othello. Connect to many other interactive games on the Web. There are so many games to play here, this one site will keep you busy forever.

Contact: Marcel van der Laan, Computer Architecture Group, Delft University of Technology, *mvdlaan@duteca.et.tudelft.nl*

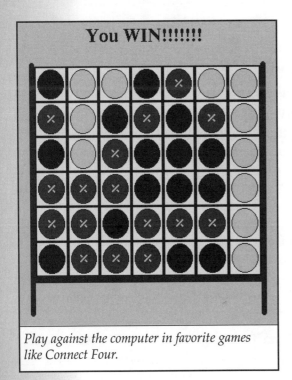

Play against the computer in favorite games like Connect Four.

Lego Information

http://legowww.homepages.com/

Lego fans will find all the information they need about the building blocks toy at this server. Catch a sneak preview of the newest product line, or find information on specific Lego sets, including parts lists. Lego designers show off their work through pictures of home-built construction projects. Lego trivia, such as a history of Lego and the

Lego theme song, is linked in. For more advanced builders, get rules for Lego games, such as Lego War, or instructions on how to build robots and other complicated projects. You can even learn how to power your Lego models with electricity or solar energy. A menu of special projects, such as animated movies and flight simulators, will provide enough ideas to fill up your spare time playing with Legos.

Contact: David Koblas, Lego Bricks Server, *koblas@netcom.com*

You'll find Legos spaceships, planes, and other constructions at the Legos home page.

Netrek

http://factoryx.factoryx.com/

Netrek is a 16-player, graphical, real-time battle simulator with a "Star Trek" theme, played over the Internet. At the WWW site, you'll find all the resources you need to begin playing, including a Netrek client that you can download through the site. Get started with Red Shirt's advice to beginners, an overview, a clue guide, and a FAQ. Basic rules, definitions, and hints are provided to familiarize you with playing. Then download the Netrek client, which can locate all games going on at many different servers and connect you to one to begin playing.

Contact: Jaime Pirnie, Netrek Home Page, *allister@factoryx.factoryx.com*

Okbridge

http://www.cts.com/~okbridge/

Okbridge is an Internet program that allows anyone anywhere on the Internet to play bridge together in real time. The program has created a 24-hour, global bridge club. Both beginners and professionals play bridge using this program, and at any time hundreds of people are playing together. From the WWW site, access a help file to learn how to play, and download the Okbridge program (for a subscription fee). You can even try the game out for free from here. You can also view a gallery of Okbridge players from around the world or connect to other bridge sites.

Contact: Dave DeMers and Matthew Clegg, CTS Network Services, *info@OKbridge.Com*

Riddler

http://www.riddler.com/

Riddler is the only entertainment network that gives you the opportunity to win cash and prizes while exploring the WWW. Playing any of the games at Riddler is free, so come in and start building your Networth while browsing fun sites. You do have to register to play any of the games, however. The game Tortoise and the Hare offers 150 trivia questions every three days to challenge your knowledge of the useless. Marlow's Crispy Challenge has three new puzzles every day for you to solve. The Quibbler sends you on a journey through the Web searching for clues to solve a riddle. Riddler's Choice 10K is a race involving some of the most exciting sites on the Web. Plus there are special pitfalls and deals along the way in all the games. You can always check out the current leaders, rules, and archives for any game. Be sure to read the rules first to understand how to play. The games are always changing, so you'll definitely want to put this site on your hotlist.

Contact: Interactive Imaginations, Riddler, *webmaster@www.riddler.com*

Try your luck with any of the challenging games at Riddler.

Role-Playing Games

http://www.acm.uiuc.edu/adnd/index.html

Gamers, look no further—here's the place for you. Get general info on role-playing games (RPGs), including an introduction and a FAQ. Download or use cool tools to make dungeon mastering a little easier. You'll find tools that create plots to spice up your game, generate random villages, and make random encounters and items. Visit a graveyard for dead characters, and memorialize your own favorite deceased hero or heroine. Post requests for games and players in a role-playing forum. You'll also find a dice roller, a spell book, a prayer book, and a list of cool character personalities. Link to home pages of many different RPGs, including Robotech, Shadow Run, Battletech, Magic, Werewolf, Vampire, and a list of free role-playing games created on the Net. Connect to discussion groups for Dungeons and Dragons, announcements of happenings in the role-playing world, a marketplace for role-playing game materials, and archives of fantasy stories. When you're not busy adventuring, you'll definitely want to explore this site.

Contact: Michael P. Duff, Association for Computing Machinery, University of Illinois at Urbana-Champaign, *duff@mcs.com*

Virtual Mystery Theater

http://www.coolsite.com/intro.html

Interact with the computer and use your creative genius to solve an online mystery. The multimedia mystery uses image maps, database searches, sounds, videos, interactive forms, passwords, and anything else you can do with your WWW browser to provide clues to the solution. Remember to follow every link, and write down every clue. Each month features a different mystery for you to solve. You'll have lots of fun playing this online game that requires all your brainpower.

Contact: Berry INFOCom, *dberry@packet.net*

Click around to find some clues......

Hunt for clues to solve a mystery in the Virtual Mystery Theater.

Web Games

http://inferno.cs.bris.ac.uk/~gid/games.html

This collection of interactive games makes use of the graphics and linking capabilities of the Web to provide you with a fun time. All of the games here even have a text-only version, except for the Cube, so you can play them with any WWW browser. If you like Tetris, you'll love Webtris. Webtris is different from the classic computer game in that everyone is playing on the same grid with the same piece at the same time, so that the game becomes a battle of bandwidth and network lag. Play a Rubick's Cube-type game where you try to solve the cube puzzle so that each side has only one color. The trick is that everyone is solving the same cube, so you can mess it up when other people are playing or solve it cooperatively. Also try out a classic marbles solitaire game or a Blobs strategy game that you play against the computer. The development of even more games is in progress, so keep checking here.

Contact: Tom Gidden, Kaleidoscope Graphics Group, University of Bristol, *gid@inferno.cs.bris.ac.uk*

WWW Addict's Pop-Culture Scavenger Hunt

http://www.galcit.caltech.edu/~ta/hunt/wwwhunt.html

Test both your WWW and pop-culture knowledge with this fun game. Each of the four levels consists of a series of questions that leads you all around the pop-culture sites on the Web. You'll find easy, medium, hard, and impossible questions that will really test your WWW know-how. The questions cover such topics as music, entertainment, and the WWW, and all the answers can be found somewhere on the Web.

Contact: Creative Internet, Graduate Aeronautical Laboratories, California Institute of Technology, *aure@galcit.caltech.edu* or *joe@galcit.caltech.edu*

Your Wacky WWW Adventure

http://ugweb.cs.ualberta.ca/~hubick/adventure/adventure.cgi

This is an interactive choose-your-own-adventure game that allows you not only to read the adventure but also to add choices that others may follow as well. On each page you'll see tons of choices added by players. Follow them to see what happens. When you get to a dead end, you can be creative and add a choice. Warning: racy language and adult situations.

Contact: Chris Hubick, Undergraduate Laboratories, University of Alberta, *hubick@cs.ualberta.ca*

For more games, visit these sites:

Aces Over the Internet

http://www.zdnet.com/~gaming/features/9510/f1/main.html

This page discusses various flight simulator games.

Crosswords FAQ

http://www.cis.ohio-state.edu/hypertext/faq/bngusenet/rec/puzzles/crosswords/top.html

This FAQ (frequently asked questions) file helps you with solving and creating crossword puzzles, including pointers to downloadable software, books, dictionaries, and tips. You can also learn more about the crossword competitions held on the newsgroup *rec.puzzles.crosswords*.

French Tarot

http://www.cs.man.ac.uk/card-games/tarot/frtarot.html

French Tarot is not a fortune-telling device, but a game played with Tarot cards. This page tells you how to play it.

The Game Room

http://www.kdcol.com/~val/games/index.html

This site contains the rules and definitions of various tabletop games, including chess variants and Eastern abstract games.

Games Questions and Answers

http://www.cis.ohio-state.edu/hypertext/faq/usenet-faqs/bygroup/rec/games/misc/top.html

This is the FAQ archive for the miscellaneous games newsgroup *rec.games.misc*. Here you'll find lots of FAQs about all aspects of gaming online. There are FAQs about instructions for specific network games, a guide to the online gaming world, and the top 100 video games, plus many more useful topics.

Hand and Foot

http://world.std.com/~ssimpson/handfoot.html

This page gives a description and the rules for a card game.

National and Regional Card Games

http://www.cs.man.ac.uk/card-games/national.html

This site discusses card games in many different countries. If you've ever wondered what they play in the Czech Republic, this is a place to find out.

On the Edge

http://www.io.com/~presage/faq.html

This page gives a description and the rules for the game, On the Edge, a trading card game.

The Puzzle Page

http://www.ditell.com/~ericward/puzzle.html

With word puzzles, riddles, math riddles, etc., this site might be more suited for adults. Poor background color choice made it difficult to read.

Rage Unlimited Edition Rules

http://www.uni-karlsruhe.de/~rz71/Private/WoD/Misc/rage.rule.html

This page gives information on the card game, Rage Unlimited. This card game is based on a popular werewolf role-playing game.

Susan

http://www.stephen.com/sue/sue.html

Susan, a subtle board game for one or two and a computer. Downloadable freeware.

Tempest of the Gods

http://mxn117.rh.psu.edu/~spud/gamer/bdp.htm

This page describes the game, Tempest of the Gods. In this game you play a tribe attempting to establish your god's pantheon as the dominant power. Any resemblence to current conservative U.S. politicians is probably coincidental.

Trading Card Games

http://www.pvv.unit.no/~toriver/deckmaster.html

This page lists and gives descriptions of many of the more popular trading card games. It also lists the producers.

WWW Entertainment Pack

http://www.dbai.tuwien.ac.at/cgi-bin/entpack

Download shareware and freeware, including Othello and Connect Four. Everything is free, but registration is required.

Hobbies

American Wine on the Web

http://www.2way.com:80/food/wine/

American Wine on the Web is an electronic magazine that reports on wine, wineries, people, and events of the rapidly growing wine regions around the United States and the Americas. The editorial stance is that wine is an everyday drink with everyday food for everyday people and that American wines are among the best in the world. Features include interviews, editorials, letters and opinions, wine in restaurants, quotables, and wine festival reports. You can read wine country reports by regional editors featuring wineries, people, events, and reviews of wines from the Southwest, the Midwest, the Southeast, Northern California, the Pacific Northwest, and Southern California. A wine glossary describes different kinds of wine, including the region where the wine is produced and descriptors. The e-zine is easy and fun to read and has just enough pictures. Look at the table of contents for new features; the contents are always changing. From here, you can also connect to the Food Center, a starting point for a tour of food and beverage sites on the WWW.

Contact: American Wine, 2 Way Systems, *wine@2way.com*

Candlemaking

http://www.interaccess.com/users/bmolo/

Get the basics for making candles here. First learn the right way to burn a candle (yes, there is a right way, according to this page). Then find out what you need to make candles, learn how to correctly melt wax, and discover what to use for molds. You'll even learn how to clean up. The page teaches an easy way to make candles with materials found around the house. After learning the basics of making candles, get some cool candlemaking ideas. You'll learn how to sandblast, make homemade chunk candles, and create ice candles. There's also a candle store here where you can order candles, but it's probably more fun to make your own.

Contact: Candles You Can Burn, Ltd., InterAccess, *bmolo@interacces.com*

Learn how to make your own candles at the candlemaking site.

Gardening and Landscaping

http://www.btw.com/garden.htm

Gardeners love this useful site. Here you'll find the tip and plant of the month to keep your garden looking beautiful. A 3D landscape garden contest lets you see online what fellow garden enthusiasts are doing. You'll also find tips and hints to create your own 3D landscape. Access a complete guide to gardening, divided by subject and searchable. Here you'll learn all the basics, including fertilizers, pest control, and seed starting. You can also order gardening books from the site or get phone numbers for organizations providing gardening products and services. Finally, a directory of related sites will point you toward tons of online gardening information, including catalogs and supplies, botanical gardens, and garden arts and letters.

Contact: Books That Work, *webmaster@btw.com*

Juggling Information Service

http://www.hal.com/services/juggle/

If you juggle or want to juggle, you have to come here. Get help with learning how to juggle and fabulous juggling tricks. There's a collection of juggling photos, drawings, and videos for you to look at. Shop for juggling supplies at various online stores. Tap into an archive of *Juggler's World* magazine for facts, help, tips, and interesting reading. An archive of the newsgroup *rec.juggling* includes a FAQ all about juggling. Find out about juggling festivals and clubs—perhaps there's one near you. A fun collection of juggling references in books, videos, articles, movies, and TV includes some good advice from Ren and Stimpy, a list of movies with juggling scenes, and a catalog of juggling-related books and videotapes. There are even juggling software programs you can download, including juggling simulators and tutorials. The whole site is searchable so you can find exactly what you're looking for among the loads of juggling information and multimedia fun.

Contact: Juggling Information Service, HAL Computer Systems, *juggle@hal.com*

Kite Site

http://www.latrobe.edu.au/Glenn/KiteSite/Kites.html

You'll find kites galore at this fun site, with pictures of all kinds of single, dual, or stunt kites. Each picture includes a short description of the type of kite. The caption also describes how the kite flies and who designed it. Just click on the small thumbnail to see the full-size picture. Get close to details of flying Deltas, Chinese dragons, Genkis, parafoils, and spinsocks. If you don't know what those terms mean, don't worry—the pictures are fun to look at for kite fliers and non-kite fliers alike. Check out some pictures of kites doing cool stunts. There are also pictures of kite buggying. This new sport involves sitting in a three-wheeled buggy and being towed by a power kite—it looks like fun. To see for yourself, check out pictures of kite buggies and buggying in action. You can also read the Buggy News newsletter to learn more about the sport. From here, connect to the *rec.kites* newsgroup for kites discussion and to other online kite pictures.

Contact: Jason Hellwege, La Trobe University, *J.Hellwege@latrobe.edu.au*

Let's go fly a kite!

Origami

http://www.cs.ubc.ca/spider/jwu/origami.html

Learn all about the art of paper folding at this fun Web page. Go to the Origami Photo Gallery for a display of impressive origami work. Connect to origami information such as a history of the art, origami associations, and the origami mailing list. Get started on your own origami activities with files and diagrams you can download to your hard drive, print out, and use. There's also a great shareware Windows program on how to fold paper airplanes. You'll find links to many more origami diagrams, articles, and home pages for loads more paper-folding fun. Join the origami mailing list to get your origami fix every day. You can share origami patterns and tips or just talk about origami all day long.

Contact: Joseph Wu, University of British Columbia Computer Sciences Department, *jwu@cs.ubc.ca*

An origami Dimetrodon on display in the Origami Photo Gallery.

The Recipe Folder

http://english-server.hss.cmu.edu/Recipes.html

You'll find all the recipes you need to cook a stellar meal at this one site. The focus is on vegetarian recipes, with a great collection culled from all over the Internet. You can also get information on vegetarian matters, including a FAQ, a list of vege-friendly organizations, and environmental data. Meat-eaters are not left out entirely, however—try out a range of meat recipes for chicken, beef, fish, pork, turkey, rabbit, and lamb. Other recipes, arranged by subject, include salads, sauces, casseroles, noodle and rice dishes, breads, appetizers, comfort foods, and beverages. Don't overlook the dessert section, with recipes for "healthy" cookies, Neiman-Marcus cookies, and truffles. The section on regional dishes includes Italian, Oriental, and Tex-Mex. After visiting this site, you'll never need to buy a cookbook again.

Contact: Recipe Folder, English-Server, Carnegie Mellon University, *terri@english-server.hss.cmu.edu*

Restaurant Le Cordon Bleu

http://sunsite.unc.edu/expo/restaurant/restaurant.html

This exhibit of French culinary arts is bound to make you ravenous by the time you finish paging through. The site is a collection of recipes taught at Le Cordon Bleu cooking school by master chefs, representing classical French cuisine. After reading a history of the school, choose from a week's worth of full menus. One sample menu might be split-pea soup with bacon, sorrel, and lettuce for starters, puff pastry cases stuffed with salmon and asparagus in a lemon butter sauce, and, for dessert, chocolate meringue cake filled with chocolate mousse. Each menu is linked to recipes for the dishes featured. You'll definitely want to try them all after viewing the full-color photographs of selected dishes that accompany them.

Contact: EXPO, Frans van Hoesel, SunSITE, University of North Carolina at Chapel Hill, *hoesel@chem.rug.nl*

Scale Model Home Page

http://msowww.anu.edu.au/~dfk/scale_model.html

This page tells you everything you could want to know about building model anythings, such as model cars, ships, and planes. Get tips from model-building experts on techniques such as airbrushing, gluing, decals, painting, and more. A color digest helps you match colors and find out what colors to use for painting your models. Read reviews and announcements of new model kits to help you decide what to buy, and download some kit plans to use. Take a look at displays of various modeling accessories to choose which to buy. You can also browse through a gallery of finished models and submit pictures of your models. You'll find listings of model clubs, model shops, mail-order shops, and kit manufacturers. An online course for beginners introduces you to modeling tools, construction, painting, finishing techniques, detailing, presentation, and display. You can also learn advanced building techniques. When you've finished looking at the page, connect to other modeling pages on the WWW.

Contact: Daniel Koehne, Mount Stromlo and Siding Spring Observatories, *dfk@mso.anu.edu.au*

Check out model airplanes and more at the Scale Model Home Page.

Weekly Crafts Project

http://mineral.galleries.com/annie/auntannie.htm

This site features a new crafts project every week, so you'll want to visit again and again. First check out the project of the week. Follow every step of the easy instructions to make the craft of the week. Each step links to a separate page with illustrations of what you do in that step. You can also link to related sites and books about the project. Look for new projects coming soon that you'll want to do, as well as recent projects you may want to try. You'll learn how to make 3D toys, paper projects, games, puppets, and more. You can also download a Windows shareware program with lots of crafts activities on it for you to do, as well as stories, poems, ideas, facts, and fun.

Contact: Aunt Annie's Crafts, Amethyst Galleries, *Aunt.Annie@dnaco.net*

The World of Internet Amateur Radio

http://www.acs.ncsu.edu/HamRadio/

All types of "hams" enjoy this informative site. The News Line feature provides the latest news in the amateur-radio world. You'll also find lots of information for both novice and experienced radio amateurs, including listings of organizations, technical information, and other resources, all searchable by keyword. The satellite news section includes an interactive form that helps you predict when a satellite will next fly over your location. Another interactive form lets you look up radio call signs. For those trying to get their licenses, FCC rules and regulations are provided, and you can even take a quiz to prepare for the exam. You can also download amateur-radio software, connect to newsgroups, or search for other hams on the Internet.

Contact: Lou Williams, North Carolina State University, *nsyslaw@acs.ncsu.edu*

World Wide Quilting Page

http://ttsw.com/MainQuiltingPage.html

Meet all your quilting information needs at this one site. Start with a brief history of quilting and some basic instructions. Then move on to more advanced techniques, such as a blocks page that shows graphics of various patterns and provides instructions for completing them. Directions for foundation-block piecing are accompanied by a collection of foundation blocks you can print out and use right away. At the design board, see computer-designed quilts and photos of real quilts created by users of the Quilting Page. You can also meet artists and teachers or connect to a bulletin board for questions, hints, and other information posted by visitors to the site. Download quilt-design software or computer-generated templates and foundations. There is even an ideas database to get you going on your own project.

Contact: Eric and Sue Traudt, T & T Software, *QHomePage@ttsw.com*

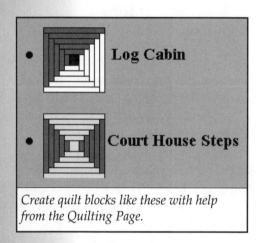

Create quilt blocks like these with help from the Quilting Page.

World-Wide Webs

http://www.ece.ucdavis.edu/~darsie/string.html

On this page, you'll find a collection of string figures from around the world. (String figures are designs you create by weaving string around your fingers.) The page teaches you how to create all the intricate string figures shown, with complete instructions and diagrams. Read descriptions of positions and movements for making the string figures. Learn some common openings and endings. Try out the beginner's string figures to get started. After mastering those, move on to more advanced string figures. Warning: This is a long page with lots of pictures that can take a while to download; save it to your hard drive for quick access.

Contact: Richard Darsie, Electrical and Computer Engineering Department, University of California at Davis, *darsie@ece.ucdavis.edu*

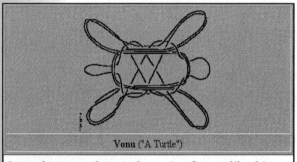

Vonu ("A Turtle")

Learn how to make complex string figures like this one at World Wide Webs.

For more information on hobbies, visit these sites:

The Arie Foundation

http://mchip00.med.nyu.edu/student-org/arie/arie.html

This site allows users to make a tax-deductible donation of baseball cards, football cards, and other sports cards and collectibles to terminally ill hospitalized children.

Atlas Online

http://www.atlasrr.com/atlasrr/

This site contains information on many aspects of model railroad constructing, designing, and enhancing. There's a catalog and a company that wouldn't mind if you bought their railroad products, but there's lots of good free information.

Beer Styles

http://www.dma.be/p/bier/0_3_uk.htm

This page covers different aspects of beer, in a manner similar to that of a wine-tasting page. Types of beer are listed, with a short description, and links to more information about each.

Birding in New England

http://www.iii.net/users/pdragon/birding.html

This site contains information on birding, including why, where (spots in New England), bird stories, and various tips and resources.

Birds at Selected Parks

http://ice.ucdavis.edu/US_National_Park_Service/NPS_birds.html

This site, from the U.S. National Park Service, lists birds one might find at various parks thoughout the United States. There is also additional information on birds at the end of the very long list of parks.

Bird-Watching

http://www.intac.com/man/faq/birds-faq/wild-birds

The FAQ (frequently asked questions) for the Usenet newsgroup *rec.birds* is perfect for the bird-watching enthusiast. This file answers questions about identifying wild birds, conservation, research into bird life, ethics for birders, equipment, good places to bird-watch, and recommendations for field guides.

Common Sense Design's Home Page

http://www.hevanet.com/berniew/index.htm

Where you can build a better boat than you can buy! This page contains information, both general and ordering, for building your own boat. While there is an order form at the end of the page, the page is worth looking at for anyone wondering what is involved in boat building.

Crafts FAQ

http://www.cis.ohio-state.edu/hypertext/faq/bngusenet/rec/crafts/misc/top.html

In this FAQ, you'll find frequently asked questions from the newsgroup *rec.crafts.misc* with answers on materials, painting, knitting, pottery, paper airplanes, crafts ideas for younger kids, and much more.

The Cyber-Plantsman

http://mirror.wwa.com/mirror/garden/cyberplt.htm#plants

This site has listings of plant societies, books, and garden-related events, as well as articles, plant descriptions, and money-saving tips. A good gardening resource.

Don't Panic It's All Organic

http://rain.org/~sals/my.html

This site discusses what organic food is and how to grow it. There are also links to other organic farm sites.

Epicurious

http://www.epicurious.com/epicurious/home.html

This is a site for everyone who really likes food. Discover where to go and what to eat when on vacation. Find out how to choose really ripe, fresh vegetables.

Food & Drink

http://www.gulf.net/~vbraun/food.html

This site contains links to cocktails, food, vegetarian recipes, restaurants, and other food-related pages. There is even a link to the Internet Law Library Code of Federal Regulations where you can find out what the U.S. standard on caramel is.

The Fuji Publishing Group Wine Page

http://www.netins.net/showcase/fujiwine/

This page covers wine shops, wine events, wine art, and other items that might interest wine afficianados.

The Garden Gate

http://www.prairienet.org/ag/garden/homepage.htm

This site contains links to a large number of garden-related sites, from online gardening magazines to the Sun Room, a page that explains how not to kill your houseplants.

The Gardener's Reading Room

http://www.prairienet.org/ag/garden/readroom.htm

This site contains links to many garden-related online zines, books, and magazines. It also includes links to plant catalogs and book reviews.

The Garlic Page

http://broadcast.com/garlic/index.htm

This page has recipies, news, and growing tips for garlic lovers.

Good Woodworking

http://www.futurenet.co.uk/crafts/goodwoodworking.html

This page describes a magazine that gives technical tips and suggestions on woodworking. Also included are reports on woodworking events and a list of contents in past issues.

Harvest Report '95

http://www.2way.com/food/wine/daily/harvest.html

This harvest report covers wine grape crop information, broken down by U.S. crop location. Great stuff for the wine-lover or for wine neophites who want to sprinkle their party conversation with phrases about the temperature fluxuations in California and their effect on Chardonney.

Herbs & Spices

http://www.teleport.com/~ronl/herbs.html

This site has an index of herbs and spices, recipes, information on growing herbs and spices, and a bit of historical trivia about them.

Hobbies and Sports

http://euclid.math.fsu.edu/FunStuff/hobbies.html

This site has links to many different hobby sites. If you aren't sure where to find a kite site or a homebrew archive, check here first.

The Hobby Centre

http://www.comprez.com/hobby/

This is a hobby catalog, with a wide range of products. It also has links to other hobby-related sites.

Hobby Madness

http://pckiso3.cs.shinshu-u.ac.jp/hobby/index-e.html

This is the hobby site of three college-age gents. It has decent music bites, a recipe, some comedy, and some cute icons.

Homebrewing Homepage

http://oeonline.com/~pbabcock/brew.html

This site contains a flea market for brewing equipment, cartoons, beer-related links, and information on homebrew clubs.

Internet Resources for Gardeners

http://mirror.wwa.com/mirror/garden/94/gs941127.htm

This site will help serious gardeners find any garden-related thing available on the Net. From Virtual Garden Tours to newsgroups and catalogs, this site provides links to all kinds of green hot spots.

Jayne's Cyber Cookbook

http://turnpike.net/metro/sapphyr/cookbook.htm

This site has recipies, cooking basics, and various conversion charts, all in easily understood prose. Good for the beginning cook.

Kite Flier's Site

http://twoshakes.kfs.org/kites/

A very cool Web site full of kite stuff.

Maelstrom Hobby's Website

http://www.bdt.com/home/mhobby/Welcome.html

This site introduces and promotes Maelstrom's gaming systems and other hobby-oriented products. It also serves as a link to other interesting Web sites, from an "X-Files" site to an anime picture archive.

The Magazine for Wooden Boat Owners and Designers

http://media1.hypernet.com/WoodenBoat.html

This page doesn't actually include a wooden boat magazine, but it does tell you how to order one and what is in the latest issue. Also, this page has links to wooden boat clubs and includes an order form for a free wooden boat catalog.

Plane Watching

http://www.dorsai.org/~aileron/planes.html

This page lists various airports across the United States and tells where the best spots to plane-watch near them are.

The Potter's Page

http://www.aztec.co.za/users/theo/

This site has practical information for both beginning and advanced potters. There's even a glaze calculation software for the user to download, as well as event and exhibition lists.

QRZ Home Page

http://www.qrz.com/

This site has lots of information for ham radio hobbyists, including a callsign database, an FTP server full of radio-related files, and a list of online amateur radio sites.

Rainbow Non-sports & Entertainment Holiday Catalog

http://www.wwcd.com/rainbow/rcc_nonsport.html

This is a hobby catalog devoted to card collectors. It has an extensive list of available cards.

Too Easy Gourmet

http://www.halcyon.com/wturner/2ez/basic.html

This page is for the truly kitchen-ignorant. There are several instructions on simple cooking activities, but the one that sums it up is the one for boiling water. Fill pot with cold water and place on stove (open side up). Turn burner under pot on high. When water boils, lower heat to medium high. Open side up? Who needs to have that pointed out?

The Vegetarian Pages

http://catless.ncl.ac.uk/Vegetarian/

This site serves as a guide to vegetarian interests on the Internet. It has links to veg-specific news, events, veggie FAQs, and organizations.

Wedding Gardens

http://www.olympus.net/gardens/gwedd.htm

This site lists and links various city gardens that can be used for weddings. Included with each is a brief description of the garden and contact (snail mail and/or phone) information for each location.

Wines on the Internet: CyberCalendar of Wine Events

http://www.wines.com/events1.html

This site lists wine-related events, including dates and physical locations.

The Woodworking Catalog

http://www.woodworking.com/

This site provides links to various woodworking manufacturers and artists. It has some free services for woodworkers interested in promoting their work, as well as some commercial services.

Humor

Calvin and Hobbes Gallery

http://eos.kub.nl:2080/calvin_hobbes/

This home page is devoted entirely to the Calvin and Hobbes comic strip. At the site, you'll find a gallery of Calvin and Hobbes cartoons in color and in black and white. Buttons make it easy to page through the gallery or return to the main page. There are also two Calvin and Hobbes stories composed of serial strips: The Ultimate Detective Story and How to Write a Term Paper. Get a biography of author Bill Watterson and a Calvin and Hobbes bibliography, complete with pictures of book covers. You'll also find news about the strip and Watterson. If you don't want to walk through the whole gallery, you can jump to an index of images in alphabetical order, over fifty images in all. If you haven't gotten your Calvin and Hobbes fix from this site, connect to the JumpStation with links to Calvin and Hobbes Web sites, FTP archives, and newsgroups.

Contact: Egon Verharen, Infolab, *egon@kub.nl*

For a daily dose of Calvin and Hobbes, make this site a daily ritual.

Doctor Fun

http://www.unitedmedia.com/comics/drfun

Laugh at the Internet's own daily cartoon at the world-famous Doctor Fun site. The single-panel, color cartoon—the Internet's own "Far Side"—has been distributed every day over the Internet since September 1993. Start with today's Doctor Fun cartoon, which you can view in 24-bit, full-color, JPEG format. At the WWW site you will find a FAQ about the cartoon and gain access to the Doctor Fun archive.

Contact: Dave Farley, United Media, *dgf1@midway.uchicago.edu*

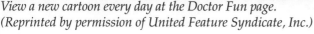

View a new cartoon every day at the Doctor Fun page.
(Reprinted by permission of United Feature Syndicate, Inc.)

The Dilbert Zone

http://www.unitedmedia.com/comics/dilbert/

Dilbert, by cartoonist Scott Adams, is fast becoming popular worldwide. Here you can get your Dilbert fix for free. Come back every day for a new Dilbert. Also visit a two-week Dilbert archive. Extras include a Scott Adams interview, a prehistory of the cartoon, and a photo tour of how Dilbert is created. You can read the Dilbert news-letter, get descriptions of characters in the cartoon, and find a news-paper in your area carrying Dilbert. Even more humorous articles are provided, so take the time to browse.

Contact: Scott Adams, United Media,

webmaster@unitedmedia.com

LaughWeb

http://www.misty.com/laughweb/

How many Microsoft engineers does it take to screw in a light bulb? None, they just define darkness as an industry standard. You'll find this joke and hundreds of others in this constantly growing online humor collection. The archives include Barney jokes, business and computer humor, political jokes, redneck jokes, and many others. Check out the laugh of the week, or look at In the News for current events humor. The Life Archive features a collection of "clean" jokes. You'll find complete scripts for comedy movies in Movie Scripts. An added bonus are warning labels that will steer you away from poten-tially offensive jokes containing strong language, sexually risque jokes, or sexist, religious, or disgusting humor. There is also a hotlist of other humor resources on the WWW.

Contact: Jascha Franklin-Hodge, Internet Market Services, *joeschmoe@world.std.com*

NetComix

http://www.phlab.missouri.edu/~c617145/comix.html

This comprehensive list is dedicated to Internet comics, comic strips, sequential art, one-panel cartoons, and editorial cartoons. The huge list is arranged alphabetically; click on the letter to jump to that point in the alphabet, or search the entire page. Most of the links are to external Internet resources, making this a large comics directory. Entries include the Art Comics Project (an ongoing weekly exhibit of comic strips by various artists), the Calvin and Hobbes archives, Dilbert, Doctor Fun, The Far Side, Fox Trot, Al Gore's cartoon gal-lery, the Mask, NetBoy, Underground Comic Reviews, and the *Wall*

Street Journal cartoons. Some of the links go to home pages, some to archives, and some are original cartoons created by Internet artists; you have to explore, but you're sure to have fun doing it. And don't forget to check out the Comic of the Week.

Contact: Christian Cosas, University of Missouri Physics Lab, *c617145@cclabs.missouri.edu*

Wrecked Humor Page

http://www.infi.net/~cashman/humor/

Access humor resources gathered from all over the Internet at this mega-humor site. Loads of canonical lists of jokes are linked in, including Michael Jackson jokes, lawyer jokes, Steven Wright jokes, O.J. Simpson jokes—you get the idea. You'll even find a canonical list of funny Unix commands that you can try out yourself; for example, ask your Unix system:

```
% If I had a ( for every $ Congress spent, what would I have?
```

And the computer will reply:

```
Too many ('s
```

In the miscellaneous humor archive, you'll discover such gems as parodies of the "I Love You" Barney song and the twelve commandments of flaming. Access top ten lists, the humor form inspired by David Letterman. Hilarious parodies include the "Star Trek: Voyager" theme song, and the Ballad of O. J. Simpson. If you exhaust all the jokes stored in this archive, you can connect from the site to other humor resources on the Internet.

Contact: Derek Cashman, InfiNet, *cashman@infi.net*

For more laughs, visit these sites:

The Atomic Cafe

http://www.sfn.saskatoon.sk.ca/current/atomic/

This page has lots of clever quotes and amusing laws. Worth a glance and a chuckle.

Binch

http://www.binch.com/

This is a humor magazine with such topics as the Power Ranger Scandal and short stories for short-minded people.

Computer Humor Page

http://www.students.uiuc.edu/~roth/comp_humor/

This page has jokes about Unix, Microsoft, and other cybertopics. If you can access this page, then you'll probably get most of the jokes.

Evil Little Brother's Excuse Generator

http://www.dtd.com/excuse

Get semi-personalized excuses for everything from skipping class to burning down someone's house. Especially fun is the excuse for, "So, you want your PowerBook back."

The Firesign Theatre

http://www.wam.umd.edu/~ljason/www/firesign.html

The Firesign Theatre is a comedy group that has been performing for years and now has their own Web site. If you've ever wondered just what they were singing, here's the place to find out.

The House of Socks

http://www.caprica.com/~jmares/house_of_socks.html/

This site leads the user through a mental sock search. Sort of.

Hypertext Humor Archives

http://www.synapse.net/~oracle/Contents/MM-Archives.html

This site has humor on everything from computers to movie scripts to general weirdness to men and women. (Note: Some rated PG-13 stuff.)

John and Rob's Evolution in Action

http://iquest.com/~rfreynol/ev/

This page contains many examples of how some of the more gratuitously stupid people in the human race take themselves out of the gene pool.

The Mole Hole Comedy Page

http://pubweb.acns.nwu.edu/~bi1874/comedy/comedy.html

This page contains computer and "Star Trek" humor, college humor, philosophical humor, and miscellaneous amusement. The question, "Why isn't 'phonetic' spelled the way it sounds?" still keeps me up nights.

Murphy's Laws and Corollaries

http://dmawww.epfl.ch/roso.mosaic/dm/murphy.html

Think you know all the aspects of Murphy's Law? Think again. Then check out this site to see the 112 you missed.

100 Ways to Confuse Your Roommate

http://www.mps.org/~rainbow/Words/ConfuseRoommate.html

This page lists 100 things you can do to drive your roommate nuts. It's funny, even if you don't have a roommate.

The Online Adventures of Ken and Glenn

http://www.xso.com/viva/

This site chronicles Ken and Glenn's attempts to combat boredom in the mid-Atlantic coast area. Check it out for instructions on polite moshing, among other things.

The Quote Book

http://www.iii.net/users/pdragon/qbook.html

This page is a list of quotes from a couple of college-age, or college-age-minded, people. It's surprisingly funny, although there is some profanity.

Rainbow Humor Page

http://www.columbia.edu/~sss31/humor.html

This page contains stories, jokes, messages for answering machines, and some R-rated jokes.

Too Much Coffee Man

http://college.antioch.edu/~pbradley/tmcm/

See Too Much Coffee Man take on his vilest enemies. Discover locations for great coffee. Tell others the location and type of your favorite coffee.

United Media

http://www.unitedmedia.com/

United Media publishes the largest collection of comic strips and editorial cartoons on the Web, including Dilbert, Peanuts, and the Inkwell.

Magazines

Alternative X

http://www.altx.com/

Alternative X is an electronic publishing company focused on the '90s alternative and countercultural scene. Founded by avant-pop novelist, musician, and essayist Mark Amerika, Alternative X features publications created by people actively engaged in the world of alternative art, writing, music, philosophy, electronic media, and anything else that's creative and alternative.

Contact: Alternative X, *x@altx.com*

Boing Boing

http://www.zeitgeist.net/Public/Boing-boing/

Boing Boing dubs itself "a blueprint for the flip side of serious culture." Published quarterly, it covers the fringes of pop and cyberculture. At the Web site, visit a gallery of comic art, read articles from past issues, and access online exclusives. You'll also find excerpts from the zine's first book, *The Happy Mutant Handbook.*

Contact: Boing Boing, Zeitgeist, *kreth@well.com*

Depth Probe

http://www.atdesign.com:80/~ake/cgi/reel/base/Studios/Eyzaguirre/

This highly Webified e-zine publishes original reviews and commentary on a wide range of topics. At the Web site, read the latest issue or access back issues with themes such as Electric Zen and Elvis Is Dead. Check out special editions that are outside of the normal weekly publication, or learn how to join the Depth Probe mailing list. You can also view a gallery of electronic art published in the magazine or leave your comments in an interactive guestbook.

Contact: Alan Eyzaguirre, @design, *ake@best.com*

Electronic Newsstand

http://www.enews.com/

This WWW interface to a huge Gopher library provides free access to a wide range of interesting articles from the world's leading publications and useful information from prestigious companies. As at a traditional newsstand, you are invited to browse at no charge through many publications. Every publisher listed in the newsstand provides a table of contents and several articles from the current issue of the magazine, journal, or periodical featured; after browsing, you can order single issues or a subscription. When you enter the newsstand, click on the "introduction" link to find out what's new, how to participate, and background information. Then browse all the titles, or search articles for specific keywords. You'll find lots of titles, including *Business Week, Discover, Games, National Review, The New Yorker, New*

Age Journal, Smithsonian, and *The Whole Earth Review.* The titles are divided by subject for easier browsing. Also featured at the newsstand are a Merchandise Mart, offering an assortment of products and services; an electronic car showroom, showcasing automobile publications, buyer's guides, and car manufacturers; and an electronic bookstore, where you can connect to publishers' catalogs.

Contact: Electronic Newsstand, *comments@enews.com*

HotWired

http://www.wired.com/

Quickly becoming the magazine of choice for many Netizens, HotWired covers issues relating to cyberspace, information technology, the communications industry, and alternative lifestyles. After becoming a member (it's free), you can access many directories of articles. Find reviews of technological products, news about the communications industry, and a gossip column. Travel around the globe, or explore issues affecting society. Visit the Piazza to interactively share comments and ideas, play in the HotWired MUD, or just rant and rave. Wander among a vast gallery of electronic art, or access the electronic sports channel. You can also read back issues of *Wired* magazine here.

Contact: Wired, *www@wired.com*

Hotwired is quickly becoming the hot magazine for Netizens.

InterText

http://ftp.etext.org/Zines/InterText/intertext.html

InterText is an electronically distributed magazine of fiction read by thousands of people on six continents. It has been in publication since March 1991, and a new issue comes out every two months. At the WWW site, you can read the current issue or access back issues from a volume library. You can also choose specific stories from a list indexed by author. You'll find in the magazine a large selection of original fiction, as well as regular columns from the editor and assistant editor. Use an interactive form at the site to subscribe to notices of new and upcoming issues. Don't miss this most established of all the Internet fiction e-zines.

Contact: Jason Snell and Geoff Duncan, ETEXT Archives, *editors@intertext.com*

Read the best original fiction on the WWW in InterText.

Hypermedia Zine List

http://www.meer.net/~johnl/e-zine-list/index.html

Zines are small, do-it-yourself publications on any topic of interest. Recently, hundreds of zines have moved onto the Internet since it costs much less to produce an electronic zine than to produce a print zine. Zines in this electronic format are popularly referred to online as *e-zines*. Even though there are so many e-zines online, they can still be hard to track down. Fortunately, this site provides a one-stop shop for e-zine access. You'll find an alphabetical list of over 600 electronic zines, located on Web, Gopher, Telnet, and FTP sites, or available through e-mail or Usenet groups. This list also includes other zine-related resources, such as Usenet newsgroups about zines.

Contact: John Labovitz, MeerNet, *johnl@meer.net*

International Teletimes

http://www.teletimes.com/

This Best of the Net winner is a global news and culture electronic magazine offered in several different languages. Each issue covers a specific theme; some recent themes have been favorite authors, travel, TV and film, history, and the environment. All back issues are archived by subject. You can also read regular columns on cuisine and wine, as well as short fiction. The magazine presents viewpoints of writers from all over the Internet to cover a variety of geographic and cultural perspectives on the topic.

Contact: Ian Wojtowicz, editor-in-chief, International Teletimes, *editor@teletimes.com*

Read about people and places all over the Internet in International Teletimes. (Copyright 1994 International Teletimes.)

Journals and Newspapers

http://english-server.hss.cmu.edu/Journals.html

Here you can browse a massive, free electronic newsstand. Access electronic editions of print magazines as well as e-zines on a variety of subjects. Links are provided to magazines ranging from *American Demographics, The New Yorker,* and *Internet World* to *The New Republic, Swanee Review,* and *The Village Voice.* Over 60 publications are available as well as an alphabetical listing of other journals accessible through the Internet.

Contact: English-Server, Carnegie Mellon University, *webmaster@english.hss.cmu.edu*

Labyrinth Electronic Publishing Project

http://www.honors.indiana.edu/lepp/index.html

For an interesting e-zine, don't miss this unique online experiment to publish creative writing and art produced by students and faculty at Indiana University. Access chapbooks of poetry by both undergraduates and faculty, all of which can be electronically searched. There is also an interesting collection of anonymous poetry. A gallery features visual art from selected artists. After viewing the pieces on exhibit, you can comment on a work or read comments others have made. You can also order print versions of *Labyrinth*, an annual publication, directly through e-mail. Connect from here to other creative sites on the Internet.

Contact: Labyrinth, Honors Division of Indiana University, *lepp@honors.indiana.edu*

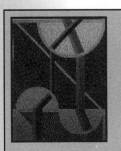

Something Like That

Gouache on 100% rag board
30 inches by 38 inches

Comment on Something Like That
View comments on Something Like That

Become an art critic at the online gallery for the Labyrinth Electronic Publishing Project. (Copyright 1994 Honors Division of Indiana University.)

Mother Jones

http://www.mojones.com/mojo_magazine.html

The print magazine of social activism and current events comes online. *Mother Jones* covers topics such as the environment, politics, crime, and so forth, and calls for social action. You can read the latest issue here or access an archive of back issues through 1993. One recent issue, for example, featured articles on women, employment, education, and Congress. Read essays, articles, and interviews, including a column by Paula Poundstone, a regular feature. One feature, Backtalk, provides an instant Internet response to ongoing articles. New issues come out every other month. The online version of the magazine is free, provided as a public service to Internet users.

Contact: Mother Jones Magazine, *webmaster@mojones.com*

Pathfinder

http://www.pathfinder.com/

Here you'll find the site of Time-Warner magazines, providing a wealth of news, information, and entertainment. News Now gives you instant access to important current events. Access popular magazines online including *Time, Life,* and *People.* Visit special sections covering ongoing events, such as Bosnia, the Middle East, campaign '96, and O. J. Simpson. You'll find financial and business information from magazines like *Money* and *Fortune,* as well as information technology news from *Information Week, Interactive Age,* and more. Sports features are provided by *Sports Illustrated* magazine. Also find a learning center, a shopping outlet, features covering arts, entertainment, home, and hobbies, plus a special section just for kids.

Contact: Time Inc. New Media, Pathfinder, *webmaster@pathfinder.com*

Stream of Consciousness

http://kzsu.stanford.edu/uwi/soc.html

Each issue of this experimental poetry zine consists of several visual poems and stories stored as GIF and JPEG files. Just click on the inline image of the poem you want to read, and launch the full image. Definitely check out this site if you're interested in visual poetry or experimental electronic publishing.

Contact: Underworld Industries, KZSU Radio at Stanford University, *jon@kzsu.stanford.edu*

The Virtual Mirror

http://sashimi.wwa.com:80/mirror

The Virtual Mirror does not aspire to be the online equivalent of a newspaper or magazine but attempts to create a new form for a new medium, the WWW. It is also a commercial publication with advertising, which is relatively rare on the Web at this time. Instead of being published in issues, the e-zine is constantly growing and evolving. Most recent features have links on the home page; after two to four weeks, these stories are moved off the home page but are still available through the index. In the index, you'll find book, CD-ROM, and movie reviews, articles on Web browsers, the "catch of the week," Net news, pointers to new sites, articles on e-mail, HTML, and listservs, pointers to virtual museums, and features on Internet tools and software, plus a lot more. Find out what's going on in cyberspace with reports from the Roving Internaut, Scout, and Webmaster Spike. One neat feature is a fractal gallery. Another interesting section, the Garden Patch, lists Internet resources for the gardener and gardening tips. There is also a business directory that lists advertisers. The Virtual Mirror is an excellent example of a dynamic, general-interest, Web magazine.

Contact: The Virtual Mirror, WorldWide Access, *mirror@wwa.com*

Webster's Weekly

http://www.awa.com/w2/

This is the first weekly, general-interest magazine to be published on the WWW. You'll find it to be a humorous, entertainment-based magazine, featuring horoscopes, cartoons, and mad ramblings, as well as articles on movies, music, photography, poetry, politics, and psychology. Regular columns include Ask the Nerd, for a nerd's perspective on life, and Intimations, a diptych of poetry and photography. Everything is archived by column name so that you can follow your favorite articles back to their beginnings. An interactive form allows you to send in feedback on the magazine as you read it. Webster's Weekly is a fun read and a good example of magazine publishing on the WWW.

Contact: Webster's Weekly, Downtown Anywhere, *w2@casagato.org*

Read Webster's Weekly for features and fun. (Art by Jon White, jon@maukau.ac.nz.)

Wimsey's Magazine Shop

http://www.wimsey.com/Magazine_Shop/

Here you'll find a huge newsstand of original electronic zines covering the arts, entertainment, fiction, and more. Connect to Pixel Pushers for digital art, Circuit Traces for fiction, Generality for surreality, and NWHQ for world-class art and literature. You'll find a starting point for the Web explorer, a literary review, a multimedia trade magazine, and a skeptics society. From here you can also connect to online newspapers around the world.

Contact: Wimsey Information Services, *webmaster@wimsey.com*

For more information on magazines, visit these sites:

The Acid-Free Paper

http://tnt.vianet.on.ca:80/pages/smithk/

This is a magazine/gallery of modern art. It includes both graphic and written artworks and accepts submissions.

Brettnews

http://pathfinder.com/@@LpBZUPEH4wMAQNZF/vibe/vibeart/ brettnews/index.html

This online magazine screams "retro" out one side of its mouth and '90s hip from the other. The entire style is in '50s "new look," but the content is quite up-to-date, with a commentary on Trump having his credit cards refused and recent road trips.

Glass Wings

http://www:aus.xanadu.com/GlassWings/welcome.html

This site has shopping, adventure essays, recipies, and a humor page. Note: It also has an R-rated sensual celebrations page.

Home Arts Online Network

http://www.homearts.com/

InfoSeek keeps saying, "This is cool. Check it out." So I did. It's a network of over 2,000 carefully edited pages, with information on all kinds of stuff. The interior homepage includes links to four magazines: *Popular Mechanics*, *Country Living*, *Redbook*, and *Good Housekeeping*. Links to tables of contents, then full text of articles. Nice design, some poor color choices, and an awful lot of submenu links, but really cool overall.

Journals Online

http://toltec.lib.utk.edu/~share/jon/

Database and links to journals online and e-journals (searching journal contents online for actual paper journals, I believe). A useful resource.

Movies

Buena Vista MoviePlex

http://www.disney.com/

Check out current and upcoming movies from Buena Vista Pictures at this online "theater." The marquee lets you enter the WWW site or go straight to currently playing movies. From the lobby you can enter various studios or go to the Magnificent Movie Brain for a movie trivia game. Once you enter a studio, click on a movie's poster to find its theater. Look at Hollywood Pictures's films such as *Judge Dredd* and *While You Were Sleeping*, Disney Pictures's films including *Pocahontas* and *The Lion King*, and films from Touchstone Pictures, such as *Ed Wood*. For each film, you get a press kit with film credits, notes and photographs, trailers, stills, and promotional video clips. You can also make comments about the movie. Go into the theater for each film to see trailers and promotional clips. For some movies, such as *Pocahontas*, you'll find extras such as a production story preview, which shows the process of animating and producing the film. The International Press Room features a wider range of movies scheduled for international release; see even more Disney movies such as *101 Dalmations, The Fox and the Hound, Mary Poppins,* and *Sleeping Beauty*. This well-designed Web site is a good place to get the low-down on new movies or to learn all about your recent favorites. There are lots of movies to check out and millions of bytes of video clips to download.

Contact: Buena Vista Web Team, Walt Disney Company

Desktop Cinema

http://www.iac.net/~flypba/movie.trailer.index.html

Movie trailers are one of the best reasons to go to the movies. Trailers are short, fast-moving, exciting film clips that give you the scoop on upcoming movies. Now check out movie trailers on the Internet without having to go to the theater. This index links directly to every one of the online movie trailers. A huge alphabetical list of all trailers lets you quickly connect to the movies you're interested in. Then you can download the trailer and watch it on your computer. You'll see trailers for *Apollo 13, Pocahontas, Waterworld, Mighty Morphin' Power Rangers, A Walk in the Clouds, The Net,* and lots more. The list connects to all of the online movie studios and many TV shows as well. You'll also find lots of information about new and upcoming movies. Link straight to the QuickTime site to learn more about the software for playing videos on your computer.

Contact: FlyPBA, Internet Access Cincinnati, *flypba@iac.net*

Early Motion Pictures

http://rs6.loc.gov/papr/mpixhome.html

This collection of early films gives a unique view of the history of turn-of-the-century America. Most of these films run only two to three minutes, and they may be downloaded and displayed on your computer. Look at some early films of San Francisco before and after the great earthquake and fire. See the last days of President McKinley and explore the life of a city through early films of New York. You'll also learn about the short-lived genre of actuality films. Each film is presented in its historical context, so you can truly understand what you're seeing. Visit here for a look at history different from the kind you get in textbooks.

Contact: American Memory, Library of Congress

Hollyweb

http://www.ingress.com/users/spease/hw/hollyweb.html

The Hollyweb site aspires to be an online film mecca. Here you can read Studio Briefing, a weekly report of current film industry news. Look over the production slate to find out what films are shooting this week. Visit this week's box office for the top ten films of the week, or take a look at all-time blockbusters, the hundred-million-dollar club. At the Hollyweb Cineplex, get a listing of film and video reviews. Be sure to browse through the Laserdisc Store, recommended videos contributed by users of the site. Stop by the Hollyweb City Hall for news, comments, and information about Hollyweb. Get on the Interstate to travel to other film-related links on the Internet: reviews, databases, cinema home pages, commercial sites, film magazines, and home pages for specific films. The online content here is updated weekly, so be sure to plan multiple visits to this site.

Contact: Scott Pease and the Hollyweb, Ingress Communications, *spease@netcom.com*

Indiana Jones Home Page

http://dialin.ind.net/~msjohnso/

Do you love Indiana Jones? Here you'll find everything you could want to know about him. There's a picture gallery of stills from all three movies and sounds from *Raiders of the Lost Ark,* including the theme, to download. You can even look at some movie clips from *Raiders*. You'll also find the latest Indy info, particularly about the upcoming fourth movie in the series. Learn about Indy novels, games, rides at Disneyworld, comics, and young Indiana Jones. Read the scripts for *Raiders* and *Temple of Doom.* Find places to buy Indy stuff and Indy-related vacation spots. Spoofs and trivia include the Simpsons spoof of the opening from *Raiders,* trivia about Indy, and other miscellaneous tidbits. There are theories about the Ark of the Covenant that you can read—some serious, some not so serious. Have lots of fun online with everyone's favorite archaeologist-adventurer.

Contact: Micah Johnson, Indiana Rural Datification Project, *msjohnso@softaid.net*

You don't have to run all over the Internet—all the best Indiana Jones stuff is on this page.

Internet Movie Database

http://www.cm.cf.ac.uk/Movies/ or http://www.msstate.edu/ Movies/

This hypertext front end to the *rec.arts.movies* database is one of the most famous WWW innovations. From here, you can search an amazing array of information on movies in a huge database of facts and trivia. Using an interactive form, search by movie title, look up the name of a film personality or character, and even search a quotes archive for keywords; you can also search titles by genre or get a whole list of titles in a genre. The database includes biographies and filmographies on just about anyone involved in movie production, as well as details on almost every movie made, including year of release, director, cast, writer, music composer, producer, plot synopsis, trivia, and soundtrack. You can also vote on movies and see how the database audience rated them on a scale of one to ten. For fun, take a movie trivia quiz, see lists of the best and worst films in the database, and get Academy Awards information.

Contact: Robert Hartill, Cardiff University and Mississippi State University, *movie@cm.cf.ac.uk*

Grab your popcorn and visit the Internet Movie Database for information on your favorite movies.

Movie Sounds

http://sunsite.unc.edu/pub/multimedia/sun-sounds/movies/

Enter a library of sounds and quotes from all sorts of movies. You can download and listen to sound files from *The Blues Brothers, Bill and Ted's Excellent Adventure, Ghostbusters, Ferris Bueller's Day Off, James Bond, Batman, The Princess Bride, Superman, The Wizard of Oz,* and many more. Some choices include "A Whole New World" from *Aladdin*, many quotes from *Star Wars*, the T-Rex's roar from *Jurassic Park,* and the *Wayne's World* theme song. Use the sounds in your multimedia home pages, or just listen to your favorite quotes. The titles are somewhat cryptic, so you may have to download files to hear what sounds they actually contain.

Contact: SunSITE, University of North Carolina at Chapel Hill

MPEG Movie Archive

http://www.eeb.ele.tue.nl/mpeg/index.html

This site offers lots of MPEG movies, ready for you to view or download to your computer. The archive is divided into different categories, such as animation, supermodels, music, movies and TV, and space. (A previously available R-rated section has been closed.) The animations and movie films include a flight through a fractal landscape, Simpsons cartoons, and segments from *Raiders of the Lost Ark.* You'll find music-video clips from Eric Clapton and Michael Jackson, among many others. Space videos include views from the Hubble Telescope, films of the Levy-Shoemaker comet, and spacewalks. The Various category is a catch-all for various MPEGs of jets, Mickey Mouse, and the bizarre. A category on racing has videos of car races. You can also download software for playing MPEG movies and get a FAQ on MPEG.

Contact: Heini Withagel, Electronic Circuit Design Home Page, *www@eeb.ele.tue.nl*

Universal Pictures

http://www.mca.com/universal_pictures/index.html

The latest WWW trend is for movie studios to build Web pages featuring upcoming movies. Universal Pictures has one of the best sites. Go to this site to get the scoop on the latest releases. You can watch video clip sneak previews before they are shown anywhere else. Or virtually attend world premieres of new films with video clips and photographs of attending stars; you'll feel as if you're actually there. Learn about the making of featured movies, and access cast and filmmaker biographies. Lots of games and fun make you feel like part of the movie and take advantage of the multimedia aspects of the WWW.

Contact: Digital Planet, MCA/Universal Pictures, *cyber@mca.com*

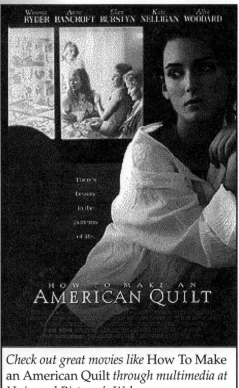

Check out great movies like How To Make an American Quilt *through multimedia at Universal Pictures's Web page.*

SCREENsite

http://www.sa.ua.edu/TCF/welcome.htm

SCREENsite facilitates the study of film and television, emphasizing teaching and research. The site is divided into four principal areas: Education, Research, Film/TV/Video Production, and Miscellanea. In

Education, you'll find teaching materials such as syllabi, sample chapters from textbooks, reading lists, and class handouts. You can also access a list of film and television studies, educators' e-mail addresses, an employment office, a list of schools with information on programs, and application procedures and information about relevant societies. Research materials at the site include bibliographies, online discussion groups, scholarly journals, publisher's online resources, and information services such as databases of film reviews, film and TV credits, and television news archives. Miscellanea connects you to other Internet resources for film and TV research. In the Film/TV/Video Production section, you'll find production courses, broadcasting sources, media e-mail contact lists, resources for screenwriters, entertainment news, and TV regulation news. You can also connect to online production companies and networks from here. Following the link for further information takes you to a comprehensive directory of film and television sources on the Internet. Any student of film or television will find something useful at this academic site.

Contact: Jeremy Butler, University of Alabama, *webmaster@tcf.ua.edu*

Unofficial Star Wars Home Page

http://force.stwing.upenn.edu:8001/~jruspini/starwars.html

This jam-packed archive contains all the information you could possibly want about the famous science fiction trilogy. Get news about the new trilogy, upcoming toy releases, and the annual convention. Multimedia files include a sound library, a sound effects archive, an image gallery, and a video archive. There is also a huge catalog of collectible books, videos, music, and toys, as well as guides to the comics, a trading card list, and a catalog of musical scores for the diehard collector. Trivia files about the actors and movies include a guide to bloopers and miscuts, a list of memorable quotes, and a catalog of missing scenes. If you become inspired to enter the *Star Wars* universe yourself, access reviews, charts, guides, and an explanation of hyperspace travel from West End Role-playing Games.

Contact: Jason Ruspini, Science and Technology Wing, University of Pennsylvania, *jruspini@force.stwing.upenn.edu*

For more information on movies, visit these sites:

Cinema Sites

http://www.webcom.com/~davidaug/Movie_Sites.html

This site has lots of nifty links, not just to movie listings and reviews, but also to information on movie production, special effects, and more.

Cinequest: The San Jose Film Festival

http://www.webcom.com/~sjfilm/

This site contains information on attending the San Jose Film Festival and submitting material to be shown there. Good for filmmakers and serious movie buffs.

The Critics

http://web3.starwave.com/showbiz/moviereviews/

This site reviews movies that are currently or have recently been in the theaters. While I disagreed with each review that I read, the organization is easy to understand, and the database seems quite up-to-date.

Cyberwalk

http://www.mca.com/

This is MCA Universal's home page. Includes links to movies, MCA records, Spencer Gifts, etc. Very nice design! Also includes Putnam publishing, home entertainment, and the Universal Studios part of Disneyworld.

Film Festivals

http://www.film.com/film/filmfests/

This site has a lot of depth to it. Not only does it provide links to more film festivals than you can imagine, it also has box office scores and listings of current films.

The Hong Kong Movies Homepage

http://www.mdstud.chalmers.se/hkmovie/

Another robust Web site, the Hong Kong Movies Homepage provides information to those who've never seen a foreign film, listings, reviews, and more.

Martial Arts: The Film and Collector's Forum

http://www.primenet.com/~martial/

This site has information on martial arts in film, the Bruce Lee Museum, and a bibliography of related works.

Movies and Films: Actors and Actresses

http://www.yahoo.com/Entertainment/Movies_and_Films/Actors_and_Actresses/

This site contains links to pages on many popular actors and actresses. Most of the links have information on all the movies, TV shows, etc., that the performer has been in.

Science Fiction and Fantasy Movies

http://sf.www.lysator.liu.se/sf_archive/sf-texts/movies/

This site covers science fiction and fantasy movies pretty throroughly. The movies are listed alphabetically by title, and each one has several reviews, by people with very different opinions on what makes a good movie.

The St. John's Anime Film Society

http://www.cs.mun.ca/~anime/afs/homepage.html

This site is both a good introduction to the unique Japanese animation artform called *anime* and a good resource for those who are already informed about the subject. There is a page for the anime-uninformed, reviews of specific movies, a gallery, and more.

Women in Film & Television

http://www.deakin.edu.au/arts/VPMA/wift.html

This is the home page for the organization Women in Film & Television. It serves primarily to tell women about the organization and to provide links to other interesting sites from Victoria, Australia.

MUDs, MOOs & MUSHes

Jay's House MOO

http://jh.ccs.neu.edu:7043/

This WWW server is a gateway to a MOO where you can interact with other players in a real-time environment. It also houses an ongoing project to investigate text-based virtual-reality systems. You enter the MOO itself through a Telnet link; an online help system at the MOO site orients you and instructs you on how to interact in the MOO. From the WWW site, you can also read about research projects, find out who's logged in to the MOO, and try out an experimental hypertext object browser with a searchable interface that gives you a preview of Jay's House. Another link allows you to meet Ron, the first hypertextified user of the MOO. This Web server is actually running inside the MOO, and all the documents are written by users inside the MOO; learn more about this innovation here.

Contact: Jay's House MOO WWW Server

The Sprawl

http://chiba.picosof.com:7777/

The Sprawl is a cyberpunk MOO that emphasizes building. Players can move and build freely within the MOO, creating a "sprawl" that has extended far into cyberspace. Using the WOO Transaction Protocol developed at Picosof, you can interact with the Sprawl through the Web. Players on the Sprawl can even add hyperlinks to their spaces, making the Sprawl the world's first multimedia MOO. Pay a visit to see the future in action. Here you can learn more about the WOO protocol and browse the MOO using your Web browser. Or take a look at some of the more interesting Web objects inside the MOO itself. You can also connect directly to the MOO through a Telnet link.

Contact: Sensemedia Publishing, The Sprawl, *sprawl@sensemedia.com*

Star Wars MUSH

http://ix.urz.uni-heidelberg.de/~jradelef/swmush.html

In this MUSH (Multi-User Shared Hallucination), you can role-play in a world based on the *Star Wars* films and books. You can do all the same things the actors do in the movies, such as flying spaceships and using the Force. You might even meet Luke Skywalker. Visit the home page to find out general information about the MUSH and its structure. You'll also learn how to play a character, a summary of recent events, rules of the MUSH, and about connections to other *Star Wars* pages online.

Contact: Star Wars MUSH Home Page, University of Heidelberg, *jradelef@ix.urz.uni-heidelberg.de*

Battle Darth Vader in the Star Wars MUSH.

TinyTIM

http://yay.tim.org/

TinyTIM is the world's oldest running MUSH, with over 9,000 rooms online and an average of 2,000 active players; usually 25 to 40 players are online together at any one time. The Web site provides information about this very large adventure game, in which players interact with other people playing in real time. At this fun site, beginners can find out about TinyTIM and MUSHes in general. Users can expand their addiction to TinyTIM by downloading pictures, documentation, and blurbs. After familiarizing yourself with TinyTIM, travel a Telnet link to the actual MUSH, and start playing.

Contact: Empedocles the Ash Ock, TinyTIM Server

TrekMUSE

http://grimmy.cnidr.org/

TrekMUSE is a text-based virtual reality owing its existence to the far-reaching vision of Gene Roddenberry. At the WWW site, find out more about the MUSE (Multi-User Shared Environment), and enter it through a Telnet link to begin exploring the "Star Trek" universe. An interactive map leads you to information on the empires, wizards, and host computer for the MUSE. Read about the seven factions or empires of TrekMUSE, including the United Federation of Planets, the Klingon empire, the Cardassians, the Ferengi, the Gorn, Independents, and the Romulans, before deciding what kind of character you want to play. Meet the TrekMUSE wizards, called Directors, who keep the MUSE running and the players happy; each presides over a different empire. You can also read the documentation for the MUSE, find out how to register, and even learn about TrekMUSE parties. After exploring the Web site, link directly to an interactive session of Trek-MUSE and "boldly go..."

Contact: TrekMUSE, Center for Networked Information Discovery and Retrieval, *webmaster@grimmy.cndir.org*

Types of MUDs

http://csugrad.cs.vt.edu/soc/mud_types.html

Are you still confused about the difference between MUDs, MOOs, MUSHes, MUSEs, and MUCKs? What about DikuMUDS and Lp-MUDs? Don't despair. Just come to this site for a basic definition of each type of MUD. You can also connect to example MUDs from each group.

Contact: Eli Burke, CS Undergraduate Web Server at Virginia Tech, *eburke@csugrad.cs.vt.edu*

WaxWeb

http://bug.village.virginia.edu/

MOOs meet the WWW in this hypermedia project based on David Blair's *WAX or Discovery of TV among the Bees*, the first movie broadcast on the Internet. WaxWeb combines the hypermedia aspect of the WWW with an authoring interface that allows users to make immediate, publicly visible links to other documents. Through WaxWeb, more than nine hundred pages of hypertext is accessible to both WWW and MOO clients. The site includes the entire film embedded as 1,500 color stills, 300 video clips, and 2,000 audio clips. When you join WaxWeb, you gain the ability to make links from word to word, insert comments, and create your own pages, adding to the narrative of Wax-Web. From the home page, read the latest news about the project, configure your viewers to access the multimedia format, and register for a character. A tutorial explains how to use tools and write hypertext in WaxWeb. You'll also find general information on VRML, the programming language of virtual reality.

Contact: Tom Meyer, WaxWeb, University of Virginia, *twm@cs.brown.edu*

For more on MUDs, MOOs, and MUSHes, visit these sites:

Angreal MOO

http://sarcazm.resnet.cornell.edu/angreal/

This is a user-participatory adventure based on the novel, *Robert Jordan's Wheel of Time.*

FredNet MOO

http://fred.net/cindy/fnmoo.html

This MOO includes a newbie tutorial, so it might be a good one to start with. Like an online civic center, FredNet MOO offers "rooms" for classes, conventions, meetings, parties, and other culturally oriented spaces.

The Jade MUD Home Page

http://www.newl.com/~quest/JadeMud/

This MUD allows the participant to make up a character and have a fast-paced, action adventure. There are good character-designing instructions and other useful information. A well set-up MUD page.

MUD List

http://www.graphcomp.com/info/mudlist.html

Interested in MUDs but want to check out more of them before choosing one? This page lists several different MUD sites and gives information on them.

MUDs

http://www2.primenet.com/bid/cybercafe/cmuds.html

This is another list of MUDs and their descriptions. There are also links to the MUDs listed.

MUD2: The Quest for Immortality

http://www.aladdin.co.uk/mud/

This Multi User Dungeon is a UK-hosted adventure. You can play with or without an account if you just want to try out MUDding.

The Realm of Phoenix MUD

http://www.nmt.edu/~crayola/homepage.html

This page gives the reader information on the MUD, The Gods of Phoenix. There are links to upcoming developments in the MUD, including something rather ominously titled, "auto sacrifice."

UTS ProgSoc MOO

http://ftoomsh.socs.uts.edu.au/~peterl/moo_www

This MOO is relatively young. Each player can become a programmer in this particular site.

Music & Dance

Alberto's Nightclub

http://albertos.com/albertos/

Finish up your evening in a genuine WWW nightclub, where you can listen to live music or dance the night away. Follow the online map to the real club's location in Mountain View, California. Access a monthly schedule of musicians playing at Alberto's, or see highlights of upcoming acts. You'll find a calendar of regular events, such as salsa classes. Join the e-mail list for free passes and late-breaking updates on events at the club. Or connect to an archive of old calendars in both ASCII and postscript forms to see what you've been missing. You can also link to many other WWW sites featuring Latin American music and dance.

Contact: Jonathan Hahn, Alberto's Nightclub, *albertos@albertos.com*

Classics World

http://www.classicalmus.com

This site is the complete online source of classical music information. At the Concert Hall, you can experience classical performances through audio and video clips; see Placido Domingo sing, or hear Harry Belafonte or the Boston Pops through the multimedia power of the WWW. Go to Mail & BBS for interactive bulletin boards discussing opera, new music, general classical music, and early music. In Opera/Vocal, learn about the origins of opera, read synopses of the 40 best-loved opera stories, meet the greatest opera singers of yesterday and today, and discuss opera at an on-site BBS. The artist area lets you read biographies, hear recordings, see tour schedules, and access audio and video clips of top classical artists; browse by name or by instrument. Go to Composers to read about the life and times of the greatest composers organized by period or by name; see pictures, hear clips of their works, and read biographies. One terrific feature of this site is the Beginner's Guide to Classical Music, which walks you through the history of classical music, with a chronological timeline, audio examples from each period, an introduction to the composers of each period, and a BBS discussion.

Contact: Classics World, *rbourne@panix.com*

COMING: A VISIT WITH JAMES GALWAY

LIVE APPEARANCES | OPERA SYNOPSES | AUDIO | LETTERS

MUSIC BRIEFS * A QUIZ * IDIOT'S GUIDE * TALK OF THE WEB

A WORD OF WELCOME TO THE NEW CLASSICS WORLD

Interactively explore the history of classical music.

Digital Tradition Folk Song Database

http://www.xerox.com/digitrad/

This invaluable resource provides a database of words and music for thousands of folk songs, the largest collection available. Search titles, full text, or keywords of all your favorite American folk songs. Many of the tunes are linked to audio files so that you can actually hear them played on your computer. You can also select song categories from a massive list or get a list of all songs organized by title or tune. This completely free resource is a great place for folk music fans to spend time.

Contact: Digital Tradition, Xerox Palo Alto Research Center, *digitrad@world.std.com*

Elvis Home Page

http://sunsite.unc.edu/elvis/elvishom.html

This home page honors Elvis and his cultural and musical heritage. Here you can tour Graceland through photographs. Check out Internet sightings of Elvis, or wander through an Elvis souvenir collection. You can also read the Elvis Space Chronicles and other documents about Elvis collected from the Internet. Fun software includes Windows applications you can download, such as a program that detects Elvis' presence in the vicinity of your computer. An interactive application allows you to read what other visitors to the site have to say about the King and to make your own comments.

Contact: Andrea Berman, SunSITE, University of North Carolina at Chapel Hill, *andrea@sunsite.unc.edu*

Take an interactive tour of Graceland at the Elvis Home Page.

The Grateful Dead

http://www.cs.cmu.edu/afs/cs.cmu.edu/user/mleone/web/ dead.html

Deadheads love visiting this home page, which is chock-full of Grateful Dead news and trivia. A Grateful Dead FAQ answers such burning questions as how the group got its name and whether "Unbroken Chain" has ever been performed live. A graphics archive features lots of images of the famous dancing bears, as well as concert photos and T-shirts. You can even download a dancing bear screen saver and Dead icons for your computer. More highlights include a searchable database of song lyrics and an archive of assorted song clips. Finally, connect to the wealth of Grateful Dead pages elsewhere on the Web.

Contact: Mark Leone, Carnegie Mellon University, *mleone@cs.cmu.edu*

Explore Dead iconography, such as these tie-dies(sic) by Mike Fowler.

Harmony Central

http://harmony-central.mit.edu/

Harmony Central is the place for musicians, whether you play an instrument, belong to a band, or just want to create music on your computer. Learn about the latest musical instruments and accessories for guitar, bass, and keyboards. Guitar players can find lessons, chord charts, and effects. There's also a multimedia guitar tutorial and a primer for jazz improvisation techniques. Find information on tube amps, building a guitar, guitar-related software, and instrument stores. Bass players can access lessons, tabulature, software, newsgroups, dealers, and help playing bass. Keyboard and synthesizer players should look at information about equipment and software. Find out more about MIDI, the music protocol that lets musical instruments talk to each other, with an easy-to-understand tutorial, software tools, and pointers to other online resources. Learn about computers and music, and download software for making music on your computer. A music services page helps you find new bands, check out prices on gear, get tickets to concerts, and place classified ads for buying or selling gear. The bands page explains publicity, getting heard online, getting gigs offline, copyright and trademarks, producing CDs, and more to help your band get started. You'll find useful information about recording, drums and percussion, composition, and lyrics sources. There are also links to tons of music-related sites for your surfing pleasure.

Contact: Scott Lehman, Harmony Central, Massachusetts Institute of Technology, *slehman@mit.edu*

Hyperreal

http://www.hyperreal.com/

This site gives a home to alternative culture, music, and expression. Here you'll find the rave culture archives, with a FAQ, a calendar, raves in the news, and much more. Use it to keep in touch with the worldwide rave scene. You'll also find a huge archive of techno and ambient music resources. Check out electronic publications on rave, techno, and alternative music. A drugs archive presents the facts (and FAQs) about illegal drugs and psychedelic culture. Finally, you can access a useful library of sound and graphics software.

Contact: Hyperreal, Mike Brown, *mike@hyperreal.com*, and Brian Behlendorf, *brian@hyperreal.com*

Internet Underground Music Archive

http://www.iuma.com/

This immense archive is the Internet's first free hi-fi music collection. You'll find lots of great features to explore on many types of music, from folk to indie rock to instrumental jazz to Japanese experimental noise. First take a guided tour to learn more about the site. Then check out the bands; you can access groups by musical genre, meet the new arrivals, and visit bands by location. There are more than six hundred independent artists to choose from, and you can hear music samples from every one. Several record labels have home pages here, including Warner Brothers and DGC. Cool extras include Ask Sue (a music industry insider and columnist), notes on underground music scenes, and users' top ten lists.

Contact: Internet Underground Music Archive (IUMA), *info@iuma.com* or *support@iuma.com*

Use this image map to sample alternative music in the Internet Underground Music Archive.

JAZZ Online

http://www.jazzonln.com/JAZZ/

JAZZ Online is the world's first interactive jazz source. It was created to provide jazz enthusiasts with a network of their own where they can communicate with each other and obtain the latest information on releases, artists, and scene happenings. In the Pocket explores the world of traditional, bebop, big band, straight ahead, progressive, and avant-garde styles of jazz. Here you can find out what's new on CD, see a gallery of cover art, get lists of jazz radio stations around the country at Jazz Radioline, read JazzTimes Online, a sampler of *Jazz-*

Times Magazine, and access a directory of jazz clubs. Visit the world's first and only online jazz jukebox, which features sound samples from new and recent CDs. Or go to Jazz Onward to find out about contemporary jazz, new age, and world music. In Onward Cyberline, read about new Onward CD releases, or visit the CD Release Zone for an in-depth look at some new CDs with text, graphics, and audio. You can also access the Onward Radioline, see cover art in the gallery, and order CDs from an online music catalog. Featured at the site is a Web site directory that lists other online jazz sites, including record labels and vendors. New jazz fans should visit the Jam Session to read about JAZZ Online and e-mail comments, read artist profiles, and get recommendations for CDs. Don't forget to stop by the JAZZ Online Bulletin Board for a grab bag of jazz news and happenings.

Contact: Joe Vella and Tim Hodges, Aimnet, *jazzonln@netcom.com*

Musi-Cal

http://www.automatrix.com/concerts/

Musi-Cal is an interactive calendar that provides easy access to the most up-to-date live music information for concerts, festivals, gigs, and special events. You can view event listings organized by geographic location, with locales worldwide, or by performer/conductor name. To use geographic listings, choose a city, state, or country (when outside the United States). Performers and places of listings are highlighted. Click on these to see listings for other performances by that group or other events in that place. You can also view all performers who have listings in an alphabetical index. An interactive form lets you search the entire database for criteria such as performer's names, locations, type of music, and dates of concerts. Search returns list the date of the concert, where it is taking place, the performer, and a phone number to call for more information. To keep the calendar updated, you can also contribute items to the listings.

Contact: Skip Montanaro, Automatrix, Inc., *concerts@automatrix.com*

Music Kitchen

http://www.nando.net/music/gm/

The Music Kitchen cooks up an eclectic blend of musical information. Visit artists such as Bonnie Raitt, the Breeders, the Meat Puppets, and more. Some artists, such as Bonnie Raitt, have free interactive software you can download, which includes audio, images, and a discography. You'll also find song lyrics and some audio examples for a recent album, as well as an extensive discography. Sample some rock-n-roll comics based on today's hottest musical acts and legendary figures in rock-n-roll. Also, independent music fans can check out a hotlist of cool links.

Contact: Fistfulayen and The Big Gun Project, NandoNet, *BigGun@biggun.com*

Access hot bands like the Breeders in the Music Kitchen.

MusicNet

http://www.next.com.au/music/

Now WWW surfers all over the world can read online *Australian Rolling Stone* magazine, featuring Australian music. Look in the Gallery for ever-changing exhibitions of photography, art, comics, and multimedia pieces, featuring an exhibition by a rock-n-roll photographer. Preview a CD-ROM from the Australian band Severed Heads, leading the world in interactive multimedia. Download samples from the first

Internet compilation album, featuring many Australian bands. Go to Earwitness, a forum for reviewing live music; you can file a report yourself, and the best reviews will be published in the Australian edition of *Rolling Stone.* Get Sydney party, rave, and club information, or access a guide to live Sydney bands. Read selected articles from past and present issues of *Australian Rolling Stone.* For a guide to music industry happenings in Australia, look at the Industry News column. Column X features pop culture snippets. You can also access features from *Connections*, Australia's entertainment technology magazine.

Contact: Next Online, *www@next.com.au*

Ohio State University Department of Dance

http://www.dance.ohio-state.edu/

This dance archive distributes material related to dance. A dance history collection includes a hypertext database of key artists, companies, and works in the development of ballet and modern dance. Follow the dance and technology link to learn about the interfacing of computers and dance. You'll also find dance documentation and information on current research projects.

Contact: David Ralley, Ohio State University Department of Dance, *ralley.2@osu.edu*

Rare Groove

http://rg.media.mit.edu/RG/RG.html

This site acts as both a magazine and radio station for hip-hop and house music. On the magazine side, features include techno and hip-hop reviews, DJ playlists, and regional reports from Boston; San Francisco; South Beach, Florida; and Raleigh, North Carolina. The radio side features a song of the week and a mix of the week, which you can listen to and immediately register your opinion of. Get various charts of top hip-hop and house tunes, sampling some of them to see what you like. Or go to the listening booth to hear a large number of song snippets. All fans of hip-hop are sure to find something they like inside Rare Groove.

Contact: Rare Groove, Massachusetts Institute of Technology, *rgmag@media.mit.edu*

Rolling Stones Web Site

http://www.stones.com/

Billing itself as the only "official" Rolling Stones WWW site, this page has all the latest information about rock-n-roll's oldest touring band. Access up-to-date tour dates, or look at live Rolling Stones concert material, such as photographs, videos, and audio clips. Check out a Stones concert broadcast live over the Internet. You'll also find interviews with the band, Stones fiction, and an image collection of album covers, band members, and "tongues."

Contact: Thinking Pictures and Sun Microsystems, Rolling Stones Server

Tango Server

http://litwww.epfl.ch/tango/

Dance away the night at this informative server. Here you'll find all the information on tango you could possibly want, such as a calendar of tango events and links to places to tango all around the world. Read the history of tango, access a lyrics collection, or just wander through the pages of audio clips, videos, and photographs. There is also an instructional manual for labanotation, the method of notating movements in dance. Meet noted people in the tango world, including performers, musicians, instructors, and composers. Finally, join an ongoing discussion of tango, and connect with tango groups and associations.

Contact: Shawn Koppenhöffer, LIT Information Services, *shawn@litsun.epfl.ch*

Dance up a storm at the Tango Server.

TicketMaster

http://www.ticketmaster.com/

Stop by TicketMaster to learn all about upcoming live events, such as concerts, sports events, family shows, and Broadway plays. Check the live event hotline to find out what's going on in the touring world. This database lists all the events available through Ticketmaster; you can browse it alphabetically, by venue, or geographically. Go Backstage with the latest Broadway news from *Variety* and other sports, music, and entertainment news, including interviews with industry icons, a concert chat section, and a showcase of unsigned musical talent. Check out the music industry's most popular acts. Get connected to Ticketmaster ticket center locations, phone numbers, and venue information, organized by state. In the store, you can order exclusive merchandise from bands, acts, Broadway shows, and sports teams. Look under Spotlight for free tickets, a sample from *LIVE!* entertainment magazine, special events, and discounts. You can also learn more about Ticketmaster at this site.

Contact: Starwave Corporation, TicketMaster Online, *luciw@starwave.com*

Ultimate Band List

http://american.recordings.com/WWWoM/ubl/ubl.shtml

Come here for the largest interactive list of music links on the Internet. You can even add the hottest music links for your favorite bands. Browse bands by name, type of music, or Internet resource. Genres listed here include pop, rock, alternative, metal, country and western, jazz, blues, classical, new age, dance, techno, and rap. There's something for every taste. Resources include newsgroups, mailing lists, FAQs, lyrics, guitar tabulatures, digital song files, and WWW pages. Each "card" for a band lists the resources in an easy-to-understand format. Get information about the artists, find out when they are touring, access the latest music news, listen to songs, and see pictures and videos. You'll find Paula Abdul, Janet Jackson, Indigo Girls, k.d. lang, Led Zeppelin, Living Colour, Aerosmith, Tori Amos, 10,000 Maniacs, Eric Clapton, Counting Crows, Guns 'n' Roses, Garth Brooks, and even the Bee Gees, plus 500 KB of more bands if you download the master list.

Contact: Ultimate Band List, American Recordings, *wwwofm@american.recordings.com.*

The Vibe

http://metaverse.com/vibe/

Access an online magazine for the latest music and entertainment industry news, published by Adam Curry, formerly of MTV. Find reviews of new albums and interviews with music stars. Get the latest tour dates for just about everyone who's on the road, or check out the recording studio for samples of hot tracks from around the world. For a daily dose of entertainment gossip, read the ongoing column Cyber-Sleaze. You'll also find movies and television information, including a home page for "Melrose Place."

Contact: On Ramp, Inc., Metaverse

Get the latest music and entertainment news at the Vibe.

Virtual Radio

http://www.microserve.net/vradio/

Tune in to this nonstop, user-definable music broadcast, bringing you the latest in new music over the WWW. Here you can find out about up-and-coming rock bands, such as Hypermarket, Metallingus, and Tin Gods, and listen to radio-quality broadcasts of entire tracks by them. For each band, read biographical information, find out about their music, and see images of the band. Then sample an entire song from each featured group. If you like what you hear, you can order through e-mail albums featured at the site. This is the new way to expose yourself to today's music, using the multimedia capabilities of the WWW to bypass the commercials and Top Forty playlists of radio.

Contact: Virtual Radio, Microserve Information Systems, *vradio@ugly.microserve.net*

World Music

http://www.unik.no/~robert/mizik/mizik.html

Sample music from all over the world and get an introduction to new types of music at this site. Regions represented include Japan, India, North Africa, Brazil, Africa, and the Caribbean. For each region, find pictures of representative musical artists, get lists of titles on their albums, listen to sampled songs, and link to other relevant information such as archives, sound samples, and discographies. You can also find out more about the artists by clicking on their names. Or check out a selection from every genre for a world music sampler. You'll find loads of links here to other places on the WWW with sound samples. Jump to jazz, Afro-Caribbean music, Australian music, and Cuban and Latin American music sites. This is a good place to begin a world music tour. From here you can also buy albums, link to popular music, find online radio stations, and listen to various sounds other than music.

Contact: Robert, Center for Technology at Kjeller, University of Oslo, *robert@unik.no*

Check out music from Africa and all around the world at World Music.

WWW Music Database

http://www.cs.uit.no/Music/

This database is a huge collection of information about albums by many different bands. You can search for album titles or artists. When you search for an artist, you'll see all of their albums, all the songs on each album, and lyrics to the songs. Some albums have cover graphics and reviews. Look up your favorite bands to see what albums are missing from your collection or to check out lyrics. There are also links to home pages, archives, and song files for some bands. You can add new entries for albums from your own collection. Not all albums have complete information, and it's easy to add missing info. You can also vote on any album or see how others have voted. You have to register to vote, but you don't have to give any personal information. Check out the lists of albums voted the best, the ones voted the worst, and the ones voted for the most. Look under Database Information to see how many artists, albums, lyrics, reviews, and cover photos are currently in the database. Already over three thousand albums are listed.

Contact: Espen Skoglund, University of Tromo, *espensk@stud.cs.uit.no*

For more information on music, visit these sites:

MTV Online

http://www.mtv.com/

Some very cool graphics (awfully big though), with links to music information (including music news, 120 minutes, bytes, etc.), animation, general credits, and a headshop. Fun for MTV or music fans.

The Music Exchange of the United Kingdom

http://www.scsn.net/~musex/exchange/Countries/ United_Kingdom/us.html

An exchange area for buying, selling, or trading anything music-related.

Music Similarities Search Engine

http://www.webcom.com/~se/

A really cool page, you ought to check it out. Enter your five favorite artists and their albums, and in a day or two, get back a long list of other artists you will probably like. The list is e-mailed and weighted as in, "you will probably like all of these albums in the range 20-30 and like maybe 2/3 of the albums weighted 10-20." I was impressed at how accurate my return list was. Many were albums I already had and loved, and some were ones I had been meaning to listen to or buy.

Nine Inch Nails Homepage

http://ibm15.scri.fsu.edu/~patters/nin.html

This fan page has past interviews with band members, parody lyrics to songs, and way too much other information about Nine Inch Nails.

Sony Music Index

http://www.sony.com/Music/MusicIndex.html

This site provides information on musicians, their tours, their recent releases, and older music—as long as it's on the Sony label.

Sony's WWW Page

http://www.sony.com/

Includes a vault of music, new releases, product information, movie info, etc. Very nice design to boot. Music links includes information about artists, tour dates, album and video clips, and more. Really cool!

WXYC Online

http://sunsite.unc.edu/wxyc/

WXYC is the first 24-hour, 7-day simulcast over the Net, brought to you by the University of North Carolina's student-run radio station.

News

CRAYON: Create Your Own Newspaper

http://spectrum.eg.bucknell.edu:80/~boulter/crayon/

Make your own newspaper using the WWW. The electronic newspaper that you create yourself is customized with the daily news information that you're most interested in. Be sure to consult How to Use CRAYON and the frequently asked questions file before beginning. Then use the online form to build your personal newspaper. First, name the newspaper using your own name. Then pick the news you want from several categories, including national, world, weather, entertainment, sports, and comics. Arrange the sections any way you want. If you want all cartoons and no news, that's fine too—this is your newspaper. Choose items for your newspaper such as Today at NASA, today's White House publications, WebWeather, PC and Macintosh news, TV listings, the current David Letterman top ten list, rock trivia, sports schedules, the deep thought of the day, zodiac forecasts, the cool site of the day, and many more. The program creates links to all of these resources that change daily and arranges them the way you choose. After you finish, save your newspaper on your hard drive. You can use it as your home page or just read it every morning over coffee.

Contact: Bucknell University, College of Engineering, Dave Maher, *dmaher@bucknell.edu*, and Jeff Boulter, *boulter@bucknell.edu*

Create your own newspaper at CRAYON.

The Daily News

http://www.cs.vu.nl/~gerben/news.html

The Daily News page links to free news services all over the world. The news services are divided into categories for easy access. At the top, you'll find information on current events; you can also link to an archive of past current events. Get news from Europe, the U.S., Asia, Africa, North and South America, Oceania, and the rest of the world. The larger areas are divided into smaller countries and regions, such as Bosnia, Britain, and Eastern Europe in the Europe section. Notes beside each listing tell you whether the resources are new, whether free registration is needed, and whether the resources are out-of-date. Types of resources you'll find here include online newspapers and news services, radio news with audio files, magazines, and news from governmental resources such as the White House and the United Nations. For example, connect to Croatian Radio News, the Irish Times, ABC hourly news update, *Time* magazine, Voice of America, China News Digest, and many more diverse services. Also connect to other lists of news sources and European weather. The Daily News could replace your morning newspaper.

Contact: Gerben Vos, Vrije Universiteit in Amsterdam, *gerben@cs.vu.nl*

Get the latest news from Slovakia and many other locations all around the world.

Internet Talk Radio

http://www.cmf.nrl.navy.mil/radio/radio.html

Tune in to Internet Talk Radio, the Internet's equivalent of National Public Radio, broadcasting interviews and news live over the Internet's own radio network, the MBONE. (To find out more about the MBONE, read the multicasting FAQ, found on this site.) Internet Talk Radio provides in-depth technical information to the Internet community, producing audio files that are freely available to the Internet from archives such as this one. One interesting feature is Geek of the Week, a weekly interview with prominent members of the technical community. Also available are excerpts from Internet Town Hall meetings, a forum on Internet issues, which include speeches by famous Netizens as well as outsiders like Janet Reno. The archive is automatically updated with new shows.

Contact: Bill Fenner, Naval Research Laboratory, *fenner@parc.xerox.com*

Hot Topics

http://www.amdahl.com/internet/hot.html

Visit an ever-changing list of hot current events on the Internet. Hot Topics contains the latest and most interesting subjects available via the WWW. Here you can find out what's going on right now in sports, the world, space, the U.S., TV and movies, and government. Also be the first to know what new hot sites are opening on the WWW. Link straight to the source to read the hot news. Events that are no longer current but may still be interesting can be found in Recent Hot Topics. You can also link to general interest topics, such as news, weather, sports, games, TV, and natural disasters. Or find special collections of events that received extensive daily coverage, such as the Persian Gulf War and the Soviet coup attempt.

Contact: Amdahl Corporation, *www@amdahl.com*

 all shuttles on the ground

launch coming up within a few days

shuttle in flight/orbit (MIR icon for docking missions)

Get the status of the Space Shuttle at a glance depending on what image is shown on the Hot Topics page. (Provided as a service for promotional purposes by the Amdahl Corporation.)

News From Around the World

http://www.funet.fi/pub/sounds/news.html

This is a collection of audio files of the latest broadcast news. Actually listen on your computer to international and national broadcasts from the CBC radio network. Get the latest broadcasts from Voice of America in English, Russian, and Chinese. There are even broadcasts in

Dutch from Radio Amsterdam. The Voice of America broadcasts are updated several times daily, and the other broadcasts are updated daily or more frequently. Visit this site to hear the radio news from all over the world whenever you want to hear it.

Contact: Kimmo Ketolainen, FUNET Network Services

The Obituary Page

http://catless.ncl.ac.uk/Obituary/README.html

For those who turn first to the obituary page when they read the newspaper, here is the WWW's own obituary page, where you'll find a repository of death notices of the famous and not-so-famous. This international service records the names of people who have died recently, their occupations, and their birth and death dates. Sometimes names are linked to information about them located elsewhere on the WWW. You can also contribute to the listing by submitting obituaries. Or connect to a virtual memorial garden. Here you can create a memorial for a pet, download genealogical resources, and find bereavement support.

Contact: Lindsay Marshall, Department of Computer Sciences, University of Newcastle, *Lindsay.Marshall@newcastle.ac.uk*.

The Omnivore

http://ukanaix.cc.ukans.edu/carrie/news_main.html

This daily news service provides coverage of events around the world as they happen. In-depth follow-ups to major events are generally available. The service is free of charge and offers global reporting. Stories come from many different sources and points of view, giving multiple perspectives from around the world. You'll also find Quick News up-to-date and all in one place. Scan headlines, and read what interests you. Find weather reports from anywhere in the world. Global and regional news comes from every location, including the South Pole. You can also access the latest news in entertainment, sports, and culture. Or link to search engines for searching world news.

Contact: Rich Rath, University of Kansas, *rath@binah.cc.brandeis.edu*

San Francisco Examiner

http://www.sfgate.com/examiner/index.html

Look here for an electronic, hypertext newspaper, updated daily, that publishes current news stories and standing features in news, business, sports, and style. Stories featured at this site are chosen as a sample from the printed newspaper, the *San Francisco Examiner,* because they are of particular interest to WWW users. The newspaper also provides many public services, such as free server space for personal home pages and political candidates. You'll also find all the other features of a print newspaper, including editorials, a Sunday magazine, a travel section, and classified advertisements.

Contact: David Dalton, San Francisco Chronicle/Examiner, *dalton@examiner.com*

Web Review

http://www-e1c.gnn.com/wr/

This electronic newspaper for the Internet community provides weekly news about the World Wide Web and the Internet. Regular features cover commerce, technology, and viewpoint. You can access all features organized by subject. Pay regular visits here to keep up with the development of the Web.

Contact: Songline Studios, Global Network Navigator, *wr-info@ora.com*

For more information on news, visit these sites:

AP News

http://www1.trib.com/NEWS/APwire.html

Updated regularly—every few minutes, apparently. Requires registration and login with username and password, but is a free service.

National Public Radio

http://www.npr.org/

Get programming guides, transcripts (audio files), news tidbits, and check out member stations across the country.

Newspage

http://www.newspage.com

News service with 500 plus sources and 25,000 plus pages updated daily. Briefs are free; full text is available for a fee and a free trial is also available. Categorized easily, with a good design.

USA Today Online

http://www.usatoday.com/

USA Today online. Very nice design.

Pets

Dog Home Page

http://www.sdsmt.edu/other/dogs/dogs.html

If you're a dog lover, and surely you are, this is the place for you. You can search for a dog breed and look at pictures of many different breeds. From there, connect to FAQs, WWW pages, further information, and pictures about the breeds you like. You'll also find frequently asked questions about owning a dog, including getting one, health care, and training. Figure out which dog you should get with a list of eighteen questions to ask a dog breeder before buying a puppy. Connect to a bunch of Usenet groups for answers to your questions and discussion about activities, breeds, behavior, rescue dogs, and more.

Then go to other WWW sites for more dog information. You can jump to general sites, breed clubs, FAQs, veterinary and medical sites, dog sledding sites, and anything else related to our best friends.

Contact: Bryan Schumacher, South Dakota School of Mines and Technology, *bschumac@silver.sdsmt.edu*

Labrador Retrievers are my favorite breed of dog. Find your favorite at the Dog Home Page.

Ferret Central

http://www.optics.rochester.edu:8080/users/pgreene/central.html

Ferrets can be the best pets because they're unusual, have great personalities, and are fun to play with. If you don't know anything about ferrets but want to learn, or if you already have a ferret and want to know more about it, this is the place to come. The extensive ferret FAQ tells you everything about ferrets as pets, including care and behavior, medical care, and more. You'll learn about ferret colors, where to get a pet ferret, what you'll need, how to ferret-proof your home, and weird things ferrets do. Visit the ferret gallery for lots of pictures; you won't believe how cute they are. There are also how-to photos for learning about basic ferret equipment such cages, collars, tags, bells, and shoulder bags. Get a list of shelters, breeders, vets, clubs, and catalogs for ferrets and ferret owners. Find out where ferrets are illegal, access a history and overview of them, read news about ferrets in the wild, and check out even more photos. Also visit ferret organizations, or meet individual ferrets through their own home pages.

Contact: Pamela Greene, University of Rochester Institute of Optics, *pgreene@optics.rochester.edu*

Fish Information Service

http://www.actwin.com/fish/index.html

Here you'll find an online archive about aquariums. The site covers freshwater, marine, tropical, and temperate aquariums, so anyone who owns fish will find something useful. Get a glossary of terms, FAQs, archives of interesting discussions, plans for do-it-yourself projects, and information about common fish diseases. You can also look at a large catalog of fish with facts, common and scientific names, and pictures. Check out photographs and movies of aquariums and underwater life. Visit aquariums on the Internet, and connect to other fish pages and related topics. This is a good resource for those who keep aquariums as a hobby or who just like to look at pictures of fish.

Contact: Mark Rosenstein, Active Windows Productions, *mar@actwin.com*

Learn all about goldfish and every other kind that can go into an aquarium at the Fish Information Service.

Herpetocultural Home Page

http://gto.ncsa.uiuc.edu/pingleto/herp.html

Loosely, herpetocultural means "all amphibians and reptiles." At this home page, you can look at photos of various herpetocultural creatures, such as crocodiles, turtles, lizards, snakes, salamanders, and frogs. Link to Internet resources for more information about these fascinating animals. Find out how to keep any of these animals as pets, something your mom, wife, or roommate is sure to love. If you have a love for the slithery and the scaly, you definitely need to pay this page a visit.

Contact: Mike Pingleton, National Center for Supercomputing Applications, University of Illinois at Urbana-Champaign, *pingleto@ncsa.uiuc.edu*

If you love the slithery and the scaly, check out this site often.

Internet Vet

http://www.zmall.com/pet_talk/tittle/pets/ivc/homepage.html

The Internet Vet, a real veterinarian, answers questions about pets through e-mail. At the Internet Vet's WWW page, you can read the archives of all questions answered by the Internet Vet. Consult the index for particular questions, or just browse through the columns. Get solutions to whatever is troubling your pet—bad habits, diseases, infections, vaccinations, etc. The column deals mainly with dogs and cats, although questions about other pets are considered.

Contact: Cindy Tittle Moore, Mall of Cyberspace, *tittle@io.com*

For more information on pets, visit these sites:

Canine Web

http://snapple.cs.washington.edu/canine/

This site contains information on dog breeds and links to other dog-related lites. Very informative!

Cat Faeries

http://www.catfaeries.com/

First, prepare yourself for an attack of "cute." When you access this page, you will be greeted by line drawings of cats with faery wings. Once you get past that, however, you will find a catelog with some very useful stuff. Cat owners may find this page very useful, if a bit much.

Cat Fanciers' Home Page

http://www.ai.mit.edu/fanciers/fanciers.html

This site has information on cat breeds, online cat clubs, and links to other cat resources.

Cats Table of Contents

http://www.zmall.com/pet_talk/cat-faqs/table-of-contents.html

Any and all the information you could ever want on cats will be linked to this site.

Cockatiels and Lovebirds

http://www.mit.edu:8001/people/rei/Tiels.html

This page contains descriptions of the care and feeding of cockatiels and lovebirds, with sketches of pet birds and ideas on how to get the birds to eat veggies.

Cybercat's Space

http://www.hooked.net/users/cybercat/

This page has bits of feline history and some cute cat pictures.

Desert Serpents Reptiles

http://www.syspac.com/~varney/index.html

This site has information on desert serpents, reptile care, reptile clubs on the Net, other reptile pages, and reptile services and suppliers.

Dr. Jim's Virtual Cat Clinic

http://rampages.onramp.net/~drjim/cats.html

This page is a "Dear Abby" for worried cat owners. Dr. Jim answers various questions from e-mail about feline health.

Electronic Zoo: Birds

http://netvet.wust1.edu/birds

This site has links to pages on poultry science, bird diseases, and a chicken gene-matching project, as well as information about pet birds.

Electronic Zoo: Cats

http://netvet.wustl.edu/cats.htm

This site provides links to as many cat-related sites as anyone can look at in one sitting. Some of the linked sites are seriously worthwhile, others humorously so.

Finding a New Home for Your Dog

http://stout.ma02.bull.com/~erics/findnewhome.html

This page has lots of useful advice for anyone who has to give up their dog. Much of the data would also apply for those giving up cats.

Good (and Bad) Beginner Fish

http://www.cco.caltech.edu/~aquaria/Faq/fish-popular.html

This page provides a great deal of information for people who are just starting out keeping pet fish. Information included covers: good first fish, good second fish, bad first fish, and what to look for in a pet fish.

Heptmed's Home Page

http://www.xmission.com/~gastown/herpmed/index.html

This site provides information on all kinds of pet care. Although the name suggests reptiles, there are pages on cats, dogs, and arachnids as well.

Hiking and Backpacking with Canines

http://snapple.cs.washington.edu/canine/backpacking/

This page provides useful information for anyone who'd like to take their dogs with them on hiking trips. Topics include what to bring, packs for your dog, and dog boots.

The Outside World

http://www.zmall.com/pet_talk/cat-faqs/outside-world.html

One of the better FAQs, this page talks about the pros and cons of indoor and outdoor cats. People considering owning cats should definitely look at this.

Pet Questions Answered

http://www.cis.ohio-state.edu/hypertext/faq/bngusenet/rec/pets/top.html

This FAQ for the newsgroup *rec.pets* answers general questions about training, behavior, and taking care of any kind of pet. There are even FAQs here for less common pets, such as ferrets, reptiles, bats, and pigs, as well as the more common cats, dogs, and birds.

Pets Are Loving Support (PALS)

http://www.sonic.net/~pals/

Get information on pets as pals.

Pet Sites

http://www.zmall.com/pet_talk/pet-faqs/homepage.html

Index of pet-related sites including FAQs, links to specific animal pages (like ferrets), and other info, such as a "virtual pet cemetery."

Reptile and Amphibian Online Magazine

http://www.pottsville.com/reptile.htm

This magazine is available online at a cost. The information that *is* online will tell you how to subscribe to the paper magazine and the information that has been published in past issues.

Reptile Solutions

http://www.reptiles.com/

This page is essentially a catalog for different types of reptiles. If you're in the market, check it out.

Snakes and Reptiles

http://www.shadeslanding.com/jas/

This site has links to a number of reptilian pages. It also features a page on snake care.

Those Wonderful Cats

http://www.eskmo.com/~panther/cats.html

This site contains links to lots of different cat pages, including the Talk to Cat Gateway, Socks on the Grass, and Virtual Reality for Cats.

Trendy's House of Herpetology

http://fovea.retina.net/~gecko/herps/

This site has information on all kinds of reptile care, from snakes to iguanas. There are lots of good links, too. Of particular interest is the theory that reptiles and computers have a natural affinity for each other.

Turtles

http://www.tietopolku.fi/teppo/konnat/turtles.html

This page has some information and several pictures on turtles.

Sports

Backcountry Home Page

http://io.datasys.swri.edu/Overview.html

Hikers and outdoors types love this archive of backcountry-related information. Get tips and recommendations on gear, suggestions for improving your backcountry skills, and advice on not getting lost. One useful feature, Distilled Wisdom, covers subjects ranging from backcountry ethics to snakebites. Tour a photographic gallery of back-country trips. You'll also find weather information for many places around the globe, camping recipes, hiking clubs, and trip reports. Don't skip the "miscellaneous" link, which has such interesting gems as Appalachian Trail videos, a backpacker's wilderness test, and a connection to the search-and-rescue BBS.

Contact: Stephen Johns, Backcountry Home Page, Southwest Research Institute, *johns@swri.edu*

Get outdoors with the help of the Backcountry Home Page.

The Baseball Server

http://www2.nando.net/SportServer/baseball/

Swing into baseball with full coverage of games and news, updated daily during the season. The archive, organized by league, includes current standings, starting pitchers, season-to-date transactions, and complete coverage of all star games. You'll also get complete coverage of events such as the World Series and any "work stoppages" that may be going on. Stay in touch with everything baseball in one handy spot at this server.

Contact: New Media Division, Nando, Raleigh News and Observer, *zonker@nando.net*

See Mickey Mantle and other baseball greats at the Baseball Server.

Cyber Cyclery

http://www.cyclery.com/

Every kind of biking is featured here, from racing to dirt biking, and lots more besides. Visit home pages for different bicycle manufacturers selected from a huge list that you can search by company or product. Take virtual bicycling tours of Alaska, the Bahamas, Italy, off-road Canada, and many more places. The Ultimate Mountain Bike Calendar has much to interest off-road bikers, including riding techniques, camping tips, a mountain bike maintenance schedule, and a birthday list of professional racers. Read a free issue of *Dirt Rag*, a mountain biking magazine, and articles from *Bike Culture Quarterly* for general cyclists. A racing link leads to information about races and events, including the Tour de France, with results of different races and a calendar of upcoming events. Under Readings, you'll find all sorts of bicycling articles, including interviews with pros, tips for maintenance and repair, product information, training tips, touring stories, and scientific facts. Travel down links to other Internet bicycling sites, such as racing sites, clubs, discussion groups, and even a random link. Every cycling enthusiast will find something of interest at this site.

Contact: Cyber Cyclery, *comments@cyclery.com*

CyberDojo

http://cswww2.essex.ac.uk/Web/karate/CyberDojo/

The CyberDojo is the main place for karate information on the Web. Get a list of recommended dojos around the world. Check out traditional karate kata and weapon kata, with exact descriptions of how to perform each kata. Find out about karate-related events all around the world, and learn karate terminology. A bibliography lists some recommended readings about the sport. There are many links to other martial arts resources, including martial arts pages, information on stretching and self defense, pictures, and home pages for karate people. You can also find out about the CyberDojo mailing list for the discussion of traditional karate. Look in the FAQ for more info about terminology, organizations, and pressure points, among other karate-related topics. The CyberDojo is one of the best karate pages on the Internet. If karate is your thing, pay a visit today.

Contact: Patrice Tarabbia, University of Essex, *tarabbia@cenatls.cena.dgac.fr*

Dirt Central

http://www.knowsys-sw.com:80/Dave/mtb/

If you love mountain biking, come to this very cool page to meet another true lover of the sport. Find out why you should ride, and read an original poem about crashing. Check out some ramblings about mountain biking and a gallery of nifty pictures. Learn all about the "dirty bike." Join a community of online mountain bikers from this site. You'll also find links to other mountain biking resources, including rules of the trail, bicycle companies, cycling services, and electronic magazines.

Contact: Dave, KnowSys Software, *Dave@KnowSys-sw.com*

ESPNET Sports Zone

http://espnet.sportszone.com/

Come to ESPN for the latest sports news, no matter what the sport. Read the top sports stories for today, or find out about ongoing events, such as the Olympics or the Tour de France. Every day there are new sports features, including polls and in-depth articles. Access scoreboards and news for professional sports such as baseball, football, and basketball. You'll find the top stories for the day, a scoreboard, overviews of teams and players, and upcoming events. Check out Sportstalk for letters to ESPN correspondents, live chat about particular sports, and letters to the Zone. Go to Zoned Out for sports biofiles, trivia, and other fun stuff. Visit the ESPN studios for up-to-the-minute program updates and TV listings. There's also a multimedia gallery with sports pictures and audio files. There's so much sports stuff to do and see here, you'll never get to it all.

Contact: ESPNET Sports Zone, *espnet.sportszone@starwave.com*

Get all the latest sports action at ESPN's Web site.

Footbag Worldwide

http://www.footbag.org/

This is the spot for information about the sport of footbag, also known as hackey sack. Get an overview of the sport, and link to a list of clubs, leagues, and organizations. You can also interactively add your own club to the list. Download information about footbag equipment, including shoes, footbags, nets, and rules for the sport. Find out how to build your own net, and get a beginner's guide to the sport. Access lists of upcoming footbag tournaments, gatherings, and festivals around the word, as well as reviews and results of recent tournaments. Link to home pages of various players, footbag newsletters, and discussion groups. A multimedia gallery with pictures, video, sounds, and even illustrated audio slide shows should get you excited about playing footbag.

Contact: Footbag Worldwide, *info@footbag.com*

GolfWeb

http://www.golfweb.com/

GolfWeb has everything related to golf that can be found on the WWW. Look in the library for interesting articles about recent championships and golf issues, photographs, and reference materials. You'll also find the official rules of golf here. A golf course database lists over 14,000 courses with extensive user comments. Or you can virtually visit golf courses all around the world. Follow the latest tour action, including pro tours, the majors, and college and amateur action. Go to the Pro Shop to buy golfing clothes, clubs, balls and tees, books and videos, travel services, shoes, and gloves. Share your favorite golf story, tip, course, or equipment recommendation on the bulletin board. There's even information and programming for the golf channel here.

Contact: Golf Digest, GolfWeb, *comments@golfweb.com*

Gymnastics

http://rainbow.rmii.com/~rachele/gymnhome.html

Connect to this home page for the archives of the lively gymnastics mailing list. The discussion includes explanations of technique, rules, routines of top gymnasts, personal stories, and anything else to do with gymnastics. You'll get detailed reports of competitions, both national and international, and a monthly calendar of gymnastics events. You'll also find gymnastics trivia, Internet resources, videos, magazines, and ASCII art at the home page.

Contact: Rachele Harless, Rocky Mountain Internet, *rachele@rmii.com*

Learn about every aspect of gymnastics at the gymnastics home page.

The Great Outdoors

http://www.gorp.com/

Tap into a huge amount of information on what to do and where to go in the great outdoors at these packed Web pages. Whether you're planning a trip or gathering information on your favorite outdoors activity, this is the place to start. The site is dedicated to people who like to be active, learn new skills, get out in the natural world, and get off the beaten path. Go to Attractions to learn about good places to go in the outdoors. You can virtually visit national parks, wildlife refuges, national monuments, recreational areas, battlefields, and more great spots all over the United States. Also listed are worldwide archaeological sites and primitive areas. Look for lots of activities, including biking, boating, climbing, fishing, hang-gliding, hiking, windsurfing, and snow sports. There are also resources on the environment, nature, and wildlife. For each sport, connect to Internet resources, photographs, magazines, clubs, books, and more. Find travel and recreational resources arranged by world location, including books and maps, traveling tips, and environmental facts. Take virtual trips to outdoors paradises all over the world, or find out how to take real adventure trips. Go to Gear to learn about equipment for any outdoor sport. The Newsstand has addresses for special interest groups, magazines, newsgroups, and e-mail newsletters for all sorts of outdoor sports and hobbies. Get some backpacking tips and recipes, learn how to stay healthy when you travel, and connect to other general travel resources on the Internet. There's lots of valuable free information for any lover of the outdoors at this one site.

Contact: Greer Consulting Services, Great Outdoors Recreation Pages, *postmaster@www.gorp.com*

Inline Online

http://galaxy.einet.net/galaxy/Leisure-and-Recreation/Sports/daniel-chick/io_org.html

Inline Online is the first digital magazine and information source entirely devoted to inline skating. Here you can get an overview of the sport and learn about the different kinds of inline skating, or browse a photo gallery of some awesome moves. From the site you can connect to various inline organizations, and get information about inline magazines. Outstanding individuals and teams are spotlighted in Who's Who. A miscellaneous news category keeps you up-to-date on the events, and rumors, in the world of inline skating. Get information about various inline-related products and the companies that make them, including a list of skate videos. This site is just getting off the ground, but it is shaping up to be a useful and complete resource.

Contact: Daniel Chick, EINet Galaxy, *3drc@qlink.queensu.ca*

The Michael Jordan Page

http://gagme.wwa.com/~boba/mj.html

This complete home page provides information on basketball's favorite son—Michael Jordan. Here you'll find information about Jordan's career, his basketball stats, links to other Jordan pages, and news about the Chicago Bulls. Get in-depth information about Jordan's career, including his return to basketball. Read Internet talk about Jordan from e-mail and Usenet newsgroups. Access a list of Jordan's basketball achievments, stats, and sports cards. Connect to other pages about Jordan and the Bulls, including stats, history, standings, wrap-ups, the team roster, and reports on the latest games. Also go to NBA information, with scoreboards, daily news reports, schedules, video highlights, and more fun stuff. You'll find links to team pages, the NBA draft, and feature stories. Expand beyond the NBA into the greater world of basketball with links to newsgroups, FAQs, and college, European, and fantasy basketball pages. There is even a collection of basketball ASCII art to view. This great page is a must-see for any Jordan or basketball fan.

Contact: Bob Allison, WorldWide Access, *boba@wwa.com*

Catch Michael live at his very own home page.

Olympic Games

http://www.atlanta.olympic.org/

Get ready for the 1996 Olympics in Atlanta, Georgia, and follow all the ceremonies at this fun site. Movies and audio files welcome you to the games. Get a FAQ about the 1996 Olympics, and check out the games at a glance. Find out what sports will occur, and take a virtual flight through the Olympic Stadium. You can read interesting sports facts and firsts and get information about a specific sport. Look at the official sports program, and find out the schedule for certain sports. You can also get travel information, find out about purchasing tickets, and look at the products and sponsors of the Games. You'll be an Olympics expert after going through this site.

Contact: 1996 Olympic Games

Professional Basketball Server

http://www.netgen.com/sis/NBA/NBA.html

This site won a Best of the Web award for Best Entertainment Site, and it's easy to see why. It is the most complete place for basketball information on the WWW. Daily coverage includes every team and player in the NBA, with up-to-date information on schedules, scores, team stats, league leaders, and team rosters. During the playoff rounds, get complete information on the brackets and series standings. In the archives, look up stats from years gone by, including championships, top ten player salaries, drafts, team histories, year-by-year award results, and all-time leaders. Get your basketball fix every day at this information-packed site.

Contact: Sports Information Server, Net.Genesis Corporation, *siscomments@netgen.com*

The Running Page

http://sunsite.unc.edu/drears/running/running.html

This is your Web source for information on running. Here you'll find resources on upcoming races, race results, places to run, products, magazines, and much more. You can connect to other online running information, including the *rec.running* FAQ. Also enter a real-time, online discussion venue for runners who want to talk to others about the sport; runners of all abilities are welcome.

Contact: SunSITE, University of North Carolina at Chapel Hill

Skateboarding

http://tumyeto.com/tydu/skatebrd/skate.htm

No aspect of skateboarding is neglected in this premier information source. Get contest results and coverage of the British and European championships. Visit skate parks all over the country through photographs. Get scene reports from everywhere, and read skateboarding fiction. Visit a skate and punk festival, or read interviews with top skaters. Check out reviews of skate videos, and access a guide on learning how to skate. Get the latest news, gossip, and events in the world of skateboarding. Connect to company home pages, skateboard organizations, and other skate sites. There are photos to view and text to read, all about skateboarding. You can also e-mail your own skateboarding experiences to the site.

Contact: Tum Yeto Ghetto

See pictures of fantastic skateboarding feats at the Skateboarding site.

SkiAmerica

http://www.skiamerica.com/biz/skiamerica

SkiAmerica is a primary online resource for information about ski resorts, lift tickets, lodging, complete travel packages, snow condition reports, and ski equipment products. SkiAmerica has been a major distributor of ski resort information for 29 years and has now emerged on the WWW so anyone in the world can access the service. Get resort information about a small number of places, accessing mountain facts, lodging, ski schools, group rates, and lift tickets. You can also get the latest ski condition reports for over 50 resorts. Purchase ski lift passes for resorts in the United States and Canada, and find out about ski lift pass specials available only on the Internet. Ski buffs should be sure to complete an interactive form to receive the *SkiAmerica* magazine free. This new service is adding pages all the time. Take a look at the White Mountains sample page to see what kind of resources will soon be available here.

Contact: SkiAmerica, UltraNet Communications, *barryh@skiamerica.com*

Soccer

http://iamwww.unibe.ch/~ftiwww/Sonstiges/Tabellen/ Eindex.html

Soccer fans can find information on the game all over the WWW. Connect to it all from this handy site. Here you'll find the latest standings for countries all over the world. You'll also get results and news from the international championships, such as the World Cup and the European Cup. An archive includes information on all World Cups, European Championships, and Intercontinental Cups, as well as records of title-holders and news on teams organized by country. For even more soccer information, link to other Internet soccer resources, such as newsgroups and WWW sites.

Contact: Reinhard Kahle, Bern University, *Kahle@iam.unibe.ch*

Sports Illustrated

http://pathfinder.com/si/greet.html

Visit the famous sports magazine's home on the Web. Here you can read this week's cover story and see the cover photo. Check out the magazine archive for past cover stories and classic stories. In the archive, you can get a retrospective of sports news with articles about tennis, baseball, basketball, football, auto racing, golf, college sports, boxing, championship games, and your favorite sports stars. The cover stories go back to February 1995, and the classic stories go further back in time for articles about important events in sports and sports figures. Check out a Wimbledon gallery with photos, news, scores, and stats from all the past Wimbledon tennis tournaments. Look at baseball photos, and tap into an Olympics site. At the SportsTalk bulletin boards, you can post messages about personalities, sports, and games (you have to register to use this feature). Who needs a subscription when you can get the best of the magazine online?

Contact: Sports Illustrated, Pathfinder

Sports Information Server

http://www.netgen.com/sis/

If you are interested in professional sports, drop by here first. Get the latest news about professional hockey, basketball, and football. The professional hockey server gives you the NHL playoffs, schedules, and scores at a glance. The professional basketball server shows the NBA playoffs, schedules, reviews of the previous season, scores, awards, and yearly statistics. You can also follow the draft and other events. Check out the Professional Football Server for an overview of the NFL draft, news, season schedules, Super Bowl history, standings, annual awards, and all the teams. The sports servers change as the season progresses, so there's always the latest info about current happenings. There are also links to international sports, such as soccer, golf, horse racing, sailing, skiing, and tennis. A discussion center lets you talk about your favorite sports or last night's game with other Internet users of the Sports Information Server.

Contact: Net.Genesis Corporation, *sis-comments@netgen.com*

Sports Library

http://www.atm.ch.cam.ac.uk/sports/sports.html

This section has covered a lot of sports sites on the Internet, but what if your favorite sport wasn't listed? Maybe you play volleyball, swim, ride horses, surf, or play laser tag. Don't worry—there's something on the Internet for you. Just check out this huge library of sports information to connect to your favorite sport. You can search the entire library for a particular word or check out the sports site of the week for something new and interesting every week. What can you connect to? WWW pages, races and championships, multimedia, news, magazines, discussion groups—everything online that has anything to do with sports. You'll find huge archives for all sorts of sports, including football, baseball, basketball, and soccer. Check out libraries of ball sports such as golf and tennis, wheel sports such as cycling and auto racing, water sports such as swimming, sailing, and fishing, and outdoors sports such as skiing and climbing. There are even obscure sports here such as underwater hockey, water polo, darts, caving, hanggliding, sky diving, cricket, hurling, and croquet. Find resources about athletics and fitness too. There's also a huge list of sports-related newsgroups. This library is so huge that it takes forever to look through it all, but it is a useful resource for almost any sport you are interested in.

Contact: Owen Garrett, Center for Atmospheric Science, University of Cambridge, *owen@atm.ch.cam.ac.uk*

Sports Schedules

http://www.cs.rochester.edu/u/ferguson/schedules/

Get schedules for all the games for any major professional sport. Schedules are included for major league hockey, baseball, football, and basketball, as well as the Canadian Football League and the Australian Football League. Just click on the sport for which you want schedules. You get back an interactive form that allows you to specify the teams or divisions you're interested in. Selecting two teams or divisions will show upcoming games between the two teams, between the team and any other team in the division, or between teams in the two divisions.

You can then print out the schedule or save it as a file on your computer for easy reference. Use the calendar to follow your favorite team or to find out about upcoming games you don't want to miss.

Contact: George Ferguson, Department of Computer Science, University of Rochester

Tennis Server

http://www.tennisserver.com/Tennis.html

Visit here for all the latest tennis news and information. You'll find the ATP Tour weekly electronic newsletter and the latest news of the sport. Get player and equipment tips from the pros, and read court-side reports on recent games and tournaments. You'll also find the rules and codes of tennis and photographs of all the hot stars. Don't forget to visit the Tennis Warehouse to order tennis equipment online. When you finish here, you can link to an even wider range of tennis information found elsewhere on the Internet.

Contact: Racquet Workshop, Tennis Server, *info.racquet@tennisserver.com*

Two-Minute Warning

http://www.dtd.com/tmw/

Play a fun NFL trivia game where you answer questions to gain yards, score points, and compete for prizes. Go to the Rulebook for a quick overview of the game. You can select easy, average, or difficult games, but you only have two minutes to complete any game you choose. The trivia questions really test your football knowledge. Take a look at the current top ten scores. If you stay in the top ten until the end of the month, you win a prize. See what prizes last month's winners received, and check out this month's prizes. Even if you don't win a prize, it's fun to play this game again and again. Also check out NFL Sidelines to visit the WWW home of the NFL.

Contact: Downtown Digital, Gigabox, *tmw@dtd.com*

Unicycling

http://www.unicycling.org/

Find everything you didn't want to know about unicycling in one spot, and have lots of fun too. Get a FAQ on unicycling, which answers all of the most common questions about this unusual sport. Connect to discussion groups such as *rec.sport.unicycling* and the unicycle mailing list. Find out how to ride a unicycle and what kind to buy. Check out lists of fun things to try and games to play with the unicycle. E-mail addresses and home pages of other unicyclists help you connect with unicyclists in your area. Read stories about unicycling experiences. Look at a photo album and a few funny movies. You'll also find links to other pastimes such as juggling and boomerangs. If you aren't already unicycling, you'll want to start after visiting this page.

Contact: Beirne Konarski, Kent University, *bkonarsk@mcs.kent.edu*

Get started unicycling at the Unicycling home page.

The Virtual Flyshop

http://www.flyshop.com/

This forum for Internet flyfishers holds lots of interesting, multimedia information about the sport. A hypermedia magazine features fictional fishing stories and real-life trip reports, complete with photographs. Find continuously updated river condition reports from all over the world. Interact with other flyfishers in an interactive forum, or enter your prize catch into the Wall of Fame. Get merchandise information, and even shop online. The site also connects to newsgroups, discussion archives, and other WWW sites on flyfishing.

Contact: Greg McDermid and Mike Tucker, Virtual Flyshop, *flyshop@flyshop.com*

World Wide Web of Sports

http://www.tns.lcs.mit.edu/cgi-bin/sports/

Come to this site for sports information to satisfy even the most avid fan. Sports covered in-depth include football, basketball, baseball, and hockey, with schedules, drafts, and video highlights of recent games. You'll also find soccer news, including international game results, and cycling information, with Tour de France reports. Link to other popular sports, such as ultimate frisbee, volleyball, rugby, golf, running, rowing, figure and speed skating, and tennis. Or go to international games such as the Olympics and the Goodwill Games. You can even create a personalized sports page using an interactive form to access only the sports information you're most interested in.

Contact: Massachusetts Institute of Technology Telemedia Lab, *webmaster@www.tns.lcs.mit.edu*

For more infomation on sports, visit these sites:

Aikido & Martial Arts Homepage

http://www.cs.uregina.ca/~romano/index.html

A very comprehensive and well-designed site for anyone interested in aikido. There are pages on a dojo, general aikido information, an aikido club, some pictures of immobilization holds, and links to a journal. There are also links to other "cool" areas.

Baseball Fantasy Camps

http://www.mcn.org/MenComNet/Community/Personals/dmca/ basfnpg1.htm

This site gives information on how to attend a baseball fantasy camp. At these camps the average sports fan can play baseball with his fantasy pro players. There are also umpire camps.

Basketball

http://www.cs.indiana.edu/hyplan/bodom/basketball.html

This site has links to all kinds of NBA sites. All information is arranged by an armchair athelete for other armchair atheletes.

Billy's Motorcycle

http://www.mindspring.com/~hume/motorcycle.html

While still under construction, this page already has links to several cool biking sites. If the contruction follows through on the "coming soon," this should be worth checking out.

The Chiu Lau Wing Chun College

http://www.worldgate.com/cybertek/wchun/

This site contains information on the available instruction in wing chun kung fu. It also has related articles, a history of the art, and links to related pages.

A Classy Twenty-Footer

http://tenthmuse.clever.net/seals/c20.html

This page has a lot of good information on the Cal20, a type of sail-boat. It also contains some well-buried sales information on Cal20 accessories, but the sales pitch is placed in an unobnoxious manner that doesn't interfere with the basic boat information.

The Climbing Dictionary

http://www.fm.bs.dlr.de/dlr/abt_12/climbing/climbing_dict.html

This page covers a long list of rock climbing terminology. The explaina-tions are easy to understand. (Example: "Watch me" is a call to indicate the climber is about to do something stupid—like fall.) Also included are some common foreign language versions of the climbing terms.

College Basketball Page

http://www.cs.cmu.edu/afs/cs.cmu.edu/user/wsr/Web/bball/bball.html

This page has much more information than either of the ESPNet col-lege basketball sites (listed below), and doesn't have a Gatoraid ad at the beginning. Information on team standings, academic information, ESPN schedules, school nicknames, season stats, and other goodies.

The Dead Runners Society

http://storm.cadcam.iupui.edu/drs/drs.html

This is the home page for a group of people who like to talk about running, developing running programs, and so forth. It also contains links to other running sites.

Enlightened Dragon Self Preservation System

http://www.cs.runet.edu/~hylton/edsps.html

This site contains brief discussions of several martial arts styles as well as links to related sites.

FIA Formula One World Championship Sporting Regulations

http://ccnga.uwaterloo.ca/~jscouria/sportingregs.html

This page describes exactly what qualifies a car to race in the Formula One Grand Prix. Car enthusiasts will either love it or already know it.

Grand Master

http://www.worldgate.com/cybertek/gmaster/

This is the electronic version of *Grand Master Magazine*, a publication covering many different martial arts. It includes articles, an online forum, and information on seminars, tournaments, and so forth.

Hapkido Homepage

http://www.cs.uregina.ca/~skagos/

This is a site maintained by a self-proclaimed geek, but it contains a very good martial arts page. The martial arts page contains links to sites for four different types of martial arts, as well as interesting miscellaneous martial arts links.

IISA News

http://www.globalone.net/lionsden/io/iisa.html

This is the home page of the International Inline Skating Association (IISA). This is the spot to find information on the Association, as well as certification information on becoming a certified inline skating instructor.

The Illuminati Biking Page

http://www.eskimo.com/~carcosa/

Information on Illuminati motorcycling events. This site also has gratuitous Kerouac quotes. For the sporty conspiracy fan in us all.

Inline Skating in Singapore

http://www.ncb.gov.sg/sif/sep94/covertwo.html

This page covers the development of inline skating in Singapore, along with a description of the Singapore Roller Skating Club.

Internet Running Related Sources

http://sunsite.unc.edu/drears/running/www.html

This page lists and links many running-related pages on the Net. A good starting place for research on the subject.

The Martial Arts as I've Learned Them

http://student-www.uchicago.edu/users/fun5/martial.html

This is one martial arts student's view of four different martial arts. He includes information on martial arts in general, with special emphasis on tang soo do, jeet kune do, qigong, and aikido. He also includes links to related sites.

The Martial Arts Clearinghouse

http://www.lehigh.edu/~sjb3/martial.html

This site has information on many types of martial arts, including many essays, interviews, book reviews and bibliographies, and historical information.

Men's College Basketball

http://espnet.sportszone.com/ncb/index.html

This site has some information for fans of men's basketball, but some of the data is only available for subscribers. Still, may be worth an occasional visit for the rankings and stats when the NCAA basketball season is underway.

Motorcycle Online

http://motorcycle.com/motorcycle.html?

This site has information on new bikes, reviews, press kits on recent motorcycle releases, motocycling events, and much more. Parental note: It also has several pictures of bikini-clad-babes-with-bikes.

The Motorcycle Page

http://www.lfbs.rwth-aachen.de/~markolf/Motorcycles.html

This site was developed by the Demons of Doom, a group that gets together to talk about bike- and nonbike-things. Lots of information on certain types of motorcycles (the ones they think are cool, mainly) and little-to-no information on others.

The Mountain Bike Pages

http://catless.ncl.ac.uk/mtb/

This site has information for kids starting to ride mountain bikes, race schedules, a routes map (without that many routes), links to other bike pages, and Olympic information.

Mountain Biking in the United States

http://xenon.stanford.edu/~rsf/mtb-usa.html

This site lists, by state, the different mountain bike-related sites and pages. Included are race lists, bike clubs, and route maps.

My Jet Skiing Page!

http://www.geopages.com/SunsetStrip/1082/js.html

This page covers one person's relationship with jet skiing. It has reviews of some jet ski models and links to other jet ski sites.

The National Women's Martial Arts Federation

http://www.en.utexas.edu/studentprojects/syverson/apin/NWMAF.html

This site includes a recognition of outstanding female martial artists, a ranking board for black belt women, a list of self-defense events, and membership information.

NetSailing Magazine

http://www.netsailing.com/

This is an online magazine devoted to sailing. Feature articles cover everything from South Sea sailing to sailing across Lake Superior. Also included is an event calendar and racing results.

New York City Inline Skating Guide

http://www.panix.com/~rbs/Skate/NYC/clubs.html

This page describes the different skating clubs in NYC and provides links to those that are online.

Nothing But Net: Basketball by the 'Net, for the 'Net.

http://www.gnn.com/gnn/meta/sports/basketball/net/index.html

This site has a basketball FAQ, e-mail lists for basketball teams, results from the NBA draft, and links to Usenet basketball newsgroups.

On the Water

http://www.hic.net/wink/boats.html

This site has links to information on buying, building, sailing, and chartering boats. There is also a link to the Safety Code of the American Whitewater Affiliation.

The Personal Watercraft Zone

http://calweb.calweb.com/~pwczone/open.html

This site is a magazine for and about jet skis. It has reviews of various models, editorials on water safety, winterizing tips, and other cool stuff.

Planet Reebok

http://planetreebok.com/

A Web page by Reebok aimed at women, with information on women's sports and fitness, an interactive mailing list, special events, and CauseNet (which links to human rights and other info). Very nice design. It doesn't appear you can order any kind of product, but it doesn't advertise them either.

Ponderosa Campground: The Home Page of Master Camper

http://www.barint.on.ca/cybermal/ponderosa/barnes4.html

This page has user questions and Master Camper's answers about camping. You can e-mail your questions to the Master Camper and, like Dear Abby of the tenting set, he will do his best to enlighten you.

PWM's Boat Page

http://www.msen.com/~pwmeek/boat.html

This page provides links to lots of sailing information, with a Great Lakes bias. A noteworthy link involves rubber-band boat racing.

Rock Climbing in Europe

http://www.oslonett.no/sp/fjell/climbing/

This site provides information on rock climbing areas in Europe, both natural and manmade. Links, arranged by country, show the user pictures of rock climbing areas and give information about each one.

Rocky Mountaineers Motorcycle Club

http://nexus.interealm.com/p/sheyl/rmmc

This site covers the activities of the Colorado gay and lesbian motorcycle club. Included are descriptions of events and membership info.

Running and Triathlon

http://canyon.epg.harris.com/~mvm/runtri.html

This site contains links to various running and triathlon newsgroups, pages, and so forth. There is also an ultrarunning bulletin board, a Florida Race Calendar, and various topical articles.

Safety Code of the American Whitewater Affiliation

http://www.rahul.net/fallside/awa/safety/safety.html

This page is a must for anyone considering doing anything around whitewater. Included is advice for rafters, canoeists, rescuing people, and universal hand/arm signals.

Skate Clubs and Organizations

http://www.terminus.com/inline/org.htm

This page has the names and addresses of skating clubs throughout the United States. Unfortunately, it doesn't include links to any of them.

Skate FAQ

http://www.cis.ohio-state.edu/hypertext/faq/usenet-faqs/ bygroup/rec/skate/top.html

There are lots of FAQs in this archive for the newsgroup *rec.skate*, but be sure to read the general info FAQ and any others that catch your fancy. You'll find FAQs about figure skating, skating tricks, roller hockey, where to skate, inline skating, and competitive skating.

Skateparks: Pros and Cons

http://web.cps.msu.edu/~dunhamda/dw/park_pc.html

This page gives some good reasons to build and not to build a park for inline skaters. If you or your community are considering building such a park, check this page out first.

Skating Around the World

http://www.cs.tulane.edu/www/Ward/inline-SK8/world.html

Ever wonder how the skating is in Vienna? Or Finland? This site will lead you to pages from skaters all over the globe, from where to skate in the U.K. to where not to skate in Amsterdam.

The Snow Page

http://rmd-www.mr.ic.ac.uk/snow/snowpage.html

This page covers every aspect of the white fluffy stuff, including sports, travel, zines, trails, and whatever else you can think of.

Spin it, Sisters! Women in Mountain Biking

http://outside.starwave.com/outside/online/disc/spinit/
index.html

This site is maintained by a couple of champion female mountian bikers. They've got a Q&A area, a roundtable, and an "about the racers" section. It's not a big site, but it's a good one.

Tai Ji

http://sunserver1.rz.uni-duesseldorf.de/~franza/taiji/sources.html

This site has links to Tai Ji (aka Taiiquan, Tai Chi, Taichicahuan) in particular and related Eastern topics in general. Included topics are Buddhism, Taoism, acupuncture, and books.

Training Tips from Coach Gordy

http://lornet.com/~asca/gordy.htm

This page provides advice on competitive swimming in a question-and-answer format.

UCL Motorcycle Club Page

http://www.ucl.ac.uk/~ucecspb/motor.html

This U.K. motocycle site has information on bikes, rides, biker gossip, links to other cool stuff, even a mission statement! Well worth a gander for anyone interested in biking from a British point of view.

Wasatch Front Rock Climbing

http://www.cs.utah.edu/~gwall/wfrc/wfrc.html

This site covers climbing sites and routes, news, area conditions, climbing shops, upcoming events, and climbing gyms. It is based in Utah, so some of the information is SW-USA specific.

Web Swim

http://alf2.tcd.ie/~smftzger/swim/header.html

This site has information on swimming as a sport, advice on shoulder injuries, links to a water polo site, and information on Masters swimming.

Wombats

http://www.wombats.org/

Wombats is the Womens' Mountain Bike and Tea Society. Here you can find out about this unique group, see the Wombat art gallery, and visit other bike sites online.

Women's College Basketball

http://espnet.sportszone.com/ncw/

This site, like the Men's College Basketball site, has some information that is only available to subscribers. There are stats and rankings, but this site is still barren compared to the men's site.

WWW Martial Arts Resource Page

http://www.middlebury.edu/~jswan/martial.arts/ma.html

This site discusses and has links to many different martial arts, from aikido to wing chun. It also has mailing lists and a "stuff to buy" section.

Television

The Late Show With David Letterman

http://bingen.cs.csbsju.edu/letterman.html

This home page gives you all the information you need on the popular late-night talk show. Find out about upcoming guests for the next week, or get up-to-date summaries of recent shows you missed. You'll always find the most recent Top Ten List on the home page, as well as an archive of all Dave's top ten lists. Browse monologues, and get the latest gossip about the show. Various images and sound bites are ready to download. From here, you can connect to other Internet resources, such as the *alt.fan.letterman* newsgroup.

Contact: Jeff Hoffmann, St. John's University and College of St. Benedict, *jahoffma@bingen.cs.csbsju.edu*

PBS Online

http://www.pbs.org/

Here you can access everything about the Public Broadcasting System (PBS). Find out what's on, including monthly listings, children's programming, news, documentaries, drama, performance, and much more. Access learning services, such as electronic field trips and instructional television. You can also link to cool educational resources from here. Visit the PBS store, selling videos, music, books, and lots more stuff related to PBS programming. Find your local PBS station. Get online news updates from MacNeil/Lehrer. Link to the home pages for PBS series, including "Frontline," "An Evening at the Pops," "Mystery!," "Masterpiece Theatre," "Lamb Chop's Play-Along," "Mr. Roger's Neighborhood," "Reading Rainbow," "Nova," and "Nature." Also link to other media literacy resources on the Net.

Contact: Public Broadcasting System, *www@pbs.org*

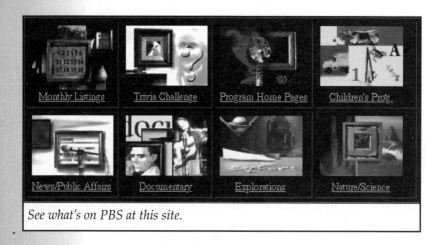

See what's on PBS at this site.

Science Fiction TV Series Guide

http://www.ee.surrey.ac.uk/Contrib/SciFi/

Science fiction fans can find here an extensive guide to sci-fi on television, with up-to-date episode summaries, cast lists, and trivia. "Star Trek" has the biggest archive, with a short history of the television show and guides to both "The Next Generation" and "Deep Space Nine," including information about the setting, cast lists, major alien species, trivia, episode summaries, and movie rumors. The "Dr. Who" guide gives up-to-date information on the long-awaited video releases of the series from the BBC. A short-form guide provides information on little-known shows no longer in production, such as "Space Rangers" and "Something Is Out There." Tour the science-fiction television universe with this useful guide.

Contact: Department of Electronic and Electrical Engineering, University of Surrey, Duncan White, *D.White@ee.surrey.ac.uk*, and Bevis King, *B.King@ee.surrey.ac.uk*

SciFi Channel: The Dominion

http://www.scifi.com/

The SciFi Channel site is one of the best examples of creative multimedia you'll find on the Web. When you first connect, you'll see what's playing right now on the SciFi Channel as it scrolls across the bottom of the screen. If you aren't immediately compelled to trade your computer for your TV set, check out SciFi Channel original programming such as "C I net Central," "Sci-Fi Buzz," "FTL Newsfeed," and more. You'll learn all about each show—when it airs, who works on it, reference guides, biographies, episode guides, and more. Of course, you can always check the current programming and search programming for the near future. You'll also find programming highlights for the current month and the following one. Look under Pulp for features from *Sci-Fi Entertainment Magazine*, science-fiction comic books, and user-created fiction. Download free stuff such as SF audio clips, video clips, and images. In Trader, buy cool merchandise featuring "The X-Files," "Doctor Who," "Babylon 5," "Star Trek," and *Star Wars*. At the Bulletin Board, talk about TV shows, movies, anime, books, zines, comics, the Internet, games, music, art, conventions, and anything else having to do with sci-fi, including the paranormal, personals, culture, and history. (There are some adults-only places in this section, but they are clearly marked.) Go into Orbit by jumping to other science-fiction sites, such as clubs, horror pages, Internet news, literature, movies, paranormal, science fact, television, and zines. Even if you aren't a diehard SciFi fan, you'll find a lot to occupy you in this fun site.

Contact: SciFi Channel

The Seinfeld Index Page

http://www.ifi.uio.no/~rubens/seinfeld/

This rich archive provides scripts, sounds, and images from the popular television show, grouped by episode. For most episodes, you can read the entire script, hear the best sound clips, and see stills of priceless moments. You can also view images and hear trademark lines from each of the main characters. Connect to over 70 sound clips grouped together in one archive, or get an archive of all the pictures. The home page will link you to other "Seinfeld" resources elsewhere on the Internet, such as the *alt.tv.seinfeld* newsgroup, an episode guide on Gopher and more pictures and sounds from the show. This is a good example of a typical WWW home page for a television show, with a wealth of useful information, all free for you to access.

Contact: Ruben Sogaard, University of Oslo, *rubens@ifi.uio.no*

Julia Louis-Dreyfus and Jason Alexander
Photo: J. Del Valle
©NBC, Inc.

See priceless moments from "Seinfeld" at the Seinfeld Index Page.

Sitcom Page

http://pmwww.cs.vu.nl/service/sitcoms/

Get information, pictures, and multimedia for your favorite television comedies at this one page. You can connect to shows such as "Saved by the Bell," "Seinfeld," "Roseanne," "Home Improvement," "Full

House," and "Blossom." Or check out old favorites such as "Growing Pains," "Family Ties," and "My Two Dads." Download complete episode guides, pictures, and occasional movies. You'll also find sound files of the theme songs. Read trivia, quotes, and interviews with cast members. Connect to newsgroups, FAQs, and other home pages about the shows. If you're a fan of a particular sitcom, this is a great place to find out more about it.

Contact: Matthijs van Doorn, Public Maintainers Page, *thijs@cs.vu.nl*

Star Trek Home Page

http://www.cosy.sbg.ac.at/rec/startrek/index.html

Visit this information-packed home page to satisfy your "Star Trek" cravings. Here you can access archived information on all "Star Trek" TV shows, including MPEG clips, still images, and sounds. Complete episode guides for the original series, "The Next Generation," "Deep Space Nine," the movies, and the animated series are linked in. You'll also turn up gems such as quotes, parodies, and a Klingon dictionary. Lists of "Star Trek" books and comics give facts on vessels, charted worlds, guest characters, and alien races found in them. You can also read "Star Trek" jokes and top ten lists, as well as a collection of original stories on the "third generation."

Contact: Brigitte Jellinek, University of Salzburg, *bjelli@cosy.sbg.ac.at*

Star Trek: The Next Generation

http://www.ugcs.caltech.edu/st-tng/

This is the definitive site for information about "Star Trek: The Next Generation." Learn all about your favorite characters, including pictures and a timeline of what happens to them in the "Star Trek" universe. You can also read about the actors who play each character. The cast list includes not only the main characters but every minor character down to the lowliest red shirt. Read about each and every episode in a huge episode guide, with a synopsis of the story, quotes, images, reviews, and even bloopers. Find out trivia about the creators, the movies, the original series, aliens, awards, and goof-ups. You can also download a timeline of the entire "Star Trek" universe here to get a tutorial in "Star Trek" history. And every time you connect to the Next Generation home page, a new random quote shows up. Even if you weren't one before, you'll be a real Trekkie after visiting this site.

Contact: Andrew Tong, California Institute of Technology, *werdna@pobox.com*

TV Net

http://tvnet.com/TVnet.html

This huge television resource provides a WWW home for TV and cable stations throughout the world. A colorful image map guides you to all the features. Connect to all the major U.S. networks for addresses, phone numbers, e-mail addresses, and home page links of network shows. You can also view the most recent network ratings. Connect as well to satellite and cable networks, and read about proposed cable networks, including launch dates. View an image map of U.S. TV stations, and get a list of TV stations' e-mail addresses. At the Virtual Agent, TV news reporters can post resumes and tape samples. Check out Shoptalk for insider news, letters, and even job listings. Finally, visit What's On Tonite, which provides free TV listings for your area, listed by time and type of show.

Contact: David Cronshaw, Cinenet, *david@tvnet.com*

The Ultimate TV List

http://www.tvnet.com/UTVL/utvl.html

The ultimate online television resource, this site links you to home pages on your favorite shows. The comprehensive TV guide lists resources alphabetically, by genre, or by Internet resource. "Cards" for each TV show in the list typically link to episode guides, newsgroups, FAQs, mailing list archives, WWW pages, and sound and film clip archives. You can also submit your favorite TV links interactively or update existing resources. When you're finished, talk about your favorite shows on the posting boards. It's easy to go channel surfing using this great resource.

Contact: David Cronshaw, TVNet, *david@tvnet.com*

 Ultimate TV List: The Simpsons

 Episode Guide:

- ftp://ftp.cs.widener.edu/pub/simpsons/episode_guide.z
- http://www.digimark.net/TheSimpsons/guides/ep.guide.html

 Newsgroups:

- news:alt.tv.simpsons
- news:alt.tv.simpsons.itchy-scratchy

 FAQ:

- http://miso.wwa.com/~mkurth/atsfaq.html
- http://www.digimark.net/TheSimpsons/faqs.html

Access "cards" like this one on all your favorite television shows at the Ultimate TV List.

TV Theme Songs

http://www.tvtrecords.com/tvbytes/tvthemes.html

Download the sound files for dozens of TV theme songs at this fun site. First you can get the free software you'll need to hear the sound files. You'll find TV themes from the fifties to the nineties. Check out the theme of the week. Also look at a double feature with many versions of a cool theme such as "The Twilight Zone." New themes are posted every week in special categories, so keep checking back. The themes are divided by genre: comedy, drama, adventure, science fiction, soaps, network intros, TV magazines, and miscellaneous shows. There's also a huge listing of themes from children's shows and even some commercials. You'll hear themes from "Pinky and the Brain," "Sesame Street," "Batman," "Star Trek" (all incarnations), "The X-Files," "Seinfeld," "Home Improvement," and many, many more. For those of you who miss Schoolhouse Rock, that's here too. From here connect to other TV-related sites. Also link to other cool sound sites on the Web, many with movie sounds.

Contact: Patrick Kenny, TVT Records, *pkenny@eecs.umich.edu*

For more information on television, visit these sites:

Babylon 5 SF References List
http://www-theory.dcs.st-and.ac.uk/~aaa/B5.Ref.html

If you would like to know all the references the television show "Babylon 5" makes to twentieth-century science-fiction authors, this is the site to visit.

CINet
http://www.cnet.com/

C I Net's homepage, great design! Includes links to 100 hot Web sites and some interesting articles (only about four though).

The David Duchovny Estrogen Brigade
http://www.egr.uh.edu/~escco/DDEB.html#faqs

This is one of the definitive fan pages on the Net and has been cited in *TV Guide* and numerous other magazines. There's lots of information on David Duchovny and links to other X-Files-related pages. (Note: This is not a page from a bunch of drooling fanatics.)

The Discovery Channel Online

http://www.discovery.com/DCO/doc/1012/online.html

Very nice design, with information on programming. This URL is awfully long; the main page URL is **http://www.discovery.com/** and will take you to the link for the Discovery Channel Online page.

Fox Prime Time Schedule

http://www.iglou.com/fox41/weekdays.html#prime

This page not only tells you what's on when, it also gives a summary of each show's plot and lets you know if an upcoming show will be pre-empted for special programming.

General Hospital Trivia Cards

http://ghwww.net.com/soaps/gh/fun/trivia.html

If you know everything that's happened on "General Hospital" since 1962, here's the place to prove it. This site provides "cards" with "General Hospital" trivia questions and answers.

NBC XtRA

http://www.nbcxtra.com/

Online newsletter/digest of the best of NBC and news. The main page includes a long questionnaire for subscribers. I don't know if the newsletter is free or not, but I would certainly hope so.

The Patrick Stewart Estrogen Brigade

http://www2.ecst.csuchico.edu/~jennifer/OTHER_PAGES/PSEB/pseb.html

This page is devoted to Patrick Stewart, aka Captain Picard, and his acting career. There is a lot of information on what he's been in other than "Star Trek." This page is also the inspiration for the David Duchovney Estrogen Brigade.

Moving On

Now that you've played your heart out, it's time to go shopping. There's no better place for hassle-free shopping that the WWW. Books, food, clothing, jewelry, computers, software, music—it's all out there somewhere behind virtual storefronts created with the aid of hypertext and multimedia, and you don't even have to get out of your chair. The next section will take you to some of the Web's best and brightest shopping stops, as well as to services that you'll find only on the Internet. And if you don't want to waste any more time, you'll also find sites in the next section to help you take care of business. Using these sites, you can find a job, buy stock, or get a mortgage, and much more besides. So make sure your charge cards are ready. We're going to enter the commercial side of the Web.

Section VI

Taking Care of Business

Shopping, Business & Consumer Sites

Taking Care of Business: Shopping, Business, & Consumer Sites

Although the WWW was originally developed for research purposes, one of its fastest growing and most exciting applications is commercial use. Visualize a world in which you can move through virtual shopping malls with the click of a mouse, browsing shops that display their goods in full-color graphics and demonstrate them in video clips. If you see something you like, order it instantly using an interactive form—no lines, no traffic, no fuss. The commercial applications of the WWW extend far beyond that, however. Even now, you can get computer support, apply for a loan, research a car, buy stock, and order flowers, all with a click of a mouse button. Soon you will be able to manage most of your finances, business, and shopping online, and the WWW is just the vehicle to make that possible.

This section will introduce you to the enormous variety of commercial services available through the Web. Whether you want to access professional services or put your own business on the Internet, you'll find services—both free and not—to help you. Professionals will discover valuable resources on the WWW, from support organizations to marketing services to secretarial help. You can even locate a job or buy a new home. Shoppers can connect to a variety of virtual stores selling computers, software, books, food items, clothing, gifts— something to suit almost any need. When your shopping trip is finished, relax in one of the WWW's restaurants or coffee shops.

This section caps your WWW tour with a well-deserved shopping spree. Why not get a souvenir to remember your trip?

Bookstores

Book Stacks Unlimited

http://www.books.com/

The virtual shelves at Book Stacks Unlimited hold more than 330,000 titles for you to choose from, but lots of "freebies" make this site a must visit for any book lover. Go to the Book Cafe to talk with authors or other book lovers in many forum choices. Discover what everyone else is reading in Bestsellers. Check the Hall of Fame for winners of awards such as the Booker Prize, the Hugo Awards, the Edgar Allan Poe awards, the Newbery Awards, and the Nobel Prize for literature. Under Novel Places, find cool book resources on the Internet, or access a huge list of online publishers. The Electronic Library holds thousands of copyright-free, electronic books to download. Rants-n-Raves tells you what's hot and what's not in general books, science fiction, reference, children's books, and computer books. Visit Author's Pen for information on all your favorite authors. You'll even find fun quotes about books. If you don't get distracted by all this free stuff, enter the store where you can search the inventory by title, author, or ISBN, or browse through more than a hundred subject areas. Thumb through the newest releases in Fresh Ink. Each book in the store features a cover GIF, reviews, the table of contents, and an excerpt. Once you find what you want (and this store is bound to have it), you can immediately make a purchase online.

Contact: Book Stacks Unlimited, *cheritag@books.com*

Book Stacks Unlimited, Inc.

Your local bookstore ~ No matter where you live

Settle down with a good book from Book Stacks Unlimited.

Future Fantasy Bookstore

http://futfan.com/home.html

Your Internet bookstore for science fiction, fantasy, and mysteries is always open. Find out about upcoming book signings at the store and order signed books ahead of time, or learn about the visiting authors. Read the store newsletter, or view covers of soon-to-be-released books. Connect to other science-fiction resources on the Internet. An interactive catalog browser lets you search the full catalog of books by genre, author, title, or date of publication. You're sure to find your favorite science fiction, fantasy, and mystery authors in this large inventory. Select the books you want to order from a hyperlinked list, and place orders online. The store also carries T-shirts, games, magazines, audio tapes, and software. Set aside plenty of time for browsing here.

Contact: Future Fantasy Bookstore, *futfan@netcom.com*

Copyright 1994, Future Fantasy

Future Fantasy is the Internet's science fiction and fantasy bookstore.

Chapter One

http://www.psi.net/chapterone/index.html

At this online bookstore, you can browse before you buy. Check out first chapters, tables of contents, and excerpts from all the books in the catalog for free before you order. One of the best sections is the children's bookstore, which contains only Newbery award-winning books. You can read the first chapter of selected Newbery award winners and decide which you'd like to buy. There are many other sections of the store as well, each tailored to a specific interest. You'll find books reviewed on C-SPAN's "Booknotes," including books by Newt Gingrich and Norman Mailer. Browse books from major university presses organized by title, subject, or publisher. You'll also find chess books, computer books, and excerpts from eleven translations of the Bible. There are sections of books reviewed by *Foreign Affairs* magazine and by *Internet World* magazine. An order form on every page makes buying a breeze. Chapter One provides a unique way to shop for books online.

Contact: Chapter One, Performance Systems International, *srg@dialabook.com*

Internet Bookshop

http://www.bookshop.co.uk/

Browse through the offerings of "the largest online bookshop in the world," as the Internet Bookshop calls itself. Search for the book you need through more than 2,000 subject categories and 780,000 titles, or look for it in the home pages of over fifty U. K. publishers. Keep track of new releases, read about the star book of the month, or get in-depth studies of featured authors. Access special promotions in the Shop Window. Check out specialty areas, with books on business, computing, language, nautical topics, psychology, and medicine. You'll also find a good reading guide, which helps you decide what to read next based on your tastes and interests. When you're done browsing, you can order books directly online.

Contact: Internet Bookshop, *gary.newbrook@bookshop.co.uk*

Intertain.Com

http://intertain.com/store/welcome.html

Intertain.Com, which calls itself "your Internet bookstore," is a huge discount bookstore accessible from the WWW. Here you can check out new releases in fiction, nonfiction, and children's books, or access a list of bestsellers. The store also features extensive listings of books, on tape. Browse through the store by searching for specific authors and titles from a selection of more than 200,000 books. You can also page through listings by subject, including mystery, espionage, history, horror, inspirational, poetry and plays, romance, science fiction, suspense, thrillers, and westerns. An online form makes ordering easy, and all prices are discounted. This store provides a great selection with many of the most popular books; shopping here can save you a trip to the mall.

Contact: Profitable Tech, Inc., Intertain.Com, *Store@intertain.com*

Macmillan's Information SuperLibrary

http://www.mcp.com/

Visit all of Macmillan's imprints, and order from more than four thousand popular computer and Internet books online. Enter the bookstore to set up custom searches for finding a specific title or to search by subject. You'll also find new releases, bestsellers, and special offers here. Descriptions of all books are included, and many have sample chapters, tables of contents, and cover graphics. Visit the Reference Desk to find out how you can stay on top of the latest computing news. The Software Library has hundreds of shareware, freeware, and demo programs for all kinds of software needs. You can also find out how to order CD-ROMs from Macmillan. Get the latest information on HTML for any skill level in the HTML Workshop. Or just browse the entire site by connecting to a site map or by selecting one of the subjects, including business, computers, education, finance, reference, and more.

Contact: Macmillan Publishing

Shishy's Kidstuff Personalized Children's Books

http://www.ot.com/kidstuff/home.html

Shishy's online store sells personalized books for children. A sample book lets you examine the products; you interactively fill in names, friends, and home town, and the book appears already personalized with illustrations. For more fun, go to the Kid's Corner for interactive hangman, a puzzle, Web sites, and a kid's art gallery submitted by online users. Kids can sign the guestbook and read what other kids have written. In the store, order books such as personalized Create-A-

Books, Presto Sticker Books, Fantasy Works, holiday and birthday books, Grace Christian publications, and special activity books. The catalog provides sample illustrations from the books, descriptions, and online ordering. You can also purchase cassettes, toys, and other items. This is a fun store to play in for both parents and children.

Contact: Shishy's Kidstuff, Oasis Telecommunications

The sample book is an example of the many personalized children's books offered by Shishy's Kidstuff select a catagory below to browse.

List of Books:
Create-A-Books® - are over 30 pages long, hard covered, full color books which are personalized throughout. They are excellent as gifts for birthdays, holidays or anytime. They will be enjoyed for a lifetime...

Presto Sticker Books - make great gifts, especially if you're not sure of all the personalization information that you need. The Sticker books are professionally-bound, hard cover, full color books that come with a personalized sheet of stickers that you put in the book. You can order your personalized version now, or just order a unpersonalized book to give as a gift and let the

You can participate in a personalized story at Shishy's Kidstuff.

UCI Bookstore

http://bookweb.cwis.uci.edu:8042/

This online student bookstore has it all: books, music, even University of California at Irvine souvenirs. First you'll find a huge inventory of both academic and general books, including a technical books section. The bookstore is particularly known for its literary criticism, philosophy, and women's studies selections, and also boasts a large stock of fiction and poetry. Next, go to the music catalog for over thirty thousand classical and jazz CDs. These book and music inventories can be searched for specific titles, and products can be ordered through e-mail. Or you can take a closer look at specialized sections, such as digital media, medical books, trade books, and UCI authors. The store also has a large collection of Japanese animation materials, including videotapes, CDs, laser discs, graphic novels, books, posters, and T-shirts. If you just like to browse, take a look at the exhibitions section, featuring such multimedia displays as a travel guide to Hawaii or West Coast jazz in photography and records.

Contact: J.K. Cohen, University of California at Irvine, *jkcohen@uci.edu*

For more online bookstores, visit these sites:

Antarctic Press Home Page

http://www.texas.net/~antarc/

This page gives information on all the latest titles from Antarctic Press, as well as a synopses of crossovers. It also lists conferences where you might find your favoite Antarctic Press artists.

Audio Club

http://www.florida.net/audio/

Try new audio books for $.99 each. You can get soundbit samples and browse the fiction library, or link to Britannica Online.

BiblioBytes Books on Computing

http://www.bb.com

This site is an online catalog for books on disk.

Bookstores Online

http://www.gov.nb.ca/hotlist/bookstor.htm

A hotlist of online bookstores, though not nearly as comprehensive as the Bookstores Online Index listing (following this one).

Bookstores Online Index

http://kbc.com/html/bookstor.htm

A huge list of linked pages that are online new and used bookstores, organized alphabetically by company. Quite impressive.

Bygone Books

http://www.lights.com/bygone/

A used bookstore in Saskatchewan, with over 7,000 titles, a couple of online books, information on ordering, and a good list of categories.

Concertina

http://www.digimark.net/iatech/books/intro.htm

This page displays recently published titles by a new Canadian children's publisher, along with a short description of each.

The Dragon and the Unicorn

http://infoweb.net/books/index.html

Specializing in science fiction and fantasy books. Cool design.

Electric Bookstore

http://www.gnn.com/gnn/bus/electric/index.html

This bookstore is searchable by author or title in subject categories. It has a database of 14,000 plus books and worldwide shipping, free in North America. Sells mostly computer books.

Electronic Newsstand Bookstore

http://www.enews.com/bookstore.html

Very nice design and a solid set of links, including several commercial publishers, which are searchable. A lot of links are to Gopher sites, though. Includes McGraw-Hill International and a link to the Ventana Press Bookstore!

Fireside Book Company

http://www.infinet.com/~fireside/

Sells used and rare books. Browse their stock, organized by category (and there are quite a few), or see images of the shop.

The Great Northwest Bookstore

http://www.teleport.com/~gnwdt/

With 150,000 used books, the store is searchable and offers a rare book search, some "cool links," and other book page links, plus an "are you from this planet?" test.

Houghton Mifflin Company

http://www.hmco.com/hmco/trade/low/index.html

This publisher's bookstore is browsable by category and includes news blurbs about recent releases and announcements. I searched on a new book and found that I could get a graphic of the cover, a blurb about the book, a link on the author's name, a "how to buy" link (so you can order online), and reviews. There are an awful lot of sub-menus, though.

Libreria al Sole

http://www.tinet.ch/sole/welcome

This page offers listings of Italian books and the chance to order them via e-mail. Some of the descriptions are in Italian.

MCW Books and Videotapes

http://www.xmission.com/~seer/mcw/

This site is essentially a book catalog. The books tend to be about weapons, military science, and so forth.

Mystery Bookstore Link Page

http://www.db.dk/dbaa/jbs/mystbook.htm

With links to specialty stores for mysteries and other cool bookstore pages.

Prentice Hall

http://www.prenhall.com/

Look here for professional technical reference books and college titles.

Resolution Press

http://www.halcyon.com/ResPress/

This site covers Resolution Press's latest releases, with a synopsis, outline, and samples of each.

Tor SF & Fantasy

http://www.tor.com/

This site contains information on Tor's books and the authors who write them. Included are release dates of upcoming books, lists of recent award winners, and links to other science fiction and fantasy-oriented pages.

University of Michigan Press

http://www.press.umich.edu/

Find scholarly works, classroom texts, and general interest books in the area of social sciences. This press is even selling books written in SGML and HTML.

University of Tennessee Books

http://www.lib.utk.edu/UTKgophers/UT-PRESS/

This site describes the types of books University of Tennessee Press publishes, as well as giving ordering information and a listing of their books.

Virtual Book Shop

http://www.virtual.bookshop.com/

This page is literally a bookshop, specializing in rare, first-edition, antiquarian, collectible, and fine books. There is a catalog, but if the book you want isn't listed, there is also a book search subscription available.

Business

BizWeb

http://www.bizweb.com/

BizWeb scours the Internet for company and product information so that you won't have to. There are over a thousand companies listed in BizWeb, all searchable or categorized by goods and services provided. Subject categories make it easy to find the service or product you want, from every kind of computing product and service to jewelry and florists. Each company listed in BizWeb includes a very short description and a direct link to that company's Internet site. Keys tell you which listings are new and at which companies you can order online. You can also register your company for free. This site makes shopping or hunting for services quick, easy, and fun.

Contact: Bob Baggerman, BizWeb, *bob@bizweb.com*

Commercial Services on the Net

http://www.directory.net/

Before you begin shopping, check this comprehensive list of commercial WWW sites. The directory lists several hundred institutions, organizations, and companies with a Web presence. You can browse an alphabetical listing of all of them or search for keywords through an interactive interface. Check back often for regular updates of new sites on the commercial Web scene. This is a free public service.

Contact: Open Market, Commercial Services on the Net, *editors@directory.net*

The Company Corporation

http://www.service.com/tcc/home.html

The Company Corporation promises to incorporate your company in forty-eight hours or less, by phone, fax, or online. At its WWW site, educate yourself about the process of incorporation with advice on why and where to incorporate, and a sample completed incorporation form. Find out about the different types of corporations, and choose the one that's best for you. Then use a form to incorporate through e-mail. The Company Corporation also provides tax identification numbers, corporation kits, IRS filing services, mail forwarding, corporate forms, and international incorporation services. New businesses will find this unique online service useful and efficient.

Contact: Company Corporation, Internet Distribution Services, *corp@incorporate.com*

Direct Marketing World

http://mainsail.com/dmworld.htm

This valuable free resource maintains information on thousands of mailing lists, list managers and brokers, ad agencies, mail houses, and other services. The site also provides up-to-date information relevant to the direct-marketing industry. A direct-mail guide introduces the beginner to direct marketing. Detailed information on many mailing lists is sorted categorically and alphabetically; each list is described in a full-page "datacard." You can also connect from here to a number of ad agencies, copywriters, consultants, merge-purge services, and list brokers, compilers, and managers. Direct-marketing professionals can place their own ads with the directory or look for jobs through a free employment service.

Contact: Mainsail Marketing Information, Mainsail Mall, *mmi@mainsail.com*

HOBIE CAT

Owners / Subscribers / Mail Order Buyers

For more information on this list, usage or update schedules call:
● Name-Finders Lists, Inc. Darlene Johnson Voice: (415) 955 8595 x225

```
110,773   Catamaran and Boat Owners    $75/M      State:   $3.50/M
 99,023   HOBIE CAT Catamaran Owners   $85/M      ZIP:     $5.00/M
 13,370   HOBIE ONE Boat Owners        *** $660

  9,993   "HOBIE HOTLINE MAGAZINE"                *** Full Run Only
          Subscribers                  $75/M      Flat fee for list
 10,632   Mail Order Buyers            *** $590
                                                  Minimum:    5,000
HOBIE CAT is the premier name in light sail
craft in America and around the world.           Mag. Tape 9T/1600
From  Auburn,  California  to  Zond Voort,          $35 Flat Fee
Holland,   water-sports  enthusiasts  sail         Mag Tape Charge
HOBIE CAT catamarans and HOBIE ONE monohulls
for  their  unmatched speed and excellence.

"HOBIE HOTLINE" Subscribers pay $25 per year
for  this bimonthly magazine published by  the
Hobie  Cat  Company.  Each  issue  features
exciting   articles  on  sailing,  colorful
action-packed  photos,  new  product  reviews,
tuning  tips,  regatta news and  hot  sailing
spots.
```

Part of a mailing list "datacard," one of thousands housed at Direct MarketingWorld. (Provided courtesy of Mainsail Marketing Info, Inc.)

Directory of Experts and Spokespersons

http://www.experts.com/index.html

This free directory offers instant access to experts and spokespersons in many fields, providing a useful service. For a fee, experts can register online to be included in the directory. You can search the directory for last names, company names, categories, or zip codes. This is a very complete resource. For example, a search for "film" turned up an entertainment-law magazine, a film archive, a school of visual arts, an attorney for actors, a child psychologist, an animations expert, and the founder of the Boring Institute. There are over 1,600 listings in the guide, each providing the contact address, phone number, and list of specialties of the expert. Every month, a top ten list demonstrates the collage of varied interests the directory offers, with people such as Dr. Joyce Brothers, the Program Director for the National Space Society, and a professor of economics at New York University.

Contact: Noble Group, The Noble Directory, *noble@sirius.com*

Entrepreneurs on the Web

http://sashimi.wwa.com/~notime/eotw/EOTW.html

Entrepreneurs can access useful information and offer their goods and services to other entrepreneurs at this online meeting place. Gathered here are business information resources from all over the Internet, including a guide to advertising on the Internet and information about WWW advertising services. You'll find resources helpful for your business in the categories of government, law, finance, business opportunities, entrepreneurial resources, and more. Many goods and services are available from other entrepreneurs on the Web here, including computers, software, business handbooks, consulting, marketing services, and financial services.

Contact: No Time Enterprises, World Wide Access, *notime@wwa.com*

Executive Secretarial Services

http://www.awa.com/ess/ess.html

Take care of all your secretarial needs online through this multipurpose service. Executive Secretarial Services does your information processing of correspondence, proposals, manuals, and theses, all produced to your specifications. They also do database management, scanning, mailings, desktop publishing, logo design, and mail forwarding. One interesting service is transcription from a phone-in dictation system; get instructions through this site. You can also obtain rate information and a client list. Send an inquiry about your needs through an easy-to-use interactive form located at the site.

Contact: Executive Secretarial Services, Downtown Anywhere, *ESS@awa.com*

Fortune Magazine

http://pathfinder.com/fortune/

Fortune Magazine's online site keeps you in touch with the business and financial worlds. Listen to the latest financial and business news of the day in online audio reports. The news reports include the latest stock market averages. Check out the Global 500, the world's largest corporations, which you can search online or download as Acrobat or Excel files. In the database, the companies are ranked by revenue, profits, assets, equity, and number of employees. See the Fortune 500 and the top fifty, as well as all the associated stories from the Fortune 500 issue. This list is searchable by revenue, industry, state, and performance. Read the annual report on information technology, including articles on politics of the Net, setting up your own home office, and cool Internet companies. The best of the magazine is available at this freely accessible site.

Contact: Pathfinder, *webmaster@pathfinder.com*

Hello Direct

http://www.hello-direct.com/

Hello Direct is your store for telephone accessories. Business customers find Hello Direct's services particularly useful. This catalog offers many products to solve telephone problems and to make your telephone system more efficient. Here you'll find prepaid calling cards, cordless phones, headsets, accessories for cellular phones, teleconferencing systems, answering systems, recording devices, and more, all of which can be ordered online. Each entry in the catalog features a photograph, details about the product, and before-you-order information that tells you exactly how the accessory will interact with your existing phone system. Internet customers can also find great specials by accessing the online catalog.

Contact: HelloDirect, *hitect@hihello.com*

The Information Center

http://greatinfo.clever.net/infocenter/

The Information Center is an online guide to business, educational, career, and financial opportunities that will help you start and build a successful business. Featured resources spotlight business-related conferences, services, and products. In the Marketplace, connect to companies offering books, computers, accounting services, 900 numbers, investment services, and more. You'll also find information on advertising services and marketing on the WWW. The business topics and articles section contains useful tips on advertising, keeping customers, and writing business plans. Also in the Information Center are loads of business, financial, and investment resources gathered from all over the Internet. Check out a schedule of business conferences and franchise shows, or do an online job search. If you want to go back to school, visit various colleges, and learn about grants, scholarships, fellowships, and financial aid. Connect to useful online magazines such as *Time, Money, NetGuide,* and *Home Office Computing.* Link to daily news and weather, even Internet news. If you want to keep track of updates to the Information Center, just register your e-mail address with the URL-Minder.

Contact: The Information Center, *infodir@sna.com*

Internet Business Center

http://www.tig.com/IBC/

This archive of resources on commercial applications of the Internet is a must-see for any professional interested in using the Internet for business purposes, such as marketing, sales, or public relations. You'll receive information customized to your Web browser and generated "on the fly." Access valuable free resources, such as information on doing business online and growth statistics of commercial Internet domains. This is also the first place to look for late-breaking Internet business news and notices of new commercial sites. Check out examples of first-rate Internet business applications. In an interaction section, you can discuss business topics ranging from marketing to security. You'll also find a listing of the best directory services on the Net here.

Contact: The Internet Group, *info@tig.com*

Master-McNeil, Inc.

http://www.naming.com/naming.html

Master-McNeil provides naming services for products and corporations. The company creates product or company names, conducts market testing, does preliminary trademark research, and more. They also perform an international analysis to approve the name in all languages and contexts. At the company's Web site you can see Master-McNeil's complete client list, with links to their home pages. Also, read about their most recent naming efforts, including explanations of how they came up with the new names. A large archive of trademark information has listings of international trademark classes and a trademark application form, among other useful resources. As another unique service, Master-McNeil publishes their company profile information in Japanese through this WWW page.

Contact: Master-McNeil, The Human Factor, *info@naming.com*

Small Business Advancement Electronic Resource
http://161.31.2.174/sbanet.html

This government resource is a useful reference for small business owners and entrepreneurs. Lots of different categories provide a variety of documents. Resource Bulletins has a hodgepodge of information, including news about the Small Business Administration and announcements of relevant conferences, forms, calls for papers, etc. There are also several journals and newsletters here. The Resource Database links to various useful databases, such as Congressional members on the Small Business or Appropriations Committees and agencies dealing with small businesses internationally. Look under Resource Proceedings for coverage of law and legislature concerning small business and proceedings of meetings. This section is divided by topic, including minority entrepreneurship, management, finance, family businesses, and many more. There is also a section of Resource Publications and Journals. There's a lot of information here; use the interactive search tool to get the most out of it. An online form lets you request additional information.

Contact: Kelly Griffin, Small Business Advancement National Center, *KellyG@cc1.uca.edu*

For more on business information, visit these sites:

Better Business Bureau
http://www.igc.apc.org/cbbb/
Includes links to local BBBs, an index, services, publications, and a directory, plus a FAQ and related sites.

Consumer Information Center Catalog
http://www.gsa.gov/staff/pa/cic/cic.htm
The main center, out of Pueblo, Colorado. Get catalogs by subject.

Consumer World

http://www.consumerworld.org/

Includes links to over 600 of the Web's best sites for consumer information, such as the Better Business Bureau, where you can file complaints, and to businesses by category. Hundred of links! I was amazed at the number of links under Consumer Resources. Two thumbs up from me, plus four stars.

Planetary Market

http://rwsa.com/market/market.html

Business opportunities for entrepreneurs, plus a link to an "executive lounge" with lots of links to great business resources, including stocks and other online business opportunities.

Cars

DealerNet

http://www.dealernet.com/

DealerNet is a virtual showroom where you can learn about all types of cars online and perhaps even buy one. Here you'll find a wide range of information about domestic and international automobiles. Virtually visit automobile procurers and dealers to learn about their cars, warranties, service, and special programs. Or visit manufacturers for information on every type of car, from Mercedes to Lexus, Saturn to Volkswagen—you'll see pictures and get lists of standard equipment, optional equipment, performance features, and specs. You can also view video footage of current models. Look at pre-owned cars for sale through the site, or visit boat and RV dealers. Also look here for financing and insurance information, to order parts and accessories online, or to get quality service. Go to Autoworld for the history, news, and future plans of the industry, or link to other automotive resources on the Internet. Image maps everywhere let you easily navigate this one-stop auto information source.

Contact: DISC, Inc., DealerNet, *info@dealernet.com*

The New Porsche 911 Carrera

A 911 Carrera is about driving in its pure state. It's about agility and handling so responsive to your reflexes that the car no longer seems to be merely a machine, but an extension of yourself. A

Research your fantasy car at DealerNet.

For more information on cars, visit these sites:

All Things Automotive Directory

http://www.webcom.com/~autodir/

They aren't kidding. Links to new car and dealer information, plus links to piles of enthusiast pages, divided by make and model name. Really useful for people who want information about cars or are enthusiasts.

AutoHelp

http://www.thesphere.com/AutoHelp/

A guide to buying used cars, "Ask Randy" automotive questions, and links to other automotive resources. Looks very helpful for car buyers.

Autoshop Online

http://autoshop-online.com/

A car repair page! With Auto 101 (a basic tour through your car and how it works), five specialists who answer questions on car repair (categorized by type of car, i.e., Japanese cars vs. GM cars), news on recalls and more.

AutoView

http://www.well.com/user/av062813/autoview.htm

Autos for sale with pictures! Gritty pictures though, and the list wasn't very long.

AutoWorld

http://www.autoworld.com/

Includes reports on new and used cars, plus a few other links. Requires a login, but it looks easy to set up an account.

Calling All Cars

http://www.cacars.com/cac/cachome.html

This is a communal used car lot in cyberspace. It allows car owners to market their vehicles all over the Net and has a list of the ten most wanted cars and links to related sites.

Cars At Cost

http://www.webcom.com/~carscost/

A service that negotiates with the dealer for you to get a new car at a discounted price. Includes a hot list of "hot" cars, cars by dealer, a comprehensive list of cars, a service request form, etc. Very user-friendly. Looks like you send in a service request and they take it from there (probably a paid service).

Cool Cars, Cool Babes, and Claudia Shiffer

http://www.planet.eon.net/~pkw/peter.html

This site continues the tradition of combining the subjects of attractive cars and attractive women. In the site author's favor, there is considerably more information, much of it useful, on cars, most of them German, than on the babes.

Exotic Car Showroom

http://vmarketing.com/autohp.html

Pick cars by model links and view them.

Ford Automobiles

http://www.ford.com/

With vehicle information and an historical library.

How to Live With a Neurotic Motorcycle

http://slack.lne.com/lemay/writings/neurotic.html

This page is a collection of Murphy's Laws for motorcycles. Good for a laugh if you or someone you love/loathe owns a motorcycle.

Motorcycle Online

http://www.mshopper.eurografix.com/welcome.htm

This online magazine lets motorcyle enthusiasts meet, talk, and place ads for buying and selling motorcycles. You'll find links to clubs, news, vendors, and a shopper magazine—motorcycles only.

Pace Publications

http://www.w2.com/pacepub.html

Sells automotive price guides, i.e., used car price guide, truck price guide, new car price guide. Seems that you can order online.

Saturn Corporation

http://www.saturncars.com/

Includes information on Saturn model year 1996 cars, the Saturn magazine, how to find a dealer, a FAQ, etc. Nice design! Good for people who want information about Saturn cars.

Used Car Net

http://www.usedcars.com/

Lists dealers, services, parts, for sale, auctions, etc. You can click on a brand to find out more.

Webfoot's Make and Model Index

http://www.webfoot.com/lots/info/make.model.html

Two thumbs up from me! Click on the make of the car, then find the model and read reviews and information about it! Surprisingly complete. This is a good place to start when looking for specific cars.

Webfoot's Useful Automotive Information

http://www.webfoot.com/lots/info/useful.info.html

This site is loaded with useful information for anyone interested in buying a car. It has information on different models of cars, what to look for when buying a car, mechanical information, and a great deal more.

Wheels Online

http://www.snsnet.net/wol/

Auto-for-sale listings, with quite comprehensive categories, pictures, and simple layout of ads. Also includes boats for sale. Nice design, too.

Classifieds & Personals

Classified Flea Market

http://www.cfm.com/

This is the online edition of San Francisco's best-read classifieds newspaper. It is published online weekly. You can learn how to place an ad yourself and see the "ad of the week." Or delve into the ads themselves; you'll find classified ads in over 90 categories, from antiques to upholstery. There are the expected categories, such as houses for sale, services offered, cars for sale, and business opportunities. There are also some unusual sections, such as a kid's column.

Contact: Offsite Web, Classified Flea Market, *sarfait@offsiteweb.com*

Face to Face

http://www.mall2000.com/face/date.html

Find that special someone whose interests, looks, and desires exactly match yours at this online dating service. When you search the database, you can be as particular as you like in selecting a match and there is no charge to browse through the database (but you do have to pay to send e-mail to someone through the service). Search for marital status, name, occupation, religion, race, country, hobbies, interests, school, age, and sex. Even search for a motivation for searching the database. You can also enter your own profile into the database, with a very complete description form.

Contact: Mall 2000, Inc., *info@mall2000.com*

Flea Market

http://info.fuw.edu.pl/market/market.html

The Flea Market is a great online bazaar where you can exchange practically anything, from interesting junk to houses. In this flea market, the "booths" are listings of items in both short and long forms. Short-form ads are one-line descriptions, including category, whether buying or selling, the language of the ad, e-mail address, and location. The long form elaborates on the short-form description. At the market you'll find listings of computers for sale, requests for research information, items wanted, jobs and people looking for jobs, cars, and much more. The listings are searchable so that you can look for a specific item you're interested in. Place your own ad, absolutely free, by using an online form. Like real-life flea markets, this one is fun to wander around in.

Contact: Kacper Nowicki, Warsaw University Physics Department, *Kacper.Nowicki@fuw.edu.pl*

Mary and Michael Wedding Photography

http://www.commerce.digital.com/palo-alto/WeddingPhoto/home.html

Learn all about the services of the only online wedding photographers through this WWW "brochure." See lots of examples of their work, including formal portraits and photos of ceremonies, churches, recessionals, and kisses. Get a listing of their rates and services; they also do computer manipulations to make the record of your wedding perfect, even if the real thing wasn't. Find out about the photographers themselves, including their techniques, philosophy, and mission. You'll also see quotes from satisfied newlyweds and a list of the weddings they've photographed. Freebies at the site include articles on how to make the wedding more special and tips for togetherness. Send an inquiry using an interactive form; they'll even make recommendations for other wedding services you might need, such as caterers, florists, and music.

Contact: Mary and Michael Wedding Photography, Digital Equipment Corporation

Mary and Michael Wedding Photography can capture that special moment for you.

Virtual Meetmarket

http://www.wwa.com:1111/

Meet that special someone, a new best friend, or just someone to talk to through this service. The Virtual Meetmarket is a unique "meeting" service that could only exist on the Web. Publish your own personal classified ad at no cost; you can use up to a full page of hypertext, including inline images. Or browse ads placed by others, and reply immediately through e-mail. Anonymity is preserved; messages in response to your ad are forwarded to you through the service. To place your own ad, just download a personal template and fill in the blanks. Even link in pictures from an archive of stock GIF images. We've all heard about couples who met, fell in love, and got married through the Internet. At the Virtual Meetmarket, that might happen to you.

Contact: Virtual Work, WorldWide Access, *virtualw@wwa.com*

---

1. **Female seeking Male**
2. **Male seeking Female**
3. **Alternative Lifestyle**

Female seeking Male:

CA1007	Los Angeles SJF
CA1948	Woman With Much Hair
GA1721	Jazz lover seeks same

Browse intriguing personals like these at the Virtual Meetmarket.

For more classifieds and personals, visit these sites:

Advertise It! Web Classifieds

http://www.netimages.com/classifieds.html

There are only nine categories and, frankly, skimpy listings.
Too bad, it was a nice page design.

American Business Classifieds

http://webcom.com/~abc/abchome.html

Looked useful, but not clear on where to go to get to the ads.
Provides free ads for personal use and nonprofits.

Americanet Classifieds

http://www.Americanet.Com/classified.html

Medium number of categories. The ads include date, region, and
topic, then full text. However, all classifieds are on one page, so
there's lots to download before the document is complete.

American Singles

http://www.as.org/as/

Straight and gay ads. Pretty straigtforward, nothing fancy.

Armondo's Personals

http://www.infohaus.com/access/by-seller/
ARMONDOs_PERSONALS

A database of gay and lesbian personal ads.

BarterNet

http://www.teleport.com/~dtpdx/bnhome.htm

A barter network. Learn about bartering, services offered, services
wanted, and even international bartering by GATT regulations.
A city directory is available to find local people.

Campus Singles

http://www.campusingles.com/

Lots of talk and a few links to personals by and for the college-age crowd. Provides some hints on first face-to-face meetings.

Christian Singles Online

http://www.netrunner.net/~gigimia/singles/index.html

Members only, but the service will match you up with your top five compatible singles. Sign up on a six-month basis for thirty dollars.

The Classified Section

http://www.webcom.com/~cyberpub/class.html

Has basic categories. Each ad links to a poster. The minimal listings are not as extensive as some of the other sites in this section.

Cupidnet

http://www.cupidnet.com/cupid/

Probably the best personal page yet. Lots of links to matchmaking, dating services, all sorts of personal ads from all over the nation and world, phone services, singles magazines and organizations, and a calendar of events. Very comprehensive. A nice design, too.

Cyberfriends

http://dare.com/fr_main

Electronic penpals (friends only, I believe).

E-mail Club

http://www.coolsite.com/e-mailclb.html

E-mail people all over the world and make new friends.

Everything Classified

http://www.cinternet.net/~aromero/cgi-bin/classified.cgi

Browse, search, or place an ad. I couldn't get the "browse" feature to do anything. Nice home page design, though.

Infoware Individual Profile System

http://digiweb.com/alc/000034/ips.html

Looks interesting! The system analyzes your personality and gives you information on how your mind works in certain ways. Worth checking out.

Internet Ad Pages

http://netmar.com/mall/ads/

Online ads, in basic categories; not terribly extensive, but possibly useful.

Internet Classifieds

http://ad.wwmedia.com/classified/main.html

Basic categories, not too extensive, with links to other pages.

Internet Personals

http://www.montagar.com/personals/index.html

Basic listings. Lists number of ads (overwhelmingly men seeking women—about eight times more than next largest) and a few helpful Personal Ad pages.

Internet Productions Worldwide Classifieds Database

http://www.ipworld.com/clasfied/homepage.htm

Searchable but not browsable. The search engine lets you limit your search every which way from Sunday to get really specific results. You can enter, update, and delete ads as well.

Love and Romance Home Page

http://home.navisoft.com/loveandromance/index.htm

Nifty! Includes love poem ideas, wedding proposal ideas, special occasion ideas, etc. Worth a look.

The Sunday Paper

http://www.sundaypaper.com/

The Sunday paper with classified ads. There are lots of categories but few ads.

The Video Dating Collection

http://www.tucson.com/dating/

This top 5-percent-of-the-Web site includes downloadable videos of singles and a "lambda collection." Paid membership required.

WebBarter

http://www.ultranet.com/~bellvill/webbarter.html

Lists members with services to offer and goods or services wanted, but lists them all on the home page, with no links and a kind of short list.

WebPersonals

http://www.webpersonals.com/

Nice design! Personals on the Web, with many categories, including "activity partners." You can read the ads, search them, or place one, including photo and sound. I'm not certain about the number of listings, but this is a nicely designed, easily navigable page.

Computer & Software Stores

Apple Computer

http://www.apple.com/

Apple's main Web site is the place to come for the latest news and information about Apple and Macintosh computers and software. Features include the most recent offerings and news. Find out more about Apple, from the corporate history to the latest press releases. Get product descriptions and support information for all of Apple's hardware and software products. Check out competitive studies comparing Macintosh computers with other personal computers or read about Apple products recently in the news. Apple customers can get customer support. You'll also find a comprehensive listing of Apple Developer technology programs, services, and support. Take a look at cool Apple technologies and current research, such as Classrooms of Tomorrow, the Dylan programming language, cool Internet tools, and virtual reality research. Visit special user communities—Apple technology applied to users' specific needs. Here you'll find tips, tours, and demos of products aimed at specialty groups such as publishers, multimedia developers, educators, librarians, and people with disabilities. Learn more about Apple's activities, plans, and products for the Internet. Link to Internet resources of interest to Apple users, from Apple shareware FTP sites to home pages of user groups and Apple vendors. You can also visit other Apple servers, such as the Apple Virtual Campus, the QuickTime Continuum, and the Apple Multimedia Program.

Contact: Apple Computer, *webmaster@apple.com*

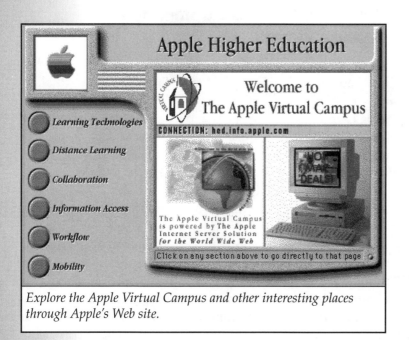

Explore the Apple Virtual Campus and other interesting places through Apple's Web site.

Center for Software Development

http://www.service.com/csd/home.html

This nonprofit organization tests developers' software products on every type of Unix, PC, Apple, Macintosh, printer, and network available. They even offer testing for Windows 95. The mission of the Center is to promote the growth of software companies. It offers the world's most comprehensive publicly available self-service computer lab. Here you'll find events to help software developers contact providers of business-related services, such as marketing, venture capital, legal, and accounting. A newsletter provides more information on these seminars and consulting services. You'll also find an inventory of hardware and software the Center provides to test software products. There is also a resource library for the software industry.

Contact: Center for Software Development, Internet Distribution Services, *info@center.org*

The Children's Software Company

http://netmedia.com/childsoft/

The Children's Software Company sells educational software for children, preschool through high school levels. From this online catalog, titles are available for Macs, PCs, and CD-ROMs at discount prices. The catalog is organized by category and by an alphabetical index. You'll find all kinds of software, including games, college prep, early learning, social sciences, math, reading, science, and many more. Detailed descriptions and reviews guide parents in selecting the programs that best suit their child's interests and developing skills. Some products even have interactive demos you can download. Order software interactively by pushing the "buy" button next to each product, which is then placed in your shopping cart; when you have finished shopping, click on the "checkout" icon to process the order. On every page, buttons let you access the index, see the items in your shopping cart, check out, go back to the home page, or get help. From the site, you can also subscribe to an electronic newsletter for announcements of sale prices, creative tips, new products, points of interest on the tzternet, and other goodies.

Contact: The Children's Software Company, Internet Media Services, Inc., *info@childsoft.com*

Find software that brings out your child's creative side at the Children's Software Company.

Computer Express

http://www.cexpress.com/

Computer Express, selling software and computer products, does all its business through an electronic storefront. Here you can shop by category, do a product search, or browse periodic specials. See the product of the week for the newest and best in high tech. Goods for sale include software, computers, modems, printers, and video games. The catalog is easy to navigate; for instance, you can easily access boutiques such as New Products, the Modem Store, or Microsoft Home Products. Put in preorders on forthcoming video games and other special items. Order instantly using an interactive form.

Contact: Computer Express, *info@cexpress.com*

Digital Equipment Corporation

http://www.service.digital.com/

Find out what's new with Digital's products and services at their Web site. Access a directory of documentation for Digital products and a complete catalog and ordering system. Digital customers can find software support and a magazine of service news. You can also get descriptions of new software products, buyers' guides, customer updates, performance reports, press releases, and more. Go shopping in the on-site Web Mall. Learn about an experiment in Web conferencing. You can also instantly search the entire site.

Contact: Digital Equipment Corporation, Digital Commercial Services, *webmaster@service.digital.com*

Investigate Digital's new products and services at their Web site.

Electronic Pricing Guide

http://www.diskovery.com/Diskovery/EPG/

The Electronic Pricing Guide provides affordable software, hardware, CD-ROMs, books, laser discs, and videos to educational customers. In the online catalog, find out about new products and special offers. Products are organized by title, category, and publisher. The guide lists all kinds of software for the major computing systems, including graphics, finance, communications, databases, fonts, multimedia, entertainment, programming, and word processing. Nationally known products from such companies as Adobe, Apple, Autodesk, Corel, IBM, Lotus, Microsoft, and WordPerfect are featured. If you're in education, add this catalog to your hotlist because you're sure to find a lot of good deals here.

Contact: Diskovery Educational Systems, *info@diskovery.com*

Emerging Business Technologies Corporation

http://www.jkcg.com/index.html

These online computer consultants assess and integrate new technologies to most effectively meet your computing needs. Read through the company literature about the many products and services the consultants provide. They specialize in Unix and Open Systems networks. They also offer networking help, including Webmaster services for making information available over the WWW.

Contact: Emerging Business Technologies Corporation, Joe Klein Consulting Group, *webmaster@gttw.com*

IBM

http://www.ibm.com/

This server provides complete access to information about IBM's products and services. Find IBM news, such as current financial information, press releases, conferences, and job openings. Access demos of IBM's Web-based experiments, including computer visualizations, and a digital library. Check out IBM products, services, and support for individuals and businesses. You'll find information on networking, Internet products, client-server computing, printing, software, educational products, personal computing, and more. A special section highlights IBM's solutions for industry computing. Tap into a showcase of recent technology and research from IBM. You can also access IBM information planetwide and read a corporate overview.

Contact: IBM, *webmaster@www.ibm.com*

Microsoft

http://www.microsoft.com/

Where do you want to go today? You'll find it all at Microsoft's Web server. Connect to a showcase of Microsoft products, and learn about support for them. Get anti-piracy information and services for educational users. Take a shortcut to the Internet, with an online tutorial, information about Microsoft's Internet products, and the facts about Microsoft Network. Virtually visit Microsoft, with corporate and stockholder information, a research directory, Microsoft events, and a library of useful links. Developers can access the latest news from Microsoft's development team and find out about useful development tools. You can also learn about Microsoft hot topics, including (of course) Windows 95; even download beta software to try out.

Contact: Microsoft Corporation, *www@microsoft.com*

Shase Shareware Virtual Library

http://vsl.cnet.com/

Tap into a huge online library that catalogues over a hundred thousand shareware computer programs available on the Internet. You can try out any of these programs for free. If you like the program, just register and pay a small fee. In the library, search all of the main software archives on the Internet for file descriptions, dates, sizes, and program names. You can choose to search the archives by platform or to search any combination of archives. Available platforms include Amiga, Atari, DOS, games, Macintosh, Windows, Novell Netware, OS/2, source code, and Unix. Or search your favorite FTP archive. One useful feature lets you quickly find the newest files in any archive. After locating the file you want, you can download it easily from the library. This search mechanism is the fastest way to locate shareware over the Internet. Before buying an expensive new software program, come here to search for inexpensive shareware that will do the same thing.

Contact: C | net Online, Virtual Software Library, *support@vsl.cnet.com*

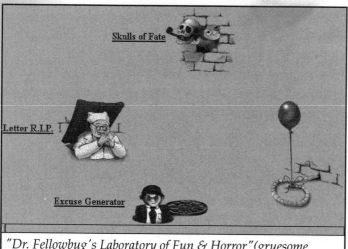

Skulls of Fate

Letter R.I.P.

Excuse Generator

"Dr. Fellowbug's Laboratory of Fun & Horror"(gruesome games played here).

Sun Microsystems

http://www.sun.com/

Find out everything there is to know about Sun's Unix-based products and solutions. You can read about Sun's offerings in hardware, software, networking, and applications, and find out what's new. Learn how to place an order and what services Sun offers, including educational services. Access Sun's research in technology and development, including the latest WWW programming language—Java. Get a corporate overview, or search the entire site for something specific. Visit Sun on the Net, with information on running the Internet on Sun products; there is a lot of useful information about setting up a commercial Internet server here. Be sure to visit the many SunSITEs around the world; these information servers were set up to provide easy access to public domain software, act as repositories for government information, promote development and research of Internet tools, and launch hot Internet applications. Each and every one will prove to be entertaining and useful to any WWW user.

Contact: Sun Microsystems, *webmaster@ sun.com*

Updata's Online CD-ROM Catalog

http://www.updata.com/

This is the home page for a huge Gopher site containing the most comprehensive catalog of CD-ROMs available. You'll find CD-ROMs listed alphabetically or by subject, including games, shareware, and educational CD-ROMs. And you'll find dozens of more specific subjects, from veterinary science to virtual reality, from animals to anatomy. If it's information you want, on almost any subject, Updata can provide it on CD-ROM. You can also search the catalog by title keyword or by a full text search. Send e-mail for answers to any question you may have about any available CD-ROM.

Contact: Updata Online CD-ROM Catalog, GeoNet, *cdrom@updata.com*

Ventana Online

http://www.vmedia.com/

To find books and software on computer programming, desktop publishing, and the Internet, among many other computer-related subjects, try this easy-to-use, graphical catalog. Navigate the pages of detailed information using a graphical button bar and pull-down menu. A graphical map of the Ventana "world" allows you to enter a number of on-site buildings. Choose the library to see the shelves of books and software for sale. You can also read about what's new and coming soon, create or update your account, and enter the help center. Selecting a particular title opens a graphic of the cover and complete information, including press releases, the introduction, the table of contents, and software supplements. If you like what you see, order immediately from the same page. As a Ventana customer, you'll also want to explore the Ventana Visitor's Center, where you will find online companions to Ventana books (including this one), free software, clip-art archives, and a link to the "nifty site of the week."

Contact: Ventana Communications Group, *help@vmedia.com*

Buy Any Ventana Product at a 15% Discount!

Featured Products

Register with Ventana Online

Register with Ventana to order products online and receive free trial issue of Internet World.

Browse the Stacks

You can find all Ventana products listed here by category.

Consult the Librarian

Choose books like these off the shelf at Ventana's virtual library.

For more computer and software stores, visit these sites:

Cisco Systems

http://www.cisco.com/

Cisco is the main provider of routers for network connections. You'll also find a lot of value-added information about networking and the Internet here.

Egghead Computers

http://www.egghead.com/

Nice design, rated in the top 5 percent of Web sites, provides secure online purchasing.

HaL Computer Systems

http://www.hal.com/

HaL sells high-performance SuperScalar RISC computers for technology, communications, and business users.

Hewlett Packard

http://www.hp.com/

Hewlett Packard is the leading provider of printers, components, medical equipment, and more. Here get news about the company and its products.

Novell

http://www.novell.com/

Novell offers operating systems, distributing services, and tools, including applications for home, business, and workgroups.

Silicon Graphics

http://www.sgi.com/

This is the place to learn about, buy, and get customer service for the 3D computers produced by Silicon Graphics.

Virgin Interactive Entertainment

http://www.worldserver.pipex.com/vie

This site describes VIE as a corporation, gives information on new releases, and offers free software.

Employment

CareerMosaic

http://www.careermosaic.com/

This huge resource is an invaluable guide to potential employers, career information, and human resource issues. A clickable map leads you to all the information inside. Learn about hot companies and new products and technologies, knowledge that can help you land a job with an up-and-coming company. Also find out about employers' benefits and lifestyles around the world to help you make career decisions. Search the jobs database for thousands of job opportunities. College students will find a listing of special opportunities at co-ops or as interns. Profiles of employers offering jobs include detailed information about the company. Online job fairs feature upcoming events with prospective employers. And a resource center provides tips on preparing your resume and help with interviewing, as well as links to resources to help you with your job search.

Contact: Bernard Hodes Advertising, CareerMosaic, *feedback@pa.hodes.com*

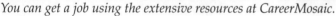

You can get a job using the extensive resources at CareerMosaic.

CareerWeb

http://www.mecklerweb.com/careerwb/careerwb.htm

CareerWeb maintains a list of career opportunities in the computing and information technology fields, divided by type of position. Whether you're an applications engineer, a software developer, or a technical writer, you'll find job opportunities here. Scan the employment listings, and then submit your resume to the Huntington Group, a professional search firm specializing in the technology industry. You can also get profiles of the companies that use this job search service and download a list of currently available positions for each one.

Contact: Huntington Group, MecklerWeb's iWORLD, *jirwin@huntington-group.com*

Employment Opportunities and Job Resources on the Internet

http://www.wpi.edu/~mfriley/jobguide.html

This huge guide lists most of the employment services available through the Internet. All the services listed can be accessed at no charge; some, however, may charge a fee to use the services. More than just job listings, this site also provides a guide to using the Internet to job hunt. Look at How to Internet for instructions on employing various Internet tools to access the job listings. Another section helps you use the Internet effectively to broaden your search and tells you how to apply for jobs listed on the Internet. The job listings themselves are divided by field to make your search easier; there is also a category for large sites with listings in more than one field. Fields you can search include arts and humanities, business, computing and technology, internships and summer jobs, engineering, government, science, agriculture, and social sciences. A miscellaneous category lists resources that do not fit in other categories, such as aviation, bus drivers, and house painters. Employment resources are also broken down by U.S. geographical region, and you'll find a category of international job listings and job resources for Canada. From this site, connect to career service centers for tips on writing resumes and conducting interviews, or link to resources that help you research the company you are targeting or the city you are moving to. This very complete and detailed guide is a good place to start any job search.

Contact: Margaret F. Riley, Worcester Polytechnic Institute, *mfriley@wpi.edu*

E-SPAN's Interactive Employment Network

http://www.espan.com/

This site, a meta-resource of information on employment, has plenty of help for the job-seeker. The Career Manager links job-seekers to the latest resume-writing tips, interview practice sessions, career strategies, salary guides, and many other resources to help you land the perfect job. Make use of practice exercises for interviewing, telephoning, and skills assessment. Resume formats and templates are also available for your use. A job-search management resource gives proven tips for organizing and shortening your job search, improving networking, developing a personal profile, and using interview notes. You can even join an online support group that shares success stories and motivational advice. Finally, the Job Library allows you to search job listings by keyword, date posted, or listings posted since your last visit, as well as post your own resume.

Contact: E-SPAN, *info@espan.com*

This online Career Manager at E-SPAN puts you on the right track to finding a job.

The Graduate's Connection

http://www.corcom.com/jsmith/graduate.html

This site creates a link between college graduates and employers worldwide. You must pay a fee to use the service, but it is free for employers to browse. Paying the fee makes you a member of the Graduate's Connection and enters your resume in the online database for employers to locate. Resumes are divided into regions where job-seekers want to locate. Employers can search all of the United States, by region, or even internationally. Then employers can pick the region they want to hire from to see a summary of each job-seeker, including their objective, the date they are available, and their educational background. After finding a resume match, employers can enter the Resume Directory to read the entire resume. Some resumes even include photographs and sound files.

Contact: The Graduate's Connection, Corcom Alaska, *Graduate@corcom.com*

Online Career Center

http://www.occ.com/occ/

With a little luck you can get a job in no time through this nonprofit employer association. The association connects the business community with faculty, students, and alumni of colleges and universities worldwide in an effort to streamline the hiring process by member corporations. A graphical map allows you to search available jobs and resumes. Post your resume at no cost, or link to information on career fairs and other events. A career assistance center lists resources on cover letters, resumes, self-employment, and so forth, as well as other valuable job-help tools. Or read about women's and minority issues in hunting for a job. As useful as a university career center, the Online Career Center serves everyone on the Internet.

Contact: Online Career Center, *occ@occ.com*

For more employment information, visit these sites:

Adams Online

http://www.adamsonline.com/

A great starting point for Internet job seekers. Includes a JobBank, resumes and cover letter examples, company profiles, grad student job listings, a career services center, Adams career books, etc.

America's Job Bank

http://www.ajb.dni.us/

Links to job search, employer services, etc.

The Business Job Finder

http://www.cob.ohio-state.edu/dept/fin/osujobs.htm

Includes links to other job sites (most of which are listed here), as well as links to job information in businesses such as accounting, insurance, investment banking, etc. This site is maintained at Ohio State University.

Career Magazine

http://www.careermag.com/careermag/

Nice design. Links to a resume bank, job search, employer profiles, and news and articles.

Career Web

http://www.cweb.com/

Includes a "career fitness test," an employers database, job search, and a library.

College Grad Job Hunter

http://www.execpc.com/~insider/

Includes resume postings, job postings, and other hints. Kind of bare.

Employment Database Search

http://www.espan.com/cgi-bin/ewais/

Search the database via keywords or category. There are no direct listings, so you must search to get results.

Employment News

http://www.ftn.net/emplnews/

Includes job listings, career help, and self-help, updated weekly. Nice design.

Finding a Job

http://www.dbisna.com/dbis/jobs/vjobhunt.htm

No listings, but includes tips on finding a job, solutions, and trends, plus information on "free charter membership," whatever that is.

Job Catapult

http://www.wm.edu/catapult/catapult.html

A springboard to many other job and employment servers, including career resources and a bibliography.

Jobcenter

http://www.jobcenter.com/

Post and edit your resume, look for jobs, and connect to other Web sites and employment resources.

JobHunt

http://rescomp.stanford.edu/jobs.html

A "meta-list" of job resources, including Internet job listings, links to other job listing services, a resume bank, and reference materials for job seekers. Rated in the top 5 percent of Web sites.

Jobsearch Via Internet Links

http://copper.ucs.indiana.edu/~dvasilef/jobsearch.html

Links are organized by company, not by job title or category.

JobWeb

http://www.jobweb.org/

Really cool home page! Select your category (such as recent graduate) and then select which documents or links you want, including a database of federal jobs, career resources, bibliographic information, a newsstand, and others. This is really easy to use, with a very, very nice design.

Navy Opportunities

http://www.navyjobs.com/

Uncle Sam recruits via the Web. Includes jobs in the fleet, medical jobs, benefits, money for college, and worldwide travel. Probably helpful to those considering military careers. (The Navy homepage is **http://www.navy.mil/.**)

Recruitment Database Ltd.

http://www.enterprise.net/recruitmentdb/

This "World Wide JobShop" has a resume and CV database, but no jobs to search for. It does put your resume or CV online immediately for free.

The Virtual Press Jobs Listing

http://tvp.com/vpjic.html

Nicely categorized, this site includes links to databases and news-groups, international employment, and business resources.

Finance

Chicago Mercantile Exchange

http://www.cme.com/

Visit the world's busiest futures exchange and the first exchange on the WWW. From the home page, get a background of the exchange, its products, its place in the economy, its history of innovation, and a glossary of futures-related terms. Page through a collection of photos and video clips of the exchange, or read a description of the trading floor. You'll also find charts of volume and membership prices, as well as an in-depth description of financial safeguards and rules on the exchange. Browse the model for federal financial regulation and lots more information related to the exchange. You'll see daily settlement prices on all CME futures and options, estimated volume, and open interest. This useful information covers stock indices, interest rates, foreign currencies, and agricultural commodities, all of which can be downloaded for local reference. Go to the marketing page for product information, a directory of members, education programs, market news, and a guide to selecting a broker. Find financial and stock market news under What's New. From here, jump to more finance-related resources.

Contact: Chicago Mercantile Exchange, *mhearn@cme.com*

FinWeb

http://www.finweb.com/

FinWeb is a meta-resource for financial and economics resources collected from all over the Internet. It should be your first stop when seeking online financial information. From here, connect to tons of resources for studying economics, including journals and working papers. Find databases covering stock market quotes and other investment resources. You can also link to other financial WWW servers, such as that of the World Bank, or make connections to legal, insurance, and government information on the Internet.

Contact: Professor James R. Garven, FINWeb Server, *jgarven@mail.utexas.edu*

GNN Personal Finance Center

http://nearnet.gnn.com/gnn/meta/finance/index.html

This page, located at the Global Network Navigator, collects resources on managing money, investment, and financial planning from across the Internet, as well as many original features and columns. Notes and News publishes recent Internet financial news, including articles on Internet advertising, new financial resources on the Internet, and other finance-related tidbits. Features and columns include articles on investing, real estate, and money matters. Most of these articles have an Internet slant, and many are written to entertain as well as inform. Move out into the Internet by browsing resources by subject, including credit cards, real estate, banking, financial planning, taxes, and investment.

Contact: Abbot Chambers, NearNet, *abcham@ora.com*

Internet Credit Bureau

http://www.aksi.net/icb/

The Internet Credit Bureau is a full-service credit agency offering unique and useful services over the Internet. The agency does charge a fee for each of its services, but accessing the site and looking over the services costs nothing. The credit bureau can supply credit reports on any company in the United States and Canada. Use the bad debt collection service to recover monies owed to you via the Internet. The bureau searches the Social Security number database to identify the owner of a particular SSN and performs a telephone number identification search to find the proper owner of a given telephone number. Use the Finder's Report to locate an individual in the United States, Puerto Rico, or the Virgin Islands. An address verification search provides you with the name of the current occupant of an address along with other information about that person. You can even learn how to become a Notary Public with a complete package that you can order with an online form. To use any of these services, you must complete an online customer application form at no charge. Handy online forms at every link let you instantly request any of the bureau's services.

Contact: Internet Credit Bureau, Acquired Knowledge Systems, Inc., *icb@aksi.net*

NETworth

http://networth.galt.com/

NETworth is a comprehensive tool for individual investors designed for interacting with today's marketplace. The site features in-depth information on over five thousand mutual funds. A searchable mutual fund market manager provides the most comprehensive online mutual fund information. Pricing is quoted directly from the markets via a real-time data feed. You'll also find samples of financial newsletters and a weekly market outlook. You can even visit an interactive question-and-answer forum with industry pros for an ongoing discussion on timely investment issues. An equities center provides free stock quotes, insider's stock resources, and a guide to finding equity resources on the Internet. A separate Internet information center features Morningstar analysis, newsletters, educational forums, and financial information databases. To get around the jam-packed site, use the NETworth Navigator to get an overview of everything inside. You must register to use the service, but it is completely free. NETworth is a valuable tool for all do-it-yourself investors.

Contact: GALT Technologies, Inc., NETworth, *comments@atlas.galt.com*

Taxing Times

http://www.scubed.com/tax/tax.html

This Best of the Net winner is an electronic compendium of almost anything you might need to file your income tax returns. Link to a huge archive of federal and state income tax forms, which you can download and print for filing; you'll even find Canadian tax forms. You can also access instructions for all forms, as well as a general guide to filing taxes. Other important tax information located here includes a personal finance resource center and *Tax Digest*. Connect to public-domain tax software, tax newsgroups, and other Internet resources. You can even download the entire tax code, if you have a lot of time on your hands.

Contact: William J. Proffer, S-Cubed Division, Maxwell Laboratories, *proffer@scubed.com*

Quote.Com

http://www.quote.com/

Get the latest financial market data over the Internet through this server, offering both free and subscription services. Here you'll find current quotes on stocks, options, commodity futures, mutual funds, and bonds. The service provides an end-of-the-day portfolio update, foreign stock and commodity data, and custom quote software. With a custom-designed personal stock portfolio, you can receive daily updates, recent news items, and e-mail alarms of important activities regarding the companies in your portfolio. You can also get access to business information services, a database of company profiles, and stock guides. Take a free test run of Quote Com's services today to determine if it should become your investment information source on the Internet.

Contact: Chris Cooper, Quote Com, *stuff@quote.com*

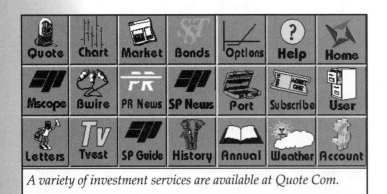

A variety of investment services are available at Quote Com.

World Bank

http://www.worldbank.org/

Visit the World Bank virtually, and learn all about the financial institution. You'll find press releases, speeches, news, and monthly business briefings here. A Public Information Center provides economic and sector reports, environmental documents, and project information. A publications catalog is a gateway to the World Bank's studies of economic and social data from developing countries. You can also tap into the World Bank's research on development, trade, economic policy, and a global economy.

Contact: World Bank

For more information on finance, visit these sites:

American Stock Exchange

http://www.amex.com/

Includes a market summary, a list of companies, news, and other information. I would think it would be extremely useful for people to keep track of their investments.

Beverly Hills Wall Street

http://www.geopages.com/cgi-bin/main/WallStreet

With resources to connect to for finance information and a helpful, nice design.

Centura Bank

http://www.centura.com/

Home page for Centura bank, the "money managers," with listings of available services.

Chase Manhattan

http://www.llnl.gov/fstc/principals/chase_manhattan.shtml

Nice design, with information on products and services, and a link to the annual report of the bank.

Citibank

http://www.citicorp.com/

Citibank's home page, with an introduction to their bank, products and services, branch locations, and regional offerings.

CyberCash

http://www.cybercash.com/

Much like DigiCash (see below), a secure financial service. Also includes a list of banks online, handy for people who want to try to find their bank, plus software downloads and merchant lists.

DigiCash

http://www.digicash.com/

For those nervous about sending their credit card numbers over the Web. As I understand it, you give them your credit card number (securely), and then they give you an "account number." All your online transactions can go through them, so that only they have your credit card number.

FDIC Home Page

http://www.fdic.gov/

Includes statistics and a corporate library. Useful for investors or people who want to know more about banking regulations.

FDIC-insured CDs

http://www.webshop.com/cbank/

Provides information on getting CDs, though I can't tell if this is affiliated with any bank.

FinanCenter

http://www.financenter.com/resources/

For individuals, ranked in the top 5 percent of Web sites and includes interactive calculations, plus interest rates, reports, and services. Looks great.

First Union

http://www.firstunion.com/

First Union bank's home page. Includes information on banking services and accounts, CyberBanking, and an application for MasterCard, among other things! Useful for FUNB customers.

JP Morgan Investments

http://www.jpmorgan.com/

Finance giant home page with information on the company, links to a corporate history, and relevant indices, such as commodities and currency. Helpful for investors investigating possibilities.

KiwiClub Web

http://kiwiclub.bus.utexas.edu/finance/kiwiserver/
kiwiserver.html

Noted as one of the best Web pages for personal finance and other really cool information. I was impressed with what was there! Check it out.

IRS

http://www.ustreas.gov/treasury/bureaus/irs/irs.html

The IRS home page! Includes tax forms, a FAQ, where to file, and where to get help.

Mastercard International

http://www.mastercard.com/

Apply via the Internet, get information, or peek into the "visionarium," whatever the heck that is.

NandO's Stock Page

http://www.nando.net/newsroom/nt/stocks.html

Links to related stories and summaries of major stock changes, but no listing of Dow Jones or NASDAQ.

NASDAQ Composite Index

http://www.secapl.com/secapl/quoteserver/nasdaq.html

Graphed all day, with only a fifteen-minute delay on updates. You can also look at the most recent day's graph and back through the last twelve months.

NationsBank

http://www.nationsbank.com/

Includes links about services and even a link about the 1996 Olympics, of which NationsBank is a sponsor.

NestEgg

http://nestegg.iddis.com/

Includes *Finance Information* magazine, Wall Street information, a calendar, and other personal investment resources. Nice design, rated in the top 5 percent of Web sites.

NETWorth

http://www.xperts.montgomery.com/

A free Internet service providing in-depth information on over 5,000 mutual funds. Wow!

Stock Research Group

http://www.stockgroup.com/

Ranked in the top 5 percent of Web sites and the #1 Web page for finance information. Great design, aimed at the individual investor, with news, company information, etc.

Wall Street

http://www.geopages.com/WallStreet/1203/

Provides links to finance and banking resources on the Internet, including Web sites, Gophers, newsgroups, and mailing lists. Helpful!

Wall Street Journal

http://update.wsj.com:443/

Great design and looks very useful. Includes links to sister publications like *Asian Economic Survey*.

Woodrow

http://woodrow.mpls.frb.fed.us/

Federal reserve bank page with plenty of good economics and U.S. banking information.

Food Stores & Restaurants

Boston Restaurant List

http://www.osf.org:8001/boston-food/boston-food.html

This list of approximately a thousand restaurant reviews tells you definitively where you should eat in Boston. The restaurant reviews are based primarily on contributions from Internet users. The reviews focus on flavor, quality, and value, but also report on service and ambiance. A restaurant has to receive two positive reviews to be included. The reviews are listed alphabetically, by geographical area and by cuisine; you can also search the entire database, access personal favorites or see other restaurants not on the list. Bonuses include reviews of Boston Sunday brunch buffets and Boston beers and ciders. Use an interactive form to submit your own reviews. This site is a model for WWW developers of review-based services, who should definitely check out the paper, "Lessons Learned from the Boston Restaurant List," presented by the maintainer at the 1994 WWW conference.

Contact: Ellis S. Cohen, Open Software Foundation, *ellis@osf.org*

Cafe Mam

http://mmink.cts.com/mmink/dossiers/cafemam.html

At Cafe Mam you can order the best organically grown, most socially responsible coffee beans available over the Web. The WWW brochure describes the coffee beans, the co-op that grows them, company efforts to support pesticide reform, rain-forest conservation, and employment practices. Read about the kinds of coffee roasts that are available, all produced from batch-roasted, certified organic, high-altitude, sun-dried, Arabica beans. You can choose from a variety of roasts and blends or order a coffee sampler. You can also purchase noncoffee items, such as T-shirts and coffee mugs. Use a form to order through e-mail or snail mail. You won't go back to Maxwell House after you browse through this gourmet coffee catalog.

Contact: Internet Ad Emporium, Multimedia Ink Designs, *rdegel@cts.com*

Guide to the Good Life

http://www-gsb.stanford.edu/goodlife/home.html

This restaurant review guide steers you toward the best restaurants in the South Bay, California, area, covering cities from San Francisco to San Jose. The restaurant reviews, culled from the books *Guide to the Good Life* and *The Peninsula and San Jose Restaurant Guide*, are searchable in many different ways; pick out a good restaurant by cuisine, geographical area, hot spots in popular downtown areas, and name. Besides the detailed reviews, listings include addresses, phone numbers, and a key to how expensive they are. You can also see ads from select restaurants and link to their reviews, or submit your own review to be included in the guide.

Contact: Todd Lone Rhino and Good Life Publications, Stanford University Graduate School of Business, *goodlife@gsb.stanford.edu*

Mothercity Espresso

http://www.halcyon.com/zipgun/mothercity/mothercity.html

What better way to top off a meal than with a good cup of coffee? That's what you'll find here in this guide to the best coffeehouses in the North American crown city of espresso—Seattle, Washington. These WWW pages will show you where in Seattle the best espresso can be found. The listings describe the coffee, atmosphere, and location of each recommended coffeehouse. You'll even see the place for yourself through huge inline photographs. The little things that make each coffeehouse unique are described, like the kind of beans they use, the way they froth their milk, or the weird artistic types who hang out there. If you can't get to Seattle but all this talk of coffee gives you a craving, you can even find out where to order the coffee beans that make these coffee houses famous.

Contact: Don Crafts, Viticulturist IT, *zipgun@halcyon.com*

Visit Seattle's coffeehouses like Caffé D'arte at Mothercity Espresso.

Pizza Hut

http://www.pizzahut.com/

Yes, now you can actually order a pizza online. Well, maybe not you, but the lucky people in Santa Cruz can, using this experimental interface to Pizza Hut. Either order a pizza with an online form, or just send in your comments. From this page, you can also learn more about the pilot program for online pizza ordering. The Pizza Hut experiment is currently on a pilot test in Santa Cruz (sorry, rest of the USA). If it's successful, it will eventually be available throughout cyberspace wherever Pizza Hut stores are within delivery distance.

So keep tabs on this exciting experiment through this Web site. When you can order a pizza without leaving your computer, you'll know the future has truly arrived.

Contact: Pizza Hut Internet Team, Pizza Hut, *webmaster@PizzaHut.COM*

S.P.S. Beer Stuff

http://www.infonet.net/showcase/spsbeer/

Visit the one-stop shop for home beer brewers on the Web. The complete online catalog at S.P.S. Beer Stuff has everything you need for homebrewing. This WWW shop is updated regularly and demands multiple visits. Be sure to check the monthly specials, or browse through a catalog stocked with starter kits, brewing equipment, beer ingredients and additives, and instructional books. A "quick reference" button bar makes navigating the catalog a snap. "More information" buttons scattered throughout link to further information about specific products. You can order immediately through an online form. Extras include answers to common questions, such as how to get started homebrewing, as well as info on brewers' clubs and competitions and complete prize-winning recipes. Be sure to use the interactive suggestion box and survey to help the store improve its WWW catalog.

Contact: S.P.S. Beer Stuff, Iowa Network Services, *SPSBEER@ins.infonet.net*

Take the Cake

http://www.cakes.com/cakes/

Take the Cake is a mail-order service now accessible over the WWW. The catalog features four varieties of cakes: apple walnut, chocolate grand marnier, lemon almond, and rum pecan. (Hungry yet?) At the WWW storefront, you can read all about the store and its founder. Enter the catalog to view pictures of all the cakes and read scrumptious-sounding descriptions. Then go to the order page where you can choose among home orders, gift orders, and corporate orders using an interactive form. Send Take the Cake your gift lists, and they'll remember important dates for your loved ones throughout the year and remind you through e-mail. Gift orders include a personalized note with the cake. Businesses can set up a corporate account through the site. Why should you send Take the Cake? A page tells you all the reasons why you would want to send a cake as a personal or business gift. Take the Cake is a convenient, one-step, hassle-free way to send a special, unique gift.

Contact: Take the Cake, Internet Information Services, *cake-info@cakes.com*

Order delicious cakes like this one at Take the Cake.

For more food stores and restaurants, visit these sites:

A la Carte Guide to North America

http://westweb.com/rest/

A guide to North American restaurants, bed and breakfasts, lodgings, hotels, etc., divided by Canada/U.S. I'm not certain of the extensiveness of the database, but it does have a nice design and is useful to a traveler, most likely.

American Supply International

http://www.dgsys.com/~asii/

Sells basic food supplies from downloadable complete catalogs. Also provides information on the company and ordering, and you can order via e-mail, phone, or fax. Includes basically everything you'd find in a supermarket or drugstore except frozen stuff. Also has a 25,000 title video library for home entertainment.

Amish Country Cheese

http://www.webcom.com/cheese/

Order holiday gift packages and individual cheeses, browse recipes, look at other Amish arts, and explore fund-raising programs.

Austin Resaurants by Type

http://www.tech.net/austin/dining/rest_ty.htm

This page lists Austin restaurants by the type of food they serve. There are listings for everything from American to Vietnamese. Included with most listings are a phone number, address, and general location (east, north, etc.)

BBQ—Smokin' the Internet

http://www.bbq.com/History.html

This is actually a serious history of barbeque, from descriptions of Hebrew sacrifices to a reference to Homer. It's linked to recipes, BBQ events, and a BBQ store.

Brothers Gourmet Coffee

http://pwr.com/brothers/brother1.html

You can order online, browse gifts and accessories, or e-mail the company. Nice design.

Celestial Seasonings

http://www.usa.net/celestial/seasonings.html

Herbal tea, apparel, and gift sets, ordered online! Nice art and great design. You can get descriptions of tea, selected by category. A favorite of mine.

Cheesecake Lady

http://dol.meer.net/catalogs/cheesecake/index.html

Order direct gourmet cheesecakes, including a sampler or gift cake. Yummy! A few good cooking suggestions here as well, with pictures and pricing.

Chrone's Virtual Diner

http://www.neb.com/noren/diner/Chrones.html

This site defines a true diner, lists several in the Northwest, and provides links to other interesting food-oriented sites.

The Coffee Shop

http://amsquare.com/coffee/homepage.html

Sells gourmet coffees, including gift sets, a "coffee-of-the-month club," coffee descriptions, and what seems to be a "discount card." You can order online by clicking on the shopping bag icon, then the order is sent when you check out. Very cool.

Cyberspace Natural Market

http://kalypso.cybercom.net/~gopher/

Sells lots and lots and lots of items, designed for convenient shopping at discount prices, including natural/healthy foodstuffs and others (personal care, cleaning products, recipes), browsable by category. You can select item and quantity to "put into your shopping cart" and then send in your complete order. Two thumbs up.

Dining Out on the Web

http://www.ird.net/diningout.html

A neat site (ranked in the top 5 percent of Web sites) of restaurant reviews and listings, searchable by outside linked databases and publications, then categorized by city and state, so you can find local stuff. Also includes international reviews.

The Dinner Co-op

http://gs216.sp.cs.cmu.edu/dinnercoop/home-page.html

Contains over 1,500 links to restaurants, food stores, shops, recipes, and other food resources—a great starting place, very comprehensive.

800 Spirits

http://owl.net/OWLspace/spirits/800.spirits.html

An expensive gift catalog, with online ordering available.

Erma's Herbs

http://www.bizcafe.com/sspecial/ermaherb.html

An online catalog of herbs, including descriptions and prices, a "make your own bath salts" option, and descriptions of the uses of various herbs. Order by filling in an order form, then printing out and snail-mailing it in with a check.

Everybody's General Store

http://www.nas.com/~goodbuy/food/food.html

Includes an odd mix of food, such as all sorts of cheese (including XXX sharp cheddar), sausages, etc. Online ordering available.

Food Trek

http://www.tisco.com/iconmall/foodtrek.htm

Sells "exceptional meat products" which appear to be mostly gift baskets with sausages and such. Online ordering.

Gourmet Gardener

http://metroux.metrobbs.com/tgg/catalog.htm

You can order online (or request a printed catalog) gourmet spices and herbs, veggies, and other stuff. I found the spice list to be a bit thin, though exotic.

Hot Hot Hot!

http://www.hot.presence.com/g/p/H3/

The Web's coolest page for hot stuff! Includes 100 plus different hot sauces, such as Rings of Fire and Nuclear Hell, catalog instructions, and online ordering. Ranked in the top 5 percent of Web sites.

International Hot Foods

http://www.xnet.com:80/~hotfoods/

Sells lots of hot food from all over the world. Includes a long list of hot sauces. Lists an 800 number for ordering the full catalog, which also includes gift baskets and lots of other food items. There's no online ordering, just catalog and shipping info, plus a list of hot sauces.

Internet Restaurant Delivery

http://www.ird.net/cgi/get?ird/index

The only delivery service on the Internet. You must register to use it.

Kosher Express Matzah Market

http://www.marketnet.com/mktnet/kosher/

Online catalog features 50 plus kosher foodstuffs, ordering online, recipes, and links to other Judaica resources.

Kosher Restaurant Database

http://shamash.nysernet.org/kosher/krestquery.html

Searchable by query only; you must input city and metro area, plus name, to get a list of kosher restaurants.

Lobster Direct

http://nova.novaweb.ca:80/lobster/

Order a lobster (or lox) and have it FedExed to your door. Includes information on Nova Scotia lobsters, how to properly eat a lobster, and a newsletter.

Long Island Restaurant Guide

http://www.macroserve.com/livrg/guide.htm

A guide to restaurants and "gustatory experiences" in the Long Island, NY, area. Searchable by location or cuisine, the list also includes a menu-browsing feature and a nice page design.

The Maples Fruit Farm

http://virtumall.com:80/MaplesFruitFarm/greeting.html

Includes specialty items, dried and fresh fruit, coffees, candies, etc. You can order online, browse selection by category, and get a history of the family owned organic farm.

Planet Earth Home Page for Food and Recipes

http://www.nosc.mil/planet_earth/food.html

Includes links to some of the other major restaurant pages already documented, plus a few recipe links, including a "mixed drinks" Gopher.

Spice Merchant

http://eMall.Com/Spice/Spice1.html

Order spices by category (from India and China), as well as teas, cookbooks, cooking wares, etc. Online ordering.

Ragu Web Page

http://www.eat.com/

With Mama Cucina's Italian cookbook featuring good recipes and a Learn to Speak Italian link.

Restaurants by Cuisine

http://albrecht.ecn.purdue.edu/~jbradfor/rest-type.html

The list is categorized by type of food and includes a few local New Orleans restaurants, but also quite a few chain restaurants and fast food places. Individual restaurant links go to a basic listing, including the local address (in Louisiana), types of food served, rating of service and cost, and maybe a couple of comments.

Taste Unlimited

http://www.ip.net/tu/home.html

Sells gourmet food stuffs and provides ordering online. Includes gift baskets, savory sauces, and company information.

Vegetarian Guide

http://catless.ncl.ac.uk/Vegetarian/Guide/

Has links and information on veggie and veggie-friendly restaurants, stores, and services. A "definitive" guide.

Virtual Vineyard

http://www.virtualvin.com/infoseek

An online guide to buying specialty foods and excellent wines, including an e-mail list, rating method, etc. The rating method is to personalize the choices so that they will be ranked according to your preferences.

Wine Net News

http://www.vino.com/wnnew.html

This page gives reviews of various wines, along with pricing information. Very descriptive.

Whole Foods International

http://www.wholefoods.com/wf.html

Includes a history of the company, a mission statement, information on the food they sell, stock and vendor information, and recipes. No ordering online, but you can electronically request a catalog and order from that. Sells organic types of food. Has a top 5 percent of Web sites ranking, too!

Your Country Cellar

http://www.interaccess.com/wineline/

This site is a catalog specializing in wine from around the world.

Game & Toy Stores

Galaxy Quest

http://virtumall.com/cgi-bin/shop?/GalaxyQuest/
gq_cat.shoppingcart.html

Go to Galaxy Quest's online store to fulfill all your "Star Trek" shopping needs. The online store adds new products as quickly as they are announced, so you can be the first on your block to own the latest "Star Trek" merchandise. The store also offers a large selection of pre-release merchandise to let you order before the items appear in stores. In the store, you can get the official Next Generation customizable card game, with a universe of more than 360 collectable cards. You'll also find "Star Trek" postage stamp sets, a universal remote shaped like a phaser, a guide to Trek life in cyberspace, a shuttlecraft clock radio, "Star Trek" CD-ROMs, limited-edition animated series cels, mouse pads, and posters—all perfect for the "Star Trek" maniac. Pictures of all the products are shown, and to order online, all you have to do is click on the gift box and follow the easy ordering procedure.

Contact: Galaxy Quest, Inc., VirtuMall, *comments@virtumall.com*

Infinite Illusions Juggling Supplies

http://pd.net/catalog/

Satisfy all your juggling-related needs at this virtual store. Through the catalog, you can order juggling supplies, books, yo-yos, boomerangs, kites, and more; you'll know what you're getting because photos accompany every description. A lot of free information on juggling makes the site well worth visiting even if you're not buying. A how-to section teaches you how to juggle three balls and use "devil sticks." You'll also find information about the American Juggling Club, downloadable pictures of jugglers, and a page of Internet juggling links. Learn all about the store as well, including its history, location, juggling conventions, and commitment to the Internet. Don't forget to join the mailing list to learn when new products are coming online.

Contact: Infinite Illusions, Paradigm Mall, *infinite@pd.net*

White Rabbit Toys

http://www.toystore.com

White Rabbit Toys is a real store in Ann Arbor, Michigan, that offers its goods for sale over the WWW. In this online catalog, you'll find a great selection of toys that encourage children to create, learn, imagine, and explore. The catalog features companies such as Brio, Ravensburger, Creativity for Kids, and Gund. Browse through the catalog, reading short descriptions of items for sale and viewing large photographs available by clicking on the "teddy bear" next to each item. One unique section features the "latest and greatest" items in the store—the newest and most popular toys. Order using a handy interactive form. All orders are confirmed by e-mail within eight hours. You'll also find a page of links to other child-related resources on the Internet as a value-added "freebie" to the catalog.

Contact: JoAnn Lilienfeld, White Rabbit Toys, *JoAnn@toystore.com*

Find adorable bears like this at White Rabbit Toys.

For more game and toy stores, visit these sites:

Amigos Toys

http://www.tradewatch.com/amigos/index.html

Includes cuddly backpacks, musical toys, and more.

CCGS

http://www.nucleus.com/~ccgs/gaming.html

This is a catalog for various role-playing games, collectible card games, and so forth. The company is Canadian, so the stock may have some items that U.S. customers have trouble finding in the States.

Cerebral Hobbies Home Page

http://www.io.com/~cerebral/

This page is a hobby catalog, but this catalog specializes in role-playing games. There are lists of new releases, a tournament and event schedule, and a newsletter, as well as the usual ordering information.

Dragon Fly Toys

http://www.magic.mb.ca/~dragon/

For children with special needs.

FAO Schwarz

http://www.faoschwarz.com/

New York's biggest and best toy store online, including an exclusively Barbie page. As far as I can tell, it only lists products, not long descriptions.

Kids World

http://supermall.com/kids/page1.html

A toy and educational materials shopping page, indexed by category, with educational toys and a free gift offer.

Hobby Haven

http://worldmall.com/hhaven/hhaven.htm

This is a catalog for hobbies. You can order, while online, items in radio control, such as planes, cars, trucks, and so forth.

Hobby Maker

http://rampages.onramp.net/~hobmaker/

This is a sales page for Hobby Maker, a Texas store that carries model kits, figurines, ceramics, painting materials, rockets, and more.

Little Toy Store on the Net

http://www.suba.com/~chicago/lts.html

Sells thoughtful toys and includes a link just for kids.

The Virtual Toy Store

http://www.halcyon.com/uncomyn/home.html

With obnoxious and hard-to-find gifts for science fiction and fantasy enthusiasts.

Gift & Clothing Stores

Appellation Spring

http://www.wilder.com/winery.html

Appellation Spring is exhibiting a selection of T-shirts featuring some of California's best wineries. So it's not the same as taking a wine-tasting tour of Sonoma Valley—it's the closest you can get on the WWW. Many of the T-shirts on display here won graphic-design awards and are well worth some browsing time. Nine wineries are represented, including Dry Creek, Mirassou, and Schransberg, and more will be added soon. Linked to each of the featured wineries is information about the winery itself and full-color GIFs of the T-shirts that represent the winery. Although the shirts are not for sale, it is still fun to view the T-shirt art and learn about the wineries.

Contact: Wilder Systems, *winery@wilder.com*

Get T-shirts from all your favorite wineries at Appellation Spring. (Copyright 1994 Wilder Systems.)

Grant's Florist and Greenhouse

http://florist.com:1080/flowers/flowers.html

At this online flower shop, you can view and order FTD flowers for delivery anywhere in the United States or Canada. You'll find here a selection of bouquets for all occasions and for general purposes, as well as a selection of exotic flowers from Hawaii. For each bouquet offered, you'll see a picture and a short description. The flowers will be delivered for you, along with a personal note that you fill out online. Grant's Florist offers a great free reminder service that would only be possible online. Register reminder dates with the florist for special occasions such as birthdays, anniversaries, or Mother's Day when you want to remember to send flowers. The florist will automatically send you an e-mail message shortly before your reminder date, in time for you to order and send flowers.

Contact: Branch Information Services, Branch Mall, *flowers-order@branch.com*

Mighty Dog Designs

http://www.awa.com/mdd/mdd_www_shirt.html

Yes, the WWW has its own T-shirt shop, where you can purchase WWW souvenir shirts to advertise your "Web walking tendencies." Large, full-color graphics allow you to preview exactly what the shirt will look like. You can also browse the full seasonal catalog for T-shirts offered by Mighty Dog Designs, ticking off what you want to order. Choose color, size, and quantity, then order your shirts immediately. You're sure to be in fashion wearing the official WWW T-shirt.

Contact: Mighty Dog Designs, Downtown Anywhere, *Downtown@awa.com*

Advertise your Web walking tendencies with this T-shirt from Mighty Dog Designs.

ImageMaker's Gifts for Dog Lovers

http://fender.onramp.net:80/imagemaker/

In this unique catalog, you'll find a wide range of gifts to delight any dog owner or dog lover. Products in the catalog include quilts and quilt kits, fabric, note cards, clothing, tote bags, towels, and photo albums, all imprinted with artistic renderings of your favorite dog breeds. You can even get a custom watercolor painted of your own pet. Select the product type you're most interested in to see images of the gift selections, descriptions, and other pertinent information. A list of available breeds allows you to custom-order anything with your favorite dog on it. An online form makes ordering a snap. You can also find out about the artist who created all these products. You're guaranteed to find a gift for someone on your Christmas list at this fun WWW store.

Contact: ImageMaker, Onramp Technologies, *townsend@onramp.net*

Nine Lives Consignment Clothing

http://chezhal.slip.netcom.com/index.html

At the only consignment store on the Internet, you can browse a large inventory of pre-owned, name-brand clothing. Use an interactive form to browse the entire inventory, choosing type of item, size, price range, and label name. Or "hire" a personal shopping assistant—an interactive form allows you to create your own clothing profile and lets the computer do the shopping for you. You have to do the buying at the real store in Los Gatos, California, however; an online order form is not available. You'll also find here a tour of the real store in photographs and information on how to sell clothing on consignment, as well as special promotions, such as online coupons.

Contact: David Butcher, Netcom, *davidb@chezhal.slip.netcom.com*

Spencer Gifts

http://www.btg.com/spencer/welcome.html

There's one in every mall—why not one in cyberspace as well? At Spencer Gifts you'll find all sorts of novelty items for sale—the amusing, the fun, the unexpected, the tacky. How about purchasing a lava lamp, a neon shark, or a "Star Trek" phone for that special someone? Get photos of all featured products along with a short description. Order with a click of your mouse. The WWW storefront maintains a working order while you shop. You can manipulate your order online by viewing the status of a previous order or changing your current order. Then send it in—the interactive form makes it easy. The current catalog is small but fun, and it will probably be expanded, so stop in often.

Contact: Spencer Gifts Internet Store, BTG Corporation, *spencer@btg.com*

For more gift and clothing stores, visit these sites:

All-Internet Shopping Directory

http://www.webcom.com/~tbrown/clos.html

On the clothes page, click on a subject link (women's clothes, accessories, jewelry, etc.), then scroll through a list of companies online, including descriptions. I linked to one company and saw that the catalog was available online.

Authentic Vintage Clothing Company

http://www.i-netWORLD.com/vintage/index.html

This is the largest wholesaler of "recycled" clothes in America, including Levi's jeans. Ordering online is available, but you have to order in bulk. This service appears aimed at smaller retailers.

Clothing Stores

http://www.scescape.com/worldlibrary/business/companies/clothing.html

A list of apparel merchandisers on the Net, organized alphabetically by business name, with one-line descriptions.

Cuba Cigar Company

http://www.webcom.com/cubacigr/

Includes descriptions of the cigars they sell, "the ins and outs of cigar smoking," and a FAQ, plus a price list.

Earth Portals

http://alive.mcn.org/earthportals/

Sells New Age gifts and products.

Ethnic Appeal

http://www.webcom.com/ethappl/

A catalog of ethnic products.

Lands' End

http://www.landsend.com/

Lands' End online! One of my favorite clothes catalogs, featuring rugged wear from Dodgeville, Wisconsin. Online catalog features online ordering, some information about the company and its services, plus some very nice design. Two thumbs up!

Levi Strauss

http://www.levi.com/menu

This awesomely designed site includes what's "hip" around the world, "how we do what we do," and other cool links. This URL is the North American Server; for the European server, you can get to it by using the simple URL: **http://www.levi.com/** and then selecting European server.

Neil Lasher Silverware Ltd.

http://www.gold.net/users/du93/index.htm

This site is a catalog of silver goods and more. Even if you aren't in the market for silver work, the descriptions of the silver-smithing process are worth a look.

ProductNet

http://www.ProductNet.com/

Sells "simple, beautifully crafted clothes that let you tell your own story."

Sharper Image

http://www.sharperimage.com/tsi/

The Sharper Image catalog online! Need I say more?

Spiegel

http://cybermart.com:80/spiegel/

The world-famous Spiegel catalog online.

Information Services

Detective Information Network

http://www.investigator.com/din/

Connect to a unique investigative information service for individuals and small businesses. These computer sleuths are "the detectives for the 21st century." The Detective Information Network provides online investigative advice and research services. Use the service to locate a missing person; research a potential business investment, when hiring a child-care provider or employee, when consulting a new doctor, lawyer, stock broker, or other professional; to search for records, in trying to settle an estate or determine the value of property, when seeking a defendant, plaintiff or expert witness, when considering a contractor, vendor, or telemarketing proposal; or when you have questions about a suitor or new friend. The online detective agency can research anything that's a matter of public record, completely with computers. At the home page you can read about the service, including newspaper comments, success stories, and testimonials from satisfied clients. The Detective Information Network provides a useful service for people who don't need a full-fledged private investigative service but do need the help of a professional investigator.

Contact: Detective Information Network, SuperNet, *din_mail@investigator.com*

Dun & Bradstreet

http://www.dbisna.com/

Dun & Bradstreet is the leading supplier of business-to-business credit, marketing, and decision support services worldwide. Now your business, no matter how large or small, can take advantage of Dun & Bradstreet's services through the Web. You'll find outlines of the service's solutions for purchasing, strategic planning, credit, marketing, research, global, and employment search. You'll also find "freebie" tips in all the above categories. Keep in touch with global business issues and with the latest business trends. You'll also find a complete overview of the company itself and learn how to receive business background reports on the Web.

Contact: Dun & Bradstreet Information Services, *webmaster@dbisna.com*

Knowledge One

http://KnowOne_WWW.Sonoma.edu/

Knowledge One offers access to timely, accurate information on any subject using the convenience and speed of the Internet. The researchers at this service have access to thousands of information sources and can provide answers to almost any question, usually within an hour. Typical questions might include, "How much money did my competitor make last year?" or "What is proper Japanese business etiquette in a certain situation?" or "What's a good restaurant in Chicago?" Knowledge One serves students, researchers, business people, and parents with a range of needs, from simple facts to in-depth research. Fill out an online form to ask your question; depending on the amount of research involved in answering, the fee can be as low as twenty dollars. You can also join an update service that allows you to stay on top of an important topic, with information updates weekly, daily, or hourly.

Contact: Knowledge One, *knowone@sonoma.edu*

LEXIS/NEXIS Communication Center

http://www.lexis-nexis.com/

LEXIS/NEXIS is an online information-search service for fast and up-to-date legal, news, and business information. The service, which has more than 650,000 active subscribers, provides information for lawyers, accountants, journalists, and marketing professionals, as well as financial, medical, and patent/trademark information that could be useful for a variety of users. At the WWW site, get the answers to all your questions about the LEXIS/NEXIS services. Educational institutions can find out how they can connect to the service. New customers can find out about the services LEXIS/NEXIS offers. A useful "freebie" here is the TimesFax, an eight-page, free, daily news summary from the pages of *The New York Times*. Those already signed up can use the Web site to contact customer service or to find local access telephone numbers.

Contact: LEXIS/NEXIS, *webmaster@lexis-nexis.com*

Stat-USA

http://www.stat-usa.gov/

Stat-USA is a division of the Economics and Statistics Department of the Chamber of Commerce. It provides an online source for business, trade, and economic information produced by the federal government. This online service gathers the most crucial business and economics information from 50 government agencies and distributes it from one central source to its customers. Here you can learn all about the service, get information on any of Stat-USA's databases, and take a free test drive. You can also place an order.

Contact: U.S. Department of Commerce, Stat-USA, *stat-usa@doc.gov*

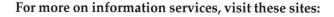

For more on information services, visit these sites:

DejaNews

http://www.dejanews.com/

The hot new research service. Researches archived information and recent news.

Search America

http://www.searchamerica.com/

Look up names, e-mail addresses, phone numbers, and mailing addresses. Members only, though there is a trial period available.

Internet Services & Commercial Use

Apollo Directory

http://apollo.co.uk/

The Apollo Directory, which links to businesses located all over the Internet, wants to become the premier advertising search engine on the WWW. When you enter the directory, select the home page for your country; the directory primarily serves the United States, Canada, the United Kingdom, Europe, and Australia. Then choose a category, location, or keyword to search for using an interactive form. The categories include business, computing, travel, the Internet, and recreation, among many more. Some ads have hyperlinks to company home pages. You can also advertise in the directory—it's free.

Contact: Gordon Wilson, Apollo Advertising, *apollo@apollo.co.uk*

Commercial Internet Exchange Association

http://www.cix.org/CIXhome.html

This nonprofit trade organization encourages development in public data communications networking. Public data network service providers who want to connect to other networks and aid in the development of the Internet are eligible to join. The exchange provides a forum for service providers to trade ideas, information, and experimental projects. At the organization's WWW site you can find out how to become a member and access a current membership list (also helpful if you're searching for an Internet service provider). The site maintains calendars and lists of conferences, conventions, and exhibitions about the Internet. You'll also find educational information about the Web and the Internet, as well as regulatory and legislative information.

Contact: Commercial Internet Exchange, CIX, *webmaster@cix.org*

Electric Press

http://www.elpress.com/homepage.html

The Electric Press designs catalogs, brochures, and newsletters for WWW display in full-color, multimedia format. Through this well-designed online "brochure," get an overview of the company, including specialized services, price lists, and information about marketing on the Internet, and let them tell you why you should use the Electric Press to meet your online marketing needs. You'll find samples of online catalogs, electronic newsletters, and product brochures designed by the company. The Electric Press also specializes in savvy marketing and offers a complete WWW server dedicated to your organization.

Contact: Duffy Mazan, Ronald Lineham, and Peg M. Dawson, Electric Press, *info@elpress.com*

Explore many teriffic Web sites designed by Electric Press.

Enterprise Integration Technologies

http://www.eit.com/

Enterprise Integration Technologies (EIT) develops and markets software products that enable electronic commerce on the Internet. Here you can get an office tour and factsheet on the company. Visit CommerceNet, founded by EIT, the first large-scale trial of Internet commerce. Access EIT research on electronic commerce, information technology, and education, as well as technical information on several Internet-related subjects, including multicasting and MPEG videos. Learn all about EIT's consulting and systems integration services, and see a sampling of past clients. Also access general goodies such as a guide to the WWW, a Webmaster's starter kit, a Web browser tune-up, and public domain icons for your Web pages. You can even download free software, such as a Web publishing tool with an HTML editor and many other useful Web publishing and electronic commerce tools.

Contact: Enterprise Integration Technologies, *webmaster@eit.com*

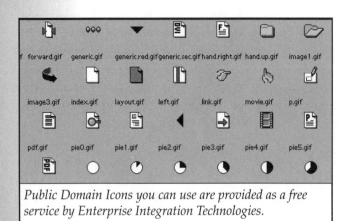

Public Domain Icons you can use are provided as a free service by Enterprise Integration Technologies.

Global Online News and Directory Service

http://www.cityscape.co.uk/gold/

This free service gives you a whole page on the WWW to advertise your company, organization, or yourself. Aiming to be a complete guide to the Internet, the directory encourages you to submit your own advertisement using an interactive form. If you're looking for a particular service, search the directory for online commercial sites or browse by selected categories. An online news service acts as a forum for what's new in the commercial resources found in the directory. Here you can page through late-breaking announcements of new products, services, and online events or submit your own announcement absolutely free.

Contact: Global Online Directory, CityScape Internet Services, *gold@cityscape.co.uk*

Internet Consultants Directory

http://www.commerce.net/directories/consultants/
consultants.html

Any company can make use of this listing of Internet consultants, whether to connect to the Internet, market goods or services, or publish company information online. Browse an alphabetical listing of consultants and organizations specializing in Internet products and services, or search the entire directory. Consultants listed here include WWW server administrators, graphic designers, networking service providers, hypermedia content authors and organizers, information brokers, and Internet applications developers. Information provided on each consultant includes the URL for his or her home page, contact information, areas of expertise, technologies used, number of years in business, and references. This public service is free both to listers and "shoppers."

Contact: CommerceNet, *feedback@commerce.net*

Internet Marketing Resources

http://arganet.tenagra.com/imr.html

Here you'll find lots of resources to help you market your business online. A list of print publications about marketing on the Internet includes relevant links. Get tips on setting up an Internet-acceptable marketing campaign or on establishing an Internet presence. Public-relations people will find helpful press release tips. Learn what sells on the Internet, and find reference sources for getting Internet demographics.

Contact: The Tenagra Corporation, *Info@Tenagra.com*

OneWorld Enterprises

http://oneworld.wa.com/

OneWorld provides value-added information services to companies and individuals who want to make their marketing and public-relations messages available over the Internet. This nonintrusive advertising service displays its WWW page designs in its virtual "port." Organizations such as Wilson WindowWare, the Asia-Pacific Chamber of Commerce, the Software Factory, and Real Estate in Seattle are located here. One extremely useful free resource hosted by OneWorld is an HTML developers' page. Get the lowdown on writing HTML documents for WWW publication, with information on HTML, server software, directory services, URLs, hypertext editors and converters, Mosaic, using graphics in HTML documents, and other general Web topics. You'll also find an overview of OneWorld's services, recommended Web consultants and artists, and a jump station to interesting WWW sites.

Contact: Charles Cooper, OneWorld Enterprises, *webmaster@oneworld.wa.com*

"Sail" into OneWorld's WWW publishing port. (Copyright 1995 OneWorld Enterprises.)

Setting Up Shop on the Internet

http://www.netrex.com/business.html

Using the Internet for commercial purposes can be tricky—there are standards for acceptable and unacceptable behavior for doing business on the Internet. Get the inside scoop at this useful home page of strategies for commercial use of the Internet. The page offers Internet history, resources, and statistics and gives an introduction to electronic commerce. It also provides advice to companies wanting to connect to the Internet, as well as solutions to the problems of marketing on the Internet. Important resources include links to the best commercial sites on the WWW, a list of the do's and don'ts of online marketing, and other business resources. You'll also find valuable information on security issues and government involvement in commercial Internet use. Before putting your business online, you should read this.

Contact: Andrew Dinsdale, Netrex, *andrewd@netrex.com*

Virtual Advertising

http://www.halcyon.com/zz/top.html

Virtual Advertising, an online advertising agency, introduces you to nonintrusive ways to advertise on the Web. At this informative site, you can read the monthly client newsletter on electronic media marketing. Check out the costs of the agency's WWW advertising services, and browse through an index of its clients, accessible through different subject areas. The agency has produced online displays for business services, retail stores, newsletters, and nonprofit organizations, all available at the site for you to look at. This online ad agency promises to be casual and informal, with no sales people and no hassle. If that's what you're looking for, stop by.

Contact: Virtual Advertising, Northwest Nexus, *arnold3a @halcyon.com*

The Virtual Press

http://www.aloha.com/~william/vphp.html

The Virtual Press meets electronic publishing needs through consulting and full-service e-publishing. This Internet publisher sells fiction in electronic format, specializing in fantasy, science fiction, and mysteries. You can order titles online. One featured electronic book is a fantasy called *At Dream's End*; check out screen shots before buying. Writers should visit here for information about electronic publishing, online writing resources, and a writing contest. Coming soon are a free Internet newspaper and technology magazine. Besides being an electronic publisher, the Virtual Press offers many online publishing services. The Internet Publishing Information Center provides software and multimedia for your online publishing efforts, as well as employment, legal, and financial resources. At the Electronic Packaging Center, you can get a professional-quality electronic newsletter, magazine, or book produced. The Virtual Press also creates home pages and Web sites and even provides help with equipment purchases, installation, and set-up. The press offers online marketing services and marketing space in Web pages. This is a good place to get electronic publishing done for you, find out more about electronic publishing, or follow trends in the industry.

Contact: The Virtual Press, William R. Stanek, Flex Information Network, *william@aloha.com*

Web Communications

http://www.webcom.com/

Web Communications offers individuals and organizations the services, tools, and resources to establish an effective WWW site. Included in the monthly fee are disk storage, the opportunity to register your own domain name, a site activity report, an access log, technical support, and more. You manage your own pages but Web Communications provides the tools for setting up and managing services, such as a file manager, a forms processor, image maps, password access, and search engines. As a guest, you can even practice making Web pages at no charge. Check out the commercial, personal, and nonprofit sites hosted by Web Communications for examples of their services. One useful extra here is a comprehensive guide to publishing on the Web, which includes an introduction to HTML, guidelines for creating a site, tips on publicizing your site, software tools, and an icon index. A WWW Power Index guides you to search tools, indices, publications, hotlists, software archives, graphics and multimedia, business, stock and financial markets, and many more useful resources on the Web.

Contact: Web Communications, *info@webcom.com*

For more Internet services and commercial use, visit these sites:

Open Market's Business Solutions

http://www.openmarket.com/omi/bussolns.html

Open Market develops and markets software, services, and solutions to facilitate business on the Internet. Find here help with doing business online, such as publishing, banking, advertising, retailing, and security. Open Market also provides an Internet index, a compilation of facts, and statistics about the Internet.

Tenagra

http://arganet.tenagra.com/Tenagra/books.html

This site contains a collection of print media references that focus on business use of the Internet. There are books, periodicals, and a subscription list included.

Web Art Publishing

http://www.webart.com/home.htm

This company offers HTML design, site development and maintenance, graphic design, and home page postcards. Here you can take a tour of Web Art's services and visit a flagship site.

Music Stores

CD Now!

http://cdnow.com/

CD Now! is a huge online music resource, offering over 140,000 CDs and cassettes, even vinyl, with a special selection of 6,000 import titles, 6,000 videos, and hundreds of T-shirts. Different Internet connection speeds can choose color, monochrome, or text versions of the online catalog. Inside, choose Find Pop to shop for everything that isn't classical, from jazz to alternative; you can search for an artist, record title, song title, or record label. When you select an artist, you'll see a listing of all their albums, with reviews and track lists for each one to help you decide what to order. Classical music fans can use the Find Classical button to enter the world's largest classical music store. Look for new releases on sale, or browse by format (VHS, laser disc, CD, vinyl, etc.) or music style, from bluegrass to reggae, Cajun to gospel, and many more. A separate section is devoted to music of the world. CD Now! carries almost every album made in the U.S. at very low prices, and it features secure online ordering. You can even keep a permanent list of albums you want to buy someday but that you don't want to order right away. Extras at the site include album reviews, artist biographies, and music magazines on pop, jazz, and classical. CD Now! also sponsors the All-Music Guide, the world's largest music database project. The guide is the combined effort of over two hundred experienced music writers, including well-known reviewers and entertainment magazine writers, who point out the most important artists and their best music. It also includes an online discussion forum. Whether you want to shop or just get some music information, CD Now! is the place to come.

Contact: CD Now!, *manager@cdnow.com*

Noteworthy Music

http://www.netmarket.com/noteworthy/bin/main/

Open a practically limitless compact disc catalog, divided into twenty music categories. You'll find all the same CDs that your local record store carries. Browse or search the inventory by artist, album, record label, music genre, or song. A multimedia directory links to items with image and sound displays. Select a checkbox to order an album; when you go to another page, the top of the screen displays the number of albums you've ordered and the total amount of your order. You can also select the Shopping button to view your current shopping list. Check out how shipping prices are calculated, or download your past order history with Noteworthy. (You have to set up an account to order.)

Contact: NetMarket Company, *staff@netmarket.com*

Windham Hill Records

http://www.windham.com/

Windham Hill is an independent record company offering innovative music. A beautiful interactive graphic leads you inside the WWW site. Take a Quick Tour to learn about Windham Hill and the Web site. Then browse the online catalog, which profiles twenty-five Windham Hill artists and forty-three of their top releases. Button bars make it easy to navigate the detailed catalog. Page through contemporary instrumental recordings, rock, roots, and blues selections, samples and compilations, and sheet music and songbooks. The catalog features such artists as Michael Hedges, George Winston, and Tuck and Patti; each artist listing provides background information, a photo, tour dates, a biography, and a discography. Album listings have the cover graphic, song clips, song lists, liner notes, and reviews. Visit the Listening Room for a selection of thirty-second sound clips. Get detailed ordering and shipping information; you must order by phone. Tune In lets you stay tuned to the world of Windham Hill, with concert information, lists of radio stations that play Windham Hill records, and a chat line that lets you interactively talk with other Windham Hill enthusiasts.

Contact: Windham Hill, *whinfo@windham.com*

Order the best in New Age music at Windham Hill Records.

For more music stores, visit these sites:

BMG and Columbia House Music Club

http://biogopher.wustl.edu:70/CGI/audio/bmg

This unofficial page offers searchable catalogs. It's quite an impressive page. You can search either database for code numbers of recordings, add in code numbers, e-mail each company's customer service, get downloads of their special offers, link to the BMG Classical Music WWW site, and even download a FileMaker Pro database specifically designed to keep up with your club membership, orders, payments, etc. A nice design and very handy for club members.

Brook Mays

http://brookmays.com/

Sells musical instruments and equipment, new and used.

CD World

http://cdworld.com/

Online ordering of 100,000 plus CDs and videos; also offers Netscape-secure transactions.

Cheap Thrills

http://www.cam.org/~thrills/

A Canadian music store, with a huge selection organized by category. The store will ship and all prices are Canadian.

Disc Drive Music

http://www.webcom.com/~screwbal/music.html

Specializes in compilations and collections not available in stores, including an X-rated collection.

Hookup Communications Music Store

http://www.hookup.net/mall/music.html

Contains links to all sorts of servers and databases. I don't think they sell music themselves, but it's nicely designed and well-organized. Even includes a "tango" database!

Hype!

http://www.hype.com/music/

Includes CDs to order, CDs to review, and CD reviews to check out.

Sheet Music Store

http://www.scinet.com/~musicbk/

Sells thousands of sheet music scores in all categories. Order by e-mail!

Sound Wire

http://soundwire.com/

Rated in the top 5 percent of Web sites, with lots of stuff and great design. You can get vinyl records here, plus zines, reviews, and audio previews.

Time Warp Vintage Music Store

http://www.vintage.com/record/

Sells rare and vintage music. Place an order or make a "want list."

Real Estate

Homebuyer's Fair

http://www.homefair.com/homepage.html

This free service not only lists houses for sale but also gives a lot of useful information about the process of buying a house. Go to the Homebuyer's Fair Information Booth for suggestions for recommended reading on current and controversial topics and links to other information resources on the Internet. You'll also find "pamphlets" on housing costs, closing, organizations that help low-income homebuyers, and a list of publications for first-time homebuyers. At the Mortgage Booth, get current mortgage rates, tips on shopping for a broker, and an electronic calculator for figuring out how large a mortgage you can qualify for. Browse through listings of available properties with experimental, Web-based interactivity to make shopping for a home easier. You can locate an apartment, get selling and relocating advice, and place your own ad. You'll find articles on Internet commerce and real estate too.

Contact: Arnold Kling, ASK Real Estate Information Services, Homebuyer's Fair, *arnoldsk@us.net*

Internet Real Estate Directory

http://www.onramp.net:80/ired/

This very attractive site provides a complete directory of real estate listings on the Internet and is a useful place to begin your online search for a new house. Site ratings help you narrow down your search by letting you know what's hot, what's worth a look, and what doesn't provide anything useful. Handy icons also tell you what type of broker you are connecting to. Real estate resources are divided by state (in the U.S.) and by country, including listings in Australia, China, Canada, France, Germany, Italy, Mexico, Sweden, Switzerland, the U.K., and many more. Connect through hyperlinks directly to the resources you most want to see. There are links to general information for buyers, sellers, agents, and brokers, such as legal issues, construction, foreclosures, and mortgages. The directory also provides e-mail contacts for buyer's agents and associations.

Contact: Buyer's Voice, Becky Swann, OnRamp Technologies, *becky@onramp.net*

Stop in here for real estate listings.

Myers Equity Express

http://www.dirs.com:80/mortgage/myers/

Once you've picked the home you want, you'll want to apply for a mortgage. You can do it through the WWW—hassle-free and no waiting. This Web site highlights Myers Equity's loan programs and provides an interactive form to apply for a home loan right away. You can even get a rebate on your loan if you use the online form. You can use the form to request mortgage information for buying a home, for refinancing, or for getting a second mortgage. Whether you're just thinking about buying a house or ready to close, this service can help you out.

Contact: Warren Myer, AAA National Directory Services, *myer@netcom.com*

RentNet

http://www.inetbiz.com:1000/

RentNet makes relocating easy through the power of the Internet. At this site, you can search a national database of furnished and unfurnished apartments and find an apartment online. Using hyperlinks, you first choose a state (those not available are coming soon). Then choose a city or area. Pick how many bedrooms you want—studio, one, two, or three. Then select a price range. The site returns a listing of available apartments that fit all the data you've entered. You can then take a look at the apartments close up to learn the price, square feet, area of city, lease term, and parking options. Take a look at a floorplan, check out the amenities, read comments about the apartment, and look at photographs. The guide always lets you backtrack to any of the options using buttons; it has a very nice design and provides a useful, free service.

Contact: RentNet, Internet Business Solutions, *rentnet@slip.net*

Apartment for rent in North Hollywood, CA, located through RentNet.

World Real Estate Listing Service

http://interchange.idc.uvic.ca/wrels/index.html

This free, public-access forum allows you to buy and sell property anywhere in the world. Property listings are organized by city, state or province, and country; a map-based, clickable interface allows you to pinpoint geographical regions. You'll find listings for Australia, Canada, the U.S., and Western Europe. Listings give brief descriptions of the properties, including price, taxes, size, zoning, utilities, and amenities; often a hyperlink leads to more information elsewhere. These are no-frills listings with very few photographs, but they span the globe, unlike other online real-estate listings. You can also place a listing yourself, using an online form. A trial run walks you through the process of posting your own listing.

Contact: World Real Estate Listing Service, West Coast Interchange, *wrels@www.wie.com*

For more information on real estate, visit these sites:

Homeowner's Finance Center

http://www.internet-is.com/homeowners/in-yahoo.html

Includes rates and analyses, forms, and mortgage databases. Helpful for new homeowners, I would assume. Nice design.

Housenet

http://205.139.162.1/housenet/

Provides resources for real estate, especially "buying a home." Looks useful.

HUD Homepage

http://www.hud.gov/

Get information on buying and improving houses, places to live, and other real estate-related stuff. Very nice design.

Internet Real Estate Directory and News

http://www.baynet.com/inman/

Includes hotlist links, news articles, and columns about real estate.

Real Estate Super Store

http://www.real-estate-ss.com/realss/

The nice design of this site lets you select a state to "shop" in. However, only two states are available to select. Maybe when it's finished, it'll be a great resource.

Virtual Malls

Branch Mall

http://www.branch.com/

The Branch Mall is a very diverse shopping mall, with both retail stores and business services. The mall also provides for secure credit card transactions. Retail stores here sell everything from novelties, food, and cosmetics to security systems, health products, and vacations. Business services include franchises, computing consulting, real estate, and office furniture. Each listing in the mall links to a virtual storefront with full catalogs and online order forms. Come here for an everything and anything WWW shopping mall.

Contact: Branch Internet Services, Branch Mall, *nan@branch.com*

Downtown Anywhere

http://www.awa.com

Enter a virtual city where you can "get access to the Internet, explore the WWW, make your own contributions available to others, sell anything worth selling, and buy anything worth buying." If you're a business owner, find out how you can purchase "real estate" in Downtown Anywhere. If you're just shopping, go to Main Street, the commercial center of the virtual city. There you can buy books, software, video games, videos, music, and more. You'll also find a variety of services, including financial services, Internet services, and computing consulting. There's even a Downtown Anywhere souvenir shop. Another shopping district, Fifth Avenue, provides even more unusual shops. Downtown Anywhere offers many public services as well, including a library, museums, ArtNetWeb, educational resources, a financial district, a travel center, and a sports arena, all with links to useful Internet resources.

Contact: Downtown Anywhere, *downtown@awa.com*

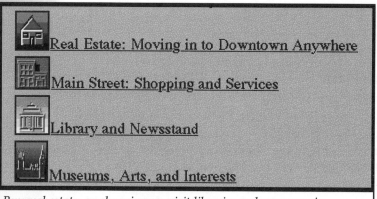

Buy real estate, go shopping, or visit libraries and museums in Downtown Anywhere.

EcoMall

http://www.ecomall.com/ecomall/

EcoMall is an online source of environmentally friendly products and services. Shop for products by category, or learn about environmentally friendly manufacturers. In the mall, you'll find ecologically sensitive merchandise such as baby products, energy-efficient appliances, food, clothing, recycled products, pet care, household products, and much more. Go to Business Services to network with other industries about new ecological products. The Classifieds offer low advertising rates for people and companies interested in the environment, where they can advertise products, magazines, or charities, or take out a personal ad. The activism section provides critical environmental information and profiles of important organizations. It also alerts you to organizations, pending legislature, and events of environmental significance and lets you make donations to environmental charities. Not only an interesting place to shop, the EcoMall publishes free news about the environment and links to other environmental resources on the Internet.

Contact: Virtual Marketing Systems Corporation, EcoMall, *eco-info@ecomall.com*

The Internet Mall

http://www.internet-mall.com/

What are you looking for? Hunting and fishing gear? Pet stores? Net banking? Educational software? Religious books? Bicycles? If it's a service or product for sale on the Internet, it's listed in the Internet Mall. This hotlist of Internet businesses includes over 1,500 cyber-shops. The Internet Mall is the most comprehensive, up-to-date, and readable listing of businesses on the Internet, and all the businesses are listed without charge. The mall is divided into different departments where you can shop for food and beverages, furniture and household items, clothes and sporting goods, personal and professional services, computer hardware and software, personal items, books and magazines, and automotive products. You can also consult the comprehensive company index or go straight to the most popular departments in the mall. Each listing includes a short description of the store and a direct connection to it, whether through a URL or an e-mail address. The Internet Mall is an invaluable starting point for any Internet shopping excursion.

Contact: The Internet Mall, Dave Taylor, MecklerWeb, *taylor@netcom.com*

eMall

http://emall.com/

eMall is a unique, electronic mall that features everything from general shopping to a food court to automotive servicing. Visit the General Store, where you'll find a variety of "unique and interesting products to make your life a little nicer," including laser discs, CD-ROMs, T-shirts, flowers, music, weight-loss products, and environmentally responsible products. When you're feeling hungry after your shopping trip, go to E.A.T.S! for all things food, including spices, hot sauces, coffee, chocolates, cakes, and tea. At the Automotive Center, you can get advice on anything to do with cars, such as selling, leasing, and maintaining. You'll also find cars and accessories for sale. The tourist can access a travel guide and information center for New York City. The business person should visit BizLink for a variety of business-to-business services, including commercial leasing, credit-card services, and telephone services. Each store in the mall is a full-service catalog,

with information about the products, images, online interactive ordering, and extras. For instance, enter the Republic of Tea for a catalog of
many different kinds of tea, a guide to the various types, a page on
brewing tea, and much more. Or go into SoundWire for music reviews, online samples, and a complete catalog of albums and videos.
All cyber-shoppers are sure to find something at the eMall.

Contact: CreationWare, eMall, *info@eMall.com*

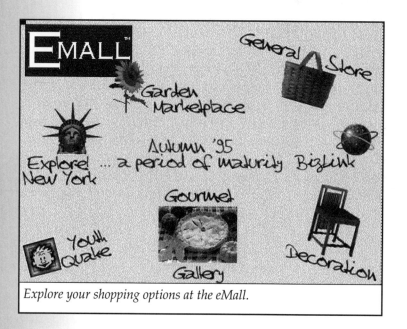

Explore your shopping options at the eMall.

Empire Mall

http://empire.na.com/

The Empire Mall features a variety of stores and services, ranging
from imported compact discs to Russian transport helicopters. The
mall even offers secure transactions and a monthly contest. A quick
index jumps to stores by what they sell. There are many interesting
stores inside the mall, including: Omaha Steaks International, selling
gourmet beef, poultry, seafood, smoked meats, and desserts; Salsa
Express, offering salsas, sauces, and dips; Tombstone Productions, the
Internet's largest retailer of horror products, ranging from costumes

and masks to props and special effects equipment; Point Communications, the premiere Web site raters; and the Virtual Irish Pub, the Internet's only authentic Irish pub. There's lots to do, see, and buy here.

Contact: Sean Moloney and Associates, Empire Mall, *ecmg@empire.na.com*

The Internet Plaza

http://storefront.xor.com/plaza/index.html

The Internet Plaza provides Internet services to companies that want to sell products or provide information on the Web. Enter the Leasing Office to learn more about its advertising procedures, price lists, and special services. Go into the Business District for professional services and products, including FinanCenter and *Career Magazine.* The stores in the Shopping District provide a complete shopping experience with interactive ordering. The Community Center supports nonprofit organizations, including the Internet Chamber of Commerce. The Plaza also offers a monthly feature highlighting an interesting customer.

Contact: XOR Network Engineering, Internet Storefront, *plaza@plaza.xor.com*

Internet Shopping Network

http://www.internet.net/

The Web's own Home Shopping Network, but with the added convenience of online ordering, the Internet Shopping Network sells a wide range of products. You'll find products from six hundred high tech companies, offering Apple software, Windows software, CD-ROMs, games, downloadable software, and hardware. Specialty stores include well-known retailers such as Hammacher Schlemmer, Sharper Image, Celestial Seasonings, and Lillian Vernon. Shop for the home and office with a wide selection of electronics. Or find super-hot deals on hardware, software, and electronics. When you find something you like, just press a button to buy. The Internet Shopping Network has something for every shopper.

Contact: Internet Shopping Network, *feedback@internet.net*

Marketplace.Com

http://marketplace.com/

Marketplace.Com features several unique shops. The mall hosts Alternative X, which presents works by dissident writers. Learn about the Internet Adaptor, a software tool for accessing the graphical WWW without a SLIP or PPP connection. Visit Cyberspace Development, a company developing software products for Internet connectivity, commerce, and publishing. Go to EmBarque for an Internet application and toolbox program. This "mall" contains a diverse and unique collection of merchandise.

Contact: Cyberspace Development, Marketplace.Com, *office@marketplace.com*

Shops.Net

http://shops.net/shops.html

This unique service is a place where people around the world can set up and manage their own virtual stores. The Internet Shopkeeper is the world's first Web-based Internet mall that allows store owners to manage their own online shops, unlike other virtual malls. At this WWW site find out all about the service, try out a demo shop, and order a shop yourself. Or just go shopping. Visit the shop of the week, or browse by category, including arts and crafts, entertainment, books, computers, gifts, and much more.

Contact: iTRiBE, Shops.Net, *signup@shops.net*

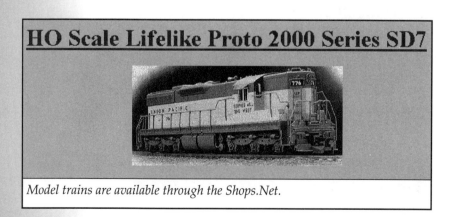

HO Scale Lifelike Proto 2000 Series SD7

Model trains are available through the Shops.Net.

VirtuMall

http://virtumall.com/

VirtuMall provides "new media marketing for the 21st century." You'll find it to be a fun online mall with lots of free "goodies." Shop by category, with hobbies, entertainment, food, computing, household, apparel, and a newsstand. Instead of going through the subject categories, you can use an interactive form to connect to a catalog directly or to search for a keyword. You can also learn about VirtuMall's development services, download free software, or play interactive games.

Contact: VirtuMall, *comments@virtumall.com*

Worldwide Marketplace

http://www.cygnus.nb.ca/

You can access this virtual shopping mall a number of different ways. An interactive map takes you around to different shop categories, including retail, travel, training and consulting services, and technology. Click on subject categories to get a listing of stores, and then click on the store you want to enter. Or take a guided tour of the entire mall. An information kiosk allows you to get a directory listing of all the mall businesses, get in touch with a specific business, or find out about leasing space in the mall. Fill out an automatic reply form for more information about the mall. Stop by the mall's administrative offices for a listing of Internet services provided by Worldwide Marketplace as well as a free arcade of video games. (What mall would be complete without one?)

Contact: Cygnus Technology, Worldwide Marketplace, *webmaster@cygnus.nb.ca*

For more virtual malls, visit these sites:

Andersen Consulting's Smart Store

http://smartstore.ac.com/smartstore/

Includes a Bargain Finder (comparison shops for CDs from eight providers) and links to really cool virtual malls. A handy gateway for shoppers.

Cybershop

http://cybershop.com/

Lots of links and some cool design.

Evergreen International

http://www.lifestyles.com/

Home page with links to various commercial catalogs including Spiegel, Sharper Image, and other stuff.

Freebie List

http://www.winternet.com/~julie/freebie.html

Lists of things you can get for free! A pretty good list, although it is organized by week listed instead of by category or company. You'll find mostly promotional stuff and instructional videos about topics like installing vinyl siding, but a thorough searcher might discover something useful.

Irish Mall

http://ireland.iol.ie/resource/imi/irishmall/

A source for Irish goods and services. Worth a look.

MegaMall

http://infotique.lm.com/cgi-bin/phpl.cgi?megamain.html

Boasting 180 plus stores with a nice design, too. You can shop by category or go to specific stores.

Milwaukee Marketplace

http://www.mixcom.com/

This online mall sells basics like software and music, as well as weird stuff like astrological counseling and hypnosis. You'll also find information about Milwaukee.

Tarheel Mall

http://netmar.com/mall/

This virtual mall received a top 5 percent of the Web rating.

Moving On

Now you have taken care of business with professional services, Internet advertising, and a wide variety of shops. Don't you think your kids deserve a WWW tour too? Although the sites in the previous sections are geared toward the family, some sites may not be appropriate for all ages. The next section reviews "clean" sites that are just for kids, from toddlers to teenagers. It also covers subjects of particular interest to kids. So move over, and let your kids have a turn.

Section VII

Just for Kids

Just for Kids

Okay, kids, now it's your turn. The sites in this section have been selected especially for you. The contents of these sites are appropriate for kids of all ages to explore. But don't worry—they're fun too!

In this section, we'll explore home pages for your favorite TV shows and cartoons, from "Sesame Street" to "Mighty Morphin' Power Rangers" to everything Disney. We'll find sites that will help you with your homework and sites that will help you with after-school recreation, like sports and reading. We'll play with toys and video games. We'll also join several kids' clubs—no adults allowed! There's even a section just for preschoolers and kindergarten kids. If all that isn't enough for you, there's also a large selection of site listings; these resources will lead you to tons more kids' places online.

A note to parents: The sites described in this section have all been thoroughly checked for content. However, hyperlinks may lead the intrepid explorer to other sites that you may not find appropriate. Also, the Web is always changing, and new content that has not been checked may be added to these sites at a future date. As with any other activity, it is best if you participate with your kids. Let them run the computer, but explore the Web together. You can check out sites before letting your kids access them, and your kids will have more fun if you are by their sides.

Kids and parents, let's start surfing. You'll discover that the Web can be both fun and educational—much better than TV anytime.

Animals

Dilophosaurus

http://ucmp1.berkeley.edu/dilophosaur/intro.html

If you've seen the movie *Jurassic Park*, then you probably already know what the dilophosaurus is (the one that spat poison). At this site you can take a narrated tour to learn all about this interesting dinosaur. Find out how the dilophosaurus was discovered and look up details about it. Learn about habits of the dinosaur. Also read about dilophosaurus the actor, as portrayed in *Jurassic Park*. All of the text is accompanied by audio files, so you can listen as the text is read aloud while you look at the pictures.

Contact: Professor Sam Welles, University of California Museum of Paleontology

The Froggy Page

http://www.cs.yale.edu/homes/sjl/froggy.html

This fun Web page links to froggy things on the Internet. Download froggy pictures and sounds. Read frog stories or learn songs about frogs. Approach frogs from a scientific angle by exploring online dissection kits and reading biological information. You can also link to famous frogs like Kermit and Keroppi or go to frog home pages. This page will point you toward everything you could possibly want to know or to find out about frogs.

Contact: Sandra Loosemore, Yale University Computing Science Department, *loosemore-sandra@cs.yale.edu*

On the Internet, it's easy being green.

Spiders of the World

http://seawifs.gsfc.nasa.gov/JASON/HTML/SPIDERS_HOME.html

Assist a scientist in spider research. This online research project asks you to determine the kind and number of spiders in your area. At the site, you'll learn how to search for spiders and how to identify spider families. You can also read all about poisonous spiders. Audio messages throughout give background and instructions for the project. A spider family key lists seventeen spider families, along with features to help you identify them. There's a drawing of each spider. Find out how to submit your spider data and set off on your spider hunt. If you don't want to participate in the research project, you can still learn a lot about spiders here. Check out a map of the earth showing all the places that have submitted spider data and see charts of their results. Find out what kinds of spiders are found at any location around the world. At this site, you'll not only learn a lot about spiders but also find out how to conduct a scientific investigation.

Contact: Gene Carl Feldman, SeaWiFS and JASON Project Home Page, *gene@seawifs.gsfc.nasa.gov*

The Lion Gallery

http://www.frontiertech.com/gall.htm

Explore a gallery full of lions created just for you. See the lion drawings of the month, all submitted by kids; if you like, you can submit one, too. You can also read the lion factoid of the month. Hear a lion roaring or look at a photo of Amon Ra, a lion at the Milwaukee County Zoo. Visit other Internet sites about lions, including *Lion King* home pages, lion pictures, lion sounds, zoos, the circus, lion stories, and more. If you're a Simba fan, you should definitely meet these other Internet lions. The gallery changes every month, so keep coming back. Submit lion-related material like photos, URLs, articles, drawings, factoids, or whatever, and you could win a free T-shirt. The site will tell you how to submit things.

Contact: Frontier Technologies, *Webmaster@FrontierTech.com*

Hunt for lions on the Internet.

Tracking Wildlife Migrations

http://ics.soe.umich.edu:85/IAPMain/

You can help build a map showing how animals migrate across North America. First, take a look at maps of the United States, Canada, and Latin America and select the country you want to view. Then select as many animals as you want from the list below. After you click on an animal's name, the computer will download a new map showing the tracks of that animal's journey. Click on a mark on the map to read observations by people who have seen the animal during its migration. Click elsewhere on the map to add your own observations. Using this site, you can track the gray whale, various birds including the peregrine falcon and bald eagle, the monarch butterfly, the sea turtle, and the caribou as they migrate north for the summer. You can also read more about the animals, such as where and when they migrate and how they are tracked.

Contact: Roger Espinosa, DeweyWeb, *roger.espinosa@umich.edu*

For more information on animals, visit these sites:

Dinosauria

http://ucmp1.berkeley.edu/expo/dinoexpo.html

One-page text with photos about dinosaur "truth is stranger than fiction."

Kid's Web Dinosaur Page

http://psych.hanover.edu/kidsweb/dino.html

Includes information, drawings, and other interesting links.

Knowledge Adventure's Dinosaur Den

http://www.adventure.com/WWW/dinosaurs/index.html

A really cool page! Includes "Create-A-Saur" (create your own dinosaur), reference information, a 3D viewing gallery, and other interesting kid-relevant links. A must visit.

National Zoo

*http://www.si.edu/organiza/museums/zoo/homepage/
nzphome.htm*

The home page for the National Zoo includes photos of animals and zoo pictures.

Photos from the New Orleans Zoo

*http://www-swiss.ai.mit.edu/philg/summer94/
new-orleans-zoo.html*

A minimal site. Just click on the animal to see the photos. (There are not that many choices.)

Safari Touch Tank

http://oberon.educ.sfu.ca/splash/tank.htm

Using this virtual touch tank, click on an animal to learn more about it. Also includes QuickTime video options.

Sea Creatures

http://www.actwin.com/fish/pictures/smithsonian.html

Smithsonian's collection of photos of sea creatures. Not a whopping lot of photos, but a start.

Sites for Turtles, Tortoises, and Terrapins!

http://www.sfc.keio.ac.jp/~s93073no/site.html

This site has pictures of turtles, some information on them, and lots of links to a great deal of data on turtles.

Tropical Rainforest Animals

http://www.ran.org/ran/kids_action/animals.html

A big, long text file in Q&A format, but obviously geared to kids' reading levels. Has some really cool information, but no pictures and no outside links.

Wombats, Marsupials, and other Animals

http://www.shicho.com/wombat/animals.html

Includes dinosaurs and Tasmanian mammals links, plus a link to the virtual zoo in St. Louis. Really cool.

The Wonderful World of Insects

http://www.ex.ac.uk/~gjlramel/six.html

This site is a good introduction to insects and would be especially good for children. It has facts and figures, along with some illustrations that lean more toward the cute than the graphically scientific.

ZooNet Photo Archives

http://www.mindspring.com/~zoonet/gallery.html

Here's where to find photos. Long lists of animal JPEGS and gallery collections, plus a few at the top of the page to whet your appetite.

Art & Writing By Kids

Art Space

http://www.uni.uiuc.edu/departments/finearts/art/artspace/uniartspace.html

This gallery displays original artwork by high school students. Click on any of the small graphics for a larger, more detailed view of the piece. You can also read the assignment descriptions that go along with the artwork. Check out drawings, including self-portraits. Look at original paintings and montages. In the 3D gallery are objects done in other media, such as masks made out of construction paper. There's also a gallery of computer imagery and photography. This student-created online art gallery might inspire your own artistic abilities.

Contact: Karen Hellyer, University Laboratory High School, *khellyer@uni.uiuc.edu*

Global Show-n-Tell

http://emma.manymedia.com:80/show-n-tell/

Global Show-n-Tell is a virtual exhibition that lets kids show off their favorite projects, possessions, accomplishments, and collections to other kids all around the world. Best of all, showing your stuff here is free. If you have work on the WWW or in an FTP site, you can enter it in the exhibition. Check out the exhibits for original artwork. (You can click on the picture for a larger one.) Some of the links go to home pages as well. Also, get information about the artist and read what the artist has to say about each exhibit. The exhibits change, so keep coming back. Check out the older exhibits if this is your first visit. Go to Other Sites of Interest to see other stuff by kids, such as artwork, activities, stories, puzzles, magazines, and multimedia. It's fun to visit all the home pages and look at other people's artwork.

Contact: Telenaut Communications and ManyMedia, *show-n-tell@manymedia.com*

Look at artwork and more by kids at the Global "Show-n-Tell page, including this picture by Douglas, who is six years old.

KidNews

http://www.umassd.edu/SpecialPrograms/ISN/KidNews.html

KidNews is a newswire service for kids around the world. Anyone can use and submit stories to this always changing online newspaper. Here, you'll read news stories, features, profiles, how-to's, reviews, sports, poetry, and fiction, all written by kids. There's also a place for kids to discuss school newspapers and some cool hangouts. All stories in KidNews are taken from school newspapers and focus on subjects of interest to you. Why don't you submit a news story? You can do it right from the WWW pages.

Contact: Dr. Peter Owens, University of Massachusetts at Dartmouth, *powens@umassd.edu*

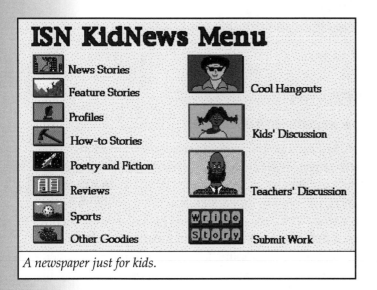

A newspaper just for kids.

Kidopedia

http://rdz.stjohns.edu/kidopedia/

Connect to an encyclopedia written by kids for kids. The articles in this online encyclopedia are sent in by kids all over the world. Find out here how to submit articles or how to start a local Kidopedia at your school; you can also visit other Kidopedias on the Internet. Or just look at the entries, which are arranged alphabetically. You'll find information on interesting people, history, animals, science, sports, important events, and other subjects. Many articles also link to pictures that illustrate the subject. After you've read articles, you can instantly send e-mail to the authors and tell them what you thought.

Contact: Tom Layton, Unibase Telecom at St. John's University

Put an encyclopedia written by kids on your virtual bookshelf.

KidPub Stories

http://www.en-garde.com/kidpub/

In this online kid's magazine, you can read stories written by kids ages five to fourteen. I saw stories about Martin Luther King Jr., a Civil War diary, murder mysteries, poems, the "Allied With Aliens" series, and many more interesting topics. One fun thing going on here is a collaborative story. You read what's already been written, then write the next paragraph and send it in to continue the story. In this way, you interact with other kids online to write a story. You can even submit your own story to be published here. Send one in, and it will be posted on the site. A template is provided for formatting your story properly. In KidPub Schools, you can link to class projects published by different schools. Maybe your class would like to publish a project on the Internet. KidPub lets you keep up with other kids online and express your own creative talents.

Contact: KidPub, En-Garde Technical Communication, *KidPub@en-garde.com*

Kids Did This!

http://sln.fi.edu/tfi/hotlists/kids.html

It's a challenge to keep up with kids on the Internet, but if you want to try, this is the place to start. Kids Did This! is a list of WWW resources created by kids in grades K-8. Topics include science, art, history, mathematics, language arts, and school newspapers. This is a great place to explore the WWW, as seen by kids.

Contact: Franklin Institute Science Museum, *baumann@fi.edu*

Press Return

http://www.scholastic.com/public/PressReturn/
Press-Return.html

Press Return is a multimedia magazine for middle and high school students. Young writers, poets, and journalists get the chance to work with professional editors and to have their work published online. Students in grades 6 to 12 can contribute essays, stories, news articles, jokes, poetry, photographs, and cartoons to the magazine. Submissions are chosen by real editors who work with you to make your work the best it can be. From the WWW site, read current and back issues of the magazine. Each issue is centered around an interesting theme. Meet the contributors to each issue, all kids. You can also read about the professional editors who work with students to publish their writing and art. If you want to get your work in the magazine, look at How to Participate to learn how to submit material. (You or your school has to be a member of Scholastic Network.) Then go to the Topic and Publication Schedule to see the themes of upcoming issues that will inspire your creative work. Even if you don't want to submit, the magazine is fun and interesting to read.

Contact: Scholastic, Inc., *staff@scholastic.com*

Peace in Pictures

http://www.macom.co.il/peace/index.html

Children of all ages are invited to join hands in a global "Peace in Pictures" project, coming to you from Jerusalem, Israel. The project is a game, contest, and collaboration involving children from all over the world that celebrates the peace process. Kids are encouraged to draw their impressions of peace, and the pictures are then placed on the Internet for everyone around the world to view, enjoy, and be inspired by. You can send your own pictures or just look at pictures already submitted. Prizes will be offered for the most expressive submissions. First check out the pictures already posted on the site, and then draw your own picture and add it to the exhibition.

Contact: MaCom Networking, *info@macom.co.il*

This peace picture is by Stephanie, age 9, from Maryland.

Plugged In's Projects

http://www.pluggedin.org/finished.html

Check out this site for all sorts of projects created on the computer by kids like you. The projects stress collaboration, creativity, fun, and use of the computer. You'll see graphics, image maps, picture books, and movies, all made by kids. The projects deal with the kids who made them, their families, their communities, and current events. There are also some purely creative works. Some projects you can explore are the artwork of the day, the illustrated story "Alien Cows," a video commercial, and holiday cards. There are lots more fun creations by kids that may inspire you to get to work on the computer. Look under World Wide Contributions for info on how you can show off your own graphics, movies, and poems.

Contact: Plugged In, *info@pluggedin.org*

Check out multimedia projects created by kids about their communities and families.

For more art and writing by kids, visit these sites:

Design an Alien Project

http://www.elk-grove.k12.il.us/schoolweb/highland/
highland.stvsp.html

This site discusses a project of some high school students who are designing an alien that they'd like to see on a "Star Trek: Voyager" show. Other students are welcome to participate.

XXX

http://cmp1.ucr.edu/exhibitions/hoffer/hoffer.homepage.html

Students at Hoffer Elementary School have created fun photography exhibits with the California Museum of Photography for you to explore. Check out collages, multimedia, videos, animations, and other cool photography projects, all by kids.

Cartoons & TV Shows

Animaniacs Reference Page

http://www2.msstate.edu/~jbp3/animx/animx.html

You'll find all sorts of references here to please any hard-core Animaniacs fan. Check out the Nifty Animaniacs Reference File (NARF) for frequently asked questions about Animaniacs, including merchandise, the cast, lyrics, and more. The Cultural References Guide lists cameos, cultural references, and random ramblings from each and every episode. Use it to get those inside jokes. The Future Episodes List will let you know what's coming up in Animaniacs broadcasts on FOX. The Mega-Lyrics file has the lyrics to every Animaniacs song, including the "Animaniacs" theme with all the variable verses, the "Pinky and the Brain" theme, "Yakko's World," "Yakko's Universe," and many more songs. Now you can sing along when you watch the show. Take the purity test to determine if you're a true fan and to learn more trivia about the Animaniacs. Download images and sound clips from the show. You can also connect to the Pointers on the Insignificant Technicalities page for everything you *didn't* want to know about Animaniacs.

Contact: Jay B. Parker, Mississippi State University, *jbp@AE.MsState.Edu*

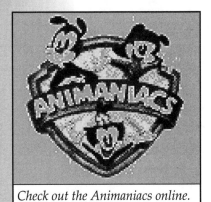

Check out the Animaniacs online.

Legion of Super-Heroes

http://www.cs.cmu.edu/afs/cs/user/vernon/www/lsh.html

At the home page for the Legion of Super-Heroes, you can learn more about the mailing list for discussing the comics—the best place online for Legion fans to meet and talk. Read the FAQ and check out back issues of the list. Also available here is a Legion timeline, a who's who in the Legion universe, a list of Legion appearances, and the gateway to the Legion-dedicated MUSH. (A MUSH is an interactive game you can play with other Internet users in real time.)

Contact: Vernon H. Harmon, Carnegie Mellon School of Computer Science, *vernon@cs.cmu.edu*

Nickelodeon Shows on the Web

http://www.ee.surrey.ac.uk/Contrib/Entertainment/ nickelodeon.html

At this unofficial Nickelodeon home page, learn a little about the television network just for kids. You can even send e-mail to Nick at Nite.

Also get guides to the Nickelodeon shows "Clarissa Explains It All," "The Adventures of Pete and Pete," and "Rugrats." The guide to "Clarissa Explains It All" has summaries of all the episodes, biographies of the cast members, video and compact disc release news, background, interviews with cast members, trivia, and other general information. You can also learn fun things about the show, such as the development of Clarissa's character and the history of Clarissa's career plans. Pete and Pete's guide has general information about the characters and special guest stars, an episode guide, notes about the music, and favorite quotes. The Rugrats page has information about the characters, some pictures, an episode guide, and a sound file of the theme song. If you're a Nickelodeon fan, you'll definitely want to browse through these guides to kids-only shows.

Contact: B. King, Department of Electronic and Electrical Engineering at the University of Surrey, *B.King@ee.surrey.ac.uk*

The Muppets Home Page

http://www.ncsa.uiuc.edu/VR/BS/Muppets/muppets.html

Everything on the Internet about Jim Henson's Muppets can be reached from here. A Muppets FAQ answers all your questions. Read episode guides to "The Muppet Show," "Fraggle Rock," "Dinosaurs," and "Sesame Street." Connect to the newsgroup *alt.tv.muppets* to talk with other Muppets fans. Get information about the Muppets' creator, Jim Henson. Look in Now Showing! to find out where you can see Muppets on TV right now. Read reviews of Muppet productions, including *The Muppet Christmas Carol* and *Labyrinth*. A Muppography lists every appearance by Muppets in books, magazines, video games, computer software, movies, TV series, videos, and more. There is also a list of Muppet albums, with song lists. Connect to other Muppet pages for Miss Piggy, Kermit, the Swedish Chef, and all the Muppets in general, with lots of pictures and songs. Muppet Movie Links has information about all the Muppet movies. Go to the Dinopage to read about the TV series "Dinosaurs." Look at Muppetabilia for pictures, quotes, and songs from "The Muppet Show" and "Sesame Street." Can you ever get enough of the Muppets? Not at this page.

Contact: Bill Sherman, National Center for Supercomputing Applications, University of Illinois at Urbana-Champaign, *wsherman@ncsa.uiuc.edu*

Meet the Muppets!

Power Rangers Home Page

http://kilp.media.mit.edu:8001/power/homepage.html

Get to know all the Mighty Morphin' Power Rangers at their very
own home page. There is a page for each of the Rangers, where you can
see pictures, learn about the Zords and power items for that Ranger,
read a history, and learn about the actor who plays that part. There are
also pages for all the bad guys, including Ivan Ooze, Lord Zedd, Rita,
and Goldar. Download lots of multimedia offerings, like movies, music, images, and a monster gallery with pictures of all your favorite
monsters from the TV show. Check out the movie page with lots of
stuff about the movie that came out in the summer of 1995, including
pictures, a trailer, a FAQ, and the official movie home page. There's
also lots more info about the Rangers, such as episode guides, a monster guide, and a toy list. Link to other sites about the movie, TV show,
and toys as well. If it's possible, you'll get your fill of Power Rangers
at this site.

Contact: Manuel Perez, Massachusetts Institute of Technology,
manny@media.mit.edu

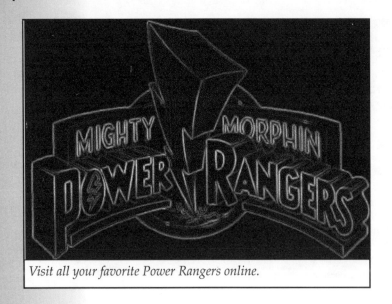

Visit all your favorite Power Rangers online.

ReBoot

http://www.inwap.com/reboot/

This is the unofficial home page for the Saturday morning cartoon about computers and the Net—a good cartoon for Internet folks like you. Get an introduction to the show by reading about the entirely computer-generated graphics used to create the animation. Meet the good and bad guys and visit places in the land of Mainframe where the cartoon takes place, with lots of color pictures. Check out the opening sequence, hear the theme song, and read a guide to each of the episodes. Find out about related toys and trading cards. Get a FAQ, learn trivia, and access a glossary of computer terms used in the show. You can also find quotes and cool things to look for in each episode. Press releases have details about the show, the characters, and the people who make "ReBoot" You can connect to other home pages for the show as well. If you're a "ReBoot" fan, be sure to visit this very cool and well-designed page. If you're not a fan yet, you probably will be one after coming here.

Contact: Joe Smith, INWAP.COM, *jsmith@inwap.com*

Sesame Street

http://weber.u.washington.edu/~lavigne/sesame.html

Take a walk down Sesame Street at this page. See pictures of "Sesame Street" friends like Grover, Bert, and Ernie. Learn all the lyrics to the Rubber Ducky song, so you can sing it over and over and annoy your parents. You can also visit more Muppets online or see a photo of the Muppets' creator, Jim Henson. From here, you can play the entire "Sesame Street" theme song and the pinball counting song. (You know: 1 2 3 4 5, 6 7 8 9 10, 11 12.) Sing along with your favorite songs from "Sesame Street" as they play on your computer. There isn't much here yet, but the author promises to add more, so keep checking back.

Contact: Rebecca Lavigne, University of Washington Computing and Communications, *lavigne@u.washington.edu*

Visit Bert and Ernie online at the Sesame Street home page.

The Simpsons Page

http://sashimi.wwa.com/hammers/comedy/simpsons/simpsons.htm

Visit all your favorite Simpsons characters in this multimedia-filled page. You can download images and sound quotes from each of the

Simpsons characters, including Homer, Bart, Krusty the Clown, Marge, Grandpa, Flanders, and more. There are also many videos clips from the show to look at. From here, link to the FAQ, the archive, and the newsgroup to learn even more about everyone's favorite cartoon family. Relive all your favorite Simpsons moments on this fun page.

Contact: Steve Rapport, WorldWide Access, *hammers@ironworks.com*

Taz-Mania

http://www.realtime.net/~lthumper/taz-mania/index.html

Taz fans come here first for the lowdown on the television show. Look in the FAQ for general information, including the lyrics to the opening song, a cast list, and more. Check out a picture gallery of Taz images. An episode list describes every episode of Taz ever aired. You can also connect to the *alt.tv.taz-mania* newsgroup for more talk about "Taz-Mania." From here, jump to the Tiny Toons and Animaniacs home pages as well.

Contact: Jeff Kramer, Real/Time Communications, *lthumper@bga.com*

Catch Taz-Mania on the World Wide Web.

The Uncanny X-Page

http://ux4.cso.uiuc.edu/~m-blase/x-page.html

Here's a resource for everything you want to know about the X-Men. Connect to loads of X-Men resources on the Internet. Find out about the people who create the comic books. In sights and sounds, look at pictures of X-Men comic characters, trading cards, and art. Read X-Men stories written by fans and listen to sound clips from the animated series. FAQs and Files has guides to the X-books, a brief history of the X-Men, information about the animated series, and even a Rogue FAQ, plus lots more trivia. Look in X-Men Lists for lists of characters, reprints, trade paperbacks, and all the known mutants in the Marvel universe. Connect to the *rec.arts.comics.xbooks* newsgroup to talk about your favorite mutants. You can also connect to other comics groups for discussion of Marvel, buying and selling comics, writing comics, and more. Join e-mail fan clubs for Gambit, Rogue, Magneto, Magik, and Blink. (Why doesn't Storm have a fan club?) Join MUSHes where you can become a mutant and play with others in ongoing role-playing games. Connect to home pages for Gambit, Rogue, Artie and Leech, Magneto, and Storm, plus lots more X-Men art. You can also connect to other comics sites from here, including Spiderman's home page.

Contact: Marty Blase, University of Illinois Student Cluster, *m-blase@students.uiuc.edu*

All your favorite mutants are on the Internet.

The Simpsons Sound Page

http://www.digitalage.com/sounds/Simpsons.html

This page is all sound, all from "The Simpsons." Check out the best-ever Simpsons sound clips. Or download sound clips organized by character, including quotes and quips from Homer, Lisa, Marge, Grandpa, Mr. Burns, Barney, Apu, Flanders, Krusty, and the Springfield police department. You'll even find theme songs for some characters.

Contact: Digital Age Communications, *Webmaster@digitalage.com*

For more on cartoons and TV shows, visit these sites:

Cartoon Factory

http://pages.prodigy.com/UT/cartoon/factory.html

Links to stuff like Disney cartoons and Warner Brothers cartoons.

Everything Nickelodeon Home Page

http://cctr.umkc.edu/user/rbarrow/nicklnx.html

Includes links to pages for individual Nick shows (quite a few of them), episode guides, FAQs, mailing lists, and fanzines.

The Fabulous Miss Piggy Page

http://www-leland.stanford.edu/~rosesage/Piggy.html

Includes photos, history, etc. What fun! Apparently has link to a Muppet Zine.

The Full House Page

http://pmwww.cs.vu.nl/service/sitcoms/FullHouse/

A favorite of some kids I know. This page contains an episode list and the title movie.

Miranda's Muppet Fest

http://www.cs.wustl.edu/~mir/muppets/

Includes photos of muppets and their handlers, song lyrics, quotes, and "Sesame Street" stuff, as well as an FTP site for archives. Cute!

Spider Man Page

http://www.met.co.nz/spiderman/index.html

More information than you'll ever need to know. Includes an unofficial newsletter and archives of information on the comic and cartoon.

Tiny Toons FAQ

http://www.swcp.com/~synth/tta-faq.html

The Tiny Toons FAQ answers lots of questions about this popular cartoon. Includes episode guides, lyrics to all the songs, trivia, characters, and pointers to places to download sounds and pictures.

Welcome To Wayne Manor

http://www.books.com/batman/batman1.htm

Holy 28.8Kbps modems, Batman! If you didn't get enough Batmania from the comics, movies, TV shows, and Saturday morning cartoons, by all means, check out this site. It includes GIFs from the comics and movies, games, and other Bat-info.

Disney

Disney Animated Features

http://www.uni-frankfurt.de/~fp/Disney/Features.html

You'll love this list of all the Disney movies with lots of fun links to explore. Check out all the animated movies from *Snow White and the Seven Dwarves* to *Pocahontas,* and even see sneak previews of upcoming Disney features. Get facts about every Disney movie and about the making of the animated classics. Read the original fairy tales or books on which movies like *Cinderella* and *Peter Pan* were based. Learn all the song lyrics from your favorite movies or look at pictures and posters from them. A link takes you straight to the Press Room at Walt Disney Pictures for more information and videos. You can also vote for your favorite Disney movies. Do you think *The Lion King* is the best Disney movie ever? Find out what others think at this site that's just for Disney animated movies.

Contact: Frank Pilhofer, Goethe University, *fp@informatik.uni-frankfurt.de*

Disney Home Page

http://www.rpi.edu/~wilmesj/disney/disney_links.html

If you can't get enough of Disney and Disney movies, come here for everything you could possibly want. Read news about upcoming Disney movies and the theme parks. Connect to places where you can talk all day about Disney, the cartoons, Disney afternoon, and the comic books. But the best part of this site is the multimedia offerings. You'll find tons of pictures of the whole Disney gang. Download stills from *The Lion King, Aladdin, The Little Mermaid, 101 Dalmations,* Disney Afternoon, and more. There are sound files from the rides at Disneyworld. Go to Movies for quotes, lyrics, videos, pictures, and sound files from all the great Disney animated movies, from *The Lion King, The Little Mermaid,* and *Beauty and the Beast* all the way back to *Snow White and the Seven Dwarves.* Connect to lots more Disney sites on the Internet from here. Be sure to visit the special *Lion King* page for trivia, pictures, music, and scripts from one of the best Disney movies ever.

Contact: Josh Wilmes, Rensselaer Polytechnic Institute, *wilmesj@rpi.edu*

Disney Theme Parks

http://www.best.com/~dijon/disney/parks/

Visit any of the world's Disney amusement parks online any time you want. Go to Disneyland in California, Disneyworld in Florida, Disneyland in Tokyo, or Disneyland in Paris. You can plan a real trip with directions, general information, and a FAQ about visiting a Disney theme park. Travel around inside the park with a map and articles about attractions, shops, restaurants, and entertainment. Preview the different attractions before you actually go. Check an entertainment schedule to learn when certain events will be happening, such as parades, fireworks, and shows from different movies like *The Lion King, Pocahantas,* and *Aladdin.* You can also find miscellaneous trivia, such as Disneyland recipes, or find out about future attractions. Be sure to read the Hidden Mickey list, a list of Mickey Mouses hidden in the designs of Disney attractions, so you can look for them when you next visit a Disney park. Go to Disneyworld again and again through the Internet.

Contact: Douglas J. Krause, Best Internet Communications, *dijon@lido.com*

Walt Disney Pictures

http://www.disney.com/

Check out current and upcoming movies from Walt Disney at this awesome site. From the lobby, you can enter various studios, jump straight to currently playing movies, or play a movie trivia game. Once you enter a studio, click on a movie's poster to enter its theater. Look at pages for Hollywood Pictures films like *Judge Dredd* and *While You Were Sleeping*, for Disney Pictures films like *Pocahontas*, and for Touchstone Pictures films like *Ed Wood*. For each movie, you can look at a press kit with film credits, notes, and photos. Download trailers, stills, and video clips from the movie. Then instantly send in your own comments about the movie. For some movies, such as *Pocahontas* and *The Lion King*, you can learn about animating and producing the film. The International Press Room features a wider range of movies. Here see even more Disney movies like *101 Dalmatians, The Fox and the Hound, Mary Poppins*, and *Sleeping Beauty*. New movies are coming out all the time, so keep coming back to see what's been added. You'll find lots of movies to explore and dozens of video clips to download in this jam-packed site.

Contact: Walt Disney Company

For more on Disney, visit these sites:

Arielholics Anonymous

http://www.csee.usf.edu/~aschenke/tlm/ariel.html

A page for Little Mermaid fans. It's G-rated; I checked it out. Nice design, including a good deal of information about the TV show and movie, such as scripts, plot summaries, and song lyrics. Also includes links to other Disney-related pages.

Dis' 'n Dat Home Page

http://www.tiac.net/users/lar3ry/dnd-HOME.html

Provides a Disney newsletter. Back issues are available. There's lots of fluffy writing on the main page, but kids might find it interesting if the news articles are written at their level.

Disney Cartoon Factory

http://pages.prodigy.com/UT/cartoon/Disney.html

Includes a long discussion of Cinderella and links to "limited editions" and "serials."

Disneyland

http://www.best.com/~dijon/disney/parks/disneyland/

The home page for the theme park in California with travel and park information, including Disneyland recipes.

A History of Disney Comics

http://www.update.uu.se/~starback/disney-comics/usa.html

A long text-only Web site with lots of history about the development of Disney comics, but no graphics and no outside links.

Mickey Mouse Club

http://rhf.bradley.edu/~russbob9/MMC.html

Includes information on the 1950s, 1970s and 1990s casts, with pictures and links to the individual club members (including Annette Funicello and nearly every single one of the 1990s cast members).

Ultimate Disney Links Page

http://www.geopages.com/hollywood/1399/

Lots and lots of links to Disney-related pages. I checked out a couple that were definitely G-rated. Boring design, but a good starting place. A few key sublinks are listed separately. You'll find links to FAQs and official and unofficial Disney pages, plus some other good resources.

Unofficial Lion King Home Page

http://www.ugcs.caltech.edu/~btman/lionking/

Very nice design and very kid-accessible, this page includes texts, sound files, and images, plus related links (such as the Hans Zimmer Worship Page).

Walt Disney World

http://www.travelweb.com/thisco/wdw/wdwhome/wdw.html

Parents can make travel arrangements and kids can check out the theme park.

Homework

The Age of Sail

http://www.cs.yale.edu/homes/sjl/sail.html

Learn the history of sailing that led to the discovery of faraway lands like America. Here you'll find three pages of clip art of ships, sailors, and pirates that you can use in reports and artwork. You can also connect to other Internet resources to satisfy your thirst for sailing, like nautical fiction, sailing songs, the history of ships, the pirate page, the America's Cup page, and more sailing pictures.

Contact: Sandra J. Loosemore, Yale University Computer Science Department, *loosemore-sandra@cs.yale.edu*

Find pirates and sailing ships at the Age of Sail site.

Ask Dr. Math!

http://forum.swarthmore.edu/dr.math/dr-math.html

A SWAT team of world-famous mathematicians will answer your most challenging math questions. This is a great service if you're stumped on a tough math problem, have a brainteaser you want help on, or just want to talk to someone who loves math. Go to this WWW page, where you'll find all the questions and answers divided by grade level and then subject. You can search the pages for a keyword. There's also an archive of challenging brainteasers and word problems. Here you'll find the e-mail address to use when sending Dr. Math your toughest math questions.

Contact: Sarah Seastone, Geometry Forum, Swarthmore College, *sarah@forum.swarthmore.edu*

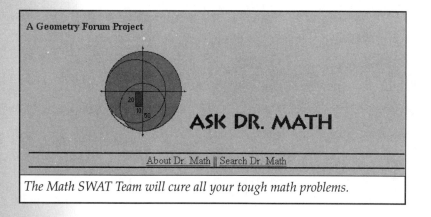

The Math SWAT Team will cure all your tough math problems.

Cool School Tools

http://www.bham.lib.al.us/cooltools/

Here you'll find an index to useful Internet resources for kids and teenagers. There are tons of links to philosophy, psychology, religion, social sciences, language, science, mathematics, technology, the arts, literature, geography, and history sites. There's also a slew of other K-12 home pages. This is a great starting point for researching a report on the Internet.

Contact: Birmingham Public Library, *aalexand@bham.lib.al.us*

Fake Out!

http://www.hmco.com/hmco/school/dictionary/

This definition guessing game lets you be creative both in trying to figure out the definitions for weird words and in making up definitions for new words. You'll see a selection of words divided by grade level. Click on the word for your grade level and try to guess the correct definition from the choices listed beneath. Press the submit button to see if you're right. If you've guessed the wrong definition, the right one will be displayed. You'll also see a list of all the definitions showing how many people chose each one. After you're done guessing the word's definition, the fun really starts. Take a look at next week's word and make up your own definition for it. Next week you can come back and see how many people chose your fake definition. You can also play the game again with a new word.

Contact: Global Network Navigator, Houghton Mifflin Company

MathMagic

http://forum.swarthmore.edu/mathmagic/

MathMagic connects students through the Internet to solve challenging math problems. The best thing about this site is the archive of current and past challenges. Read through them and try to stump yourself. The problems in the archive are divided by age group so you can easily find the appropriate level of difficulty. Try to solve fun brainteasers, word problems, and puzzles that really challenge your math know-how.

Contact: Alan Hodson, Geometry Forum, Swarthmore College, *alanh@laguna.epcc.edu*

Pyramid Crossword Puzzle

http://www.mtlake.com/cyberkids/Issue1/Crossword.html

Have fun filling out a crossword puzzle and learn something about Egyptian pyramids and mythology. First read the article, which discusses Egyptian mythology, the *Book of the Dead*, hieroglyphics, and King Tut. Then test your knowledge with the Pyramid Crossword

Puzzle (you'll have to print it out first). You can check your answers online. The puzzle is a fun way to learn about the ancient Egyptians.

Contact: Julie Richer, Mountain Lake Software

Science Bytes

http://loki.ur.utk.edu/ut2kids/science.html

Read an e-zine (electronic 'zine or magazine) just for kids that describes the work of scientists at the University of Tennessee. The magazine explores current science questions and issues and pursues all-new questions and projects. Fun topics to read about include animals, insects, maps, and geography. This is also a great place to find out what scientists do and how they do it.

Contact: University of Tennessee, *tina@novell.ur.utk.edu*

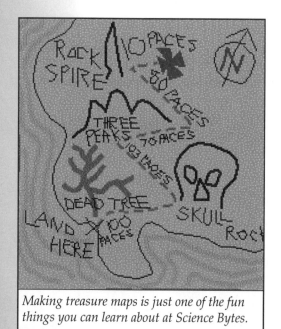

Making treasure maps is just one of the fun things you can learn about at Science Bytes.

Let's Learn Science

http://www.ed.gov/pubs/parents/Science/index.html

This online science book is meant for parents and kids to explore together. It describes lots of activities that parents can do with their kids at home and in the community to learn more about science. The activities are organized from easiest to most difficult, and most are suitable for young children. They are designed to teach some basic concepts about science and conducting scientific research. All the activities use only simple home materials. Learn about bugs, bubbles, buoyancy, and many more fun science concepts. You can even make slime and sticky stuff. The book also tells kids and parents how to keep a science journal together. And it describes field trips to the zoo, museum, planetarium, aquarium, library, bookstore, and nature hikes, all designed with methods of learning science in mind. This is a fun way to learn science and spend time together.

Contact: U.S. Department of Education, *webmaster@inet.ed.gov*

Science Fair

http://www.scri.fsu.edu/~dennisl/special/sciencefair95.html

Here's a place where you can get help with those science fair projects. You'll find practical hints for selecting and completing a science fair project. You can also read descriptions of possible projects and try them out; maybe you'll want to use one for your next science fair. Look at a reference source of technical tips you might need, such as finding averages, graphing, or handling data. You can also ask questions about science fair projects by sending e-mail. Send a description of your own science project, and it will be posted on the page for others to look at.

Contact: Cyberspace Middle School, Supercomputer Computations Research Institute, University of Florida, *larry@fsulcd.physics.fsu.edu*

Space Scavenger Hunt

http://198.150.8.9/space.html

Study along with other students to find out what space is, how we explore it, and whether we're really alone in the universe. You can complete space searches and scavenger hunts to get acquainted with

WWW space resources. Try to answer questions about space voyages, satellites, planets, comets, and the solar system. All the answers are online; all you have to do is search for them. Use the hotlinks on the page to find the answers. These link to information about the solar system and planets, the space shuttle, the Hubble space telescope, space art and photographs, space museums, NASA, and much more. When you're done, maybe you should try to make up your own space search. You'll certainly be a space expert after finishing these online scavenger hunts.

Contact: Mr. Mitchener and his sixth-grade students, Madison Middle School

StarChild Project

http://guinan.gsfc.nasa.gov/K12/StarChild.html

Here's an easy way to learn about astronomy, space, and space travel. This site is filled with pictures, and it will teach you exactly what astronomers do. Learn more about the earth and see a simulation of the earth's rotation. Check out photos of galaxies or look at a video of colliding galaxies. Visit the moon by viewing a movie of the moon's craters. Take a tour of the solar system. Learn about stars, including our sun. See a simulation of the Big Bang and the creation of the universe. All the new terms in the text are hyperlinked to a glossary for easy explanations. The pictures and movies throughout make this a fun introduction to astronomy.

Contact: WebStars, NASA, *StarTraxhelp@athena.gsfc.nasa.gov*

Visit the sun and many other attractions in the universe at StarChild.

Spanish Counting Book

http://davinci.vancouver.wsu.edu/buckman/SpanishBook.html

Look here for a very cute book to teach you how to count in Spanish from one to fifteen. Each number is illustrated with a picture drawn by kindergarten students using KidPics. For some numbers, there are audio links that let you hear the students reading the numbers out loud. You can even download an entire self-running slide show of the project for the Macintosh.

Contact: Tim Lauer, Buckman School, *timlauer@teleport.com*

Trees of the World

http://www.hipark.austin.isd.tenet.edu/home/trees/main.html

Learn about trees in different places all over the world, from Texas to Canada, South Africa to Norway. The descriptions of the different trees are contributed by students who live in those places. You'll see a picture of the tree and learn something about it, such as where it's found, what kind of leaves it has, how tall it gets, and other characteristics. You can even get your class to contribute information about trees where you live.

Contact: Highland Park Elementary School, *scottie@hipark.austin.isd.tenet.edu*

Where on the Globe Is Roger?

http://gsn.org/gsn/roger.home.html

If you've ever wanted to travel around the world, now's your chance. Learn about history, culture, and geography as you electronically travel along with Roger Williams, who is driving his truck, Bubba, from continent to continent around the world. He's already gone to South America and Australia. Now he's heading to Japan, China, Russia, Europe, and Africa. At the WWW site, you can read his reports about the places he visits and see photos of his trip. Meet other kids around the world as Roger visits their schools, and read their letters to Roger. You can even learn all about Bubba the truck.

Contact: Global SchoolNet Foundation, *andresyv@cerf.net*

U.S. Map Game

http://www2.opennet.com/schoolhouse/map/Welcome.html

Here you'll see a map of the United States. When you click on any state, its capital will appear. You can try to guess the capitals and then click on the state to see if you're right. Test yourself before your next big geography quiz, play capitals with a friend, or teach your younger brother or sister about U.S. geography.

Contact: Latitude28 Schoolhouse, OpenNet Technologies, *webmaster@opennet.com*

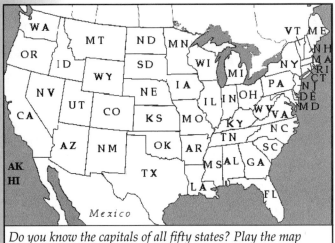

Do you know the capitals of all fifty states? Play the map game and find out.

For more homework ideas, visit these sites:

Hands-On Children's Museum

http://www.wln.com/~deltapac/hocm.html

Includes the Ocean Odyssey, which has quite a bit of good resources and links to ocean animal photos.

NPR Science Friday for Kids

http://www.npr.org/sfkids/

Information on science stories on National Public Radio for kids, with resources and forums. On bottom of page is info on KIDSNET, including how to join it, but no other outside links.

Kids' Clubs

Electronic Scouting

http://www.HiWAAY.net/hyper/Scouts/

This home page provides an interactive way to find any kind of scouting information online. You'll find lots of resources on your type of scouting or the scouting group you want to join. Connect to Cub Scouts, Boy Scouts, Varsity Scouts, Explorers, Sea Exploring, Order of the Arrow, Girl Scouts, and International Scouting programs. Learn the oaths and laws of each scouting group. Find out about the different ranks of Cub and Boy Scouts. Get a guide to safe scouting. Download fun stuff like games, skits, songs, yells, cheers, skills, and crafts. Get scouting clip art and a Scout songbook. Connect to links of interest for citizenship, hobbies, crafts, and outdoor activities. Learn about skills like cooking, camping, making fires, and hiking. Find out how to tie knots and understand Morse code. Visit the NetWoods Virtual

Campsite for interesting ceremonies and activities. Link to other troops, councils, and lodges on the Web. Find out how to join discussion groups for your particular scouting group. There's also a huge list of online resources for software, learning about scouting, and training.

Contact: U.S. Scouting Service, HiWAAY Information Services, *hyper@hiwaay.net.*

Learn about any kind of scouting group at the home page for scouting.

CyberKids Home

http://www.woodwind.com/mtlake/CyberKids/CyberKids.html

Here's a cool place for kids to hang out, learn, and have fun. This free online magazine contains stories and art created by kids. You'll find contests, educational articles, and games. The Launchpad will take you to cool kids' sites for art, business, books, fun and games, history, math, museums and libraries, nature, science and technology, and just kids' stuff. Have fun doing puzzles, playing games, and more. Tell the world about yourself and find keypals from around the world in CyberKids Interactive. (A keypal is an electronic penpal; you exchange letters with your keypal through electronic mail.) Here you can share your thoughts and ideas with each other, discuss what you've seen in CyberKids, and make suggestions. It's easy to post your own comments. You can even download a free Dracula font to use on your computer, but first you have to fill out a form telling about yourself (get your parents to help).

Contact: Mountain Lake Software, Woodwind Consulting, *cyberkids@mtlake.com*

In the CyberKids magazine, you can read stories, look at art, and learn new things.

FishNet

http://www.jayi.com/jayi/

FishNet is a cool place for teens to hang out and get information relevant to their lives. You have to register, but it's free, and your e-mail address or phone number will never be made public. The resources are geared especially toward high school students. Access a useful college guide with information on different colleges, a place to ask questions of an admissions expert, and sage advice on the college admissions process. This huge guide is guaranteed to soothe your application jitters. Check out *Edge*, an electronic magazine with news and features on the Internet, careers, trends, getting into college, sports, school, book reviews, and more. In Threads, you can say what you want about the topics that are most important to you or read what others are saying. Dive into a Chunk and add your nuggets of wisdom. You can start your own topics, ask questions, or let the conversation go wherever you like. Talk about technology, schools, relationships, sports, and philosophy. Go to KnowBase for information on a whole slew of subjects, including stuff to do, your body and fitness, cool stuff, tidbits of interesting news, new slang, and books. Ed/Op links to places for beyond-school educational programs. The Moola

Mall has cool stuff to buy. FishNet is such a great site, you won't ever want to leave.

Contact: Webb Howell, WebPress, *whowell@interpath.com*

FishNet is one of the coolest places to hang out on the Internet.

Keypals

http://www.reedbooks.com.au/heinemann/global/keypal.html

Are you looking for a keypal? Come to this site, and you're sure to find one. This service acts as a bulletin board for posting messages from people looking for keypals. Read through the messages already posted at the bottom of the page. If you find somebody you think you'd like, just click on the top line to instantly send that person an e-mail message. You can also post your own message by clicking on that option and then typing a message in the window that opens. There are messages on the bulletin board from kids ages five to fourteen. Each message has a short description of interests, so you can match up with someone like you. Classes can also connect to other classes using this service. If you're looking for an Internet friend, send an e-mail message right now and you might get a new keypal.

Contact: Reed Interactive, *heinemann@reedbooks.com.au*

KidLink Chat

http://www.kidlink.org/IRC/

The KidLink project is aimed at getting kids ages ten to fifteen talking over the Internet in a global dialogue. So far, more than 37,000 kids in 71 countries have participated. You can join the project and talk with other kids in real time using Internet Relay Chat, or IRC. You must register by e-mail to use the Chat service. First connect to the KidLink WWW page, where you can learn about Chat, get examples of lessons and activities, and find out who is chatting right now. Look at the documentation for help with using IRC and to find out how to register and connect. You'll also find a command guide, a brief tutorial, and IRC software. Look at the template and registration example to find out how to register with KidLink. You can also go to the KidLink home page for more information about the KidLink project.

Contact: KidLink, *irc-mgr@kidlink.org*

Kids' Club

http://mack.rt66.com/kidsclub/home.htm

This online club is just for kids ages five to sixteen. You do have to pay membership fees to join, so look over the introduction before deciding whether you want to be a member. One activity going on is an Internet beauty pageant, where members vote on the winners. Another contest is the Over-Achiever Contest, where you share something fantastic you have done recently with other members. Go shopping in the club's store. Find lots of activities, including puzzles, games, jokes, and 3D pictures. You can check out all these features without becoming a member of the club. As a member, you interact with other Kids' Club members all over the world through a gallery of photos and automatic e-mail forms.

Contact: Kids' Club, Rt66.COM, *kidsclub@rt66.com*

KidsCom

http://www.kidscom.com/

Visit KidsCom for a communication playground for kids ages eight to fourteen. You have to register, but it's free. The registration is just to make sure that only kids use KidsCom. Here you can find a keypal—a boy or girl with similar interests to write to on the Internet. There's a graffiti wall where you can express yourself legally. Ask an Internet guru a question you have about the Internet and see your question and the answer posted on KidsCom. Play a fun geography game— perhaps you'll learn something. Follow links to other fun kids' sites. Talk about your favorite things with other kids your age. Play for KidsKash by answering trivia questions. You can spend the KidsKash in the Loot Locker, where prizes change every month. Post pictures and stories about your pets in the Pet Arena. Participate in a storywriting game each week, then vote on which story you like best. Go to New Stuff for Kids to find out about the newest and coolest toys, video games, and other kids' stuff. There's lots of fun stuff to do in this online playground. If you want to see what's in KidsCom before you register, just look at the preview in the Parents' and Teachers' Place. You should also show this to your parents so they can see what is in KidsCom, since they aren't allowed inside.

Contact: KidsCom, SpectraCom

Kids' Crossing

http://rmii.com/~pachecod/kidsnet/ckids.html

At Kids' Crossing, you can participate in interactive games that involve working with other kids around the world through the Internet. If you're under twelve, you have to register to use Kids' Crossing. (Be sure to get your parents' help with registering.) There are lots of places to visit in Kids' Crossing: the Lunch Room, the Block, Interactivity, the Library, Computers, and Adventures. In the Lunch Room, post messages on a bulletin board just for kids and meet other kids through e-mail. On the Block, connect to other kids' home pages on the Internet, visit online schools, and enter your own home page if you have one. Go to Interactivity to play games like Madlibs, Hangman, Othello, Mr. Potato Head, and more on your computer or to get videos from Disney films. You can also tell about fun places you have visited on the Net. In the Library, learn more about the Internet and find stuff online. Go to the Computer room to learn how to write HTML, download free graphics to use in your home page, and get help with making your first home page. Visit Adventures for more fun places to see on the Web.

Contact: Dan Pacheco and Parallel Publishing, Rocky Mountain Internet, *pachecod@rmii.com*

Kids' Space

http://plaza.interport.net/kids_space/

Kids' Space is a home page for all kids on the Internet. You can show pictures, write stories, share music, chat with new friends, and find fun places to visit on the Internet. Just click on the map or the words to go wherever you like. Visit the gallery to see pictures by young artists or to submit your own pictures for viewing. Story Book has lots of stories by kids. There's a place for you to type your own story straight into the computer, using pictures for inspiration. The On Air Concert has music by kids played on different instruments. In Beanstalk, you can write a story based on a picture someone else has submitted or draw a picture for another person's story. Go Outside to find great kids' places on the Internet—there's a new list every month. In the Mail Office, share your thoughts with friends on the bulletin board, find a penpal, or send a letter about the site. Go to the Doctor's Office or click on the help icon at any time for help with using Kids' Space. There are lots of fun things to see, read, hear, and do and cool places to go in this great site. You could hang out here all day.

Contact: Sachiko Oba, Interport Communications

See drawings by kids, like this one by Nicole Scott, age 9, from Montreal, Canada.

Midlink Magazine

http://longwood.cs.ucf.edu/~MidLink/

Midlink is an electronic magazine just for kids in the middle grades. Enjoy art and writing that link middle school kids all over the world. Connect to fun projects like the International Book Fair, where you can share your favorite books. Read exciting articles about science, math, the environment, animals, and the earth. Link to cool school home pages and the home pages of other kids. Check out "portfolios" on all sorts of fun subjects created by other kids. Take a magical mystery tour of hometowns across America. Look at spectacular computer art and read fantastic stories by kids. You'll even find jokes in the LaughLink section. You can also submit your own stuff. Finally, try out the list of favorite Web sites. The magazine is published every other month and each issue has a new and exciting theme, so keep coming back.

Contact: Caroline McCullen, University of Central Florida, Department of Computer Science, *Caroliine_McCullen@ncsu.edu*

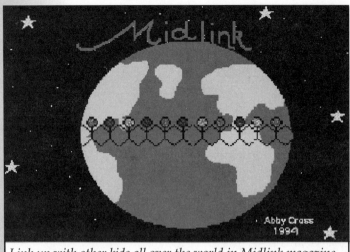

Link up with other kids all over the world in Midlink magazine.

For more kids' clubs, visit these sites:

Girl Scout Home Page

http://www.hiwaay.net/hyper/Scouts/gshp.html

Disappointing. Only has links to individual councils—no archived information, nothing.

Girl Scout Law

http://www.ptgirlscouts.org/gslaw.html

Boring page of text only—no images, no links! But it does contain the Girl Scout pledge and law, etc.

Girl Scouts USA

http://www.gsusa.org/

Unfortunately, there's nothing here but an image and a counter. The page is still under construction and hopefully will have some cool links and information for kids as well as troop leaders.

InterNETional Scouting Resources

http://scoutwww.strw.leidenuniv.nl/scout/

Links to archives of information on scouting, the World Jamboree, and other pages. Includes images for downloading, but has a relatively dull page design.

The Kid Club

http://huizen.dds.nl/~ink/

Based out of Holland and very new, this club is for kids ages 10-15 only. Not much there yet, but has the potential to be pretty cool.

The Kids Internet Club

http://www.cam.org/~hanyz/kic.html

Provides information about the page maintainer and links to Internet "safe places for kids" (but doesn't tell what links are).

Scouting FAQ

http://www.cis.ohio-state.edu/hypertext/faq/usenet/scouting/top.html

Besides the general FAQ for the newsgroup *rec.scouting*, there are FAQs here about scouting around the world, skits, yells, campfires, games, fund-raising ideas, and scouting resources on the World Wide Web.

Scouting Resource Page

http://www.hiwaay.net/hyper/Scouts/

Scouting resource page with lots of scouting links; no information on Girl Scouts, though.

ScoutNet International

http://chnet.ch/~scout/scoutnet/world/countrys.html

Links to scouting pages all over the world! Categorized by country with good graphics and includes boys' and girls' organizations.

Spidey's Web

http://www.aonline.com/spideys/spideys.html

A playground for kids of all ages. Has lots of cool kid-to-kid links, games, and other stuff kids would like.

TECC Kid Page

http://www.tecc.co.uk/homepages/kids.html

For kids only! A few links, but explains things so younger children can understand them.

Preschool & Kindergarten

Blue Dog Can Count

http://kao.ini.cmu.edu:5550/bdf.html

This Web site provides a fun way to learn basic math. All you have to do is type two numbers in the blank boxes and then choose whether to add, multiply, or divide them. Then click on the button Go Blue Go, and Blue Dog will bark the correct answer. Test your math skills by seeing if you can come up with the right answer before you listen to Blue Dog bark. You can also click on Blue Dog's cool picture to hear her bark. (Blue Dog is a she.)

Contact: The Void, *honus+@cmu.edu*

If Blue Dog can count, so can you.

Dr. Seuss Home Page

http://klinzhai.iuma.com/~drseuss/seuss/

Learn all about the famous Dr. Seuss books at this home page. Read a
short biography of Theodor Seuss Geisel—Dr. Seuss—then look at a
list of all of Dr. Seuss' books, including special collections, cassettes,
and books in Spanish. Visit Dr. Seuss at the movies and get a listing of
all Dr. Seuss films and videos. The Dr. Seuss parody page (more for
the parents than the kids) has parodies of Dr. Seuss' works and style.
My favorite is Dr. Seuss' Inferno. The What's New page lets you find
new additions each time you check in at the site. There's not a lot here
yet, but it is growing.

Contact: David Bedno, Klinzhai, *drseuss@gorn.iuma.com*

Julia's Home Page

http://www.iii.net/users/juliafb.html

If you think preschoolers aren't ready for the computer or the Internet, check out Julia's page. Julia, 4 years old, made her own home page on the World Wide Web. Find out about Julia's interests, including dancing, creating art, and playing. Hear Julia say her name. And connect to all of Julia's favorite sites on the Internet. There are links to Barbie, coloring books, *The Lion King*, teddy bears, Mr. Potato Head, games, Cinderella, *Star Wars*, dinosaurs, Legos, and many more fun sites perfect for preschoolers to explore.

Contact: Julia Frances Becker, intuitive information, inc., *ralphb@iii.net*

Learn Your Alphabet

http://www.klsc.com/children/

At this site there are several fun games to help younger kids learn the alphabet and start reading. The games progress from easy to difficult as reading level increases. Match pictures with words and letters to learn the alphabet and whole words. Then play Pick a Letter to further match letters with words and pictures. The last game will help kids start reading. Pick the word that goes with each picture. There's also a game to help kids start counting by matching numbers with pictures, colors, and words. These educational games are completely free, but if your kids like them, you can treat them as shareware; see the note to parents for more information.

Contact: ABC Educational Games, Colorado SuperNet, *msb@klsc.com* \

Online Coloring Book

http://robot0.ge.uiuc.edu/~carlosp/color/

Color pictures online at this fun Web site. Select the picture you want to color from the choices of Birthday, Christmas, Clown, Flower, House, and Snowman. You can use lots of different colors to decorate your picture. Just choose the color you want, then click the area in the picture you want to color, and the program fills it in. When you're done coloring, you can download the picture you made and save it or print it out. And you never have to worry about coloring outside of the lines. There's a simple and an expert version, depending on how good a computer user you are. The expert program colors multiple areas at once, so you can color many parts of the picture, then click on Process Image to see what it looks like. This way takes less time, too. Try out both methods for lots of online fun.

Contact: Carlos A. Pero, College of Engineering, University of Illinois, *c-pero@uiuc.edu*

The Refrigerator

http://users.aimnet.com/%7Ejennings/refrigerator/

Mom and Dad always hang your artwork on the refrigerator at home, right? Now put your artistic creations on the "refrigerator" of the WWW. This site is an art gallery just for masterpieces by very young kids. Find out how you can submit artwork to the refrigerator (get your parents to help). Your masterpiece will be published along with your name, age, date of birth, and anything you want to say about it. From here, you can also connect to other kids' artwork online or look at artwork already hanging on the refrigerator.

Contact: Mike Jennings, Aimnet, *jennings@biohazard.org*

See & Say

http://www.pencom.com/~ph/sas.html

Play with your own See & Say toy on the Internet. All you have to do is click on an animal on the See & Say picture to hear what it sounds like. This is a fun way to learn about animals, and it's free.

Contact: Patrick Hester, Pencom, *ph@pencom.com*

Theodore Tugboat

http://www.screen.com/

Here's a fun online activity center based on a TV show from Canada, "Theodore Tugboat." Read an interactive story called "Theodore's Surprise Friend." You get to decide what Theodore should do next by clicking on the underlined words. Each page is illustrated with a color picture. You can learn about the characters and locations in Theodore's world as you read. Download a page from an online coloring book to print out and color. Fill out a form to receive a postcard from Theodore in the mail. You can also read about the TV show, including the characters and the location of the show, the Big Harbor. There are lots of fun things to do here in one of the best WWW pages for young kids.

Contact: Theodore Tugboat, Cochran International, Andrew Hartlen, *ajh@cochran.com*

For more preschool and kindergarten places, visit these sites:

Christmas in Cyberspace
http://193.65.230.1/mp/rec/santa/

Includes a history of Christmas and its origins, some great artwork, and an "e-mail Santa" feature for kids to send their Christmas list directly.

Humor & Inspiration
http://www.gnn.com/gnn/meta/edu/dept/humor/index.html

This is a humor site appropriate for younger children. It includes a comic strip called "Hoo's School," the world according to student bloopers, and a playground survey on love.

Reading

Alice in Cyberspace
http://www.germany.eu.net/books/carroll/alice.html

Read both of Lewis Carroll's classics online. Here you'll find *Alice's Adventures in Wonderland* and *Through the Looking-Glass*, with all the original illustrations by Sir John Tenniel—almost 100 pictures in all. You can look at the books online or download them to your local hard drive through the FTP link. You'll also find biographical notes and references

in addition to the text. For an adventure, download the colorized Jab-
berwocky, a full-screen color image of the famous drawing.

Contact: WindSpiel Company, EUNet Germany

Follow all of Alice's adventures online.

Chapter One Award Winners

http://www.psi.net/ChapterOne/children/index.html

Visit an online bookstore and browse Newbery Award winners for
free. You can read the first chapter of selected Newbery winners and
decide which ones you'd like to buy. But first, find out more about the
Newberry Awards program, including the terms and criteria on
which the awards are based. Then check out sample chapters from
books like *The Giver* by Lois Lowry, *Missing May* by Cynthia Rylant,
The Whipping Boy by Sid Fleischman, and many more. Simply click on
a title to read the first chapter. You'll also see a short description that

gives the publisher, author, and price for each book. This is a great way to try out books before buying them. Many of the books are available from the online bookstore. You can order them with the click of a mouse. Others you'll have to visit your local bookstore to purchase.

Contact: Chapter One, Performance Systems International, *srg@dialabook.com*

Children's Literature Web Guide

http://www.ucalgary.ca/~dkbrown/index.html

This wonderful site is a well-organized collection of Internet resources related to books for children and young adults. Page through many different categories of interest: conferences and book events; favorite books and must-reads from *rec.arts.books.children*; online children's stories; resources for parents, teachers, storytellers, writers, and illustrators; children's publishers and booksellers online; research guides; and other related Internet sites. You'll also find an archive of children's book award winners, including international awards, children's choice awards, and awards from the U.S., Canada, Britain, and Australia. Scan lists of recommended books and bestsellers, including book lists by grade level, young adult lists, various bibliographies, and many more lists to start off your reading adventures. A resource on authors of children's books, their characters, and their settings points to author home pages and sites about characters and places, like Nancy Drew, Oz, or Winnie the Pooh. The section about movies based on children's books links to reviews and home pages of children's movies currently playing in theaters or available on video. Access a list of electronic journals and discussion groups devoted mostly to book reviews. Go to Children's Writings for a guide to publications by children on the Internet. You'll find no pictures here, but there are lots of entertaining and informative links, making this site a terrific guide for beginning online reading or before a trip to the bookstore.

Contact: David K. Brown, University of Calgary, *dkbrown@acs.ucalgary.ca*

The Cinderella Project

*http://www.usm.edu/usmhburg/lib_arts/english/cinderella/
inventory.html*

How many versions of the classic fairy tale "Cinderella" can there be?
There are twelve different versions in this archive, complete with pictures. If you love the Cinderella story, these should keep you busy for
a while. The versions range from one published in 1729 to one published in 1912. You can compare the versions and see how they changed
over time. Switch between different versions by following a link at the
end of every episode, and click on the "page" link whenever you want
to see a picture. There are nine episodes in every story, and you won't
believe the differences between them.

Contact: University of Southern Mississippi, *webmaster@cc.usm.edu*

*Read the Cinderella story over and over in
this online archive.*

Goosebumps Forever

http://scholastic.com:2005/public/Stine-Home.html

Connect to the home page for the popular writer of scary stories, R. L.
Stine. Here you can get all the information you could want about Stine

and his books in the popular Goosebumps series. Read the latest Stine biography, including a photograph of the author. Take a look at a transcript of Stine's live online chat from Halloween 1994, during which he talked with students about his writing, his ideas, and his life. You can read the whole conversation. Also read a sample chapter from a new book by Stine. Come here for the lowdown on a great writer.

Contact: Scholastic, Inc., *staff@scholastic.com*

Great Family Read-Alouds

http://picard.dartmouth.edu/~cam/ReadAloud.html

Check here for a list of books in different genres, all perfect for the family to read aloud together. All of the titles on the list are generally available at bookstores, schools, or public libraries. Pick from the genres of fantasy, folklore, historical fiction, imaginary animals, mythology, poetry, and timeless stories. Or read them all. Each book listing includes a short description and recommends appropriate grade levels, but I think all children will enjoy this collection of classic books. The books on this list make an engaging alternative to television.

Contact: Marion Cross School PTA, Ted Jerome, *ted.jerome@valley.net*

Grin's Message

http://www2.opennet.com/schoolhouse/grin/Welcome.html

Grin's Message is an online picture book by Carlton Scott. The story is about a cute dolphin named Grin and other sea animals who are his friends, like an octopus and a manatee. There's poetry to read and pictures to look at on every one of the seven virtual pages. Grin's Message is fun for parents and kids to read aloud together.

Contact: Latitude28 Schoolhouse, OpenNet Technologies, *webmaster@opennet.com*

Illustrated Poetry

http://www.digimark.net/iatech/books/rafttoc.htm

In this online book, there are nine poems to read and look at. Each poem is illustrated with a beautiful picture. The poems are very short and easy to read. This picture book is perfect for younger kids, but older people, even adults, will enjoy the poetry. Once you've read the poetry, you can send feedback right away using an online form. You can also order the book to have for your very own. Although the book is free to look at online, you can treat it as shareware to support other electronic publishing ventures.

Contact: DigiMark Center, Interaccess Technology Corporation, *info@interaccess.ca*

Learning to Read

http://www.ed.gov/pubs/parents/Reading/index.html

This online textbook has lots of tips and activities for helping kids learn to read. The site offers suggestions, for everyone from babies up to beginning readers, about getting to know books. There are lots of activities parents and young children can do together to develop reading, talking, communication, and writing skills. Learn how parents and children can share reading fun together. Get suggestions on some great books for different ages. Find out how to set up a family reading time and discussions about stories you are reading. You'll find activities for writing names, sharing family stories, cooking, making a book, and creating a dictionary. The whole family will have lots of fun completing these reading and writing activities in an online pamphlet for beginning readers.

Contact: U.S. Department of Education, *webmaster@inet.ed.gov*

Online Picture Books

http://www.digimark.net/iatech/books/

This site contains four complete picture books for kids and parents to read together. The best of the bunch is *Waking in Jerusalem* by Sharon Katz, an illustrated book with some audio accompaniments. It is the story of a young child who watches the city of Jerusalem wake up, and it will quickly become a favorite. *I Live on a Raft* is a collection of short poems, with a picture on every page. Read the story of *My Blue Suitcase*, also by Sharon Katz, about a well-loved suitcase that travels on its own. *The Song of Moses* has readings and interpretations of Bible stories like the Flood and the Garden of Eden. If you like the books, you can order hard-copy versions over the Internet for moderate prices. You might like to read the comments by the illustrators on design techniques for creating the book. Or find out more about the writers. You can also make comments about the stories. This nice site is always a pleasant place to visit.

Contact: Interaccess Technology Corporation, DigiMark Center, *info@interaccess.ca*

Read wonderful online picture books like Waking in Jerusalem *by Sharon Katz.*

Reading Rainbow

http://www.pbs.org/readingrainbow/rr.html

If "Reading Rainbow" is a favorite TV program, visit the show's home page to find out even more about it. Read about each episode and get activity suggestions for each book. You'll learn about the author and illustrator of the book featured in each show. There's a description of the story and an activity that goes with each book. The site suggests lots of fun things to do and new books to discover. Check out great "Reading Rainbow" programs on VHS or products like T-shirts, posters, buttons, and stickers that you can buy. You can also send comments about the series through e-mail from this site.

Contact: Public Broadcasting System, *www@pbs.org*

Visit the "Reading Rainbow" home page.

Young Adult Reading

http://www.docker.com/~whiteheadm/yaread.html

Get book reviews and lists of books just for teens. You can use these lists of recommended books to plan a trip to the library or bookstore. The reviews include a brief description of the story, opinions about the book, and a list of other books by the same author. I found reviews of books by Carol Ellis and Bebe Faas Rice, as well as *Diana: My Autobiography*. Also be sure to check out the young adult reading lists for other reading suggestions.

Contact: Murray Whitehead, Docker Services, Ltd., *whiteheadm@docker.com*

Storybook Library

http://www2.northstar.k12.ak.us/schools/upk/books/
books.html

You can visit this library of stories on the WWW anytime. All the stories here were written and drawn for kids by kids. Most of the stories are by fourth, fifth, and sixth graders. Read picture stories like "Meany the Dragon," "A Christmas Tree's Adventure," and "The Bus That Fell Down." First-grade classes created an alphabet book and a book about winter. There's also a book of poetry by a fifth-grader. All the stories are illustrated and easy to read. There are fifteen books here, so make time for hours of online reading.

Contact: University Park Elementary, FNSBSD School Home Page Directory

Read about dragons and other fantastic things at the Storybook Library; this drawing is from the story "Meany the Dragon" by Nephi Hirt, grade 6.

For more information on reading, visit these sites:

Baby-Sitters Club

http://www.scholastic.com/public/Baby-sitters/Baby-sitters.html

With links on the movie, book series, etc., for fans of the BSC series.

Harper Collins Kids Books Page

http://www.harpercollins.com/kids/

Designed for kids to explore with a very nice design. Looks like a lot of cool information on Harper Collins's books and authors, plus a link to "how a book is made."

How the Grinch Stole Christmas Page

http://www.webb.com/grinch

Two thumbs up! Awesome design! You can read the book (includes sound bite narration, images, and songs), enter a contest, "mail the grinch," or peek at the Dr. Seuss biography. Very cool.

Scholastic Publications

http://www.scholastic.com/public/Home-Page.html

Includes educational network projects and a link to the R. L. Stine (Goosebumps) page.

Site Listings for Kids

Berit's Best Sites for Children

http://www.cochran.com/theosite/KSites.html

Berit Erickson has put together a huge list of cool Internet places. The sites are divided by subject and even rated, so you can quickly find the hottest sites. This list goes with the Theodore Tugboat Web pages.

Contact: Berit Erickson, Theodore Tugboat, *berit@cochran.com*

The Bowen Family's Children's Page

http://www.comlab.ox.ac.uk/oucl/users/jonathan.bowen/children/index.html

Here you will find links to the Bowen children's home pages, which are fun to explore just by themselves. But there are also many links to sites the Bowen kids like, such as games, movies, other children's pages, museums, and more.

Contact: Jonathan Bowen, Oxford University Computing Laboratory, *J.P.Bowen@reading.ac.uk*

Canadian Kids Home Page

http://www.onramp.ca/~lowens/107kids.htm

Look here for a collection of interesting sites for kids, most of them Canadian in flavor. The list was compiled entirely by kid cybernauts from Canada, and it emphasizes pages with lots of graphics and sounds.

Contact: Leslie Owens, Onramp Network Services, *lowens@csdcorp.com*

The Children Page

http://www.pd.astro.it/local-cgi-bin/kids.cgi/forms

This is a short list of links put together by children in Italy. From here you can enter the green world of frogs or make a visit to Mars, and lots more.

Contact: Astronomical Observatory of Padova, *web@www.pd.astro.it*

Children's Pages at WombatNet

http://www.batnet.com/wombat/children.html

Here you'll discover lots of links to online sites covering animals, dinosaurs, hobbies, libraries, magazines, museums, news, space, toys, and travel, plus many online high schools.

Contact: WombatNet, *info@batnet.com*

Kidding Around

http://alexia.lis.uiuc.edu/~watts/kiddin.html

Kidding Around is the place to explore strange and wonderful new places on the Internet. The page was created just for middle school kids and teenagers. If you are new to the Internet, go to the Rules of the Road, where you can get an introduction to using the Internet. On the Roadmap, you can visit fantastic lands and spooky stops. Learn about science, technology, and the earth. Take a road trip or go on safari to see wild animals. Meet penpals, visit famous people, and explore Toon Town. Hearth and Home lets you visit pets and families. There are amusement parks, library reading rooms, sports stadiums, movie theaters, TV rooms, and museums to check out. See weird wonders and puzzling places. You can also find out how to write and publish your own work on the Web and learn more about cyberspace. There are fun things to read, see, and do at the end of every link.

Contact: Heather McCammond-Watts, Graduate School of Library and Information Science, University of Illinois, *watts@alexia.lis.uiuc.edu*

Travel to fantastic lands all over the Internet with Kidding Around as your starting place.

CyberKids Launchpad

http://www.woodwind.com/cyberkids/Launchpad.html

This "launchpad" to the Internet links to educational and fun places to visit online. Look for sites in subjects like art, nature, math, fun, and games. You'll also find more launchpads with even more cool sites.

Contact: Mountain Lake Software, Woodwind Consulting, *webmaster@mtlake.com*

Interesting Places for Kids

http://www.crc.ricoh.com/people/steve/kids.html

This is a list of sites that are especially interesting to kids. The list was primarily put together for the author's ten-year-old daughter, Katy. You'll find links to art, literature, museums, toys and games, movies and TV, and more.

Contact: Stephen R. Savitzky, Ricoh California Resarch Center, *steve@crc.ricoh.com*

Kids & Parents on the Web

http://www.halcyon.com/ResPress/kids.htm

This huge list contains over 700 resources packed with info for school and family use. The sites are arranged by subject, with short descriptions.

Contact: Resolution Business Press, Northwest Nexus, *rbpress@halcyon.com*

Kids' Corner

http://www.ot.com/kids/surfin.html

The Web Surfin' section of this fun kids' stop links to sites for science, reading, history, art, reference, sports, and games. Most of the sites in the list are briefly described, so that you can quickly locate what you're interested in.

Contact: Oasis Telecommunications

Kid's Internet Delight (KID) List

http://www.clark.net/pub/journalism/kid.html

This is a list of over 60 useful sites for kids to visit, in alphabetical order. There are no descriptions of the sites, so you'll just have to follow the links to see what's at the end of each.

Contact: John Makulowich, Clark Internet Services, *makulow@trainer.com*

Kids on Campus

http://www.tc.cornell.edu:80/Kids.on.Campus/

Every year a group of kids visits Cornell University to learn more about the Internet and computers. They put together an annual WWW tour for other kids like you to use. This list makes a great place to look for cool Web sites.

Contact: Cornell Theory Center, Cornell University, *doc-comments@tc.cornell.edu*

Kids on the Web

http://www.zen.org/~brendan/kids.html

This list of sites for and about kids is always growing, so you'll want to put it in your Bookmarks. You'll find lots of online toys and gizmos to play with, as well as educational sites that may not be as interesting.

Contact: Brendan Kehoe, Zen Internet Group, *brendan@zen.org*

Kids' Web

http://www.primenet.com/~sburr/

This is a collection of sites that parents and younger children can explore together. The sites were originally collected for Emma and Simon, the children of the page's author. Links gathered here include educational sites, fun stops, software recommendations, and more.

Contact: S. Burr, Primenet Services, *sburr@primenet.com*

Kids' Web Digital Library

http://www.npac.syr.edu/textbook/kidsweb/

This second Kids' Web is a digital library for schoolkids, with links to Internet sites about the arts, science, social science, fun and games, reference books, and sports. There are lots of fun places to explore here.

Contact: Paul Coddington, Northeast Parallel Architectures Center, Syracuse University, *kidsweb@npac.syr.edu*

Latitude28 Schoolhouse

http://lido.packet.net/schoolhouse/inside.html

This online "schoolhouse" makes educational materials accessible to students of all ages. If you let them know what your favorite educational resource on the Internet is, they'll publish it in their list of good educational sites. (Maybe you'll want to suggest something you found in this book.)

Contact: Latitude28 Schoolhouse, OpenNet Technologies, *webmaster@opennet.com*

Midlink's Best Web Sites in Cyberspace

http://longwood.cs.ucf.edu:80/~MidLink/web.sites.html

From Midlink magazine comes a list of World Wide Web sites chosen just for kids. These may be the best Web sites you'll ever find—I don't know. Try them out and decide for yourself.

Contact: Caroline McCullen, University of Central Florida, Department of Computer Science, *Caroline_McCullen@ncsu.edu*

Primenet Links

http://www.primenet.com/links/education.html

Here the focus is on educational sites—math, science, history, astronomy, computers, archaeology, and more. This is a good place to come when you're doing homework or researching a school project.

Contact: Primenet Services, *webmaster@primenet.com*

Safe Surf Kids' Wave

http://www.safesurf.com/wave/sskwave.html

This is a listing of kids' sites on the Internet that have been determined to be "safe" for all ages to visit. The sites are divided by age level.

Contact: Safe Surf Organization, *SafeSurf@aol.com*

Uncle Bob's Kids' Page

http://gagme.wwa.com/~boba/kidsi.html

Uncle Bob's page is a treasure chest of links that have been cleaned, checked, and annotated. The page was even a pick for Cool Site of the Day, so you know it's good. There's so much to explore here, you can't possibly get through it all. But you'll have fun trying.

Contact: Bob Allison, WorldWide Access, *boba@wwa.com*

For more listings for kids, visit these sites:

The Kid's Page

http://www.prgone.com/more/kidspage.html

With lots of fun links, including educational, Legos, Muppets, and the kids' clubs.

Rollanet's Kid Corner

http://www.rollanet.org/kids/

Quite a few really cool links, with big easy-to-use buttons and some pretty cool graphics.

Toys & Games

Choose Your Own

http://hillside.coled.umn.edu/class1/Buzz/Story.html

Play a Choose Your Own Adventure game created by sixth-grade students. First read the introduction to the story. Then click on the Random Space-Time Warp button at the bottom of the page to find out what happens. The introduction was written by all the students collaboratively, but each student made up a different ending to the story. See if you can collect all the story endings. The story includes pictures drawn by students, sounds, and hyperlinks to the students' home pages.

Contact: Hillside Elementary School, *events@hillside.coled.umn.edu*

Choose random endings to a story written and illustrated by sixth graders.

Crafts for Kids

http://ucunix.san.uc.edu/~edavis/kids-list/crafts.html

Find all sorts of crafts ideas at this fun page. Get instructions for making Christmas crafts such as ornaments, wreaths, decorations, cards, and wrapping paper—all easy and fun to do. There are lots of art projects that use baby food jars left over from a younger sibling. Useful crafts to make include juggling balls, T-shirts, bird feeders, bookmarks, jewelry, stationery, potholders, and candles. Fun and easy crafts include Indian vests, handmade flowers, macaroni necklaces, puppets, and many more. You'll also find recipes for homemade silly putty, Play-doh, fingerpaints, clay, slime, and dough. Keep yourself occupied for hours with these fun things to make at home.

Contact: Ellen Davis, University of Cincinnati, *Ellen.Davis@UC.EDU*

Dogsled Racing

http://academy.la.ca.us/wms/idt.html

Link to a site that tells you all about the Iditarod, a 1,049-mile dogsled race across Alaska. Here you can follow along with the race. Get the latest race standings, results, and weather reports. See pictures and a map of the race course. Meet some of the mushers who participated in the race. The three mushers you'll meet are 17, 15, and 11 years old, and they have all been racing since the age of 3. You can send the mushers your own questions about dogsled racing. Learn about the dog teams that are the real heroes of the Iditarod, and see photos of them. It's fun to follow this exciting and unusual sport, in which kids and dogs are the champions.

Contact: Academy One, Willoughby Middle School, *xx144@nptn.org*

Games Kids Play

http://www.corpcomm.net/~gnieboer/gamehome.htm

This site has the official rules to many fun outdoors games like Duck Duck Goose and Red Rover. Look here and you'll find out how to play Red Light Green Light and Tag, with variations like Freeze Tag and TV Tag. The games are fun for two people or for whole groups. Also check out some jump-rope rhymes and the rules to Marbles, with a link to a list of marble types. If you're looking for something to do to while away a summer afternoon, check here for an outdoors game to play.

Contact: Geoff Nieboer, Corporate Communications, *gnieboer@corpcomm.net*

Puzzles for Kids

http://www.teleport.com/~halfmoon/puzzles.html

Here you'll find a collection of handmade puzzles just for younger kids. You can look at and order all the puzzles online. All the puzzles are designed and hand painted by a craftsperson. They are field tested by preschool students. The puzzles are best for two-to-five-year-olds, but the appropriate ages are listed beside each puzzle. You can look at each puzzle in detail, then order using an online form.

Contact: Beverly's Craft Page, Teleport Internet Services, *halfmoon@teleport.com*

Cute puzzles like this dinosaur are available for purchase online.

Soccer for Kids

http://www.cts.com/browse/jsent/kid.html

A cool place for soccer news and information is this kids' soccer page. Here you can read about soccer experiences, learn great tips for playing, and see soccer photos and drawings. Check out an interview with a collegiate player from Africa, written by kids. Link to a penpal connection for meeting and writing to other kids all over the world who also love soccer. Fill out a form to be placed on the penpal page so you can hook up with other soccer fans and players your own age. Or you can look at other possible penpals and send them an e-mail message. You can also contribute to the Web page by sending in stuff about soccer. Finally, go to the Soccer Cybertour to connect to tons of soccer info online. On the Soccer Cybertour, you can take an international tour of soccer sites, learn about the teams and players in different countries, check out college leagues and youth soccer, and read about the history of soccer. Get international soccer results, World Cup reports, and soccer rules. This one site covers all of the soccer information on the Web.

Contact: JS Enterprises. CTS Network Services, *jsent@cts.com*

TeleOlympics

http://www.nptn.org/cyber.serv/AOneP/TO.html

The TeleOlympics project is open to students worldwide on the Internet. On the same day, students compete with other students around the world in events involving running, jumping, and throwing. The results are sent out electronically. Also, access a history of the Olympics and a word search to help you learn more about the games. Check out the six-week training program to prepare for the TeleOlympics. Learn about the students who hold the TeleOlympics records, including what schools they go to and their ages. Go through the TeleOlympics opening ceremonies, where you can learn what schools and countries participated. Maybe you'll want to get your school to participate next year, so check the registrations and discussions as they begin for next year's TeleOlympics. You can also read about Math Olympics, which goes on at the same time as TeleOlympics. Or connect to other Olympics Web sites, including a FAQ and a calendar of upcoming events.

Contact: National Public Telecomputing Network, Shelly Benner, *sdb@nptn.org*, and Linda Delzeit, *linda@nptn.org*

Teddy Bears

http://www.rhein.de/Mailing-Lists/teddy-bears/

Enter the cuddly world of teddy bears at this home page just for our furry friends. There's not much here yet, but soon there will be a history of teddy bears and information about teddy manufacturers and designers. Now you can read a teddy bear bibliography to find out about teddy-bear books, magazines, and other publications. Connect to places online that sell teddy bears, as well as teddy bear–related sites like Pooh Corner. You can also read lots of articles, all about teddy bears.

Contact: Andreas Oesterhelt, Rhein Information Services, *webmaster@www.rhein.de*

Tor's Game Page

http://www.ii.uib.no/~tor/games.html

This page was created by Tor Bjørstad, a kid living in Norway. It includes links to online interactive games like Madlibs, Hyper Jeopardy, Choose-Your-Own-Adventure, Name That Tune, and many more. You'll also find interactive toys here—toys that you can fool around with but that don't really do anything. These include the Magic 8-Ball, a Ouija Board, the Graffiti Wall, and more. And link to other Web sites about games, as well as to Tor's favorite MUDs. Helpful icons tell you what your browser and computer system need to play the games, such as sound cards and fill-out forms. You'll have lots of fun exploring this huge collection of online games.

Contact: Tor E. Bjørstad, University of Bergen, *tor@ii.uib.no*

Vocabulary & Word Puzzles

http://syndicate.com/

There are lots of word puzzles here for you to try. The puzzles are fun and also teach vocabulary. Read about the different kinds of puzzles, each with a different animal character, under Word Puzzles Descriptions. The puzzles will help you learn word definitions, roots of words, opposites, synonyms, definitions, and analogies. Power Puzzles has more challenging word puzzles for advanced puzzlesmiths.

Read a comic strip to learn more about vocabulary. Enter word puzzle contests for free. There are new contests every month, each with a chance to win prizes. Also connect to a hotlist of crossword puzzle sites for more puzzles to work. The pictures are large and slow to download, so you might want to save the puzzle pages as a local file on your computer and solve them there.

Contact: Rich Encounter, Syndicate.Com, *rich@syndicate.com*

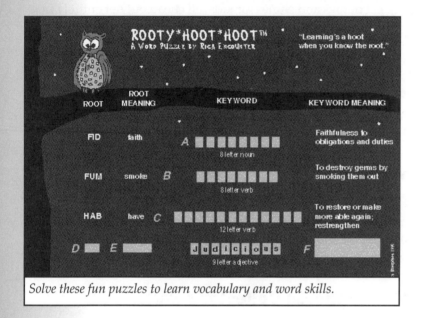

Solve these fun puzzles to learn vocabulary and word skills.

For more toys and games, visit these sites:

Action Figure Home Page

http://www.aloha.com/~randym/action_figures/

This looks really cool! Get information on action figures, links to other toy pages, and discussion.

Crayola Home Page

http://www.ot.com/crayola/

Includes Crayola kids' magazine, how crayons are made, Crayola trivia, and other stuff. Really nifty.

Free Stuff from Alvin Peters for Kids

http://www.winternet.com/~julie/freealpe.html

A long list of toys and games for kids, all cheap but not entirely free. Includes how to order and shipping and handling charges.

GI Joe

http://www.gijoe.com/

GI Joe is now officially online! Very cool design, with links to games and stuff.

Irwin Toys

http://www.irwin-toy.com/

Irwin Toys, makers of Slinky, ReBoot, and Power Ranger toys. This is actually a cool site, with good design, a toy-buying guide, and trivia quizzes.

Plastic Princess Collector's Page

http://deeptht.armory.com/~zenugirl/barbie.html

For those who really like Barbie and similar dolls. Rated in the top 5 percent of Web sites, with lots of links to other related pages, plus some nice pictures.

Playmates

http://www.playmatestoys.com/

Playmates home page, with the "coolest" toys and games around, plus an interactive thingy.

Toys R Us

*http://www.tru.com:80/cgi-bin/coins/_813959236-31527_/
toyshome.html*

The online store includes a hotlist of selling items, a store tour, and
baby items. Designed especially for kids.

The Unofficial Happy Meal Page

http://www.ionet.net/~saylor/happy.shtml

With summaries of Happy Meal themes and toys available, plus a
buy/sell listing for those who want to get or get rid of their Happy
Meal toys.

Virtual Barbie

http://silver.ucs.indiana.edu/~jwarf/barbie.html

One woman's collection of Barbies and links to other Barbie sites.
Aimed more toward collectors rather than kids, but there's not much
else "Barbie" stuff out there.

Video Games & Software

Nintendo Home Page

http://www.nintendo.com/

Here you'll find the official source for Nintendo information. Learn
about brand-new video game releases and about Nintendo systems
such as Super NES, Virtual Boy, and Game Boy. You'll also find information on current hot titles and future attractions for all these systems. Each of these includes screen shots of the game, the release date,
and a review so you can decide just what to buy. Visit cool related sites
for hardware, video games, and fan-created home pages for specific
games. Keep an eye on the Net through a frequently updated section
that separates fact from the rumors, innuendo, and gossip you so often see flying around the Internet. Check out Internet gimmicks, such

as a software program for chatting on the Web. You can also help save Mario by following Yoshi's Island adventures online.

Contact: Nintendo, *nintendo@www.nintendo.com*

Bert's Coloring Programs

http://www.xmission.com/~wwwads/berts.html

This site gives an introduction to shareware coloring programs that are a good way to have fun with the computer. The best thing about the site is that you can try out the programs before you buy them. The software lets you place images on a variety of backgrounds and easily create your own picture before coloring. It also has a voice feature that allows pictures to speak their names. You can even write a short story about the picture. From the site, automatically download shareware copies of Bert's Dinosaurs, Bert's African Animals, Bert's Christmas, Bert's Prehistoric Animals, and Bert's Whales and Dolphins. Unfortunately, there are only MS-DOS versions of the programs. Try them all and pay shareware fees only if you like them.

Contact: Theron Wierenga, XMission Internet Access, *mups_wiereng@wmich.edu*

You can not only color fun pictures, but also create them, write stories about them, and make them talk using Bert's Coloring Programs.

Direct Download

http://wcl-rs.bham.ac.uk/GamesDomain/directd/directd.html

Download freeware and shareware video games for many platforms right away at this site. The best and most popular games have a smiley face next to them so you know what's hot and what's not. You can even vote for your favorite games. You'll find lots of games for Amiga, Macintosh, and PC platforms. There are over 2,500 games in all, and more are being added all the time. The games are divided into different categories, so you can quickly find card, arcade, adventure, strategy, board, and educational games. There are also some game demos for brand-new, just-released, commercial video games. For each game in the archive, you can check out a description, file statistics, and version info, then follow direct links to download it right away. Some games also have screen shots. These games are all free or cost little and are sure to give you hours of fun.

Contact: Dave Stanworth, Wolfson Computer Laboratory, *djh@gamesdom.demon.co.uk*

Download popular shareware games directly from this site.

Sega of America

http://www.segaoa.com/

This fun Web page will take you inside Sega of America. Learn all about the latest and hottest video games for all Sega systems. Get a history of Sega, read the latest news, and find out about new enterprises, such as Sega Music and the Sega channel. Visit Sega Live, where you can chat interactively with other Sega players and with game developers. You can also link to the best independent gaming resources on the Web. Visit Sega Sports for news on upcoming games, current scores and schedules, and live chat groups. Other fun stuff includes visiting Bug's dressing room, Sherman's Lagoon, or Vector Man, with videos and screen shots from the games.

Contact: Sega of America, *webmaster@segoa.com*

TotWare

http://www.het.brown.edu/people/mende/totware.html

TotWare is an entire page of pointers to great freeware and shareware programs for kids. All the computer programs are available online for the PC and Mac. You can immediately download and start using the computer programs. There are banger programs for the littlest children. Painting software includes coloring books, drawing programs aimed at all kids, and programs for making animations. Download software for learning about nature and for learning letters and numbers, as well as lots of games every kid will love. You'll find loads of fun and educational software here that's free or practically free.

Contact: Benjamin and Paul Mende, Brown High Energy Physics, *mende@het.brown.edu*

Video Game Reviews

http://wcl-rs.bham.ac.uk/gdreview

Check here for a quick reference guide to video games being discussed around the Net. Here you'll find a huge archive of reviews of video, computer, and shareware games, and reviews of hardware for the most popular computer and video gaming platforms. New reviews are updated within 24 hours, so you'll get games news fast.

The reviews are written by gamers who know what they're talking about. You'll also find all the latest news, rumors, and opinions from inside the video gaming industry. Look at screen shots of new games for a visual preview before you buy. Go to the Games Index for a quick-access list of every game reviewed. You can also add to the site by submitting reviews of games you have recently tried or of shareware games you've discovered. Send in news and rumors about the gaming industry. Or just write a letter on any games subject you want and read what other people are debating in the Letters area.

Contact: Dave Stanworth, Wolfson Computer Laboratory, *djh@gamesdom.demon.co.uk*

Check out previews of new games like *Ring Cycle*.

For more video games and software, visit these sites:

The Gaming Page

http://sdcc8.ucsd.edu/~kkilzer/arcade.html

With links to all sorts of arcade games, computer games, magazines, and system information.

Nintendo Questions

http://sbh.cse.bris.ac.uk/Nintendo.html

A fairly complete page of information and questions on the Nintendo Super NES system.

Nintendo Super Game Boy Home Page

http://reality.sgi.com/employees/portuesi/sgb.html

This page contains tips and tricks for Super Game Boy, reviews of SGB games, favorite SGB color schemes, and a catalog of SGB games.

The 3D Gaming Scene

http://www.pol.umu.se/html/ac/spel.htm

This site contains information on Doom, Heretic, Dark Forces, Cyber-mage, and other popular video games. There are descriptions of each game so you can get an idea what it's about before buying it and some helpful instructions on some of them.

Moving On

Congratulations! You have now completed your WWW tour, and you can consider yourself an experienced Webwalker. The following appendices will guide you to some resources on the WWW that can expand your Webwalking skills. Appendix C is a tutorial for using Netscape that will walk you step by step through using the browser. If you want to interactively search the Web for something particular or just find out what's new on the Web, use Appendix D, which lists many WWW searching engines and databases to help you find additional Web resources. Remember, the World Wide Web is constantly changing. Keep revisiting any of the sites listed in this book to see new innovations and useful updates. And have fun exploring the WWW on your own.

Appendix A: About the Online Companion

By purchasing this book you have access to the *Walking the World Wide Web Online Companion,* a unique feature offered exclusively by Ventana. To use this online companion, you first must connect to the Internet and then must register with Ventana. After you are online, you can register from the home page on your CD-ROM version of the book by simply double-clicking the link that says "Register." An interactive form appears requesting some personal information. The form asks you for a *code key.* Your unique code key is printed on a card located behind the CD-ROM at the back of this book. You only need to enter the code key once; after that, it is added to your "key ring" at Ventana, allowing you access to the online companion whenever you want. Entering the code key grants you access only to that particular online companion and only for three months from the date you enter the code key.

The registration form also asks you to enter an account name and password. You can use whatever name and password you want, but you'll need to remember them for future use. Every time you want to use the online companion, you'll need to enter your account name and password. If you have obtained access to other online companions and are now registering for a new one, click on the "Register" link and select the option for users who have already established accounts. You'll be able to use the same account and password for the online companion you're adding, after you enter your code key for that product.

During the registration process, you will have the option of entering credit card account information. This optional service makes it easy and convenient to purchase Ventana products from the Ventana catalog and to add more time to your online companion access. An optional questionnaire requesting demographic information and data on your service provider, usage patterns, and so on is also included as part of the registration procedure. You are not required to fill out the questionnaire; doing so will help us to serve you more effectively.

You can connect to the *Walking the World Wide Web Online Companion* by following a link from the home page on the CD-ROM version of the book. Or connect directly by typing in the following URL:

http://www.vmedia.com/wwww2nd.html

(Readers without CD-ROM capabilities can also register with Ventana and use the online companion by connecting to this URL.)

The online companion has many great and useful features. Check there often for updates to the listings in the book, including new or changed URLs, additions to the listings already featured, and brand-new listings for you to explore. Look at the "What's New" page to see what changes have been made since you last visited. You can also search the entire hypertext for a keyword or send e-mail to Shannon Turlington using an interactive form.

Appendix B: About the Companion CD

Installing the CD-ROM

The CD-ROM included with your copy of *Walking the World Wide Web, Second Edition,* contains a complete hypertext version of the hard-copy book and a copy of Netscape Navigator 2.0, which you can use to read the hypertext version and access all the online sites.

This CD-ROM enables you to`browse the entire text of the book locally so that you can plan your Web-walking excursions before spending a penny on online time. Then after you fire up your Internet connection, you can link directly to any of the sites reviewed in the book.

Windows 3.11 Users

To install the CD-ROM, load the CD and with Windows running, select File, Run from the Program Manager. Then type **D:\VIEWER** (where D: is your CD-ROM drive) in the command-line box and press Enter. You'll see a menu screen offering several choices. See "Navigating the CD" below for your option choices.

Windows 95 Users

If you are running Windows 95, insert the CD into the CD-ROM drive and double-click on the My Computer icon. Double-click on the Walking the WWW icon. Then double-click on the Viewer icon. You'll see a menu screen offering several choices. See "Navigating the CD" below for your option choices.

Navigating the CD

Your choices for navigating the CD appear at the side of the opening screen. You can exit from the CD, get Help on navigating, view the Book Contents, learn more about Ventana, or view the Hot Picks.

To launch the HTML content, click on the Book Contents button. You will have the option of installing Netscape 2.0 or locating your existing Netscape 2.0 version located on your hard drive. After launching Netscape from the CD-ROM, the Ventana home page automatically appears and allows you to browse the entire text of the book locally so that you can plan your Web-walking excursions before incurring any online costs.

Appendix C: Netscape & the World Wide Web

"Surfing the Net" has become a cliché for describing many kinds of Internet activities. The World Wide Web (WWW) takes the analogy a step further. Using what are called *hyperlinks*, you can jump from topic to topic, finding information, software, pictures, sounds, and even movies, all with a single click of your mouse.

One of the best software tools for exploring the power of the World Wide Web is Netscape Navigator. Netscape is available for Macintosh and Windows systems, we've included the Windows version on the Companion CD-ROM at the back of this book.

What Is Netscape?

Netscape Navigator, developed by the Netscape Communications Corporation, is a software *front end*, or interface, used to access the World Wide Web. It is based on NCSA Mosaic, the original graphical WWW browser. Netscape was designed specifically to simplify navigation through the millions of pages that constitute the Web, and many of its features make it the ideal browser to use with a SLIP or PPP Internet connection. This appendix describes Netscape Version 2.0, the latest version at the time of this writing. You will always find the latest version of Netscape ready to download from the Ventana Online Software Archive at *http://kells.vmedia.com/archives/index.html*.

Netscape Requirements

As mentioned above, the Windows version of Netscape is included on the Companion CD-ROM. To effectively run Netscape, you will need a PC running Windows and, ideally, a color monitor. Netscape for Windows will operate on a PC running either Microsoft Windows, Windows for Workgroups, or Windows NT; you'll also need the Winsock TCP/IP stack.

XWindows users can also use Netscape, but a Unix version is not included on the CD-ROM. For more information about the XWindows version of Netscape, connect to the Netscape FTP site at *ftp://ftp.netscape.com/*.

In addition to the above computer requirements, Netscape will not operate without a direct connection to the Internet. This means that your computer needs to be connected to the Internet over a direct line or via modem with a SLIP or PPP connection (Netscape will not work with a standard dial-up connection). If you are using a modem, Netscape will operate at speeds as low as 9600 bps, but a 14.4 Kbps or better modem is recommended. Contact your Internet service provider about upgrading to a SLIP or PPP connection.

Browsing the Web With Netscape

Netscape will open directly from the Companion CD-ROM. (See Appendix A, "About the Companion CD-ROM," for instructions on installing and opening Netscape.) The first time you use Netscape from the CD-ROM (and every time thereafter, until you set up a new home page), the introductory page will appear as shown in Figure C-1.

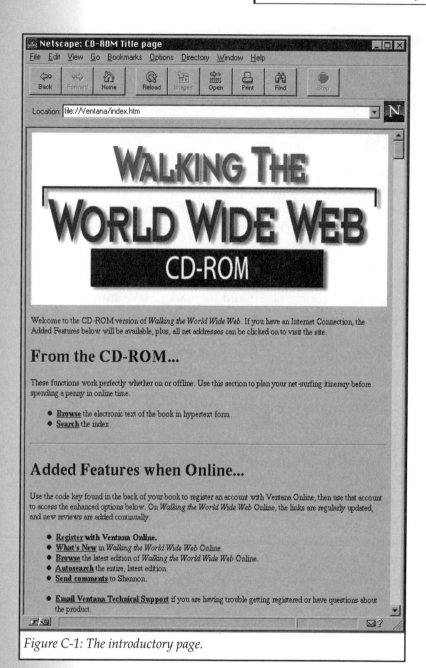

Figure C-1: The introductory page.

At this point, you really haven't connected to a location on the WWW yet; the page shown in Figure C-1 actually resides on your hard drive rather than on the Web. To get out on the Web, go to the File menu, select Open Location, and enter the following into the text field:

http://home.netscape.com/

Make sure you type this exactly as shown and don't insert any spaces. After a few seconds, the Netscape home page should appear (see Figure C-2). Every Web server site has a *home page*, or main document, that introduces you to the site. From this page you can jump to other resources by simply clicking on the embedded hypertext links on the screen, indicated by colored, underlined text. If the home page doesn't appear, or you get a message saying that no connection could be made, make sure that you are properly connected to the Internet either by modem or direct connection, and that the connection is active. You may also not be able to connect because the site is too busy or not accepting connections; in that case, just try again later.

You can also access this page by choosing Netscape's Home from the Directory menu. The Directory menu and the Help menu in Netscape have links to many documents with information about Netscape and the Internet. Some of the most useful of these are also reached by clicking on the buttons in the directory toolbar (these are located at the top of the window).

Figure C-2: The Netscape home page.

So that you don't have to type in that URL again, select Add Bookmark from the Bookmarks menu. The next time you want to access the Netscape home page, all you will have to do is open the Bookmarks menu. You should see the Netscape home page listed at the bottom of the menu along with any other Bookmarks you may have added. Simply select it to connect to that page. Bookmarks are one of Netscape's most powerful features. Your Bookmarks are your own personal hotlist for navigating the Web; here you can add URLs for the pages that you find most useful or that you want to return to at a later time. Use the Bookmarks feature to keep from having to remember or write down lengthy URLs.

Also under the Bookmarks menu, choose Go to Bookmarks to customize your Bookmarks list. This will open a window displaying all your Bookmarks and some useful features. You can move Bookmarks around and create custom folders and separators to organize your list, or add descriptions to help you remember what's on the page.

Navigating in the Document Window

"Pages" in Netscape can be any length. You can scroll through a page by clicking on the up or down arrow on the scroll bar at the right of the page window. If the page is wider than your window, you can move across it by clicking on the left or right arrow on the scroll bar at the bottom of the page window. If you resize your window, the text will automatically reflow. To customize the size of the window, drag the bottom right square around until the window is a new size.

You can increase the amount of screen "real estate" you get by hiding or showing items on the window. Open the Options menu. There, choose whether or not to show certain items on the Netscape window, such as the toolbar, location field, and directory buttons. The fewer things you have selected, the more of your Netscape window is available to display a document.

All About Links

Links are the core of the WWW. A link, also called a *hyperlink,* is a word or phrase (sometimes a picture) that connects you to another page. Netscape allows you to traverse these links simply by clicking on these words or phrases. Links appear as underlined text (pictures usually have informative captions describing the link). Links that you haven't clicked on yet appear as blue; links that you have taken appear as purple. You can customize the colors you'd like links to appear by opening the Options menu and then selecting Colors under General Preferences. You can even choose what color you'd like the background of Netscape to appear.

Netscape remembers the links you have chosen from session to session, so you can follow previously explored links like a trail of bread crumbs to pages you'd like to revisit. You can choose how long you'd like Netscape to mark these followed links by choosing General Preferences, found under the Options menu. Select Appearance, and choose from the options given.

A Quick Tour Through the Web

This section contains a sample trip through the World Wide Web that you can follow along with. The top of each new Web page (and lower sections where applicable) is shown so that you can be sure you're in the right place.

We'll start at the home page shown in Figure C-2. Look at the top of the Netscape window. You'll see some text that says "Welcome to Netscape." This is the title of the page that you have currently downloaded. Every time you download a new WWW page, a new title will appear.

One of the best places to begin exploring is in the section called "Exploring the Net." Scroll down the page until you see the Exploring the Net heading. This page is accessible by clicking on the link Exploring the Net, shown in Figure C-3. When you position the mouse's pointer over the link, a URL will appear in the status message field at the bottom of the Netscape window. This is the URL of the link.

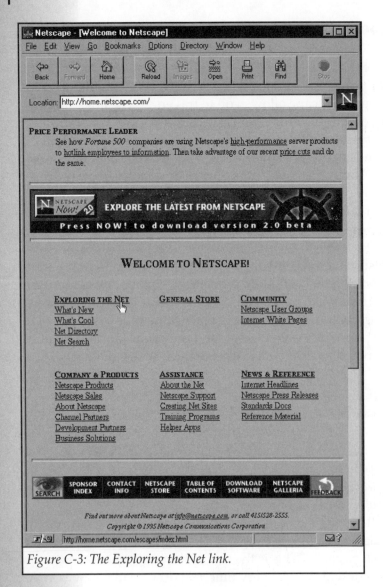

Figure C-3: The Exploring the Net link.

Click on the link. The "N" at the top right corner, called the *status indicator*, will animate, indicating that the program is transferring data. The status message field at the bottom of the window will display information about the transfer, such as how much of the document has transferred and the size in kilobytes of the document. Shortly thereafter (the time it takes depends on your type of Internet connection), the Exploring the Net page will appear, as shown in Figure C-4. When the transfer is complete, the progress bar in the lower right corner of the Netscape window will fill with color.

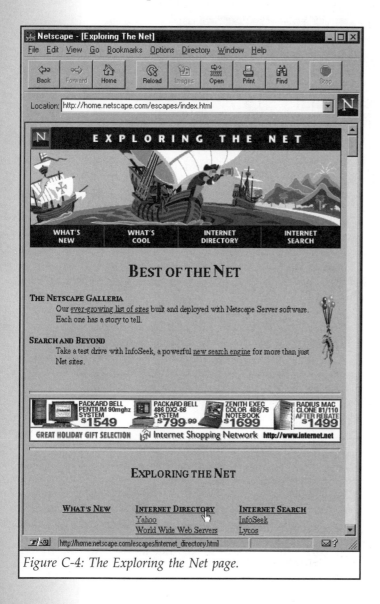

Figure C-4: *The Exploring the Net page.*

Scroll down this page until you see the link to Internet Directory at the bottom, and then click on that link. The Internet Directory page will appear, as shown in Figure C-5.

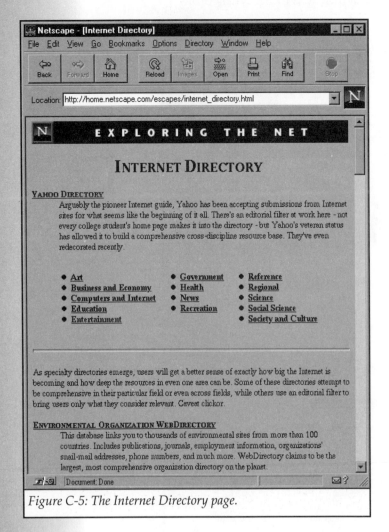

Figure C-5: The Internet Directory page.

At the bottom of the page, you should see a link that says, World-Wide Web Servers. Click on this link. Once again, the "N" in the top corner will animate, indicating that Netscape is looking for the next page. When it appears, it should look like the page shown in Figure C-6.

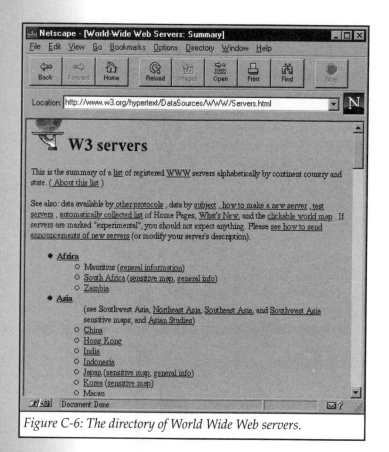

Figure C-6: The directory of World Wide Web servers.

This page is a directory of WWW sites divided by the country, city, or state where the site is located. It can be useful for finding many interesting WWW sites. If you like, browse through the list and visit any site that catches your interest.

Notice at the top of the page the paragraph that says that data is also divided by other protocols and by subject. Click on the "subject" link. The WWW Virtual Library will appear, as shown in Figure C-7. This is a directory of WWW sites catalogued by subject, as in an actual library.

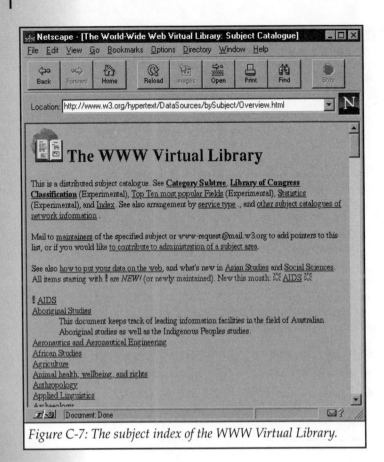

Figure C-7: The subject index of the WWW Virtual Library.

Once the page appears, take some time to look through the different subjects that are available. New categories are added all the time, so venture to this page as often as you can, looking for new entries. New entries are indicated by an exclamation point (!). In this particular case, let's check out something fun—games.

The categories are listed in alphabetical order, so scroll down until you see games. Click on the Games link. After a few seconds the Games and Recreation page will appear, as shown in Figure C-8.

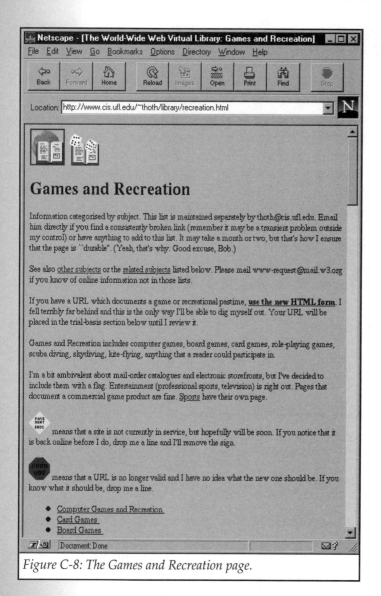

Figure C-8: The Games and Recreation page.

There are all sorts of categories of games listed here, from computer games that can be played on the Internet to pages for card, role-playing, and board games. Let's take a look at the Table Games section, and specifically the link for the Foosball archive, shown in Figure C-9.

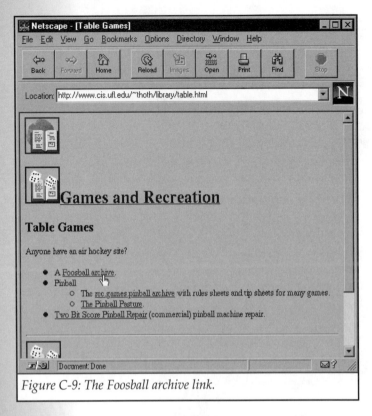

Figure C-9: The Foosball archive link.

Click on the Foosball archive link, and the Foosball page will appear. This page contains a long list of files and subdirectories, as shown in Figure C-10.

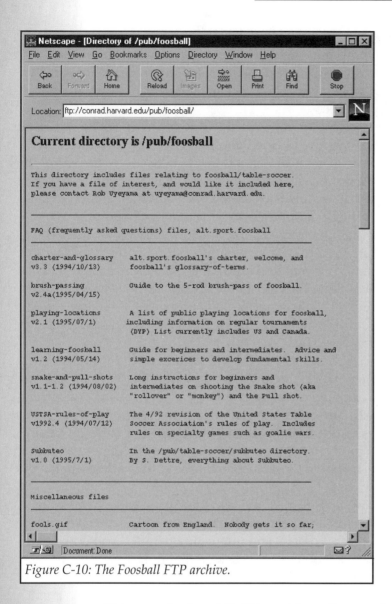

Figure C-10: The Foosball FTP archive.

This page looks a bit different from the previous ones. That's because it is actually the directory listing from an FTP (File Transfer Protocol) server. As you can see, Netscape can access FTP files as easily as accessing HTML pages; each file in the FTP server is hyperlinked just as HTML links are. If you click on one of the files, it will be sent automatically to your computer using the FTP protocol that's built right into Netscape. (Further instructions for using Netscape to access other types of Internet resources, including FTP, Gopher, Usenet news, and electronic mail, are given later in this appendix.)

But let's say you don't want to download one of those files. In fact, let's say you've decided you're really not the slightest bit interested in foosball and would like to take a look at some of the other game options instead. To go back to a page you were previously viewing, simply click on the Back button at the top of the window. (The Back button is the first in a line of buttons called the *toolbar* that you can use to access the Netscape features you'll use most frequently.) Clicking on this button will return you to the last page you were looking at, the Table Games page. You can keep backtracking through all the documents you've seen using this button and click on new links at any point. Similarly, the Forward button will move you forward through documents you've already visited.

There's another way to move back and forth through documents. Open the Go menu. At the bottom of the menu, you'll see a complete list of all the pages you have visited during the current session with Netscape. You can select any of them to return to that page. This history list only remains during your current session; after you quit Netscape, this list will disappear. To permanently save links to any of these documents, be sure to add them to your Bookmarks list.

For now, let's go back twice to the World Wide Web Virtual Library: Games and Recreation page. This time, let's take a look at one of the more colorful and interesting pages. Scroll down to Miscellaneous Hobbies, and click on that link. You'll see the Juggling Information Service link, shown in Figure C-11.

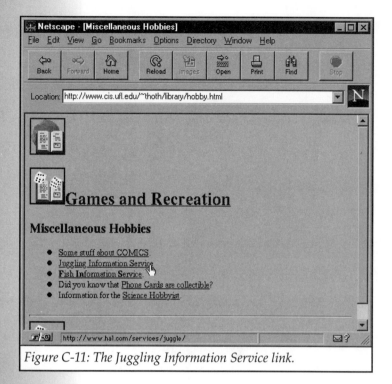

Figure C-11: The Juggling Information Service link.

Click on the Juggling Information Service link to visit that site, as shown in Figure C-12. As you scroll through the list of different options, you'll see that all sorts of things are available, like movies (in QuickTime or MPEG format), pictures, text files, and even merchandise.

Figure C-12: The Juggling Information Service page.

Retrieving Files

If you do want to download a file, it couldn't be simpler. To demonstrate the process, let's click on the Movie Theater link on the Juggling page. This link is actually a graphic, but you can click on it just like a text link. The Movie Theater page is shown in Figure C-13.

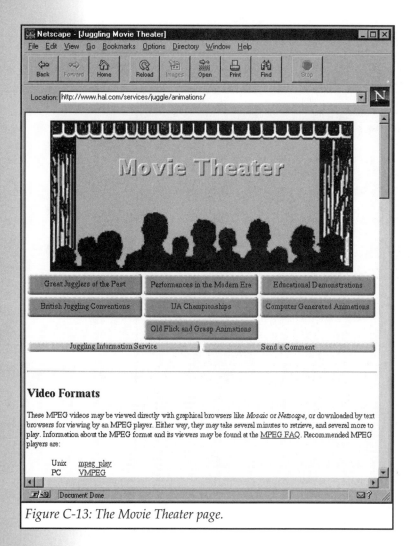

Figure C-13: The Movie Theater page.

Find the Performances in the Modern Era link, another graphic at the top of the page, and click on it. The Performances in the Modern Era page will appear, as shown in Figure C-14.

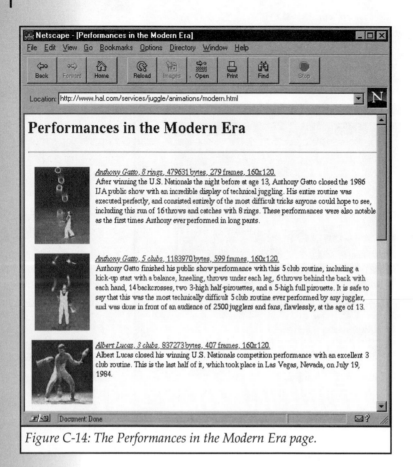

Figure C-14: The Performances in the Modern Era page.

To download any of the MPEG movies, just click on the picture next to the description. **Note:** If you have a SLIP or PPP modem connection, one of these downloads could take several minutes, since movie files are very large. Suppose you started loading the file without realizing how big it was, and now you want to stop loading. All you have to do is click on the Stop button in the toolbar.

If you stop loading a WWW page midway through transfer, you will probably only see a portion of the page, with a notice at the bottom that says, "Transfer interrupted!" If you change your mind and decide you do want to see the whole page, click on the Reload button. Netscape will then reload the page in its entirety.

If you decide you do want to play the movie on your computer, you must have an *external player* or *helper application* that is able to read and display the file. This is also true of audio files that you might try to download. These players are generally available as freeware over the Internet; check the Ventana Online Visitor's Center (*http://kells.vmedia.com/archives/index.html*) for an archive of any external players you might need. You must tell Netscape where to find these external players. To do this, select Preferences under the Options menu. You'll see an option called Helpers. Here there are fields that tell Netscape where on your hard drive to locate external players for movies and audio files.

Even though Netscape requires external players for movie and audio files, you can display all GIF and JPEG graphics by using the program itself. Many of these graphics are *inline graphics*, which means that they display on the same page as the text (look at Figure C-14 for an example of an inline graphic). Sometimes small graphics, called *thumbnails*, are linked to full-size versions, often in GIF or JPEG format. Simply click on the linked image and Netscape will display the full-size graphic on its own page. You must then click on the Back button to get back to the original page.

Unfortunately, the ease of retrieving files using Netscape doesn't make up for the general difficulty of finding specific files. There is no search function within Netscape to find a specific file on the WWW, nor is there a guarantee that you will be able to download files (a few are password-protected). See Appendix D for a listing of Internet directories and search tools that may make your search for a particular file easier.

Although you can't use Netscape to find a particular file on the Internet, you can use the Find feature to search for keywords within a document once you've downloaded it. To do this, simply click on the Find button and enter the keyword you want to search for in the dialog window that opens. This can be useful when looking for something specific in long documents. For instance, if you wanted to quickly find the listing for games in the WWW Virtual Library, you can use Find to locate it right away.

Going Directly to Another Page

If you know the URL of any WWW page, you can go there directly instead of following a chain of links as we did above. For instance, to go directly to the Juggling Information Service page, you can enter the URL for that page as follows:

1. Click on the Open button in the toolbar.

2. Enter **http://www.hal.com/services/juggle/** into the text field that appears, and click the OK button or press Return.

Netscape gives you a shorthand way of opening documents too. At the top of the window, you'll see a field called Location. This field displays the URL of the document you are currently viewing. Use your mouse to highlight the text in this field, and then type in the URL you want to go to. Press Return and Netscape will open the document.

Throughout the Internet, you'll see all sorts of WWW pages noted by various groups and individuals. Because these URLs are often long, the best thing to do is highlight the URL and copy it, and then paste it into a document (I use the Clipboard). You could also copy the URL and paste it directly to the Location field (the Copy and Paste features are located under the Edit menu in Netscape). This way you won't misspell or incorrectly type a URL.

Setting Up a New Home Page

Now that we're at the end of the tour, suppose you want to go back where we started from, the home page shown in Figure C-1. To get there, all you have to do is click on the Home button in the toolbar. This button takes you directly home, the home page that Netscape opens automatically whenever you start the program. The page shown in Figure C-1 is the default home page, but if you want to configure a different home page, that's easy.

Let's say you always use the WWW Virtual Library to explore the Web. There's no need for you to have to click through the other pages to get to it each time you use Netscape. To remedy this situation, you can designate the Virtual Library as your home page. It's easy to make this change.

1. Go to the page you want to start as your new home page.
2. Highlight the URL that appears in the Location field at the top of the window, and copy it using the Clipboard or the Stickies.
3. Select General Preferences from the Options menu.
4. Select the Appearance option.
5. Place your cursor in the Home Page location field, and then paste in the URL you copied.
6. Click the OK button.

That's it. The next time you run Netscape, the program will automatically open the WWW Virtual Library page. If you ever want to use a different home page, just enter its URL as you did above. Any page on the Internet can be your home page, as long as you know its URL.

Perhaps you would like to create your own home page, resident on your hard drive. To open a file on your hard drive, choose Open File from the File menu, then select the file from the window that appears. To set this as your home page, look at the URL given in the Location field. Select and copy this URL using the Edit menu, then paste it into the Home Page location field as described earlier. (For tips on creating your own HTML page, see "Building Your Own Home Pages" at the end of this appendix.)

The Pop-up Menu

The pop-up menu contains some key commands for using Netscape, hold down the right mouse button to bring up the pop-up menu. With the pop-up menu, you can go back or forward among documents. If the cursor is positioned over a highlighted link, you can use the pop-up menu to open the link, add the link as a Bookmark, or open a new window with the link. You can also save the link as a file on your hard drive or copy the link's URL to paste somewhere else, as described earlier. If the cursor is positioned over an image icon or link, you can use the pop-up menu to view the image, save the image as a file on your hard drive, or copy the image's location (URL). The pop-up menu can be a great shortcut for some of Netscape's more useful commands.

Graphics & Modem Connections

If you're connected to the Internet via a SLIP or PPP modem connection, some of the graphics that are part of many WWW pages can take quite a while to reach your screen. In fact, some of them may not be worth the wait! It's easy to configure Netscape so that it does not automatically download inline images. Open the Options menu, and de-select Auto Load Images. When Auto Load Images is turned off, you'll see an image icon where the image should be. You can click on this to load the one image. You may also see text beside the image icon, called *alt text*, which tells you what the image is. If you want to load all the images on a page when auto load of images is turned off, just click on the Images button in the toolbar.

Using Forms With Netscape

Interactive forms are one of the most powerful features of the WWW. You will often run into forms as a way of ordering products, giving feedback on a site, filling out a questionnaire, or interacting with the site, such as with games or databases. Many Web sites also provide forms as a way of searching the site for particular information. One example of a WWW form is the registration form to use the Online Companion to *Walking the World Wide Web*. Take a look at this form now; you can connect to it from the home page on the Companion CD-ROM or from the URL of the Online Companion: **http://www.vmedia.com/ restricted/wwww/** (just follow the Register link). If you scroll down the page, you'll see boxes where you can type and buttons that you can select (see Figure C-15). Click in a text field with your mouse, and then start typing to answer the form's questions. When you're done, click on the Send button at the bottom of the form. This will automatically send the form the correct e-mail address. Filling out this form will let you access the Online Companion, with updates and new sites added all the time. (For more information about connecting to the Online Companion, see Appendix B," About the Online Companion.")

Figure C-15: Part of the Online Companion registration form.

Sending forms over the Internet can be potentially dangerous. Anywhere along the route from your computer to the form's destination, someone can intercept the form and read its contents, such as credit card numbers. Although this is not likely to happen, it is a possibility. To help protect you, Netscape provides many security features that let you know whether the form you're sending is secure or insecure. At the bottom of the Netscape window, you'll see a security indicator. A broken key and a gray colorbar indicate that the document you are currently downloading is an insecure document; a whole key and a blue colorbar indicate a secure document.

You'll find choices under the Options menu for displaying secure documents. Select Security Preferences to choose whether you want an alert when entering, leaving, or viewing secure documents or when submitting insecure forms. If you want to learn more about Netscape's security features, choose On Security under the Help menu.

Accessing FTP Sites With Netscape

Earlier we saw that Netscape uses the FTP protocol to retrieve files with a simple mouse click from whatever Web page you may be browsing. But you can also use Netscape to download files directly from any of the literally thousands of servers that provide files to Internet users via the FTP protocol, even servers that may not have WWW home pages. Typically, you access FTP sites using a stand-alone FTP client program. But since Netscape has FTP built right in, you may never again need to use a stand-alone FTP program unless you want to upload files.

In the steps that follow, we'll use Netscape to get a file from the Netscape FTP server:

1. When your Internet connection has been established, launch Netscape by double-clicking on its icon.
2. Click on the Open button in the toolbar.
3. Enter **ftp://ftp.netscape.com/** in the URL field.
4. Hit the OK button to activate your URL selection. The directory listing for the Netscape FTP server will appear in the Netscape window after a few seconds.
5. Clicking on the name of a directory takes you to that directory, where other files will be listed. Clicking on a file name downloads that file. Text files will be displayed in the Netscape window (look beside the file name to see what type of file it is). If you select a file for downloading that is not a text file, such as a compressed software file, a dialog box will appear where you may specify a new name and location for the file. Click OK to proceed with the download.

Acessing Gopher Sites With Netscape

What if you don't know exactly what you're looking for on the Net and want to refine your search carefully as you explore? What if you want to delve deeply into a particular area of interest? Typical Web sites may not help you, for often the links to other information are as arbitrary, whimsical, and wild as the imagination of the page's author. Gopher servers, on the other hand, serve up information in tidy hierarchical menus and submenus, sticking to a subject and presenting it in top-down outline format. With HTML documents you leap rapidly from peak to peak; using Gopher, you follow logically related information trails. There is a time and place for both methods, and fortunately Netscape supports them both.

Gopher servers are usually accessed with specialized Gopher programs, but Netscape makes extra software unnecessary. Netscape can log onto a Gopher server and then present you with the information so that it looks very much like any Web page. Menu items are blue like other Web links, and clicking on them brings up the appropriate submenus. Let's give it a try using the WELL Gopher as an example. The WELL (Whole Earth 'Lectronic Link) is an information service known for the variety of its online forums and the lively interactions of its users, but it also maintains a very interesting Gopher site. To begin exploring it,

1. With your Internet connection established, launch Netscape by double-clicking its icon.

Note: For the purposes of this exercise, it doesn't matter what Web page is currently displayed.

2. Click on the Open button. The Open URL dialog box will appear.

3. Type **gopher://gopher.well.com/** in the URL field and click OK. In a few seconds, the top level menu of the WELL Gopher appears.

Notice that when you connect to a Gopher server, virtually all the text in the Netscape window is comprised of hotlinks.

4. Click the top menu item, About this gopherspace. A new submenu appears.

5. Click the top item, What is this place? (The basic story). This time a text file appears.

6. After reading the file, use Netscape's Back button to return to the top-level WELL Gopher menu. From there you can begin to explore many different areas. Feel free to browse. The WELL Gopher is especially known for its information on media, communications, and cyberpunk literature.

Although every Gopher site looks about the same in terms of structure, the content varies greatly. There are Gopher sites that specialize in just about any academic field you can think of, from art to astrophysics. In addition there are some Gopher sites that are just plain fun.

While exploring the Web, you may run into hyperlinks that lead to FTP, Gopher, Telnet, and even Usenet news sites. If you want to explore one of these, just click on the link. Netscape will transport you seamlessly to any of these Internet protocols.

Accessing Usenet Newsgroups With Netscape

Usenet News is a fantastic Internet resource that lets you read and post messages on literally thousands of topics. The number and subjects of newsgroups you can access depend on what your Internet service provider makes available. Generally, you would use a newsreader program to access Usenet newsgroups. Netscape is the only WWW browser that allows you to both read and post to Usenet, making additional newsreaders unnecessary. Before you can access Usenet with Netscape, however, you must tell Netscape what Usenet server to access. To do this, select the Options menu and choose Mail and News Preferences. Under Servers you will see a text field where you can enter the IP address of your news (NNTP) server. If you don't know the IP address of your news server, your Internet service provider should be able to give it to you.

You can access all Usenet newsgroups by choosing Netscape News, under the Window menu. You can also access a specific newsgroup with a Usenet URL. For example, if you wanted to access the newsgroup that discusses the World Wide Web, you would click on the Open button and type in this URL: **news:comp.infosystems.www**. Notice that this URL looks different from the URLs you use to access WWW, Gopher, and FTP sites; there are no slashes after the first colon.

If you choose to look at all newsgroups, Netscape will open a screen showing all the newsgroups that you are subscribed to. Here you can subscribe and unsubscribe to specific newsgroups. Double-click on the newsgroup in your list of subscribed newsgroups that you want to access. Double-click on the titles of articles that have been posted to the newsgroup to read them. Once you enter a specific newsgroup, you can move back and forth between different threads, reply either to the entire group or via e-mail, or forward the posting to someone through e-mail. Netscape also creates links to any URL mentioned in a newsgroup posting, so you can visit that URL immediately. (See Figure C-16 for a newsgroup displayed in Netscape.)

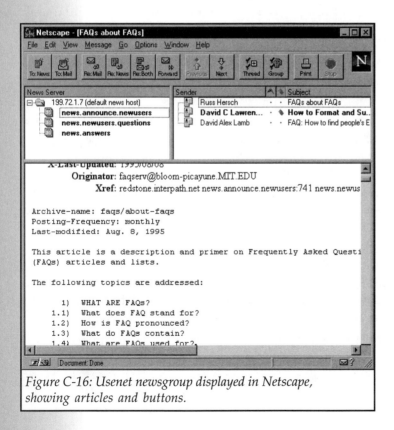

Figure C-16: Usenet newsgroup displayed in Netscape, showing articles and buttons.

Sending Internet E-Mail With Netscape

Version 2.0 of Netscape is the first Web browser that lets you send, receive, and organize Internet e-mail. You can even create an address book, organize your e-mail into folders, and do everything else with Netscape that you can do with a typical e-mail program. To access this feature, choose Netscape Mail under the Window menu.

Before you can send e-mail with Netscape, you must tell the program what mail server to use. First, select Mail and News Preferences under the Options menu, then choose Server. You will see a text field where you can fill in the name of your mail server. If you don't know the name of your mail server, ask your Internet service provider. You must also fill in the options under Identity (also located in the Mail and News preferences) to send e-mail with Netscape.

A special link, called a *mailto* link, allows you to send e-mail from a Web site with a click of your mouse. Mailto links look like this: **mailto:shannon@vmedia.com.** Notice that this URL is different from standard WWW, Gopher, and FTP URLs; there are no slashes after the first colon, and the second part of the URL is actually an Internet e-mail address.

To send e-mail about a Web page you are looking at, choose Mail Document from the File menu. Netscape automatically fills in the title and URL of the document currently displayed in the Netscape window. This makes it easy to tell all your friends about nifty WWW pages you have discovered. You must fill in the To address yourself, and you can add comments to the body of the message.

Obviously, I cannot completely go over all the great features of Netscape in this appendix. For instance, 3D and animation capabilities have recently been incorporated into the browser. To learn more about Netscape Navigator and its latest features, check the items under the Help menu or visit Netscape's home page (*http://www.netscape.com/*).

Building Your Own Web Pages

Now that you've traveled the Web, you may want to start creating your own Web pages. All Web pages are written in a language called HTML (HyperText Markup Language), a subset of SGML (Standard Generalized Markup Language, a system designed for typesetting and document page description). HTML is simply ASCII text with embedded codes expressing instructions for the proper display of that text. The most basic HTML commands instruct the Web browser client program regarding the display of the information (what size and style of type, etc.).

More important, HTML commands can include display information and links to other data types (video, graphics, and audio) and even other servers. This is the real power of the Web—its ability to let you access an amazingly wide variety of information types, across the entire Internet, with a click of the mouse.

A good starting point for HTML authoring is creating a local home page for yourself—a file on your hard drive that's loaded when you start Netscape and that contains some of your favorite links. After you feel comfortable with your authoring skills, you may want to set up your own server, or at least your own home page area on one, so that everyone on the Web can access your pages. If you have access to a server site, it's a relatively simple matter. Some SLIP/PPP service providers even let you start up Web pages on their system as part of an account.

I have found that the best way to start learning the HTML techniques for creating Web pages is to study the content and structure of the pages you visit. You can look at the source code for the page you're on by selecting Document Source from the View menu. This opens the file in a word processor on your computer, showing all the HTML tags; you can then save the document and use it as a template for your new HTML file. There are even some special editors designed specifically for automating the process of applying HTML tags to text. HTML Assistant, for instance, is available on many anonymous FTP sites. Netscape lets you preview or test any HTML documents you create. To view a local HTML file in Netscape, select Open File from the File menu.

You can also save HTML pages directly to your hard disk using Save As... from the File menu. (A shortcut way to save HTML documents to your hard drive is to drag a link directly onto the desktop with your mouse.) If you would like to print an HTML document from Netscape, choose Print from the File menu or click on the Print button. Print Setup, under the File menu, lets you choose options for printing.

HTML files on most Web servers have the extension .html. Since DOS does not support file-name extensions of more than three characters, Windows HTML files end with the extension .htm. If you do not use the .html or .htm extension, Netscape and other WWW browsers will not recognize your files as valid HTML pages.

There are several excellent HTML reference areas online, as shown in Table C-1. These pages will teach you the basics of HTML authoring.

Site	URL
CERN HTML Reference	http://www.w3.org/hypertext/WWW/MarkUp/MarkUp.html
Peter Flynn's How to Write HTML	http://kcgl1.eng.ohio-state.edu:80/www/doc/htmldoc.html
NCSA Beginner's Guide to HTML	http://www.ncsa.uiuc.edu/General/Internet/WWW/HTMLPrimer.html

Table C-1: Popular HTML references.

Another good place to look for HTML authoring tips is Netscape's own Help menu. Choose the option Creating Your Own Web Services to connect to a document describing HTML tags, including the special tags unique to Netscape.

If you want to start with more general information regarding the World Wide Web (straight from the horse's mouth), the best resource is the CERN Web server (*http://www.w3.org/*). CERN engineers developed the Web, and this is a great clearinghouse for software information.

Appendix D: World Wide Web Search Tools

The listings and reviews of sites in this book take you deep into the WWW. Should you want to go further, though, and explore on your own, the Web has its own assortment of search tools to help you. Although none of these tools has catalogued every document you can connect to through the WWW, together they give a fairly complete picture of the Web. With different methods of cataloguing WWW resources and building URL databases, each of these tools has something unique to offer. Using one or many of them, you should be able to locate Internet information on any subject you're interested in.

CUI W3 Catalog

This searchable catalog of WWW resources provides a useful way to find new sites on the Web. The CUI W3 Catalog uses a search engine called HTGREP to plow through a huge database of thousands of entries culled from the NCSA What's New archives and the Virtual Library at CERN, as well as from many other regularly maintained Internet lists. To use it, enter a keyword describing the topic you're interested in, and the catalog returns pages and pages of results, often within seconds. Because the catalog performs keyword searches not only on titles of documents but also on descriptions of WWW pages, searches can return an amazing amount of information, all of it fully hyperlinked. The CUI W3 Catalog is maintained by the University of Geneva. To access, use the URL **http://cuiwww.unige.ch/w3catalog/**.

Inter-Links Internet Access

Inter-Links is a searchable, privately maintained database; it features "lighter" fare, indexing mostly entertainment-based resources. It is maintained as a labor of love by Rob Kabascoff at Nova Southeastern University, Fort Lauderdale, Florida. Designed to be used with Lynx, Inter-Links searches all Internet resources, not just WWW documents. The database is divided into subject categories such as Fun and Games, News and Weather, Library Resources, and Reference Shelf. Inter-Links also supplies an introduction to Internet services, a beginner's tutorial to using different Internet tools. Browsing Inter-Links is like browsing the top 100 "hits" of the Web. It is located at **http://www.nova.edu/Inter-Links/**.

JumpStation II

At JumpStation II, you'll find a searchable database of WWW documents created by a robot program. Using an interactive form, you can choose to search for keywords contained in document titles, headers, or URLs. Although your search is limited to the scanty information found in document titles and URLs, the database created by the robot program is huge, with over 275,000 documents indexed. You can also search for a partial address—useful if you can't remember all of a URL. JumpStation was written by Jonathan Fletcher and is located at **http://js.stir.ac.uk/jsbin/jsii/**.

Lycos

The spider programs at Lycos catalog over 90 percent of the Web, all searchable here. This is by far the largest robot-created catalog of resources you will find. The search typically returns a lot of information with the results, including the URL and title of relevant documents and an excerpt from the document showing the keyword you were searching for. This information can help you narrow down resources to those most relevant to your needs but can also be jumbled and confusing. However, you'll find some interesting lists of resources at Lycos, including the Lycos 250, the 250 hottest sites on the Web as determined by how many other sites link to them. Lycos is located at **http://lycos.cs.cmu.edu/**.

The Mother-of-All-BBS

This unique resource collects home pages for companies, universities, research centers, government agencies, and many more, all posted by users as if tacked to a bulletin board. At the top level, you'll find an assortment of general subject listings, such as business services, computer products, financial aid, Internet training, literature, odds and ends, real estate, travel clubs, and zoos, to name a few. Click on a subject to descend deeper into the tree where you'll find more specialized subjects and links to appropriate home pages. At any time, you can perform a WAIS search for a keyword. The Global List gives quick access to the most recent additions to the bulletin board. Because the items are all contributed by users, this database of WWW resources is a very eclectic collection. Developed by Oliver McBryan at the University of Colorado at Boulder, you'll find the Mother-of-all-BBS at **http://www.cs.colorado.edu/homes/mcbryan/public_html/bb/summary.html**.

Net Happenings

Net Happenings, originally a mailing list, now has a WWW page. The purpose of Net Happenings is to announce new resources of interest to the Internet community. At this Web page, you can quickly access today's articles, this month's articles, or past articles by month. You can also search the entire archive by title, keywords, and subject. You can even fill out a handy form to announce your new Internet resources. Each announcement is preceded by a keyword, such as WWW, software, book, emag, lists, conference, or Gopher, to help you quickly locate resources of interest. Each article has a short description of the new resource and a hotlinked URL to connect you to resources you find. Net Happenings is a valuable service for finding new Net resources. The service is maintained by Gleason Sackman and is located at **http://www.mid.net/net/**.

Planet Earth Home Page

This page is a one-stop shop for Internet resources. It links to geographic locations all over the WWW, as well as to universities, science spots, community information, multimedia resources, and international government. This mass of information is organized into an easy-to-use, interactive format and is accompanied by homemade graphics. A comprehensive image map divides the site into different "rooms," which you enter to access different subjects. If you are just getting started on the Internet, you'll find links to Internet information, search engines for the WWW, and popular WWW resources. If travel is more your bag, the world is divided into two regions, with links to server maps, maps of WWW sites, and country home pages. You can also link to resources for community, education, multimedia, government, reference, and science. The Planet Earth Home Page is maintained by Richard P. Bocker and is located at **http://www.nosc.mil/planet_earth/info.html**.

Starting Points for Internet Exploration

This site contains hyperlinks to many popular Internet-based information resources that you may want to access frequently, including some of the navigational resources listed in this appendix. Other places that Starting Points takes you include the Web Overview at CERN, Web news, and interesting home pages, as well as to frequently visited sites in Gopherspace and FTP archives. You'll also find ways to search for a Usenet newsgroup or find information about people on the Internet. Starting Points is maintained by NCSA and can be found at the URL **http://www.ncsa.uiuc.edu/SDG/Software/Mosaic/StartingPoints/NetworkStartingPoints.html**.

TradeWave Galaxy

While WWW robots search externally for Web resources, this "galaxy" of resources is a database in itself, with its own searching mechanism. Intended as a free guide to WWW resources and to services provided by TradeWave, the Galaxy includes public and commercial Internet information. (TradeWave is an Internet consulting firm.) The database is arranged by topic, including business, community, government, law, and recreation. Searches return an excerpt from the site's description, frequent words, an outline of the site, and a hyperlink to the site. Only items already in the Galaxy database are searched. You can control the search by entering keywords and limiting the search to only

WWW, Gopher, or Telnet resources. Finally, you can add your own WWW documents to the Galaxy database, using a forms interface. The TradeWave Galaxy is located at **http://galaxy.einet.net/ galaxy.html**.

The Virtual Town

Visit your hometown in cyberspace. This unique information resource is set up like an actual small town would be, with links to information all over the WWW. Move around through an interactive map of the town that shows the layout of all the different "buildings." The map is really large, so you may want to bypass to the text version, which presents the town layout in a menued interface. Where can you go in the virtual town? Just imagine the places in a real town, and you'll probably find them here. Travel all around town via the bus and light-rail terminal (owned by the Virtual Town Transit Authority). The City Hall links to home pages for everyone who helped build the Virtual Town, the "town council," as well as a suggestion box and town charter. Public services include a post office, a public library, and the Virtual Town University. For entertainment, visit the games arcade, the Cinema Paradiso or the CyberSound Music Studio. Finish up your day by dining at one of the restaurants or having a drink at the White Stag. There are many more places to explore, and new construction is under way all the time. Go to the URL **http://www.cs.ucdavis.edu/virt-town/ welcome.html**.

W3 Search Engines

This page gathers many of the most popular and useful WWW and Internet searching tools into one handy resource. Here you'll find interactive searching tools for information servers, software, people on the Internet, online publications, news, and FAQs, documentation, and miscellaneous fun stuff such as acronyms and hacking jargon. In addition to listing useful searching tools, an interactive form allows you to enter keywords and search with that tool immediately. The most useful section is the information servers sections, with direct interfaces to tools like InfoSeek, the CUI W3 Catalog, the WebCrawler, the WWW Worm, the JumpStation, and many more. You can also search WAIS indices, Gopher servers, or *The Whole Internet Catalog* to extend further into the Internet. Connect to this meta-index at **http://cuiwww.unige.ch/meta-index.html**.

WebCrawler

The WebCrawler is another robot program, but this one indexes the content of WWW documents, not just their titles and URLs. The Web-Crawler burrows through the Web, building a huge database of fully indexed WWW documents. By indexing content as well as document titles and URLs, WebCrawler's search returns are likely to be closer to what you wanted than the WWW Worm's or the JumpStation's returns. However, the search does not return excerpts, so all you receive is the site's title. You can search for one or more keywords; a numbering system included with the search returns gives you an idea of how relevant the found document is to the keyword you were looking for. You can also enter multiple keywords to narrow down your search. The WebCrawler program is provided by America Online at **http://webcrawler.com/**.

What's New

What's New is the unofficial newspaper of the WWW. It announces new servers and Web-related tools as well as exciting new sites on the Web or updates to existing ones. The announcements link directly to the Web pages and sites referenced. Listings are divided by day, and the archive for one month's announcements often contains several hundred thousand bytes of information. You can search the entire archives or check out the pick of the week. The What's New page can be a gold mine for discovering brand-new WWW sites. It is maintained by NCSA. Look for it at **http://www.ncsa.uiuc.edu/SDG/Software/Mosaic/Docs/whats-new.html**.

World Wide Web Worm

The WWW Worm is an automatic robot program that scours the WWW for available resources. It was the winner of the Best Navigational Tool award from Best of the Web '94. The robot searches on a keyword provided by the user, scanning HTML document titles and URLs. Because the search is limited to titles and URLs, excluding document content, returns may not include everything available on the subject. And since the database searched is essentially the entire WWW, over three million multimedia resources, the robot may take a long time to return results over slower modem connections. The WWW Worm was developed by Oliver McBryan at the University of Colorado at Boulder. To access it, use the URL **http://www.cs.colorado.edu/home/mcbryan/WWWW.html**.

The WWW Virtual Library

The Virtual Library represents the first attempt to create a library of WWW-published information, and it is the first and best-known of the subject catalogs. The subjects range from Aboriginal studies to zoos, with everything else you can think of in between. Although there is a lot of information available here, the list is by no means complete. Still, the Virtual Library is a good place to begin a subject search. Each subject is maintained by a volunteer; so some lists are more complete than others. The project is an experiment by CERN to demonstrate the library capabilities of the WWW; think of each subject index as a shelf in a library, containing lots of "books," or WWW documents, on that particular subject. To access the Virtual Library, use the URL **http://www.w3.org/hypertext/DataSources/bySubject/Overview.html**.

Yahoo

Yahoo is a huge WWW database that is growing all the time. You'll quickly find it invaluable for searching for Web resources. Browse through the major categories of art, business, computers, economy, education, entertainment, environment and nature, events, government, health, humanities, law, news, politics, reference, regional information, science, social science, and society and culture. Or search the entire database for keywords. Everything is cross-referenced to make finding a particular resource easy. You can also access what's new, what's cool, and what's popular to get to the newest and the best on the Web. Or, for fun, follow a random link. Yahoo is located at **http://www.yahoo.com/**.

Index

B

D

E

F

G

J

M

Q

R

S

T

U

V

W

X

Y

Z

Ride the Windows Wave

Looking Good in Color

$29.95, 272 pages, illustrated in full color, Part #: 219-4

Like effective design, using color properly is an essential part of a desktop publishing investment. This richly illustrated four-color book addresses basic issues from color theory— through computer technologies, printing processes and budget issues—to final design. Even the graphically challenged can make immediate use of the practical advice in *Looking Good in Color*.

The Microsoft Network Tour Guide

$24.95, 336 pages, illustrated, Part #: 256-9

In the entertaining, informative tradition of Ventana's bestselling *Tour Guides*, this new title takes readers on a pleasure cruise of Microsoft's new online service. The introduction to MSN's innovative content includes a look at customizable menus, shortcut icons and integration with Windows 95.

Microsoft Office 96 Power Toolkit

$49.95, 800 pages, illustrated, Part #: 290-9

Microsoft's Office's integrated programming tools are showcased in this guide to customizing Office. More than a mere manual, it's packed with hints, little-known techniques, and advice on effective strategies for using Visual Basic for Applications and OLE 2.0 to make all your applications become partners in workgroup solutions. The companion CD-ROM contains selected tools, programming examples, graphic and audio elements, demos and more.

Books marked with this logo include a free Internet *Online Companion*™, featuring archives of free utilities plus a software archive and links to other Internet resources.

Internet Resources

The Web Server Book

$49.95, 680 pages, illustrated, Part #: 234-8

The cornerstone of Internet publishing is a set of UNIX tools, which transform a computer into a "server" that can be accessed by networked "clients." This step-by-step in-depth guide to the tools also features a look at key issues—including content development, services and security. The companion CD-ROM contains Linux™, Netscape Navigator™, ready-to-run server software and more.

Internet Business 500

$29.95, 360 pages, illustrated, Part #: 287-9

This authoritative list of the most useful, most valuable online resources for business is also the most current list, linked to a regularly updated *Online Companion* on the Internet. The companion CD-ROM features the latest version of *Netscape Navigator*, plus a hyperlinked version of the entire text of the book.

Internet Roadside Attractions

$29.95, 376 pages, illustrated, Part #: 197-3

Why take the word of one when you can get a quorum? Seven experienced Internauts—teachers and bestselling authors—share their favorite Web sites, Gophers, FTP sites, chats, games, newsgroups and mailing lists. In-depth descriptions are organized alphabetically by category for easy browsing. The companion CD-ROM contains the entire text of the book, hyperlinked for off-line browsing and Web hopping.

Internet Guide for Windows 95

$24.95, 552 pages, illustrated, Part #: 260-7

The *Internet Guide for Windows 95* shows how to use Windows 95's built-in communications tools to access and navigate the Net. Whether you're using The Microsoft Network or an independent Internet provider and Microsoft *Plus!*, this easy-to-read guide helps you started quickly and easily. Learn how to e-mail, download files, and navigate the World Wide Web and take a tour of top sites. An *Online Companion* on Ventana Online features hypertext links to top sites listed in the book.

PGP Companion for Windows

$29.95, 208 pages, illustrated, Part #: 304-2

Pretty Good Privacy (PGP) is a practically perfect way to protect online information from unwanted intrusion. Complete instructions cover encryption, public and private keys, digital signatures and security issues. Introduces a graphical interface—Win PGP—freely available on the Internet just like PGP itself.

The Windows Internet Tour Guide, Second Edition

$29.95, 424 pages, illustrated, Part #: 174-0

This runaway bestseller has been updated to include Ventana Mosaic™, the hot new Web reader, along with graphical software for e-mail, file downloading, newsreading and more. Noted for its down-to-earth documentation, the new edition features expanded listings and a look at Net developments. Includes three companion disks.

Check your local bookstore or software retailer for these and other bestselling titles, or call toll free:

800/743-5369

To order any Ventana title, complete this order form and mail or fax it to us, with payment, for quick shipment.

TITLE	PART #	QTY	PRICE	TOTAL

SHIPPING

For all standard orders, please ADD $4.50/first book, $1.35/each additional.
For *Internet Publishing Kit* orders, ADD $6.50/first kit, $2.00/each additional.
For "two-day air," ADD $8.25/first book/$2.25/each additional.
For "two-day air" on the kits, ADD $10.50/first kit, $4.00/each additional.
For orders to Canada, ADD $6.50/book.
For orders sent C.O.D., ADD $4.50 to your shipping rate.
North Carolina residents must ADD 6% sales tax.
International orders require additional shipping charges.

SUBTOTAL = $ _____

SHIPPING = $ _____

TOTAL = $ _____

Name _____ Daytime telephone _____

Company _____

Address (No PO Box) _____

City_____ State_____ Zip_____

Payment enclosed ____VISA ____MC ____ Acc't # _____ Exp. date_____

Signature _____ Exact name on card _____

Mail to: Ventana • PO Box 13964 • Research Triangle Park, NC 27709-3964 ☎ 800/743-5369 • Fax 919/544-9472

Check your local bookstore or software retailer for these and other bestselling titles, or call toll free: **800/743-5369**

Readers Survey ... Tell us what you think!

For a FREE Ventana catalog, please answer the following reader-satisfaction survey.
Your assistance will help us produce better computer productivity guides.

1. How did you learn about this book?
- ❑ Ventana Online
- ❑ Book review
- ❑ Recommendation: ❑ bookstore ❑ friend
- ❑ Other: _____
- ❑ Advertisement (please specify) _____
- ❑ Bookstore (please specify) _____

2. What type of computer do you use?
- ❑ 386 ❑ 486 ❑ Quadra ❑ Pentium ❑ PowerMac ❑ Mac II ❑ Other _____

3. Please rate the following features of this book, on a scale of 1 to 5. (5 is excellent, 1 is poor.)

Organization	5	4	3	2	1	Depth of material	5	4	3	2	1
Relevant illustrations/examples	5	4	3	2	1	Value of companion disk/CD-ROM	5	4	3	2	1
Online Companion	5	4	3	2	1	Special features	5	4	3	2	1
Timesaving tips	5	4	3	2	1	Cover design and attractiveness	5	4	3	2	1
Other (please specify) _____							5	4	3	2	1

4. Where do you use this book most often?
- ❑ Home (personal)
- ❑ Business office
- ❑ Home office

5. Please indicate your job function
- ❑ Engineering
- ❑ PR/Publishing/Advertising
- ❑ Software Development
- ❑ Finance/Accounting
- ❑ Product Management
- ❑ Research and Development
- ❑ Management
- ❑ Purchasing/Buying
- ❑ MIS/DP/IS
- ❑ Sales/Marketing
- ❑ Other _____

6. How many years have you used a computer?

Personal use	❑ 1	❑ 2	❑ 3	❑ 4	❑ 5-10	❑ 10+
Business use	❑ 1	❑ 2	❑ 3	❑ 4	❑ 5-10	❑ 10+

7. How many years have you been online? ❑ 1 ❑ 2 ❑ 3 ❑ 4 ❑ 5-10 ❑ 10+

8. What computer magazines do you frequently read?
- ❑ Byte
- ❑ Home PC
- ❑ MacUser
- ❑ PC Magazine
- ❑ Windows Sources
- ❑ Communications Week
- ❑ Inter@ctive Week
- ❑ Macworld
- ❑ PC Computing
- ❑ Windows Magazine
- ❑ Computer Shopper
- ❑ Internet World
- ❑ NetGuide
- ❑ PC WEEK
- ❑ Others (please specify) _____
- ❑ Computer Life
- ❑ Mac Week
- ❑ Online Access
- ❑ Web Week

9. What is your age?
- ❑ Under 21
- ❑ 21-30
- ❑ 31-40
- ❑ 41-50
- ❑ 51-60
- ❑ Over 60

10. Gender ❑ Male ❑ Female

Name _____
Address _____
City _____
State _____ Zip _____

Please fax to: (919) 544-9472
or mail to: VENTANA
PO Box 13964
Research Triangle Park, NC 27709-3964